W0013874

Freshwater Fishing

Erratum
p. 479 and p. 483 should be transposed.

An eel-bobber of Battersea, c. 1800.

Eel-bobbing, or babbing: a centuries-old method of catching eels. Lobworms were threaded on worsted and tied in a bunch (known as a 'bob' or 'bab') to the end of the line. No hook was used. When an eel bit at the worm its teeth got caught in the worsted and it was hoisted out of the water; sometimes (as shown) straight into a tub. The customary tackle was a large cork float; but the old woman eel-bobber of Battersea has dispensed with such a refinement—obviously preferring to fish by touch.

Falkus and Buller's Freshwater Fishing

A book of tackles and techniques, with some notes on various fishes; fish recipes; fishing safety and sundry other matters by Fred Buller and Hugh Falkus

Macdonald and Jane's · London

First published in 1975 by Macdonald and Jane's
(Macdonald & Co. (Publishers) Ltd.)
Paulton House, 8 Shepherdess Walk, London N1 7LB

Printed in Great Britain by
REDWOOD BURN LIMITED
Trowbridge & Esher

Designed by Barrie Carr

ISBN 0 356 04612 5

Contents

Acknowledgements

To all those scientists, experimenters, bibliographers, authors and fellow travellers from whom, during our two lifetimes of angling we have derived so much, we owe our thanks. Despite the demands of courtesy, to list them all as individuals would be impossible, since (although their deeds or sayings are remembered) their names in many cases are unknown.

There are some, however, to whom we owe a special debt, and for whose help we can, and must, express our gratitude.

Mr Alwyne Wheeler, of The British Museum (Natural History).
Dr Michael Kennedy of The Inland Fisheries Trust, Dublin.
Mr Ronald Coleby, of Nottingham, most kind and knowledgeable of angling bibliophiles.
Dr Winifred Frost and the late Mr George Thompson, of the Freshwater Biological Association, Windermere.
Mr William Hardy and Mr James Hardy, of Hardy Bros. Alnwick.
Mr Peter Collins.
Mr Gerry Hughes.
Mr Jack Thorndike.
Mr David Jacques.
Mr Jos Milbourn.
The members of Oxford Scientific Films.
The staff of Scientific Anglers, U.S.A.
Dr H. Thirlaway, librarian of the Piscatorial Society.
The Reverend Edward Alston.
Mr T. R. Collins, of The Stewartry Museum, Kirkcudbrightshire.
Mr Albert Dixon.
Mr Frank Plum.
Mr Fred J. Taylor.
Mr Peter Thomas.

In particular we should like to thank four people. Our publishing editor, Patrick Annesley, for his informed criticism and unfailing good humour. Our secretary, Mrs M. G. Lewin, who patiently typed until we finally abandoned, rather than completed, our task. Our estimable contributor Ken Sutton, who also read the proofs and last of all Richard Walker, a man of the highest learning in matters of angling.

F.B. and H.F.

Introduction

This is a book of simple purpose. Our object has been to describe a few tested rigs and methods which we hope will lead the reader towards a better understanding and enjoyment of his sport.

The book is not of course complete. Nor can it ever be, such is the speed of modern tackle development and the complexity of angling. Fishing tackle and techniques are discussed weekly by a host of writers. Any attempt at making a comprehensive survey of so much material would be absurd. We have, therefore, confined our comments to various aspects of the sport which gave us pleasure to write about; which we think are important or may be little known, or to which we wish to draw special attention.

Not the least of our pleasure has been the study of angling history. In a practical work a discussion of historical details may be questioned. But not only is the enjoyment of angling enriched by a knowledge of its background, such knowledge is imperative if the basic values of angling are to be fully appreciated. Evidence of this can be found in our notes on sportsmanship.

Broadly we have arranged the book into two parts. First, a section on the fishes themselves, placed alphabetically – except that, not being mere slaves to system, we have allowed the Silver Bream to follow the Bream; the Brown Trout, Rainbow Trout and Sea-Trout to group themselves under 'T' for *Trout*; and the Gwyniad, Powan, Pollan, Vendace and Skelly to come together under the general title *The Whitefishes*. That this section is prefaced with some remarks on fish as food is because, historically, man's whole relationship with fishes is based on their culinary value, however much that relationship has been obscured by the sophistries and sentiment of anglers.

The second part of the book, for lack of any better inspiration, we have called *Ways and Means*. Here the arrangement follows no particular pattern, being by turns lyrical, discursive and didactic. Our principal claim for it is simply that we have tried to say only things which we believe are worth saying.

We have made frequent use of quotation; not through any reluctance to write our own copy, but to acquaint the reader with writers we admire; in particular those who, in addition to being fine anglers, wrote with knowledge, wit and (above all) charm – a quality seldom encountered in the angling literature of today.

Finally, we are aware that angling lore results from experience accumulated over many centuries; that every angler owes a debt to others both past and present. In consequence, we have done our best to trace the originators of the rigs and methods described and to give credit where it is due.

Dedicated to our friends

The Fishes

Preamble
Fish as Food

. . . the austere, scrupulous regulations of the Romish Church, have tended more than any other circumstances, to enhance the value, and increase the quantity of this species of food: so rigid was the precept upon this point, that in the year 1629, *Claude Guillon* was beheaded at *St Claude* in *Burgundy*, for eating a morsel of *Horseflesh* on a *Fish*-day . . .
THE REV. W. B. DANIEL, *Rural Sports* (1801)

Thursday.
Tomorrow will be Friday, so we'll fish the stream today. (Painted by Dendy Sadler, 1880).

One of the rewards of fishing is that with few exceptions fish are good to eat. For centuries this has been taken for granted, but in ancient times it was the subject of great argument. The fathers of medicine recommended certain species of fish as being very wholesome, and disparaged others as being decidedly unwholesome. Unfortunately, when it came to deciding which species were good and which were bad, the early physicians were seldom in agreement.

One old thinker divided fish into clean and unclean species by their habitat: 'Those which keep near the rocks are easily digested, but not very nutritious. Those which haunt deep water are very nutritious, but upsetting to the internal economy.'

He had it both ways.

On the grounds that some fish didn't get enough exercise, another early intellectual wrote:

> All fish that standing pools frequent,
> Do ever yield bad juice and nourishment.

This was an interesting point, since that great physician, Xenocrates, had stated emphatically: 'The tail end of *all* fishes is the most wholesome part, on account of it being most frequently exercised.'

But although the great medical minds of long ago disagreed over dietary values, they were united in prescribing fish – in one form or another – as a nostrum for most human ills and disorders.

If you were bitten by a mad dog, 'Pickled fish, applied topically,' would be found 'sufficiently effectual'.

Toothache? Then, 'Rub your teeth with the brains of a dog-fish boiled in oil'.

If your wife became hysterical, 'Lint, greased with a dolphin's fat, and then ignited . . .' proved instantly effective.

For easy deliverance in pregnancy, the '. . . fragrance of burnt eel' took some beating; or, 'A torpedo fish, caught when the moon is in Libra and kept in the open air for three days before being placed in the patient's room' would be sure to do the trick. (In hot weather, one might think, it certainly would!)

Superfluous hair? The choice of depilatories was fairly wide. 'Tunny guts, fresh or pickled,' were pretty good; or 'fish brains, applied with alum on the sixteenth day of the moon' – just as effective.

For carbuncles there was nothing better than 'burnt mullet mixed with honey'.

The best aphrodisiac? Fish every time. Fish, it seems, was an essential part of the wedding feast.

But to more recent times. In medieval England, fish was very valuable. In the 13th century, the pike (although, seemingly, without magical properties) was in great demand and very expensive. Its price, as fixed by Edward I, was double that of salmon, and more than ten times that of either turbot or cod. Even in the 16th century, a big pike fetched as much as a lamb, and a small pickerel was dearer than a fat capon.

It is unlikely that this prodigious demand for pike had any direct connection with the flavour of the fish itself. 'Days of abstinence' – which occurred almost every other day – made fish a necessity. Roads were very bad; transport difficult and tedious. Saltwater species were not readily available to people living far inland. The pike was a large fish, obtainable nearly everywhere and at any time. It is not surprising that in Elizabethan England, when Fast Days numbered no fewer than 145, the pike was so popular.

Religious festivals notwithstanding, there is no doubt that most species of freshwater fish were eagerly sought, and much care lavished on their preparation. Thus Walton wrote, with relish, of the carp (at the end of a complicated recipe which included marjoram, thyme, rosemary, parsley, onions, oysters, oranges, anchovies, claret and cloves):

> . . . lay it with the broth, into the dish; and pour upon it a quarter of a pound of the best fresh butter, melted, and beaten with half a dozen spoonfuls of the broth, the yolks of two or three eggs, and some of the herbs shred. Garnish your dish with lemons, and serve it up. And much good do you.

Doubtless, the primary function of such elaborations was to conceal the muddy flavour. All the same, as Arthur Ransome said:

> There are fashions in fish. It is possible in angling literature to watch, for example, the decline and fall of the pike from the eminence he once enjoyed. He was once for the angler 'my joy of all the scaly shoal' and when cooked 'too good' for any but those who fished for him 'or very honest men'. With the pike the other coarse fish have lost their kitchen reputations. Yet once upon a time a pike would be the chief dish at a banquet and many another fish now seldom cooked was valued as highly as trout or salmon. At the Assizes in Derby in 1613, the bill of fare included: '15 different sorts of fowl, among others young swans, knots, herns, bitterns, etc., three venison pasties appointed for every meal, 13 several sorts of sea-fish, *14 several sorts of freshwater fish*, each appointed to be ordered a different way . . .' [Our italics].

Today, most coarse anglers return their catch alive. They are missing little. In this age of pre-packaged and frozen foods, few housewives can be bothered to carry out the complicated preparations that so many old recipes demand. Nevertheless, certain freshwater fishes make excellent eating, and since we feel that an effort should be made to keep some of these recipes in print, we have added a selection to our notes on the various species.

Above: *Barbel, 12¼ lb, caught on the river Kennet at Newbury in July 1894, by R. C. Blundell of the Piscatorial Society.*

Below: *Aylmer Tryon's record-sharing barbel* *(see p. 11)*.

1 · The Barbel

Barbus barbus

In the great carp family of fishes, the Cyprinidae, there is a genus of fishes, *Barbus*, very rich in species. Of these, the mahseer of India, *Barbus tor*, is perhaps the best known. In Africa there are at least 100 different species. In Europe there are three species and four sub-species, only one of which is found in Britain: *Barbus barbus*, the barbel.

In Britain the barbel is mainly confined to one northern habitat centred on the Trent river system and one southern habitat centred on the Thames river system. Southern barbel rivers include the Thames, Kennet, Lea, Colne, Wey, Loddon and Great Ouse. Northern barbel rivers include the Trent, Nidd, Wharfe, Ure, Swale, Dove and Derwent. It has, however, been successfully introduced to other rivers, notably the Severn, Wye, Medway, Wiltshire Avon, Hampshire Avon and Dorset Stour.

It is distinguishable from all other British species by the presence of four barbules attached to the upper lip and jaw. These barbules are touch and taste organs. Whereas predatory fish and plankton-feeding fish rely mainly on visual aids in their search for food, most species that live and feed on the bottom use touch and taste organs.

During the course of evolution the barbel has adapted itself to live close to the bottom in swift-flowing streams of moderately deep rivers; the significance of the body structure when related to its feeding habits was appreciated by Richard Walker when he wrote in *Still-Water Angling*:

> The barbel has a reputation of being capricious largely because too few anglers take the trouble to study it. This may be because all barbuled fish probably feed by touch rather than by sight, and can feed in darkness when they are difficult to observe and relatively few anglers are about.

Although big strides have been made in most modern fishing techniques, present day barbel specialists are unlikely to take the quantities of barbel caught by earlier anglers. In the old days colossal bags were landed. Individual daily catches of 97, 100 and 123 barbel have been recorded. During eight days on the River Trent an angler once caught 300 barbel to his own rod. Most of these old timers pre-baited their swims, or had them pre-baited by professionals, with prodigious quantities of groundbait, as many as three or four thousand lobworms sometimes being used for this purpose.

Today, although huge bags are probably a thing of the past, barbel fishing is en-

Barbel, 12 lb 12 oz (top) and 10 lb 12 oz. This beautiful brace was taken from Ham Mill Pool on the river Kennet by W. Kelsey on 11th August 1894. The heavier fish measured 30½ in. and the lighter 29½ in. The fish are the property of the Piscatorial Society.

joyed by more anglers than ever before. Since the last war two new angling techniques have emerged. The first of these – a truly remarkable concept – was to groundbait a small patch of river-bed very heavily with cooked hempseeds. This was done by means of a large bait-dropper. A *No. 6 hook* was then baited with one or two grains of hempseed! The tackle, with just sufficient lead to hold bottom, was ledger-fished *on top* of the groundbait seeds. The angler sat, rod in hand, waiting for a hungry barbel to find the little heap of hemp and suck up the two 'armed' hempseeds along with the decoy seeds.

We have nothing but admiration for the angler who conceived this astonishing method of fishing. He must have persevered, without the benefit of previous success until such time as Stour barbel came to accept hempseeds as foodstuff. The method was developed on the Throop fishery of the Dorset Stour. It has now been banned by the riparian owners. In our opinion, unnecessarily.

The second technique was developed on the Royalty Fishery of the Hampshire Avon.

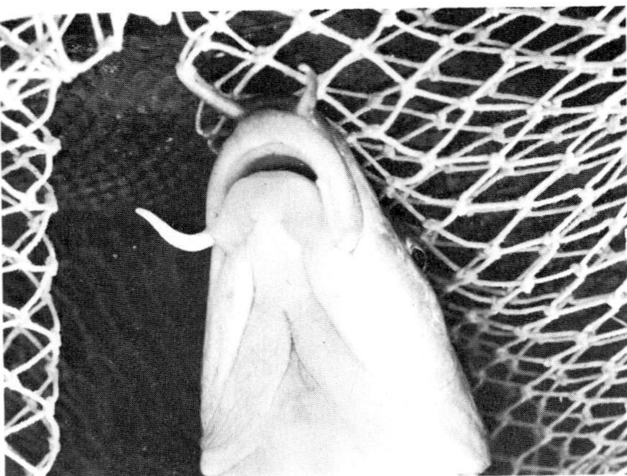

The four barbules, two near the tip of the nose and a pair at the angle of the jaw, show that the barbel is exclusively a bottom feeder.
(Photograph: Richard Walker)

A three ounce Avon barbel. Although F.B. was not wildly excited when he caught this tiny fish instead of the hoped-for ten pounder, he was encouraged to read that he had made one of 'the rarest of catches'! In Coarse Fish *(1943) E. Marshall-Hardy writes: 'Very small barbel (gudgeon size) are unbelievably scarce. To the best of my knowledge I have not caught one in forty years' angling, and I have sought them diligently, for their rarity has always fascinated and mystified me.'*

This evolved from the traditional rolling-ledger method, where baits like breadcrust, breadcrumb, bran-paste, lobs and bunches of maggots were fished (on size 4, 6 or 8 hooks tied to 6 or 7 lb B.S. lines) in fast swims that had been heavily groundbaited with large balls of bread-and-bran mixture. In time, small hooks (sizes 14 and 16) baited with single maggot, tied to lines of from 2 to 4 lb B.S., replaced the traditional gear. Very large quantities of maggots were used as groundbait, with the result that the barbel gradually became preoccupied maggot feeders. Generally the maggots were accurately delivered into the quieter runs close to the bank by means of a swimfeeder or a bait-dropper.

Another significant post-war development has been the discovery of several new barbel and chub baits. In some rivers barbel will take lumps of sausage or Spam, and other items from the delicatessen store.

Apart from these new methods and baits there are, of course, the traditional laying-on, float ledgering, ledgering and swimming-the-stream methods. These are the same as for roach fishing but used with stronger tackle. A big barbel is a powerful fish in most waters: it will break light tackle if it can reach weed cover. If 5 lb B.S. line is acceptable to the barbel never use lighter. Whenever possible we prefer to fish with 6 lb B.S. line.

It is always exciting to know that there are bigger fish in the water than have ever been taken out. D. Cummins, one of England's most experienced skin divers, recently stated that the remains of the original supports for the old Chertsey Bridge hold barbel of record size. He has used the ancient 'tickling' technique to bring them to the surface in order to convince anglers who doubted their existence!

Near London, the Thames, from Putney upwards, produces Barbel in great quantities, and of large size; but they are held in little estimation, except as affording sport to the angler. During summer this fish frequents the weedy parts of the river in shoals, but as soon as the weeds begin to decay in autumn, it seeks deeper water, and shelters itself near piles, locks, and bridges, where it remains till the following spring. The Lea, in Essex, also produces this fish. It has not been found in Ireland . . .

So numerous are the Barbel about Shepperton and Walton, that one hundred and fifty pounds' weight have been taken in five hours; and on one occasion it is said that two hundred and eighty pounds' weight of large-sized Barbel were taken in one day. The largest fish I can find recorded weighed fifteen and a half pounds. Mr Jesse, and other anglers, have occasionally caught Barbel when trolling or spinning with Bleak, Gudgeon, or Minnow, for large Thames Trout.

WILLIAM YARRELL, *A History of British Fishes* (3rd edition, 1859).

A BRITISH RECORD BARBEL

On September 13th, 1934, Aylmer Tryon, then a novice coarse fisherman, was ledgering in the Hampshire Avon from a moored boat with his father, the late G. C. Tryon, and Mr Hayter, warden of the Christchurch Royalty Fishery. He was receiving instruction on barbel fishing from a parent who was one of the best all-round fishermen of his time; indeed, although G. C. Tryon shared a trout beat on the River Test with Sir Edward Grey, author of the classic book *Fly Fishing*, his preference was for pike and barbel.

Aylmer Tryon remembers how perplexed he felt when his first catch – a 4 lb barbel, to him a splendidly large fish – was described by his companions as 'only a small one'. He remembers Hayter taking the fish some distance upstream before releasing it 'so that it shouldn't disturb the swim'. Minutes later he hooked a second barbel – which broke him. A misfortune which in Aylmer Tryon's own words 'made me not at all popular with my companions'.

With a thicker gut leader fitted he fished on, and his lobworm bait was soon taken by another fish. Although this third fish felt much heavier than the first, Aylmer Tryon was slow to call attention to it and when he did, his father and Hayter failed to respond.

They were amusing themselves trying to catch some large perch which could be seen clearly on that lovely sunny day just downstream of the boat. However, as soon as he mentioned that he was into a big salmon, his companions suddenly lost interest in the

The bridge pool on the Hampshire Avon at Ibsley. The two largest barbel landed in recent times came from the Hampshire Avon. Both were foulhooked by salmon anglers. The larger fish, caught at Avon-Tyrell by Lady Rothes, weighed 17 lb. The other, taken by Mr C. Cassey from the bridge pool at Ibsley, weighed 16 lb 1 oz. This fish created considerable interest as members of the Prince of Wales Hanwell Club gathered round Colonel Crow, the famous bailiff of Lord Normanton's water at Ibsley, to see it weighed.

Barbel 16 lb 1 oz. Taken from the bridge pool at Ibsley on March 6th 1960 by C. Cassey.

perch. With one accord they began to give advice on how to play it.

Eventually the fish was netted. It proved to be a magnificent barbel: 14 lb 6 oz when weighed by Hayter at the Royalty hut. This weight was confirmed when the fish was re-weighed at a butcher's shop.

Knowing that a 16 lb 4 oz barbel had been foul-hooked by Roy Beddington when salmon fishing during the 1931 coarse-fish close season, the Tryons had no thought of their fish being in record class. Nevertheless it was sent to the taxidermists, J. Cooper & Sons, who set it up.

Subsequently this fish was recognised as the (equal) British record. Today the fish is still preserved at the home of the Tryon family at Great Durnford, Wiltshire. Its modest captor, nowadays a great exponent of salmon and trout fishing, is still very much alive. He told F.B. that nobody else had made enquiries about it since its capture nearly forty years ago.

He has one regret. 'It was a pity my father didn't catch it. He had long dreamed of a big barbel. In fact, that was our reason for going to the Royalty.'

The mighty mahseer (a cousin of the barbel) is India's finest freshwater game fish. This one was caught near Bombay.

COOKING THE BARBEL

The barbel is a swete fysshe; but it is a quasy meete and a perylous, for mannys body.
DAME JULIANA BERNERS, *The Treatyse of Fysshynge wyth an Angle* (1496).

Despite Dame Juliana's caveat, Michel Duborgel, in *La Pêche et les Poissons de Rivière*, offers the following:

1 *Boiled Barbel in Court Bouillon*

Court bouillon
Parsley
Butter
Capers

Clean the fish and boil in court bouillon. Serve in a sauce made by reducing two cupfuls of the court bouillon, thickened with a nut of butter, some chopped parsley, and capers. If served cold,[1] provide Mayonnaise or vinaigrette sauce.

2 *Stuffed Barbel*

Mushrooms
Hardboiled egg
Bechamel sauce

Clean and split the fish and stuff with chopped mushrooms and hardboiled egg. Cook in a fireproof dish and serve covered with white sauce.

1 God forbid!

2 · The Bleak

Alburnus alburnus

Although of little value to the angler as sport fish, the bleak and other small fry deserve some notice. Dr J. J. Manley wrote about them with great charm in *Fish and Fishing*. He thought that anglers should know something of angling literature, of the natural history of fishes, gastronomic merits and demerits, and nomenclature – so that they should not '. . . pursue their quarry as mere savages'. His book was published in 1877, but it has a timeless appeal.

The bleak with its green-tinted back and glittering coat of scales was once the subject of a commercial fishery which supported a French industry dating back to 1656. A substance called nacre, derived from the scales, was used for the coating of imitation pearls (and still is in eastern Europe). Four thousand bleak are required to produce four ounces of pearl essence.

The bleak is widely distributed throughout Europe, north of the Alps and Pyrenees and eastwards to the Caspian Basin. It is absent from Norway, Ireland, Scotland and the English Lake District. Its normal adult length is between five and six inches, although exceptionally it will grow to eight inches.

Its small size makes it scarcely worth the angler's attention. Walton, with customary clarity, called it 'the freshwater sprat'. Bleak tend to swim near the surface and if the angler wishes to *avoid* catching them – as usually he does – he should fish with sufficient weight to take his bait through the shoal as quickly as possible. Before the cult of 'all-in' match angling, the Thames match angler would rid his swim of these little fish by throwing in a handful of chrysalids (casters) – which floated downstream taking the bleak shoal with them.

Prior to the 20th century, bleak were popular table fish. According to Cholmondeley-Pennell, bleak '. . . dressed and eaten like whitebait make a very good dish'. Another Victorian, Francis Francis, thought bleak '. . . very delicate eating when cooked in the way in which sprats are cooked'. A modern author, Alwyne Wheeler thinks them: 'palatable, if somewhat bony'.

Perch, pike and trout, however, regard them highly. In consequence the bleak is an excellent bait for these freshwater predators.

3 · The Bream

Abramis brama

The Bream being at full growth is a large and stately fish, he will breed both in rivers and ponds, and where, if he likes the water and air, he will grow not only to be very large, but as fat as a hog.
IZAAK WALTON, *The Compleat Angler* (Part I, 1653).

Bream angler (1972) (Photograph: Alfred Pond).

Common bream currently recognised as the British Record, caught in July 1970 by Will Gollins (a member of the 3 Counties specimen group). This 11 lb 12 oz fish was the culmination of a programme of fishing by the group in which several bream over 10 lb were caught in a Shropshire mere (Photograph: Don Bridgewood).

The bream is essentially a fish of lowland lakes and sluggish rivers. According to Alwyne Wheeler in *The Fishes of The British Isles and N.W. Europe* (1969) it is *always* gregarious, and this propensity for shoaling goes a long way to explain its popularity with anglers: the arrival of one bream implies the presence of many others. The experienced match-angler is well aware of this and will attempt to hold a bream shoal within the confines of his swim by heavy ground baiting.

But bream are great wanderers. Although they may be taken by the stone from a particular swim on one occasion, this in no way guarantees their appearance in that swim on any future occasion.

Were it not for anglers the adult bream would be almost entirely a bottom feeder, for its natural food is the flora and fauna of the bottom, which it obtains by grubbing in the mud or silt. When bream are feeding like this in a lake they will seldom take a bait that is not resting on the bottom. In these circumstances the angler is restricted to methods such as ledgering, float-ledgering and laying-on.

In rivers, however, when the angler's maggots, casters and particles of other forms of groundbait are brought to a shoal by means of the current, bream may intercept these items. On such occasions they can be caught by 'swimming the stream' or by 'long-trotting'. Sometimes when bream can see these acceptable offerings drifting down from above, they will even move some way towards the surface to intercept them – and can then be taken 'on the drop'.

The 'big five' bream baits are lobworms,

Britain's largest bream: 13 lb 12 oz found dead in Startops End Reservoir, Tring, on November 19th 1931. It was weighed 2 hours after being taken from the water; the weight verified by Dr Jordan, Curator of Tring Museum. The 50 pence piece resting on the tail fin gives some idea of the size of the bream's 'rudder'.

paste, pinched-crumb, and bunches of maggots or brandlings. The best fishing in some bream waters is to be had at night. Although still-water bream fishing is generally considered to be a sport of the summer and autumn months, many good bream are now taken in winter. F. B. has taken bream from Wilstone reservoir (a big-bream water at Tring) on a day when groundbait was used to free the float from newly formed ice. When the water temperature is low the slightest sign of a bite, be it registered on dough-bobbin, swingtip or float, should receive the angler's immediate attention.

Although the bream is a poor fighter it must be struck and played carefully on light tackle. This is particularly so when hooked in the swollen waters of flooded rivers, where the pressure of the stream increases the fish's resistance.

A perplexing aspect of bream fishing is the sudden disappearance of quality fish after several increasingly good seasons. The Tring complex of reservoirs in Hertfordshire, the most famous of all big-bream waters, provides an example of this. After producing a series of big bream during the period 1931–33 the reservoirs of Startops End and Marsworth produced nothing of note until the period 1938–40 when again they were responsible for many near-record and one new record fish. The best years for big fish were the years 1933 and 1940. In 1933 there were fish of 12 lb 14 oz, 12 lb, 11 lb 12 oz, 11 lb 11½ oz, 10 lb 15 oz, 10 lb 14 oz, 10 lb 12 oz, 10 lb 11 oz, 10 lb 9 oz, 10 lb 8 oz, 10 lb 8 oz, 10 lb 7 oz, 10 lb 4 oz, 10 lb 4 oz and 10 lb 3 oz. In 1934 not a single double-figure fish was taken.

The most notable catch was from Startops

Vic Evans, a familar figure in the London tackle trade but a fly fisherman by persuasion, tries his hand for coarse fish on Tring's Wilstone Reservoir.

End on July 31st 1939, when Frank Bench of Coventry took bream of 8 lb, 9 lb, 10 lb, 11 lb, 12 lb, 12½ lb, and 12 lb 15 oz – which broke the previous record.

A few large fish survived to be caught during 1940, then once again these reservoirs lived on their reputations until the next double-figure bream was caught in 1945.

A probable explanation of the temporary disappearance of big bream may be found in a brief study of population dynamics. Although the stock of bream in any given water may consist of individuals varying from one to twelve or thirteen years old, each shoal usually consists of survivors from a certain year-class, i.e. fish surviving from one season's spawning. Due to death from various natural causes the number of fish in each succeeding year-class diminishes. As a result the population pattern of bream (like that of other fish) can be compared to the formation of stones in a pyramid.

The first-year fish, being the most numerous, are represented by the stones that make up the base layer of the pyramid. Succeeding years are represented by the gradually diminishing numbers of stones that make up the succeeding layers. The last surviving fish in the oldest year-class is represented by the apex stone. From this pattern of a progressively diminishing number of fish in each year-class we can see why large fish are comparatively rare. From time to time, however, one particular year-class, survives in unusually large numbers. This flourishing year-class remains as a population bulge throughout the shoal-members' lifespan, and during the later years of its existence provides anglers with unusually good sport. When these fish have died, many years may elapse before replacement shoals of the same quality fish occur. During its tenancy the year-class of a population bulge represents such an enormous burden on the food supply that for a time subsequent year-classes are impoverished and diminished.

COOKING THE BREAM

The bream is considered of little consequence as food – at least in Britain. H. F. once breakfasted on fried bream while camping near the Broads . . . he was very hungry. But for those who want to make what they can of it, here are three other recipes – for which we are grateful to *The Sporting Wife* by Barbara Hargreaves (2nd edition, 1971).

1 *Stuffed Bream*

1 bream, 1½–2 lb
1 oz butter
Flour
1 tablespoonful, lemon juice
Forcemeat
Salt and pepper

Forcemeat
½ small onion, grated
1 oz grated cheese
2 oz sliced mushrooms
1 small cupful cooked rice
1 tablespoonful chopped chives
1 dessertspoonful chopped parsley
Grated lemon rind
Nutmeg
Cayenne pepper
1 oz butter
4 tablespoonsful cream
1 beaten egg
Salt and pepper

Fry the onion and mushrooms in butter and mix the rice and cheese. Add all other ingredients and blend well. Put nearly all the butter in a fireproof dish. Stuff the fish with the forcemeat and place in the dish. Sprinkle with flour and seasoning and dot with the rest of the butter; then sprinkle with lemon juice. Cover dish with greased paper or foil. Bake in a moderate oven for 40–50 minutes according to size of fish.

2 *Brème à la Mode du Pêcheur*

1 bream
Shallots
White wine
Butter
Breadcrumbs

Place the cleaned fish upon a bed of chopped shallots and breadcrumbs, in a fireproof dish, and cover the fish with the same mixture. Add the white wine and part of butter and cook in a medium oven for 25 minutes, adding wine and butter as needed to keep the fish moist.

3 *Baked Bream*

Clean the fish and remove head and fins. Score the sides. Chop onion and garlic and place in bottom of a fireproof dish. Slice a lemon thinly and put one slice in each of the scores. Lay the fish in the dish and squeeze the juice from any of the lemon that is left over on to the fish. Pour two tablespoonfuls of oil over the fish and sprinkle with breadcrumbs. Cover with lid or foil and cook in a moderate oven for 30 minutes. Remove foil and leave the fish in the oven until the breadcrumbs are browned and the fish is cooked right through. Serve very hot.

In Europe the bream had, and indeed still has, some sort of reputation as a table fish. As Walton said: 'Though some do not, yet the French esteem this fish highly, and to that end have a proverb: "He that hath breams in his pond is able to bid his friend welcome." '

Well – maybe.

4 · The Silver Bream

Blicca bjoerkna

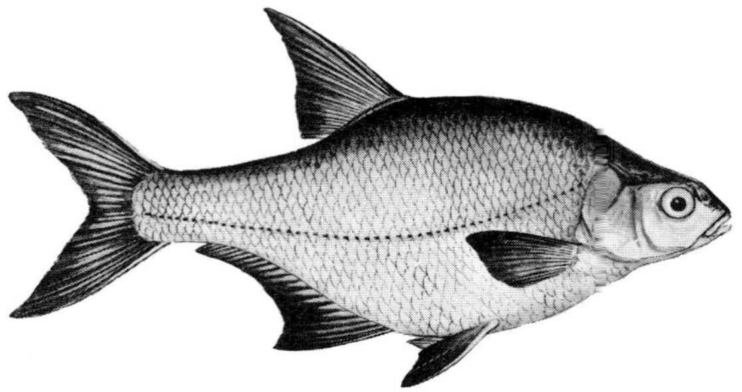

The silver bream, also known as white bream or bream-flat, is widely distributed in lakes and slow-running rivers throughout Europe north of the Alps and Pyrenees and eastwards to the U.S.S.R. It is absent from Norway and occurs in the British Isles only in the eastern countries of England, north of the Thames.

That two separate species of bream exist was recognized over five hundred years ago by Dame Juliana Berners.[1] Nevertheless, few anglers seem able to differentiate between them. The following extract comes from *Fish and Fishing* (1877) by Dr J. J. Manley.

> The white bream is a fish hardly worth pen, ink and paper. It seldom exceeds a pound in weight, and though its colouring is pretty enough, being very silvery, it is covered with an indescribably nasty slime, something like starch, and almost as difficult to get off the fingers as bird lime.

Manley was wrong. The silver bream is *not* a slimy fish. What he has described is, in fact, a small common, bronze bream (*Abramis brama*). The following points of recognition refer to the silver bream:

1. It seldom exceeds ten inches in length.
2. It is not a slimy fish. As a result, its scales readily become detached when handled.
3. It is a much more slender fish than the common bream.
4. Its eye is noticeably large.
5. With its silvery sides and green-tinted back, it closely resembles the bleak in colouring.

Since it has been said that silver bream occur in the Royalty Fishery on the Hampshire Avon, and that common bream are absent from the Throop Fishery on the Dorset Stour, it is worth recording that Richard Walker (for whose opinion we have the highest regard) states that all the bream he has caught in the Housepool on the Royalty have been common bream, and that he has caught common bream and roach/common bream hybrids from the Throop Fishery, at Nettlebed.

1 'It was long doubted whether what was supposed to be a second species of Bream in our lakes was truly distinct. . . . Yet that they [breamflats or silver bream] were believed to be distinct fishes in very early times appears from the *Book of St Albans*, where Bremettis are mentioned separately, as to be fished for with some difference of baits; and that they are distinct fishes is now generally admitted. . . .' JONATHAN COUCH, *British Fishes* (Vol. 4, 1877).

5 · The Bullhead or Miller's Thumb

Cottus gobio

Notwithstanding the disgust which the form of the *Bull-head* creates, the largest, when the heads are cut off, are very delicious eating . . .
THE REV. W. B. DANIEL, *Rural Sports* (1801).

This aggressive little fish grows to a length of three to four inches. It is of no angling interest, save that it may compete with other species for food such as bottom-living invertebrates and fly larvae. It lives a solitary life, fiercely defending a small hole or crevice under rock or stones – from which it seldom emerges except at night. It dislikes company, and emits a distinctive threat call – a sharp 'barking' sound – when approached too closely by another bullhead.

The fish called Loches, and the other called Millers-thumbes or Culles, they always feede in the bottome of brookes, and rivers. They are fish holesome to be eaten of feeble persons having an ague, or other sicknesse.
LEONARD MASCALL, *A Booke of Fishing with Hooke and Line* (1590).

There is indisputable evidence that bullheads are occasionally eaten by pike. Dr J. Paling, of Oxford Scientific Films, has taken some remarkable film of a small pike seizing a bullhead from its lair. The pike seemed to have difficulty in swallowing the bullhead owing to the spiny nature of this prey. Eventually it succeeded in doing so, after regurgitating and then re-swallowing. Altogether, the operation took about half-an-hour.

6 · The Burbot

Lota lota

We Londoners very seldom see or hear of a burbolt, and they are such a stupid and ugly fish that I cannot advise trouble to be taken with their dissemination, though doubtless they would thrive in many of our ponds and lakes . . .
The flesh is said to be good, especially the liver when fried, but it is indigestible.
FRANK BUCKLAND, *The Natural History of British Fishes* (1880).

A specimen of a British burbot (Lota lota), *burbot or 'eel pout'. It was caught on a ledgered worm by the Rev E. C. Alston in 1936 in the stream that runs out of Stamford Water near Thetford in Norfolk. One of his fishing companions at that time, the late W. Griggs, proprietor of the most famous of all fish taxidermist firms J. Cooper & Sons, later caught three of these little fishes.*

A burbot or burbolt from Couch's British Fishes *(1862). Specimens of three feet or more have been recorded in Siberia, but the length of a typical adult would be 12–14 in.*

The burbot, pout, or eel-pout was once common in most of the East Anglian streams and although local in distribution, was not uncommon in the rivers of Durham, Yorkshire, Lincolnshire and Cambridgeshire. It is now very rare.

Anglers fortunate enough to catch one should not be put off by the unknown author of *The Arte of Angling (1577)*, one of the earliest fishing books, who described the pout as 'an ill-favoured fish': 'Rather give me the carpe, than the poute . . . for the head of the one is better than the liver of the other.' We can guess that the author was probably alluding to the ugliness of the pout's head (more particularly to its protruding lips) and to the excellent flavour of its liver, since the pout's liver was considered a great delicacy at that time. The ancients were no fools: modern science reveals that the pout's liver is rich in vitamin A.

Shakespeare, the most famous contemporary of this unknown author, also referred to the appearance of our little fish when he said: 'Like a misbehaved and sullen wench, Thou pout'st upon thy fortune and thy love'.

We can think of nothing else to say about the burbot. Never having caught or tasted one, we can offer no advice on how to catch or cook it.

7 · The Carp

Cyprinus carpio

It is generally believed that the common carp was introduced into Britain from the Continent during the Middle Ages. In *A Treatyse of Fysshynge wyth an Angle*, published in 1496, but in all probability written sometime between 1406 and 1425, the author (supposedly Dame Juliana Berners) wrote:

> The carpe is a deyntous fysshe: but there ben but fewe in Englonde. And therefore I wryte the lasse of hym.

It is interesting, therefore, to learn from Arthur Bryant's *The Age of Chivalry*, that in 1248, John Pechum, an Oxford friar, when created Archbishop of Canterbury, had to provide for his enthronement feast (in addition to other items):

> . . . 300 ling, 600 cod, 40 fresh salmon, 7 barrels of salt salmon, 5 barrels of salt sturgeon, 600 fresh eels, 8,000 whelks, 100 pike, 400 tench, *100 carp* [our italics], 800 bream, 1,400 lampreys, 200 large roach, besides seals, porpoises and 'pophyns'!

If there were indeed 'but fewe' English carp about at the beginning of the 15th century, the provision of a *hundred* for a 13th century feast seems a pretty stiff order.

How Pechum solved his problem is not recorded, but his enthronement seems to have been responsible for the first mention of the carp in English history.

> Twice the carp shot off with such speed that the reel overran, checked and gave [them] warning. On the fourth occasion one of the monsters made a direct run of thirty yards and then broke me, the fine gut cast parting above the float. There then occurred an incident that illustrates the uncanny nature of these fish. My float, lying out in the middle of the pond, turned and sailed slowly in again to my very feet, towed by the monster who then in some manner freed himself, thus returning me my tackle with a sardonic invitation to try again. No other fish is capable of putting so fine a point on irony.
>
> ARTHUR RANSOME, *Rod and Line* (1929).

A common carp of 12 lb – outwitted by Bill Keal.

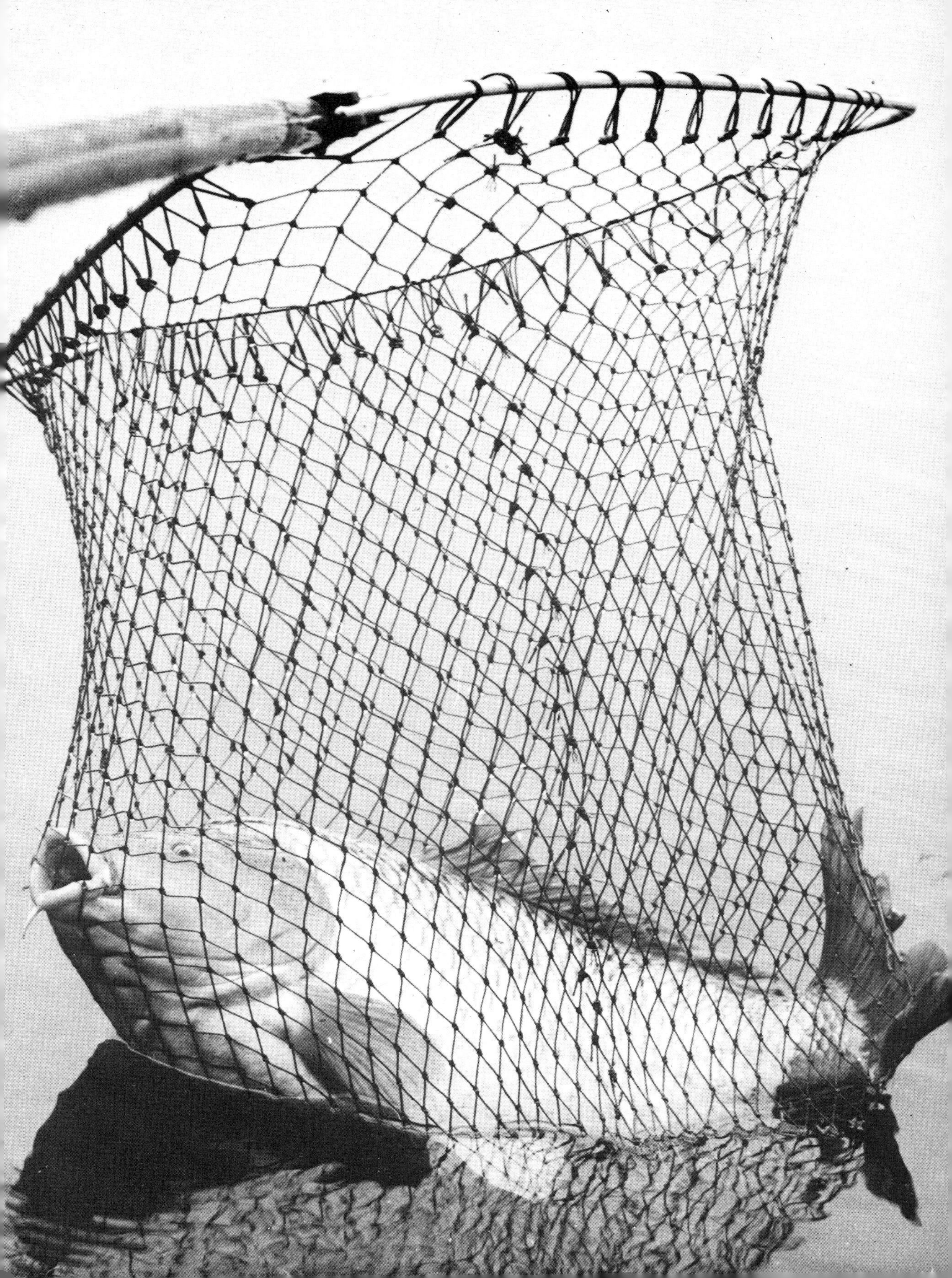

Playing a $31\frac{1}{4}$ lb carp in Redmire Pool (1954). Note the kneeling position – to keep out of sight of the fish.

Below: *The fish immediately after landing. In spite of its immense size, it is most comfortably accommodated within the net frame.* *(See Richard Walker's comments on p. 392.)*

Since its introduction, the carp has survived in its preferred habitat of small lakes and certain sections of a few slow-flowing rivers. Although nowadays treated as a sport fish, it was originally cultivated by members of religious orders, as one of the fish foods which was allowable on the numerous 'days of abstinence'.

Except for a few new colonies that have become established as a result of fish making good their escape from flooded ponds or stews, all British carp populations appear to have been man-made.

Carp spawn during the late spring or summer if and when the water temperature rises to 64–68°F. Because of their intolerance of low temperature at spawning time, carp living in water whose temperature in certain years does not reach the required temperature level are unable to spawn. This must occasionally happen in Britain.

Carp fishing, at least in temperate latitudes, is essentially a pursuit of the summer and autumn months. Although in mild winters sport may be obtained with fish that have not yet started their hibernation, or with fish that have broken their hibernation, winter carp fishing is undesirable.

Winter hibernation is characterized by a cessation, or at least a sharp reduction of food consumption, and a consequent fall in the level of metabolism. These combine to reduce the demand on the energy that has been accumulated in the carp's body in the form of fat deposits. Hibernation results from the fish's need to adapt to the absence of vegetating plants and to the relatively low oxygen content of the water during a period of ice cover. Even with minimal activity, an overwintering fish must be in good condition with sufficient reserves of fat if it is to survive. In an experiment, Kirpichnikov (1958), demonstrated that small carp with a 1·92 condition factor survived for only six days when kept at a temperature of 0°C, whereas those with a 2·40 to 2·50 condition factor[1] survived for over 40 days at the same temperature.

Perhaps the problem of overwintering explains the failure of the common carp to penetrate our river systems. It is likely that extremely cold winters make demands on the fat reserves of river carp that prove fatal, in which case it is easy to understand why the best river-carp fisheries are found in areas downstream of hot-water effluents.

That the common carp sustains itself in Great Britain rather uneasily is not surprising when one remembers that it is an exotic species 'planted' beyond its natural boundaries[2]. In recent years, however, the carp's promotion to the status of a major

1 The condition of a fish can be assessed by relating the ratio of its length to its weight. The larger the ratio the better the condition.

Thus: $$\Omega = \frac{W\,100}{L^3}$$

Where W is the weight of the fish
L is its length　　Ω is the condition coefficient

2 The case of the crucian carp (p. 34) is somewhat different. This species can actually survive freezing. From the evidence available – its tolerance of low temperatures, of low oxygen requirement, and the spread of habitat – there is every reason to suspect that the crucian carp is indigenous.

sport fish has resulted in many attempts at starting new carp fisheries.

The main problem when creating a carp fishery in a temperate climate is the difficulty of reconciling the carp's need for deep water in winter (so that it can escape the deoxygenation of shallow water when ice cover is prolonged), with its need for very warm water during the breeding season (high temperature is only regularly achieved in water that warms up quickly – i.e. *shallow* water). From this it will be seen that the ideal carp water is a shallow lake or pond containing at least one sizeable pocket of deep water.

The carp is an extremely cautious fish. So much so that until the 1940s, the main problem of catching carp was finding a line strong enough to hold the fish, yet fine enough to escape its notice. To the old school of carp fishermen this problem was insoluble – so they fished with light tackle and banked on their skill to land the fish. The result was that they caught many carp but very few large ones. Albert Buckley's record carp of 26 lb caught in 1930, on 4x gut and a size 10 hook, represented the very pinnacle of achievement using the old methods. Today the record stands at 44 lb, and hardly a season passes without a thirty pounder being caught: that record has, however, stood since 1952.

From what has been said, a reader who has yet to fish for carp might suspect that the carp is strong as well as cunning. He would be right. The strength and cunning of carp are both prodigous and legendary.

Nearly 400 years ago the anonymous author of the second known angling book in the English language, *The Arte of Angling*, offered this timeless advice to the carp angler:

> The best bait that ever I did know for the killing of Carpe, is, a quantitie of sufference, with a good deale of patience, and as much silence as may be possible, all these mingled together.

Several books have been written on the subject of carp fishing; the most notable being Richard Walker's *Still-Water Angling*, and James Gibbinson's *Carp*[1]. The modern carp-angler uses a powerful rod like the Hardy 'R. W.' carp rod, a monofilament line of 10–14 lb B.S. and a straight-eyed hook tied direct to the main line. He takes with him a landing-net capable of enclosing a 50 pounder and a sack to keep the fish in. Another important item is an electric bite alarm, or a glowbobbin (see page 380). Leads and floats are rarely used nowadays although the leaded tackle described on page 456 is an excellent rig when the angler is fishing into the wind.

Margin-fishing with floating crust is a technique specially associated with carp. One of the biggest thrills an angler can experience is to see a big carp suck down his piece of crust – a moment of palpitating excitement. Whatever method is used to catch carp (and there are times when most of the methods described in this book are possible), *the tackle must be free-running*. A carp *must* be allowed to run with the bait

1 RICHARD WALKER, *Still-Water Angling*, MacGibbon & Kee, 1953. JAMES GIBBINSON, *Carp*, Macdonald, 1968.

without feeling any drag. Carp fishing demands a fixed-spool reel – and until the moment of the strike the bale arm must always be left open.

Because carp fishing is a waiting game many carp fishermen take their beds with them.

The three varieties of carp. Left: *fully-scaled common carp.* Right: *scaleless mirror carp.* Bottom: *partially-scaled leather carp.*

Opercular bone from Walker's record 44 lb carp.

Opercular bone from a fifteen-year-old pike.

Although scientists prefer to have an opercular bone for determining the age of a fish, an opercular can only be obtained if the fish is dead. An alternative method is to read a scale taken from a fish's shoulder. Both photographs show the annuli or growth checks with remarkable clarity.

DETERMINING THE AGE OF FISH

Scientists use one of three methods for determining the age of fish.

1. Scale reading.
2. Otolith (ear bone) reading.
3. Opercular (gill bone) reading.

All three methods are based on the principle that a fish grows at a faster rate during the summer than it does during the winter, and that *it continues to grow throughout its life.*

Each year of growth produces a series of rings (or circuli) on a fish's scales and bones (unlike a tree that produces one ring each year). During a period of quick summer-growth these rings are well spaced, whereas

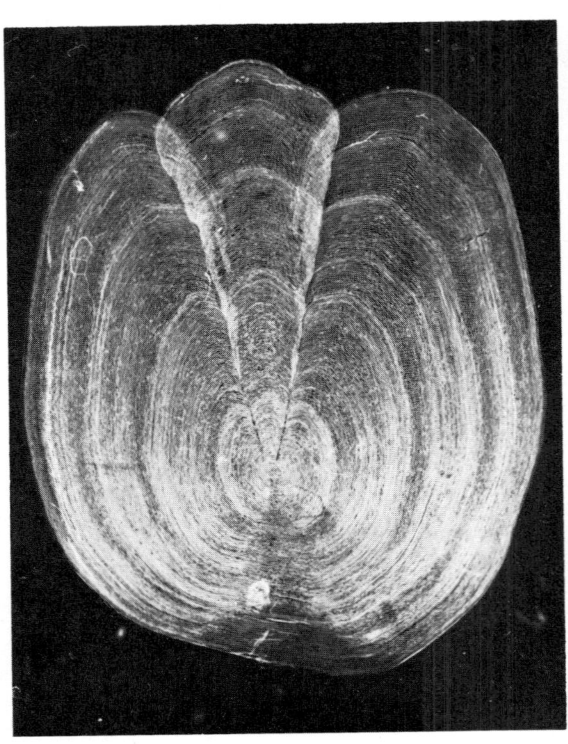

Scale from a five-year-old pike.

(Photographs: The Freshwater Biological Association.)

during a period of slow winter-growth the rings are close together and form what is known as a 'growth check'.

Counting these checks (or annuli) is commonly the basis for determining the age of a fish. But in *Pike* (published in 1971) F.B. suggested that it is possible for a fish to go on living after it has stopped growing, and that this last phase of its life would not be recorded on its bones. Hoping that Richard Walker's record carp might one day provide the necessary evidence he wrote (in 1968):

This fish weighed 44 lb at the time of capture (1952) and its scale reading indicated an age of 15 years. Nevertheless, Walker's fish has survived a further 16 years at the London Zoo and is still alive. This fish now weighs a lot less than it did when it was caught. In the circumstances we can hardly expect the scales or opercular bones to record the non-growing phase of its life. We expect the reading to indicate an age of 15 but we know the fish to be at least 31 years old.

F.B. was right. After the carp's death in 1971, when it was 34 years old, he was able to obtain one of its opercular bones (see previous page). A reading of this bone showed *no indication of the last 19 years of the carp's life*.

Note: It should be remembered that the carp in question was living in an unnatural environment, with limited space and fairly constant water temperature, incidence of light and food availability. Until further research has been made it would be unwise to apply this finding to fish living in natural conditions. It is, however, permissible to say that *in certain circumstances a fish can live for a period of time without linear growth and without recording this non-growing phase of life on its scales and bones*.

Peter Thomas holding Richard Walker's record carp; from an original painting by Maurice Ingham.

Mirror carp from Redmire Pool.

It is common practice in *Holland* to keep *carp* alive for three weeks or a month, by placing them in a *net*, well wrapped up with *wet moss*, hanging them up in a cellar or cool place, and feeding them with *bread* and *milk* . . .
THE REV W. B. DANIEL, *Rural Sports* (1801).

COOKING THE CARP

Walton's Carp

Marjoram
Thyme
Parsley
Rosemary
Savoury
Onions
Pickled oysters
Anchovies
Claret wine
Salt
Cloves
Mace
Oranges
Lemons
Butter
3 egg yolks
1 carp

Take a carp and rub him clean with water and salt, but scale him not; then open him; and put him, with his blood and his liver, which you must save when you open him, into a small pot or kettle; then take sweet marjoram, thyme, and parsley, of each half a handful, a sprig of rosemary, and another of savoury; bind them into two or three small bundles and put them in your Carp, with four or five whole onions, twenty pickled oysters, and three anchovies. Then pour upon your Carp as much claret wine as will only cover him; and season your claret well with salt, cloves, and mace, and the rinds of oranges and lemons. That done, cover your pot and set it on a quick fire till it be sufficiently boiled. Then take out the Carp; and lay it with the broth, into the dish; and pour upon it a quarter of a pound of the best fresh butter, melted and beaten with half a dozen spoonfuls of the broth, the yolks of two or three eggs, and some of the herbs shred. Garnish your dish with lemons, and so serve it up. And much good do you.

IZAAK WALTON, *The Compleat Angler*.

Carp Delicious

Handful of chopped sorrel
Bread
Shallots
Cream
Salt and pepper
Garlic
Bayleaf
Plain flour
Chopped anchovies
Butter
Chopped chives
Parsley
3 eggs, hardboiled
3 raw yolks
Thyme
Mushrooms
Capers
Fish stock
Lemon juice

[After this lot a carp seems superfluous. However, we will press on.]

Put a handful of prepared, washed and chopped sorrel, a piece of butter, a piece of bread, chopped chives, parsley, and shallots into a saucepan and simmer for ten minutes. Add some cream and simmer till mixed. Hardboil three eggs; chop the yolks and add to the mixture with three raw yolks, salt and black pepper. Stuff the cleaned carp with this mixture and sew it up; put the whole to marinate in oil seasoned with salt, pepper, chives, garlic, thyme, and bayleaf. When ready, grill, basting with marinade.

Put chopped mushrooms in a saucepan and simmer in a little butter; let them cool and add a pinch of flour, capers, chopped anchovies, parsley, chives, shallots, butter, stock, salt and pepper. Cook gently and finish with a little lemon juice or a dash of vinegar.

Serve the carp on a hot dish with this sauce.

Recipe by MANUEL DE LA FRIANDAISE (1796) cited in *The Sporting Wife*.

8 · The Crucian Carp

Carassius carassius

Although the crucian carp was reported as having been caught in the Thames during the 19th century, it is essentially a fish of lowland still-water ponds and lakes. It is said to be found in certain slow-flowing rivers in south-west England, but we have not heard of this being confirmed.

The crucian is a hardy fish, tolerant of extremely cold water and water of comparatively low oxygen content. It can be distinguished from the common carp by the following means:

1. It lacks the barbules of the common carp.
2. It is deeper in the body than the common carp; its depth of body being equal to half its length.
3. It has an elevated convex dorsal fin, the trailing edge of which points to the origin of the tail.
4. It has a characteristic hump-back.

In favourable conditions it attains a length of ten to twelve inches and a weight of about two pounds. Exceptionally (in Europe) it grows to 18 inches and a weight of seven pounds.

The British record crucian carp is 4 lb 11 oz. It was taken by H. C. Hinson from Broadwater lake at Godalming in September, 1938.

Crucian carp fishing is a summer/autumn activity. The bait should be fished on or near the bottom. All the usual roach baits (with the exception of hemp) can be tried with hope of success.

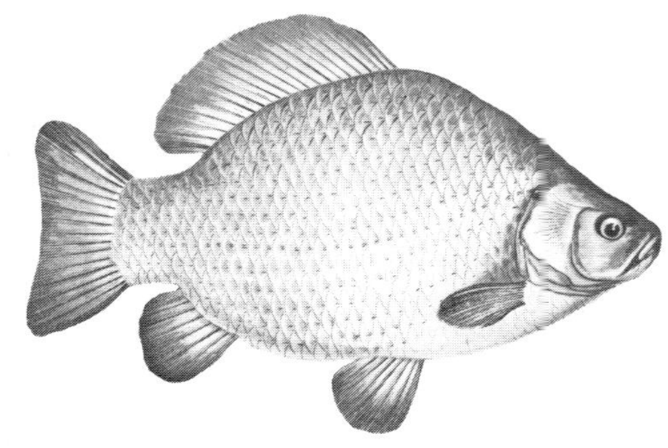

Crucian carp, from Couch's British Fishes *(1862).*

One of the London Angling Association's lakes near Rickmansworth, Hertfordshire, provides capital sport for crucians. The officers of this association, being far-sighted, offer Associate Membership to all-comers. By calling at one of the main London tackle shops, anglers from anywhere in Britain can join the L.A.A., with a view to catching (among other species) big crucian carp.

9 · The Catfish

Silurus glanis

Another fish that would do well in this country is the Cat-fish (Pimelodus). It is a species of Silurus, also called the Bullhead and Bull-pout. They are found in all the waters of North America. In some places it is esteemed a great delicacy, equal to an eel. FRANK BUCKLAND, *The Natural History of British Fishes* (1881).

Record catfish, 43 lb 8 oz, caught by Richard Bray of Chesham, Bucks, on a four inch dead roach-bait intended for pike. It was taken from Wilstone Reservoir at Tring in September, 1970. According to B. Double, bailiff at Tring, catfish have never been introduced into Wilstone Reservoir. It seems likely that small catfish found their way from Marsworth into the canal and thence into Wilstone. The Tring complex of lakes: Wilstone, Marsworth and Startops End are connected as part of a water supply system for the nearby Grand Union Canal (Photograph: Frank Guttfield).

Catfish are often described as having six whiskers. This description fits the American catfish, but not the European, the wels. The latter has two large feelers on the top side of the mouth, and four small barbules, ½ in. to 1 in. long, underneath the chin (Photograph: Bob Rolph).

The European catfish (*Silurus glanis*), sometimes known as the 'wels', was introduced into a number of British lakes including the lake complexes at Claydon in Buckinghamshire, Tring in Hertfordshire and Woburn Abbey in Bedfordshire. It has perpetuated itself in all three waters and at Claydon lake is regularly caught by a few specialist 'cat' anglers.

The wels catfish in suitable conditions can grow to a remarkable size. Specimens measuring 16½ ft and weighing up to 660 lb have been recorded from the U.S.S.R. It is an active night feeder and like most night feeding fishes possesses very small eyes. It has two long feelers (8 in. long for a 20 lb fish) on the top side of the jaw and four small barbules (½ in. to 1 in.) on the underside of the chin; these indicate its preference for bottom feeding. Of all types of bottoms it prefers mud. The name 'wels' derives from the German 'walzen' (English 'wallow') from its habit of wallowing in mud.

The wels is mainly a lake dweller, although it also flourishes in the deep parts of large rivers. In eastern Europe the catfish spawns between May and July in the marshy areas of lakes. River catfish usually migrate upstream before or during a flood in order to spawn over suitable areas of flooded land.

Although its scavenging habits are well known, the catfish is undoubtedly predatory and piscivorous (fish eating) and many are caught on fish baits.

Three British anglers, R. Rolph, R. Blackmore and D. Cruickshank are known to be specialist cat-anglers and we are indebted to them for guidance on catfishing techniques.

These three anglers prepare their swims by pre-baiting with freshwater mussels. Of all baits they have found mussel to be the most effective, although *continued* use of this bait has resulted in a drop-off in catches. Settled periods of warm, windless weather have been the most productive. Early in the season the period between dusk and 2 a.m. produces most bites, but as the season progresses feeding times become more irregular, with fish sometimes taking during the hours of daylight.

Their tackle has consisted of a carp rod and fixed-spool reel with 10–12 lb B.S. nylon. Hooks, sizes 1 or 2, were used to lip-hook a variety of deadbaits: rudd, perch, roach and small bream. The angling method was ledgering – carp style – with balearm pickup left open to allow the 'cats' to run with the

Robert A. Rolph with a 21 lb wels. It is generally supposed that the first British water to hold the wels catfish was Woburn Abbey lake – where catfish were introduced at the request of the Russell family in 1880. But according to Dr Albert Gunther, one time curator of the Ichthyological Department of the British Museum, there were specimens of the wels catfish in Britain before 1866. Gunther, who was opposed to the introduction of the zander but in favour of introducing the wels, stated that the Acclimatisation Society of Great Britain possessed live specimens of the wels in 1864.

bait. Premature striking invariably resulted in failure to hook the fish.

By such methods these three anglers accounted for 38 catfish over 10 lb in three seasons. A remarkable achievement – and a just reward for their keenness and perseverance.

Note: Enthusiastic catfish-anglers may be interested to know that West African catfish can be caught on ledgered cubes of bar soap. These catfish often feed on palm nuts. Palm nuts are made into palm oil, which is used in soap manufacture. Hence this somewhat unusual bait!

This catfish, estimated weight 40–45 lb, was found in Marsworth Reservoir, c. 1934. Holding the fish are C. E. Double, grandfather of the present Tring Bailiff, and T. Plumridge. This huge 'cat' was probably one of the seven small catfish put into Marsworth Reservoir many years before; the seven were probably descendants of the seventy catfish originally introduced into Woburn Abbey, from Germany in 1880. Another huge catfish, estimated weight 50 lb, was found dead in Marsworth Reservoir, c. 1943 (Photograph: B. Double).

COOKING THE CATFISH

Although the prospect of eating catfish seems rather daunting, Alwyne Wheeler in *The Fishes of The British Isles and North-West Europe*, states that the wels is a valuable commercial fish in Russia, where the eggs are said to be used as a substitute for caviar or to adulterate genuine caviar. The Russians have a high opinion of catfish flesh (as have the Americans for their own species of catfish *Amiurus lacustris*); indeed they find a use for the whole body since they process catfish skin into leather.

Photograph: *The Angler's Mail.*

10 · The Charr

Salvelinus alpinus

The boat drifts on. The rise for the moment is done. Then, suddenly, I am playing another, but? But? The quarter-pounder that comes fighting to the net is scarlet and green and orange – oh surely here is such a capture as never man made before! And yet, 'It's just a bit char,' says Chisholm dispassionately. 'There's ay an odd yin in here.'

There is a pannikin, a bailer, in the boat and, moved by some precocious sense of beauty, the angler scoops the same full of the cold, deep, water, enlarges the char in it alive, and desires that the boat may be rowed to the beach that the elder person may at once wonder and mark.

And wonder and mark he does, telling the while of the loveliness and antiquity of chars.

And, 'What are you going to do with it?' he asks. An awkward question that. 'Oh, I dunno; kill it, I suppose.'

'Nonsense,' says the elder person. 'Why, you've made a pet of it now, one simply doesn't kill pets – far better put the poor little chap back into the loch again.'

So, a trifle perhaps, in the devotional spirit of David the King, when he 'coupit'

the water of the well of Bethlehem,
outboard the bailer is inverted, and, with a
kick of colour, the char is gone.

PATRICK CHALMERS, *The Angler's England* (1938).

The charr[1] populations of the British Isles are a series of non-migratory, lake dwelling colonies of fishes belonging to the salmon family (Salmonidae). They are found in several deep lakes of the English Lake District and north Wales, and in many of the deep lakes in Scotland and Ireland.

Whether these charr populations represent a number of different species and subspecies (as classified by Tate Regan and other authorities) remains undetermined. The present taxonomic situation is one of considerable confusion. Until further studies have been completed it seems reasonable to consider the British and Irish charr as varieties of the charr found in alpine lakes of the northern hemisphere, in countries as widely separated as Greenland, Russia, Japan and North America. In the arctic, the charr is migratory, and like salmon and sea-trout is an anadromous fish (that is, the adult fish feeds in the sea, enters freshwater rivers to spawn and returns to sea after breeding).

All lake-dwelling charr are probably descended from a migratory stock whose extensive habitat shrank to its present size some 11,500 years ago when during the last ice age the ice retreated north. It has been suggested that the migratory charr became a freshwater species as a result of being land-locked in lakes which formed behind terminal moraines when these were deposited by melting glaciers. It seems more likely, however, that the evolution was more gradual, and that a true lake-dwelling variety came about as a result of certain migratory charr exploiting these lakes.

A similar instance of an originally anadromous fish adapting itself to a freshwater situation is provided by the offspring of the coho salmon introduced into Lake Michigan which have apparently accepted this new environment as a 'sea' feeding ground, and spawn in rivers which flow into the lake. As a result, a purely freshwater variety of the coho salmon has been established.

Adult lake charr in Britain average 10 to 12 inches in length; but in favourable conditions will attain 16 inches. In the exceptional conditions of Lac Leman (Geneva), charr reach a length of 31 inches and a weight of 22 lb. This size is similar to that recorded for the sea-fed migratory race of charr.

Charr usually live in deep water. Alwyne Wheeler in *The Fishes of the British Isles and North-West Europe*, records that in Lac Leman charr are mostly found at depths of 100 to 230 feet, and sometimes as deep as 325 feet. R. P. Hardie in *Ferox and Char* (1940), his work on charr distribution in Scotland, quotes James Murray who, in enumerating the animals found in the 'abyssal' region of Loch Ness, mentions a small charr 'dredged at a depth of over 500 feet'.

1 Though the spelling *char* has been commonly used – and seems to be endemic in Ireland – we prefer the older form.

◁ *Windermere charr taken on a deep-trailing rig.*

Tim Dinsdale who is at present (May 1971) investigating Loch Ness, states that charr are abundant in the loch and swim at depths down to 400 feet. (Were the existence of a 'monster' verified, and should it prove to be a fish-eater, charr could constitute its basic diet).

R. P. Hardie was of the opinion that charr were the diet of the mighty *Salmo-ferox*, and in his book traced the link between these fish. Studies at Konigsee Lake in Austria reveal that the charr is the staple diet of the large Konigsee trout.

In the main, charr feed on planktonic crustacea, although insect larvae, shrimps, molluscs and small fish also feature in their diet.

THE HABITS OF WINDERMERE CHARR

The best known British charr are those of Lake Windermere, which have been intensively studied by Dr W. E. Frost of the Freshwater Biological Association. Windermere holds two distinct charr populations: the *autumn* spawners and the *spring* spawners. The autumn spawners breed on gravel shallows in three to twelve feet of water near the shore during November and December. The spring spawners breed on stony ground in 50 to 70 feet of water during February and March. A small number of charr also run from the lake into the river Brathay and spawn there. These, too, are autumn spawners.

By tagging charr on their breeding grounds it has been established that autumn and spring fish remain true to their respective spawning times and places.

For many years the annual charr run up the river Brathay ceased, or was too small to be noticed. This situation prevailed for some time before, and during, the period when perch trapping (started 1939) and pike netting (started 1945) were in operation. After the removal of many tons of pike and perch the charr population increased, and since 1948 the annual charr run has again become a feature of the Brathay.

Charr normally keep to the deeps and repair to the shallows only to spawn. For this reason they have few opportunities to feed on small fish, and their principal diet is plankton. When small fish also take to the deeps, however, the charr feed on them as greedily as the trout do. Many charr have been seen to regurgitate small perch about an inch long. In a statement given before the Fishery Commissioners at Bowness in 1878, one Mr Jackson declared that he took a three-inch perch from a charr's stomach.

The year 1970 marked what seems to be a change in the traditional behaviour of Windermere charr. According to Albert Dixon, a veteran Windermere charr fisherman, it was the first year he had ever known it possible to catch charr throughout the season without proceeding south of Red Knab – a point midway down the north basin. Perhaps this change in charr behaviour can be linked with the basic change in the whole economy of Windermere. The oligotrophic state (poor in dissolved nutrient salts) of the majority of British mountain lakes, extending

Two charr from Lough Melvin, presented to the Piscatorial Society in 1866 by T. R. Sachs.

from the end of the ice-age, has now changed with relative rapidity in lakes where the human population has increased in the catchment area. Such lakes have been enriched by sewage and crop dressings to the point where they have become eutrophic in character (rich in dissolved nutrient salts). If the process continues at the same rate, lakes that were once ideally suited to members of the Salmonidae – brown trout, sea-trout, salmon, charr and white-fish – will open themselves to members of the Cyprinidae: roach, bream, rudd and tench.

Windermere charr weigh from five ounces to about one pound. Larger fish are occasionally taken, but in a lifetime of fishing, Dixon has had only eight charr over 1 lb. Of these the best was a cock fish of $1\frac{1}{4}$ lb. Although there are records of charr weighing up to 3 lb, a charr of $1\frac{1}{2}$ lb is an exceptional fish. It is therefore interesting to note that a T. Upton, of Sedbergh, introduced some $\frac{1}{2}$ lb Windermere charr into Lilleymere (a lake presumably rich in food) in the autumn of 1839. Two caught on a fly the following August weighed 2 lb apiece.

Following this demonstration of growth rate, it might be interesting to introduce charr fingerlings into one of the deeper and more fertile southern reservoirs.

Nowadays, although fishermen flood into the Lake District in their hundreds, only three boat crews regularly patrol the north basin of Windermere – home of the old sport of plumb-line fishing for charr. And yet – charr fishing on Windermere has never been better than it is today, something that can be said about no other naturally bred freshwater British sportfish. During the 1970 season, Albert Dixon caught 625 of these beautiful vermillion-tinted fish; a figure which compares favourably with the best days of the nineteenth century when (in 1863) a famous Lakeland fisherman caught 509 Windermere charr and trout.

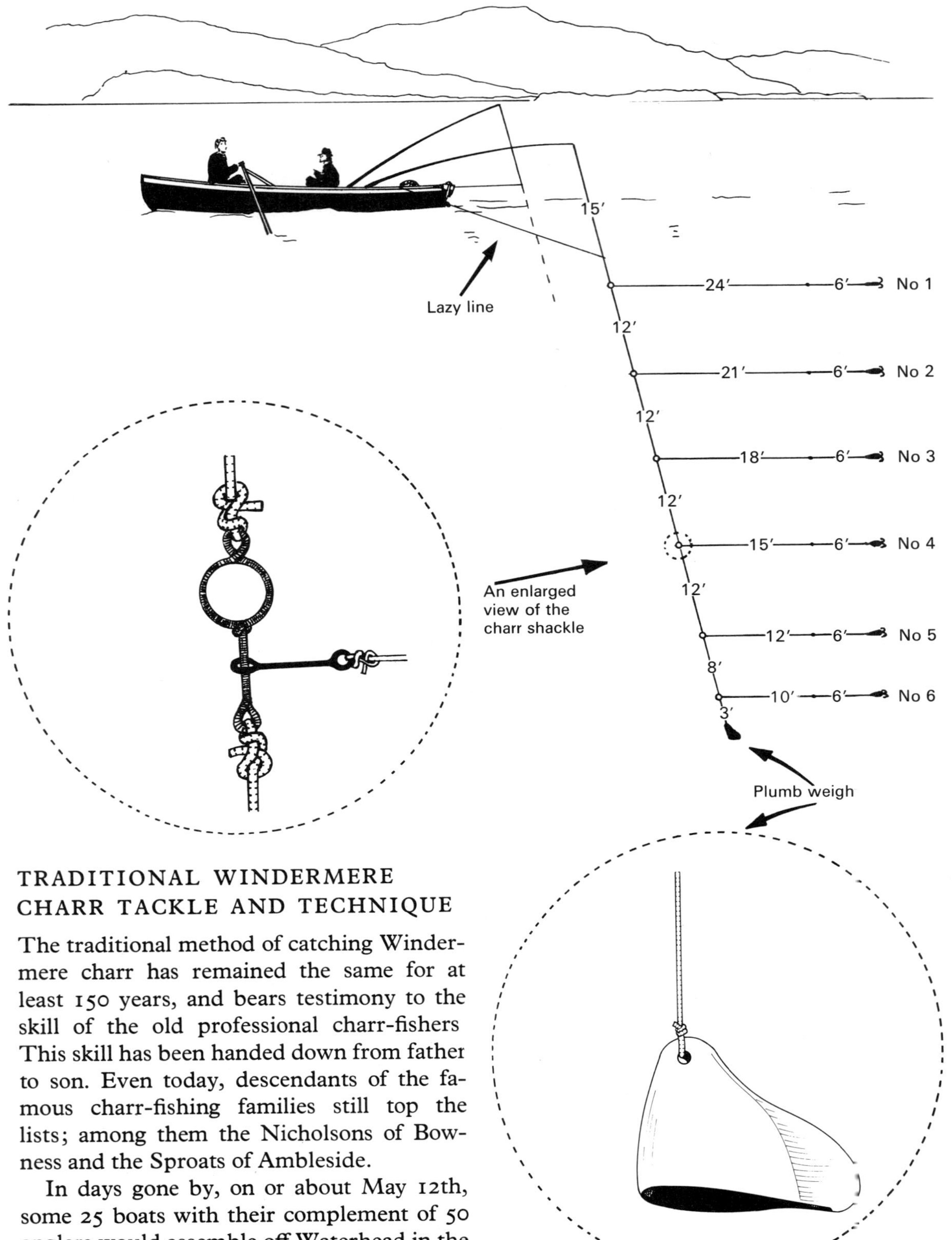

TRADITIONAL WINDERMERE CHARR TACKLE AND TECHNIQUE

The traditional method of catching Windermere charr has remained the same for at least 150 years, and bears testimony to the skill of the old professional charr-fishers This skill has been handed down from father to son. Even today, descendants of the famous charr-fishing families still top the lists; among them the Nicholsons of Bowness and the Sproats of Ambleside.

In days gone by, on or about May 12th, some 25 boats with their complement of 50 anglers would assemble off Waterhead in the North Basin where most of the charr were

Fig. 10.1. Traditional charr trailing tackle.

congregated. This meeting was called The Carnival, and good fishing was expected by all. As the old-time charr fisherman said: 'They'll take a flat-iron in May!' And May is still one of the best fishing months of the season.

Tackle

The basis of the traditional charr trailing-rig is a heavy lead, about 1½ lb, cone shaped in section, and fashioned like a rudder to keep it from twisting. This lead hangs straight down from the boat like a plumbline – hence the phrase 'plumb-lining for charr'.

The lead is suspended at depth from a rod, or spreader, about 18 ft long. Formerly one-piece ash saplings were used, but nowadays one-piece East India canes are the most popular.

The 26 yards of mainline that connects the tip of the rod to the lead is a braided cotton, or cuttyhunk, between 60 and 80 lb B.S., soaked in a mixture of lampblack and boiled linseed oil. After a thorough soaking the the line is hung out under cover for about three weeks to dry. This dressing helps to preserve cotton lines for a number of years. It also stiffens the texture of the line and closes the braid, so that it becomes much easier to handle.

Six droppers are attached to the mainline. The top dropper is tied 15 feet down from the rod tip; the second, third, fourth and fifth at intervals of 12 feet. The sixth and last dropper is tied eight feet below the fifth dropper. The lead is attached two to three feet below the sixth dropper.

The droppers which are not tied directly to the line but to a brass wire charr-shackle, vary in length. The top dropper is 24 feet long, with a six-foot leader, making 30 feet in all. Each lower dropper, proceeding downwards, is three feet shorter than the previous one. This has the effect of making the baits fish vertically in line rather than in echelon.

The line used on the droppers is about 30 lb B.S. and dressed in the same manner as the mainline. The leader (nowadays) is 8 lb B.S. nylon, and incorporates three swivels: one at each end and one in the middle. The spinners are armed with a size 8 treble hook which is fastened to the terminal swivel by means of an oval link.

A set consisting of two sides of charr tackle is carried in a case with three drawers. Two drawers are for the made-up tackle, and the other for various spares; leads, leader material, spinners and hooks. The drawers that contain the complete rig are fitted with a cork shoulder which ensures that the hooks can be seated without snarling

This highly specialized rig, devised by generations of charr fishermen, cannot be purchased. Even the spinners are handmade. These are of two basic types: head spinners and tail spinners (tail spinners are preferred). All baits are made of thin sheet-metal. The finish can be plain silver; or copper and silver (copper on one side and electroplated silver on the other); or brass and silver; or silver and gold-leaf.

For generations, real gold was used in the making of charr baits – a thin gold strip which covered the side of a silver bait. Gold from a sovereign was preferred, and the instructions for using it are quite clear:

'The gold must be beaten out to the thickness of a butterfly wing.'

The old charr fishermen believed that gold from Australian sovereigns had some special charr-catching properties. The last fisherman to own genuine Australian gold baits is believed to have been the late Bruce Squires of Ambleside. These baits were so precious to him that after the 1940 season he never chanced them in the lake again where, as he said: 'Those terrible pike abound!'

Traditional charr tackle case.

Technique

The lead is dropped over the side of the boat and allowed to sink until the first shackle is reached. The big half-inch ring on the shackle is then placed over the nail that projects upwards from the gunwale.

The sixth bait is tossed overboard, the dropper held until the bait is seen to be spinning freely, then released.

As soon as the boat's forward speed tensions the dropper the shackle is lifted off the nail and the next section of mainline fed out until the next shackle is reached – and the process repeated. When the top shackle is reached it is left on the nail until the line has been fastened to the rod tip.

A sleigh-bell which has been soldered on to two strips of springy wire is then bound on to the rod top. (Most charr fishermen leave this bell permanently fixed.)

The butt of the rod is now slotted into position and the top shackle released.

A charr often strikes a spinner without hooking itself, but the ringing of the bell caused by the shaking of a well-hooked fish

Charr baits are kept highly polished since every glimmer of reflected light is needed in the deeps where sunlight barely penetrates. Baits are polished the night before use. Some fishermen even re-polish their baits during the lunch break. Like Irish trout fishermen on Lough Mask, Windermere charr fishermen traditionally meet and brew tea at certain places on the lake shore.

gives evidence of a proper strike. The angler now pulls on the lazy-line until he can reach the mainline. One end of the lazy-line is attached to the mainline some two feet above the top shackle and the other end to a convenient brass screw-eye in the gunwale.

Coiling the mainline and droppers neatly on the stern sheet he pulls up the mainline until the appropriate dropper is reached. This is placed over the nail. He can then pull in the dropper and net the fish.

The line must never be allowed to go slack when a fish is being brought up. Charr fishermen expect to land only three fish out of five, so that carelessness will lead to a much lower average.

The landing net should have the same dressing recommended for the lines. This helps to prevent treble hooks from penetrating the braid.

The skill in fishing single-handed is to keep the boat moving while the tackle is taken up and let out again. This is made possible by the design of Windermere boats. These are fitted with pin rowlocks to allow an angler to pull on each oar in turn with one hand (proprietors of South of England reservoirs please note).

The best trailing speed is between one and one-and-a-half m.p.h.

Charr may take a bait at any time of the day from first light until late evening. Sometimes fish are taken mostly on the top bait 15 to 20 feet down; sometimes on the lower baits – ranging from 15 feet to 70 feet. During hot weather, fish are seldom taken on the top two baits.

May and June are the peak months for

A view of the charr fisherman's trailing rod in action. Note the sleigh-bell fitted to the extreme tip. The lazy-line is out of sight.

Above: *The rod is held in position by the two specially made fittings. It has been lifted out of the 'V' shaped fitting to show how this is bolted on the gunwale.*
Note the lashing, which provides additional security.

Below: *Pin rowlocks. A necessity if the fisherman is to work the boat single-handed. Note the size of the net – an insurance against hooking a large brown trout.*

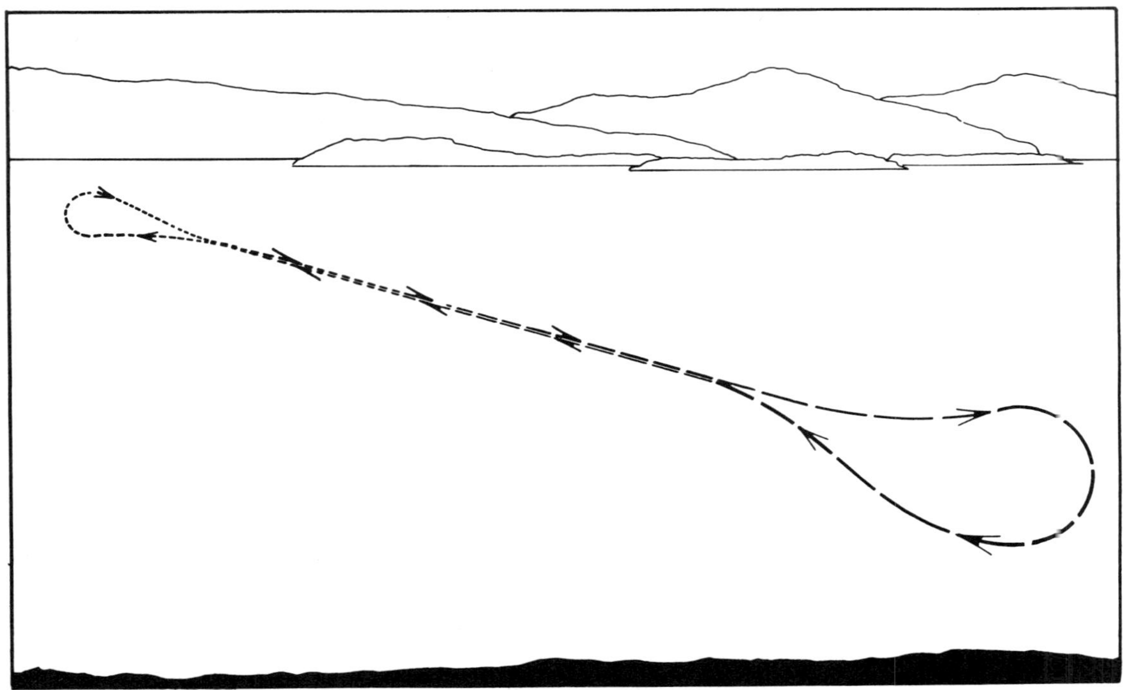

Fig. 10.2 (above). *A typical repetitive course maintained by a charr-fisherman once he has found taking fish.*

Below: *Albert Dixon fishing the north basin of Windermere.*

charr fishing. At this time of the year the angler can expect any or all of his baits to catch fish. July is usually the poorest month, but in August and September the fish begin to take more freely again. At this time of the season the bottom baits produce the bulk of the catch.

Year after year an individual bag for the season is directly related to the order of merit established among charr fishermen. Albert Dixon's explanation of this is rather surprising: 'I fish according to my diary.' That is to say he directs his boat (on a lake ten miles long and nearly a mile wide at its widest point) along the very same line that he followed on that date the previous year! There is an unwritten law which inhibits a charr fisherman from fishing along another man's line.

Formerly, some good trout were taken on charr tackle, but fewer are taken nowadays. It may be that the big Windermere trout (though never present in large numbers) have succumbed to the gill-nets used to reduce the pike population. Most trout taken on charr tackle are caught on the third bait from the top, about 40 feet below the surface. When a big trout is hooked the angler makes a long turn and comes downwind before attempting to land the fish.

*The downrigger set up for charr trailing (*above*). Today there is no need to fish for charr with a heavily leaded hand-line. An angler using a modified form of downrigger has excellent opportunities of sport on a light rod, with no lead between him and the fish.*

The Hardy 'Wanless' trout spinning rod, shown above, is fitted with 6lb B.S. *nylon. The plumb-lead-line on the centrepin downrigger reel is trapped at the required depth by a turn round the reel handle.* *(For a full description of this method of trailing see pp. 478–80.)*

Albert Dixon, with charr 'rods' outside his boat-house.

So far as we know only two English lakes besides Windermere have been fished with Windermere plumb-line charr tackle: Crummock and Coniston. In 1971, F. B. – with permission of Ireland's Inland Fisheries Trust – fished Lough Currane and Lough Mask for charr and trout with plumb-line tackle of his own make as an experiment. Fishing on Mask during a two-day period of hot, dry weather when, according to all reports the fishing was 'dead', he caught 13 trout. Ten were caught 60 feet down – confirming evidence of lack of activity at the surface during these difficult conditions.

Significantly, studies of Lough Mask by Patrick Fitzmaurice of the Inland Fisheries Trust, during 1968 and 1969, show that the oxygen content of the water at depths of up to 70 feet from the surface was never less than it was near the surface. Even at the greatest depth – 192 feet, the deepest sounding ever made on an Irish lough – the dissolved oxygen value never fell below five parts per million.

Because of this favourable oxygen profile, the trout and charr of Lough Mask, have freedom to feed at greater depth than fish occupying deep lakes where the *thermocline* is of the classic pattern.

THERMAL STRATIFICATION

When the coldest part of the winter has passed, deep lakes in cold and temperate regions develop a uniform temperature from top to bottom (approximately 39 – 42°F. – that is 4–6°C).

As the summer advances, the surface layer – unlike the lower layer which has no source of heat – absorbs heat from the sun's rays. This upper layer of warmed water is known as the *epilimnion*.

The lower layer of cold water is known as the *hypolimnion*.

The 'sandwich' in between these two layers – a region of rapidly dropping temperature – is known as the *thermocline*.

Since warm water is lighter than cold water it floats on top; so that during windy spells, when surface water is blown across a lake, the warm water of the epilimnion circulates independently (see Fig. 10.3)

Most living organisms in a temperature-stratified lake live in the warm epilimnion where the oxygen supply is constantly replenished from contact with the surface. All dead organisms, however, sink into the hypolimnion where the process of decay uses up the oxygen. Since there is no source from which this oxygen can be replenished, the hypolimnion gradually becomes more deoxygenated as the summer advances.

In *Life in Lakes and Rivers* (1961), Worthington and Macan record a typical example of summer depth of epilimnion and thermocline, in Windermere, July 1948:

Epilimnion: 0 – 30 feet.

Thermocline: 33 – 50 feet.

From this it can be seen that thermal stratification has a considerable effect on the activities of fish. American anglers have long been aware of this. As a result, echo-sounders and deepwater thermometers form a standard part of their fishing equipment.

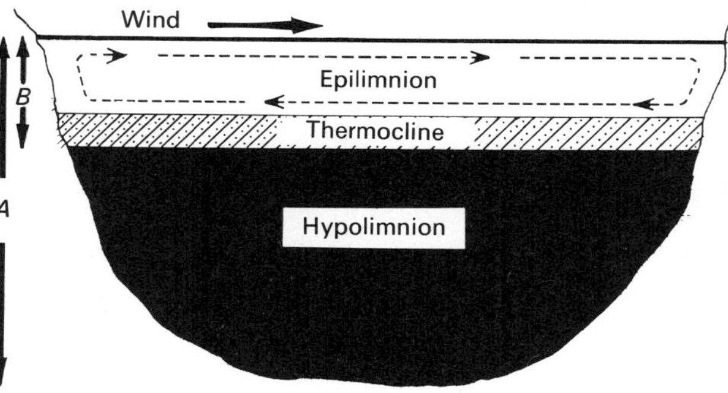

Fig. 10.3.

Modern equipment for deep-water trailing. left: *electric outboard-motor.* top-right: *echo-sounder and transducer.* centre-bottom: *deep-water temperature gauge.*

An angler fishing a lake or loch from the bank might think that since he is casting into relatively shallow water (say, 20 feet deep), he will always be casting into the fish-holding epilimnion. He would be wrong. Although water stratifies horizontally, prolonged spells of wind from one direction can tilt the layers into the shape of a wedge. When this happens, the warm, oxygenated epilimnion is extra-deep on the lee shore of the lake, and the cold oxygen-starved hypolimnion reaches up towards the surface on the windward shore. It is mainly for this reason that, in summer, anglers should fish on the lee shore on all lakes that are subject to the formation of a thermocline.

In winter months the lee shore offers no such advantage. In autumn, as soon as the air temperature begins to fall, the epilimnion starts to cool down and with the advent of a gale is obliterated.

Above: *Echo-sounder, an essential piece of equipment for recording depth and the underwater contours of a lake.*

Remember: *Each lake has its own particular characteristics. The readings given by deep-water instruments need careful interpretation. Their true value can only be determined from a series of experiments, with data recorded, on each individual lake.*

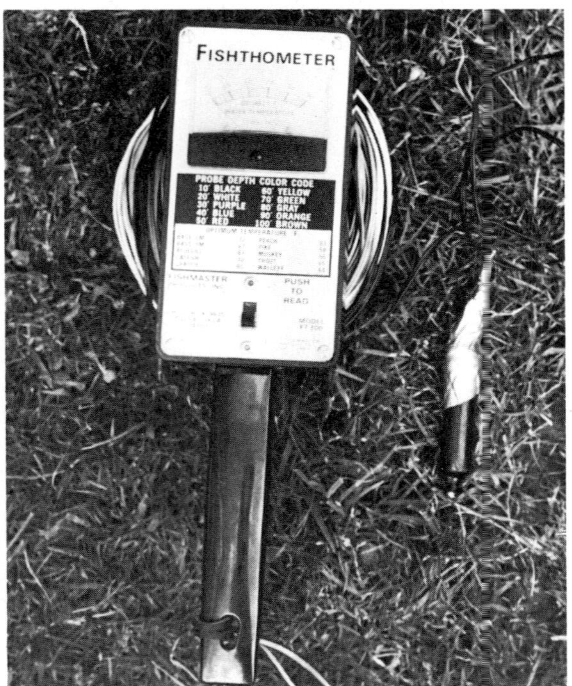

Above: *Deep-water thermometer. The temperature 'dolly' (right of picture) is lowered into the water on a colour-coded cable, and the temperature shown on the dial when a switch is pressed.*

Below: *The result of one day's fishing on Lough Mask with plumb-line technique at 60 feet: eight trout of up to $5\frac{1}{2}$lb.*

Below: *Lough Mask; water of great fish, and swiftly changing mood.*

Charr pot. The charr has been praised by gourmets for centuries. In 1769, Defoe wrote: 'It is a curious fish, and as a dainty, is potted and sent far and near by way of present.' Charr pies were once a favourite luxury. In 1662, Sir Daniel Fleming of Rydal, near Windermere, sent one to his aunt and duly noted in his account book: '. . . for the carryage of a charr-pie unto my Aunt Dudley at London. At 2d per lb, £0 6s. 0d.'

COOKING THE CHARR

John Davy in *The Angler in the Lake District* (1857) gives a recipe for Potted Charr which he obtained from a 'worthy neighbour' who was

. . . so esteemed for higher qualities, that her portrait in her old age has been painted, paid for by a friendly subscription, and presented to her daughter.

Here it is in her own words:

One dozen of charr, dress and wipe with a dry cloth; strew a little salt in and over them, and let them lie all night; then wipe them with a dry cloth, and season with one ounce of white pepper, quarter of an ounce of cayenne, half an ounce of pounded cloves, and a little mace. Clarify two pounds of butter. Then put them with their backs down into a pot lined with paper; and then pour the butter over, and bake four hours in a slow oven.

Potted Charr

Cook in the oven with the head on and when the eyes go white, then it is ready. Flake fish off the bones, mix into a paste with cream or white sauce, adding seasoning as required. Put into a pot and press down tight, then pour melted butter over the top and allow to set.
Old Windermere recipe.

I have heard say that no man may discuss the salmon, in print, unless he has caught twelve of them for each year of his own life. And as for trout, it is laid down that the man who would write concerning trout must abstain from ink until he has qualified for his task by catching, on artificial fly, a weight of trouts which is three times greater that that at which he himself tips the bathroom scales. Counsels of perfection both.

What the ruling on char may be I do not know, but I am confident that I now contravene it; for only once have I caught a char, and then he was only a very little one. But he was as beautiful as a butterfly.
PATRICK CHALMERS, *A Fisherman's Angles* (1931).

11 · The Chub

Leuciscus cephalus

Cruising down the Severn, we had moored our canoe under some bushes in a secluded spot to take our mid-day rest. Presently we saw two men in coracles coming down the river. They stopped opposite us and commenced to net the river. They played out their net in a semi-circle, and then, beating the water with their paddles, they closed in and with their coracles side by side, handed the net in.

It was a caution to see the fish they had caught. Roach, pike and dace; in half an hour they caught a great number: great chub of five pounds and one of nine pounds in weight.

The 'Angler's Souvenir,' (1877). Quoted by A. COURTNEY-WILLIAMS, *Angling Diversions* (1945).

The chub, together with three sub-species, is widely distributed throughout mainland Europe except in the extreme north. Although in Great Britain the chub is absent from Ireland, west Wales, the Cornish peninsula, and in Scotland north of the Firth of Forth, it is nevertheless widely distributed throughout the rest of England and Scotland.

Very occasionally the chub flourishes in still waters but its usual habitat is clean running water. It spawns in May, June or July when the water temperature reaches 59°F. Its choice of diet is catholic, the range of baits that an angler may usefully take with him grows with the reading of every book.

From just a few books we have culled the following. Worms of every sort; frogs; insect larvae; flies of all descriptions (live and artificial); water weeds; spinners; plugs; grasshoppers; slugs; crayfish; breadpaste; dough; crust; crumb; cheese; cheese-paste; wheat; barley; hemp; elderberry; cherries; sultanas; raisins; maggots; caterpillars; bullock's brains; the pith from the backbone of an ox; wasp grubs; bacon rind; snails; withey grubs; shrimps (sea or freshwater); dock grubs; greaves; bumble bees; cockchafers; salmon roe; caddis grub; beetles; water bugs; algae; macaroni; small water voles; small eels; gudgeon; small dace; prides; roachlets; young chub; small trout; bullheads; minnows, and sausage! In a swim where a game-keeper friend habitually discarded rabbit paunches, E. Marshall-Hardy caught many splendid chub on pieces of rabbit gut.

The chub's habit of bold biting endears him to the angler – even though a highly developed sense of self-preservation makes

Mrs Louie Thompson of Sheffield, with a magnificent 6 lb chub. The background of vegetation provided good cover while the fish was being played.

him difficult to approach. There is a passage in *The Compleat Angler*, that describes these seemingly paradoxical traits in the chub's character. 'The chub is the fearfullest of fishes' and 'he will infallibly take the bait'.

Quoted at length the same passage also provides an unsurpassed description of dapping:

Go to the same hole in which I caught my Chub, where in most hot days you will find a dozen or twenty Chevens floating near the top of the water. Get two or three grasshoppers as you go over the meadow; and get secretly behind the tree, and stand as free from motion as is possible. Then put a grasshopper on your hook, and let your hook hang a quarter of a yard short of the water, to which end you must rest your rod on some bough of the tree. But it is likely the Chubs will sink down towards the bottom of the water at the first shadow of your rod, for a Chub is the fearfullest of fishes, and will do so if but a bird flies over him, and makes the least shadow on the water; but they will presently rise up to the top again, and there lie soaring till some shadow affrights them again. I say when they lie upon the top of the water, look out the best Chub, which you, setting yourself in a fit place, may very easily see, and move your rod as softly as a snail moves, to that Chub you intend to catch; let your bait fall gently upon the water three or four inches before him, and he will infallibly take the bait.

The deadliest method for catching chub – dapping apart – is with an artificial fly. Some idea of its effectiveness can be gleaned from the following account. Sir Hugh Lucas-Tooth M.P., owner of the Hampshire Avon fishing at Burgate, has allowed three crack angling clubs to fish his water for many years, both to enjoy good sport and, at the same time, to rid his section of the river of as many coarse fish as possible. During the last 20 years tons of coarse fish have been caught and removed to other waters. In all this time only a few chub over four pounds have been taken by bait-fishing methods; whereas during the same period Sir Hugh has caught many heavier fish to his own rod – all on fly (albeit in the coarse fish close season).

Special big bushy flies are tied for chub fishing. A chub fly doesn't imitate any kind of fly that one expects to find floating on the water, but rather a fly that comes to the water by way of mishap – a fat moth, for example. Not that a chub will neglect an olive, or a sedge (or their artificial counterparts) if these are the best on offer, but on the whole the big chub is an economical feeder who prefers to eat well, rather than often.

When appropriate, the deadliest of all bait-fishing methods is unquestionably long-trotting. This takes the bait so far away that even the 'fearfullest of fishes' cannot perceive the angler.

One of the finest ploys for catching chub is *resting the swim*. If several chub are quickly taken from a swim, the angler is advised to move on and fish other swims until the first swim has recovered. If this is not possible then we suggest a walk down the river while the swim is rested for half an hour.

Bryanston weir on Dorset's river Stour.

The British chub record stands at $10\frac{1}{2}$ lb[1], but on the Continent chub have been caught up to a weight of 18 lb. Some anglers will swear that there are waters in Britain holding fish almost as big. Noted chub rivers like the Hampshire Avon, the Wye, the Dorset Stour, the Annan and the Great Ouse are waters likely to hold a record fish. Mr Harding, one time master-fisherman of the Dorset Stour, who fished the Blandford section of the river between the two wars almost every day of his life, maintained that the biggest chub in Britain lived below the weir in the grounds of Bryanston School.

1 This chub was caught in 1875 on the River Crane with a live minnow by W. Cockburn, and another big chub of $8\frac{1}{2}$ lb was caught from the Sussex Rother by D. Deekes.

*The chub, 'skelly' to the Scots and Cumbrians. Although a fine sporting fish it is often persecuted where it shares living space with fish of a higher economic value such as trout. The 3 lb chub seen in the picture (*above*) was caught in that most famous of all trout-streams – the river Test. Notice the perfect shape and immaculate scaling of a fish that has fed well and never seen the inside of a keepnet.*

Right: *A brace of fine chub: 5 lb and 4 lb, taken on the dry fly by F.B.*

Bottom: *Only a novice would confuse a dace with a chub upwards of $1\frac{1}{2}$ lb, since the size of the chub and its bronze tinge of colour contrasts with the size (rarely more than a pound) and silver colour of the dace. It is much easier to confuse a large dace with a small chub, since both are silvery. Although there are many points of identification, a very simple one is* the shape of the anal fin. *In the chub (as pictured above) the leading edge of the anal fin is convex. That of the dace is concave.*

COOKING THE CHUB

The chub . . . is objected against, not only for being full of small forked bones, dispersed through all his body, but that he eats waterish, and that the flesh of him is not firm, but short and tasteless.
IZAAK WALTON, *The Compleat Angler*.

For those who feel they can face it, we offer the possibility of roast chub (culled from *The Compleat Angler*).

First scale him, and then wash him clean, and then take out his guts; and to that end make the hole as little and near to his gills as you may conveniently, and especially make clean his throat from the grass and weeds that are usually in it, for if that be not very clean, it will make him to taste very sour. Having so done, put some sweet herbs into his belly; and then tie him with two or three splinters to a spit, and roast him, basted often with vinegar, or rather verjuice and butter, with good store of salt mixed with it.

In *A Handbook of Angling* (1847), Edward Fitzgibbon, 'Ephemera', writes of the chub as follows: 'His burnished gold outside hides a miserable interior. He is neither fish, flesh, nor good red herring. He is, to all intents and purposes, save in appearance, what the French call him, *un villain*, that is, a downright chaw-bacon, or clod-hopper. Though M. A. Soyer, of the Reform Club should condescend to dress him, I doubt whether he would make him fit to appear at any dinner table.'

I don't say it is quite the English thing, don't know if it really goes perfectly with beer and tea and a cold climate. Doubt if it does. But a good freshwater bouillabaisse is quite a thing to try. As the poet said:

A freshwater bouillabaisse
Includes dace.
Even if you can't spell it
You can smell it.

You can indeed. But I wouldn't say it really and truly *has* to include dace – a bit of poetic licence, please – though you can chuck 'em in if you have them handy. Everything helps – except bream, of course. Bream are *persona non grata* in this as in everything else. Talk about *slime*. But almost anything else goes – perch, roach, gudgeon pre-eminently, dace, rudd, ruffe, eels, even minnows if you can stoop so low. Pike, bleak, and even chub if you are very pushed. I wouldn't personally include carp in anything, but some would. In fact carp are considered a delicacy by many.

I think the first fact about a freshwater bouillabaisse is *the more the merrier*. The more mixed the bag, the more intriguing the final flavour. Or flavours. Cut them all up, fairly small, some smaller than others. You need a couple of pounds for a fair sitting. Then get busy on the trimmings. With a couple of pounds of fish, give or take half a pound, you will need two goodish onions, which you should slice; four tomatoes, skinned and crushed; a clove of garlic; a bay leaf; a pinch of saffron; parsley and fennel; and enough olive oil to cover the pieces of fish.

If you can't stand olive oil, try your luck

with something else. I think the general technique is this, more or less . . . You put the firmer, solider bits of fish, and all the trimmings, into the pan and pour in enough olive oil just to cover the fish. You *then* pour boiling water over the whole lot and cook fairly furiously for five minutes. You must cook this lot very fast. Then you add the softer fish flesh, *and* a glass of white wine, and boil the lot hard for seven minutes more.

To serve, pour off the liquid into soup bowls containing pieces of bread; whether fresh or toasted, I leave it to you. Put the fish flesh into a dish and sprinkle with parsley. Serve both at once, the liquid and the flesh, and let joy be unrestrained. It may well be so, provided you have also put on the table generous quantities of white wine, the best you can buy. Failing that, I suppose, beer of the lighter sorts, or stout. I have eaten this dish with stout. Or after stout. I'm not sure that I'd face it all – the labour, the complexity, the smells – without something to drink.

MAURICE WIGGIN, *Troubled Waters* (1960).

12 · The Dace

Leuciscus leuciscus

Except in Norway where it is confined to one area, the dace is widely distributed throughout Europe north of the Alps and the Pyrenees. It inhabits most British rivers, except those in Cornwall, west Wales and Scotland. In the Lake District it is found only in the river Eden. In Ireland it was accidentally introduced when an English pike angler's live-bait can tipped over! Since then it has become established in the Cork Blackwater system.

During the 18th and 19th centuries Lancashire anglers were thought to be blessed with a species unique to that country – the graining – a belief shared by the naturalist, Yarrell. This was discounted by C. Tate Regan and the 'graining' is known to be none other than the dace.

Since the dace is generally associated with clear, fairly fast running rivers and streams, some anglers may wonder why it fails to exploit the higher streams and the spate rivers with the trout, sea-trout, grayling and salmon. The reason is that the eggs of these Salmonidae are buried by the female fish, and thus gain some protection during the spate. The eggs of the dace are laid on, and adhere to, water plants of the type which seldom gain a footing in spate streams. Dace usually spawn in February and March, although after a severe winter, spawning may be delayed until April or May. During the spawning period the male dace assumes its spawning livery – when the head and body is covered with white tubercles while the fish becomes very rough to the touch.

The largest bags of dace are likely to be made in February and March when the shoals migrate upstream from the deeps into a shallow spawning area. The record match bag of 251 dace weighing 64 lb, caught by F. B. in the Hampshire Avon on March 10th 1957, were possibly fish that had assembled in this way prior to spawning.

Though small in stature the dace gives a good account of itself on fine tackle. It can be caught on almost any bait with almost any method save livebaiting, although even this reservation must be discarded if one accepts the Rev. W. B. Daniel's claim that he 'caught dace of upwards of a pound weight, upon night lines, baited with minnows for eels'. Perhaps Daniel made the common error of confusing the dace with the chub (see page 57).

The dace is a free-rising fish capable of testing the reflexes of the best fly-fisherman. Its quick take and equally quick rejection of a fly or bait is sometimes too much for the contemplative type of angler. Indeed a

Dace 1 lb 3$\frac{3}{4}$ oz, 1 lb 2 oz, 1 lb 1$\frac{1}{2}$ oz, 1 lb 1$\frac{1}{4}$ oz, 1 lb 1 oz, 1 lb $\frac{1}{2}$ oz, 1 lb and 1 lb (photographed by permission of A. G. Davies, Curator of the Hertford Museum). *Between 1898 and 1900, E. Steinhart caught eight dace of one pound or over from the river Beane at Waterford Marsh, Hertfordshire. An astonishing performance. Nevertheless, the all-time dace champion must surely be W. H. Clarke, of Barnham, Norfolk. In 25 years' fishing on the Little Ouse near Thetford, he has caught 42 dace weighing over the pound! His best fish (1 lb 3$\frac{1}{2}$ oz) was caught in the summer of 1958. Had it been taken during the following winter it could well have weighed an extra two ounces.*

lightning strike is essential when hempseed is used as a hookbait.

Large dace of the order of 9 to 12 in. are more deliberate biters and more deliberate risers. Hugh Sheringham summed it up nicely when he wrote: 'All fish become rather more dignified in their behaviour as they get bigger.'

Although the rod-caught record is 1 lb 8 oz 5 dr, few anglers have caught dace weighing more than a pound. The record dace was taken by R. W. Humphrey from the river Wylye – a tributary of the Hampshire Avon, in September 1932. Sheringham caught five dace that weighed over one pound apiece. All of these were taken on fly, which is some indication of the effectiveness of this method for catching big dace. The most famous English waters for big dace are: the Hertfordshire rivers Beane, Rib and Gade; the Kennet, the Kennet and Avon Canal, the Hampshire Avon, the Wiltshire Wylye, the Test, the Usk, the Dorset Stour, and the Bedfordshire Ivel.

During November, December and January dace are likely to be found in the deeper runs. At other times, if not disturbed, they will move into relatively shallow water. At all times they are more likely to be found in gravelly runs, whether fast, slow, shallow or deep, than elsewhere. When in very shallow runs, dace are easily frightened into deep water if groundbait, other than the lightest sprinkling of maggots or casters, is thrown to them.

In small rivers and in streams the best way to prepare a dace swim is to wade in some 15 or 20 yards above the fish and cause a cloud of mud and silt to be sent downstream together with a sprinkling of maggots. The angler can achieve this by stirring the bottom with his feet – an alternative to *raking* the bottom, which is the traditional method of small-stream dace fishing.

Matthews's account of his exploit is so interesting and vivid that we include it for the enjoyment of our readers.[1]

'The little River Beane was to be seen some time before we reached the eventful spot, its serpentine course being plainly discernible through the many old pollards and alders growing upon its banks. Just before my visit refreshing rains had been experienced, but in not sufficient volume to put any land water into the Beane, and we found that river not only on the bright side, but rather slow-running.

'Nothing daunted, I jointed my roach-pole, put on a brand new line and hook length and a very old favourite float, and having nicked on a good bunch of gentles, made my initial cast. The swim was in a bend, and my friend walking well above me, now produced his box of gentles and used them for ground-bait. Just then, too, I saw a man walking across the field with a rake over his shoulder, and motioning him to hurry on, and pointing to a certain piece of water about 30 yards from where I was crouched on a camp stool, my friend rejoined me, telling me that, as the water was not naturally coloured it would have to be made so artificially, and when I next looked upstream the man I had seen with the rake was already at work with that implement. The local mill now also began to work, and no sooner had the stream received an impetus than down went the float. I promptly responded, felt a heavy drag, saw the glittering sides of an immense dace, and – then the line came back! My feelings under such circumstances can be better imagined than described, and, knowing that I must have disturbed the fish, I suggested a walk, and off downstream my friend and I tramped, leaving the man plying the rake stealthily.

'When we returned to the spot the water was showing a nice colour and had risen, and there was quite a fast stream running. "Now look out," I thought, "no bungling or missing fish this time!" My friend again stole above the swim with the ground-baiting gentles, and I had not had more than five swims down when the float disappeared in a slanting position. Once more I struck, and found I had hooked another splendid dace. The fish ran upstream and then started boring, but the whalebone-spliced top piece on my rod had very fortunately plenty of "give" in it, and the fish was soon in mid-water. "A beauty indeed," exclaimed my friend, as the next moment he slipped skilfully my V-shaped landing net under the dace and lifted it on to the bank. It certainly was the largest dace I had ever seen alive out of a river, and on my friend's steelyards it weighed 1 lb ½ oz good. He next measured

1 Reprinted from A. R. MATTHEWS'S, *How to Catch Coarse Fish* (1921).

Dace, 1 lb 4 oz, taken from the Beane in 1899 by A. R. Matthews. This fish held the rod-caught record until 1905 (photographed by permission of the Piscatorial Society).

the fish, its dimensions being: length 13 in., girth 8 in. The man with the rake (who I ascertained was a clever old angler himself) had noted my bent rod, and had further heard the splashing in the water and seen the dace netted, came up to admire it, while, what with the sight of the notable fish and the congratulations of my friend, my readers can better imagine than I can describe my feelings. I had caught a fish which thousands of anglers had never been able to secure, and it was a very proud moment for me, indeed, I can tell you.

'Giving the swim another rest, I restarted operations in the course of half an hour, and found the faithful raker still at his post. For the third time my friend resorted to his gentle-box, and once more in went the "ground-bait" all alive-O! There was now a beautiful stream, and my friend prophesied that I would catch further dace. And, what was more thrilling to me, that I might get a larger dace than the one lying in the grass at the side of the hedge! But, strange to say, I fished for quite a quarter of an hour without the slightest sign of a dace bite. It then occurred to me to try a red worm, and when I had baited I fished a different part of the swim where, the water and stream having increased in height and pace, a little "boily" eddy had been created.

'Once or twice did the float go round and round the swim quietly, and then – such a lovely bite! I was on the fish in a second with one of those clean strikes that extract from the pole a kind of "tung", and was soon doing battle with another monster of the dace tribe. First up and then downstream the fish rushed, now across it, now back in a vain endeavour to reach a bunch of lily roots at my feet.

'I don't think he's quite as large as the first, I remarked to my friend – I had not obtained a clear view of the fish then – but I promptly a bit later recalled the words, and when I gazed at the fish in the dripping landing-net, I felt that I could scarcely believe my eyes.

'"Now you've done something," exclaimed my friend, as he put the fish on the steelyards.

'"Bigger? Here! Wait a minute! Good gracious! You lucky beggar! Why, it weighs 1 lb 4 oz!"

'"And don't it bump the weight, too," chimed in the old man with the rake. "If that ain't the champion dace," he added, "I never seed such dace, and I have had werry near 50 years of dodging about the river and seed millions of big daces."

'The dimensions of this fish, as taken on the bank by my friend, were: length 13½ in., girth 8½ in. It was a shapely, elegant-looking fish, and beautiful in colouring.'

COOKING THE DACE

Dace are by no means to be scorned as table fish. How could they fail to be sweet eating, when their own tastes are so pellucid and aerial? A fine dish of them fried in delicate fats, as soon as the happy angler comes home, makes a royal banquet, with a suspicion of vinegar, a little cress, and some brown bread and butter. You could not do better, believe me, if they were troutlets which hissed and spat in the pan. A little white wine – Chablis shall we say – goes well with them. Indeed, there is a proper vintage for every kind of fish that swims, but to enlarge upon this theme would be either to speak to ears too gross to understand it, or else it would be to insult the fine spirits to whom this knowledge is native and instinctive.

CHARLES MARSON, *Super Flumina* (1905).

On the preparation of a dace for the table, Dr J. J. Manley remarked 'perhaps the more you disguise it the better'. Nevertheless he records the following old Thames-side recipe:

Without scaling the fish, lay him on a grid-iron, over a slow fire, and strew on him a little flour; when he begins to grow brown, make a slit not more than skin deep, in his back from head to tail, and lay him on again; when he is broiled enough, his skin, scales and all, will peel off, and leave the flesh, which will have become very firm, perfectly clean, then open the belly, and take out the inside, and use anchovy and butter for sauce.

13 · The Eel

Anguilla anguilla

There are those who denigrate the eel. Indeed, is any fish so badly treated? For many an angler reeling in that slimy, twisting knot, one look is enough: with his scissors he snips the leader and bends to his tackle-bag to repair the damage – leaving the eel to writhe among the rushes, wrapped in nylon with a hook in its gullet.

No creature should be so barbarously treated.

The eel is as mysterious in its habits as those other migratory fishes: salmon and sea-trout. It has a history which is second to none. Besides, whether fried, stewed or smoked, it is delicious to eat. That enchanting writer, Arthur Ransome, knew its gastronomic value. Of a day when after big carp, he writes: 'Four times the baits were taken by eels, landed amid anathemas, tempered by the thought of next day's breakfast.' Catch *him* cutting them adrift!

The angler who is ignorant of the eel's

'The eel, as is well known, will live a long time out of water. This habit is of the greatest service to him, as sometimes it is necessary for him to migrate from place to place by an overland route.' (Frank Buckland, The Natural History of British Fishes).

table qualities is a fool. But the angler who leaves an eel writhing with a hook in its stomach is worse than a fool. It is hoped that the following notes will enlighten such an unfeeling oaf, and encourage him to treat this remarkable animal with more respect.

It seems that the eel was the first fish to achieve the dignity of a name. A distinction it fully deserves. Few other fish have been so highly praised or so highly prized. Certainly no fish has been the subject of more scientific controversy and conjecture. Indeed, the story of this quiet, mysterious creature is touched with a strange wonder and romance; a story not untinged with humour. As an 18th century writer put it:

> There is a greater variety in the eel than in any other fish of the river, and it is not yet determined how to treat them, whether as a fish or as a reptile. Some who have no good will to them, put them as no better than a species of serpent and will call them water snakes.

Of course, not everyone has been in sympathy with this animal. Even to-day not everyone is deeply conscious of the eel and the riddle of its life cycle – which for so many centuries remained unsolved. Many people, unmoved by the mystery of its birth, have abused the eel, treating it as a freshwater vermin. It has been dismissed as 'a nasty, slimy creature; nothing but an invigorated putrefaction'. But not by the ancient Greeks.

To them it was 'The King of Fish; the white-skinned Nymph; a goddess, all clothed in beet' – with which, on beech leaves, it was often served. And, highest of all honours: 'The Helen of the Feast'.

The Greeks were inordinately fond of eels. They paid vast sums of money for the luxury of eating them – while the voluptuous Sybarites were so addicted that all persons catching eels were exempt from paying taxes and tributes.

By some of the more credulous, the eel was considered a prophylactic, preventing all kinds of maladies; a panacea; a tonic for the voice. The smoke of burnt eel was said to ease the pangs of childbirth; whereas the fragrance of it, cooking, restored the sense of smell to a dead man.

By the Boeotians it was thought worthy of sacrificial offering to the gods. Agatharchides of Knidos relates:

> The largest eels from Lake Copais are sacrificed by the Boeotians, who crown them like human victims and, after sprinkling them with meal, offer prayers over them.

The Boeotians were proverbially stupid; but the Egyptians went even further in their adoration of the eel. To them it was sacred – apropos of which, Antiphanes makes an ironic comparison between the value of a god and the exhorbitant prices paid for an eel in Athens:

> They say that the Egyptians are clever in that they rank the eel equal to a god; but in reality it is held in esteem and value far higher than gods, for them we can propitiate with a prayer or two, while to get even a smell of an eel at Athens we have to spend 12 drachmae or more!

To the Athenians, a dish of eels was the greatest of all delicacies. There was simply nothing to touch it. As one of them lamented: 'When you are dead, you cannot then eat eels!' But for all these panegyrics, no one knew where the eels came from or how they bred. The supply of eels seemed inexhaustible – and yet, no eel had ever been observed to spawn.

This is not surprising; for, as we know to-day, the European eel does not originate in European waters. Together with its close relative the American eel, it breeds thousands of miles away in the depths of the Sargasso Sea, outside the Gulf of Mexico.

Its story is indeed touched with wonder. From the Sargasso Sea, the eel larva starts off in the springtime as a tiny leaf-shaped creature called a leptocephalus, which drifts north-eastwards with the Gulf Stream. Three years later it turns up on our shores as an elver, or miniature eel: a slender creature about three inches long.

Practically no piece of fresh water is without its complement of eels, and each year a new stock arrives. During April and May the elvers enter our estuaries in vast numbers, and make their way up towards their destination in river, stream, lake, pond and mere. From then on, the eel lives in fresh water; until finally, it returns to sea.

That, very briefly, is the life-story of the eel. But until the present century little of this was known, and the riddle of the eel's breeding-cycle was the subject of continuous debate. From Aristotle onwards, pretty well every zoologist and fishing writer produced a theory. Aristotle himself records the first really important observation:

> Some fish leave the sea to go to the pools and rivers. The eel on the contrary, leaves them to do down to the sea.

But as eels had never been found with ova or milt inside them, and were seemingly lacking in generative organs, he thought they came from inside the earth: 'They form spontaneously. In mud.'

On the other hand Oppian thought that little eels came from eel slime:

> Strange the formation of the eely race,
> That knows no sex, yet loves the close embrace.
> Their folded lengths they round each other twine,
> Twist amorous knots, and slimy bodies join;
> Till the close strife brings off a frothy juice,
> The seed that must the wriggling kind produce.
> That genial bed impregnates all the heap,
> And little eelets soon begin to creep.

In Pliny's opinion, eels were sexless – being neither male nor female:

> They have no other mode of procreation than by rubbing themselves against rocks – and their scrapings come to life.

Other thinkers attributed the birth of eels to the dew of May mornings; the hair of horses; the gills of fishes; and to various forms of 'spontaneous generation'. So, through the ages, theory followed theory.

Doing no better himself, the great Izaak Walton summed up the situation in *The Compleat Angler*.

> Most men differ about their breeding. Some say they are bred by generation as other fish do; and others, that they breed as some worms do, of mud, as rats and mice, and many other living creatures, by the sun's heat, or out of the putrefaction of the earth, and divers other ways. And others say that eels growing old breed other eels out of the corruption of their own age. And

others say that as pearls are made of glutinous dew drops, which are condensed by the sun's heat, so eels are bred of a particular dew, falling in the months of May or June on the banks of some particular ponds or rivers – adapted by nature for that end – which in a few days are by the sun's heat turned into eels: and some of the ancients have called the eels that are thus bred, the offspring of Jove.

A poor naturalist, whatever his skill as a fisherman, old Izaak fell into the common trap of drawing false conclusions from data equally false:

But that eels may be bred as some worms, and some kinds of bees and wasps are, either of dew, or out of the corruption of the earth, seems to be made probable by the barnacles and the young goslings bred by the sun's heat, and the rotten planks of an old ship, and hatched of trees.

It is known to-day that there is only one species of European eel: *Anguilla anguilla.* But its change of shape and colouring – notably the change from yellow belly to silver belly – which takes place shortly before its return to sea – led early observers to believe that there were several different species. And so, accordingly, error was heaped on error. Each of these supposedly different species was thought to breed in a different way. Walton again:

Let me tell you that some curious searchers into the nature of fish observe that there be several kinds of eels, as the silver eel, and green or greenish eel, with which the river of Thames abounds . . . and a blackish eel, whose head is more flat and bigger than ordinary eels: and also an eel whose fins are reddish – These several kinds of eels are, say some, diversely bred, as namely: out of the corruption of the earth, and some by dew and other ways . . . and yet it is affirmed by some for a certain, that the silver eel is bred not by spawning as other fish do, but that her brood come alive from her, being

Alan Dart's record eel- weight 8 lb 10 oz – caught 1969, from Hunstrete Lake in Gloucestershire, on dace deadbait (Photograph: Angling Times).

then little live eels no bigger nor longer than a pin: and I have had too many testimonies of this to doubt the truth of it myself, and if I thought it needful I might prove it, but I think it needless.

Perhaps Izaak Walton's belief in the spontaneous generation of silver eels is hardly surprising in an age when the study of natural history rested on such shaky foundations. Consider his views on the procreation of pike:

Tis not to be doubted, but that they are bred of a weed called Pickerel Weed, unless learned Gesner is much mistaken, for he says: this weed and other glutinous matter with the help of the sun's heat in some particular months, do becomes pikes.

A century or so later, we were little further forward. In *The Fisherman: or The Art of Angling made Easy*, Guiniad Charfy observed:

Others dispute their generation, and tell us they are produced not by any spawn, or ova, but by the slime of the earth, impregnated by the heat of the sun; so that they will have them to be only an invigorated corruption and putrefaction. These and many other nasty notions these squeamish people have about eels, in order to help their stomachs to loathe them, or at least to justify a pretended aversion to them.

But after all, the eel, let him be engendered how he may, it is a very good, rich, nourishing and wholesome fish, when well digested, but is not so proper for weak and indisposed stomachs. They distinguish them into several sorts, but we generally know no more than two, namely, the Silver Eel, and the Black Eel; and these seem to be of no specific difference in kind, only as the water is less clear or muddy in which they are nourished. The eel has this property, that although they breed in rivers, yet as they grow bigger, those of them that remove and go down the stream never attempt to go back again, and those that reach into the sea, never return, but continue there till they die, or till they grow to an extraordinary size, and are then called Congers.

That Congers were simply overgrown freshwater eels was a common belief at the time. But reference to the seaward movement of eels recalls Izaak Walton's brilliant non-sequitur:

It is said that eels that are bred in rivers that relate to the sea, never return to the fresh water when once they have tasted the salt water; and I do the more easily believe this, because I am certain that powdered beef is a most excellent bait to catch an eel.[1]

Gradually, as the years went by, a little light began to dawn. The Rev. W. Richardson, writing in 1793 was of the opinion that eels descending a river went down to the sea to breed. Of the Cumberland Derwent, he remarks: 'The young eels come up the river in April, in size about the thickness of a common knitting needle.'

He was right. But naturalists in this country were lagging far behind those on the Continent. That adult eels disappeared into the sea, and young eels came out of it had been noted in Italy a century earlier by Francesco Redi, a gentleman of Tuscany:

1 Patrick Annesley has pointed out that 'powdered beef' probably means beef cured with powdered salt. In which case, presumably, it was the salty taste that the eels found irresistible.

I can affirm, following my long observations, that each year with the first August rains, and by night when it is dark and cloudy, the eels begin to descend from the lakes and rivers in compact groups towards the sea. Here, the female lays her eggs from which, after a variable time depending on the rigours of the sea, hatch elvers or young eels, which then ascend the fresh waters by way of the estuaries.

This very important and accurate piece of original observation was published in Italy in 1684. But in this country, as late as 1862, in the *Origin of the Silver Eel* – a work based on observations extending over 60 years – we find a Mr D. Cairncross blithely asserting:

The progenitor of the silver eel is a small beetle. Of this, I feel fully satisfied in my own mind, from a rigid and extensive comparison of its structure and habits with those of other insects.

And even the famous Frank Buckland, in his *Familiar History of British Fishes*, published in 1873, writes:

There are three or four distinct species of the freshwater eel inhabiting this country. It is, strictly speaking, a fresh-water fish, and undoubtedly remains all the year in ponds, and breeds there; but when following its natural instinct, it migrates towards the sea in autumn and lives in the brackish waters at the mouths of rivers.

On the subject of breeding he seems rather confused, for he also says:

The old eels run down the rivers in the autumn and deposit their ova. It is a disputed point whether the parent eels ever return up rivers. My own opinion is that they do.

Referring to elvers, he says:

Some argue that they are the spawn of the Conger. This is, of course, ridiculous. There can be no doubt that they are the young of fresh-water eels – I should think these little fish to be about a week or ten days old.

Well, he was about three years out. Regarding the actual birth of eels, he records a remarkable observation:

The roe of the eel is exceedingly minute, and is often taken to be simply fat. I once, and once only, found some young eels hatching out; this was on the rocks near the entrance of the harbour at Guernsey.

Buckland's little eels were almost certainly parasitic worms. The first recorded capture of an immature eel, before it had reached the elver stage, was made by a German scientist in the Straits of Messina in 1856. But, not realizing that the strange leaf-like little creature he had found was a young eel, he named it *Leptocephalus brevirostris* – or, Short-snouted thinhead.

That this *Leptocephalus brevirostris* was in fact the larva of the eel was discovered by two Italian scientists in 1896. But it was not until some years later that the eel's spawning ground in the Sargasso Sea was located – a classic piece of research carried out by a young Danish marine biologist, Johannes Schmidt, who published his findings in 1921.

By means of intensive netting with fine-meshed nets in the North Atlantic, and examining haul after haul, he was able to draw up a chart showing that the *leptocephali* he caught became progressively smaller and smaller in size as he approached the Sargasso Sea – where he found the smallest larvae of all. It is from this far-off Atlantic birthplace that the tiny eels set off with the Gulf Stream on their three-year eastward drift, during the latter stages of which occurs the metamorphosis from *leptocephalus* to elver. The elvers reach our shores in the late spring and early summer. Then comes the determined thrust into river and stream as millions of little eels fight their way up towards the freshwater destinations where they will spend their lives.

St. John, in his *Wild Sports of the Highlands*, writes of elvers running up the Findhorn:

> I was much interested one day in May in watching the thousands of small eels which were making their way up the river. It was some distance from the mouth, and where the stream, confined by a narrow rocky channel, ran with great strength. Nevertheless, these little eels persevered in swimming against the stream. When they came to a fall, where they could not possibly ascend, they wriggled out of the water, and gliding along the rock close to the edge where the stone was constantly wet from the splashing and spray of the fall, they made their way up till they got above the difficulty and then again slipping into the water, they continued their course.
>
> For several hours there was a continued succession of these little fish going up in the same way; and for more than a week, the same thing was to be seen every day. The perseverance they displayed was very great, for frequently, although washed back several times, an eel would always continue its efforts till it managed to ascend.

As the Polish biologist, Opuszynski, has observed: nothing it seems, can stop them.

> Their urge to undertake this journey is unconquerable. They are not deterred by any obstacle such as sluice or waterfall. They have been seen mounting a vertical wall. Even the bodies of the elver which die in doing so and adhere to the wall, serve as a kind of rung for succeeding elvers.

From data recorded by Dr Winifred Frost at Windermere, it transpires that the male eel stays in fresh water for seven to nine years, the female for 10 to 12 years – although in one exceptional case, a stay of 19 years has been recorded. Almost invariably the mature female eel is larger than the male. Female silver eels – that is, eels on the point of seaward migration – average about one pound, while the males average three to four ounces, and very rarely exceed 18 inches in length. Large eels are almost certainly females.[1] The British rod-caught record stands at 8 lb 10 oz – although many larger eels caught by other methods have been recorded.

Richardson mentions eels upwards of 9 lb from Ullswater, and John Watson, in his *English Lake District Fisheries* (1899), refers to a 9 lb eel from Windermere. Buckland lists one of 8¾ lb from the pond of Dutford Mill,

1 In very few other British species is the mature male smaller than the female. One exception is the pike (*Esox lucius*). Pike spawn while moving forward and are known to adopt an eye-to-eye orientation during the spawning act (see *Pike*, F. Buller, 1971). It is interesting to consider the possibility that this disparity in size of eels may indicate that the eel, too, is a mobile spawner.

and another of 9 lb from the river Arun. And there are stories of a huge eel captured in the river Kennet. On the subject of a 36 lb eel taken from the river Ouse near Denver Sluice, Buckland says:

The man who secured it left for Cambridge with his prize, and obtained upwards of three pounds by showing it. I cannot help thinking this eel must have been a Conger.

And he was probably right. He also has a droll account of a large eel taken from the Serpentine when the lake was cleaned out in 1869.

It was a fine specimen, and weighed over 6 lb. A cast of it is now in my museum. This eel was served up for dinner by my assistant, who stuffed it. It made the whole family ill for some hours.

After their long years in fresh water, the eels return to the sea. In preparation for this migration the snouts of both sexes become more pointed; the eyes enlarge; the back becomes black; the belly changes from yellow to silver, and the gut degenerates; so that like many other migrational fishes (e.g. salmon and lamprey), the eel does little or no feeding during its arduous journey home.

On some dark autumn night, the European eels begin to nose their way seawards, seemingly towards their distant spawning ground. At least, they go to sea; this much is certain. But little more is known. As Leon Bertin says in his biological study of the eel, published in 1956:

The eels virtually disappear once they have reached the sea, and we are almost completely in the dark concerning the tremendous journey of many thousands of miles which they accomplish in their passage to the Sargasso Sea.

Do they, in fact, ever reach the Sargasso Sea? In this respect, even to-day, the story of the eel is still incomplete. It has been suggested that the European eel is not equipped for such a journey, and that European stocks derive from the American eel – which provides larvae for both American and European waters:

The principal distinction between the American and the European eel is an average difference in the number of vertebrae: about 115 for the European eel, and 107 for the American.

If it is possible that a difference in the water temperature at which the eggs develop and hatch can result in a difference in vertebrae, then the eggs that hatch in the westerly waters of the Sargasso Sea may drift off to the north-west and become American eels, while those that hatch in the eastern waters of the Sargasso drift north-east and become European eels. If this is so, the European eel population comes from America. It seems unlikely. Nevertheless, at the present time this vital part of the eel's life-cycle remains to be resolved.

The eels' migrational changes take about six months to complete, and their journey seawards begins during late summer and autumn. But migrating eels seldom move down river if there is a glimmer of light. They are creatures of darkness. They tend to travel only on dark, cloudy nights, and usually when the river is rising. As Buckland observed: 'Not in calm, clear nights: the darker and stormier the night, the greater the exodus.'

And nearly 100 years before, referring to silver eels descending from Ullswater, Richardson noted:

> Immense quantities of silver eels are taken in August, September and October, in nets at Eel-Stank, about half a mile down the river Eamont. In five or six hours, eight or ten horse loads have been caught; but such large quantities only on the darkest and stormiest nights. The largest eels commonly go last; some have weighed upwards of 9 lb. It is worthy of remark that they scarcely stir if the moon peeps out, or when there is lightning; the fishermen even think the light of a candle prevents their motion.

Not so far-fetched as it may seem, that candle-light. Hanging a piece of glowing turf over the gap while they emptied their nets in the darkness, was an old Irish eel-fishermen's dodge to prevent eels running past before the nets had been re-set.

Whether migrating eels ever wriggle overland during any stage of their journey from fresh water to the sea has been the subject of much controversy. Buckland writes:

> There is no doubt indeed that eels occasionally quit the water and travel during the night over the moist meadows.

But some people are sceptical. Reliable eye-witness accounts are few, and very little evidence is available. Of great interest, therefore, is the following account written by an experienced fisherman and naturalist, who, while trout fishing one evening, witnessed an extraordinary overland mass migration of silver eels to the river Petterill near the village of Greystoke, in Cumberland; a movement made all the more remarkable by the fact that it happened in bright moonlight:

> It was a warm, damp autumn evening with a low mist over the river. The sky was clear, with a full moon and very few clouds. The river was at normal height. Between 11 p.m. and midnight, while walking from one part of the river to another, I saw a moving, shimmering mass in the moonlight.
>
> As I approached this mass I saw that it was a stream of silver eels, none of which was more than about a foot long. They kept moving steadily forward through the long wet meadow grass and were not halted by my walking among them; in fact, several of them passed over my waders. I followed them to the river and saw them dropping into the water from a steep bank about four feet high. The movement lasted for perhaps five minutes and must have involved several hundred eels.

Three very interesting points emerge from this account. First, the *size* of the eels. None was more than about a foot long – which seems to indicate a mass migration of *males*. Secondly, the moonlight. That eels should move at all on a bright moonlit night – let alone overland – is remarkable. And thirdly, the quantity of eels involved.

Joscelyn Lane also gives an excellent first-hand account in *Lake and Loch Fishing*:

> Apparently there is still some difference of opinion among anglers as to whether eels can travel overland when migrating or are restricted to following streams and rivulets. As luck would have it, I once came upon quite a large colony of eels just about to set out on their

transatlantic trek. I was in a car at the time on my way to Itchenor for a day's sailing in the estuary. There had been a few showers, and not far from the town the car was held up by a wide column of eels crossing the road. I got out to investigate and found they were coming along a deep ditch on the right-hand side of the road from a spot about 20 yards higher up, where they could be seen wriggling through the grass of an adjoining field on their way down to the ditch. On returning to the car I found that the eels were still crossing the road and streaming along the bottom of a ditch on the opposite side for some 30 yards, where I lost sight of them as the ditch diverged from the road. By the time I got back to the car again the tail of the procession had passed. There was no water in either of these ditches, along which several hundreds of eels must have travelled while I was there. Unfortunately I was not well acquainted with the countryside, nor, much to my regret, had I time to discover the source of the migration.

These are extremely valuable eye-witness accounts which affirm that migrating silver eels not only travel overland, but will do so together in large numbers – sometimes even in bright moonlight.

There is no biological reason why the eel *shouldn't* move overland if it wishes. In water, three-fifths of an eel's oxygen uptake is through the skin. The carbon dioxide excretion in water is mainly through the gills; but in air, ten-elevenths of this excretion is through the skin.

Experiments have shown that at a temperature of about 16°C, an eel out of water can take up as much oxygen when its mouth and gill openings are closed as when they are open and the gills able to function. Thus in damp conditions, such as long, dew-wet grass, with a temperature of around 15°C, an eel by breathing through its skin can stay alive out of water for a considerable time. As Bertin remarks:

There are pools which do not communicate directly or indirectly with any river. What happens to the silver eels of these pools? In the first place, they do all try to go. It is then that they are seen wandering at night in the damp meadows, profiting by their resistance to asphyxiation and dessication.

Altogether, a very remarkable animal, the eel, and worthy of the angler's respect.

Finally, in the words of Izaak Walton:

Gesner quotes Venerable Bede to say that in England there is an island called Ely, by reason of the innumerable number of eels that breed in it.

On the subject of which, that 17th-century cleric, Thomas Fuller, observed:

It is said that when the priests of this part of the country would still retain their wives in spite of what Pope and Monks could do to the contrary, their wives and children were miraculously turned into eels. I consider it a lie.

Never mind what he considered. Next time you see an eel, reflect that what you are looking at is a creature whose fantastic life-cycle remained for centuries an unsolved riddle that is still not fully solved even to-day; a creature for whom the Greeks beggared themselves, and the Sybarites escaped their taxes; a tonic for the voice; a panacea; a Boeothian sacrifice; an Egyptian god. And, perhaps, even the descendant of some incontinent priest.

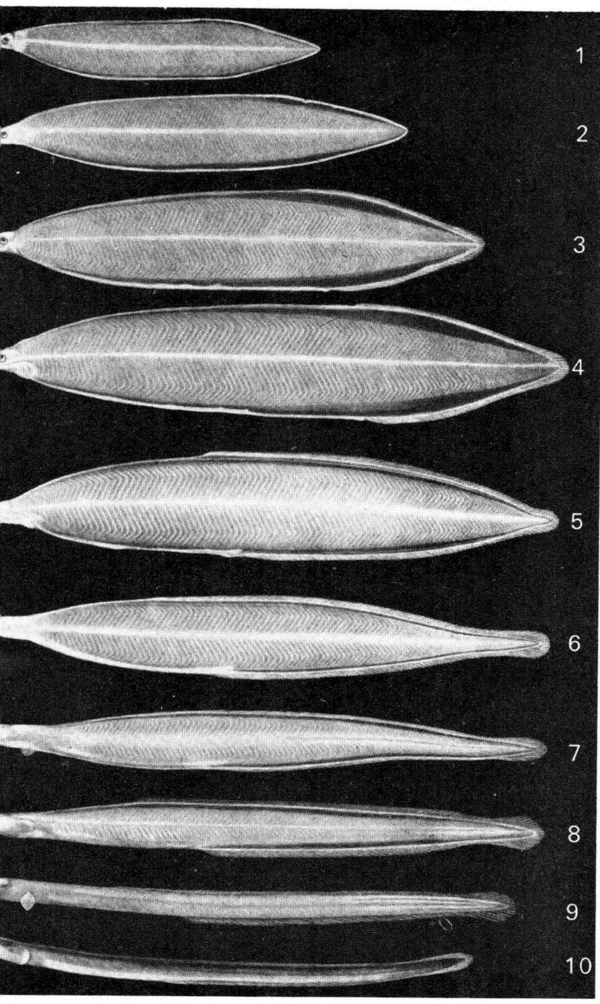

The development of the European eel (after Murray and Hjørt).

1–5. The leaf-shaped leptocephali *increasing in size during their long journey eastwards across the Atlantic.*

6–8. Stages in metamorphosis from leptocephalus *to glass-eel.*

9. Glass-eel.

10. Elver.

EEL FISHING

As for the various methods of catching eels, it has all been written before. 'Catholic in his tastes', writes Guiniad Charfy,[1]

The eel may be caught with divers baits, namely, powdered Beef, Garden Worms, or Lobs, Minnows, Hen's or Chicken's Guts, Fish Garbage, etc., but their best bait is a small kind of Lamprey, called a Pride. . . . The Ledger Bait, and Lying on the Grabble are the Methods chiefly in use in angling for these fish. He bites best in a fall of rain, in windy or gloomy weather, and after a thunderstorm.

Of passing interest is his description of Lying on the Grabble.

Above the hook a cut Shot is to be fixed . . . and next to this a small bored Bullet; thus the bullet will be prevented from slipping, and the hook Link have liberty to play in the water.

An adequate description of one of our modern ledgering techniques (see p. 459). Charfy's 'Ledger bait', however, was quite different from what is known as ledgering today (see pp. 459–60).

'As [eels] seldom stir in the daytime *unless by force*', says Charfy (our italics), 'they are generally catched at Night . . .' He mentions a method of bringing eels out in the daytime by 'raking the mud'. This will work as well today as it did in the 18th century – or indeed as it did over 2,000 years ago; stirring up the mud was an ancient device. Aristophanes's sausage seller outbawls Cleon with: 'Yes, it is with you as with the eel-

1 'Guiniad Charfy' was a pseudonym. The full story is given on page 428.

catchers; when the lake is still, they do not take anything, but if they stir up the mud, they do. So it is with you, when you disturb the State.' (There is little new in the fishing literature of any age!)

To all this we have very little to add. Both float and ledger tackle can be used with success, and boiled shrimp is an excellent bait.

HOW TO HANDLE, STUN, KILL AND SKIN AN EEL

An eel will live for a very long time out of water and if it is to be killed this should be done as quickly and humanely as possible. But to jab with a knife at a wriggling eel frequently results in injury to the angler. The eel should always be stunned before any attempt is made to kill it.

With the grip shown in the picture, hold the eel with three fingers. This is the only grip that will overcome the eel's sliminess. If you happen to have a dry newspaper handy, place the eel on it first: contact with dry paper makes an eel lie quiescent.

To stun an eel, hold it as shown and strike its *tail* (the portion downwards of the vent) hard against a rock; or hit it with a priest.

Kill the eel by severing the vertebrae in the neck. If you wish to skin the eel, *don't cut off its head.* A headless eel is much more difficult to skin.

What fisshe is slipperer than an ele?
Ffor whan thow hym grippist and wenest wele
Too haue hym siker right as the list,
Than faylist thou off hym, he is owte of thy fyst . . .

PIERS OF FULHAM, *Manuscript poem* (c. 1400).

1. Clench the live eel firmly under the middle finger. Stun it by striking it by the tail. Sever the neck vertebrae : do not *cut off the head.*
2. Tie a string round the neck of the eel and fasten to a nail. Using a razor blade or very sharp knife slice the skin right round the neck. Be careful not to cut too far into the neck. Note: *A cotton work-glove is useful for handling eels.*
3. Grasp the edge of the cut skin with a pair of pliers and pull downwards. Pull the skin right off over the tail.
4. Skinned eel with skin held alongside.

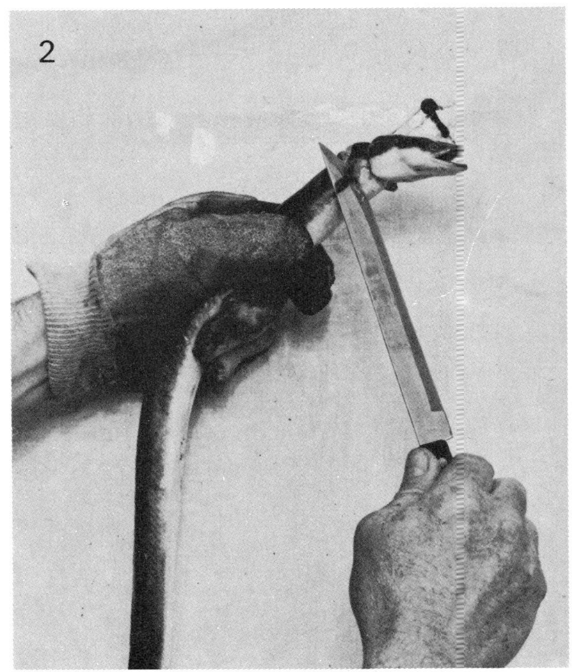

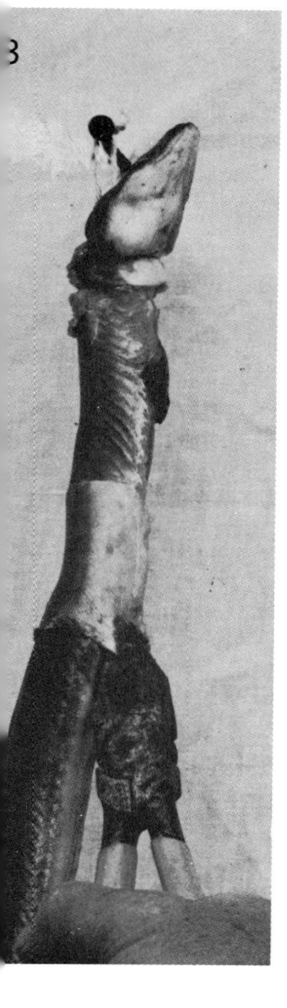

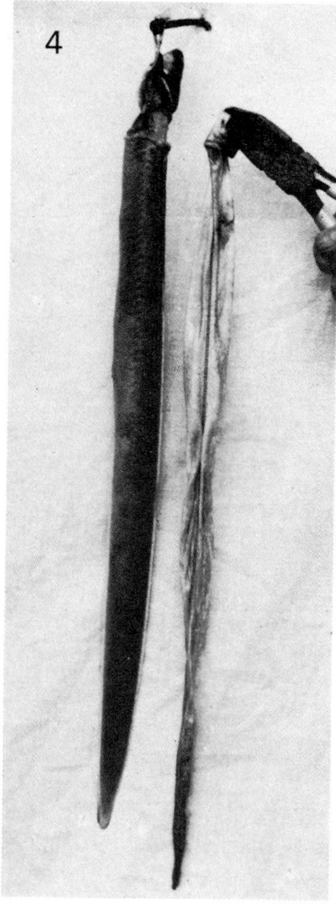

Above: *Eel spears (or 'glaives') from the Border Country* (Photographed by kind permission of J. Milbourn).

A Wicker Eel Trap, advertised in Farlow's catalogue of 1930.

'The bait – worms, fresh or salt water mussels with the shells crushed, small fish and many kinds of offal – is put in at the small end of the basket which is then closed with the cap provided, and the trap covered with sacking. The bait may be enclosed in a special receptacle of woven or perforated material, and should be changed frequently.

'The basket can be weighted with a brick or piece of iron and should have a stout cord attached for recovery and placed in the stream where the eels are known to run. The large inverted neck of the basket prevents any eels secured escaping from the trap.'

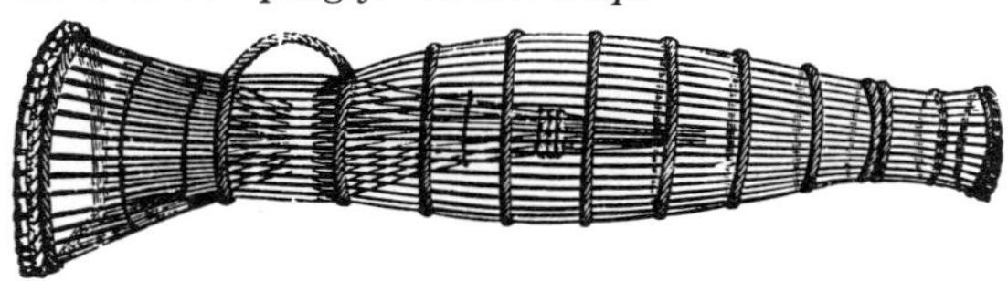

There is also a practice adopted for killing eels . . . that of spearing for them . . . and this is so extensively practised, that when the rushes grow up, there is a regular flotilla of spearmen. A man stands on his bundle, poking before him with his long-handled spear. When he takes an eel, he bites its head between his teeth, and then strings it up with a needle on a long cord. Anything so hideous as the appearance of these fellows, their faces begrimed with blood and dirt, can hardly be imagined.
O'GORMAN, *The Practice of Angling* (Vol. 1, 1845).

COOKING THE EEL

First, wash him in water and salt; then pull off his skin below his vent or navel, and not much further; having done that, take out his guts as clean as you can, but wash him not; then give him three or four scotches with a knife; and then put into his belly and those scotches, sweet herbs, an anchovy, and a little nutmeg grated or cut very small; and your herbs and anchovies must also be cut very small, and be mixed with good butter and salt: having done this, then pull his skin over him all but his head, which you are to cut off, to the end you may tie his skin about that part where his head grew, and it must be so tied as to keep all his moisture within his skin: and having done this, tie him with tape or packthread to a spit, and roast him leisurely, and baste him with water and salt till his skin breaks, and then with butter: and having roasted him enough, let what was put into his belly, and what he drips, be his sauce.

IZAAK WALTON, *The Compleat Angler*.

1 *Grilled Eel*

Cut the eel into chunks. Dip in flour or bread-crumbs, and grill or fry. Serve with tomato sauce, or with lemon slices and chopped parsley.

2 *Jellied Eel*

Several 2 lb eels
1 large onion
1 bay leaf
1 tablespoonful vinegar
2 oz gelatine
1 sprig of parsley
2 pints cold water
Whites of two eggs plus crushed egg shells
Salt and pepper

Clean and skin the eels. Put into a saucepan with the water and all the ingredients except the eggs and gelatine. Simmer until the eels are tender. Take out the fish, cut into pieces and remove the bones. Strain the liquid and return to the pan. Add the crushed egg shells and lightly whisked whites of the eggs. Add the gelatine and bring to the boil. Simmer for two minutes and strain again. Line a mould with the pieces of eel, add jelly and leave to set.

14 · The Grayling

Thymallus thymallus

The Grayling. 'The long, brownish dorsal fin is beautifully marked with stripes of darker hue. The adipose fin is velvety in texture. The head and back are deep purple, while the sides are a riot of purple, blue and copper, with here and there a tinge of pink and palest blue. . . . Trout may be called handsome – grayling are beautiful fish.' (E. Marshall-Hardy).

It had a deceptive because only superficial likeness to a pool in another river that I happened to know very well. As a result I started to fish it at the wrong place and so scared grayling instead of catching them. As I moved off with only half or less than half the grayling I ought to have taken from that pool, I knew that I had failed and badly failed to meet the true test of a fisherman, which is, that he shall be able to catch his share of fish in water that he is fishing for the first time.
ARTHUR RANSOME, *Rod and Line* (1929).

The grayling, like its cousins the trout and the salmon, belongs to the Salmonoidei, a sub-order of fishes which have existed for 70 million years, since the beginning of the Eocene period. Of the seven characters that distinguish Salmonoid fishes from other groups of fishes, two are familiar to anglers: the adipose fin and the pyloric caeca – worm-like appendages attached to the gut. The characteristic that distinguishes the grayling from all other Salmonoids is the possession of a large, dappled, sail-like dorsal fin.

The grayling has a wide distribution in the rivers of Britain and Northern Europe principally because of its introduction to waters where previously it never existed. Prior to widespread introduction it was confined to a few east-flowing rivers. It does not occur in Ireland.

Grayling 2 lb 9 oz. Taken from the river Test on shot-link ledger by F.B.

In the upper reaches of most clean and unpolluted rivers, where water turbulence and high rate of fall are typical features, the trout reigns supreme. Conversely in the middle reaches of such rivers, where the current is a bit slower and where glides, shallows and deeps alternate, the grayling seems to have a decided advantage over the trout. Provided there is an abundant weed growth, the middle reaches are also favoured by chub and dace, although these fishes extend even farther downstream than the grayling.

Not surprisingly, where the habitats of several species overlap, some species will suffer due to competition for food and spawning areas. A probable explanation for the separate niches enjoyed by the trout and the grayling lies in the different spawning techniques. Trout eggs are buried in gravel by the parent fish and are thus protected from the strong force of the current, whereas grayling eggs are merely 'dropped' on to the gravel bottom and in consequence would be more likely to be swept away by the currents of headwater streams.

In Britain, grayling rarely attain a weight of 4 lb, although grayling of twice this weight have been recorded from northern Scandinavia. The British Record rod-caught grayling was caught in 1883 by Dr T. Sanctuary on the river Wylye. It weighed 4 lb 9 oz. Other large grayling include a 4 lb 4 oz fish from the river Itchen and three more, each over 4 lb, taken from the river Test in 1905. The best bag of heavy grayling – 15 weighing 30 lb – was taken by H. J. Mordaunt, also from the River Test. All these fish were taken from chalkstreams and it is interesting to note that in his book *Grayling* (1968), R. V. Righyni states that grayling flourish and grow big in alkaline waters. A glance at a list of big-grayling rivers would appear to endorse this: Test, Itchen, Hampshire Avon, Wylye, Driffield Beck, Driffield Canal, Chess, Kennet and Dove.

The grayling's large dorsal fin, reminiscent of the fin of the sailfish, is used in a unique way. At spawning time – usually May or June – the cock fish wraps his fin over the back of the hen. This behaviour, it seems, stimulates the hen grayling to oviposit while keeping the cockfish 'on station' – or as the scientists say 'properly orientated' – so that its milt is accurately deposited.

The grayling's eye is different from that of any other native fish, its pupil being pear-shaped. Writers have conjectured that this may account for the grayling's curious behaviour when it rises to take a fly at the surface. During a hatch, trout and most other surface-feeding river fish either feed in shallow water or, if in deep water, 'keep station' a few inches below the surface. Not the grayling. It keeps station near the bottom, rises almost perpendicularly to take a fly and then returns to its lie with the celerity of a dive-bomber.

There is yet another facet of the grayling's behaviour; when hooked it often gyrates like a propellor. This manœuvre does nothing to inspire an angler's confidence. He knows from experience that any but a well-hooked fish will quickly regain its freedom.

One of the pleasantest ways to catch grayling is with the artificial fly. Trout fly-fishing pundits argue that 'this, or that, way' is the most sporting technique. Fortunately no purist dogma has attached itself to the grayling. No fisherman need feel guilty in following his inclination to fish 'up' or 'down' with either wet or dry flies.

Fishing the cockspur worm on float tackle is the classic style of the Yorkshireman – who fishes in the knowledge that this method will interest fewer spawning or ill-conditioned trout than that of the maggot angler with his liberal dosings of maggot groundbait.

F. B., who has enjoyed grayling fishing for most of his fishing life, obtains great pleasure when he 'works up' a swim with groundbait in the traditional style of the roach-fisherman. For this style of fishing – long-trotting – he fishes a single maggot, or sometimes two maggots, on a short-shanked size 10 spade-end hook and prefers to use a four-inch fluted float rather than the traditional grayling float.

He has found the shot link-ledger method excellent for covering swims that vary in depth and has taken his largest grayling on this rig – including three of 2 lb (best 2 lb 9 oz), all from swims of the same character, six to eight feet deep and close to the bank.

Grayling are obliging fish: they seem to feed for a period even during the coldest weather, sometimes on days when the river seems dead where other species are concerned. In autumn they tend to form into shoals, and the very best time for catching them is when it is almost dark.

Compared with the trout, which has received considerable attention from scientists, the grayling has been largely neglected. However, Roy Shaw, the Yorkshire naturalist has done much to redress this state of affairs, having spent a great deal of time observing and photographing the grayling's spawning behaviour. We are grateful to him for permission to reproduce these splendid pictures.

1. In March and April the grayling of the Driffield Canal congregate on the spawning shallows.

2. Material from the spawning site, sand, fine gravel and snail shells.

3. In as little as six inches of water the males, who are mostly larger, and noticeably darker than the females, perform their courtship ceremonies and shepherd the ripe females into position. Pairs of competing males frequently clash in a flurry of spray. Shaw says: 'At times several battles are enacted simultaneously and large dorsals cleave the water side by side'.

4. Once over the chosen site, the cock fish moves close to the female and leans towards her. This movement enables him to wrap his huge dorsal fin over her back – thus ensuring correct orientation during the spawning act.

5. Although grayling frequently share a habitat with trout they occupy a different niche, and although it is often said that grayling flourish to the detriment of trout, it is sometimes forgotten that trout can sometimes flourish to the detriment of grayling. As the grayling's eggs are dropped a brown trout moves in to take them.

COOKING THE GRAYLING

The grayling besides offering good sport for nine months of the year is an excellent fish for the table. Indeed the flesh of the grayling, taken in season (it comes in with the pheasant in October), is more predictably good than that of the trout. Before cooking grayling it is advisable to remove the scales.

1 *Baked Grayling*

Clean and wash the fish. Dry it well, place it in a baking dish in which a little butter has been previously melted. Season with salt and pepper, cover with a greased paper, and bake gently from 25 to 35 minutes, basting occasionally. Or wrap the fish in greaseproof paper and bake in a tin.

I. P. MORETON & W. A. HUNTER, *Fisherman's Manual* (1932).

2 *Grilled Grayling*

Anoint them with olive oil, season with salt and pepper and grill for seven to ten minutes. A squeeze of lemon will prove a pleasant addition when the fish is served.

E. MARSHALL-HARDY, *Coarse Fish.*

Finally a point for the gourmet. Grayling, like all freshwater fish except the salmon, should be cooked on the day of capture. When this is impossible – deep freeze them rather than put them in a refrigerator. In his book *Grayling* (1968), that skilful angler R. V. Righyni, offers this advice:

An expert in the freezing of food once told me that the slow reduction in temperature in a refrigerator separates certain fluids from the flesh of fish and these form into small frozen globules. When the temperature is raised again, the fluids remain separate and the result is that the cooked fish is of a poor consistency and flavour. Quick, deep freezing, he said, was different. The flesh undergoes no physical change and when thawed out again, it is in the same state as before the freezing.

15 · The Gudgeon

Gobio gobio

The adult gudgeon is often mistaken for an immature barbel. This is surprising since the barbel can be recognised at a glance by its four barbules on lip and upper jaw. The gudgeon has only two – at the angle of the mouth. Recent research carried out on the river Mole by Stott, Elsdon and Johnson (1962), proved that some gudgeon possess a strong homing instinct. After a number of gudgeon had been transferred as far as one third of a mile upstream or downstream, over 50% of those recaptured had returned to the home range within 2 or 3 weeks.

Finally, the GUDGEON. Now this is another little fish that deserves better of anglers than he gets. True, he stays small – a two-ounce gudgeon is good, and three ounces is enormous – but he has a number of virtues. First, he will go on biting on the hottest day, when everything in the river seems to have called it a day and gone to sleep. . . . Secondly, the gudgeon is the most undemanding of fish – he will go on biting even when you are standing in the river with your feet in the middle of a shoal of him. Thirdly, he is delicious eating. . . . But it seems to have been forgotten, and you hear more curses than praise when an angler has happened to get among a mob of these drab-looking little fish. If only they would accept their luck, catch a panful, and try them fried in breadcrumbs, they might change their tune.
MAURICE WIGGIN, *Fishing for Beginners* (1958).

The British record rod-caught gudgeon weighed 4 oz 4 dr. But in spite of its diminutive size, this 'toothsome morsel' as Dr J. J. Manley wrote, 'is well worth a Note all to himself'.

Since it feeds at ground the gudgeon lives close to the bottom and prefers a depth of from three to six feet in a stream just strong enough to keep a gravelly or sandy bottom lightly scoured. Although its natural habitat is running water, it sometimes flourishes and breeds when introduced into still waters.

For gudgeon fishing, a size 14 or 16 hook is tied on a 2–3 lb B.S. line; nothing finer should be used for fear of breaking on the strike. The float should be big enough to support at least 4 BB shots. This will enable the leads to get the bait right down to the river bed at the *head* of the swim. The fishing depth should be adjusted so that the bait 'trips' along the bottom. Given time, a gudgeon is capable of swallowing a sizeable worm, but a *small* bait – whether a pellet of paste, a pinch of bread, a maggot or a piece of worm – is more effective since it allows an immediate strike.

Experienced gudgeon anglers, realizing that gudgeon soon satisfy their appetites, do no groundbaiting. Instead, they rake the gravel at the head of the swim with a huge rake. The gudgeon's exploitation of a newly-raked swim can be compared to the seagull's exploitation of fresh plough.

Victorian and Edwardian professional Thames fishermen who took out gudgeon-fishing parties called this practice of raking, 'scratching their backs'. By these means, presumably, gudgeon were so easily caught that the Oxford Dictionary defines the gudgeon as 'A gullible person . . . One that will swallow anything'. Jonathan Swift defined a (human) gudgeon as 'A person easily cheated and ensnared'. Jay goes even further:

What gudgeons are we men,
Every woman's easy prey!
Though we've felt the hook, again
We bite, and then betray.

Gudgeon fishing was once regarded as a social grace and some gallants even went so far as to claim that ladies made better gudgeon-fishers than men; their light touch, it was thought, fitted them for the delicate strike – the merest twist of the wrist – required to hook a gudgeon. Weller, however, was a realist. 'Beware of lady gudgeon-fishers', he warned; and Manley, pointing to the dangers of taking women to the river bank, noted that 'Many a heart has been irretrievably lost when gudgeon fishing.'

COOKING THE GUDGEON

Let me say, then, that, in my humble opinion, however mean a fish the gudgeon may be thought whereon to exercise the angler's skill, he is worthy of all commendation as a fish for the angler's table, and indeed the board of the most fastidious *gourmet*. There are few fresh-water fish worth the salt with which they must be eaten, if eaten at all, but oesophagistically I am enthusiastic about our *Gobio fluviatilis*. The ancients highly prized it. Galen places it in a conspicuous position among edible fish, both for the delicacy and sweetness of its taste and its digestibility.

The whole matter is one of extreme simplicity, just as boiling a potato, grilling a chop, or making melted butter; and hence, perhaps, the very general failure. To the wives of professional Thames fishermen it seems specially to have been given to master the art of cooking gudgeon successfully. The chief secret, as with the cooking of all coarse fresh-water fish, is to allow the gudgeon, after being cleaned, to become dry and almost hard by exposure to sun and wind. The next important point is the quick and delicate manipulation to which he should be subjected in the frying-pan, as he becomes encrusted with egg and breadcrumbs; but a verbal description of this could not be given even by the most learned and versatile author of a most exhaustive cookery book. It is a question of fine and dexterous *touch*, and the operator could hardly say more of his performance than Dr Lynn says of his tricks, 'And that's how it's done.'

J. J. MANLEY, *Fish and Fishing* (1877).

16 · The Lampreys

The eel may be caught with divers baits . . .
but their best bait is a small kind of
Lamprey, called a Pride.
GUINIAD CHARFY, *The Fisherman.*

Sea lamprey 3 lb taken from the Cumberland Esk.

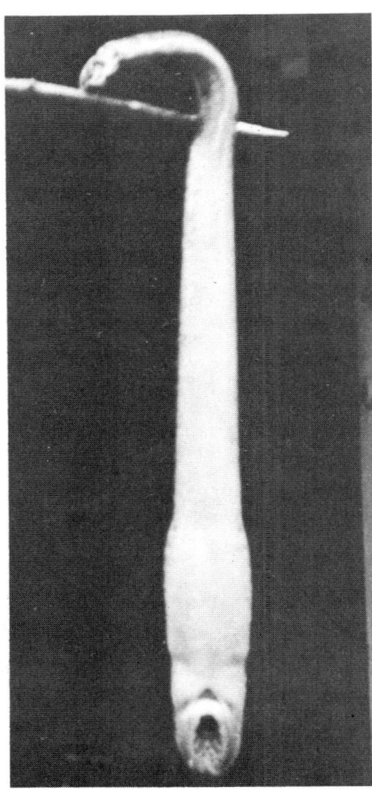

There are three species of lamprey. All spawn in freshwater, and all spend their first five or six years in freshwater. During this period of their lives – when they are non-parasitic – they are called 'prides'.

Prides are blind, toothless, and bear little resemblance to their parents. As larvae they live in the mud or sand at the bottom of a pool somewhere downstream of the natal site, where they feed on organic matter and detritus.

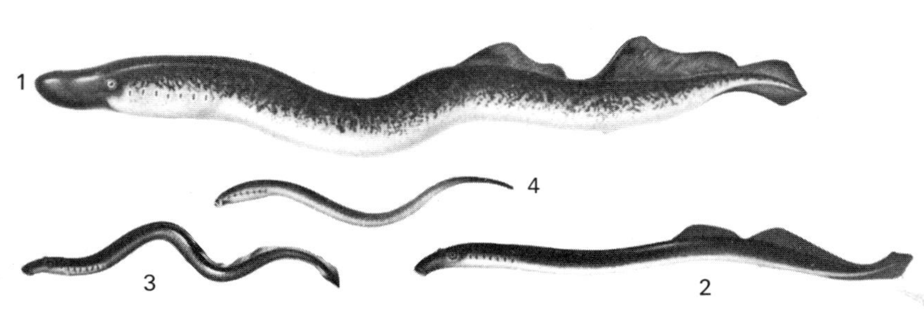

Lampreys: 1. Sea lamprey; 2. River lamprey; 3. Brook lamprey; 4. Pride.

When adult, all three species of lamprey are jawless, eel-like fishes with round suctorial mouths. All spawn in gravelly streams or rivers, where they clear a place in the gravel to deposit their eggs. All three species die shortly after spawning.

1 *The Sea Lamprey (Petromyzon marinus)*

After its metamorphosis to its adult form (which takes place after six to eight years), it migrates to the sea. Here it attacks a wide range of fishes, including cod, haddock, salmon and basking shark, with its powerful sucking apparatus, causing death to the less robust species. After a sea life of one to two years, it returns to fresh water to spawn. Sea lampreys grow to three feet in length and may weigh up to 5 or 6 lb.

2 *The River Lamprey or Lampern (Lampetra fluviatilis)*

This species is smaller than the sea lamprey, reaching a maximum length of about 20 inches. The prides undergo a metamorphosis when they are about five inches long and then migrate to salt water. Although little is known about their marine life, it is thought that river lampreys do not move far out to sea. They stay in salt water for about a year, and are parasitic, feeding on the blood and body tissues of their hosts – mainly estuarine species. According to Tate Regan, a number of river lampreys:

> . . . reside permanently in freshwater, while the rest, like the sea lamprey, spend the greater part of their adult life in the sea and enter the rivers chiefly in order to spawn.

Loch Lomond swarms with river lampreys which attack sea-trout and powan. Perhaps in such large stretches of water lampreys use the lake as the 'sea' and its feeder streams as spawning rivers. Henry Lamond, Loch Lomond's greatest chronicler and fisherman, found lampreys spawning in the lower reaches of the Luss Water. He also recorded the finding of lampreys on sea-trout netted from the loch, but never on any netted from the river Leven (Loch Lomond's outflow) or in the Clyde estuary.

The late Andrew Colquhoun, of Luss, held a unique record – the capture of a lamprey on fly. Lamond quotes the incident in his book *Loch Lomond* (1931): 'In striking a rising sea-trout on one occasion he missed the sea-trout but hooked and landed its attendant lamprey!'

3 *The Brook Lamprey, or Planer's Lamprey (Lampetra planeri)*

The brook lamprey differs in three respects from the others.

(a) It spends its entire life in freshwater, usually in the headwaters of the stream.

(b) It is non-parasitic, using its suctorial disc for holding on to stones.

(c) The adult does not feed. It spawns in the year it matures.

The brook lamprey is the most common lamprey in Britain now that the migratory species are unable to penetrate the pollution barriers existing in the lower reaches of many rivers. It is seldom larger than eight inches in length and is classed highly as a hookbait for trout, chub, perch, pike and eels.

The Lamprey is a Sea fish. . . . It is reckoned a great delicacy, either when potted or stewed, but is said to occasion surfeits; a fatal instance of this occurred to Henry I.
THE REV. W. B. DANIEL, *Rural Sports* (1801).

COOKING LAMPREYS

According to Professor J. M. D. Meiklejohn (*A New History of England and Great Britain*, 1903), Henry I died in Normandy in 1135:

He was very fond of lampreys and after a day spent in hunting he ate very heartily of them. His body was brought to England and buried in Reading Minster which he had himself built.

Here, for the curious, are two recipes.

1 *Baked Lamprey*

1 medium-sized lamprey
Suet farce
1 egg
Breadcrumbs
Fat for basting
Anchovy sauce, or any other fish sauce preferred
1 lemon

Rub the fish well with salt, wash it in warm water, and remove the cartilage and strings which run down the back. Fill the body with the prepared farce, sew it up securely, and fasten round two or three thicknesses of buttered or greased paper. Cover the fish with hot water, boil gently for 20 minutes, then drain and dry well. Put it into a baking dish, in which a little butter or fat has been previously melted, and baste well. Bake gently for about half an hour, basting frequently, then strip off the skin, brush the fish over with beaten egg, and coat it lightly with breadcrumbs. Bake the fish for about 20 minutes longer, or until nicely browned, then serve it garnished with sliced lemon, and send the sauce to table in a tureen.

2 *Stewed Lamprey*

1 medium-sized lamprey
¾ pint of stock or water
1 glass of port or sherry
1 oz of butter
1 oz of flour
1 lemon sliced
1 teaspoonful of lemon-juice
2 small onions sliced
2 or 3 mushrooms, or 6 button mushrooms
1 bay-leaf
Salt and pepper

Wash thoroughly in salted warm water, remove the head, tail and fins, and cut the fish across into two-inch lengths. Bring the stock or water to boiling point, put in the fish with the bay-leaf and necessary seasoning, and simmer gently for three-quarters of an hour. Meanwhile, melt the butter in another saucepan, fry the onion slightly then add the flour, and fry slowly until well browned. When the fish has stewed one hour, pour the liquor from it over the prepared butter and flour, stir until boiling, then put in the mushrooms, wine and lemon-juice. Place the fish in the prepared sauce, simmer gently for half an hour longer, serve with the sauce strained over, and garnish with slices of lemon.

17 · The Stone Loach

Noemacheilus barbatulus

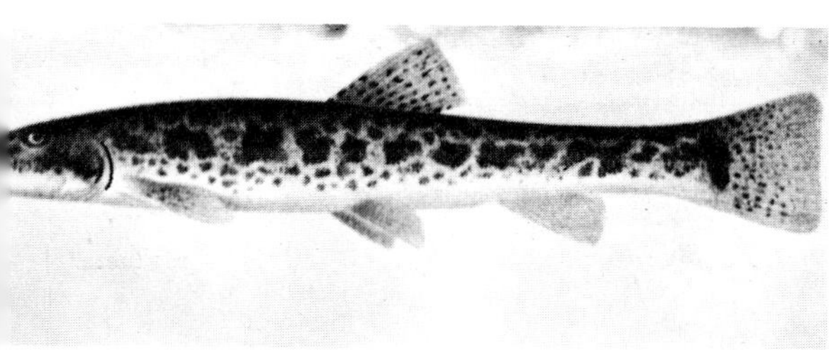

Loach are of small interest to the angler except insofar as they compete with the young of other species for food, and provide food for larger fishes. R. Lawson, Fisheries Officer of the Piscatorial Society, who keeps records of the stomach contents of pike taken from a River Kennet trout fishery, found stones in the stomach of a small pike (2–3 lb) together with unidentifiable fish remains. F. B. suggested that these remains were likely to be those of a bullhead or a loach, since one would expect a pike to pick up an occasional stone when attacking either of these bottom-haunting species. Strange to relate, the next pike examined had stones in its stomach–together with a stone loach.

18 · The Spined Loach

Cobitis taenia

The spined loach is rarely observed because, unlike the stone loach, it prefers a deep-water habitat. The spines from which it takes its name are situated on each side of the head, just below the eye. By projecting these spines sideways and outwards, the loach can 'lock' itself in its burrow – a hole in silk weed, mud or sand, from which it seldom emerges except to feed. This 'locking' device prevents other fishes from sucking the loach from its lair.

19 · The Minnow

Phoxinus phoxinus

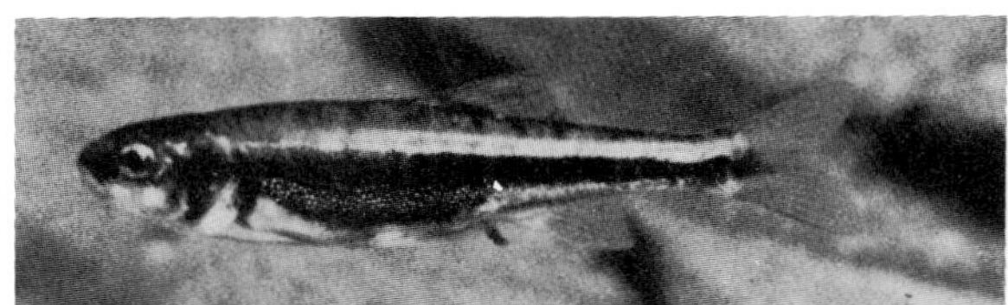

The minnow is of some interest to the angler as a baitfish, since it features in the diet of pike, perch, trout, chub and eels. Fried like whitebait, minnows are very tasty. They are easily caught on a fragment of worm or paste on a small hook, or in traps such as those shown in Figs 19.1*a* and *b*.

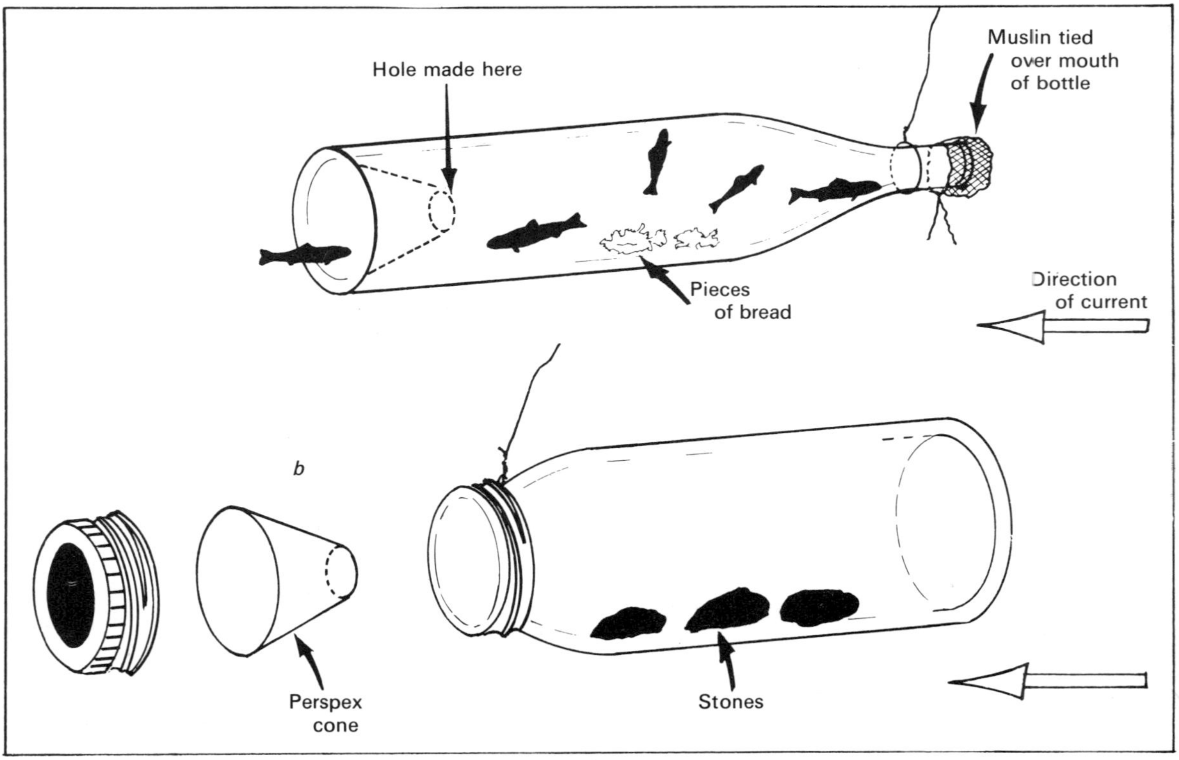

Hole made here

Muslin tied over mouth of bottle

Pieces of bread

Direction of current

b

Perspex cone

Stones

Minnows taken in a Kilner trap.
Photograph: Edwin Grant/*The Angler's Mail.*

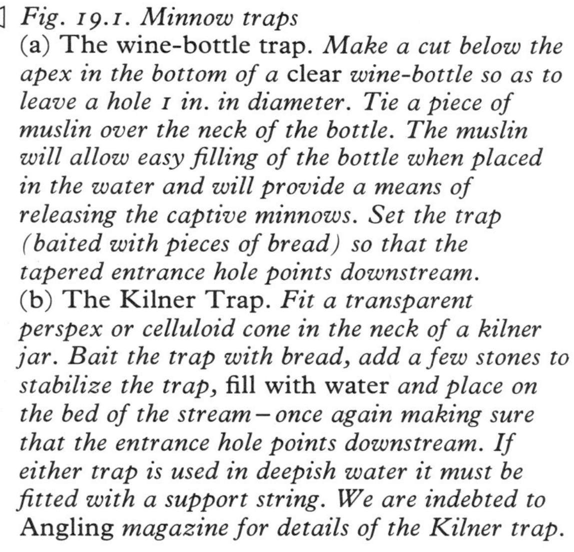

◁ *Fig. 19.1. Minnow traps*
(a) The wine-bottle trap. *Make a cut below the apex in the bottom of a* clear *wine-bottle so as to leave a hole 1 in. in diameter. Tie a piece of muslin over the neck of the bottle. The muslin will allow easy filling of the bottle when placed in the water and will provide a means of releasing the captive minnows. Set the trap (baited with pieces of bread) so that the tapered entrance hole points downstream.*
(b) The Kilner Trap. *Fit a transparent perspex or celluloid cone in the neck of a kilner jar. Bait the trap with bread, add a few stones to stabilize the trap,* fill with water *and place on the bed of the stream – once again making sure that the entrance hole points downstream. If either trap is used in deepish water it must be fitted with a support string. We are indebted to* Angling *magazine for details of the Kilner trap.*

20 · The Perch

Perca fluviatilis

. . . but my mind was on the perch. This was the fish of my childhood – and I suspect yours – this was the fish I began on, the first fish I ever caught. Perhaps it is the first fish to all men, perhaps all men get the same thrill as I do whenever I see a perch, perhaps their minds go back as mine does to that first day, that first tremendous thrill as the float bobbed and I pulled hard and there on the hook kicked a striped green fish with a silver tummy and red fins.
BRIAN VESEY-FITZGERALD, *The Hampshire Avon* (1950).

Perch . . . like noise, and are fond of music, which attracts them to the surface. One of my sons (now I hope happy) assured me that he saw a vast shoal of them appear over water, attracted by the sound of bag-pipes, when a Scotch regiment were marching over a neighbouring bridge, and that they remained there until the sound died away in the distance.

How much superior the ear of perch to that of Paganini, who, on hearing the Scotch pipe, prostrated himself on the floor, declaring that it must have been invented by the devil.
O'GORMAN, *The Practice of Angling* (Vol. 2, 1845).

Note the strong prickly dorsal spines. As many a young angler has learnt through painful experience, the proper way to hold a perch is to stroke back these dorsal spines with one hand before securing the fish with the other. (From T. F. Salter, *The Angler's Guide,* (8th edition, 1833.)

The perch is widely distributed across the northern temperate parts of Asia and Europe, although absent from northern Scotland, northern Scandinavia, Spain and southern Italy. It spawns in April or May; the female laying her spawn on strands of weed or on sunken objects such as tree branches or roots. Unlike most other European piscivorous freshwater fishes, it can survive in a body of water which contains no other species of fish. Nikolsky, in *The Ecology of Fishes* (1963), states that adult perch, although not able to sustain themselves by feeding directly on plankton, nevertheless live at its expense by feeding on their own plankton-eating young. This habit is thought to explain those populations of stunted perch which exist in various lakes. When one season's crop of perch survives in great abundance, it can dominate as a year-class for up to 15 years (see pp. 17–18 for a discussion of the same phenomenon with regard to bream populations).

Perch are usually found in shoals of the same age group, the males outnumbering the females by ratios of up to 9:1.

A bold biter, the perch has been popular with generations of anglers; many a novice has been grateful for its attention when other species proved more reticent. It is also very good to eat.

The perch bait *par excellence* is the worm. Although all species of worms will tempt a hungry perch the two largest British species, the lobworm and the blue-headed lobworm (see p. 435) are best for large perch. The Rev. W. B. Daniel in his *Rural Sports* (1801) suggests '. . . small lobworms which have no knot'. (This is the famous 'maiden lob' of early angling literature: in reality an immature lobworm – neither male nor female, since worms are hermaphrodites, having both male and female reproductive organs.) Live minnows and gudgeon are also excellent baits for perch.

Although Pennant lists an 8 lb perch from the Serpentine (Daniel records 9 lb for the same fish) and mentions another eight-pounder taken from Dagenham Breach, and Colonel Thornton describes the catching of a 7 lb 3 oz Loch Lomond perch, a two-pounder represents a handsome catch for most anglers. A three-pounder is considered a very good fish, while a four-pounder is the peak of most anglers' expectations. In Britain, few anglers have landed a perch over 5 lb.

There are two angling methods that, although not exclusive to perch fishing, are distinctly associated with it. One is sink-and-draw method, used with worm bait; the other, a paternoster baited with worm or minnow. Both methods display a bait a foot or two off the bottom, which is where the perch normally expects to dine.

From his experience of fishing Arlesey lake in Bedfordshire, noted home of big perch, Richard Walker is of the opinion that the big fellows haunt (particularly in winter) the proximity of underwater ridges, or any place where there is a sudden discontinuity of depth, such places providing suitable cover for the sudden pounce which is characteristic of the hunting perch.

Spinning is a good method of taking perch but suffers from one drawback: the need to use a fairly heavy mainline, and a wire

4 lb perch caught by R. Weston of Bletchley, Bucks, on 4 lb line and size 12 hook. At time of going to press this fine perch is a record for Wilstone reservoir.

leader in case a pike should be hooked. Unless the wire leader is used, a pike is likely to bite through the line and escape with a spinner in its mouth.

The perch prefers a bait that is spinning evenly rather than wobbling. The most deadly spinner is one made with a mother-of pearl spinning blade.

Perch will take an artificial fly, or lure, retrieved with the same irregular jerk (or sink-and-draw) used for mackerel feathering. This sink-and-draw procedure can also be applied to spinning, if a perch has followed a bait without taking it. In these circumstances the spinner is allowed to fall close to the bottom, given a jerk and then let fall again. This is repeated until the perch is provoked into taking. By this method, F. B. once hooked three 2 lb Hampshire Avon perch that previously had merely followed his fly-spoon close into the bank.

Perch are bold biters. Even so, the loss of one hooked perch back to the shoal usually heralds the end of sport for a time so far as that particular shoal is concerned. 'Faddist' (Edward Ensom), in *Coarse Fish 'Briefs'* (1957), quotes J. H. R. Bazley, England's

The best of a bag of perch, including some two pounders, taken on the fly at Hanningfield by Peter Thomas and F. B., 1968.

finest-ever match fisherman. Bazley suggested that the fear communicated by a broken-free perch to the rest of the shoal is simply one of panic, which causes a 'stampede', and is not to be confused with an awareness or suspicion of the angler's wiles:

Immediately the fish is hooked, the others follow it about. When the hook comes away, the fortunate fish swims off full tilt – goodness knows where – and the others dovetail behind it, so that when the next bait is dropped in, there are no perch to take it. Sometimes a perch which has regained its liberty does not dash away any great distance, but after a swim round, comes back to the original spot, when the fish bite just as freely as if they had received no warning of what might be in store for them.

Every so often one hears about a fishing experience which in retrospect takes on a dream-like quality. An example is the following account of an astonishing season with giant perch – for which we are grateful to Gerry Hughes, features editor of a fishing weekly: *The Angler's Mail.*

'When the perch fishing in our club pit really hit peak form it was "fantastic". In the course of one short season Brazier's Pit an old gravel pit near Nazeing in Essex, roughly an acre in size, produced at least six perch of over 4 lb, and three-pounders by the score.

'The pit was square in shape, with tall trees overhanging one bank. The other three sides were bordered by hedges. The water was up to about ten feet in depth, going to 16 feet in places. When the club first took it over, a few years prior to this wonderful season, it was thought to hold very few fish, and since it looked right for carp, several hundred were put in.

'We knew nothing about the stock of perch until the opening of the 1966 season. Then, within a few weeks, some hairy stories began to circulate.

'Knowing how rumours build up, particularly over the size of fish, I ignored them for a couple of weeks. Then came an accidental meeting with another club member, who told of an astonishing experience the previous Sunday. He was watching a fellow angler playing a big perch, when, a few yards from the bank, the fish suddenly stopped coming in. Through the clear water he saw what appeared to be *two* perch on the end of the line, one holding the other by the tail. Eventually the bigger fish released its hold and the perch that had taken the minnow livebait was netted – it weighed $2\frac{3}{4}$ lb!

'That story convinced me that I should investigate immediately. The most successful bait, it seemed, was live minnow, or a bunch of minnows, fished on float tackle. I hadn't time to catch any on my first visit, so had to make do with lobworms. When I got to the water, soon after dawn, I found at least 20 other members already there. When the sun came up the perch fed ravenously on their minnow baits. Most of the fish caught were round the 1 lb mark or under; but at midday word got round that a big one had been caught by a teenager fishing under the overhanging trees on the far bank, and with the sun now blazing down and the perch ignoring my lobworm I wandered round to have a look.

'Yes, said the lad, he had caught a big perch several hours before. It had taken two minnows floatfished, just a few yards from the bank, at a spot where the water was deepest. Then he pulled up his keepnet and showed me the most impressive fish I have ever seen in my life.

'Its spiky dorsal was raised like the crest on an angry dragon, its eyes were like marbles and it had a mouth like a small bucket. Weighed on a set of accurate scales it went 4 lb 10 oz and it made every big fish I had ever seen before look like small fry.

'With shaking hands I went back to my rod but very little was caught during that hot, sultry afternoon. Then, just before sunset something else happened that made me tremble as I watched.

'As the air temperature dropped, shoals of bleak slashed on the surface, chased by some very large perch. The perch were so determined to get their evening meal that on occasion huge dorsals, and mouths like teacups came clear of the water.

'On my next visit I stopped at the river – only half a mile from the pit – and caught a dozen bleak. These were hastily transported in a canvas bucket and transferred to my

A shoal of perch. (Photograph from *Fine Angling for Coarse Fish*, Seeley Service).

keepnet, once I arrived. Only four survived the journey but I knew I was in with a better chance than on my previous visit.

'I tackled up with a large balsa-bodied Avon trotting-float, liphooked a big bleak on a size 6 spade-end, and with other anglers arriving in steady numbers, cast out as far as I could to avoid bankside disturbance.

'Just five minutes later the float vanished. It didn't wobble or dip, it just vanished, and line poured off the spool of my reel, which had been left with the bale arm open.

'I took a deep breath, lifted the rod from the rests, closed the pickup and struck. There was a mighty plunge on the end of the line. The perch made several strong rushes out in the depths and then began to give ground. I brought it in close enough to see its dim, shadowy shape when everything went slack and I reeled in an empty hook.

'An hour later, with a fresh bait in the same spot, the float vanished again. It went down so fast you could almost hear the "pop". Once more I had the perch within a few yards of the bank when the hook came away. One of the bleak had died in the keep net so I put the sole survivor on the hook and cast out again. "This time," I thought, "I'll give the perch plenty of time before striking."

'The next bite was just like the other two. Down went the float with line pouring off the spool. This time I counted to ten, then picked up the rod, and struck. There was a violent plunging at the other end and I really bent the rod into that fish.

'But it seemed that the bleak I was using were a shade too big for the perch to manage comfortably. This time I got the bait back – without a scale left on it. It must have lodged across the perch's mouth.

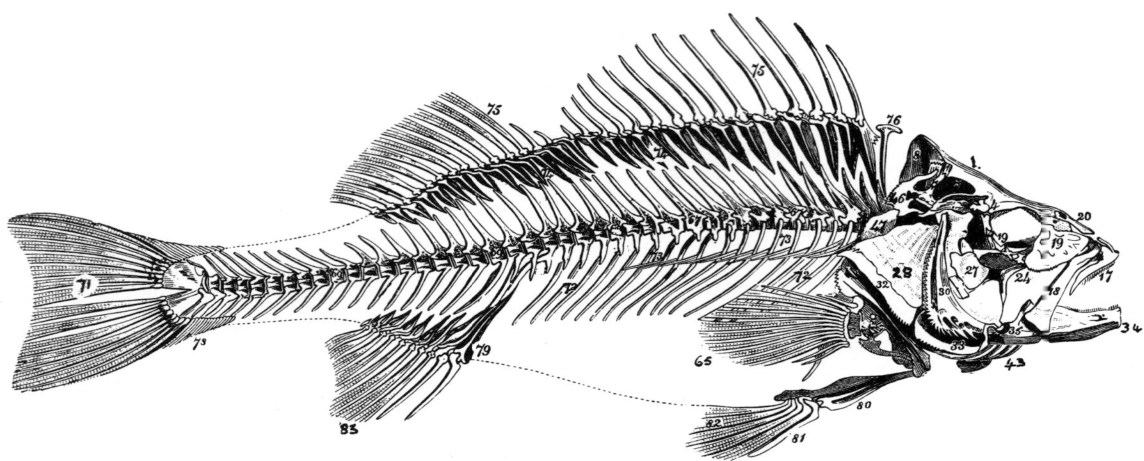

The Skeleton of a Fish (Perch) after Gunther

1. *Frontal bone*
4. *Post frontal*
8. *Supraoccipital*
17. *Premaxillary*
18. *Maxillary*
19. *Proeorbital*
20. *Nasal*
24. *Pterygoid*
27. *Pretympanic*
28. *Operculum*
30. *Proeoperculum*
32. *Suboperculum*
33. *Interoperculum*
34. *Dentary (of the mandible)*
35. *Articulary*
43. *Branchiostegals*
46. *Post-temporal*
47. *Scapula*
53. *Carpals*
65. *Pectoral rays*
67. *Abdominal vertebrae*
69. *Caudal vertebrae*
71. *Caudal rays*
72. *Ribs*
73. *Epipleural spines*
74. *Interneural spines*
75. *Dorsal spines and dorsal ray*
76. *First interneural*
79. *Interhaemal spines*
80. *Pubic bone*
81. *Ventral spine*
82. *Ventral rays*
83. *Anal rays*

'Two days later I had a phone call saying that a 4 lb 6 oz perch had been taken on a fly spoon, so I was there again the following weekend. I took along a friend, John Piper, who was keen on perch fishing and gave him the swim where I'd had the three stupendous runs on the previous Sunday.

'Thinking I would try for either perch or carp, I baited up with a very big lobworm, and dropped an Arlesey-bomb ledger rig on to a gravel bar that rose to within five feet of the surface about twenty feet out. As I put the rod on its rests, with the bale arm of the reel still open, I noticed that line was still trickling over the lip of the spool. Then the rod tip bounced and the trickle of line became a rush.

'I struck immediately and my first thought was that I was into a carp. The fish ran to my left, changed its mind and doubled back, circled round and kited in towards the bank down to my right. There matters came to a halt for lying upside down in the water was a large thorn bush, presumably uprooted from the hedge the previous winter. It made a safe sanctuary for whatever was on the end of my 4 lb line.

'I put the rod back in the rest and opened

the bale arm hoping that if left to its own devices the carp would swim out again. Ten minutes later it hadn't budged so I wandered along to John Piper. I asked if he would give me some assistance. "It's a small carp," I said as I explained the situation.

'But it wasn't. When we got back I closed the bale arm, lifted the rod and there, just below the surface, was a huge perch, my worm hanging from the corner of its jaw. Miraculously it had untanged itself from the underwater branches and within a minute or two it was safely in the landing net.

'Piper, a very experienced angler, was speechless. By far the biggest perch he had ever seen, and certainly the biggest I had ever caught. 4 lb 5 oz – the fish of a lifetime.

'I remember little else about that day. In the evening, the bleak shoals fled for their lives once again as the big perch chased them, but I don't think I caught another fish.

'Two weeks later another friend of mine "twitched" a lobworm slowly along the bottom, close by the bankside and landed a perch of 4 lb 6 oz. Before the season ended several more were reported and there were whispers of others, their captors preferring to keep quiet.

'Sadly, the fishing went down after that. We must have caught it at its very peak. The following year the size of the fish fell off rapidly and the year after that sport was almost non-existent, except with carp.

'We had just that one astonishing season. But I shall never forget it. I'll never see perch fishing like it again.'

COOKING THE PERCH

1 *At the Lakeside*

Take each perch separately, merely wiping him dry – not cutting or scraping him in the least, as that would break the skin and let out his juices; then take a piece of paper, and wet it in the lake and roll the perch in it, in three or four folds. Screw up the ends and thrust perch, paper and all, into embers. In five to ten minutes your fish is cooked. Rake him out; take off the charred paper, and carefully remove his scales which will come off *en masse*; rub the white succulent side with butter, pepper and salt to taste; make an incision along the backbone and flake off all the firm white flesh; turn the carcass over and serve the other side of the fish in the same way; throw away the bones and interior and eat the remainder. It is a dish for a king, or an angler. A salmon or big trout may be filleted and served in the same way, or roasted upon skewers.

FRANCIS FRANCIS, *A Month in the West* (1886).

2 *Fried Perch*

4 perch
Eggs
Breadcrumbs
Frying-fat
Salt, pepper and flour

Scale, clean, wash and dry the fish thoroughly. Sprinkle with salt and pepper, dredge well with flour, brush over with beaten egg, and cover with breadcrumbs. Have ready some hot fat, fry the fish until nicely browned, drain well, and serve with anchovy, shrimp, or melted butter sauce.

Mrs Beeton's Every-Day Cookery.

21 · The Pike

Esox lucius

The fish was evidently a huge one; the chance of tempting him to be caught *secundum artem* was *nil*. Tizard earnestly assured me his master was most anxious to have a large pike for the table – and so – I yielded to the tempter. . . . The boat glides noiselessly down to the unconscious esox and now the gaff is steadily but surely stretched over the spot where the leviathan's shoulder is likely to be, giving him an imaginary length of about four feet . . . whish! There was a rapid stroke, a plunge, and with a rush sufficient to upset a whaleboat the stricken monster dashed for the bottom of the river, at that point at least twenty feet deep.

It was an exciting moment. I found myself being incontinently pulled over the boat's side, which was taking in water freely and clutched at the nearest available support, which happened to be the seat of the keeper's corduroy nether garments. It came bodily away in my grasp. At this juncture, nothing I believe, could have saved the boat from capsizing, if the gaff, yielding to the excessive strain, had not first twisted in the socket, and then straightened out, thus, of course, releasing the enemy who, though struck deep, may, I would fain hope, have yet survived in the indefensible attack upon him *contra bonos mores* and lived on to attain a still greater age and yet vaster breadth of tail.

Tizard, the keeper, was the only one who did not laugh heartily, but on a hint that we should contribute to his next tailor's bill his countenance assumed its wonted serenity.

H. CHOLMONDELEY-PENNELL, *Fishing, Pike and Other Coarse Fish* (1885).

The pike, commonly called jack when under three or four pounds in weight, is a well-known fish; like many of us, better known than trusted or treated. He is a greedy, unsociable, tyrannising savage, and is hated like a Blue Beard. Everybody girds at him with spear, gaff, hook, net, snare, and even with powder and shot. He has not a friend in the world. The horrible gorge hook is specially invented for the torment of his maw. Notwithstanding, he fights his way vigorously, grows into immense strength, despite his many enemies, and lives longer than his greatest foe, man. His voracity is unbounded; and, like the most accomplished corporate officers, he is nearly omnivorous, his palate giving the preference, however, to fish, flesh, and fowl. Dyspepsia never interferes with his

Pike, 40 lb, caught in Suffolk and presented to the Piscatorial Society in 1882 by R. S. Fennings. It measures 44¼ inches long, 12¼ inches from nose to gill cover; its flanks are 10 inches deep.

digestion; and he possesses a quality that would have been valuable at La Trappe – he can fast without inconvenience for a se'nnight. He can gorge himself then to beyond the gills without the slightest derangement of the stomach. He is shark and ostrich combined. His body is comely to look at; and if he could hide his head – by no means a diminished one – his green and silver vesture would attract many admirers. His intemperate habits, however, render him an object of disgust and dread. He devours his own children; but strange to say, likes better (for eating) the children of his neighbours. Heat spoils his appetite, cold sharpens it; and this very day (30th December, 1846) a friend has sent me a gormandising specimen, caught by an armed gudgeon, amidst the ice and snow of the Thames, near Marlow. I envy his constitution.

'EPHEMERA' [EDWARD FITZGIBBON], *A Handbook of Angling* (1847).

There are six living species which represent the genus *Esocidae* (the Pikes and Pickerels), in the order *Clupeiformes.* The three larger species (the Pikes), consist of the pike, *Esox lucius,* known in America as the northern pike; the muskellunge, *Esox musquinongy*; and the amur pike, *Esox reicherti.* The three smaller species (the Pickerels), are the chain pickerel, *Esox niger*; the redfin pickerel, *Esox americanus*; and the grass pickerel, *Esox vermiculatus. Esox lucius* is the only species found in the British Isles, and it occurs in still waters and the slower-moving parts of many rivers throughout England, Scotland, Wales and Ireland.

The head of the famous Dowdeswell pike. This fish was found dead in Dowdeswell Reservoir, near Cheltenham, in 1896. Its weight was recorded as 60 lb.

DIET AND APPETITE

Before considering the various pike tackles and techniques it is worthwhile to study the means by which pike satisfy their appetites. When an angler knows what pike feed on, and understands how they locate, select and capture their prey, he will fish with a much greater chance of success.

The pike is a fish of catholic tastes. Waterfowl, chickens, frogs, rats, mice, voles, puppies, kittens and many other species have been known to pass through those cavernous jaws; but although it will grab any creature it can swallow, the pike is mainly a fish eater. It is this aspect of its diet which is responsible for its age-old reputation as a relentless killer.

'He murders all he meets with', wrote Richard Franck, 300 years ago.

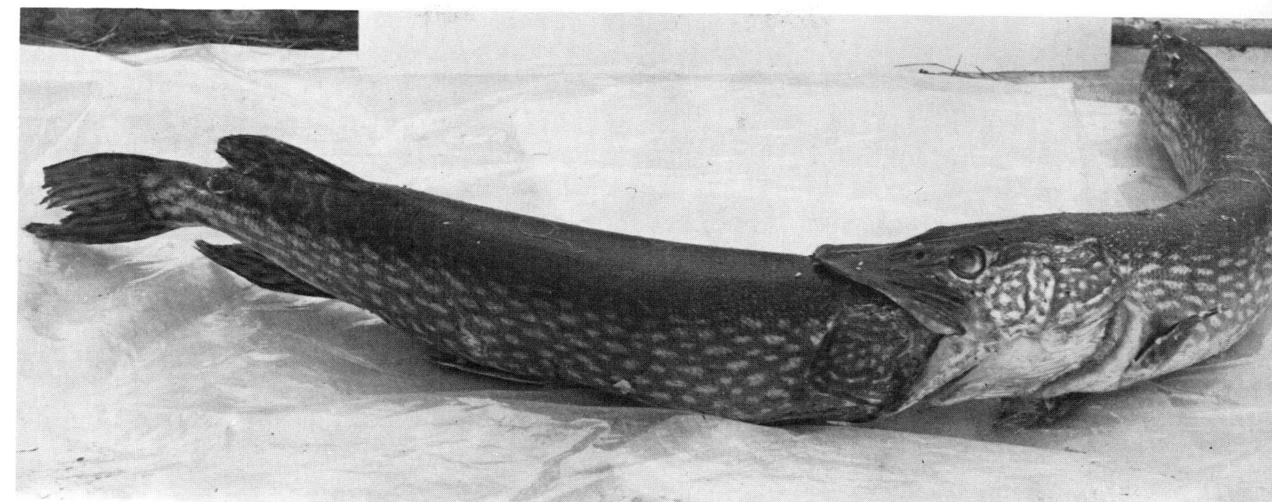

The two pike in this remarkable picture – which was given to us by Sir Frederick Hoare – were found dead in Staines South Reservoir in April 1972. Each fish was about 2 ft 6 in long and weighed just over 6 lb. The attacking fish had its jaws extended to their limit and since a pike's mouth contains a large number of sharp backward-facing teeth it was quite unable to release its prey. As a result, both fish died. (Photograph by courtesy of G. F. Mugele, Metropolitan Water Board.)

From his fierce looks the frightened trembling fry,
To holes and sedgy pits for safety fly.

Ever since the first pike fishing story was told there have been accounts of the pike's enormous gluttony, tales of a cunning and rapacious monster unequalled in ferocity, a veritable fish of blood.

Though the salmon is called the King of Fresh-water Fish, yet the Pike is, and the more justly, styled the King of the Fresh Water. . . . Nor is he barely king of the river, but, as a monarch, that makes by arbitrary power, and delights in the blood of his subjects, he becomes the tyrant thereof; for justly may he be said to be the terror of the watery people.

So wrote an 18th-century angler, whose summing-up of the general regard for pike was echoed by another writer 100 years later:

The pike is a systematic and professional marauder; he respects not his own kith and kin; he prowls up and down seeking what he may devour.

Dramatic stuff. But the reference to cannibalism is certainly true. Dr E. D. Toner, investigating the food of Lough Mask pike, reported the finding of 13 small pike among 323 fish taken from the stomachs of larger pike.

Alfred Jardine wrote of an incident witnessed on Loch Tay in 1870. Two pike were found together, one fish having the head of the other jammed inside its jaws. They were gaffed by a boatman and sent, undivided in death, to the great Frank Buckland – who made a cast of them for his fish museum. Together, they weighed 19 lb, an example of gluttony indeed. But there are many similar examples as our picture shows.

The pike's gastronomic excesses do not end with the eating of its own kind. A list of further victims is given by another in the long line of angling writers:

> Shrouded from observation in his solitary retreat, he follows with his eye the shoals of fish that wander heedlessly along; he marks the water rat swimming in his burrow; the ducklings paddling among the water weeds, the dabchick and the moorhen swimming leisurely on the surface; he selects his victim, and like a tiger springing from the jungle he rushes forth, seldom missing his aim, there is a sudden swirl and splash; circle after circle forms on the surface of the water, and all is still in an instant.

There is no doubt that ducks and other wildfowl feature in the pike's diet. Jardine writes of a visit to Sonning-on-Thames where the landlord of his hostelry informed him of a pike which had swallowed, one by one, twelve from a brood of 15 half-grown ducks. Jardine witnessed the demise of yet another of the brood, before setting out to fish with a gudgeon-baited paternoster. The pike was duly caught. It weighed 15 lb, and inside it Jardine found 'the recently swallowed duck with its feathers scarcely rumpled'.

But how often do such incidents occur?

Dr Michael Kennedy, of the Inland Fisheries Trust, Dublin, states that birds are seldom discovered among the stomach contents of Irish pike. It seems that by the time Irish pike attain a weight of two pounds and over, they are almost exclusively fish eaters.

Dr Winifred Frost found rodent remains inside Windermere pike on only one occasion; and a solitary duckling – in a Blenham Tarn pike.

That *Esox* is a rapacious glutton has been stated in unequivocal terms by nearly every pike angler who has obeyed the urge to write about his sport. Typical of this view was an estimate (published by Cholmondeley-Pennell in 1865) which suggested that a pike was capable of consuming twice its own weight of fish in a week. By this reckoning, the yearly food consumption of a 10 lb pike would be roughly 1,040 lb. Many freshwater anglers would accept this figure as being a reasonable assessment of the pike's annual depredations. And they would be wrong.

From experiments conducted by Dr L. Johnson of the Freshwater Biological Association on Lake Windermere, it may be inferred that a 10 lb pike can be kept alive on an annual food intake of only 14 lb of fish. This amount of food will not permit any increase in the pike's weight, but it will keep the pike alive. Similarly, a 10 lb pike, offered as much as it can eat, will show a normal yearly growth increment while consuming as little as 35 lb of small fish.

These experiments were made on captive pike. But even so, it seems likely that the

Powan (Coregonus clupeoides), *found only in Loch Lomond and Loch Eck. This species is the staple diet of the Loch Lomond pike.*

annual food intake of a pike living in its natural habitat is not more than five to six times its own weight. This means that in one year a 10 lb pike consumes 50–60 lb of food. Almost 1,000 lb less than Cholmondeley-Pennell's estimate!

William Kendall, an American, was the first writer to take a more favourable view of pike:

It is beginning to be recognised that there are still places for them in both the human and natural economy . . . there have been waters in which some pike and other fishes have lived in reciprocal counterpoise from time immemorial, notwithstanding the condemned characteristic voracity of the pike.

With regard to this 'condemned characteristic voracity', Dr Johnson's research has revealed some interesting facts. In its ability to turn food into body maintenance and growth, the pike compares favourably with certain species; for instance, plaice and trout.

This turning of food into body maintenance and growth is known as the gross conversion rate. This, for the pike, is 3·41. In simple terms it means that to maintain life and increase its body weight by one pound, a pike must eat 3·41 lb of food. To do likewise, a plaice must consume 5 lb of food, and a trout 7·1 lb.

From these figures it is evident that, compared with some of the other fishes, nature has equipped the pike with a gut which functions with great economy, a fact not appreciated by Walton when he pronounced:

All pikes that live long prove chargeable to their keepers, because their life is maintained by the death of so many other fish.

On the contrary, the pike, with its gross conversion rate of only 3·41, seems to be a most reasonable fellow – unlike the 7·1 trout, who murders all he meets with!

AGE AND FECUNDITY

It is not only the pike's gastronomic excesses that have been exaggerated. Most early writers were in error when they speculated on the number of years that pike will live. In 1653, Walton published the story of the 267-year-old Mannheim pike. His predecessor, Sir Francis Bacon, in *A History of Life and Death* (1623), wrote: '. . . forty years is likely to be a maximum'. A century later, Pennant referred to a 90-year-old pike.

The Victorian naturalist, Frank Buckland, was the first writer to produce some facts. He describes the taking of a pike from a Windsor Park lake 12 years after it had been introduced as a one-and-a-half-pounder. It weighed 35 lb, and by Buckland's calculation was 14 years old.

Dr Kennedy has given us details of the pike's amazingly rapid growth rate in Ireland's great limestone loughs. Some incidental determinations are as follows:

50½ lb female pike netted from Lough Mask in 1966 age 8 years +.

41 lb female pike netted from Lough Mask in 1966 age 8 years +.

36 lb female pike netted from Lough Cloone in 1963 age 8 years +.

Dr Winifred Frost, who has developed an accurate method of reading the age of pike from their opercular (gill cover) bones, has also given us some incidental determinations. These are:

35 lb female pike netted from Windermere in 1960 age 14 years.

33¼ lb female pike netted from Windermere in 1960 age 18 years.

The former was the heaviest pike taken from the lake during 25 years of netting operations, and the latter was the oldest pike taken during the same period.

William Giles, who has read the scales of many Norfolk pike for the Norfolk river authority, tells us that he has never known a pike to be older than about eighteen years.

Determining a pike's age from an opercular bone is more reliable than scale reading. Dr Frost's method is as follows:–

Remove the left operculum from the dead pike with a scalpel or knife. Soak it in hot water and then clean off the skin with a cloth. To improve its 'reading' quality, keep the bone in storage for a month or two. View the bone by reflected light, on a dark background, under a low-power microscope.

Seasonal differences in the pike's rate of growth affect the bone structure of the operculum, so that reflected light, and to some extent transmitted light, give the bone appearance of being made up from a series of concentric bands, differing in their degree of whiteness from the white matrix of the background. A count of these growth checks (annuli), gives the age of the pike. Some caution is necessary if six or more annuli are counted, since a brown glutinous tissue usually obscures at least one annulus near the point of attachment.

It will have been noted that of the big pike netted from Loughs Mask, Cloone, and Windermere, all five were female. This is not surprising. Male pike rarely exceed 10 lb in weight. The largest male pike taken in Ireland after many years of gill-netting weighed 14 lb. The largest taken in a sample

The correct way to measure a fish. *Lay the fish flat on measuring board, or stick, its snout just touching the riser. Smooth the tail fin into its normal shape and measure to the fork.*

of 7,000 Windermere pike weighed 12½ lb. In three generations, the largest to pass through the hands of London taxidermists, John Cooper and Sons, weighed 12 lb.

Reports of 20 and 30 lb male pike can be discounted. All 'male' pike of this size have been wrongly sexed. Various organs within the female's body cavity are sometimes mistaken for male glands – a mistake usually made during the early stages of ovary development.

So far as we are aware, no scientist has attempted to explain why male pike are unable to match the growth rate and ultimate size of female pike. Having studied an account of the spawning behaviour of pike (Fabricius and Gustafson, 1956), it occurs to us that, historically, male body length may have been an important factor in the process of natural selection. Our reasons are these:

During the spawning act, male and female pike *move forward together*. While moving, the male pike is accurately located beside the female by means of an eye to eye orientation. The natural displacement of water caused by both fish moving forward causes a current to flow in the opposite direction. If the male were bigger than the female, its vent would be positioned to the rear of the female's vent and its milt cloud would be *swept away* from the falling eggs, rather than over them. Thus, spawning acts would tend to be unsuccessful. As a result, smaller and shorter-bodied male pike would tend to become the more successful progenitors.

Although most pike spawn for the first time in their second or third year, it seems that size rather than age is the determining factor. Usually, pike spawn in relatively shallow water. Lake pike prefer sheltered bays within the 12-foot contour. They tend to use the same spawning sites year after year, and these are likely to be near their normal feeding grounds. Exceptionally, pike have been known to travel up to five miles from their spawning sites.

The fecundity of pike is legendary. Buckland counted 595,200 eggs in the ovaries of a 32 lb pike. Frost and Kipling found that the weight of the female gonads, expressed as a percentage of the total

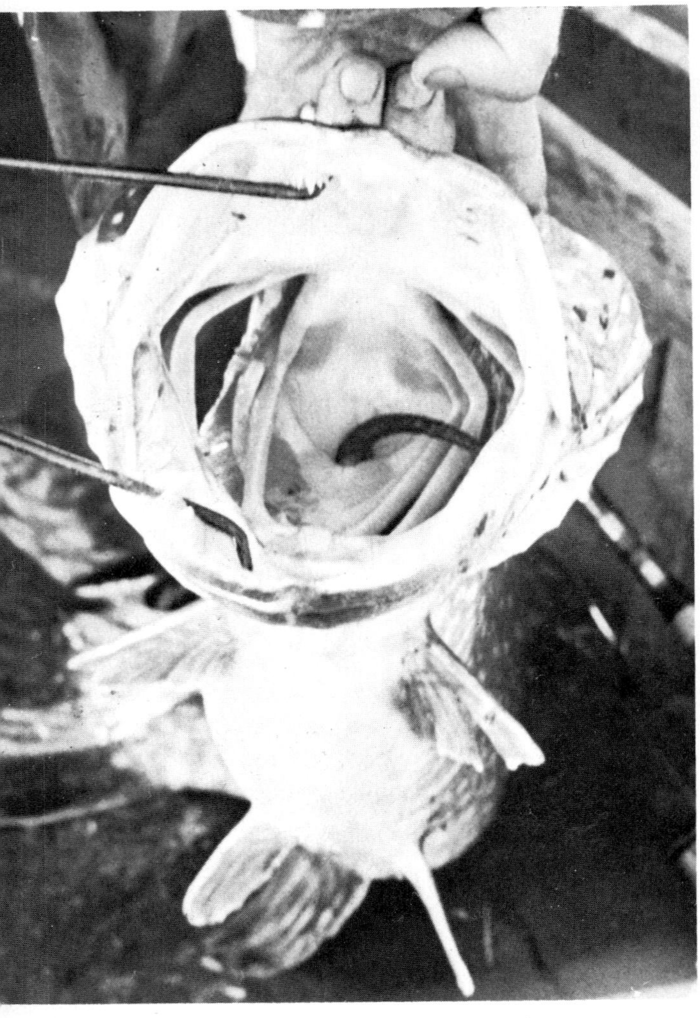

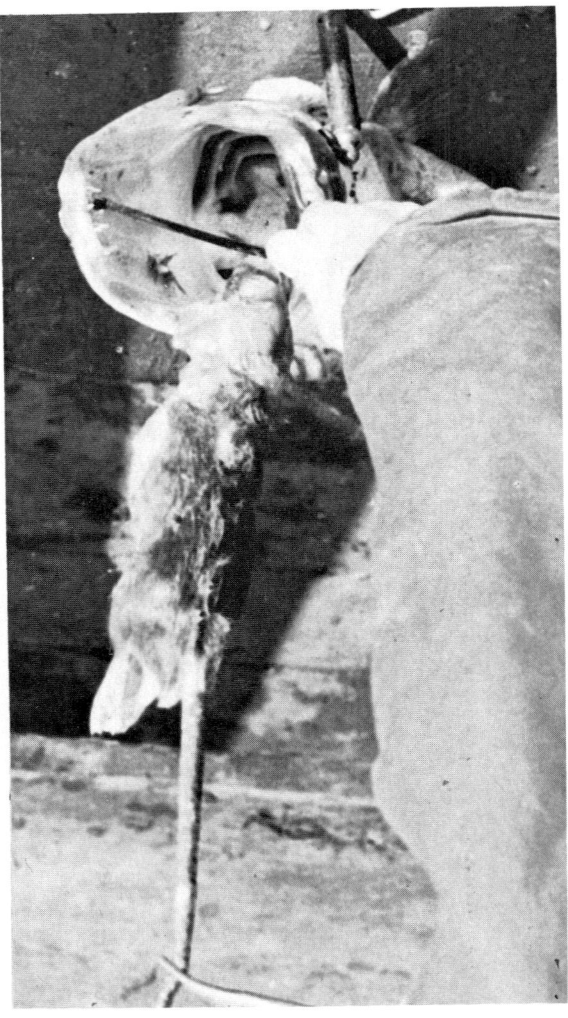

Above: *pike showing tail of brown rat sticking out of its throat.* Above right: *a full grown rat is retrieved from the pike. Examination of an adult pike's stomach normally reveals evidence of a fish diet; examination of a large sample of pike stomachs usually reflects the availability, relative abundance, and variety of fish found in the habitat. From time to time, however, more bizarre dietary items are recorded, which include mice, rats, voles, ducklings, moorhens, dab-chicks, etc. The finding of curious food items indicates that pike, like most other creatures, are opportunists when it comes to satisfying their hunger.*

This enormous pike was taken on rod and line by Herr Friedrick Witzany from a gravel pit near Goslar in West Germany, September 1971. It weighed 52 lb 4 oz at the time of capture. Had this fish survived until the following March – when the weight of its fully developed ovaries would have represented approximately 20% of its body weight – it could have weighed as much as 65 lb! (Photograph: Kurt Tempes)

bodyweight, increases from 2% in August to 7% in October, 10% in November, 12% in December, 14% in January, 15% in February, and when fully ripe, prior to spawning, to as much as 20%.

In May, 1905, *The Field* reported the gaffing of a spent 48 lb female pike from one of the inlets of Lough Corrib. It was thought that, prior to spawning, this pike must have weighed about 60 lb! An astonishing figure, but there is every reason to believe it.

Esox lucius, like all the Pikes and Pickerels (with the exception of the Amur pike), strikes at its prey from ambush. The Amur pike – named after its native valley which lies between Russia and Mongolia – is the one species endowed with an instinct to hunt in open water.

The pike's hunting technique of striking from ambush is helped by its coloration: dark olive-green when viewed from above, lighter green and mottled when viewed from the side, and white when viewed from below. This colour combination is an excellent camouflage and enables a pike to lurk unseen in a green jungle of weeds and lily pads, until an unsuspecting victim has moved within range of its powerful dash.

SALARIO: Why I am sure, if he forfeit, thou wil not take his flesh? What's that good for?
SHYLOCK: To bait fish withal.
THE MERCHANT OF VENICE, *Act III, Sc. I.*

Above: *The skull of John Garvin's record Irish pike: 53 lb 12 oz.*

Below: *Peter Hancock's record English pike: 40 lb 1 oz.*

SENSES AND FEEDING HABITS

A pike's awareness of a bait, and ability to locate it, can be achieved only by the use of one or more of three senses: sight, smell and hearing. If an angler suspects which of these senses he is appealing to on any occasion, he should be able to present his bait with a good deal more confidence than he has felt hitherto.

A pike tends to use the minimum of effort in hunting its food. Its eyes are set high in the head and provide an extensive field of view forwards and upwards. Many of its attacks on other fish are made from ambush. Once a prey fish swims into the striking zone, even if it is a wary and speedy trout, it has little chance of eluding the pike's short but powerful dash from the bottom.

The pike, then, is well equipped to hunt by sight. But it is certainly not vision that plays the *major* part in the pike's feeding routine. The netting of a totally blind but otherwise healthy pike in Lake Windermere proved that it is possible for pike to obtain sufficient food by the use of senses other than sight.

Is it possible to evaluate the degree with which the pike's different senses are used for the purpose of getting a meal? One thing is certain, a livebait has a much greater chance of being taken by a pike than a freely-swimming fish of the same size and species. Is the attraction of the live-bait simply visual, or does the pike become aware of the bait's presence because of some emitted sound or scent? Does a tethered livebait cause distress signals (vibrations) which are picked up by the pike's listening equipment? Does it emit a fear substance which a pike can home on by sense of smell? Is it merely a display of physical distress which catches a pike's eye?

Vigorous livebaits are more effective than ailing ones. Perhaps their *signals* are more vigorous, and extend over a greater range.

Like other fishes, pike do not possess hearing organs similar to mammals. The 'ear' seems to be used mainly as a balancing device. Nevertheless, many species of fish emit underwater sounds. The meaning of these sounds is not yet known; but it seems reasonable to suppose that they have some specific function, and that in some way or another they can be received and understood by other fishes.

What is beyond doubt is that most species of fish are extremely sensitive to vibrations. And the pike is no exception. If a bait is cast so that it falls a little way behind a stationary pike, the pike may swim away – presumably frightened – or it may *turn round and face the bait.* Both reactions demonstrate the pike's ability to 'hear', but the latter indicates that the pike's sense of 'hearing' may sometimes help it to locate its prey.

But what of ledgered deadbaits? They emit no vibrations whatever. And yet deadbaits fished stationary on the bottom are extremely effective. Why? The answer is almost certainly – smell.

The sense of smell in most fishes is exceptionally acute. It has been demonstrated that salmon, returning from the sea to spawn in fresh water, detect their 'home' rivers entirely by scent. The ability of sea

Mid-winter (Photograph: Angling News Services).

fishes to follow a scent trail is equally well established: as a result, the rubby-dubby bag has become a valuable item of sea-angling equipment. During the breeding season, a male pike is able to track down a female pike by sense of smell. And although, as yet, no one has produced scientific proof, it is almost certain that pike are able to locate their prey by the same means.

Since there is little doubt that a deadbait gives off a stronger scent than a livebait, it seems probable that pike approach deadbait as a result of picking up the trail of this scent – in the same way that a shark picks up and follows the scent of the rubby-dubby, although, needless to say, over a very much shorter range.

This may explain why, in locations which permit satisfactory presentation, deadbait often proves more successful than livebait.

DEADBAIT LEDGERING FOR PIKE

Although many claims are made for new methods and tackles, most are simply old ones re-discovered: for example, that beloved contraption of the modern match angler – the swingtip.[1]

Several anglers claim to have introduced the ledger method of fishing a stationary deadbait, and not a few claim to have been the first to use herrings for this purpose. But the method and the bait were described by Dame Juliana Berners. Here is an extract from her book, *A Treatyse of Fysshynge wyth an Angle* (1496), with the spelling brought up to date.

1 See p. 384.

> Take a codling hook, and take a roach or a fresh herring, and a wire with an hole in the end, and put it in at the mouth, and out at the tail, down by the ridge of the fresh herring; and then put the hook in after, and draw the hook into the cheek of the fresh herring; then put a plumb of lead upon your line a yard long from your hook, and a float in midway between; and cast it in a pit where the pike useth, and this is the best and most surest craft of taking the pike.

What more can be said? She knew it all hundreds of years ago!

But since those far-off days stationary deadbaits have been little used; at least, not until recent years when Fred J. Taylor developed improved rigs for this style of fishing. From his writings a new school of pike fishing has grown up, so that today stationary deadbait fishing has once again become a major method in the pike angler's repertoire.

For preference, herring deadbaits should be ledgered on a leadless tackle over a hard, weed-free bottom. Unlike herring, whose bladders are collapsed, roach and rudd sink slowly and are superior when fished over soft weed or mud.

Cast the bait close to the margins or close to weed-beds. Open the reel bale-arm and allow the pike to make its first run unimpeded. Tighten on the fish at the start of the second run.

Deadbait fishing, more particularly herring deadbait fishing, accounts for many big pike. Most anglers would agree that the sample of pike it produces is better than that produced by spinning. Perhaps its growing popularity is bound up with its appeal to

Loch Lomond pike.

those who consider livebaiting cruel. It is of course an advantage to be able to buy supplies of bait in advance of a fishing trip. Ready access to herring bait provides an opportunity to prebait and groundbait and, for those with an experimental turn of mind, a chance to locate pike by using a series of hookless search-trimmers.

The search-trimmer is used on big 'dour' lochs and lakes, and consists of a bulky, readily visible float supporting a deadbait on a $1\frac{1}{2}$ lb B.S. line. Such fine line ensures that a break occurs soon after a pike takes the bait.

In this way a feeding area is pinpointed, and although the angler is faced with a great expanse of water he can fish these pinpointed areas with confidence.

The Search-Trimmer

No better pattern for a trimmer exists than the one that has been in use for centuries. It is shaped like a compressed cotton bobbin with a diameter of about 4½ in. and depth of about 1½ in. The bobbin is deeply grooved to receive a reservoir of strong line (about 30 ft). A tapered peg is fitted in a tight-fitting tapered hole drilled through the centre of the bobbin. A small hole drilled through the base of the peg provides an anchorage for the line which is then wound into the groove on the bobbin. The pointed end of the peg is provided with a split that traps the line so long as the point of the peg is directed skywards.

The terminal tackle consists of a 1 oz. anchoring weight fitted direct to the mainline, and a 6 ft link of 1½ lb B.S. nylon, to which is tied the deadbait: herring, sprat, dace or roach.

A three-way swivel is tied on the mainline three feet up from the anchoring lead to provide an easy means of attaching the bait-link to the mainline.

Directions for Setting a Search-Trimmer

Lower the bait over the side of the boat. Then, holding the bobbin in the left hand, lower the lead – releasing enough line for the lead to touch bottom. Pull off another three feet of line and then trap the line in the split peg.

When a pike takes the bait and moves off, it will overturn the trimmer and release the trapped line. The pike can then pull off a further twenty to twenty-five feet of line,

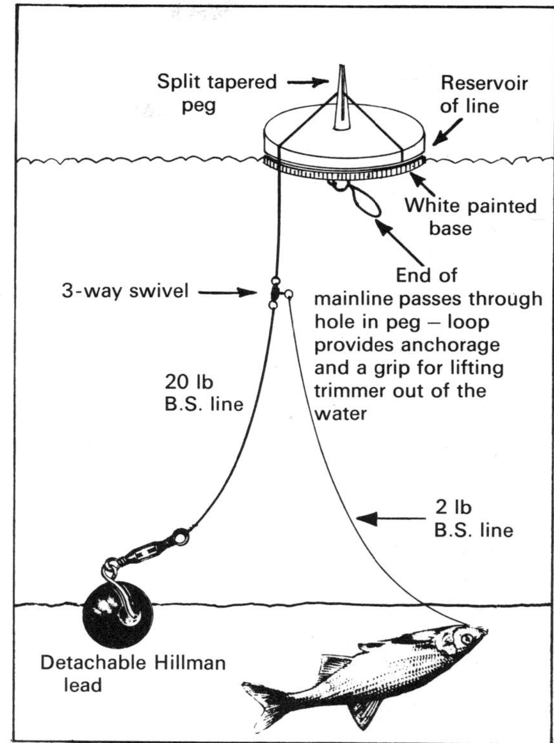

Fig. 21.1. The search-trimmer.

which will allow time for the bait-link to break before the pike becomes alarmed by resistance of the trimmer.

If the underside of the trimmer is painted white and the topside red, an angler will know instantly from a distance when he has had a run.

The F. J. Taylor Deadbait Tackle

Take a 2–3 ft length of 14 or 20 lb alasticum wire; bend it over and slip the bend behind a size 2 or 4 treble hook (see Fig. 21.2.*a* and *b*).

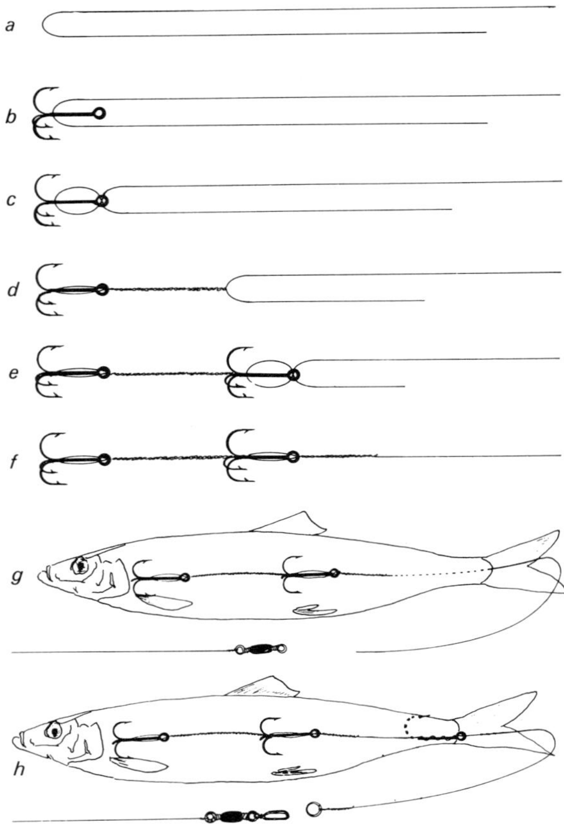

Fig. 21.2. The Fred J. Taylor deadbait tackle.

Pass both ends of the wire through the eye of the treble, from opposite sides (*c*). Pull tight and twist the wire (*d*) right up to the second treble, slipping the bend of the wire behind it in the same way as the first. Push the ends of the wire through the eye of the second treble (*e*), pull tight and finish off with a twisted section of about 1 in. (*f*).

The distance between the trebles should fit the size of the deadbait. Half a dozen tackles made up with varied distances between hooks will accommodate any variation in the size of the herring or other deadbait used.

Taylor prefers to pass the end of the wire through the fish with the help of a baiting needle (dotted line in Fig. 21.2.*g*). This prevents the bait from being flung off the hooks during the cast.

Finally, trim the emergent wire to between 9 and 12 in., before connecting up to a swivel on the main line.

For anglers who blench at the mention of a baiting needle, Taylor suggests the rig illustrated in *h*. The business end is the same as before, but the free end of the wire is twisted four times round the shank of a large Model Perfect hook before it is passed through the eye. The hook is slid along the wire according to the length of the deadbait, then pulled through the fleshy part of the tail.

A split-ring is twisted on 12 in. or so up the leader and the wire trimmed off.

To allow for the quick changing of mounts a link-swivel is attached to the main line.

Lough Mask pike netted in March, 1957, by the Inland Fisheries Trust. Weight: 46 lb. Length: 45 in. Holding the fish is Dr Michael Kennedy, one of the Trust's scientists. This picture enables one to imagine the magnificent proportions of the Dowdeswell pike (see p. 104), which at 51 inches was six inches longer than the Mask pike! (Photograph by courtesy of *The Irish Times.*)

Two famous pike fishermen, Bill Giles and Reg Sandys, on Loch Lomond.

The Loch Lomond Pike Rig

There are few lakes in Britain so beautiful as Loch Lomond and few which hold pike so large and so powerful. An angler fishing Lomond is always in with a chance of hooking a 40 or even a 50 pounder. His tackle deserves special attention.

When dealing with powerful loch pike hooked close to dangerous ground, a 5 ft naked ORM wire 30 lb leader is essential. This extra-long leader reduces the chance of a pike's teeth coming into contact with the nylon line, should the leader take a turn or two round the pike's body. The wire should be a dull bronze colour – simply because most anglers fish less confidently with a bright reflective wire. A size 1 or 1/0 treble is fastened to one end of the leader and a loop whip-finished at the other end. If preferred, two trebles can be used, set some 4 or 5 inches apart.

One arm of the treble is hooked through the fleshy tail of the deadbait.

If two trebles are in use, the upper treble is hooked in the deadbait's tail and the lower treble hooked just forward of the pectoral fin.

A 6 in. celluloid sliding float is preferred for its streamline qualities. Above the float a sliding nylon stop-knot is fitted. This is best tied with a 6 in. slip of 35 lb nylon.

A small-bored bead can be fitted between the stop-knot and the float. This will allow a less bulky stop-knot to be equally effective.

A Catherine lead is used because the line

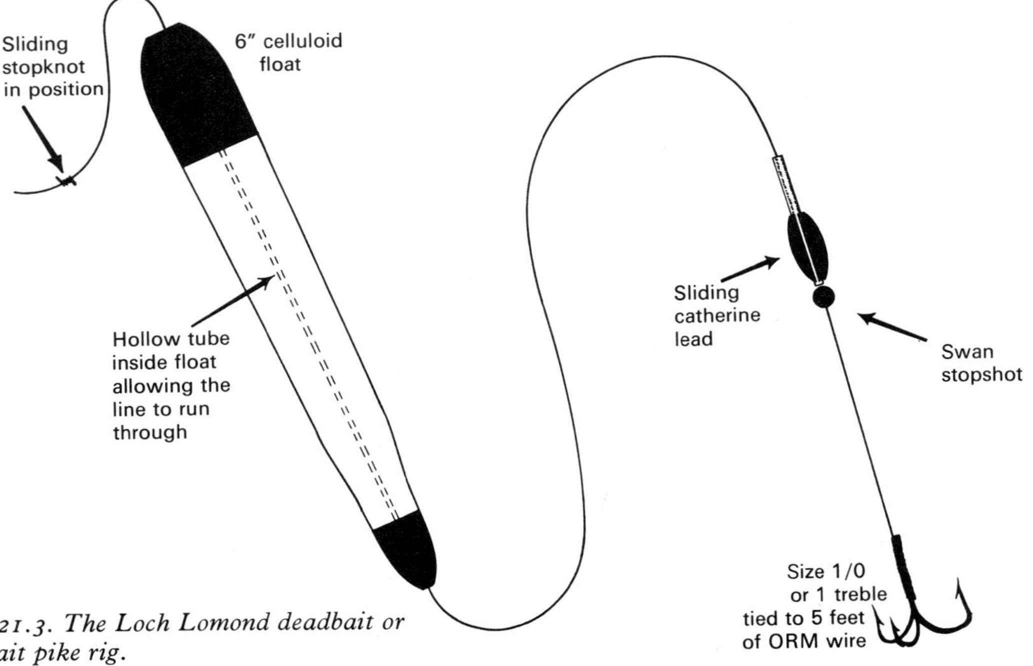

Fig. 21.3. The Loch Lomond deadbait or livebait pike rig.

runs through it freely and it can be changed to vary the weight in an instant. The lead is stopped by a swanshot pinched on to the wire. A sliding lead enables a pike to take the deadbait away without hindrance even if the lead has fallen in a bad lie on a stony bottom.

A lead is not always used when deadbaiting in calm water. On these occasions care must be taken to pierce the swim-bladder of a dead roach, otherwise the bait may not sink to the bottom. No lead need be used when the rig is fished as a livebaiting rig in shallow water, or in very clear water under 5 ft deep.

Pilot floats are optional. They are necessary, perhaps, with monofil main line in order to prevent the line from sinking to the stony bottom – in which case, six half-inch pilots are better than one large one. Better still, because of its excellent floating properties, is a main line of 30 lb *braided* nylon (used without pilots).

Braided nylon must be fastened to the leader swivel or loop with a hangman's jam knot (see p. 416). Any other knot may result in breakage due to line strangulation. This could lose a pike angler the fish of a lifetime (as it did F. B. – a huge Loch Lomond pike estimated by four experienced observers to be no less than 45 to 50 lb!).

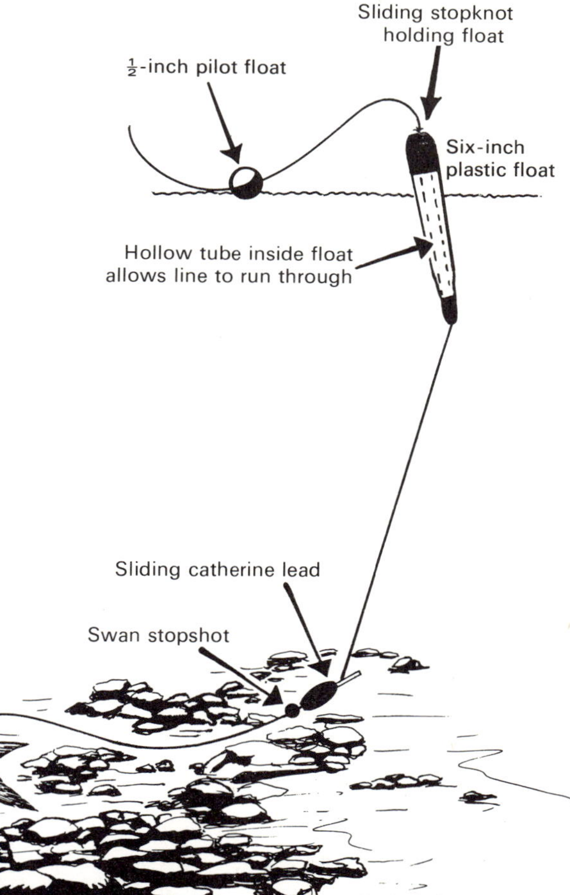

Fig. 21.4. Float-ledgering with the Loch Lomond pike rig.

By this the Pike, cleane wearied underneath
A willow lies and pants (if Fishes breath)
Wherewith the Angler gently puls him to him
And, lest his hast might happen to undoe him,
Lays downe his rod, then takes his line in hand.
And, by degrees getting the Fishe to land . . .
WILLIAM BROWNE, *Britannia's Pastorals* (1613).

A New Method of Deadbait Fishing

Mr B. B. Clements of Canada has given us an interesting note on deadbait fishing. For the last few years his usual method has been to wobble a dead smelt in the manner of Fred Wagstaffe, who had kindly sent him a rig to copy (see p. 129). This method was so successful that he seldom used any other. It had its off-days, however, and during one of these he discovered a new way of presenting a deadbait – which consistently brings large pike into the boat.

'Having been persuaded by my neighbour to take him "after big pike", we fished steadily for most of the morning with only moderate success when he hooked a small fish of about a pound. Swinging it into the boat he inadvertently stuck one of the trebles into my trousers beyond hope of extracting it without tearing the cloth. So I put my rod down with the smelt I was wobbling hanging over the side. Having dealt with the hook I turned, picked up my rod, and found a fighting 12 lb pike on the other end, much to my surprise.

'A week or so later in the same area, having wobbled a smelt all morning with no success, I stuck the rod in the holder hanging over the stern and lowered the bait to just off the bottom. Five minutes later it was doing a merry dance and I had another double-figure fish.

'These experiences set me thinking and after a few trials an exceedingly simple and rewarding method appeared. Any pike rod about seven feet long will do. It is put in a rod-holder over the stern and equipped with a centre-pin reel and braided line. A standard deadbait ledger type flight completes the tackle with a small weight added to get the bait down close to the bottom. The boat is anchored at the bow only, so that it will slowly swing to and fro.

'This method gives a simulation of a preoccupied, headdown fish feeding off the bottom, rising and sinking with the motion of the boat and moving as the boat swings.

'The centre-pin reel is set with the check on and the drag off. When a fish takes, the tell-tale music of the check is heard and the fun starts. Usually the best method is to give the fish line for a few seconds, then tighten up and strike. This method is delicate and fast enough to prevent gorging. Occasionally a fish will swallow the bait without moving, but mostly however they grab the bait and make off at a steady speed.

'When moving the boat a spectacular take often happens. The movement of the boat slowly brings the bait towards the surface and the fish will often leap out of the water on the strike. I am sure the jack must lie looking at the bait and when they see it

Pike: 33 lb. Caught March 1967, by Dick Barder in a lake near Maidstone, Kent. This superb pike took a No. 4 copper Mepps spinner at 4 p.m. Conditions were windy, after a day of tremendous storm. It was landed after a twenty minute fight on a 7 ft glass rod, Altex reel, $9\frac{1}{2}$ *lb line and 8 lb Alasticum trace. Length of fish:* $46\frac{1}{2}$ *in.*

disappearing charge after it. My bait has even been taken when starting to move my boat by its very noisy 35 h.p. engine.

'Another variation of this technique is to swim the bait out from the boat by float and trotting technique. On one occasion we were fishing at the base of a waterfall in a big back eddy over a very rocky bottom and in about four to five feet of water. Having no success wobbling for pike I decided to float the deadbait just off the bottom and away from the canoe using the current, whilst I fished for walleyes under the boat with another rod. Within the next hour I had two double-figure pike. This trotting method is similar to that being used by Bill Giles and mentioned in Fred Buller's book [*Pike*] except my bait is suspended head downward in a feeding attitude rather than horizontal as though swimming.'

Note: This is really a form of trolling, or sink-and-draw, (see pp. 474–7).

As the year advances from winter, a pike's food requirements increase. They become nearly double in late spring, and reach a maximum in June. Although temperature is significant, daylight is the main factor which governs a pike's food intake. From this it might be thought that late June/July should provide an angler with his best sport. This could well be the case in large lochs; but not in smaller shallower waters, where weed cover is profuse. The pike's technique of attacking from ambush is most successful in conditions of abundant weed, and in this situation fewer hungry pike are available to the angler.

And nigh this toppling reed, still as the dead
The great pike lies, the murderous patriarch
Watching the waterpit sheer-shelving dark,
Where through the plash his lithe bright
  vassals thread.

The rose-finned roach and bluish bream
And staring ruffe steal up the stream
Hard by their glutted tyrant, now
Still as a sunken bough.

He on the sandbank lies,
Sunning himself long hours
With stony gorgon eyes;
Westward the hot sun lowers.

From EDMUND BLUNDEN, *The Pike.*

Major W. H. Booth's fine 37 lb Wye pike shared the English record with Alfred Jardine's pike for 23 years. This pike was caught on a phantom bait.

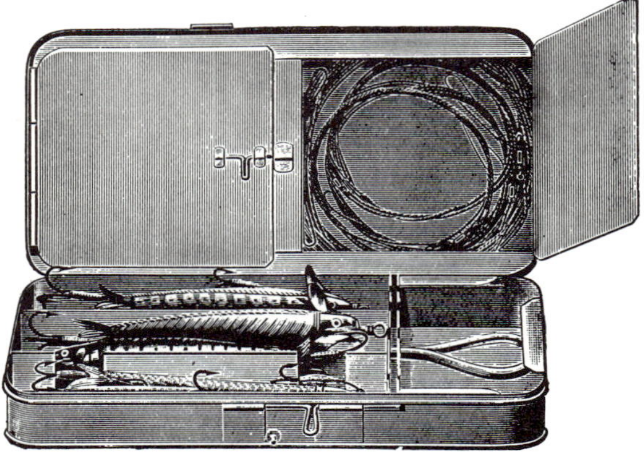

19th century phantom bait and leader box.

Flights and Mounts for Deadbaits

The terms 'flight' and 'mount' are often confused. There is, however, an important distinction. A spinning 'flight' is an arrangement of hooks which will put a curve in a natural bait, and so cause it to revolve when drawn through the water. A spinning 'mount' uses means other than a curve (vanes, etc) to induce the bait to spin or wobble.

Note: Most of the flights and mounts we describe have not been marketed during recent years. This is not the fault of the tackles themselves. The reason why they are not on offer in a modern catalogue is *not* because they are wanting in appeal either to fish or fishermen, but because of the harsh modern commercial climate that demands a reduction in tackle items. The tackles used so successfully by our grandfathers will, given the chance, kill fish equally well today. Hence our illustration and description of spinning flights and mounts which the unthinking angler might otherwise reject as being 'out of date'.

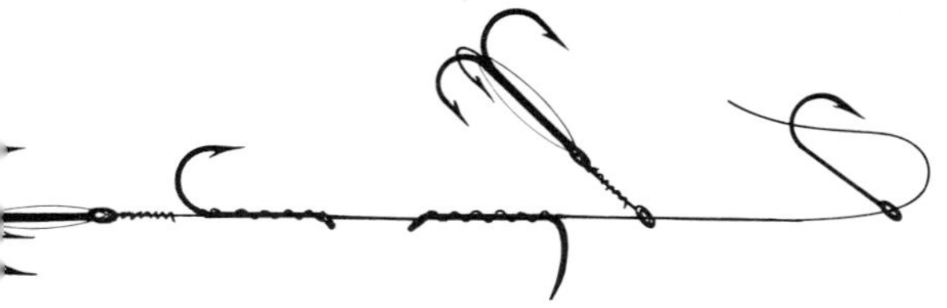

Fig. 21.5.a. The Bromley-Pennell Flight.

Fig. 21.5.b.

The Bromley-Pennell Deadbait Flight

There exists, still, a spinning flight which has been condemned by almost every writer on the subject: the Thames flight. It deserves a brief mention for its historical interest since it taught our grandfathers and great-grandfathers how to attract pike with a natural bait – even though their pike frequently came unhooked!

The Bromley-Pennell spinning flight (Fig. 21.5), legitimate heir to the Thames flight, incorporates only two trebles instead of the Thames flight's outmoded four. Both these trebles are free-flying – which allows them to find an attachment in the pike's mouth the moment the angler strikes.

This is not the case with most other flights (including the Thames flight), where the strike power has first to overcome the hold which the trebles have in the bait, before freeing them to find an attachment in the pike's jaw.

The Bromley-Pennell flight can easily be made up with alasticum wire, the trebles being attached in the way described for the Nottingham flight (p. 128). The curiously shaped 'holding' hook, seen in the illustrations, is a normal hook straightened out and trimmed with pliers. The lip hook is put on after the wire has been pushed through the gill cover and out through the mouth. It is secured in the correct position by a few turns of wire on the shank before being pulled through both lips of the bait. Should extra casting weight be needed, a barrel lead is pushed down the throat of the bait before the lip hook is fitted.

If the bait is required to spin, it is curved by setting the hooks as shown in Fig. 12.5.*b*; otherwise, very good results can be obtained by setting the bait 'straight', and employing a jerky retrieve. This excellent deadbait tackle will probably regain its former popularity when more anglers take up loch and reservoir fishing and become conscious of the need to cover a lot of water.

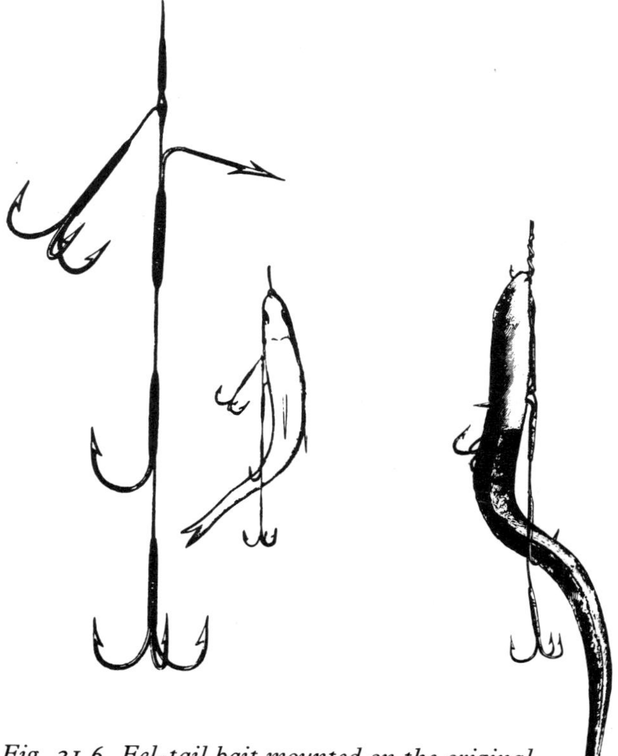

Fig. 21.6. Eel-tail bait mounted on the original Bromley-Pennell flight. On Corrib, H. Cholmondeley-Pennell, fishing the eel-tail, hooked – and lost – the largest pike he contacted during his lifetime.

Cholmondeley-Pennell had this to say about the preparation of a natural eel-bait for use on his mount.

The fresh eel (and tail) makes an excellent spinning bait, tough and enduring. I have used fresh eel-bait dressed in a great many different fashions, from the whole eel (where the latter is not above seven or eight inches long), to six inches or so of the tail cut off a larger specimen. In this case the eel from which the bait is taken, is best rather small, and should not, for ordinary river and lake spinning, exceed a foot in length (9 in. better). For great lochs, like L. Corrib where pike are scarce and run sometimes to an extra-ordinary size, larger eels may be used with advantage. The most perfect eel-tail bait for pike spinning is, I consider, one about 7 inches long, made from an eel of say, three-quarters of a foot, an artificial head – which is more durable than the natural head – being formed out of the turned-back skin. This turned-back skin, besides being so much stronger by being doubled, has a blue colour which looks thoroughly fish-like in the water, and has apparently an appetising effect on the pike's taste.

In forming the head, skin the eel backwards towards the tail as far as the point where the bait is to commence, trimming off the flesh round the spinal bone 'cone-shaped'. Then tie the skin tightly round, close above the bone, and cut it off to within about an inch and a half of the ligature, turning the flap then downwards again, towards the tail. The pin-hook will eventually pass through both the turned down flap and the under-skin, and keep the flap fixed.

To skin an eel:

Make a circular incision through the skin below the pectoral fin. This is best done by passing the blade of a sharp penknife under the skin, bit by bit, in a circular direction. Then pin the head of the eel tightly down to a kitchen table with a steel fork, and having got hold of the edge of the skin with the finger nails [we prefer to use pliers], turn it, or rather pull it, down a little way; now take hold of it with a dry cloth, and it will generally peel backwards with ease.

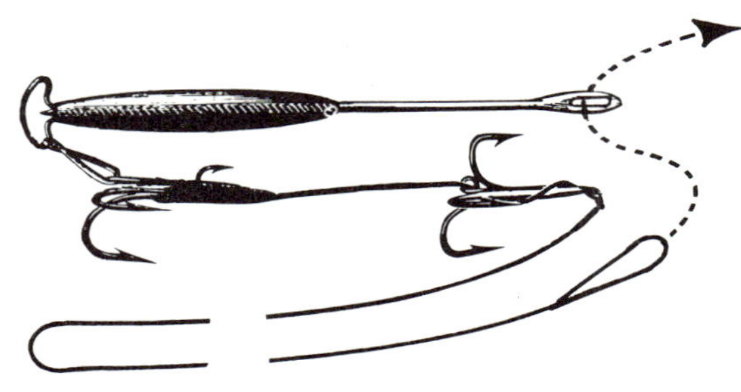

Fig. 21.7.

Marston's Deadbait Snap Tackle (or Flight) This can be used either as a snap tackle or as a spinning flight. It was invented by R. B. Marston, editor of *The Fishing Gazette.*

Alfred Jardine (in *Pike and Perch*, 1898) described its make-up:

To bait this tackle, screw out the needle until the end of lead to the needle eye measures the same length as the bait from tip of nose to entre of tail. Insert the needle in the mouth of bait, and push it with the lead quite through, being careful to keep in the centre until the eye protrudes from the tail sufficiently to admit loop of gimp passing through it; then turn up the hooks, fixing one of the first triangles in the gill-cover, then fix one of the next set midway between tail and the first set, and complete by making a half-hitch round the root of the tail with the gimp, and pass loop through the needle eye. Or the hooks may be detached from the lead and used as a livebait snap. It can also be used for spinning by threading the gimp in at the side, above but rather behind the vent and out at the mouth, by the aid of the needle; then thread through the centre of lead which is pushed into the bait, the triangle of hooks being drawn up tightly, to give the necessary curve to make the bait spin: at the same time make a half-hitch round the wire eye of the lead, and pass through the lips of the bait by puncturing them with the needle.

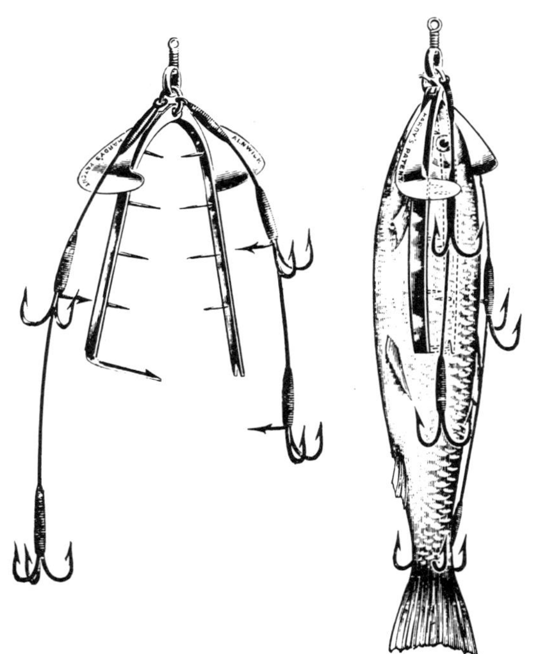

Fig. 21.8.

The Hardy 'Crocodile' Deadbait-Spinning Mount

Place the nose of the bait against the hinge, close the side clips against the bait until the prong of one passes through the body and engages with the end of the other. Push the spiked hooks into the bait and bind the bait to the mount with a length of fine copper wire.

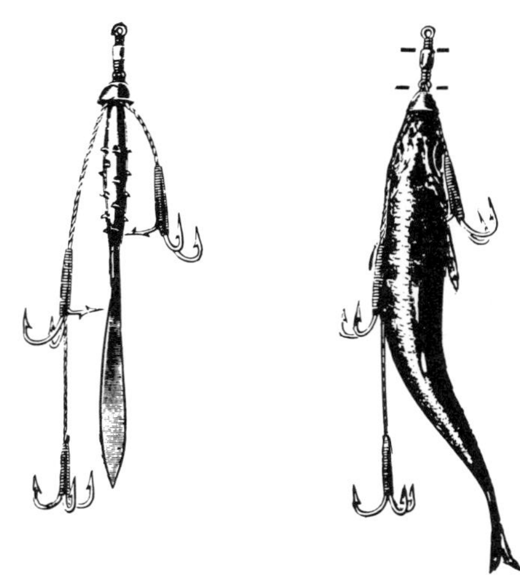

Fig. 21.9.

Farlow's Wobbling Flight

This flight, which was produced well into the 1930s, is extremely easy to bait-up. The flattened copper spear is forced through the mouth into the body of the deadbait, and the two spiked hooks pushed into its sides. The tail is then bent to produce a deadly wobbling action.

As a safety precaution it is always advisable to bind a natural bait on to a flight with a length of copper wire.

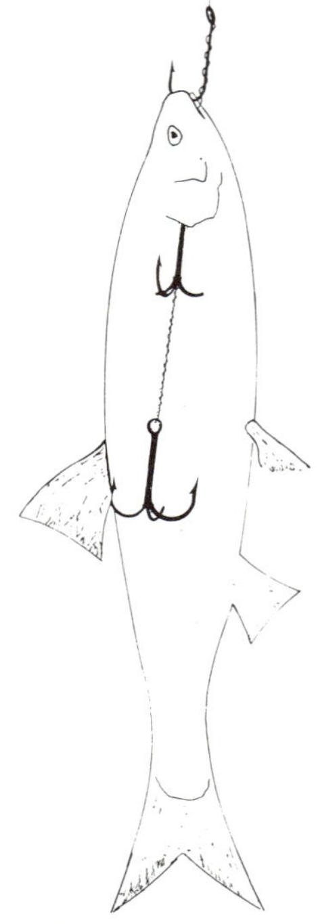

Fig. 21.10.

The Nottingham Deadbait Spinning Flight

If you are looking for a tackle which will hold a herring firmly while it is being trailed, allow it either to tack and dive or to spin, give good hooking power and allow you to fish for long periods without renewing the bait, you will find all these qualities in the Nottingham flight.

This splendid flight was developed early in the 19th century by the Nottingham pike spinners. It is one of the few flights which will make a roach spin well – a bait otherwise considered inferior to dace, sprats, gudgeon and bleak whose more streamlined bodies are more conducive to a regular and even spin (although nowadays pike anglers put less store on such matters).

To make a Nottingham flight with alasticum wire is a simple matter.

Take a 30 in. length of 14 or 20 lb breaking strain wire and bend about ten inches back. Slip the bend behind a No. 2 or 4 treble hook; pass the ends of the wire through the eye of the treble from each side, and pull tight.

Twist the wire right up to the back of a second treble; pass both ends of the wire through the eye of the second treble, and pull tight. Twist the wires for a further half inch. Retain the longer of the two wires, but trim the short one back to the twisted section.

Make up a set of these tackles by varying the distance between the trebles.

You now have a range of flights capable of accommodating a wide variety of deadbaits.

To bait up, choose a flight appropriate to the bait-size. Reference to Fig. 12.10 will establish the relationship between bait-size and flight for positioning the hooks correctly.

Pull *one* arm of the bottom treble deep into the side of the bait, below and behind the dorsal fin.

Bend the body of the fish to the required shape (it is this bend which causes the bait to spin), before pressing *two* arms of the top treble into the bait just to the rear of the gill cover.

Pass the wire through the gill and out through the mouth, then through the eye of a short-shanked size 1, 2, or 4 single-eyed hook. Slip the hook down to within a quarter of an inch of the bait's mouth.

Secure the hook with a few twists round the shank, before pulling it through both lips of the bait.

A swivel, or a swivelled Wye-lead is used as a link between flight and main line.

Fred Wagstaffe suggests sliding a barrel-lead down through the bait's mouth before fitting the lip hook. This is sound advice, for, as he says, it gives an attractive wobbling and diving action to the bait. This, of course, applies when the flight is used as a wobbling tackle. When the flight is used as a spinning tackle, put the lead up-trace where it is more accessible for adjustment.

Wobbling

Unlike a bait that revolves with a *regular* action when retrieved through water, a wobbling bait is not intended to spin and its progress is irregular.

Mostly, wobbling is confined to deadbait fishing when the bait is twitched or jerked by the dropping and lifting of the rod-top, or by an irregular winding of the reel or both. Some artificial baits can also be fished with a wobbling action – e.g. a kidney bar-spoon and long-bladed spoons such as the Toby.

Normally wobbled deadbaits are retrieved head first i.e. in the head-up position prior to the cast. If the bait is reversed so that it hangs head-down prior to the cast – the mode of fishing is the classic trolling style (see p. 475).

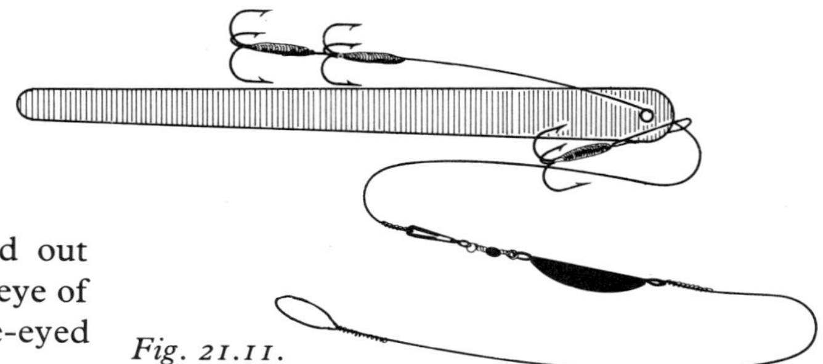

Fig. 21.11.

Martin's Deadbait Flight

'Trent Otter', that great all-round coarse angler, J. W. Martin, writing in 1906, had this to say of pike spinning with natural and artificial baits.

> If there was one thing more than another that I delighted in, that one was spinning for pike; and I should say, at a rough guess, that four fifths of my pike have been so captured.

In another part of his book he writes:

> Quite ninety per cent of the hundreds and hundreds of Jack which I have landed at one time or other have been taken on spinning tackles.

From these comments it is clear that Martin really understood something about pike spinning; indeed, his favourite tackle was of his own design. This tackle (Fig. 21.11) is a development of the old Trent flight, where two trebles (size 4 or 6) are fitted close together on a 16 in. length of wire.

With the aid of a baiting needle, the wire is threaded completely through the bait from the vent to the mouth and the hooks pulled up until the first treble buries itself in the vent, leaving the second treble to hang underneath the fish towards the tail. The wire is then passed through the eye of the tapered strip of zinc ($4\frac{1}{2}$–6 in. long, $\frac{3}{8}$ in. wide, tapering to $\frac{1}{8}$ in.). Then the zinc strip is pushed down the throat of the deadbait – dace, roach, bleak or sprat – until it emerges at the tail end, where half an inch of the strip is bent back to grip the bait at the root of the tail. Finally, the loose-looped treble is dropped into position.

The zinc strip should always be a little longer than the bait, which should not exceed $2\frac{1}{2}$ oz in weight.

Martin reckoned there was no better flight on which to mount a deadbait. He found that it was not only a great killer of pike, but held up well to long sessions of casting which caused most other baits to disintegrate.

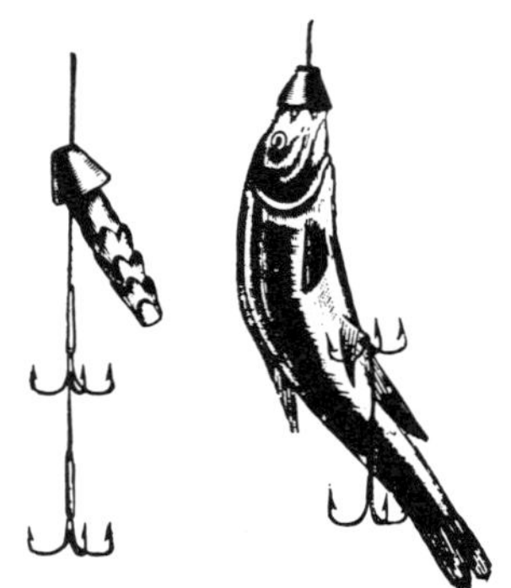

Fig. 21.12.

The Dee Flight

With the Dee flight (now obsolete) it was necessary to detach the lead from the tackle before passing the leader through the bait with a baiting needle via the vent and mouth. The lead was then slipped back on to the leader and pushed down the bait's throat. Finally, the hooks were attached with the bait in a bent position as in the figure.

The Drop-Minnow Aerial Flight

This is a development of the Dee flight. A bait can be fitted to the Aerial flight without the aid of a baiting needle. The

Fig. 21.13.

spiked lead is pushed down the throat of a dead minnow and a single hook from each of the two forward trebles is pushed into the minnow to provide the necessary anchorage.

The Archer Deadbait Spinning Mount

Like most of the commercial deadbait pike spinning mounts manufactured during the last 100 years, the Archer mount (Fig. 12.14) is really a modified version of the original Chapman mount.

The Chapman mount consisted of a wire spike, sharpened at one end to facilitate penetration of the bait, and leaded at the other to increase casting potential. The mount incorporated two spinning blades or vanes which fitted close to the head of the bait. Since the efficacy of the vanes depended on the size of the bait they were expected to set in motion, it was vital to have either a bait which suited the mount, or a mount which suited the bait.

The mount was armed with a complement of up to six trebles. Gradually, over the years, it became evident that although a lot of trebles ensure a secure grip of the bait – which means that the bait lasts longer – a correspondingly heavy price is paid in lost fish. The chances of a pike being firmly hooked are greatly reduced when the force of the strike is dissipated by a forest of trebles. On the other hand, although the use of

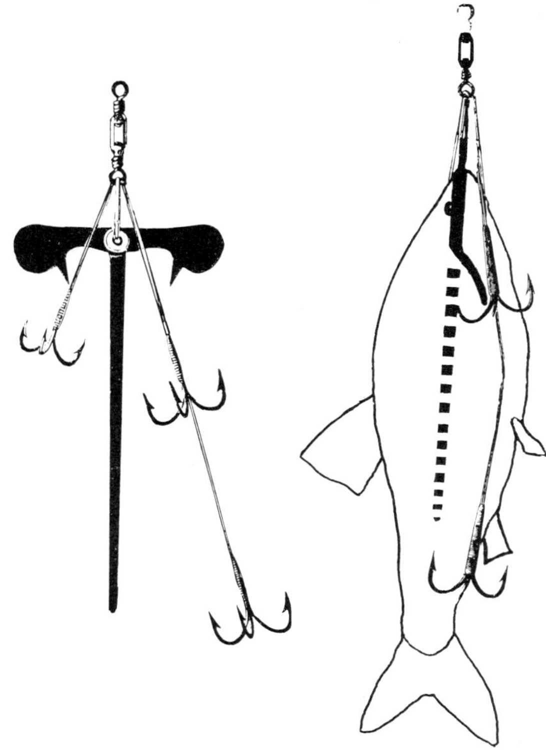

Fig. 21.14.

fewer trebles means that a bait is less securely held and needs replacing more often, it also results in a higher proportion of hooked fish being landed.

As these mechanical difficulties became more widely understood, the Archer mount, incorporating just three trebles, found universal favour. Or perhaps it might be truer to say that the Archer's popularity was due to the greater facility with which a bait could be put on. At any rate, Jardine spoke highly of it – which was praise indeed.

As can be seen in Fig. 12.14.*a*, the spinning-blades are hinged forward prior to the bait being mounted. When the vanes are pushed back into position they grip the bait behind the head. The trebles are then attached to the bait with cotton-elastic, or by pressing in lightly. Fig. 12.14.*b* shows the mounted bait.

LIVEBAITING FOR PIKE

A Note on Livebaits

Although some anglers remain convinced that pike never eat tench, they have been found in pike stomach's on many occasions, and we may hazard a guess that they didn't get there by accident. A taxidermist records taking several tench between two and three pounds each from the stomachs of three 20 pounders. Nevertheless, we can find no reference to an angler having used them successfully as livebaits – and have never done so ourselves.

Loch anglers seldom use perch as livebaits. This could be a mistake. Undoubtedly, a loch pike prefers trout or roach or whitefish if it can get them, but there is no doubt that perch are eaten in large numbers.

The old livebaiter's trick of cutting off the perch's spiky dorsal fin is both barbarous and unnecessary. A pike will hardly become aware that this fin is missing until *after* it has taken the bait – by which time the angler has had a chance to hook his fish. A more commendable method of using this bait was evolved by Windermere pike anglers who trail a dead perch on late summer evenings.

Some of the scales on the perch's flanks are scraped off leaving a whitish patch. Baits so treated produce a higher quota of strikes than natural baits.

The success of this little ruse may be due to the similarity of the scraped patch to a patch of fungus, indicating a wounded and easy-to-catch prey or it may simply serve as a more efficient signal and increase the range at which the bait can be seen in poor (evening) light.

Dace and gudgeon have always been popular livebaits. The convenience of carrying a dozen or so of these in a livebait can has probably outweighed other considerations, yet it is difficult to ignore the opinion of Jardine, who took so many good pike on the dace – his favourite bait.

It is a good plan to fish with a bait which is fairly selective: say, a roach or chub of not less than ¾ lb. This size of livebait, or deadbait for that matter, tends to select pike upwards of six to seven pounds, and if properly presented is large enough to tempt the really big pike.

Rigs and Tackles

The Pye Livebaiting Float Rig

An angler whose record qualifies him to describe pike livebaiting methods and tackle is that famous Broadsman, Dennis Pye. Although he is one of the few big-fish catching anglers to retain the use of the Jardine snap-tackle, he completes his rig with an individual choice of float.

For Norfolk waters, he uses a two-piece, 10 ft, built-cane rod with a test curve of 4 lb together with a 4 in. centre-pin reel

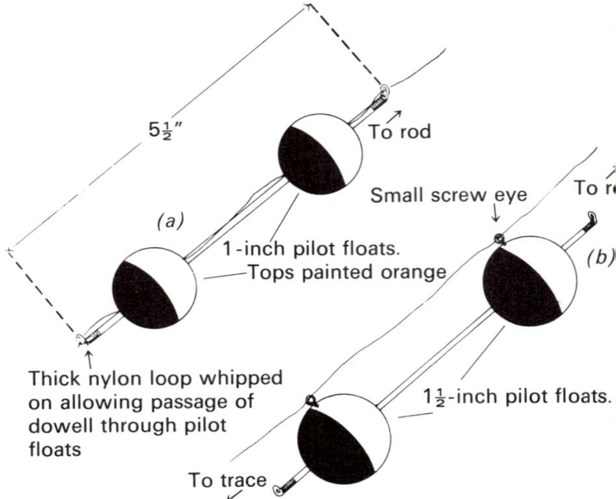

Fig. 21.15. Dennis Pye's floats.

loaded with 200 yards of 10 lb braided nylon. The business end consists of an 18 in., 10 lb steel leader, attached to a No. 2 Jardine snap-tackle. For shallow water, or water of medium depth, his rig is completed with the float illustrated in Fig. 21.15.*a*. For deep water fishing, he uses the float illustrated in Fig. 21.15.*b*.

Pye's method is to lob the float rig, complete with large livebait, *into* the wind, on the principle that the livebait will swim away from the boat as soon as it feels wind-drag on the line. By this method, distances up to 60 yards can be covered. To ensure such extensive coverage, the line is well greased to keep it floating. A sunk line creates excessive drag, which diminishes the power of a strike. There is the added danger of the line becoming fouled on underwater objects, which may cause a break.

For float-fishing in shallow water, Pye leaves the tackle un-leaded, observing that, with no lead to drag about, the bait will be

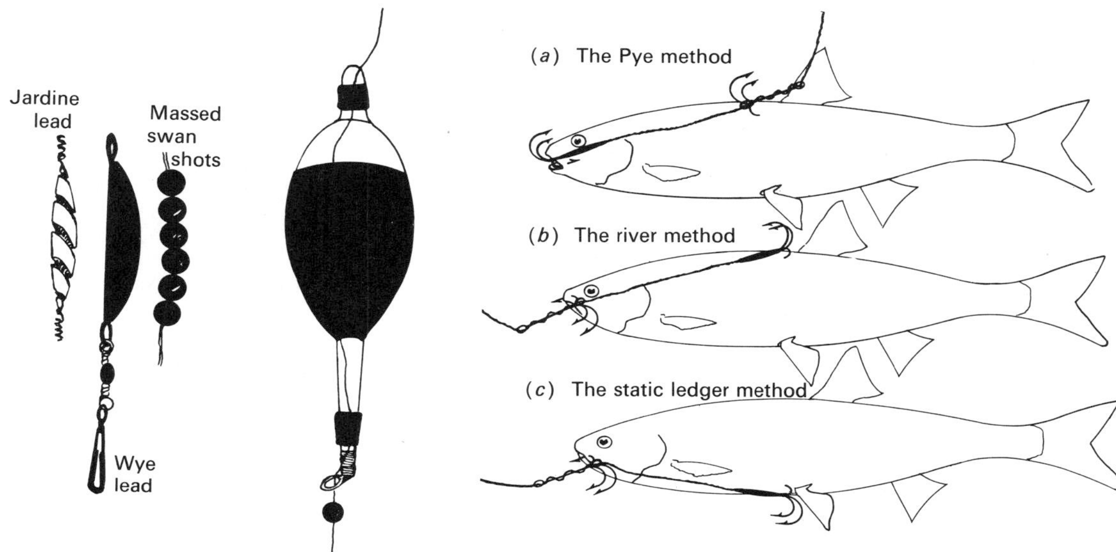

Figs. 21.16 and (right) *21.17.*

Fig. 21.18. Livebaiting rigs.

more active. This activity, he thinks, creates vibrations that attract a pike's attention.

Pye's special floats have sufficient buoyancy to keep the bait operating high in the water and at the same time, due to their slimness, prevent a pike from becoming alarmed when its slashing attack drags the floats back on to its own flank. He has noticed that a bulbous float, when fished in shallow water, often alarms a pike for this reason.

The sliding-float rig is preferred for deep water fishing. The float is stopped at the appropriate depth by a small shot fastened to the line, and a weight attached about four feet from the bait.

Alternative lead designs are illustrated in Fig. 21.16.

The float in Fig. 21.17, is a compromise design for those fishermen who still hanker after the 'bung' type of pike float.

Pye advocates mounting the snap-tackles as depicted in Fig. 21.18.*a*. His treatment of livebait is worth noting:

'When hooking a livebait on the trebles, I always put the small hook on the first treble through the side of the mouth in the soft sinew which is very thin. My second hook is placed just in front of the dorsal fin, but first I remove a scale with the point of the hook before gently inserting the treble just under the skin. A bait hooked like this will not stand a great deal of casting, before being flung off the hook. But I don't advocate casting long distances; my method is a gentle lob in the direction I wish my bait to travel, then a slight pressure so that the bait feels the drag of the line. It will then swim away. After my bait has been out and retrieved without being taken by a pike, I always release it, and it will swim away with only slight injury from which it generally recovers.'

The method illustrated in Fig. 21.18*b*, is a better method of attaching a bait for streamy water, since during recovery, after it has been trotted down a fast run, the bait is retrieved nose first. If the attachment shown in Fig. 18*a* is used, however, the bait has a tendency to revolve propeller-wise during retrieval.

The attachment illustrated in Fig. 18*c*, has not yet become popular; but it is a very useful method to use with a static ledger: it ensures that the bait points head upstream once foraging ceases. That it does not provide a secure hook hold for frequent casting can be discounted, since much casting is not required with the static ledger.

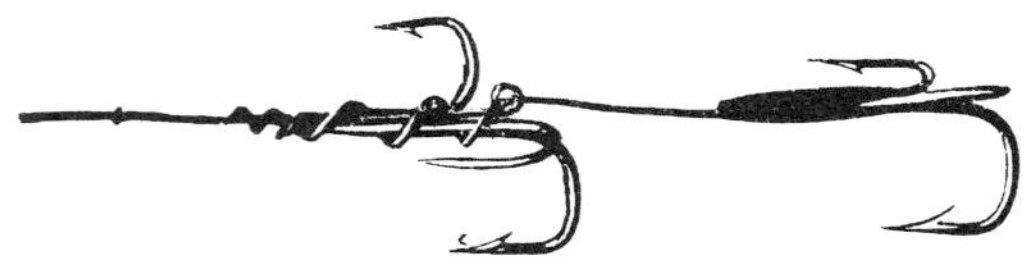

Fig. 21.19.
The Jardine Snap-Tackle
Although described by Jardine in the late 19th century this most famous of all pike tackles has survived unchanged until the present time. Jardine designed the tackle for his favourite pike-bait – the dace.

Saddle Tackles

Salter's tackle (Fig. 21.20) was invented some time between 1814 and 1833. His instructions for making it are as follows:

Take two hooks of the size No. 3, and tie each of them to about an inch-and-a-quarter of twisted wire; then take a hook, of the size No. 8, and about ten inches of gimp; put one end of the gimp to the wire that the aforesaid hooks are tied to; lay the hook No. 8 on the wire and gimp, and tie the whole very securely together; then make a loop at the other end of the gimp, and the whole is ready to receive the bait. To bait this snap; act as follows: take a proper-sized live Gudgeon, Roach, or Dace, and run the small hook through the flesh just under the back fin, and let the two large hooks hang one on each side of the bait-fish, and all is complete. When a Jack seizes your bait, and runs off, strike smartly, and you will seldom fail hooking him.

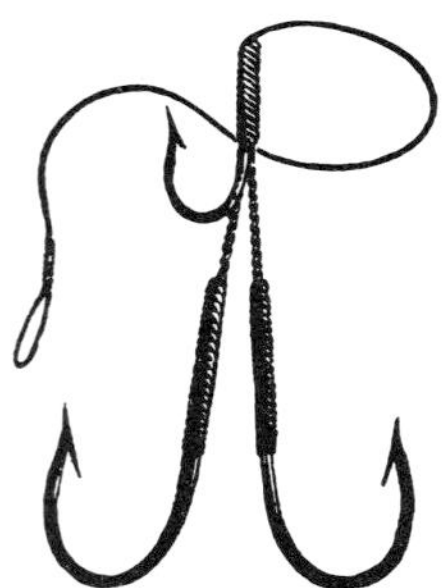

Fig. 21.20.

Salter's tackle was the precursor of a number of livebait saddle tackles.

Saddle tackles are effective if casting is restricted to a gentle swing. More powerful casting results in a lost bait. The last saddle tackle to be marketed was the *Mullins* tackle, made by Hardy Bros. It survived until after the 1939–1945 war. In the Mullins tackle the lower hooks were kept in position by an elastic band.

According to Charles Marson in *Super Flumina* (1905) it was the Duke of Wellington who first tried elastic as a means of securing a livebait. Marson's attempts to

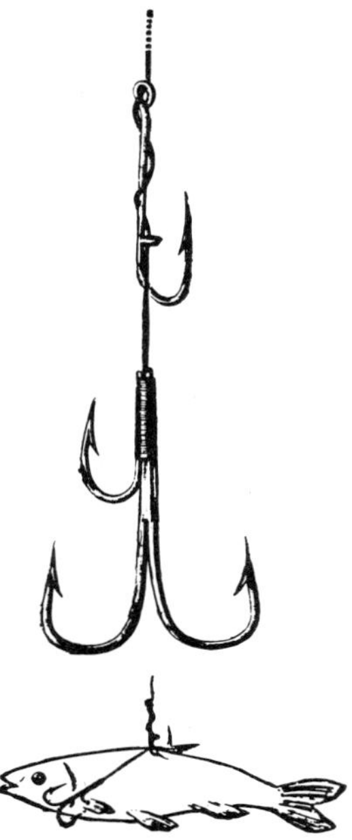

Fig. 21.21. Cholmondeley-Pennell's Adjustable Side-Saddle Tackle was described in his Pike and Other Coarse Fish. *third edition, 1889.*

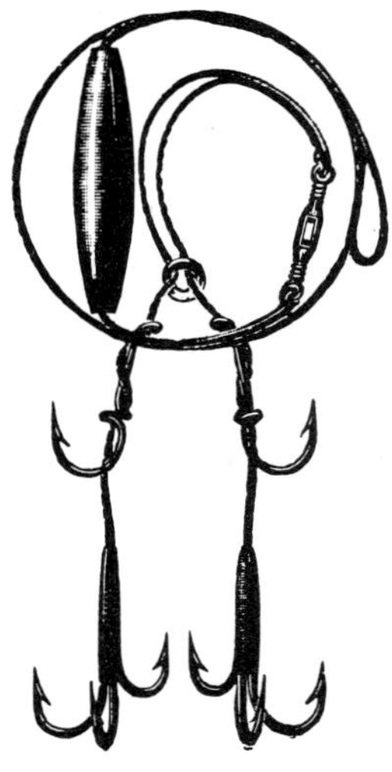

Fig. 21.22. Allcock's Saddle Tackle. The two single bait-supporting hooks pass through the same nick in the body of the bait near its dorsal fin, but in opposite directions. Alas, this excellent saddle-tackle is no longer made commercially.

emulate the Iron Duke brought forth this classic grizzle:

Out of humble imitation of him I have lost many valuable and rare dace, until his memory becomes odious to me.

Marson preferred a variation of Salter's original saddle-tackle:

The bait wears a brace of triangles as an ass wears a pannier; but a single hook is caught in the back fin. The girth prevents the gear from breaking loose at the cast; and the enemy has a choice of seven hooks.

In spite of having seven hooks, only one secures the bait, an arrangement which provoked this comment from Marson:

We know that the fewer pricks given to the bait the better both for mercy and business.

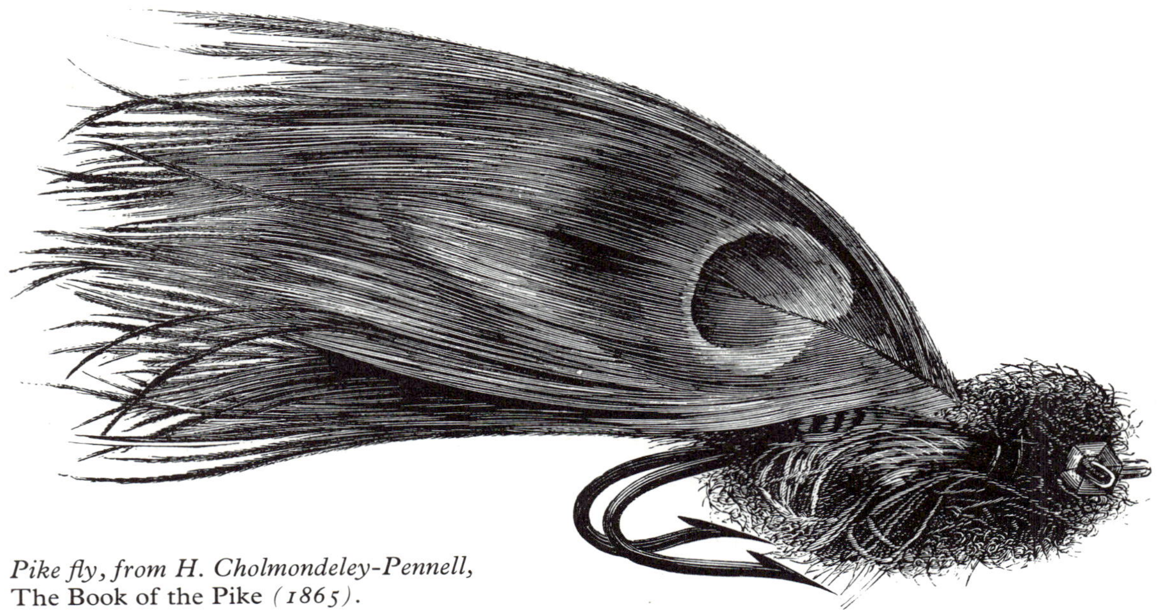

Pike fly, from H. Cholmondeley-Pennell, The Book of the Pike *(1865).*

In the late summer months and fine days in autumn, when the deeps are curled by a fine breeze, pike are to be taken very pleasantly by means of a fly. The best imitation is a very large one of a dragon fly. . . . An imitation of the sand-martin or swallow, dressed by means of feathers on a large hook, will prove an attractive bait for pike in the seasons last mentioned.
'EPHEMERA' (EDWARD FITZGIBBON), *A Handbook of Angling* (1847).

The late J. St. John, well known to Berkshire sportsmen, used to take numbers of pike in the Loddon with the end of a calf's tail tied to a triangle. He occasionally used a squirrel's tail. The latter I have tried with some success. No doubt these baits are taken for rats. They should be drawn along the surface at a fair speed.
ANON. (c. 1901).

I know some do angle for bream and pike with artificial flies, but I judge that labour lost, and the knowledge a needless curiosity, these being fish taken much easier (especially the Pike) by other ways.
COLONEL ROBERT VENABLES, *The Experienc'd Angler* (1662).

Scene of a spectacular battle (above)*: the bay where T. Morgan caught his huge 47 lb 11 oz Loch Lomond pike. The battle started in the bottom right hand corner. The pike then towed man and boat towards the wooded peninsula (right middle foreground) until it reached the deep channel that lies beyond the tiny one-tree island; there, it turned left and headed out into deep water. Later the pike retraced its route and was finally killed close to the spot where it had been hooked.* Note: *For reasons which we find incomprehensible, Morgan's pike is not accepted as the British Rod-Caught Record.*

(Below) *24 lb Loch Lomond pike caught from 'Tommy Morgan's Island'.*

Ireland is studded with small but prolific pike waters – like this little lough near Tulla in Co. Clare. To the pike angler, fishing grounds are available almost anywhere in the whole of the Northern Hemisphere, from Siberia to North America.

Pike fishing c. 1805.

GAFFING A PIKE

When gaffing a pike, most anglers hold the gaff incorrectly. The best place to gaff a pike is through the lower jaw, and to be effective the point of the gaff should be lifted in the vertical plane. Used in this way the gaff point will easily penetrate the soft skin between the lower jawbones *without harming the pike*.

A gaff held incorrectly and brought up at 45 degrees delivers a glancing blow to the pike's chin and may cause considerable damage. Even when a pike is to be killed, and a belly stroke is made, the gaff may fail to penetrate if the blow is not delivered correctly. The gaff should be held as shown: this enables an angler to lift it vertically. To hold it as a broom is held can produce numerous abortive and embarrassing strokes.

A CASE OF NEUTRAL DEFORMITY?

In February 1971 Mr David Mason caught a remarkable pike in the River Witham. It was only $38\frac{1}{2}$ in. long yet it weighed 30 lb! There can be no doubt that it weighed at least 30 lb since four competent witnesses, including Mr Albert Ibbotson, secretary of The Yorkshire Specimen Group, were present at the weighing-in. Nevertheless, some anglers found it impossible to believe that a pike measuring a mere $38\frac{1}{2}$ in. could weigh as much as 30 lb. They were partly justified in their criticism since it turned out that the length measurement had been taken,

Photograph: Angling News Services.

A pike from the river Witham: 27½ lb, caught by Deryck Naylor of Sheffield. This pike, which took a herring bait ledgered with float tackle, has the characteristic look of fish with coalesced vertebrae (Photograph: Angling News Services). Right: *X-ray photograph of fish with coalesced vertebrae* (British Museum).

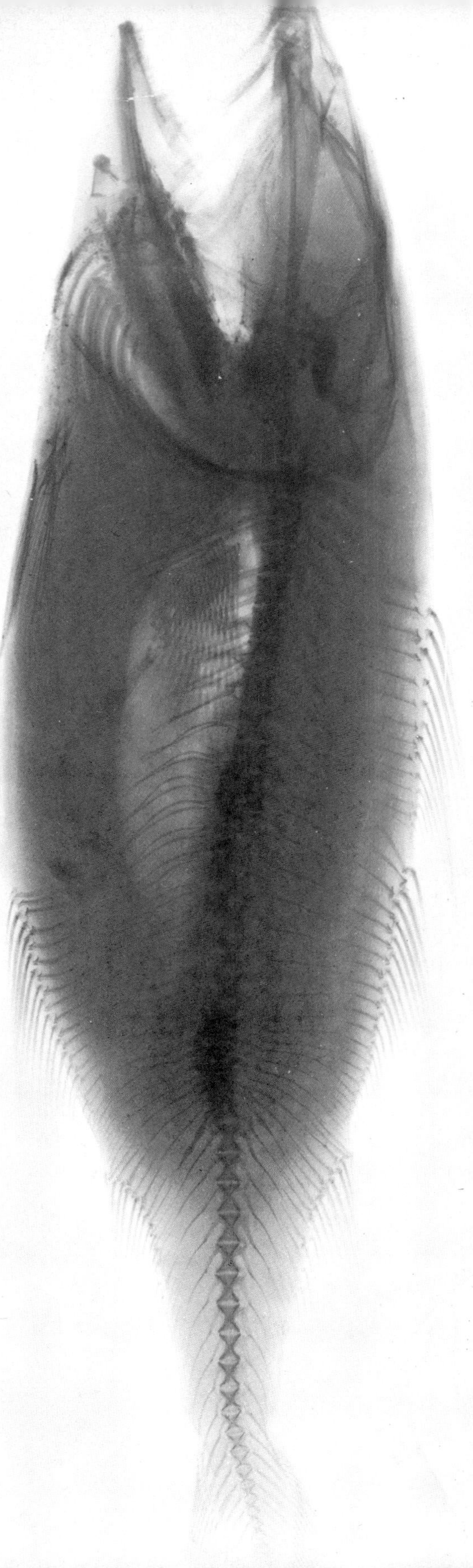

'from the tip of the pike's nose to the stub of the tail, instead of the cleft'. In order to compute the probable true length of this pike it is necessary to add a further 2 inches to the original measurement – making 40½ in. in all.

This brown trout (photograph by Angling News Services) *is another example of a fish with coalesced vertebrae.* Right: *its deformity revealed in an X-ray photograph.*

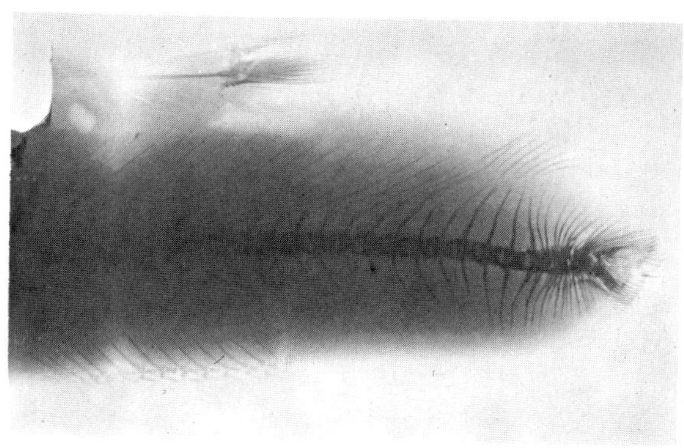

It can be argued that even 40½ in. is still very short for such a heavy pike. According to Mona's scale a 40½ in. pike in good condition should weigh only 20–21 lb – while F.B.'s scale indicates an approximate weight of no more than 26 lb.[1] A *possible* explanation of the unusual length/weight ratio of this fish is that it possessed a shortened vertebral column. Due to a deformity known as 'coalesced vertebrae' a fish of normal weight will have a shortened body length. Such a fish has a sawn-off appearance – as if the tail were attached to the body without the tapered 'wrist' associated with most fishes. (See X-ray photograph on p. 140.)

Mr Albert Ibbotson writing to the *Angling Times* gave measurements taken from other pike caught from the River Witham in the area where the controversial pike was caught. Two sets of these measurements are appended for comparison with the measurements of Mason's pike.

Mason's pike (after adjustment): 40½ in. length, 23 in. girth, 30 lb weight;
Pike 2: 36 in. length, 30 in. girth, 32 lb weight;
Pike 3: 42 in. length, 23 in. girth, 33 lb weight.

These figures come from a reliable witness, and it seems likely that the River Witham contains a local race of pike suffering (quite happily it appears) from a congenital deformity – coalesced vertebrae.

Many of the roach that inhabited the River Lea near Hertford in the 1950s displayed a similar characteristic.

1 As F. B. points out in his book *Pike*, in *special circumstances* a 40½ in. pike could weigh *more* than 30 lb. But in the case of Mason's pike these circumstances did not exist since the fish was not fully ripe with spawn nor had it just swallowed the largest food morsel that it was capable of swallowing.

PIKE IN ANTIQUITY

Judging by the evidence of fossils, the pike, *Esox lucius*, is almost identical with its ancient and extinct forebear, *Esox lepidotus*, which living during the upper Miocene period. Fossils of *Esox lepidotus*, believed to be about 20 million years old, have been found in deposits at Oeningen, in Baden. Fossils of *Esox papyraceus* have been found in the lignites of Rott, near Bonn, in Germany. These fossils belong to the Upper Oligocene period, and are therefore some 30 million years old.

The oldest fossils of *Esox lucius* found in Britain have come from the Cromer Forest beds at West Runton, in Norfolk. According to modern carbon-dating methods, the Cromer Forest flourished during an interglacial period just over 500,000 years ago. At that time, much ocean water was contained in glaciers; accordingly, sea levels were slightly lower than they are today. Even now, when tides are exceptionally low, fossilized tree stumps of the old Cromer Forest can still be seen. The pike of long ago would have lived in lakes and rivers within the forest area.

During the passage of time freshwater fishes show a remarkable stability in their physical character. The photographs opposite kindly sent to us by Professor G. V. Nikolski of Moscow University, show bream and perch fossils from the Likhvinsk interglacial deposits laid down some 500,000 years ago.

1) A bream fossil 2) A modern bream
3) A perch fossil 4) A modern perch

The pike fossil below is even older. It was found in the Upper Miocene deposits (about 20 million years old) at Oeningen in Baden, Germany. The appearance of this ancient pike *Esox lepidotus* shows a remarkable similarity to the modern pike *Esox lucius*.

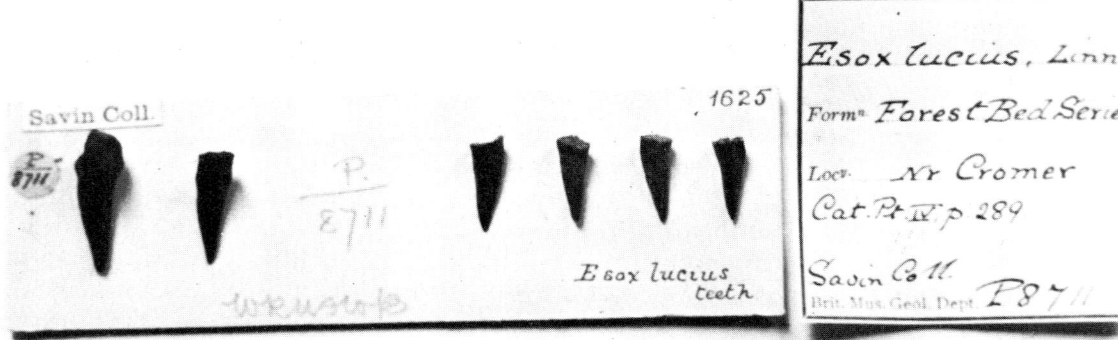

Photograph: British Museum.

Fossil pike (Esox lepidotus) (Photograph: British Museum).

COOKING THE PIKE

The Victorians cared little for pike as food, even though Victorian writers concocted numerous recipes for cooking them. In her *Dictionary of Cookery* (1872), Mrs Beeton offers the following:

Pike – à la Genevese.

Divide a 4 or 5 lb pike into slices or cutlets one-and-a-half inches thick; two chopped shallots, a little parsley, a small bunch of herbs, two bay leaves, two carrots, pounded mace, pepper and salt to taste, four tablespoonfuls of madeira or sherry, half-a-pint of white stock, thickening of flour and butter, one teaspoonful of essence of anchovies, the juice of one lemon, cayenne and salt to taste. Rub the bottom of a stewpan over with butter, and put in the shallots, herbs, bay leaves, carrots, mace, and seasoning; stir them for ten minutes over a clear fire, and add the madeira or sherry; simmer gently half an hour, and strain through a sieve over the fish, which stews in this gravy. As soon as the fish is sufficiently cooked take away all the liquor, except a little to keep the pike moist, and put it into another stewpan; add the stock, thicken with butter and flour, and put lemon-juice, cayenne and salt, lay the pike on a hot dish, pour over it part of the sauce, and serve the remainder in a tureen. Time, 1¼ hours. Sufficient for six or eight persons.

Pike Fishcakes

Since there is no pleasure in munching a mouthful of bones, a pike should be filleted before any attempt is made to cook it. Although difficult to describe, this operation is very easy to perform.

Two knives are required: one, pointed, the other, broad. Place the pike belly down on a table. Press the point of the gutting (or pointed) knife into the pike's back at the rear of the skull, and make a cut about an inch deep along one side of the backbone until the cut passes alongside and beyond the dorsal fin (Fig. A). Repeat the same stroke on the other side of the backbone (the cuts should be about ⅛ in. apart), which will bring the blade past and beyond the other side of the dorsal fin. In Fig. B, the backbone is just revealed. Lay the pike on its side, and with the same knife make a cut down the body immediately behind the gill-cover, and another a few inches forward of the tail fin (see the position of the knives in Fig. C). Still using the same knife, slit open the belly from the vent until both cuts are reached.

Lay the pike on its side with its back towards you and place the broad flat knife in the uppermost cut (one of the two cuts made along the backbone); draw the knife gently from end to end in a flowing motion; the blade follows the ribs until the whole side falls away complete (Fig. D).

Note: Wearing a cotton gardening glove helps when cleaning very slippery fish, like pike.

Turn the pike over, still with its back towards you, and repeat the same operation until the other side falls away. Cut out the ventral fins with the gutting knife, as shown in Fig. E. Now grip the thin end of the fillet, after laying it skin down on the table, and proceed to cut through the flesh down to the skin. Once down to the skin, change the

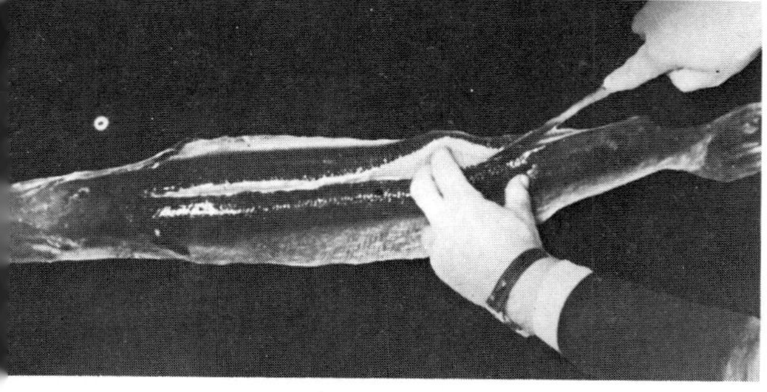

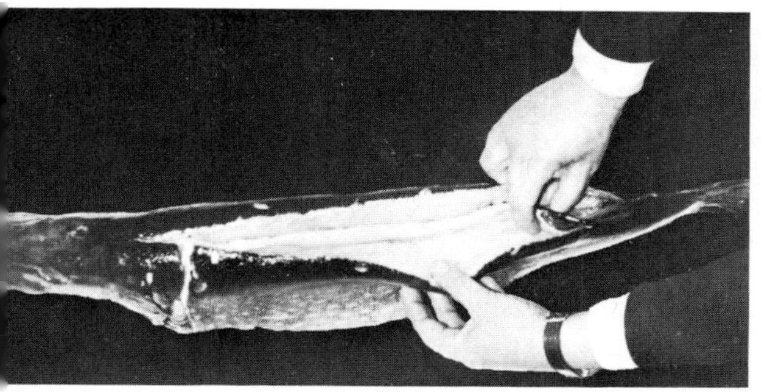

F

G

angle of the knife so as to make it run almost parallel to the skin, but taking care not to cut through the skin (Fig. F). The unusable remains, except for the skin and ventral fins, are left intact (Fig. G). Once the fillets are isolated and washed, hold them up for a minute to drain; then place them on a large plate and sprinkle with a fine layer of salt. Two or three hours' salting is sufficient if the pike is to be cooked the same day. Otherwise, place the salted fillets in a domestic refrigerator.

Cooking, Boil the fillets for ten minutes; drain off and mash. Mix the cooked fish with an equal amount of boiled, mashed potatoes; season with parsley. Shape the fish/potato mash into fish cakes and dip in breadcrumbs or flour. Fry until crisp and brown on the outside. Serve with a knob of butter on each fish-cake and add a fine sprinkling of salt with a dash of sauce according to palate.

Izaak Walton said of pike: 'This dish of meat is too good for any but Anglers, or very honest men.' After eating five of these fish cakes, contemplate Walton's statement and consider whether even honest men should qualify for such a feast.

A Recipe for Pike

I suppose that the usual way to cook pike is to bake it. That is quite a job, but the result can be delicious. First of all you must scale the fish and then dry it carefully with a clean towel. Then you need a pound of beef suet and a pound of grated bread, and mix and season with salt, pepper and nutmeg; work into this some shredded lemon peel and some thyme and some chopped anchovies and the yolk of eggs (three eggs to an eight-pound fish), and then squeeze lemon juice over the whole, and place it in the stomach of the fish. Sew the fish up, and bake in an oven until the skin cracks. And now you need a sauce. This sauce is the real secret of baked pike. And the best sauce is compounded thus: a pint of beef gravy, a pint of skinned shrimps, half a pint of stewed mushrooms, a quart of stewed oysters, a wineglass full of port; mix this into a pound of melted butter. Now take the thread out of your pike, pour the sauce over him, and enjoy yourself.

But the best way of all, in my opinion, to cook pike is this: Clean and scale your fish, and then boil or parboil it and then bone it: cut the white flakes of flesh into strips of an inch or so, and fry them in bread crumbs (if you have an egg so much the better). That served hot (with a lemon if possible) and thin bread and butter is a dish for a king.

BRIAN VESEY-FITZGERALD *The Hampshire Avon.*

Pike Quenelles

In 1898, Georges Auguste Escoffier, sometime chef de cuisine at the Carlton Hotel and one of the best chefs of his time, began writing notes for a book which was to become the classic work on French cuisine: *A Guide to Modern Cookery*.

Since Escoffier is regarded as *the* master in matters of cuisine, anglers may be interested to know that he described a special dish (No. 1040) – *Quenelles de Brochet à la Lyonnaise* – the details of which we are happy to provide.

Pound separately 1 lb of the meat of pike, cleared of all skin and bones, and 1 lb of the fat of kidney of beef, very dry, cleaned, and cut into small pieces. If desired, half the weight of the fat of kidney of beef may be replaced by ½ lb of beef marrow.

Put the pounded meat of the pike and the kidney fat on separate plates. Now pound 1 lb frangipane Panada (No. 192) and add thereto, little by little, the white of 4 little eggs. Put the pike meat and the fat back in the mortar, and finely pound the whole until a fine smooth paste is obtained. Rub the latter through a sieve; put the resulting puree in a basin, and work it well with a wooden spoon in order to smooth it.

With this forcemeat, mould some quenelles with a spoon and poach them in salted water.

If these quenelles are to be served with an

ordinary fish sauce, put them into it as soon as they are poached and drained, and simmer them in it for 10 minutes that they may swell.

If the sauce intended for them is to be thickened with egg yolks and buttered at the last moment, put them into a saucepan with a few tablespoons of fumet, and simmer them as directed in the case of an ordinary fish sauce, taking care to keep the saucepan well covered that the concentrated steam may assist the swelling of the quenelles. In this case they are added to the sauce at the last moment.

N.B. – Slices of truffle may always be added to the sauce. The quenelles are dished either in a silver timbale, in a shallow timbale crust, or in a fine vol-au-vent crust, in accordance with the arrangement of the menu.

192 – C. Frangipane Panada

Put into a stewpan 4 oz sifted flour, the yolks of four eggs, a little salt, pepper and nutmeg. Now add by degrees 3 oz melted butter and dilute with ½ pint boiled milk. Pass through a strainer, stir over the fire until the boil is reached; set to cook for five minutes whilst gently wielding the whisk. Lightly butter the surface of the panada in order to avoid its drying while it cools.

22 · The Roach

Rutilus rutilus

The roach, in common with the bream, the dace, the tench and most other freshwater species, is a member of the carp family (Cyprinidae). Although absent from Norway and other high regions including those of Scotland and Wales, it is generally distributed throughout the temperate parts of western and central Europe, and eastern Europe as far as the U.S.S.R. According to the celebrated icthyologist, Tate Regan, it is also found in Russian Turkestan and throughout Siberia.

It is not thought to be indigenous to Ireland. According to Alwyne Wheeler, Britain's foremost fish taxonomist, the only native Irish freshwater fish are sticklebacks, eels and shads. It has, however, established itself in the Foyle and Erne systems of northern Ireland and the river Blackwater of southern Ireland. There are reports of roach being caught at different points on Ireland's longest river – the Shannon. This should lead to wonderful roach fishing on the lakes and rivers of the Shannon system within five years, for that is time it took for roach to become established after the first reports of their appearance on the river Erne. The Irish match-record bag of roach (64 lb 7½ oz) was taken by an angler fishing the Erne below Belturbet in October, 1970 – just five years after the first appearance of roach in that river.

The true home of British roach is in the sluggish waters of the eastern rivers of England where the land is low lying, but colonies have established themselves as far north as Loch Lomond and Teith in Scotland, and recently in Esthwaite lake in the English Lake District.

The penetration of roach to these mountain areas seems to be linked with the changes that have occurred in some mountain lakes due to a process known as 'eutrophication' – becoming richer in dissolved nutrient salts (see p. 43).

The roach is a shoal fish and tends to swim in a shoal throughout its life: a point of considerable importance to the angler. A roach shoal usually consists of fish that have collected together soon after hatching, and have subsequently kept together although, when shoals are reduced in size by natural hazards, some mixing is noticeable, particularly in small waters.

The roach has no mouth teeth. Instead, it possesses pharyngeal or throat teeth, a feature of all Cyprinids. These throat teeth enable the roach to crush food particles against a hard plate attached to the basal part of the skull.

The bottom roach in the case is the British Record Roach, 3 lb 14 oz. Caught by W. Penney at Molesey Reservoir, 6th September, 1938 (Photograph: G. Berth-Jones).

Every roach angler must at some time or another have suffered the indignity of retrieving a bunch of maggot skins, the contents of which were sucked 'dry' without so much as a warning tremble of the float. This is the work of the pharyngeal teeth.

Roach are omnivorous, that is to say they subsist on a mixed diet of animal and plant life. Adult roach find most of their food on or near the bottom, or (as bygone writers put it) 'at ground'. Their animal diet has been found to include the larvae of midges (*Chironomids*), caddis (*Trichoptera*), mayflies (*Ephemeroptera*), as well as invertebrates such as shrimps (*Gammarus*), snails (*Mollusca*) and the water louse (*Asellus*). Their plant diet includes filamentous algae and some of the higher plants. Roach also feed on the pupae of many insects, either in midwater or at sub-surface levels. During spells of warm weather they will take flies at the surface.

Anglers contribute enormously to the diet of roach. Literally tons of groundbait, both animal and vegetable, are thrown into heavily fished waters – and eaten by the fish.

Roach reach their peak condition in winter. During this period their ovaries and testes develop in weight, until by late spring the eggs and milt are ripe for spawning. By this time, male roach have developed numerous white conical tubercles on the

A famous angler : W. F. Hardy ledgering for roach from Balmaha Pier, Loch Lomond. Above right: *Bill Hardy shows his catch to H.F.*

head, on the fin rays and even on the scales. They are now noticeably rough to the touch – or, as the Reverend W. B. Daniel put it in *Rural Sports* (1801), 'They feel like the rough side of an oyster shell.'

Spawning is carried out in the weedy shallows when the water temperature reaches about 15°C (59°F). The eggs adhere to the vegetation and usually hatch within nine to 12 days. After spawning, river roach migrate to the streamy runs. The reason for this migration has yet to be established.

In a favourable habitat, with good feeding, roach commonly grow to a weight of 2 lb. A weight of 4 lb is likely to be the upper limit, but even in extremely favourable conditions such a weight is a rarity. To date the British Rod-Caught Record roach is a 3 lb 14 oz fish, caught by W. Penney, in Molesey Reservoir in 1938. Another fish, although officially recognised by the British Record Fish Committee as the joint equal record, is still the subject of debate, since one of Britain's most experienced anglers believes it to be a hybrid. (For notes on hybridization, see p. 166.)

The roach is not highly esteemed as a table fish. Accordingly, it has a low economic value – except in those few European countries that do not enjoy access to a supply of fresh sea fish. In these countries, where freshwater fish are prized for food, there is usually a long record of fish cultivation.

A great deal is known about the roach in Czechoslovakia, where written records of fish cultivation go back to the 11th and 12th centuries, and some 96% of all marketable fish is supplied from freshwater fish farms. Most countries try to benefit from the study and application of advanced agricultural techniques. It is sad to record that although United Kingdom authorities should be looking to countries like Czechoslovakia for guidance in the techniques of coarse fish cultivation, they do not do so. On the subject of coarse fish culture, Britain is truly backward. Where else, when dealing with the problems of poor fishing, would roach (netted from one water where they are unwanted) be transferred to another water without due thought for the infertile condition of that new water, or of the limitations of its productive capacity, or of the fate of the freshly introduced inmates? And the roach is by no means the only species to suffer such treatment.

If the importance of a fish species depended not on its commercial value but on the number of anglers who derived pleasure from catching it, the roach would deserve special consideration. It is the most popular sport-fish in Britain. It gives enjoyment to more anglers than any other species. No record is so coveted as that of the biggest rod-caught roach.

ROACH AS SPORTFISH

The successful roach fisher is not to be sneezed at. He is an artist. His tackle is fine, his 'strike' is delicate and true, as swift and polished as the action of the fly fisher. He casts beautifully with unerring aim.
DENYS WATKINS PITCHFORD.

By contrast to present-day enthusiasm for roach, Guiniad Charfy, writing two hundred years ago, thought them:

. . . notorious for their simplicity and being easily taken. When they are hooked you have no more trouble with them; and therefore they are called the Water Sheep, being so mild and so ready to yield.

It must be conceded that the roach is not the most furious of fighters. Further, one must agree that small roach are exceedingly easy to catch. But the catching of *big* roach is altogether another matter. Specimen-roach fishing is as difficult as small-roach fishing is easy: it demands considerable skill and places an angler high in any piscatorial order of merit. J. W. Martin ('Trent Otter'), famous champion of roach fishing, said:

There is a large class of anglers who confine their attention exclusively to this branch of fishing; they are never tempted to try any other, and I have fancied more than once that they rather prided themselves on the fact. But there is one thing certain; a successful roach fisherman stands on the very highest rung of the angling ladder.

Roach angling methods have been developed over hundreds of years. They can be applied to practically every sort of fresh-

water fishing – and most of them to certain branches of sea fishing, too. Ledgering, float/ledgering, laying-on, lift-fishing, stret-pegging, trotting, poling, fly-fishing with artificials, both wet and dry, dapping with the natural insect, all are highly skilled techniques. The angler who has mastered these and can catch big roach can catch anything.

Trotting

In running water the most popular method of catching roach is swimming the stream, or trotting. From a stretch of riverside the angler selects a swim of a dozen yards or so. When he does so he is making use of an established principle: fish are not evenly spread out along a water-course but, for reasons of safety, comfort and food availability, concentrated in certain favourable pockets.

After judicious groundbaiting, the angler begins his routine of casting to the head of the swim just a little upstream of him, and retrieving from the downstream end. In the course of a day's fishing he will almost certainly make many alterations to his tackle in an attempt to meet the changing demands of the fish. He may try a different bait; change the hook size; alter the fishing depth by increasing or decreasing the distance between float and hook; substitute a float carrying more lead shot to make the bait sink faster,

Trotting: an expert in action. Dave Steuart brings a fine roach to the net.

or a float carrying less shot to allow the bait to go down more slowly.

When the water is clear and the fish extremely shy, it is essential for the angler to keep out of sight. In these conditions he will stand 20 to 40 years upstream of the fish and 'trot' his float and bait down to them. The longer the range, the greater the strain imposed on his tackle by the strike. Because of this, and because heavier floats with more shotting are normally used, a stronger, more supple rod is recommended for this type of fishing.

Roach poling

1. Tackling up. 2. Baiting – with boiled wheat. 3. Now – wait for it. 4. Got him! (Continued over page.)

1

2

3

4

5

6

7

5. Keep out of sight and let the net do the work. 6. Lift the fish straight up with the minimum of disturbance. 7. A nice catch of medium sized roach.

A Roach-Pole Technique

Practitioners of the old River Thames and River Lea roach-poling tradition, are being joined by a steady flow of new pole-fishing enthusiasts. This enthusiasm for pole-fishing is inspired by the brilliant example of Continental (mostly French) anglers, who use this technique so successfully in international competition. Although it would be unwise to regard the roach-pole technique as the complete answer to a match fisherman's problems, we must concede that the fixed-float, pole-fishing technique is a deadly one to use when fish are feeding in deep water.

To float-fish such water with the traditional 14-foot rod demands a sliding float, which results in a considerable loss of hooking efficiency. This loss is due to slack line, and is greatest at maximum range and depth – when the line is bent at full ninety degrees to the float (see Fig. 32. , p. 346).

The strike achieves its greatest efficiency when the rod-tip is directly above the float.

The roach-pole enables an angler to float-fish, float-ledger, or lay-on effectively in water which is otherwise held to be swing-tip or ledger territory.

Because of the powerful lever action of any long rod, it has always been difficult to make

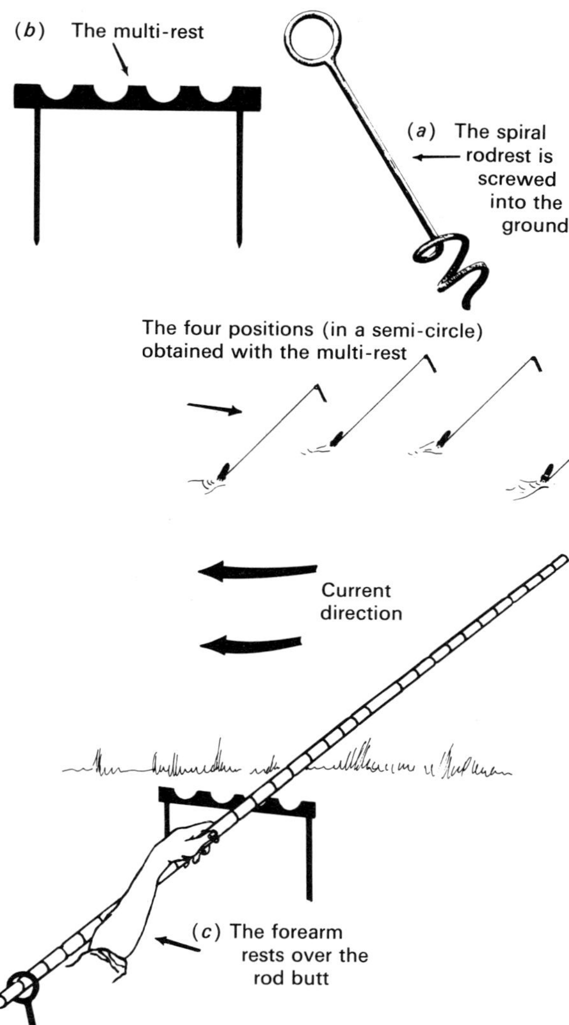

Fig. 22.1. Back rod-rest invented by R. Crosbie of the Harlesden Angling Society.

full use of the exceptional length of a roach-pole. If an attempt is made to hold most of the rod out over the water, ordinary rod-rests get pulled out of the ground. An ingenious back rod-rest (Fig. 22.1) eliminates this problem. Used in conjunction with a multiple front rod-rest (Fig. 22.1.*b*), several spots in a swim can be searched with a laying-on or float-ledger technique. With these items, some 20 feet of a 23-foot roach-pole can be made to overhang the river.

Fig. 1*c* illustrates how the forearm is used to counteract the leverage of the rod at the moment of striking. Experienced 'polers', swimming the stream from a sitting position make use of their knee and thigh to augment the support given by the forearm: the thigh is moved in unison with the arm as the rod follows the float from the head to the tail of the swim. Doubtless, some of the newer super-lightweight glass-fibre poles will not need this extra support.

A Ledgering Technique for Hampshire Avon Roach

Although the rolling ledger is a well established and effective method of fishing the lower Hampshire Avon, it is often less rewarding when used on the middle Avon. After trying many variations on the theme, in the course of which he reluctantly discarded the often invaluable swimfeeder, F. B. began to think that ledgering in these waters took second place to float fishing.

A walk down the river bank early one morning, on a day favourable for seeing fish, made him think again. In that low clear

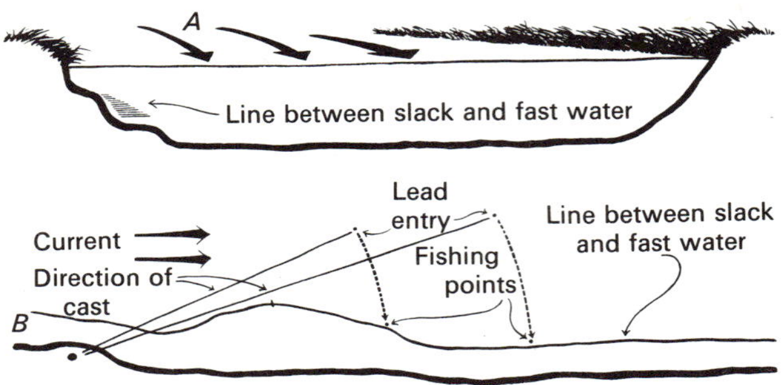

Fig. 22.2. Fishing at ground provides a better chance of coming to terms with large roach. The big fish are inclined to feed on the bottom. Small fish tend to search for food particles in suspension.

water he saw many shoals of large roach lying close to the bank. So long as these fish remained undisturbed, they concentrated in swims along a line between the flowing water and the dead water at the edge (see Fig. 22.2). Moreover, a chance conversation with a very successful Avon roach fisher revealed that, after dark, a number of three-pound roach had been taken very close to the bank.

Generally speaking, deep water provides security for fish and, as a consequence, can be searched by them for food at any time of the day or night. On the other hand, shallow water – particularly the shallow strip close to the bank – provides no security except at night, or during floods, or when the water is completely undisturbed. As a result, shallow waters can be cropped only when one or more of these special conditions obtain. Because they are seldom visited, the shallow areas must offer better feeding – and so becomes a great attraction. Water-borne food particles temporarily coming to rest somewhere in an area where streamy water fades into slack, add to this attraction.

To fish a ledgered bait into such an area is anything but straightforward. Apart from the difficulty of pinpointing the shoal without alarming it, Avon roach in particular are very sensitive to splash (perhaps because of the absence of boat traffic) so that a direct cast frightens them back into the faster and deeper water. After experiment the following technique was evolved and has proved itself to be the most selective and deadly of all methods for catching large roach from the Hampshire Avon.

Select a known roach swim. Stalk carefully to a point 30 feet above the head of it. Take portions from the inside of a new loaf, wetted and pressed sufficiently to sink, and release them quietly into the run with the aid of a landing net.

Because of its sensitivity and flexibility, use a medium fly rod for this type of fishing rather than the usual Avon-type rod. The latter is not needed because a long line is never fished.

The most important item of tackle is an ultra-light casting lead – an $\frac{1}{8}$ oz, or $\frac{1}{4}$ oz Arlesey bomb.

Tackle up well back from the water's edge. Approach the head of the swim with great care. Cast a little more than halfway across the river at an angle of 45° downstream. As soon as the lead enters the water, hold the rod high while the current swings the lead and crust-baited hook round in an arc. With a normal winter flow, and such a light lead, the terminal tackle hardly touches bottom. Holding the rod high helps to speed up the

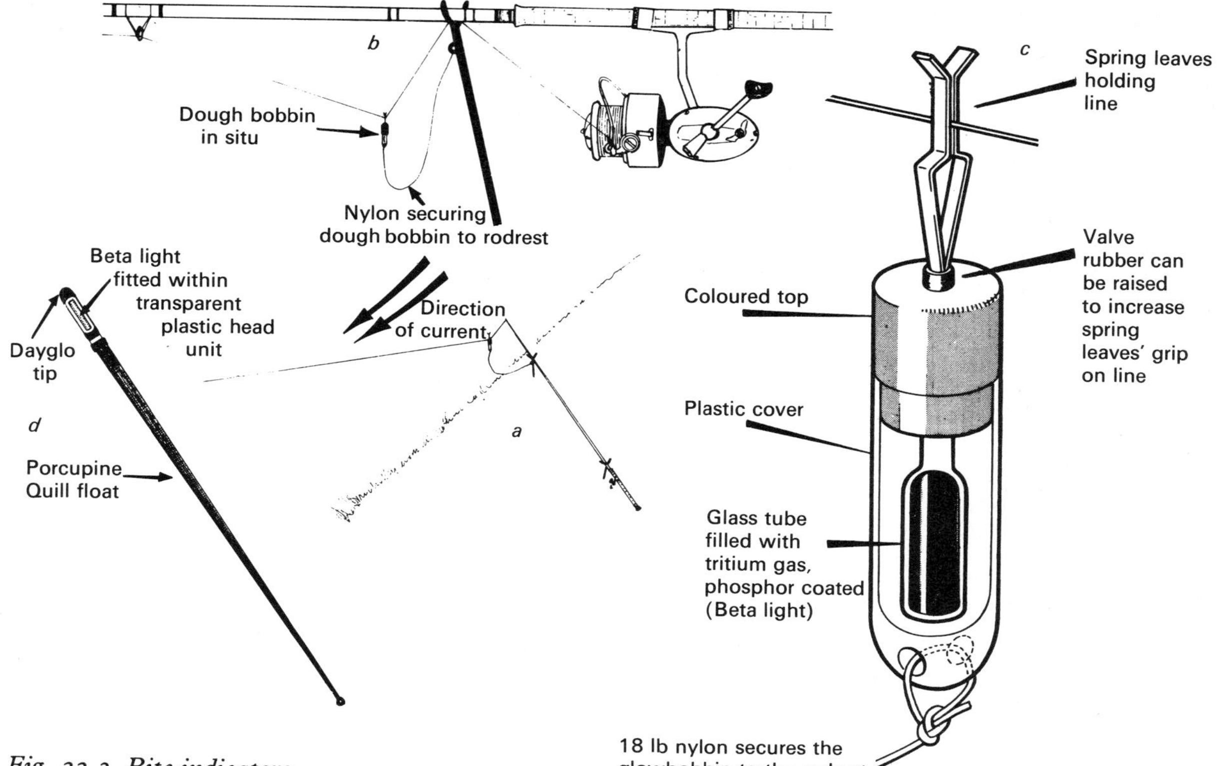

Fig. 22.3. Bite indicators.

swing round. This ensures that the bread will not saturate fully and part company with the hook before coming to rest.

Provided you have not chosen to fish an outside bend of the river, the baited hook should now be resting in an area where the current fades into slack water (see Fig. 22.2).

Put the rod in a rest at right angles to the direction of the flow and fit a natural dough-bobbin bite indicator on to the line (Fig. 22.3*a*). An alternative lay-out for the bite indicator is shown in Fig. 22.3*b*. The utmost caution is necessary if the fish are not to be frightened; indeed, it is well to emulate the trout fly-fisherman – and *kneel*.

Disturbance caused by catching one or two roach will make it necessary to move a few yards down the swim. At once repeat the groundbaiting process. This time expect the bites to come quickly, because the first groundbaiting will have activated roach throughout the swim.

Because roach, even big roach, have small mouths compared with most other fish, it is advisable to use very small pieces of crust on a size 10 Mackenzie (or other fine, round bend) hook. Although bites are just as frequent on bigger pieces of crust, fewer fish are hooked. On the Avon, breadcrumb tends to be a selective bait. When using it, you will rarely be bothered by small fish.

All roach over a pound are exciting to play on a fly rod. When hooked, heavy roach give a characteristic bump-bump sensation quite different from that of the occasional rogue chub, which tends to make a sudden dart.

Use crust from the top corners of an under-baked tin loaf. The rest can be broken up into

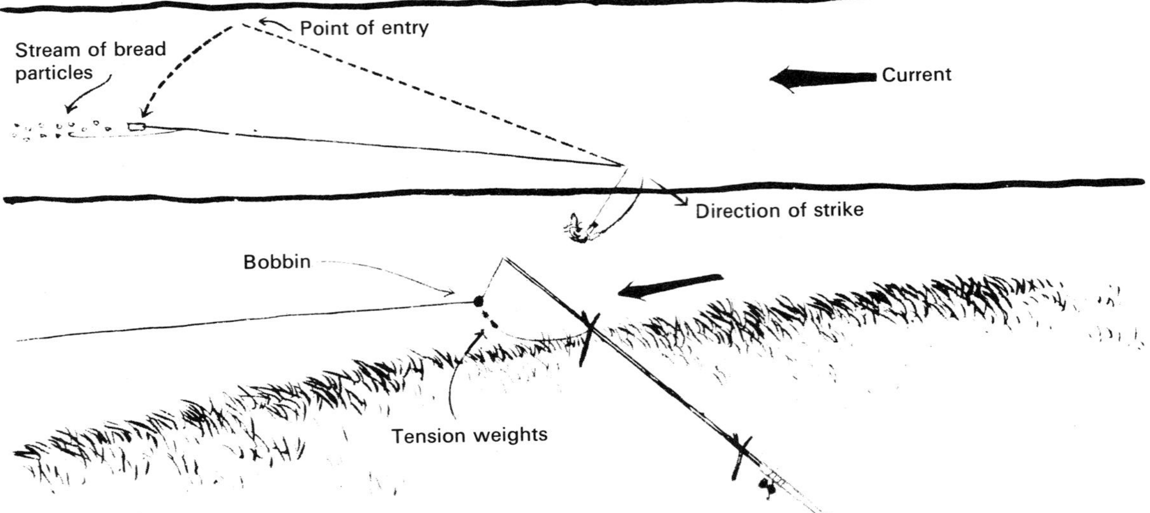

Fig. 22.4. A swimfeeder technique for roach.

small pieces and added sparingly to the crumb-groundbait. Never use secondary groundbaits such as bran or cloud. Unlike their lesser brethren, big roach do not feed on one kind of groundbait and take another kind of hookbait – unless of course they are very hungry.

Crust is the deadliest of all baits for big Avon roach or, indeed, for big roach anywhere. Although it is true that big roach are sometimes caught on maggots, most maggot fishing anglers will have to catch many hundreds of small roach before they tighten on a two-pounder.

The big roach are usually the last to start feeding. Don't spoil your chance of catching them by trying to liven things up in the meantime. Small roach well on the feed are easily caught, but the disturbance caused by hooking and landing them one after the other puts the big roach down. So – be patient.

Fig. 22.3*c* shows an enlarged view of a modern dough-bobbin bite indicator. The Beta-light contained within the body of the indicator enables an angler to see a bite in total darkness just as well as in daylight. Fig. 22.3*d* shows a Beta-light fitted to a float.

A Swimfeeder Technique on the Dorset Stour

Sometimes in the written word, and often in the minds of anglers, the Dorset Stour is coupled with the Hampshire Avon. But although it holds the same species of fish, and although it drains a neighbouring watershed before entering the sea as one with the Avon, the Stour is a river that demands a separate understanding. It has a greater variation of mood and character. The upper and middle reaches, in particular, have sections of lazy, muddy-bottomed deeps, frequently alternating with gravelly shallows. There is less urgency in the stream. This slower current is essentially the difference between the two rivers.

Many anglers who have enjoyed success on the Avon find themselves in difficulty when they fish the Stour. A bag of chub is commonplace on the Avon; on the middle and upper Stour it is a rarity. So is the heavy mixed bag of fish taken by any one method and any one bait. Each of the many Stour species has its own special needs and the roach is no exception.

If you wish to catch roach, you must fish for roach. But first you must locate them.

To this end, the Stour is an accommodating river. In times of low water it displays its fish temptingly for all to see. A careful drift in a boat on a summer's day will reveal a host of fishes – likely to cause tackle-fumbling excitement to all but the steadiest of anglers.

As you walk the bank you may notice the absence of roach from likely looking pieces of water, but here and there find them in 'pockets'. Normally they lie in the deeper runs, in the permanent open waters of bridge pools and mill pools, where they find their much-needed security. Such places often hold their own local shoals of roach – large, educated and hard to catch.

When the water is low and crystal clear, you are able to locate and lay siege to a shoal of good roach – preferably using fine, floatless (and sometimes weightless) tackle. This style of fishing demands a stealthy approach, sometimes even a belly-crawl. If success results, the pleasure comes not so much from taking a bag of fish – whatever its size – but from the manner in which it is taken.

In the tinted streams of autumn and winter, when the eye can no longer detect the quarry, you can usually expect roach to be occupying the first substantial deeps beyond a stretch of shallows. In these conditions you are fishing 'blind', and must change your technique accordingly.

Start fishing about eight yards above a known roach swim and, if the river is narrow, contrive to fish from the shallow side into the deep. This is important, since it is the deepest part of a swim which gives maximum security to the fish – and you must not be too close.

For groundbait, tear up two new loaves into hook-size pieces. These should be kept in a screw-lid sweet-shop bottle, so as to retain their original freshness.

Fill a swimfeeder straight from the bottle, in the manner of the pipe smoker who fills his pipe from a pouch – but press gently. Fresh crust and crumb will grip easily on the inside of the feeder.

The hookbait should be taken from the corners of a fresh, underbaked tin loaf – also kept fresh in a sealed container. Let the loaded feeder hang clear while you bait a No. 10 round bend hook. Do this by biting off an irregular piece of crust, say about $\frac{5}{8}$ in. × $\frac{3}{8}$ in. × $\frac{3}{8}$ in., and pulling the hook right through the bait until the barb is exposed on the opposite side.

A light, medium length, all-action rod is used to put the swimfeeder and bait approximately 30 degrees downstream of an imaginary line drawn straight across the river. Cast accurately to a chosen point each time, and let the stream take the feeder round in an arc on a tight line until it settles. Allow the contents of the feeder to soak for a few seconds; then make a long forearm strike to clear the feeder. Repeat the process at least a

Ranunculus on the Dorset Stour (Photograph: D. Steuart).

dozen times. This will ensure that the river bed is carpeted with pieces of bread that are indistinguishable from the hookbait. When roach start to feed, they invariably work upstream to the food source. And if your crust-baited hook is lying nicely among many similar pieces of crust, it will cause the downfall of even the most suspicious roach.

A light, supple rod is essential for this style of ledgering, for it helps you to achieve slowly-accelerated and accurate casts. Slow acceleration prevents the groundbait from being flung out of the feeder during casting. Even more important is the ability of the rod to function as an efficient shock absorber, since the fish must not be frightened by clumsy splashes. The feeder should be slowed down just before it hits the water by trapping line coming off the spool.

Five-pound breaking strain monofil as the main line is about right, with a three-pound hook-link. The distance between the feeder and the bottom eye of a three-way swivel should remain at fourteen inches. The distance between hook and swivel can be varied to suit conditions; but three feet is usual. These proportions ensure that when pieces of groundbait are washed out of the feeder by the current, they lay a trail downstream directly over the hookbait.

On most Stour roach swims it is possible to use a bite indicator. The most sensitive type of indicator is one which incorporates the dough-bobbin principle. This signals a warning tremble, and provides a biting fish with at least a foot of slack line. This slack line is important, for it permits time for a bite to develop and gives the angler a chance to 'read' the bite. Recommended, is a Hardy 'Dobob' – painted in contrasting colours, so that it can be seen regardless of background. When necessary, lead shot is added to the bottom compartment of the 'Dobob'. Suitably leaded, the 'Dobob' just counteracts the pull of the stream and gives the line the right amount of sag.

With this style of ledgering, the rod should be set up at right angles to the line so that a sideways strike 'mends' the line immediately. If you ledger, as some anglers do, with the rod pointing straight at the line, quick hook penetration is unlikely, since the line cannot be recovered at the same speed as the rodtip until the latter has been raised through 90 degrees. Simple geometry will illustrate the point. In practice, having the rod correctly angled means that the rod points 30 degrees upstream while the line points 60 degrees downstream.

Resist the temptation to ginger up proceedings by using maggots. Maggots will encourage the small fish. If these are caught in numbers, the suspicions of the big roach will be aroused.

Using this method F.B. has caught good bags of large roach: 'On one memorable occasion even the smallest capture weighed 1 lb 7 oz, and the best was well over 2 lb. On this particular day I resisted the temptation to use maggots, even though my companions were using them successfully to catch numbers of fine quality roach. My pleasure came later that evening . . . There is only one sight better than a good bag of fine quality roach: a better bag of even finer quality roach.'

ROACH ON THE FLY

There are times and places, both much commoner than most anglers imagine, when roach can be caught by fly-fishing, sometimes more successfully than by any other method.

'In very hot weather', writes Richard Walker, 'shoals of roach may rise to the surface and then they can be caught with a dry fly, J. W. Dunne's dressing for the black gnat being a very successful fly, though there are times when really big roach will rise to a much larger fly. I have caught roach between 1 and 2 lb on sedge imitations tied on hooks as large as size 10, and once or twice on artificial daddy long-legs on size 10 longshank hooks.

'It is much more common to find roach catchable with a sunk fly, however, and there are two outstandingly successful patterns, both nymphs. One is the Pheasant Tail, the other a little olive nymph with its abdomen ribbed with the narrowest gauge flat gold tinsel. Sixteen is the most useful size, though sometimes a size 14 is taken readily.

'I have caught literally hundreds of good roach on one or other of these nymph patterns, from many different rivers and lakes, from the Hampshire Avon to the Tweed, from South-country gravel pits to Loch Lomond. By introducing more or less of fine copper wire into the nymph dressing, it can be made to fish at almost any desired depth. The secret of success in using it is to let it sink as far as conditions demand and then to retrieve it slowly and steadily without any jerks, being prepared to strike instantly if the slightest pluck or check is felt.

'I believe that it is advantageous to use a knotless tapered leader, down to 4X or 5X at the point, because roach will often nip at the knots in an ordinary leader.

'I do not suggest for a moment that fly-fishing will ever supersede the normal methods of roach-fishing like trotting, ledgering, laying-on, lift-method and stret-pegging. I do say that the roach fisher who does not possess and has not learned to use a fly rod is handicapped. He will miss many opportunities to catch roach that could have been taken in satisfactory numbers with fly-fishing equipment.

'Using it does not necessarily involve artificial flies. There are times when a small hook, about size 16, tied to the end of a fine leader and baited with a single maggot, will catch roach after roach, often in hot weather and gin-clear water, where the splash of the lightest float tackle or ledger lead would scare the fish.

'I also believe that up to the present we have only touched the fringe of the possibilities that fly-fishing can offer for roach and indeed other coarse fish, and that the angler who experiments will find exploration of these possibilities quite fascinating.'

ROACH IN THE KITCHEN

Roach are just eatable if filleted, dipped in milk, rolled in flour and fried in butter. Serve with slices of lemon.

Unfortunately, few writers give instructions for coping with the tiny, needle-sharp bones with which most coarse species abound. There seems to be no alternative to picking them out one by one, either before the fish is served or between each mouthful! Even Mrs Beeton has ducked this one.

23 . The Rudd

Scardinius erythrophthalmus

The Rudd: a kind of Roach all tinged with gold,
Strong, broad and thick, most lovely to behold.
(ANON.)

Confusion between roach and rudd has for long existed. Even the specific name for the rudd is itself tinged with error, an error perpetuated by so eminent an angler as H. Cholmondeley-Pennell, who, in *The Fisherman's Magazine* (Vol. 1, 1864), wrote of the rudd:

From these peculiarities of colouring it is unnecessary to say that it derives its name. The specific name, *erythrophthalmus* (from the Greek *erythros*, red, and *ophthalmos*, the eye) has also a similar origin.

In Walton's time, the rudd, or 'red-eye' as it was often called, was thought to be a bastard roach – the product of mixing the eggs and milt of two different species: roach and bream. As late as 1833, T. F. Salter, in *The Angler's Guide*, states:

I have no doubt that the fish called a Rudd is a true Roach, but a little altered in shape, by being put into ponds not congenial to their habits and nature.

And even today, the rudd of Ireland are known locally as 'roach'.

For notes on identification of roach and rudd, and roach/rudd hybrids, see p. 167.

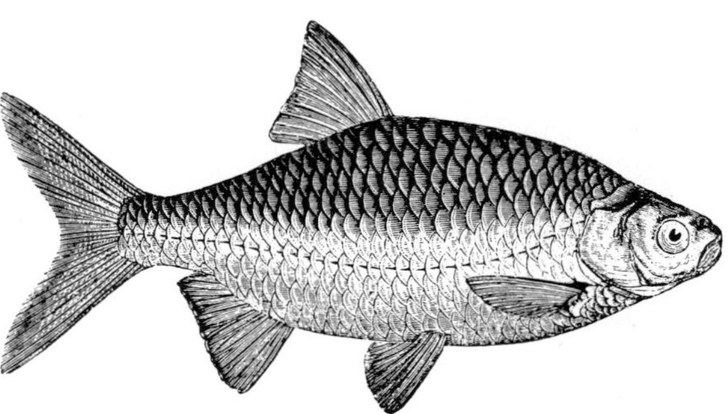

'The Red-eye, or Rudd' from Yarrell's British Fishes *(Vol. I, 1841.)*
Note: *The red-eye is a misnomer. It is the roach that has an iris of deep red, whereas the iris of the rudd is a brassy yellow.*

With the exception of the Iberian peninsula, the rudd is irregularly but extensively distributed through central Europe and through central Asia eastwards to Siberia. It is absent from Scotland but is widely distributed and very abundant in Ireland.

The rudd is a roach-like fish, capable of growing to a weight of over 4 lb. It occurs mostly in ponds, but occasionally in sluggish rivers like the Great Ouse. Noted rudd waters are the Norfolk Broads and Slapton Ley in Devonshire.

Our description of the rudd as 'a roach-like fish', and the poet's description 'The rudd; a kind of roach', have been chosen deliberately for two reasons: first because

The record rod caught rudd of $4\frac{1}{2}$ lb (top left) *and the other rudd of $4\frac{1}{4}$ lb were caught by the Rev. E. C. Alston at Ringmere in the parish of Wretham, near Thetford, Norfolk in June 1933. These fish were survivors of a stock of small rudd he had introduced to Ringmere in 1929 when the lake had re-flooded after being dried up. The rudd, together with some tench, roach and pike had come from nearby Stamford Water – a lake beyond the reach of modern anglers, since it lies in what is now a tank-testing area. Ringmere itself no longer exists: the water table has been lowered through water abstraction.*

Alston well remembers that astonishing day when he caught 30 fish including five rudd of over 4 lb each! A light breeze kept blowing his float back towards him. He had ground-baited with bread and bran, but all the rudd took small redworms suspended two feet below the float which drifted back in four feet of water. When the news broke, anglers came from all parts of Britain to try for the big Ringmere rudd. None was caught, or at least none that weighed more than 3 lb.

they are apposite; secondly because they explain the dilemma that exists in the minds of many anglers – the difficulty of differentiating between the roach and the rudd, and the even greater difficulty of differentiating between the hybrid roach/rudd and its parents.

Although the famous 19th-century icthyologist, Yarrel, dismissed the possibility of *hybrid* fishes, they are now known to be common. Indeed, the current 'authenticated' British Co-Record Rod-Caught Roach, is thought by some authorities to be a roach/rudd hybrid.

The rudd prefers a weedy habitat. Its feeding habits are very similar to those of the roach, but in warm sunny weather it rises even more readily to the fly. Some of the best-ever bags of rudd have been taken by fly-fishermen. John Bickerdyke once caught

29 rudd from Lough Derg; all were taken on the fly, and the bag included specimens weighing up to 3 lb.

Some idea of the opportunities that come the way of the fly-fisherman can be seen from details of a catch made on one day in June 1906, by two anglers, R. L. White and R. C. Hardy Corfe, who between them caught 170 lb of rudd from Ravensthorpe Reservoir in Northamptonshire. Most of the fish were taken on the dry-fly, and the bag included many fish weighing from 2 lb to 2½ lb apiece.

H. T. Sheringham who loved the rudd, wrote of it in his famous book *Coarse Fishing*: 'Were it as common as the chub it would be one of the most popular and sought after fishes, for it bites heartily and fights with power'. Sheringham recommended the following flies. Wet patterns: Alder, Palmer, Coachman (all dressed as for chub fishing – with the small white kid tag). Dry patterns: Wickhams Fancy, Coachman, Black Gnat, Soldier Palmer and Red Tag.

Marshall-Hardy held strong views as to the best times for catching rudd. He believed that rudd were most active when water temperatures were high. Accordingly he preferred to fish in high summer – during early morning and late evening. His favourite time was a still evening after a blazing hot day.

Although most bait-fishing methods used for roach are suitable for rudd, it must be remembered that most good rudd fishing is to be found in inaccessible, weedy, reed or rush-fringed lakes, ponds, broads and meres, where to fish from the bank is extremely difficult. In such waters boat-fishing is the answer. In shallow waters, however, fishing must be carried out at long range since rudd are very wary of an approaching boat. The acceptable fishing range is about 25 yards. An angler should anchor his boat across the wind so as to leave himself a downwind cast into the rudd swim.

Groundbait should consist of *floating* materials like unsqueezed bread-mush and floating crusts to bring rudd to the surface. A small self-cocking float, set about 18 inches above the hook (size 8 or 10), provides the casting weight that carries the bait (floating crust or slow-sinking crumb) up to the reed-beds or rushes, close to which the fish will be feeding.

As a sporting fish the rudd has long been neglected. Recently, however, a few small groups of highly competent anglers have taken a renewed interest in the species. In recent years, Peter Butler has led parties of anglers on very successful rudd-fishing trips to Ireland, and some Lancastrians have had considerable success with rudd in Esthwaite lake in the English Lake District. They have had their best successes when fishing with ledger tackle. They found night fishing more productive than day fishing, and the months of September and October better than the generally accepted 'rudd-biting' months of June, July and August.

Margin-fishing is a comparatively new method of angling for rudd. Richard Walker admits that success with this method came by accident when he caught rudd on tackle designed for carp. The use of suitably scaled-down tackle – 4 lb B.S. line and a size 8 hook – later proved that carp-style margin-fishing was an excellent method for taking rudd.

Another good method, which is also very exciting, is described by Walker in *Still Water Angling* (1953):

Where a boat is available, or the fish can be covered from the bank, a deadly way of fishing is to use a fly-rod with a hook-to-nylon instead of a fly, carrying a bunch of six or eight gentles. Get out as long a line as you can comfortably. It must be well-greased and so should all but the last link of the cast. Strike on seeing the line pulled along the surface. Ground-bait can take the form of crusts of bread anchored to the bottom,[1] or you can throw in loose crusts and follow them down-wind in a boat, keeping as far away as you can cast.

COOKING THE RUDD

Of the few who have tasted rudd fewer still speak kindly of its flavour. The best recipe is that recommended by Anthony Bridges:

Cut the fillets, and after covering them with plenty of eggs and breadcrumbs, fry them over a brisk fire till thoroughly browned. Then pour over them a gravy made thus:

After removing the fillets, lay the bone and trimmings in a stew-pan with two shallots and a small bunch of parsley, stew them for one hour, and strain the liquor, which add to the following sauce. Put 2 oz of butter over the fire; when melted, add the above liquor, and also one tablespoon of flour, one teaspoonful of soy, one dessertspoonful of anchovy, one of Worcestershire sauce, and a little salt.

But watch those bones.

1 Marshall-Hardy's method of anchoring crusts is still a very good one. 'Bread buoys' are made by filling ladies' hair-nets with dry crusts (which act as a float). The buoys are attached to lengths of nylon and anchored close to the reeds or lily pads by means of suitable lead weights.

IDENTIFICATION OF ROACH, RUDD, BREAM, AND THEIR HYBRIDS

Since roach, rudd and bream are all members of the carp family (Cyprinidae), all three species are closely related. The closeness of that relationship is exemplified by their ability to hybridize.

The best known hybrid of the animal world is the mule – offspring of a he-ass and a mare. A mule is incapable of reproducing its kind. Similarly, the hybrids of roach/rudd, roach/bream and rudd/bream cannot breed successfully with their own or any other hybrids. It is for this reason that our waters are not teeming with these 'in-between' fishes; it explains why hybrids never supplant the parent species.

There are, of course, many other hybrids Chub/bleak, dace/bleak, dace/rudd, roach bleak, roach/bream, roach/silver bream, rudd silver bream, rudd/bleak, bream/silver bream, carp/crucian carp, have all been recorded.

Hybrids are not given scientific names, but first generation hybrids like those listed above are known as F_1 hybrids of two named parent species.

Although little research other than routine taxonomic work has been done on fish

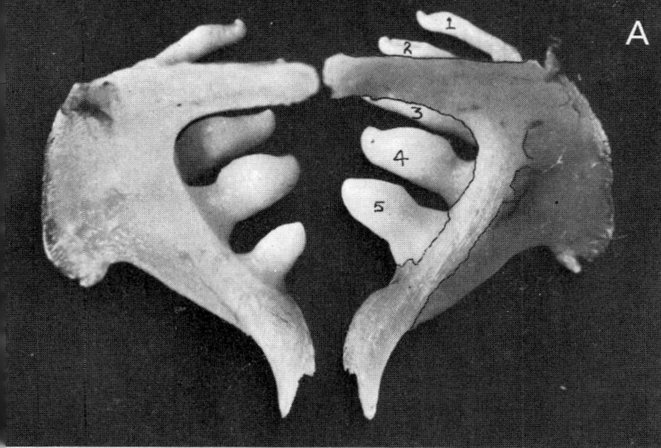

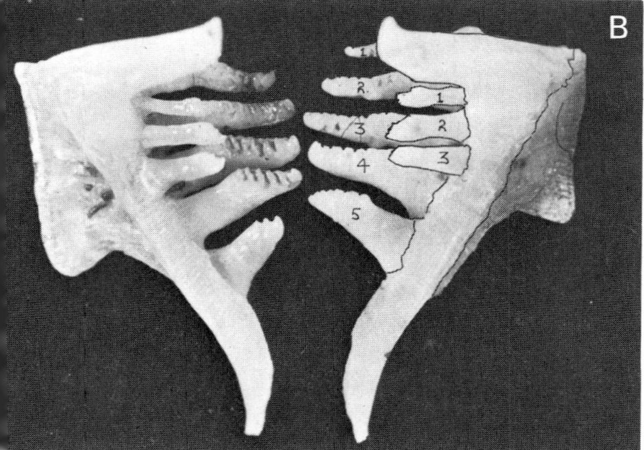

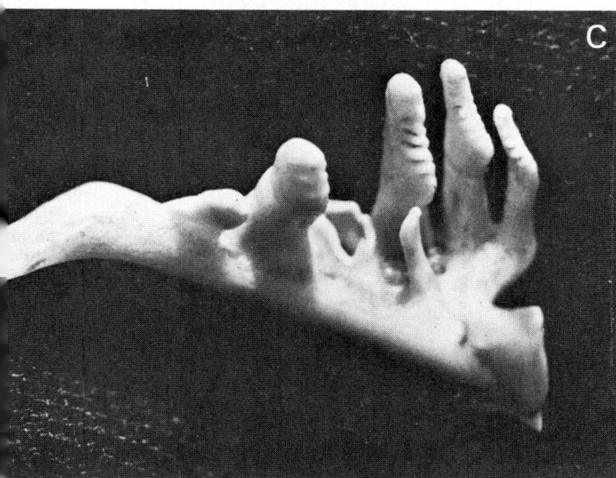

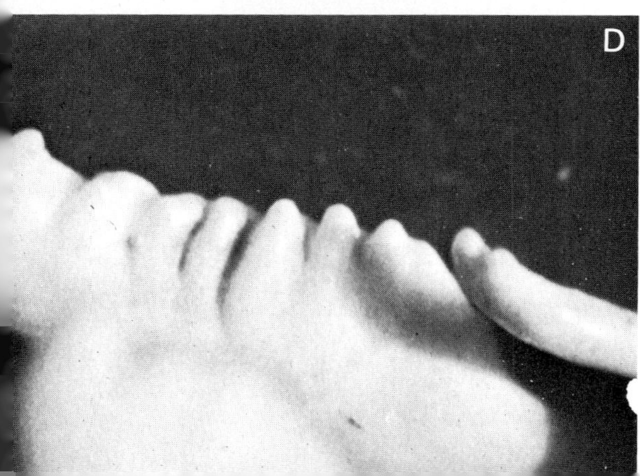

Pharyngeal teeth ('fingerprints' of identity). A. Roach: 1 row; 5 or 6 teeth each side; smooth edges.
B. Rudd: 2 rows. Back row, 5 teeth each side, serrated edges; *Front row, 3 smaller teeth each side,* serrated edges.
C. Roach/Rudd hybrid: 2 rows; back row, 5 slightly serrated teeth each side; front row, 3 smaller serrated teeth each side (Note the broken main row tooth. Broken pharyngeal teeth regenerate). D. Close-up of the serrations of the roach/rudd hybrid. These are absent in the true roach but present in the true rudd.

hybridism in Britain, American and Canadian scientists have shown that although the hybrids of species belonging to the family Esocidae (the pikes) cannot reproduce their own kind, they can in certain instances become successful parents when back-crossed with one or other of the original parent species. But if wild second generation F_2 cyprinid hybrids exist in Britain, they are as yet unrecorded. For anglers, the problem so far as roach, rudd and bream are concerned is the identification of these species and the hybrids that can result.

To reduce the chance of further controversies of this nature we suggest that all 'record' fish should be identified by the supreme authority – The British Museum (Natural History). Only there do we find full facilities for the work of fish identification: trained staff, and a unique collection of specimens including hybrids.

One of the invariable questions asked when a record claim is made on behalf of a roach, or a crucian carp, is whether the roach is a true roach or a hybrid between a roach and a bream, or whether the crucian carp is a true crucian or a hybrid between a crucian carp and common carp. (There are, of course, many other Cyprinid hybrids, but these are either less common or do not become the subject of a record claim).

The authority on hybridization among British fishes is Alwyne Wheeler, fish taxonomist to The British Museum (Natural History). Wheeler has made an extensive study of his subject and the facilities of his department are available to anglers for a more positive identification of doubtful fish. It must be remembered, however, that 100% accuracy is impossible.

(It has always been supposed that hybrids occur when spawn *accidentally* mixes on the spawning grounds. In North America, however, it has been demonstrated that natural hybrids have resulted from the deliberate mating of the male of one species with the female of another. So far as the U.K. is concerned, it is known that the male rudd mixes with apparent deliberation with spawning fish of another species.)

Roach, Rudd and Roach/Rudd Hybrids

Hitherto, identification of the roach/rudd hybrid has defeated all but the most experienced and practised observers. Richard Walker, who has done a great deal of work in this field, has used pharyngeal (throat) teeth to establish positive identification. He states – and Alwyne Wheeler agrees – that it is not possible to distinguish between roach, rudd or roach/rudd hybrids by means of scale counts or fin ray counts alone, on account of the overlap in numbers. For example: Tate Regan gives the count of branched rays in the anal fin as follows:

Roach: 9–12.
Rudd: 10–13.
Hybrid: 11.

Pharyngeal teeth are the 'fingerprints' of identity to the taxonomic detective. If pharyngeals are not available (e.g. when fish are returned alive to the water) it is not possible to identify a true roach, or a true rudd, or a hybrid roach/rudd by reference to any *single* distinguishing characteristic. *True identity can be decided only by an accumulation of evidence.* The characteristic differences are summarized as follows:

1. *Position of the dorsal fin.*

Roach. The dorsal fin originates *slightly behind* a line raised from the frontal end of the base of the pelvic fins at right angles to a line drawn from the centre of the fish's eye to the fork of its tail.

Rudd. The dorsal fin originates *well behind* a line raised from the frontal end of the base of the pelvic fins.

Hybrid. The dorsal fin originates midway between the points of origin specified for the roach and the rudd.

2. *The juxtaposition of the lips.*

Roach. Upper lip protrudes slightly beyond lower lip (semi-ventral mouth).

Rudd. Lower lip protrudes beyond upper lip (dorsal mouth).

Hybrid. Lips are level (terminal mouth).

3. *Abdominal keel.*

Roach. Keel non-existent. A section

Photograph of the rudd, the roach and the roach/rudd F_1 hybrid showing how the position of the dorsal fin-relative to the root of the pelvic fin – varies in the three fishes. The close up views of the head give the juxtaposition of the lips.

through the body immediately in front of the frontal ray of the anal fin is oval.

Rudd. The section through the body is pointed.

Hybrid. The section through the body is pointed.

Note: This keel is very clear to an experienced observer.

4. *Colour.*

Roach. A young fish has an overall silvery tinge in its scales. An older fish is shot with coppery reflections when turned in the light. The fins are crimson.
The iris of the eye is red.

Rudd. The scales have a polished brassy or bronze tinge about them.
The fins are tinted yellow.
The iris of the eye is yellow.

Hybrid. The scales have a brassy tinge reminiscent of the true rudd.
The fins are tinted orange.
The iris of the eye is orange.

Rudd were first differentiated from roach in 1600. In his book *Certaine experiments concerning fish and fruite; practised by John Taverner, gentleman, and by him published for the benefit of others,* Taverner differentiated between 'The shallow or pond Roch with red fins' and 'the river Roch' by the latter fish's inability to spawn in ponds. At least this is how Turrell in *Ancient Angling Authors* interprets Taverner's comments.

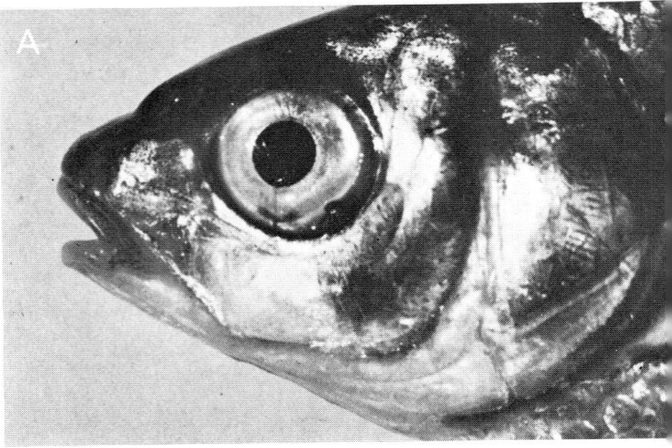

Roach/Common Bream Hybrid

This hybrid, often called the Pomeranian bream, is found in practically all waters containing the parent species, and in some locations is frequently caught. F. B. has taken many from the canal at Slough and the river Cam above Cambridge. Provided no rudd are present to complicate matters, a ray count of the anal fin will identify this hybrid which has the appearance of a rather deep roach.

Number of rays in anal fin
Roach: 9–12.
Bream: 23–29.
Hybrid: 15–19.

In addition, the abdominal keel of the hybrid is not very pronounced. The upper lip protrudes slightly beyond lower lip.

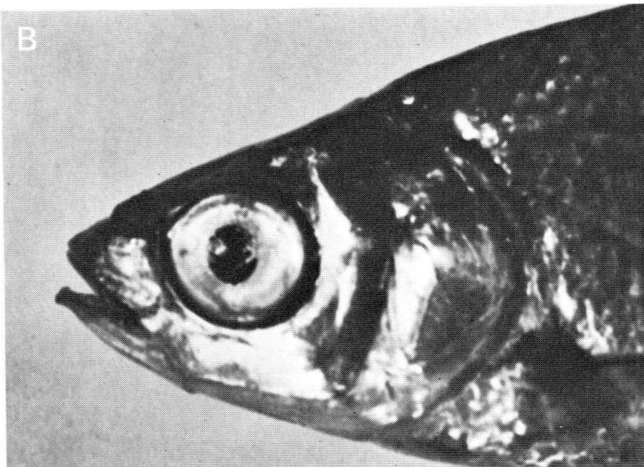

Rudd/Common Bream Hybrid

This hybrid differs from the roach/common bream hybrid in the same way that the rudd does from the roach: the body is deeper. The lower lip projects slightly. The abdominal keel is well defined – as one might expect when both parents are well keeled.

Number of rays in anal fin
Rudd: 10–13.
Bream: 23–29.
Hybrid: 15–18.

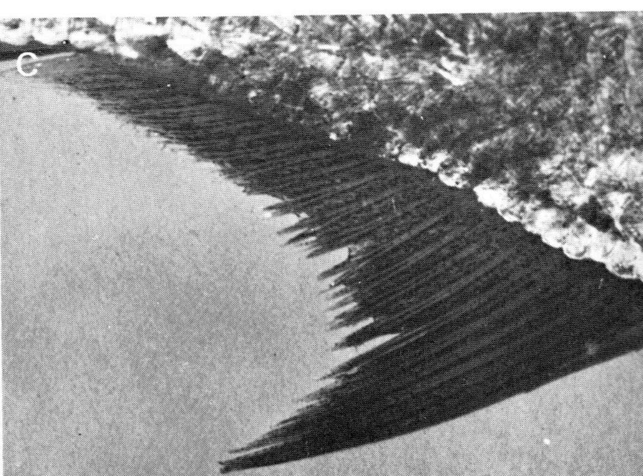

A. Head of common bream.

B. Head of rudd/common bream hybrid. Note projecting lower lip.

C. Anal fin of common bream.

D. Anal fin of rudd/common bream hybrid.

Pharyngeal teeth of other common cyprinids

A. Common bream. Single row long curling teeth.

B. Roach/bream. Mild serrations compared with bream.

C. Barbel. Characteristic triple row of teeth.

D. Chub. 2 rows.

E. Tench. 1 row.

F. Carp. Showing characteristic coral-like grinding surfaces.

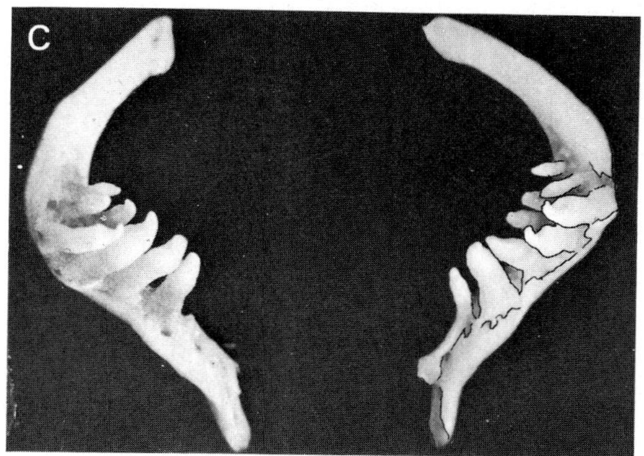

C

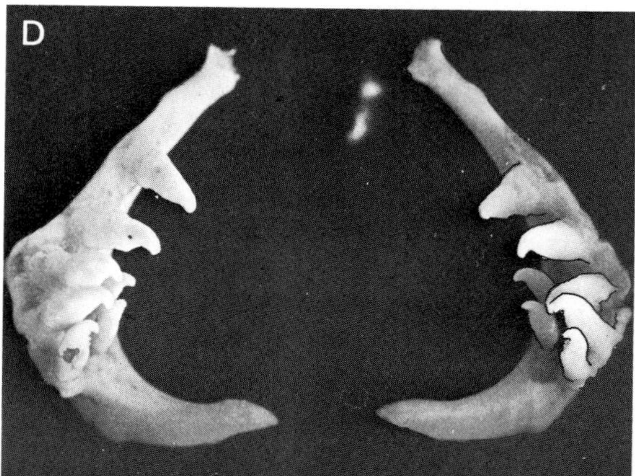

D

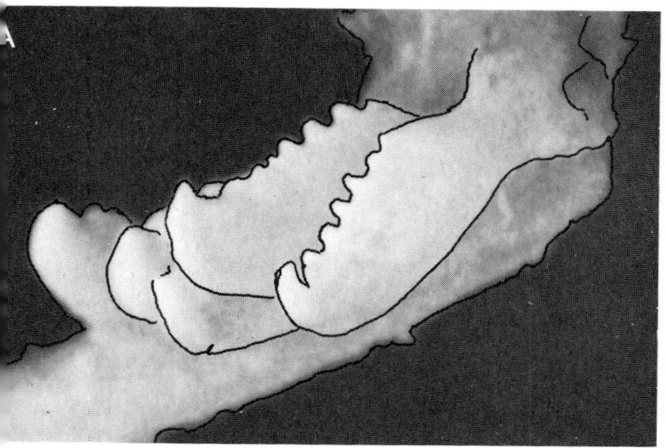

A

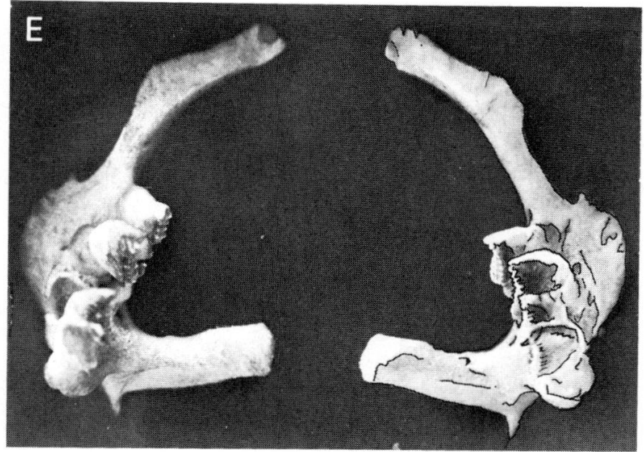

E

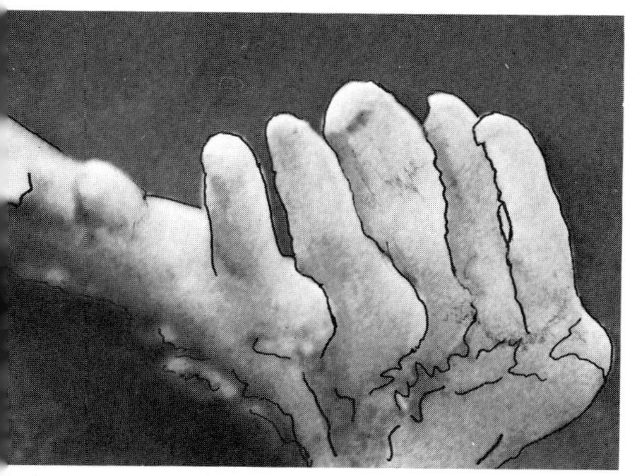

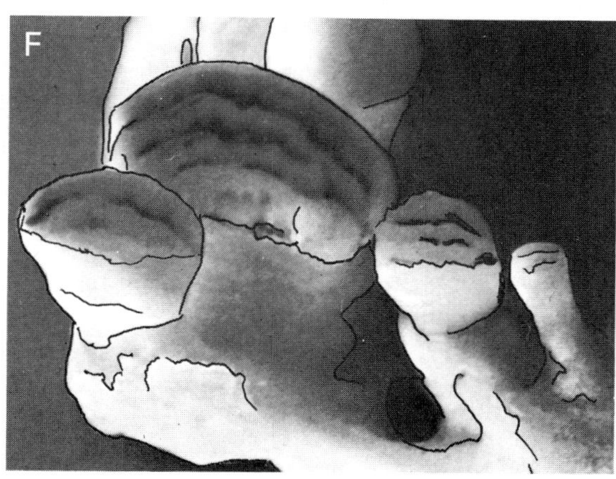

F

It has been noticed that shoaling cyprinids such as roach, dace, bream and rudd frequently hybridize when there is a shortage of suitable weed. In the absence of an abundant weed growth there is competition for spawning sites, so that spawning shoals of different species get mixed up on the available sites. As a result, sperm from one species may accidentally fertilize the ova from another.

The fact that hybrids are rare or non-existent in some waters, even where many cyprinid species share the habitat, may be due to ample spawning accommodation; or it may be due to the various species attaining ripeness at different times.

That different species of fish become active spawners at different temperatures is another factor favouring the production of pure-bred fishes. According to Wheeler, in *The Fishes of the British Isles and North West Europe*, common bream favour a temperature of 59°F (15°C) whereas roach and rudd prefer a temperature of 64°F (18°C).

Note. It should be remembered that the foregoing notes represent only a very brief study of hybridization. We hope, however, that they will stimulate the coarse angler to take an interest in the results of future scientific research into this extremely complex subject.

24 · The Ruffe or Pope

Gymnocephalus cernus

The ruffe is the grossest at his bite of any fish that biteth, and is taken with the red worm on the ground, and where he lieth, there is he commonly alone . . . But surely an wholesome fish! . . . There cannot be a better, and chiefly for a sick body. I count him better than either gudgeon or perch, for he eateth faster and pleasanter . . . I have been well content to deal with them, for this property they have, as is seen among the wicked: that though they see their fellows perish never so fast, yet will they not be warned, so that you shall have them as long as one is left, especially a little before a rain or in the bite time. And if you close some small worms in a ball of old black dung or earth, and cast it in where you angle for them, you shall have the better sport, for at that will they lie like little hogs.

A modernized excerpt from the second book on angling published in English: *The Arte of Angling* (1577). Author unknown.

The name 'Ruffe' or 'Ruff', a variant of 'rough', alludes to this little fish's prickly scales. 'Pope' is of unknown origin, although according to one authority the barbarous practice of pressing a ruffe's spiky dorsal fin into a piece of cork before putting the fish back into the water (so that it would die a lingering death) was once connected with the anti-papists of Tudor Britain who, wishing to find a means of expressing their hatred of the Pope, sent little substitute 'Popes' sailing to their deaths from starvation.

The ruffe rarely grows to a length of more than seven inches. It is closely related to the perch, proof of which exists in the form of perch/ruffe hybrids. These hybrids (F_1), like the hybrids between two different pike species cannot breed *inter se*, but are fertile when back-crossed with either parent species to produce F_2 hybrids.

The ruffe is at home in still waters or slow-flowing rivers, and like the perch shoals readily. Again, like the perch it is a bold biter – an unpopular habit, since it invariably pouches the angler's bait, making it difficult to unhook.

Many anglers believe that if a swim produces ruffe it is unlikely to produce anything else, and try to avoid this little fish. But were fashions to change, anglers might think differently since the ruffe has a high culinary reputation; its flesh is white, succulent and easily digested.

During the late 1960s, when the perch in the Metropolitan Barn Elms Reservoir died from an epidemic of perch-ulcer, ruffe also died in their thousands. Due to this disease, the ruffe has almost disappeared from many southern waters.

The pope annoys the perch-fisher more than the bleak annoys the roach-fisher. Pope are chiefly remarkable for an appetite which cannot be appeased and for never growing any bigger. They could not be any smaller.

H. T. SHERINGHAM, *Fishing: Its Cause, Treatment and Cure* (1925).

25 · The Atlantic Salmon

Salmo salar

For Salmon being Fish of Prey, and great Feeders, Nature directs them to the salt Waters, as Physick to purge and cleanse them, not only from their Impurities after Spawning, but from all their muddy terrene Particles and gross Humours, acquired by their extraordinary, excessive Feeding all the Summer in fresh Rivers. . . . And when they are fatted and glutted with their long, excessive Feeding in fresh Rivers, and have spawn'd in the latter end of the Year, repair to the Sea for Warmness, and to be purged from the gross Humours by the Calidity of the Saline Water; and when Winter is over, return to their Summer Habitations.
ROBERT HOWLETT, *The Angler's Sure Guide* (1706).

It is difficult to understand how such nonsense ever comes to be written. Howlett's salmon feeding-habits in fresh water cannot have been based on observation, yet they are stated as fact! But, needless to say, Howlett was by no means the only angler to prove himself a poor naturalist. (See the story of the eel, pp. 66*ff*.)

There is no mention of a salmon by the early Greeks, but the invading Romans knew him well enough. He was leaping in the Thames when Agricola marched north. From the banks of so many rivers they glimpsed his flashing beauty, and they named him *Salmo* – which means 'The Leaper'.

His origin is shrouded in mystery. But it is generally agreed that the several species of salmon, both the Pacific species and the Atlantic salmon, came from a common ancestor about 500,000 years ago. Whether this ancestor originated in fresh or salt water is uncertain. Biological evidence favours fresh, since most members of the Salmonidae are unable to breed in salt water. Newly-hatched salmon cannot tolerate salinity.

The Atlantic salmon's life cycle starts in fresh water when the eggs are laid during November and December in the gravel bed of some well oxygenated and fairly fast-flowing stream. An egg takes between three and four months to hatch, and the product – known as an alevin – is a tiny translucent creature with an umbilical sac hanging below its throat.

During the alevin stage the little salmon lives on the contents of its yolk sac – which contains upwards of a month's rations. And when the yolk sac has been absorbed the alevin becomes a fry.

Now, forced to fend for itself, it hunts

actively for food, gradually acquiring a form of camouflage in the shape of dark 'finger' marks along its sides. At this stage of its development it is known as a parr, and in looks is very similar to a small brown trout.

Parr feed on insects, nymphs, fly larvae, tiny crustacea and other forms of life, depending on the food supply available. In turn they are preyed on by a host of enemies. In quiet backwaters the watchful heron lurks like a sentinel at the water's edge – rising at the first hint of danger with its harsh cry of alarm. On many British rivers nowadays, feral mink hunt like small fierce otters; cormorants, mergansers and goosanders dive in the pools, while in the shallower stretches even the beautiful little kingfisher takes its toll of tiny fish. Pike, perch, chub, eels and other coarse fish, together with brown trout, have all been known to take their share of immature salmon. On one occasion 134 tags – originally attached to salmon parr by freshwater research biologists – were taken from the stomachs of 20 brown trout which ranged in size from nine to thirteen inches long. So that the salmon's cousin, the brown trout, is undoubtedly one of its worst enemies.

When the parr is anything between one and four or five years old – usually two – certain physiological changes take place to fit it for a new environment. And during May or June, as a slender, fork-tailed, silvery little fish of about six inches in length, now known as a smolt, it migrates to salt water.

In the estuary the young salmon meet further enemies: herring-gulls, pollack, coalfish, congers and many more. But they hurry on towards the rich feeding grounds of the sea. And they go there in order to grow.

In the Gorge d'Enfer, at Les Eyzies, is a little shelter : Abri de Poisson, so named because it contains this relief carving of a salmon – one of the earliest records of pre-historic association between salmon and man. It was probably the invention of the flint-tipped spear, the bow and arrow and the bone harpoon (see p. 364), that enabled early man to get on terms with the migrating salmon.

They grow very quickly. By the end of their first year at sea they will be 20 to 30 times their original weight, although after this the growth rate lessens. Some salmon return to fresh water as grilse – fish of 3 to 10 lb that have stayed little over a year at sea. Some return as maiden salmon after a sea life of two or more years. Some may even return, after an absence of four years, as 30 or 40 pounders; indeed several years may separate the homecoming of fish which left the river together. But at whatever age they return – whether as grilse after one year at sea, or as maiden salmon of two sea years or longer – return they must, since they cannot spawn in salt water.

The recapture of tagged fish indicates that salmon returning to Britain move in from the Atlantic at many points, and on arrival in coastal waters swim close inshore up or down the coast until they reach their destined rivers. Although a small percentage find their way into strange rivers, the majority return to spawn in the rivers of their birth. It is not known how a salmon navigates from the distant ocean to the coast, but experiments have established that it selects its destined river by the particular *odour* of that river.

Salmon have a very acute sense of smell and are able to recognise certain predators by scent. For instance, fish running up a Canadian river have been seen to scatter rapidly when a bear put its paw into the water upstream of them. Anglers may be interested to know that the odour of human skin certainly affects salmon. Even when extremely dilute it has caused fish to show distinct alarm reactions lasting for several minutes.

The returning salmon bring their rations with them; they enter a river with a sufficient food reserve in their tissues to sustain them for upwards of twelve months, in addition to supplying the food necessary for their developing milt and ova. Of course, not all salmon endure so long a period of waiting. They don't enter their various rivers all at the same time. There is no month of the year during which, in one river or another, fresh salmon are not running. And while those that arrive in late winter and early spring will wait for many months before spawning, others spawn only a short time after their summer or autumn arrival.

During their long migration up river towards the spawning redds, driven by a ripening sexual urge, salmon force their way past the most formidable obstacles. And what they cannot swim over they try to jump. As an early writer noted:

> In spawning time, when they repair from the sea up the river, scarce anything can stop their progress. They have been seen to leap up cataracts or precipices many yards high.

Not without good reason the Romans dubbed them 'The Leapers', but even up to less than a couple of hundred years ago the question of *how Salmo* managed to perform its leap was a matter of some controversy. According to one school of thought:

> The salmon will throw herself over cataracts or waterfalls by taking her tail in her mouth and bending her backbone downwards, till the letting it go all at once gives her strength enough to throw herself over the cataract at a leap.

But a more astute observer wrote:

> I very much question the truth of this fact, as to the *manner* – namely, the taking hold of her tail, for neither does the salmon's mouth, which is small and weak, nor the tail, which is large and slippery, allow the thing in itself. But that they *will* leap, or throw themselves out of the water perpendicularly is certain, and I affirm that I have seen a very large salmon leap as near as I could judge five or six feet high – and some say they leap much higher. But so high as mentioned I can assert from my own knowledge.

He was right. The leaping of salmon at waterfalls has often been exaggerated, but the truth is sufficiently dramatic. A leap of 11 feet has been measured over a perpendicular waterfall.

By late October many of the salmon have arrived in or close to those parts of the river, or feeder streams, where they are going to spawn. And from then until the end of December most of the spawning takes place.

Now, with the late autumn leaves drifting overhead, the salmon's silver streamlined beauty has quite vanished. The once sleek females are dark, almost black, with bulging bellies; the males rust-red, their heads ugly and misshapen, with huge pointed knobs or 'kypes', curving upwards from their lower jaws.

After a period of exploratory wandering in a stretch of clean, shallow, streamy water with a bottom of gravel and small stones, the female prepares the spawning bed by movements of her tail. Meanwhile the male fish waits in close attendance, ready to drive off any intruders.

Eventually, perhaps after days of preparation, the male joins the female on the bed, and while he quivers violently the eggs and milt are extruded almost simultaneously. Immediately afterwards, the male swims away some little distance downstream; while the female, by going a foot or two above the bed, covers the eggs with gravel by vigorous movements of her tail.

Several more similar sequences may be carried out before the female has deposited all her eggs. Nature prepares for huge losses. A hen fish carries an average of 700 eggs per pound of her body weight.

By the time spawning is finished the fish are emaciated and very weak. These spent fish, or 'kelts' as they are called, are little more than two thirds of their original weight. The once juicy pink flesh is pale and flaccid: and often enough their hollow-flanked and ragged-finned bodies are smothered in fungus.

Only a few survive. Once their all-important task is done most salmon die of exhaustion and disease. For reasons which are unknown the surviving females greatly outnumber the males. Those fish that regain the rich feeding pastures of the sea recover their condition surprisingly quickly, and it is strange that on their subsequent return to the river for a second spawning, the fat content is as high as – or in some cases even higher than – that of virgin fish.

The proportion of fish that survive for a third spawning is very small indeed. Only an exceptional fish returns to spawn for a fourth time.

It is interesting that surviving kelts do not all leave the river together – even when seemingly able to do so – but over a period which may extend into several months. Again, as with the incoming fish, nature seems to insure against total disaster. Were all fresh fish to enter a river during the same week or month, some catastrophe such as river blockage, drought or disease, might wipe out a complete annual run. As it is, those fish still at sea, destined to make their homecoming during a later month, or even another year, form an insurance against total loss. And so, even, with the returning kelts: should some meet with disaster – perhaps seals or porpoises waiting at the river mouth – there are others to follow, and there are those that have already gone ahead.

But gone where? What is the salmon's destination? Where do the young smolts go, to put on weight so rapidly, when they hurry seawards?

Until the late 1950s the story of the Atlantic Salmon's pelagic wandering was a mystery. Although it was known that once salmon reached the sea they grew very quickly, nobody knew what they fed on or where they went. But eventually, alas, two of their main feeding grounds were located: one in the Baltic, and the other, a much larger area, off the west coast of Greenland. And to date, the result of this discovery has (for the salmon) been most unfortunate.

Commercial salmon fishing started on the Greenland coast in 1957, and the tremendous catches made during recent years have caused considerable alarm. Since there are no rivers in West Greenland capable of maintaining such numbers of salmon, it is clear that most of these fish are being provided by other countries. Supporting evidence of this is the number of fish caught off Greenland which were originally tagged as smolts by fishery research stations in Great Britain, Sweden, Canada and the U.S.A.

But the wave of indignation that has followed the ruthless exploitation of the sea-feeding salmon should not be allowed to obscure the danger which lurks in our own rivers. Certainly, if *Salmo salar* is to survive as a species, catches at sea *must* be regulated by international agreement, otherwise its decline is inevitable; at the same time, however, Britain should redouble her efforts to put her own house in order.

Since the 18th century the threat to salmon stocks has been threefold: river obstruction by weirs, locks or dams; water abstraction, and pollution. Salmon can tolerate scarcely any pollution at all.

The pollution that has turned clear waterways into the open sewers which so many of our rivers are today is of two kinds, equally disastrous: pollution by directly toxic substances, and pollution by substances which, although not inherently poisonous, suffocate a river by depriving it of dissolved oxygen.

All the main British rivers once held huge runs of salmon. Salmon figured largely in commissariats for military campaigns – Edward II, during his war with Bruce, ordered thousands of dried salmon to feed his army; farmers fed salmon fry to their swine; even as late as the Reformation, salmon was only half the price of pike. They were still great salmon rivers less than 200 years ago, when special teams of horses transported fish from northern counties to the London markets; but few of them hold big runs of salmon today. The industrial revolution destroyed their beauty, and now the pollution of waste matter pours from towns and factories along their banks. Their lower reaches are open drains and the effluent vomits from estuary mouths to stain the tide.

Three hundred years ago, Walton wrote:

There is no better salmon than in England; and that although some of our northern rivers have salmon as fat and as large as the River Thames, yet none are of so excellent a taste.

A century later, the Thames is quoted as being:

The greatest and chiefest of all the rivers of Britain – for the prodigious quantity of its fish, the variety of their sorts and the goodness of their kind, preferable to all the other rivers in Europe; and the prime of the English salmon is found in the Thames.

Later, a member of London City Corporation, a Mr Binnell, said:

The Thames abounds with salmon, flounders, plaice, mullet, whiting, smelts, eels, perch, trout, carp, tench, bream, chub, roach, dace and gudgeons, beside *oysters* – the finest in the world.

Look at the Thames today!

In 1816 the Thames had an exceptional run of salmon, so many being caught that they fetched only threepence a pound in Billingsgate market. Twenty years later, the Thames salmon had almost vanished. The locks and weirs that made the river navigable blocked the passage of salmon to their spawning redds – and pollution finished the job. Today, the London river, like so many of our rivers, is a national disgrace.

The essential river requirements of salmon are: water containing sufficient oxygen, and ready access to the spawning redds. The provision of fish ladders beside lock or weir, and cessation from using the river as a common drain, would bring back a run of fish even to the Thames.

Most salmon return from the sea to spawn in the rivers of their birth. But not all. Each year, a small but vital number find their way to the redds of strange rivers. Quite apart from fresh stocks introduced by man, these wanderers would explore and eventually re-stock the Thames, as they would our other barren rivers, if not repelled by the present outflow of filth.

Is there no place today for *Salmo* – the Leaper, creature of beauty and fascination? It seems a pity to ignore the beauty at our feet; to be so poor in spirit that we deny him even the encouragement of clean water.[1]

. . . however delightful Angling may be, it ceases to be innocent when used otherwise than as a mere recreation.
RICHARD BROOKES, *The Art of Angling* (1766).

Sir Joseph Bankes it has been said, attempted to produce lobsters from fleas, but failed; and, in a rage, exclaimed – 'Fleas are not lobsters, damn their souls!' I hope the Scotch breeders will fare better, and not have to exclaim – 'Par are not salmon, damn their souls!'
O'GORMAN, *The Practice of Angling* (Vol. 2, 1845).

1 The Port of London Authority (April 1973) states that as a result of the recent drive against pollution the water of the Thames is now clean enough to permit a run of salmon. Already, it seems, sea-trout have been recorded at Teddington. Soon, perhaps, sooner than we dared to hope, an observer on the Embankment may witness the near miracle of *Salmo salar* leaping once again in Chelsea Reach.

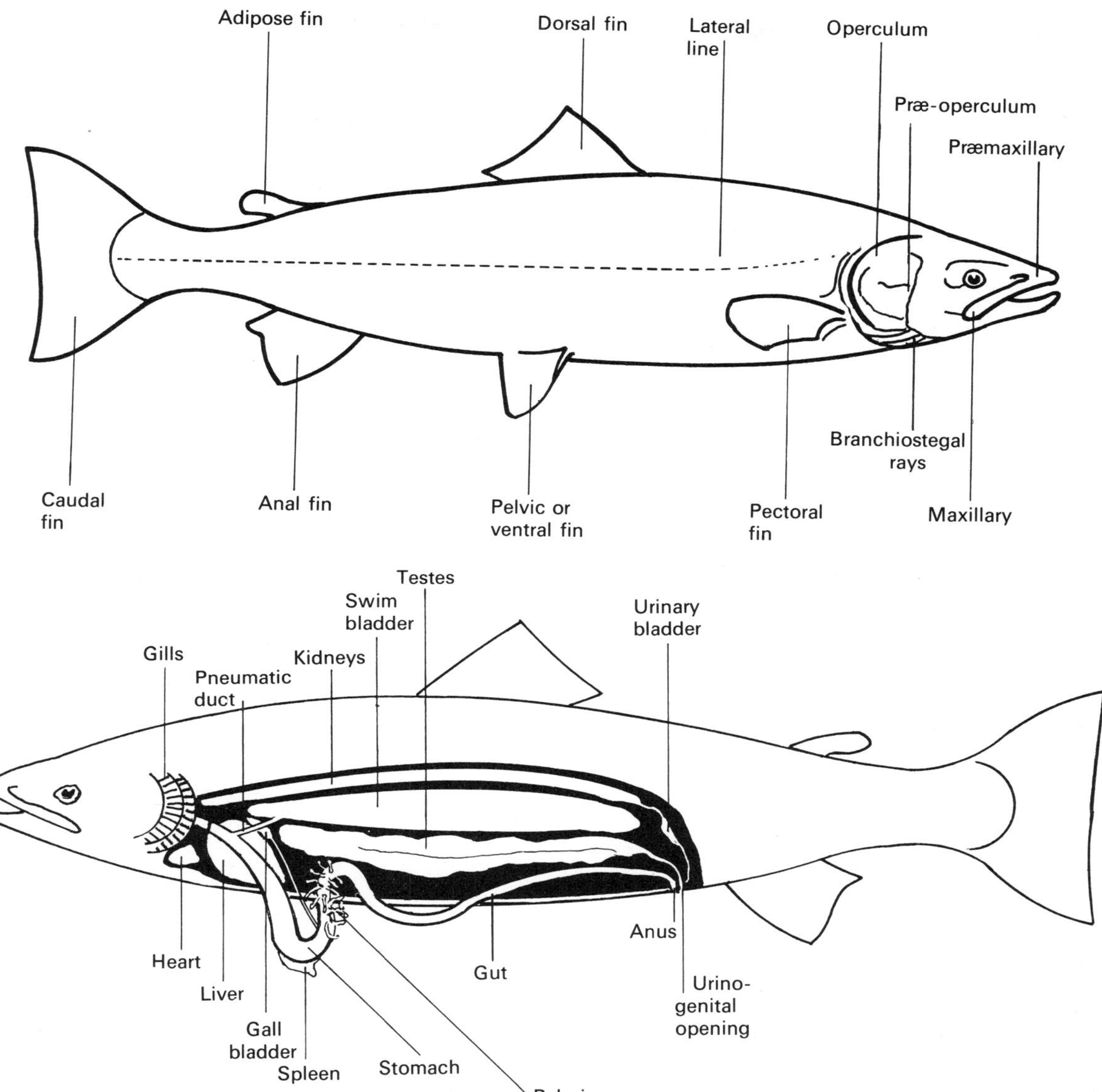

Fig. 25.1. Top: *Diagram of a salmon showing the various fins, lateral line, operculum and prae-operculum, maxillary and prae-maxillary, and branchiostegal rays.*

Bottom: *Anatomy of a salmonid (diagrammatic).*

So much has been said of the breeding of fish, particularly of salmon, that I did not think any occasion could occur to call forth any observations of mine: but I have, within a short time, seen extracts from a treatise, by a Scotchman, on this subject, and in this treatise it is gravely asserted, first – that salmon breed with a fish called par – next, that salmon do not become what we call fry, the first season they are produced, but rather have a kind of tadpole existence the first spring, and, in fact do not attain the shape of fry till the second spring.

Now, to my mind, these are monstrous doctrines and, I think, incapable of being proved. . . . As to what par may be, I know not – it is possible that fish of different kinds, when closely confined, may produce an odd breed of some kind; but it must be somewhat like the breeding of cats and badgers in the Caves of Blarney:

And there are caves where no daylight enters,
But cats and badgers do for ever breed.

Since writing the above, I have discovered what is meant by par; they are what we call gravelin, and we suppose them to be produced from some part of the pea of the salmon which had been imperfect, or been carried away without due impregnation. . . .

I regret to find that some of my most particular friends are imbued with what I call – 'the tadpole heresy'. For my part, nothing but the evidence of my senses will persuade me.

O'GORMAN, *The Practice of Angling* (Vol. 2, 1845).

Make not a daily practice (which is nothing else but a profession) of any recreation, lest your immoderate love and delight therein, bring a cross with it, and blast all your content and pleasure in the same.

COLONEL ROBERT VENABLES, *The Experienc'd Angler* (1662).

SALMON FISHING

A hundred years ago, Alexander Kelso, a perplexed though very experienced salmon angler wrote:

There is no accounting for the humour of a salmon. You do not know when he will take it into his head to rise. The angler must make up his mind to have many blank days. He must never tire of throwing his fly, and never be put out by failure. It is impossible to lay down any hard and fast rule for selecting a fly. The art of doing so is only acquired by long experience, and the best of us are often at our wits' end to know what fly to select.

Well – despite all that has been written since, and despite all the fine theories, no one is really very much further forward today. Admittedly modern 'greased-line' tactics have made late spring and summer fishing much more refined and enjoyable – and indeed more successful, certainly in conditions of low water. And the same can be said for modern spinning techniques. But the modern angler still doesn't know *why a salmon takes a lure*.

By 'lure' we mean any of the various spinners and baits a salmon is offered – including the so-called 'fly'. 'So-called' because nobody knows exactly what this thing called a salmon 'fly' is supposed to represent.

When the matter is given thought, the catching of a salmon on rod and line – whether with fly or anything else – seems highly improbable. After all, why on earth should anyone expect to hook a fish that eats nothing or almost nothing, and has no appetite? But that in effect is the problem confronting every salmon angler; for what he is trying to do is to catch a fish that is not hungry; that while lying in the river waiting to spawn lives on the supply of nourishment stored in its tissues, and has no need for food.

When a salmon enters a river it contains sufficient nourishment to sustain it for over twelve months, in addition to providing for the developing spawn. It makes no effort to search for food, and because of this it is a difficult fish to catch on rod and line. Indeed what seems remarkable is that any are caught at all.

Nevertheless, salmon *are* caught on rod and line because, surprisingly, there are times when they will react to and take various baits or lures. Nobody knows why they behave in this unexpected manner, although a number of theories have been propounded. The most attractive and plausible theory is that the salmon takes from *habit* – the feeding habit formed during its life at sea; and, perhaps, during its earlier river life as a parr; a habit triggered-off by the sight of something which is, or seems to be, alive. It is also possible that anger, curiosity or irritation plays a part.

The experienced angler has learned that a salmon's reactions to any sort of lure depend largely on the prevailing conditions of weather and water, and that he must vary his lure and method of fishing accordingly. Salmon fishing is largely a matter of luck; but the skilful fisherman will, in the long run, catch more fish than the novice simply because in addition to his ration of luck, he has the knowledge born of experience.

He knows that in early spring fishing he may fail to catch fish because his lure is too small, and in summer he may fail because his lure is too big. When the water temperature is low – as it is in early spring or late autumn – he will fish with a sunk line and a large sunk lure, perhaps 3 or 4 inches long. And when the water temperature rises above 48°–50°F, he changes to a greased (or floating) line and a very small lure, perhaps three-quarters of an inch long or even smaller, fished close to the surface. Indeed, if the air temperature is higher than the water temperature, he may do so in conditions of 45°–48°F. He has learned all this from experience. He doesn't know the reasons for it. And at best, it is only a rough guide.

There are no certainties in salmon fishing. Every salmon lie in every pool in every river is a separate study in itself. Each lie presents problems to be solved afresh each time the fisherman visits the river and tries in the face of varying conditions to forecast how on that occasion the salmon are going to behave.

He may note the wind speed and direction, take a look at the sky and the thermometer and the barometer and the light and the height and colour of the water, and say: 'To-day seems a good day. If I put on such and such a lure and fish down this pool I will catch a salmon.' And sometimes he will. And very often he won't.

During the summer there is a better chance of catching a salmon on the greased line if the air temperature is higher than the water temperature; when the air is cold the fish usually tend to stay down. But sometimes they will show a determined reluctance to rise to a fly even on what seems to be the perfect day. And what salmon fisherman hasn't been surprised to hook a fish on some seemingly hopeless day when he was only casting for the fun of it?

And surely it is this very uncertainty that lends the sport of salmon fishing such tremendous fascination and charm. It provides a limitless field of speculation and conjecture, and the novice can always feel that he is in with a chance.

If there is anyone alive who can unfailingly predict when and why salmon will or will not take, we can only say that we have never met him.

On a certain stretch of fishing there is a pool which at one time attracted the attention of a cormorant. The salmon in this pool seemed exceptionally dour, and everyone agreed that these fish wouldn't take because the cormorant disturbed them. One afternoon the fishery owner went down to the pool with his gun, and waited for the cormorant. When it turned up he shot it, and tossed the empty cartridge case into the pool. As the spent case slowly sank, a salmon rose and took it.

This episode is similar in essence to the story of the child (later an admiral) who caught a 40 lb pike on the head of a croquet mallet. He was playing boats with it on the edge of a lake in Warwickshire, throwing it out a yard or two and pulling it in on a string. The pike seized the mallet head, got its teeth embedded in the wood and was pulled ashore by the child's father: Colonel R. Purefoy Fitzgerald.

Salmon. A woodcarving on display at the Nith Hotel, Dumfriesshire.

Now, we do not for one moment suggest that anyone should bait with broken croquet mallets or empty cartridge cases, but there is a moral to be drawn. Such incidents emphasize that in fishing almost nothing is impossible. If the fisherman persists, there is always a chance of catching a fish – however hopeless the conditions; however bizarre his tackle or technique.

'Never be put out by failure.' They are wise words. But it is not easy for the salmon fisherman to be philosophical after a blank day which, with one thing and another, may have set him back ten or fifteen pounds; a

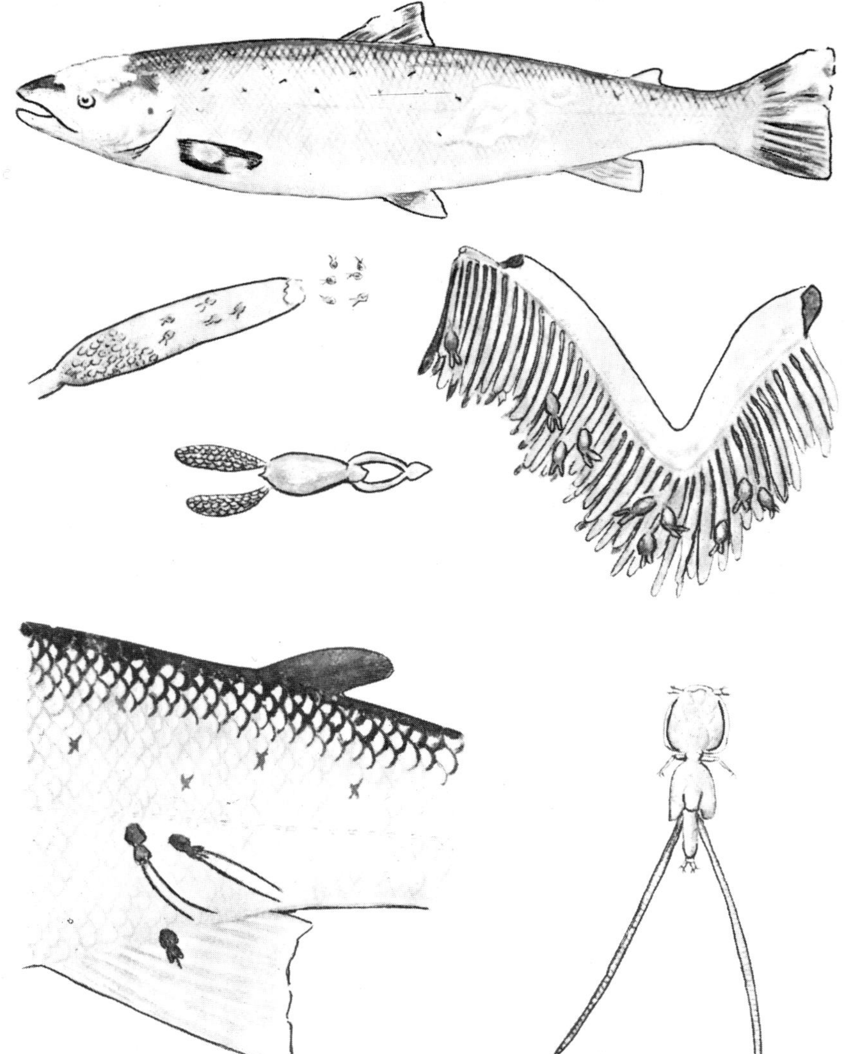

Fig. 25.2. Parasites of the salmon. (Top) *salmon with parasite fungus,* Saprolegnia. (Centre, above and left) *reproductive tip of a fungus filament, discharging spores (greatly enlarged).* (Centre, below and left) *gill-maggot (enlarged).* (Centre right) *gill-maggots attached to gill.* (Bottom left), *sea lice attached above anal fin of salmon,* (Bottom right), *a female sea louse (enlarged).* (Reproduced from *The Sea Angler's Fishes* by Michael Kennedy.)

failure which is made no more bearable by the heavy humour of his wife and friends.

But take heart. There are plenty of excuses for not catching salmon. Here are just a few to choose from:

The weather was too settled, or unsettled. It was too hot, too cold, too bright or too dull. There was thunder about, or mist on the water. The wind was too strong, or from the wrong direction, or there was no wind. The river was too high, too low, too coloured or too clear. There was foam on the surface. The fish were running through. There were no fish. The glass was falling or rising too quickly. There was too much grue. Air and water temperatures were all to hell. The pool had been disturbed by poachers, predators, canoeists, swimmers, or the fellow on the other bank. You had forgotten your lucky charm.

There are times when you may think that only the last excuse is valid.

On a summer's day twenty years ago, one of the authors of this book was ghillying for two famous (and articulate) salmon fishermen. It was about three o'clock in the afternoon; very warm, very bright, very still. The two experts had flogged the hours away with various patterns and sizes of greased-line fly; and now sat, exhausted, on a river-side seat, analysing their failure.

Conditions, they agreed, were impossible. The river was too low; the light too strong; there was no ripple. The fish were 'potted'. It was absurd to think that a salmon would take anything at that time of the day – unless the sky clouded over, or a breeze came up, or it rained. There was a chance, just the faintest chance that a very tiny fly might get an offer at dusk. But until then it was hopeless. There was no point in fishing.

A boy appeared from behind some trees on the opposite bank. He carried a cheap fibre-glass rod; from it, on stout nylon, dangled a three-inch blue-and-silver Devon. He released the bale-arm of his reel and swung the Devon out across the pool. A salmon took it at once.

The boy skulldragged the fish ashore, knocked it on the head, put a cord through its gills, slung it over his shoulder and disappeared in the bushes. There was a brief but blinding flow of obscenity from the two experts after which they fell silent and sat staring across the sun-flecked water, each alone with his thoughts. For the first time in their respective forty-odd years of fishing, neither of them could think of anything else to say.

Of such moments is the very stuff of salmon fishing composed.

PRINCIPLES OF SALMON FLY-FISHING

No sport is basically so simple as the exasperating, illogical but altogether delightful sport of fly-fishing for salmon. A rod, reel, line, leader, lure. These are the few essentials. All spare tackle can be carried in the pockets: a case of lures, a reel or two of nylon; scissors; priest; polaroid glasses. What else? Since on most rivers a salmon can be tailed by hand, a gaff, net or tailer is unnecessary. If a bag is needed it is only for carrying lunch.

There are two ways of fishing fly for salmon:

1. With the small fly (length approximately $\frac{3}{8}$ in to $1\frac{1}{4}$ in) fished close to the surface on floating line known to salmon fishermen as the 'greased line' method.
2. With the big fly (length approximately $2\frac{1}{2}$ in to 4 in) fished close to the bottom on sunk (or ungreased) line.

Nowadays, silk lines are seldom used and it is no longer necessary to grease or ungrease a line in order to make it float or sink.

There is a range of floating and sinking lines that will serve for any type of water. Each pool on each river has its own characteristics, and a salmon fisherman should choose the line or lines that will suit the particular water he is going to fish at the time of year he will be fishing it.

Whether he fishes a big fly or a small fly depends on the air and water temperatures. As a rough guide, the big fly is fished when the water temperature is *below* 48–50°F. The small fly when the water temperature is *above* 48–50°F. But the air temperature too is important. When the air is warmer than the water the small fly is always in with a chance, even with a water temperature as low as 42–44°F. When the air is appreciably colder than the water, the big fly will take fish even when the water temperature is up to 52–54°F. Generally speaking, however, from April/May until late autumn only the small fly kills.

Very much the same applies to salmon spinning: deep down near the bottom with a big lure in early spring and autumn. High up near the surface with a small lure in summer.

Fishing in mid-water with either fly or spinner is seldom profitable.

Choice and Presentation of the Small Fly

In so unlikely a sport as salmon fishing – which consists of offering a meal to a fish that has no appetite – it is obviously important for the angler to bolster his confidence with some sort of theory. And so over the years, in an attempt to meet this demand, writers on salmon fishing have set out to explain why and when a salmon will take a fly. In consequence a vast amount of mumbo-jumbo has been amassed, not the least of which concerns the *choice* of fly.

Few salmon fishermen are as honest as that man of long ago who wrote: 'It is impossible to lay down any hard and fast rule for selecting a fly . . . the best of us are at our wits' end to know what fly to select.' Frequently, the best of us *are* at our wits' end. But few of us care to admit it.

This reluctance is understandable. Confidence in a fly is the key to success, because only if an angler has confidence in his fly will he fish it with sufficient care and concentration; only if he is confident will he persist, and in the long run it is the most careful and persistent angler who catches the most salmon. Success, then, depends on confidence. And what confidence can anyone have in a fly that has not been chosen for some particular reason – be it fact or fancy?

But *what* reason? Size? Shape? Colour?

Certain colours in salmon flies are sometimes recommended on the grounds that they enable a fish to see the fly better, and that brightly coloured flies will therefore result in more offers. This is very doubtful. Salmon have excellent vision. They may refuse a fly for a number of reasons, but however drab it may be an inability to see it well enough – even in spate water – is unlikely to be among them. And anyway, why should a salmon be more eager to take a manufactured 'fly' simply because it can be *seen* more clearly? The reverse, one could argue, is more likely to be the case. Again, salmon are undoubtedly colour conscious;

(see Salmon and the Prawn, p. 198) but does anyone know what fly colour (if any) is likely to stimulate them at any given moment?

Theories have been advanced concerning colour and light. Some pundits advocate a bright fly for a bright day and a dull fly for a dull day; while others prefer a dull fly on a bright day and a bright fly on a dull day. Does it really make any difference? The angler who, whatever the conditions, cocks a snook at colour altogether and relies on a plain Stoat's Tail seems to catch his share of fish.

It is probable that if you select any one pattern of fly that gives you confidence (because your friends have done well on it, or you fancy the name, or it has your lucky colour) and you fish it in varying sizes and degrees of dressing throughout the season, you will do just as well as you would if you had a host of different patterns to choose from. Indeed, you are likely to do better, since you will not waste so much time wondering which pattern to choose, or whether what you have on is really the best fly for that particular moment.

If you are a believer in the bright-light bright-fly theory, or what-have-you, choose two basic patterns: a light pattern and a dark pattern. They should be carried in a comprehensive size range, say: 4, 6, 8, 10, 12; a number of each size with varying amounts of dressing: slender, medium, fat. They should be tied on single hooks, double hooks, and (if you can find reliable treble hooks) on tubes, too. Will this do you?

No, you object, it will not! You have no wish to be restricted to one or two patterns. Like most other salmon fishermen, you already own several cases crammed with flies of every shape and size and colour. What you want is a simple method of choosing one. Very well. Number them all and get your wife to call a number. Very nearly as good as any other method.

No? Not scientific enough? Perhaps you are right. Let us examine it all a little more closely.

You have, we will imagine, arrived at the river and, because the water temperature is, say 54°F, and the air temperature 60°F, have put aside your sunk line and big lures and decided to fish with a small fly and 'greased-line' tackle. And quite right, too. The air temperature is higher than the water temperature, and the water temperature is higher than 48–50°F. (See p. 187.)

You have not yet attached a leader to your line. Again, quite right, since the thickness of leader will depend on the size of fly – and the fly has not yet been chosen. (It could also be said that until you have judged the strength of the current in the stretch you are going to fish, the line itself could not have been chosen from three possibilities: floating, sink-tip; slow sinker. But we will come to that in a minute).

The most important point to consider when choosing a fly for any given piece of water is the depth at which you want the fly to swim. A fish will take a fly that is swimming at a certain depth but refuse the same fly if it is swimming higher or lower. Hypotheses abound, but no one knows the reason for this. And on the question of the depth at which a greased-line fly should swim, most writers are very cagey. Nevertheless everything hinges on it, and the answer is: from three to five inches. In summer, a salmon will sometimes take a fly that is swimming on or almost on the surface; but usually will simply swirl at it. If the fly is swimming too deep, the fish will pay no attention to it. For fishing the small fly the *ideal* depth is four inches.

A slender, lightly dressed fly will sink faster than a bushy dressing on a similar hook. And since weight usually decreases as the size of the hook diminishes, it follows that a lightly dressed size 8 may fish at the same height as, say, a bushy size 6 on the same length of leader on the same type of fly-line in the same current.

Dressing, then, is of the greatest importance – but not for the reasons usually attributed. What is of primary importance in a fly dressing is neither the colours nor the materials, it is the *quantity*.

So, irrespective of its colour, you will start by choosing flies with dressings that will suit a certain size of hook and allow it to swim at the right depth in the water you are going to fish.

And how do you determine size? As a rough guide, the size of a fly depends on the height of the river. The higher the water the stronger the current, and, therefore, the larger the fly. Conversely, the lower the river the slacker the current and the smaller the fly – until, in conditions of summer low, you should be fishing a fly as small as size 10, 12, or even 14.[1]

But will this one selected size suit all the water in any particular pool? Probably not. The current varies from a fast run-in to a slack middle and a streamy tail. To fish it properly – that is to say to give yourself the best chance of hooking a fish at every cast – you will need to make at least one change of fly, possibly two or three; start perhaps with a size 4 in the neck; change to a size 8 in the middle, and change again to a size 6 in the tail.

The size of the fly is related directly to the speed at which the fly should be fished. It is wise to present a fly to a salmon at a speed not in excess of that which a living creature of the fly's size (perhaps a shrimp or a tiny fish) could move. Say, 1–1½ m.p.h.

From this it is clear that correct fly presentation consists of controlling the depth and the speed of the fly all the way down the pool. Only by careful study of the water can you work out how to do this. So, your first task is to examine the water, bearing in mind that the fly is to be fished at an average depth of four inches.

Note the strength of the current and where it changes; the amount of ripple (line-tip, leader and fly go under more readily in a ripple than in a smooth glide); observe the position of all likely salmon lies; the swirl and eddy that occur near sunken rocks – which themselves often form lies for salmon. Most important of all, note that narrow strip of water between fast current and slack on the inside bend of a pool. Almost without exception these pieces of water provide

1 When this size of fly is fished we strongly recommend the use of double hooks. A double even as small as a number 12 or 14 has a very strong hold when embedded in the gristle at the side of a salmon's mouth.

taking lies for salmon. But remember that a fly's speed and depth must be maintained as it swings out of a current into slack water, otherwise it will falter and begin to sink. A salmon will move to but refuse a fly that behaves in this manner.

As you 'read' the water an idea of fly size and dressing will begin to take shape. And as you progress down the pool it soon becomes evident how often, if at all, you will need to change the fly in sympathy with the current.

Broadly speaking the depth at which a fly will swim depends on the current, the weight of the fly and the type of fly-line. A rough and ready guide for choice of line is as follows:

Slack or sluggish water: floating line.

Medium to fast current: floating line with sink-tip.

Very fast current: slow sinking line.

Unless more than one rod is in use, it is obviously impracticable to change the line as you fish down a pool, whereas it is a simple matter to change the fly.

Now to the fly itself. From your various fly boxes a multitude of variegated single, double and tube flies look up at you. Which one to choose?

Well, you have examined and 'read' the water. A sink-tip floating line has been fitted to the rod, and you intend to use a nine-foot leader. You have a clear picture of fly size and amount of dressing, so already your choice has been considerably narrowed.

27 lb Tay Salmon taken by FB in September on $\frac{3}{7}$ oz black and brass Toby fished–deep and slow–good medicine in the conditions; water high but clear, temperature 49°F after the first snow shower of the season.

A fresh-run 18 lb summer salmon from the Cumberland Derwent, taken before breakfast in very low water on No. 12 double (see p. 191). Ghillie: Kathleen Falkus.

Next, the pattern of fly. Light or dark? Take a look at the sky. Is the light hard or soft? If you believe in bright flies for bright days, or whatever, select only those flies which seem to fit your particular bill. This reduces the number still further. From the remainder select only those whose hairs or feather fibres are soft and flexible; which, when the fly moves through the water, will tend to flicker and give it life. A straggly, chewed-looking fly is vastly more attractive than something neat and stiff and 'over-stuffed'.

You have now whittled your original choice down to perhaps three or four possibles. Tip these into your hat, close your eyes and pick one out.

Good. You have now chosen a fly. And what have you come up with? A rather battered size 6 Blue Charm. And a very good fly to start with.

You can now select the thickness of leader that will enable this fly to swim in a life-like manner.

What it all boils down to is this: there is no substitute for experience when it comes to choosing a fly. Experience merely reduces the number of flies an angler tips into his hat. When he is very experienced he may not need to tip any into his hat at all. Even then, whatever fly he chooses, what really matters is how he presents it to the fish.

Double Hooks

Double hooks are also a comparative novelty.
JOHN BICKERDYKE, *Angling for Game Fish* (1889).

Not so.

Young Salmons under a quarter of a yard

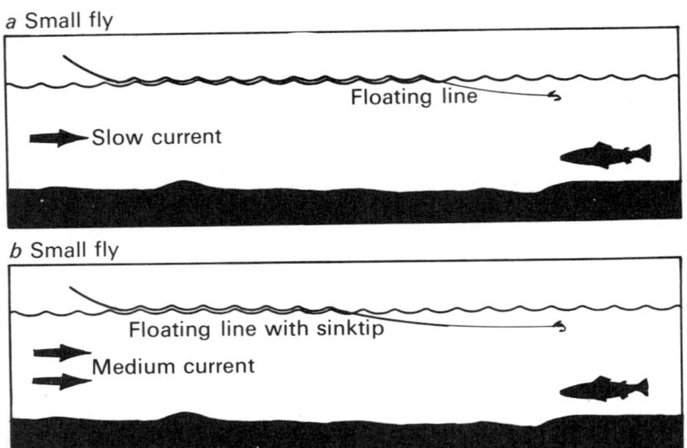

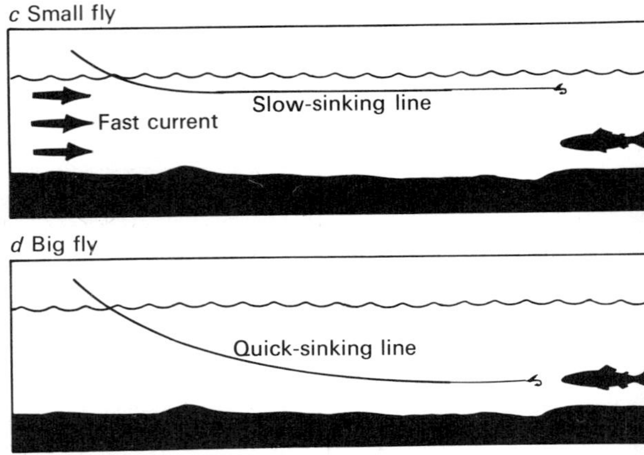

Fig. 25.2. a, b and c show choice of line for summer small-fly fishing. Choice depends on strength of current. The angler's object is to fish the fly at an average depth of four inches irrespective of current speed.
For early spring and autumn fishing (d) a big fly is fished deep on fully sunk line.

long, have tender mouths, [1] so as they are apt to break their hold: to obviate which inconvenience, I have known some that use to fasten two hooks together, in like manner as some double Pike hooks lately used in Trowling are made, not with the points opposite to one another, but about a quarter of a Circle from each other, and on them they make their Flie, that if one Hook break hold, the other may not fail.
COLONEL ROBERT VENABLES,
The Experienc'd Angler (fourth edition, 1676).

1 These sound like sea-trout. The softness of mouth of a fresh-run sea-trout is discussed on p. 310.

Choice of Fly Line

For the various methods of fishing fly we suggest the following lines:

1. Early spring and autumn fishing (with big fly):
   Wet-cel, quick-sinking.
2. Summer fishing (with small fly):
   Fast current: Wet-cel, slow-sinking.
   Medium current: Air-cel with sink-tip.
   Slow current or slack water: Air-cel.

'Tis not so wide as a church-door', he reflected with Mercutio, 'but 'twill suffice – if I can only land him.'
JOHN BUCHAN, *John MacNab* (1925).

Patrick Annesley on the Cumberland Derwent, working the fly by hand in conditions of dead low water (see Fig. 25.3 a, p. 194). Exposed tree roots indicate how low the river has dropped during the prolonged drought of 1972. The line of normal water level is clearly visible just underneath the tree branches. In such conditions salmon fly-fishing is often considered hopeless. Nevertheless, seconds after this picture was taken a salmon took the fly – a very sparsely dressed No. 12 Logie, on an extra-fine leader point.

. . . perhaps as yet there has been no rain in the valley. A man from the hills has told us of it; we have seen it in the distance as a vast veil of greyness, hung in a moving heaven so that it swept gently over the screes, the bogs and mountain ploughland, the grateful upturned face of the earth. All we know of it and much more is already old news to the salmon. As soon as rain is in the offing, the salmon in the pools become restless and often will not look at a fly. Conversely, this persistent refusal to rise is frequently taken as a sign of the coming of rain.

ERIC TAVERNER, *Salmon Fishing* (1931).

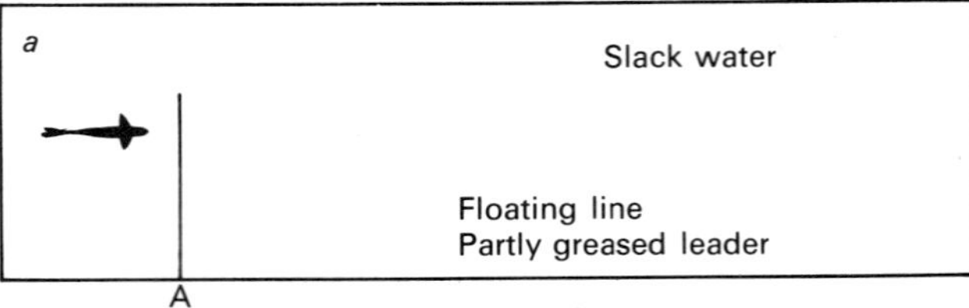

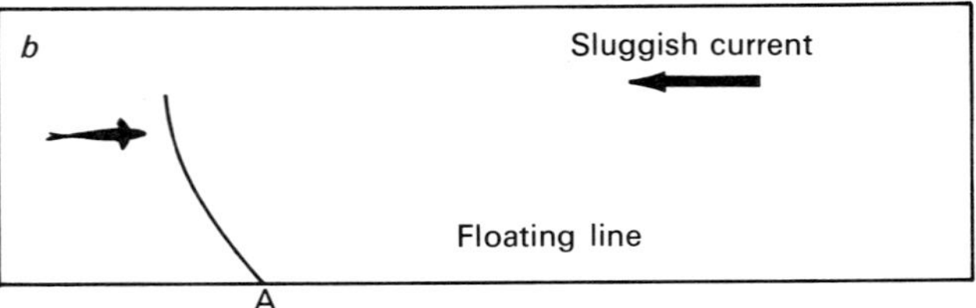

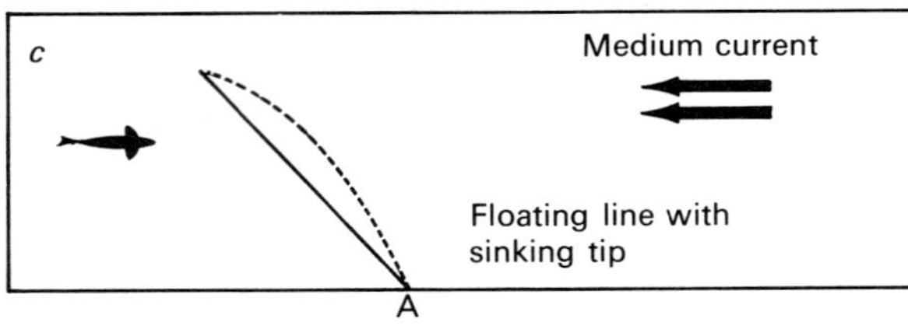

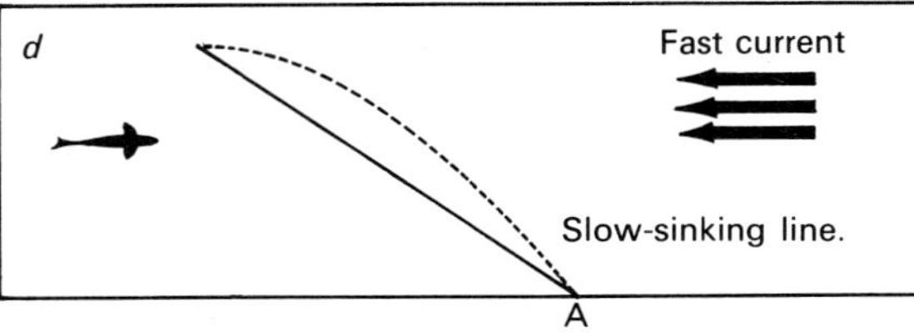

Fig. 25.3. The diagrams show a salmon lying in the same position relative to the bank, but in water varying from dead slack to very fast. The angler is casting from point 'A'. In each case he is using a small 'greased' line fly ranging in length from $\frac{3}{8}$ inch in the slack water, to $1\frac{1}{4}$ inch in the fast water. His length of leader remains the same: 9 ft.

Angle of Presentation

Since the object of floating-line fishing for salmon is to present a small fly ($\frac{3}{8}$ in–$1\frac{1}{4}$ in) to a salmon at a depth of four inches, and a speed of between one and one-and-a-half miles per hour, it follows that the angle at which the fly is cast depends largely on the strength of current.

In slack water (Fig. 25.3.*a*) the fly is cast square to the bank and line is stripped in to give the fly movement. This is how a fly has to be fished on some pools in conditions of dead low water. A modern floating line is used. Such conditions of low, still water are extremely difficult to overcome. The ability to catch a fish in these circumstances is one of the skills that separate the expert salmon angler from the rest.

In a sluggish current (Fig. 25.3.*b*) the fly is cast at a slightly more acute angle. This means that a longer line will have to be cast. No mend is made in the line. Instead, a slight belly is allowed to form, and the current is used to swing the fly over the fish. The angler is still fishing a floating line.

In a medium current (Fig. 25.3.*c*) the cast is made at an even more acute angle, which necessitates casting an even longer line. Now, in order to control the fly's depth and speed as it passes over the fish, a mend is made in the line as soon as a belly has formed. The line used in this strength of current is a floating line with sinking tip.

In a fast current (Fig. 25.3.*d*) the angler must go still further upstream and cast a very long line indeed, mending as soon as the cast is completed – shooting an extra yard or two of line as he does so. In water of this strength, a sinking tip is not sufficient to keep the fly at

Salmon fishing in low water conditions. *Having cast, the angler raises his rod point to form a belly of slack line. This slack helps to cushion any 'snatch' that may occur as a fish takes, and prevents the fly from being pulled out of the fish's mouth.*

Low water salmon fishing usually means a gentle current. Here, the angler is drawing in line with his left hand as the fly reaches slack water at the end of its swing. To keep the fly moving through the water, and therefore lifelike, will often succeed in hooking a fish that would otherwise move to the fly but refuse it. As a salmon takes, the line is released, so that the yard or two of slack can slide smoothly out. A salmon hooks itself.

the proper depth; to prevent it skidding, a modern slow sinking line is used. To mend such a line at long range is far from easy. If the current is really strong this is a very difficult fish to hook. All too often the fly simply skids ineffectually over the taking area.

It will be seen that (as in Fig. 25.3.*a*) the fish could easily be covered by casting more squarely. But to do so is quite pointless since the fly cannot be prevented from fishing at excessive speed.

Very occasionally a fly that is cast from square on, or slightly downstream, in a strong current, and stripped back over the salmon's head, will be taken. But this 'take' occurs very rarely, and in our experience results almost invariably in a poorly hooked fish.

Note. Mending a line should be done only in rippled water. In the smooth, glassy water of a pool tail it is likely to do more harm than good owing to the disturbance caused by the splash of the line turning over. In these circumstances there is no alternative to throwing a long line from as far upstream as possible.

Effective Casting Range

Although there is a considerable element of luck in salmon fishing, some anglers catch many more fish than others. Their success is not due mainly to good fortune. It derives from attention to detail – which reduces reliance on the element of luck.

1. By using water sense and intuition.
2. Making a stealthy approach to the riverside. Concealment. Taking care not to cause vibration or shadow.
3. Using well balanced tackle, suitable for the water in question.
4. Correct choice and presentation of a lure.
5. Ability to wade stealthily, and deep.
6. Ability to cast and *effectively control* a long line. Factors 1 to 5 being equal, the angler who consistently achieves the greatest *effective casting range* will catch the most fish.

In Fig. 25.4.*a*, an angler at A casts to B1. His fly swings round on the arc B1, C1. It covers three fish: Y, X and W. Owing to the speed of the current, however, with its resultant drag on the line, the fly will not be fishing effectively (i.e. at the right depth and speed) until it reaches the horizontal dotted line. Thus, although he has cast to B1, the angler's *effective casting range* is only the distance between R1 and the bank. Although the fly has passed over salmon Y and X, it has not done so in a manner that would induce them to take. The only fish that is being effectively covered is the salmon at W.

In Fig. 25.4.*b*, the angler casts again to B1. This time, however, he mends his line. His effective casting range is now between R2 and the bank. A considerable advantage has been gained, since he can now effectively cover two extra salmon: Y and X.

In Fig. 25.4.*c*, the angler wades out to A2 and casts again, this time to B2. Again he mends his line correctly. His fly now traverses the arc B2, C2, and he can cover the salmon at Z.

By long casting, mending and wading, he can, therefore, effectively cover all four fish. *Note:* If he *starts* by wading out to A2 and

Effective casting range

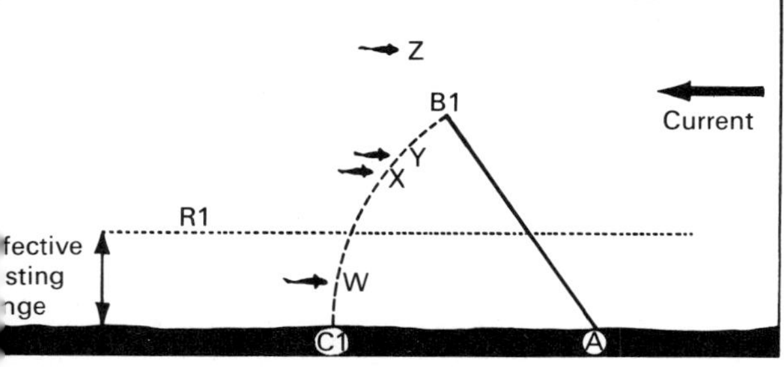

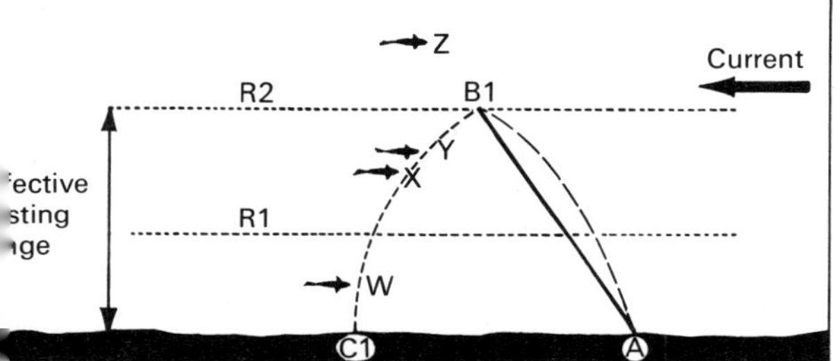

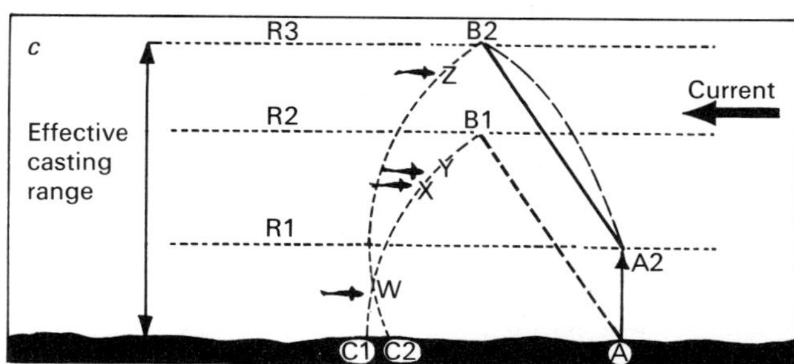

Fig. 25.4. The increase in effective casting range *in Figs. (b) and (c), has been exaggerated for the sake of clarity. It is the principle of the thing that matters. Once the novice salmon-angler appreciates the simple point that his lure is effective only when it is fishing at the correct depth and speed, he will start to catch many more salmon.*

casting to B2 in order to cover the fish at Z, he will over-cast the fish at X and Y.

To wade straight into a pool and start off by casting as far as possible across the river is a very common mistake. *Always fish the nearer water first.*

There is a further point of interest in Fig. 25.4.*c*.

If the angler at A2 fishes his cast right out towards the point C2 – by moving his rod across to his left as far as he can reach, and leading the fly inshore – he can also cover the fish at W.

When an angler is wading deep, he should always fish a cast right out in this manner. Many opportunities of catching fish are missed because when the fly is straight downstream, at the dangle, it is retrieved and cast again.

Hooking a Salmon

According to our observation at the waterside a salmon usually takes a 'greased-line' fly in one of three ways (see Fig. 25.5).

(*a*) It will rise from its lie, move forwards and upwards intercept the fly, take the fly in its mouth and sink back to its lie without turning. This fish is hooked in the right-hand side of the mouth when the angler is casting from the left bank (and *vice versa*).

(*b*) It will rise to intercept and take the fly, turn *against* the direction in which the fly is travelling, and describe a circle as it returns to its lie. When the angler is casting from the left bank this fish, too, is hooked in the right-hand side of the mouth. Like the fish in (*a*), it is usually well hooked.

(*c*) Occasionally a salmon will turn in the

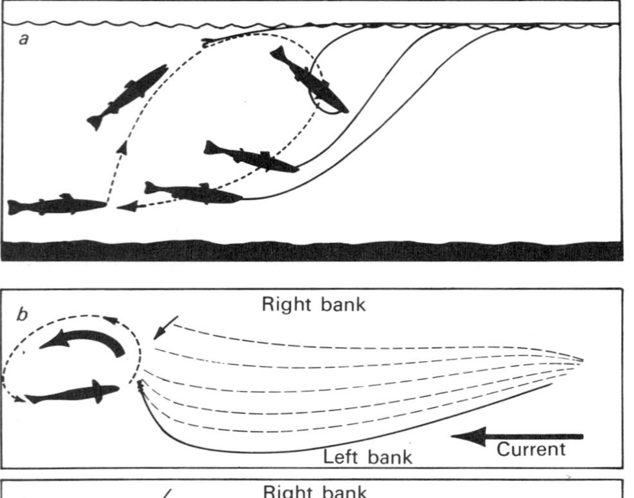

Fig. 25.5.

same direction as that in which the fly is travelling and, having taken the fly, circle away downstream. Unlike the fish in (*a*) and (*b*) it will have the fly in the left side of its mouth when the angler is on the left bank (and *vice versa*). In our experience the fish that takes like this is *poorly* hooked. Indeed what often happens is that it runs out a few yards of line – and then comes off.

Note: Salmon have been seen to chase a fly for many yards across a pool before taking it (in the same way that a prawn on a spinner is sometimes chased) but such a reaction to the fly is unusual. We ourselves have witnessed it only twice.

Overfishing of Lies

A great deal has been said on this subject. We agree with very little of it. Almost invariably, the angler is advised to fish a lie sparingly and to rest it often. In our experience this is unsound advice.

Provided a salmon lie is properly fished (meaning that the fish has not been frightened out of it) *there is no such thing as over-fishing it.* So long as the angler remains out of sight and avoids casting shadow either with rod or line, a salmon remains catchable however many times it may have been covered unsuccessfully. On numerous occasions we have known salmon – which, since the water was clear, could be identified individually – caught from lies that had been fished consistently all day long.

THE SALMON AND THE PRAWN

Most aspects of salmon fishing have received lavish attention from other writers, and we have no wish to cover ground that has already been combed bare. There are, however, certain features that have not been fully explored, one of which is the vexed question of the salmon and the prawn.

In general the prawn has had a poor press. It is not an 'in' lure. Many writers have considered it, and almost without exception they have condemned it. Some, throwing up their hands in horror, have denounced it as being harmful, and even 'unsporting'; a method of fishing quite beyond the pale.

We do not share this view. In our opinion the harmful effects of prawn fishing have been greatly exaggerated; furthermore, we think that far from being an 'unsporting' method (whatever that may mean) it is a skilful and fascinating technique, especially in low clear water when both prawn and salmon can be seen during every moment of the encounter.

That much of what we have to say on the subject (including the Falkus low-water prawning technique) has not been said before is, perhaps, because few fishermen have had the opportunity to observe and experiment in water of such crystal clarity as that of H. F.'s stretch of fishing. He writes as follows:

Although I have often been told that a prawn will sometimes empty a salmon pool I have never witnessed it. My own river provides unique opportunities for observing sea-trout and salmon behaviour, and for many years I have taken advantage of this. Time and again I have watched the reactions of salmon to a prawn, but never once have I seen a salmon actually *leave* a pool because of a prawn.

We do not of course suggest that it *never* happens (the behaviour of migratory fishes varies from river to river, the reason for which may well be that suggested on p. 286), merely that if it does happen (and there is evidence that it does) it is on rivers outside our experience. On many rivers the prawn does little or no harm, and although it is by no means always successful there are times when it can serve the angler well.

Being without inhibitions, H. F. has experimented with boiled prawns of different colours, painting them (in the absence of suitable dyes) with dabs of oil pigment.

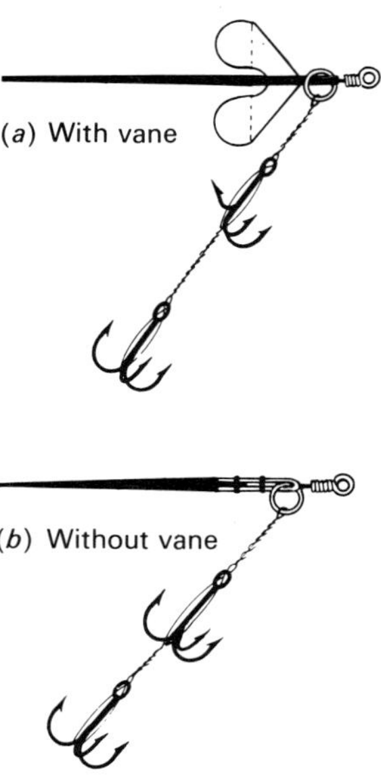

Fig. 25.6. Prawn mounts.

Although the olfactory sense of salmon is known to be extremely acute, the scent of oil paint seems to be no deterrent. A freshly painted prawn is very messy to use, but the salmon has no objection to taking it.

Experiments indicate that the best colour is a rich magenta – better than yellow or orange or green or blue or any other colour. The second most successful colour is the boiled prawn's natural pink.

There are several ways in which a prawn can be presented to a salmon.

1. Mounted with spinning vane (Fig. 25.6.*a*), it can be fished across a pool in the same way as any other spinner.

2. Without vane (Fig. 25.6.*b* and Fig. 25.7), it can be fished across a pool like a fly; or by sink-and-draw.

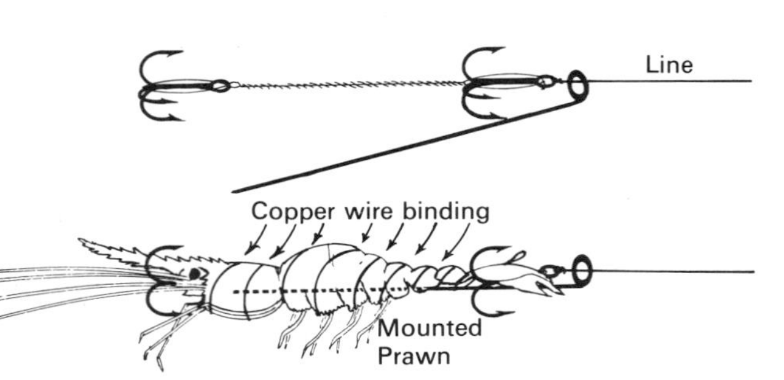

Fig. 25.7. Home-made prawn mount.

Fig. 25.8. Float fishing with a prawn.

3. Either with or without vane, it can be let down on the current under the angler's own bank a yard at a time, brought back a foot or so, and then allowed to go still further downstream, until the length of pool has been covered; and then slowly withdrawn.
4. Without vane, it can be drift-lined.
5. Without vane, it can be left motionless (ledgered) on the bottom for a salmon to pick up – like a deadbait for pike.
6. Without vane, it can be fished on a float and allowed to drift unimpeded down a pool from top to tail. (*Very* deadly at times.)

A salmon reacts to a prawn as follows.

1. It remains in its lie and ignores the prawn completely.
2. It shows signs of agitation as the prawn approaches, eventually abandoning its lie. (It is probably this behaviour that has given rise to some of the hair-raising stories about salmon fleeing from a prawn.) The salmon does not often stay away from its lie for very long – usually, from two to five minutes.
3. It swims up as though to intercept the prawn, but turns away without touching it and returns to its lie.
4. It sucks the prawn into its mouth and immediately blows it out again, leaving no mark on it whatever.
5. It takes the prawn with the very front of its mouth and gives it a little nip, removing a tiny piece from the back, or the eggs from the belly. At other times it contrives to shave off the whiskers and sometimes part of the head as cleanly as if they had been cut by a razor.
6. It takes the prawn in its mouth, crushes it, and then blows it out again.
7. It takes the prawn fiercely (sometimes halfway down its throat), either by grabbing it as it swings past or by sucking it up off the bottom.
8. It chases the length or width of a pool to grab a prawn.

Probably the most effective way of fishing a prawn is to let it drift unchecked through a pool, suspended from a float (Fig. 25.8). But by far the most exciting method is in low clear water, when the prawn is drift-lined (with no float, and the very minimum of lead) to a particular fish, and both prawn and salmon are kept in view.

Sometimes, if the prawn can be swung round well below a salmon, then manoeuvred upstream into the position shown in Fig. 25.10 . . . and left to lie there, the salmon, after

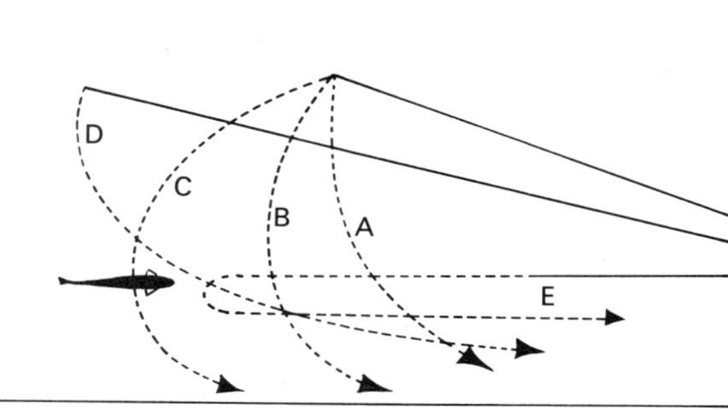

Fig. 25.9. Each cast over a known lie should be different. A fish can sometimes be induced to take if a prawn it has already seen and refused suddenly behaves differently. A. B. C. D. and E. show ways of presenting a prawn with or without spinning vane.

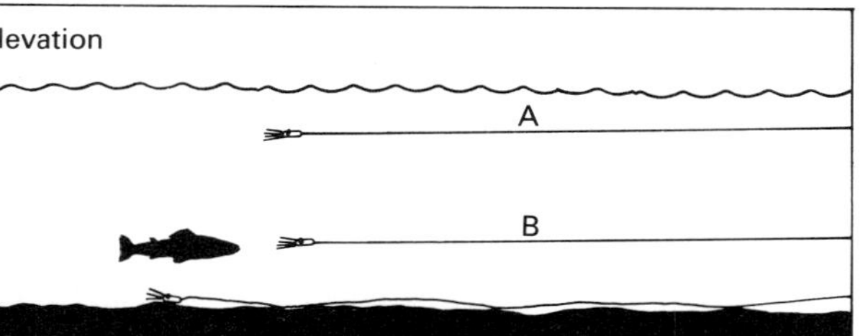

Fig. 29.9. A salmon will sometimes rise to a prawn fished near to the surface as shown in A. More often, however, it takes a prawn that is fished deep (B). The various paths of the prawn are shown in plan view in Fig. 25.9.
Below: *A stationary prawn positioned just on the edge of the salmon's backward vision (see dotted lines) will sometimes induce a savage take.*

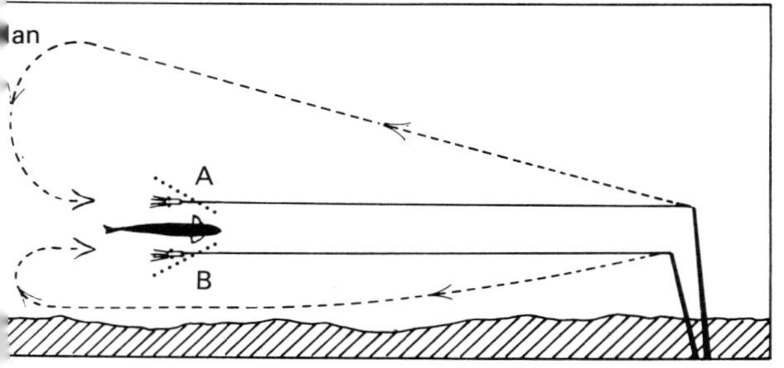

a few minutes of increasing agitation, will suddenly turn and make a ferocious grab at it. A most exciting moment for the angler, and anyone else who happens to be watching. Needless to say, both angler and watchers should remain well concealed.

Anyone who considers prawn fishing to be 'unsporting' may care to reflect that this low-water technique demands the highest degree of angling skill.

There is however, one very important aspect of prawn fishing. Whatever one's own opinion may be, it is not the effect of the prawn on the fish that matters, it is the effect of the prawn on other fishermen.

No sportsman should wittingly spoil someone else's pleasure. If your companions think that prawn will interfere with their chances of catching salmon, *don't fish it.* If the rules of the beat forbid prawn, observe them. It is a question of good manners. Always, when fishing as a guest, enquire first before using prawn.

To bag a hen on a 'cocks only' day will not brighten your chances of another shooting invitation. So with salmon fishing. Unless your host is a very enlightened fisherman, or just doesn't care, 'the carriage' will soon be waiting if he comes down to fish a fly and finds you putting a prawn through the pool.

SHRIMP FISHING

Spinning

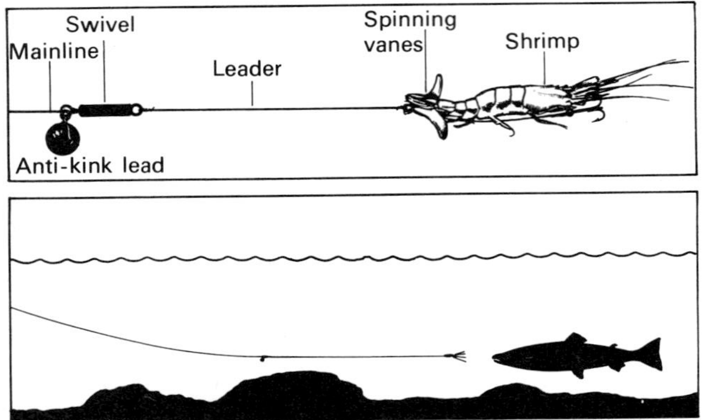

Fig. 25.11. Spinning a shrimp.

The shrimp fishes in clear water during the summer months. Like a sunk fly, it should be presented close to the bottom and as slowly as possible.

The three best methods of fishing shrimp are: spinning, rolling-ledger and stret-pegging. Spinning is not the most productive method, but it is certainly the most practical, since it can be used in water which – owing to an uneven bottom – prohibits the use of rolling-ledger or stret-pegging.

The best colour for a shrimp is a dark, rich magenta. (See prawn fishing, p. 199.)

Rolling Ledger

Provided the river has a bed of fine gravel where fish are lying, the rolling-ledger is the best method of presenting shrimp in *fast* water. The angler casts from A to B and fishes the shrimp across the noses of the fish on the arc BC. The lead should be heavy enough to bump slowly round, thereby controlling the speed of the swing – with the shrimp 'swimming' an inch or two off the bottom. The use of a long rod assists in controlling speed.

To fish the shrimp too fast and with too short a rod is a common mistake. In strong water a long line should be cast from well upstream. This will lessen the angle B.A.C. and help to slow down the speed of the swing.

When the shrimp stops, the angler should tighten instantly. This is the reverse of worm fishing (see p. 205).

When a salmon takes a worm: *wait*.

When a salmon takes prawn or shrimp: *tighten at once*.

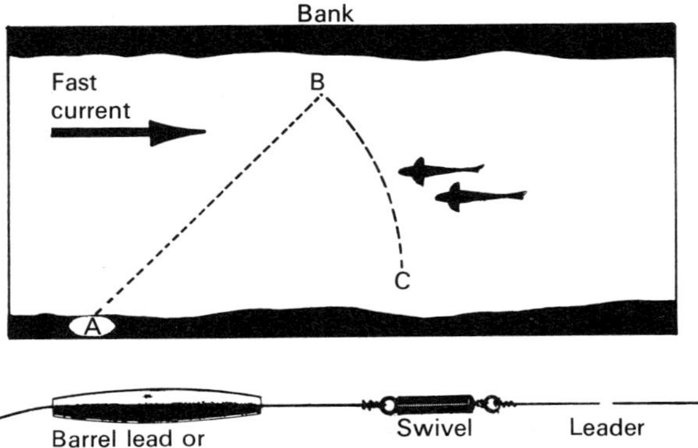

Fig. 25.12. Rolling ledger.

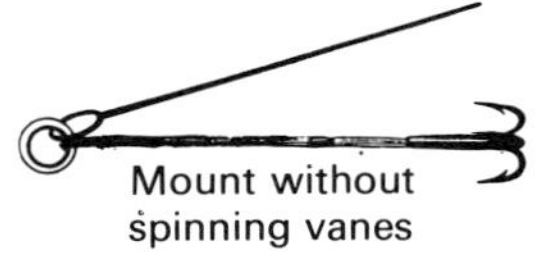

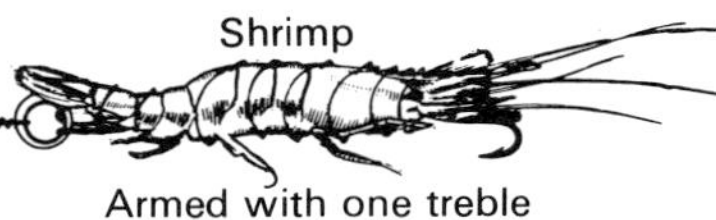

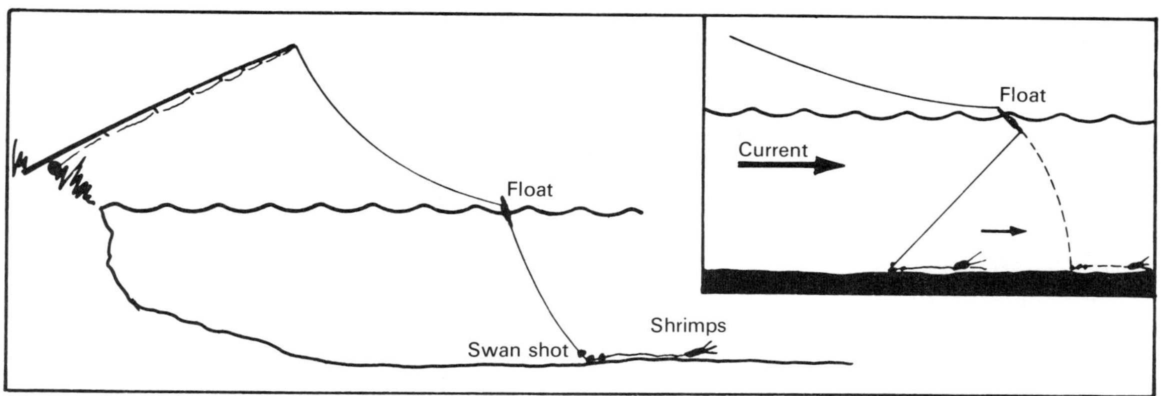

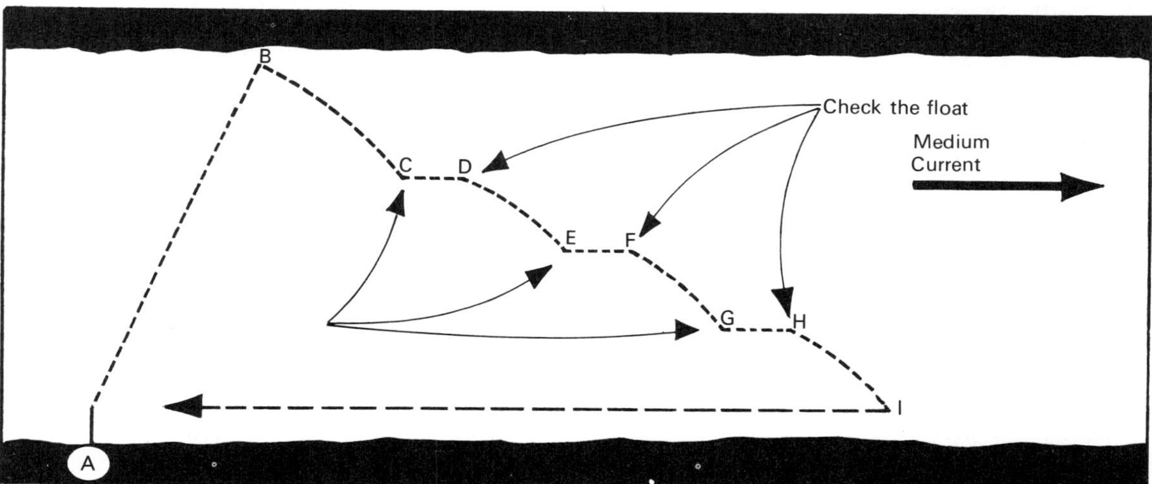

Fig. 25.13. Stret-pegging.

Stret-pegging

Of all methods of fishing a shrimp this is the most deadly. But like rolling-ledger, it can be used only where the bottom is suitable.

An angler at A. casts to B. and allows the shrimp to swing round *as slowly as possible* to C. At this point line is released, so that the float drifts down on the current to D. The float is then checked, which allows the shrimp to swing round to E. And so on – until the shrimp finishes up in slack water under the angler's bank at I. – via E. F. G. H. (For other notes on stret-pegging, see p. 467.)

WATER-SENSE

The shaping hand of evolution that once fashioned man as a hunter has gradually adapted him to a new way of living. Even so, eleven thousand years of farming, manufacturing, trading and other substitute activities, have not succeeded entirely in eradicating his hunting instinct – the urge to stalk and kill his prey, be it fur, feather or fin. So that although the newcomer to angling is sometimes perplexed to find that he harbours an urge to hunt, such a desire is not really surprising.

Nor is it surprising that some persons, however eager, remain forever duffers, while others (in whom the hunting instinct is more strongly developed) quickly become accomplished anglers.

Regardless of what comes naturally, however, the most successful anglers are those who have developed their water-sense: that ability to 'read' water; to examine a stretch of fishing and decide unerringly where, how and with what to fish it.

By those fortunate enough to have the opportunity, water-sense begins to be absorbed during childhood. To the late starter it is not so easily acquired, and books alone are of little help. There is simply so substitute for experience at the waterside, preferably in the company of a top-class fisherman.

We urge the novice to miss no opportunity of learning to 'read' water. It is like learning a new language. Gradually, what has seemed meaningless becomes significant. Even water as seemingly featureless as a canal will assume a new appearance, and certain spots will stand out as being more attractive than others. Aided by water-sense, the novice will find himself taking salmon and sea-trout with the upstream-worm from water which, previously, he would have walked past without a second glance.

Those anglers who despise worm-fishing as a thing so simple as to be quite unworthy of their attention, would quickly discover their mistake if brought to a small clear water on a warm sunny day in June or July.
W. C. STEWART, *The Practical Angler* (1857).

LOW-WATER UPSTREAM WORM FISHING

During summer, in conditions of low water and high temperature, salmon (and sea-trout) often lie in fast, shallow, broken runs and glides no more than two or three feet deep. That they do so is almost certainly because of the increased oxygenation of this type of water.

In these conditions a worm offers an angler the best chance of success, since it can be fished with less disturbance than any other method.

The object is to present the worm in such a way that it behaves as naturally as possible – drifting with the current without drag or hindrance. A fixed-spool reel can of course be used for the job, but in these fast, shallow runs the most suitable tackle is a centre-pin. A light 10–11 ft single-handed rod should be used with a centre-pin reel holding up to 200 yards of 16–20 lb B.S. monofilament nylon. On the end of this mainline is tied a small swivel, and on the other end of the swivel a 3 ft leader of much lighter nylon. On the end of the leader is either a Stewart tackle (three hooks in tandem) or a single hook (see p. 439).

In our experience, few anglers have mastered the art of upstream worming for salmon. Most use a fixed-spool reel, unaware of the problems involved. As we have witnessed on numerous occasions, a salmon frequently touches a worm a number of times before properly taking it inside its mouth. It is when a fish is toying with a bait in this fashion that the advantage of the centre-pin reel becomes apparent. Time and time again the worm must cover exactly the same spot. This is extremely difficult to accomplish with anything but a reel which has the exact length of line already stripped off.

Cast from a position that is roughly at right angles to, or just above the lie you wish to cover. Drop the worm a sufficient distance upstream for it to sink within two or three inches of the bottom by the time it reaches the fish. This distance depends on the depth of water and strength of current.

Whenever possible dispense with extra weight. If the current is very strong, a swan shot or a twist or two of lead wire can be put on the leader about 18 inches above the worm. But *always use as little as you can.*

When a fish is lying in fast, shallow water and takes the worm opposite to or just below the rod, the Stewart tackle is the best. In quiet water towards the tail of a deep pool a fish will take as the worm floats slowly past or bumps gently round in front of it. Here, a single hook is preferable.

Tackles are very easy to make. Home-made worming tackles if properly tied are more reliable than any professional tackle we have seen. This is because the 'bought' tackle is made up with eyeless hooks. Even when the tackle is brand new an eyeless hook whipped to the leader is unsafe, the hook is liable to 'draw'. When the whipping on the hook shank becomes frayed the hook will certainly 'draw', and we have known more salmon lost for this reason than any other (except striking too quickly!). We recommend the use of eyed hooks tied with the Stewart-tackle knot shown on p. 418.

It is true that the Stewart is a sort of snap-tackle. *But* when the bait suddenly stops on its passage down stream, *don't jerk it.* It may have snagged, and a jerk may simply increase the hold. *Wait.* If it is a fish you will feel a slight 'grating' sensation. Tighten the moment the fish moves.

All the time the worm is fishing try to gauge exactly where it is and what it is doing. Guide it over or round rocks. (This is where a long rod is so useful.) If the worm is heading for an unavoidable snag, retrieve it and cast again.

Hold the line between the fingers of the non-casting hand, and learn to detect the difference between the touch of a rock and a salmon – which may 'nudge' the bait several times before actually taking it. *Always 'feel' a line with wetted fingers. Finger-tips are more sensitive wet than dry.* (A point which inexperienced coarse fishermen may profitably note. And fly fishermen, too, for that matter.)

Don't expect salmon to be lying behind rocks that are close to the surface or partly exposed. There is too much turbulence. Fish only lie behind rocks which have a smooth flow of water over them; even then they usually lie on top. Fish lie in front of rocks, beside rocks, or between rocks in a steady glide, seldom behind them.

Don't start by fishing the distant water. Always fish the lies close to your own bank before casting farther out.

The fish are lying in water which is two or three feet deep. Most of it will be wadeable. But keep out of the water as much as possible. Don't wade unless you are sure you can do so without disturbance. Upstream worming in fast shallows is quite different from fly fishing in deep runs and pools. In a pool, a fish disturbed by a wading angler will soon return to its lie. In a shallow run it will not.

Keep a supply of spare tackles in your pocket ready tied and wound on frames (see p. 360). If a tackle snags on the bottom, don't wade out to free it. Break it and tie on another. Tackles are expendable. You are bound to lose a lot in shallow, rocky water. But if you stumble about among the lies you will simply drive the fish away.

Don't be in too much of a hurry. Fish slowly and carefully. *You cannot over-fish a salmon lie – provided you fish properly.* Although you have covered a salmon a number of times unsuccessfully, it may take later in the day – if you haven't walked on top of it!

Presenting a Worm (1)

The angler stands just upstream of the lie and casts to B. The worm sinks as it washes down with the current between B and C. AC is shorter than AB, so that the angler must shorten line as the worm comes downstream, by drawing in with the non-casting hand over the forefinger of the hand holding the rod.

Note: If the angler stands too far upstream of the fish it is difficult to prevent drag. Too far downstream, and the worm will not precede the line.

Fig. 25.14. Presenting a worm (1).

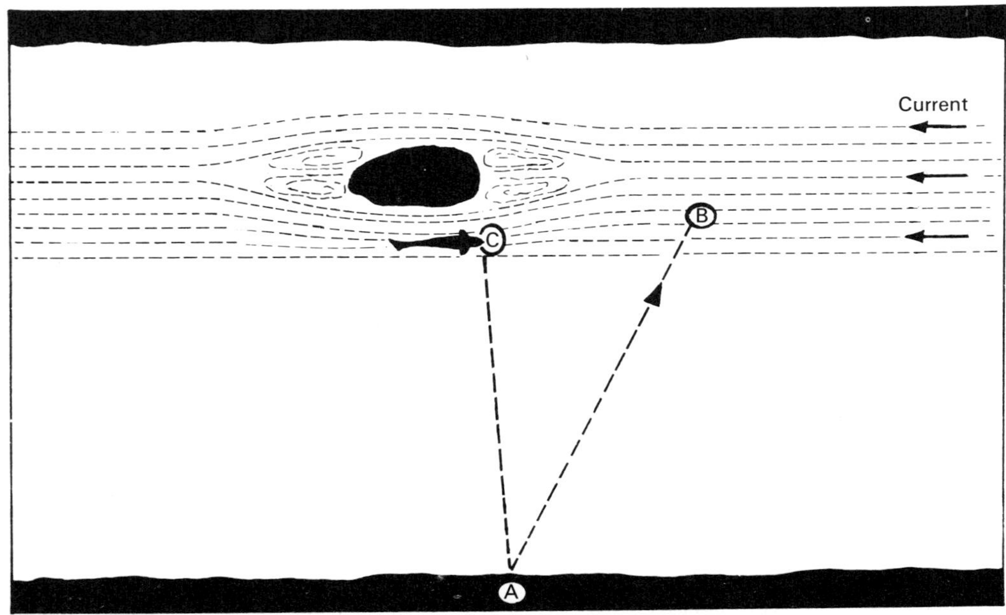

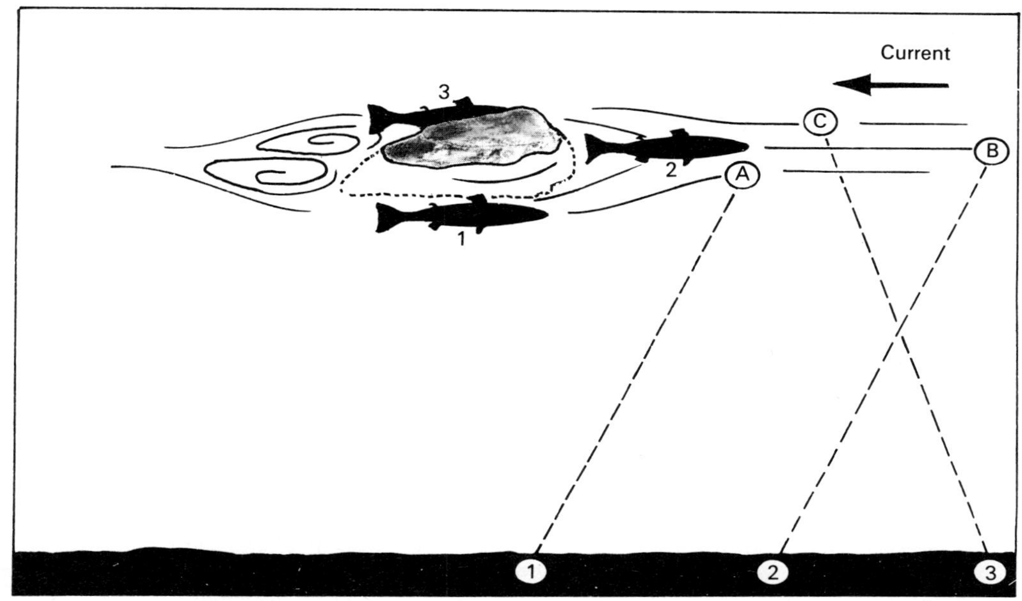

Fig. 25.15. Presenting a worm (2).

Presenting a Worm (2)

The order in which to fish three possible salmon lies by a rock.

1. Cast to point A for No. 1, the nearest fish, first. This operation, if unsuccessful, will not disturb the other lies.
2. Move upstream and fish for No. 2, by casting to point B.
3. No. 3 is an extremely difficult fish to catch – except from the opposite bank. Move still further upstream and cast *downstream* to point C., letting go some slack line. If the fish refuses the worm, guide the line over the rock by holding the rod at arm's length above your head. When fishing lies of this nature, a long, light rod is a great advantage.

Presenting a Worm (3)

Fig. 25.16 shows ten salmon lying in a stretch of fast, shallow, clear, broken water. The tops of the rocks are very close to or above the surface. None of the fish would be visible to an observer on the bank. Only by using his water-sense, by 'reading' the stretch, could an angler decide where the fish were lying.

Before starting to fish water of this sort, time should always be spent in careful examination: snags and probable lies being memorized.

Very seldom is such water fished straight down from top to bottom, or straight up from bottom to top. The angler should move

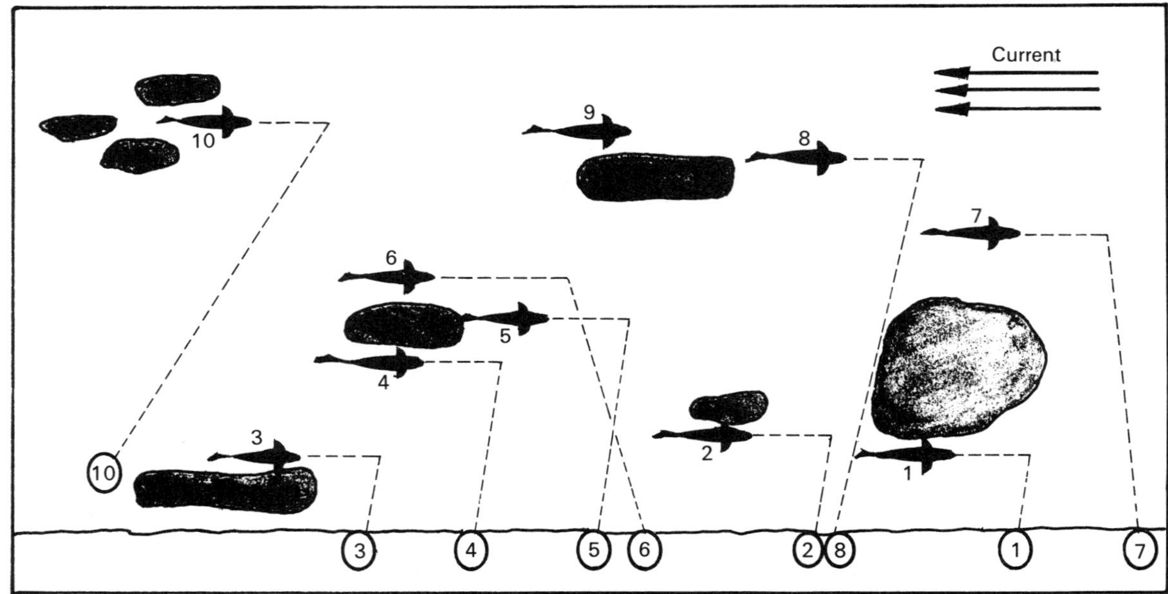

Fig. 25.16. Presenting a worm (3).

about, now up, now down, according to the particular lie he wishes to cover. The order in which the lies are fished is of the greatest importance.

In our imaginary piece of water, lies 1, 2 and 3 should be fished first.

Then lies 4, 5 and 6.

After this, the farther lies can be fished: 7 and 8.

The fish lying at 9 is virtually uncatchable (except from the opposite bank) unless the angler wades well in above lie 2. But if he does this he will certainly frighten away the fish lying at 1 and 2, which, if they have already refused the worm but remain undisturbed, may take later in the day. In addition, he is almost certain to get snagged on the long rock. This fish is best left alone.

There is, however, a good chance of covering 10 satisfactorily. It is now safe for the angler to wade, since he is well below the fish in lie 3. He can turn a long and difficult cast into a relatively easy one.

Of a number of salmon at any particular moment, only one or two (if any) may be *taking* fish. Obviously, the more fish the angler covers correctly, the more chance he has of covering a *taker*. Although every salmon refuses his worm the first time he fishes the water, he may very well hook one later in the day – *provided he has not frightened it out of its lie.*

Presenting a Worm (4)

A method of fishing the moving worm in

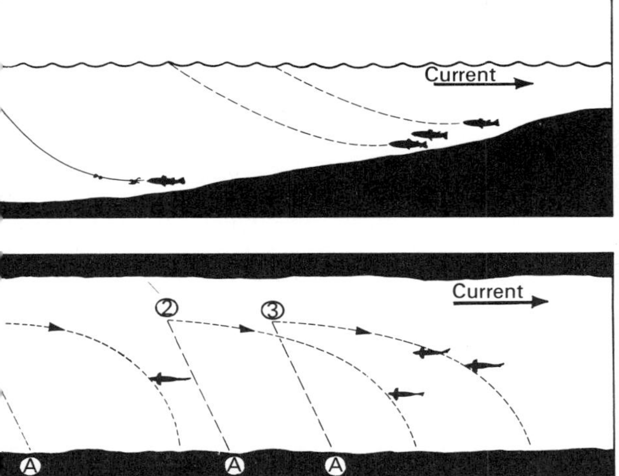

Fig. 25.17. Presenting a worm (4).

deep water is to cast well upstream with a swan-shot or twist or two of lead wire on the leader. The worm is allowed to sink, then to swing slowly round in front of the fish, just off the bottom. It can work well in a deep pool where fish are lying just in front of a steeply rising tail.

Salmon will sometimes nudge a worm more than once before actually taking it. It is essential that the angler is able to 'feel' the worm during every moment of the cast. As it comes downstream he must draw in line with the non-casting hand, letting it slip again at just the right speed as the worm goes past towards the tail of the pool.

This method of fishing looks easy and (by those who have not tried it) is often derided. It is, in fact, extremely difficult.

Tailing a salmon by hand. *The back of the angler's hand points towards the fish's head. Pressure is exerted by thumb and index finger only; the other fingers curl loosely round the tail.*

LOST AT THE GAFF

Unless you are a very experienced salmon fisherman do not carry a gaff.

To many fishermen a gaff is a vital piece of equipment; but it is not without good reason that the woeful cry: 'Lost at the gaff!' has become a cliché. The barbless steel hook is an uncertain instrument and many are the fish that would be landed except for its inexpert use.

A gaff is of value in places where it is impossible to beach a fish or bring its nose in close to the side; where a strong back-eddy and a high bank make tailing difficult; when fishing from a boat; or when the line is caught on some obstruction and the fish, although beaten, cannot be brought closer to hand. And in almost every case a large net is preferable.

Why violate a fish of such beauty by sticking a meat hook into it? Why run the risk of losing it by trying to land it in this uncivilized manner? The time to approach a salmon and take it from the water is when it is lying on its side, exhausted. If a gaff is to be used that is the time to use it, not before. But if the fish is beaten, such treatment is seldom necessary. Nature has equipped the salmon with a tail by which it may be lifted, and to land a fish by hand is in every way more satisfactory. The fish is undamaged, and any danger of the leader being cut by a hasty gaff stroke is avoided. But of course there is more to it than that.

The use of the hand demands that a salmon is lying beaten and ready to land. Only too often the possession of a gaff lures a fisherman into the fatal error of trying to land his fish too quickly. As soon as the salmon is reachable some misguided helper, or the angler himself, rushes forward with the gaff and slashes at it. This has one of three results:

1. He misses the fish and breaks the leader.
2. The fish sees him and dashes away in alarm, thus prolonging the fight and giving itself more time to get rid of the hook.
3. He gaffs and lands the fish. This is, perhaps, the worst of all, for it leaves a novice with an entirely erroneous impression of how a fish should be landed, and encourages him to try this unhappy trick again.

Sometimes when a fish swings into the side shortly after being hooked the angler is tempted to try to gaff it out at once. But such an incautious procedure results in many more losses than gains. It should be tried only in emergency.

There are two golden rules when playing a salmon (which, for that matter, apply to all other species): *never let it see you*, and *never force it*. Keep well away from the water and *don't* try to bring the fish in too soon. Sometimes a fish allows itself to be brought close in during the initial stages of the fight. This apparent submission is quite usual and may be described as the danger time. At this moment, far from lunging at the fish with a gaff, you should take special precaution to remain out of sight. The fish is only dimly aware of what is happening, but once it sees you and becomes frightened it will resist to the limit of its strength. There are exceptions, of course, but a frightened fish will fight far longer than the fish that never sees the fisherman. Provided they have not been scared by the sight of the angler, many salmon abandon the struggle quite quickly–especially if they have been treated to a 'walking' session up a pool. (See p. 213.)

Wherever there is a place convenient for beaching a salmon no landing tackle of any sort is necessary. The exact landing spot is selected before fishing starts. When the salmon is beaten it is drawn ashore at this place–not by reeling in, but by walking backwards.

When the fish is lying on its side with its head aground the fight is ended and you can relax. The fish will not move again. To close matters, approach the salmon from down stream, reeling in as you go. Then, keeping a good length of line out by holding the rod at arm's length inshore, take the wrist of the tail firmly with thumb and forefinger, the back of the hand uppermost and pointing towards the head. First, push the fish forward up the shore clear of the water, then pick it up. It is a very simple operation.

STEALTH

VIATOR: . . . May a man take a stool and sit down on the ground by you?

PISCATOR: Yea, so that you sit not over near the water.

VIATOR: Nay, I trow, I will sit far enough off for slipping in.

PISCATOR: I do not mean therefor, but I would not have you sit so that the fish may see either your shadow, your face, or any part of you.

VIATOR: And why? Are they so quick of sight?

PISCATOR: Look, what they lack in hearing, it is supplied into them in seeing chiefly . . .

VIATOR: Well, now I am set, may I then talk and not hinder your fishing?

PISCATOR: Spare not, but not too loud.

VIATOR: Do the fish then hear?

PISCATOR: No, you may talk, whoop, or hallo and never stir them, but I would not gladly by your loud talking that either some bungler, idle person, or jester might resort unto us . . .

This exerpt from *The Arte of Angling* (1577) shows Piscator to be an angler of rare perception. This is the second known angling book to be published in the English language (following only Dame Juliana Berners's *A Treatyse of Fysshynge wyth an Angle*, 1496). The author is unknown.

In spite of the natural reluctance of salmon and sea-trout to take a lure, failure is by no means always the fault of the fish. Many a fisherman would improve his catch if he cultivated a more stealthy approach.

Thumping along against the skyline; rattling about on rocks in nailed waders; a noisy descent of a shingle bank; poking the bottom with an iron-shod wading staff; slashing the water of a smooth pool tail by unskilful (and sometimes unnecessary) mending of the line; fishing with sun or moon behind him, so that his shadow and the shadow of the rod precedes him down a pool . . . none of this is likely to be *helpful*.

Casting is often held to be the most important aspect of fly-fishing. It is not.

Ian Blagburn and Barrie Welham with a fine fresh-run twenty pounder from the Stanley Water, River Tay (Photograph: G.T. Sports Pictures).

Good casting is important, but more important is *stealth*.

The effect of a faulty approach to the sport of fishing is twofold:

1. It affects the fish; so that no matter how skilfully a fly is cast, no fish are going to take it. They have fled.
2. It affects the fisherman. Anyone behaving in such an insensitive manner is unlikely to recognize and interpret the subtle signals constantly relayed by wind, weather, light, temperature and water: signals he should be relying on to tell him when to change tackle or method.

The novice who wants to become a good fisherman should study the basic elements of good hunting. When he has learned to think and act like a hunter he will no longer worry about being a good fisherman. He will already have become one.

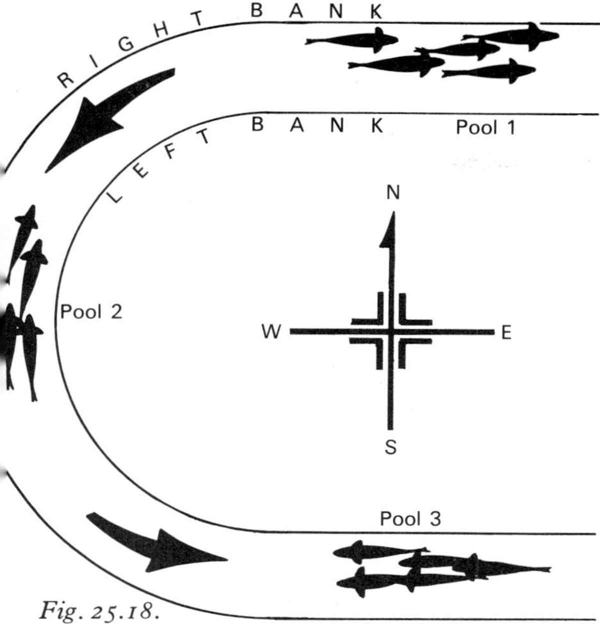

Fig. 25.18.

Avoidance of Shadow

Fish are frightened by the sudden movement of shadow across the water. When the sun is behind the angler, shadow is thrown by the angler himself or the movement of his rod.

In Fig. 25.18, a salmon fisherman – who is allowed to fish from the left bank only – has three pools at his disposal during a day's fishing. In order to minimize the risk of causing shadow, he should start in the morning on pool 3 – while the sun moves from east to south. Then, at mid-day and during the afternoon, when the sun is moving from south to west, he should fish pool 2. In the evening, with the sun in the west, he can move on to pool 1.

The sea-trout night fly-fisherman should make a similar approach during conditions of bright moonlight.

Note: Almost always, careful wading causes less disturbance than casting from a high bank.

'WALKING' A FISH

It is advisable to 'walk' a fish, whether salmon or trout, whenever you are in a position to do so. It takes the heart out of the fish and, by reducing his resistance, shortens the fight. 'Walking' can sometimes prevent a fish from running into a weed bed or snag; more particularly it is a method of preventing a fish from rejoining and scaring other members of a shoal. Fish have an extremely sensitive sense of smell. Odours from the skin of an injured fish have been known to produce a fright reaction among a shoal.

The moment the fish is hooked, turn away and begin to walk upstream. The rod is held absolutely steady with the butt set firmly against the body, the point at an angle of about 45 degrees to the water and at right angles to the river. The fish is *not* towed up the pool. No attempt is made to pull him along, or indeed to bully him in any way. You are not indulging in a trial of strength but the art of gentle persuasion. You do not haul, or jerk, or allow the rod to vibrate, or hold the line tightly against the rod. At the first gentle pressure the fish either comes with you or he doesn't. If your move is made soon enough he usually *does*, but there is no question of trying to force him.

When he comes forward his weight on the line is scarcely felt, for he swims steadily upstream, urged on by the slight belly of line which forms between him and the rod, and only the drag of the line through the water is felt.

Sometimes you may think the fish has escaped, and in sudden despair tighten the line too savagely. This has disastrous results: he will go tearing off, and to interfere with such a run is to invite a breakage.

If a steady but unhurried progress is maintained upstream, the fish will follow quietly. He will often, in fact, gain ground, so that by the time a previously selected landing place is reached, he is somewhere out in the middle of the river and conveniently opposite the rod. You are now in the best place for playing the fish and bringing matters to a conclusion. Indeed, if he has been 'walked' far, most of the playing has been done.

After a 'walking' session a fish is not usually inclined to run far. Stay where you are and keep well back from the water. If there is a background of bank and foliage behind you so much the better.

The flash of his flank will signal defeat. Sink your landing net, when the fish turns on its side shorten line and draw him firmly over the net with one steady movement.

In the case of a big fish hooked on light tackle, it frequently pays to walk him up and down a section of river bank a number of times. It is surprising how docile he will become and, *provided he doesn't see you*, how easily he can be landed.

In still water a big fish can (so to speak) be 'walked' by rowing the boat gently and steadily in one direction.

Remember: A fish cannot be 'walked' if:

1. You try to bully it.
2. It *sees* you.

When playing a fish, *keep out of sight*. The sight of a human being is very frightening. A fish that never sees the angler can be landed in half the time.

Solway 'Haaf' netting.

GHILLIES

The ghillie, as a type, reminds us of the little girl with the curl. When he is good he is very, very good, but when he is bad . . .

He is not often very, very good. After all, why should he be? The ghillie's job is no holier than any other trade and only a naïve angler would consider his engagement of a ghillie an automatic key to success. Nevertheless, whatever a ghillie's qualifications for the job, at modern rates he is an expensive item on the salmon fisherman's account. The rate is fairly standard, but although there is little variation in his cost there is considerable variation in his value. At his best he is priceless. At his worst he is a pest. A word or two about him may be helpful.

If on a beat where wading is necessary, he turns up in hob-nailed boots carrying only his lunch, despatch him at once for his waders. You have not employed him to sit idly on the bank (as so many of them do) while you stumble about in strange water by yourself. He should arrive in body waders – or bring them with him – ready to wade at your elbow if you require him to do so. And if you are sensible you will.

To wade beside you is the duty of any ghillie worth the name. But the true value of a *good* ghillie is not merely his willingness to wade or shoulder your bag or row the boat, it is his ability to give good advice; the advice of an expert who knows his water and something about the behaviour of the fish it holds.

Besides having a thorough knowledge of the contours of the river bottom, this paragon will know the way of the river itself with its swirls and eddies, and the effect these will have on your lure. He will know every salmon lie in the beat and how these lies alter according to the height of water. It is this expert knowledge that (hopefully) you pay for when you employ him. And if he really *does* know his stuff you should pay him well. Quite simply, it is a good investment.

In all probability you will have laid out a considerable sum of money for your salmon beat. If you have a good ghillie who is also a happy ghillie you will know that, no matter how unhelpful the conditions, *all the time you are fishing* you are giving yourself the best chance of hooking a salmon, because you will be presenting your lure in the way most likely to hook it in the lies most likely to hold it.

You will not often meet a very good ghillie. If you ever do, grapple him to your heart with hoops of gold – and treasure what he says, for it is all too seldom heard.

Contrary to general belief, it is *not* the ghillie's job to set up your tackle and tie on your lure. *Always* do this for yourself. Only by doing so will you be sure that the reel is firmly attached; the line correctly threaded, and the lure securely tied. Similarly, you should seldom permit your ghillie to land a fish for you. Again, *do it yourself*. All too frequently does the eager but inexperienced helper – with gaff extended – crane forward at the water's edge, ready to swipe at the earliest opportunity.

The good ghillie can, of course, perform all of these elementary tasks as well as any angler and better than most. But in fairness to him, as well as yourself, you should be responsible for landing your own fish and setting up your own tackle. Then, if a knot slips, or the reel drops off in the heat of action while a fish is running, or a hasty gaff stroke breaks the leader . . . you have only yourself to blame. It is better that way.

The 'Dee' otter.

THE 'DEE' OTTER

This boon to the salmon fisherman who spins for his fish and leaves a small fortune in spinners on the river bottom each season, was developed by Willie Hogg of Castle Douglas. Particularly keen on sea-trout and salmon fishing, Hogg was a fine all-round angler who fished the Kirkcudbrightshire Dee with great success. In our opinion, the 'Dee' otter is the best ever produced. As the pictures show, it is very simple, and easily made.

The Dee otter consists of a wooden disc, with a slit in it, and two lead weights. A thick rubber band fits inside the slit. When putting it on the line to free a snagged spinner, the rubber band is slipped along the edge of the wooden disc. The line can then pass along the slit (between the two lead weights) into the centre hole (see top picture).

The rubber band is then replaced so that the otter is prevented from coming off the line – which can now run freely through the hole (see bottom picture).

The rod is raised. The otter slides down the line into the river. It is worked out into the current by pulling on the line from slightly upstream of the snagged spinner.

Poaching implements. Salmon leisters from the Border country.

Below: *Curiously enough, an instrument remarkably like a leister – the* bâton fourchie – *was used in otter hunting during medieval times. Our illustration is from* Livre de Chasse, *most famous of all hunting treatises, written by Gaston de Foix, a fourteenth century feudal lord of the Pyrenees. The following passage comes from* Sport in Art *(second edition, 1920) by W. A. Baillie-Grohman.*

'Otter-hunting, as Gaston writes, required "Great Mastery", it required "lyners" and four experienced huntsmen, and he considered that it was a very fine chase . . . the bâton fourchie, *as we see, carried still three iron prongs, while in later centuries the two-pronged iron came into use.'*

Gaston de Foix's exploits were recorded by the medieval chronicler Jean Froissart; he died, it seems, in 1391 of apoplexy after a day-long bear hunt.

Cy apres deuise comment on doit chacier et prendre la loutre.

FISHING MANNERS

No matter whether you are fishing fly or spinner, *don't* go in half way down a pool, look round at the angler above in feigned surprise and say: 'Oh, sorry! Didn't see you. You don't mind if I have a dip in, now I'm here, do you?'

This doesn't fool anybody.

The fisherman above *does* mind, whatever he may say. Having started first he has the right to fish down the pool first. If you want to fish it too, wait either until he has fished it out, or until he gives you the nod to start.

And again, if you are fishing spinner from one bank with a fisherman opposite fishing fly, wait for him to get a reasonable distance down the pool. He will find it very disconcerting to have your piece of ironmongery hooking his line or flying round his ears. If his fly hooked you in the back of the neck you would be the first to whine – but he can't cast as far across the river as you can.

You may think we exaggerate. We don't. On much ticket and association water today, fishing manners are appalling. Plop, plop, plop – in go those bloody spinners not a yard away; and fly fishermen, pushing in ahead without even as much as 'By your leave'!

And while we are on the subject of thoughtless and selfish behaviour, who are the faceless anglers who leave the waterside littered with empty tins, beer bottles, plastic bags, food wrappings and cigarette cartons? It is commonplace to find yards of discarded nylon draped along river banks – an enduring threat to wildlife (see p. 362). *Someone* must leave it there. But who? And come to that, who defecates at the riverside – without even the courtesy of interment?

COOKING THE SALMON

Fresh Salmon Steaks

1 salmon 6–12 lb
Chopped parsley
Unsalted butter
Olive oil, 1 teaspoonful per steak
Slices of cucumber in the skin
Salt and black pepper

Cut the salmon into steaks 1¼–1½ inches thick.
Sprinkle with salt and pepper.
Melt butter.
Add steaks and simmer gently.
Turn steaks after about five minutes (or when slightly brown).
Place steaks on a hot dish.
Clean pan. Fry the sliced cucumber in fresh butter. Pour over the steaks.
Note: Sliced cucumber in vinegar or soured cream is delicious with most salmon dishes.

Salmon Kedgeree

1 lb poached salmon
¼ lb rice
4 tablespoonsful butter
2 hard-boiled eggs
Salted water
Salt and black pepper
½ pint hot cream sauce

Cook rice in boiling salted water until tender.
Drain and keep warm.
Flake fish, removing bones and skin.
Melt butter in saucepan; add fish and sauté gently.

Add $\frac{1}{4}$ pint fresh cream to 1 pint Bechamel Sauce and bring to boiling point. Add a few drops of lemon juice.

Finely chop whites of hard-boiled eggs and combine with rice and fish. Season to taste with salt and black pepper. Fold in hot cream sauce. Serve with yolks of hard-boiled eggs, pressed through a sieve or finely chopped, sprinkled over the top.

Poached Salmon

Clean fish and place in a fish kettle with salt and a dash of vinegar or a squeeze of lemon juice.

Cover with boiling water and simmer until the flesh can be separated easily from the bone (approximately 10 minutes per lb).

If the fish is to be eaten hot, drain and serve with shrimp sauce, sliced cucumber and brown bread and butter.

If it is to be eaten cold, leave it in the liquor. Serve with mayonnaise, lemon and salad.

Traditional Dunkeld whisky pots.

26 · The Three-Spined Stickleback

Gasterosteus aculeatus

The three-spined stickleback, or tiddler, is one of the most widespread, prolific and (behaviourally) most interesting of all North European freshwater fishes. Although some populations live and breed wholly in freshwater, others are anadromous – breeding in freshwater, migrating to sea, and then returning to freshwater to spawn. Yet others are wholly marine. (Its relative, the ten-spined stickleback (*Gasterosteus pungitius*), is much less tolerant of salinity.)

Having studied this fascinating little fish both in Britain and on the Continent, we are tempted to write at length about it. We desist, since the subject is of little direct interest to the angler, but encourage anyone interested in fish behaviour to pursue the matter for himself.

Recommended reading: *Territory in the Three-Spined Stickleback (Gasterosteus aculeatus L.) An Experimental Study in Intraspecific Competition*, J. van den Assem: Leiden, E. J. Brill (1967). Also, the appropriate passages in *Animal Behaviour*, Niko Tinbergen: Life Nature Library (1965).

Photograph: Oxford Scientific Films.

27 · The Tench

Tinca tinca

A cork float with a crimson tip is very necessary to proper angling for tench; it supplies the one touch of colour that is wanting in the landscape and it is a satisfying thing to look upon. A severely practical mind might argue that it is as visible to the fish as to the fisherman, and might suggest a fragment of porcupine quill as being less ostentatious, but however one regards it, tench fishing is a lengthy occupation, and must be approached with leisurely mind. The sordid yearning for bites should not be put in the balance against artistic effect. Besides, it may be said of tench more emphatically than of most other fish; if they are going to feed they are and if they are not, they most certainly are not. As a rule they are not, and their feelings are therefore not so important as the angler's. In this canal at any rate, their feelings receive but the scantiest consideration. Evening by evening the villagers come forth, each armed with a beanpole to which is attached a stout window cord, the bung of a beer cask, and a huge hook on the stoutest gimp. A lobworm is affixed to the hook and flung with much force and splashing into some little opening among the weeds, where it remains until night draws down her veil. The villagers sit in a contemplative row under this ancient grey wall, which once enclosed a grange fortressed against unquiet times. But now all is peace, and the cooing of doves in the garden trees has replaced the clash of arms. About once a week the villagers have a bite; a beanpole is lifted by stalwart arms, and a two-pound tench is summarily brought to the bank; but for the most part evening's solemn stillness is undisturbed by rude conflict. This is not surprising. Apart from the uncompromising nature of the tackle, there are other reasons against success. The canal is here one solid mass of weed. No barge has passed this way for years, and so there is no object in keeping the channel clear in the summer. If the angler wishes to fish, he must make a clear space for himself with the end of his beanpole. Hence it comes that the villagers angle in two feet of water not more than six feet away from the bank, while the tench live secure out of reach.

H. T. SHERINGHAM, *An Angler's Hours* (1905).

This 11 lb 9¼ oz tench was found in Colonel Thornton's lake at Thornville Royal, Yorkshire, when the lake was drained in 1801. It measured 2 ft 9 in. from eye to fork and had a girth of 27 in. A diseased tench weighing 12 lb 8 oz was caught by R. Blaber in the river Kennet in 1951. This fish was suffering from dropsy and would have weighed much less had it been in good health.

The tench is another member of the Carp family, and like the carp has a wide distribution in Asia, Europe and Britain – apart from Scotland and the Cornish Peninsula.

Although tench are pre-eminently a fish of still waters, Alwyne Wheeler is right when he describes them as occurring occasionally 'in the lower reaches of rivers, most often in backwaters'. Even in the Test – because of its fast current a most un-characteristic tench water – they are to be found in a backwater below Romsey.

Dr J. J. Manley states in *Fish and Fishing* (1877) that he netted five tench averaging over 5 lb from a backwater in the lower reaches of a very fast flowing river – the Hampshire Avon.

Although the colour of tench varies much with the locality, green is the characteristic colour. An exotic variety of tench, the golden tench, occasionally reported in the angling press, may be descendants of golden tench successfully bred and distributed by Mr Burr, of Aldermaston Park, Reading, from a pair given to him by Frank Buckland in 1862.

Tench usually spawn in June, although the necessary combination of ripeness, and an optimum spawning temperature of 64°F, may advance or retard the spawning act by a month or more. The fecundity of tench is prodigious. According to Gunther, 297,000 eggs have been taken from one female.

'A tenche is a good fysshe.' Prior to this statement, which appeared with some notes of tench fishing in *A Treatyse of Fysshynge*

A fine Lincolnshire tench caught by F. J. Taylor. It weighed 5½ lb (3 lb short of the British rod-caught record of 8 lb 8 oz, caught by M. Foode in the Leicester canal in 1950).

wyth an Angle (1496), the tench was rarely mentioned by the ancients. This omission, according to Couch in *British Fishes* (1862–5), is due to its lack of esteem as a table fish; nevertheless, to anglers and non-anglers alike, the tench is famous for its role as physician to other fishes – especially to the pike. Until recently, generations of anglers believed that a tench had the power to heal wounded fish – if they rubbed against its slime or if it licked or sucked their wounds. Walton wrote: 'The tyrant pike will not be a wolf to his physician, but forbears to devour him though he be never so hungry.' Here, Walton was wrong (see p. 131). But that tench are extremely hardy fish is undoubtedly true; that they escape the ravages of the commoner fish diseases like fungus and fin rot is also probable.

As J. J. Manley observed:

It has long been said that the tench, unlike other fish, is free from liability to all diseases; and certainly when carefully observing the fresh-water fish at the Westminster Aquarium soon after it was opened, I noticed that tench alone seemed perfectly free from that unnatural coating of slimy excrescence which more or less affected the other fish, and so sorely puzzled the ichthyologists of the Aquarium. But whether this freedom from disease, presuming the fact established, is to be attributed to the natural slime on the tench, and whether this really has the healing virtue so long credited to it, may be questioned.

That another species of fish, namely the perch, has been seen to rub itself against the tench is beyond question. Dr Tate Regan, Britain's most famous ichthyologist, wrote in *British Freshwater Fishes* (1911):

My friend, the late Dr Bowdler Sharpe, told me

A recent find of a bag of tench caught in low-water conditions by James Bendall from Elstree Reservoir in 1874 perfectly illustrates J. J. Manley's remarks (p. 225). This beautiful case of fish – now the property of F.B. – was thrown out by the brewers when the famous Fisheries Inn beside Elstree Reservoir was recently rebuilt. Such important ornaments of the history of angling – and there are many in Britain today – should be preserved in a national sporting museum.

that one day in May he stood on the bridge over the lake at Avington and watched a large Tench lying in the water below; a shoal of Perch swam up and lay round and above the Tench and appeared to be rubbing against him; on being disturbed they swam back under the bridge, but soon repaired again to the Tench and repeated this manoeuvre several times. The meaning of this is obscure, but there can be little doubt that observation of similar incidents has led to belief in the healing powers of the Tench.

Tench appear to be resistant to quite severe pollution, and deoxygenation. Indeed it is quite probable that tench are the last fish to die whenever these diabolical twins of human ingenuity intensify their choking grasp. The largest tench that F. B. has ever seen, fish of between 8 and 10 lb, were on Mr Pierrepoint Morgan's estate near Watford. These were the progeny of tench that had survived a wartime pollution of the upper Colne which killed all other species of fish. Later, in 1953, the estate keeper picked up an $8\frac{1}{2}$ lb tench which had grounded itself in some shallows.

Still-water tench fishing is essentially a summer activity; although when the weather is mild, it is sometimes enjoyed during late autumn and winter in sluggish rivers.

According to most authors tench hibernate during periods of cold weather by burying themselves in the mud; but proof of this hibernating behaviour is still wanting.

Certainly tench unlike most other fish can survive in wet mud during periods of drought. John Bickerdyke in *The Book of The All-Round Angler*, (1888) gives a personal experience:

In my youthful days I used to fish a small farm horse-pond, which, though shallow and muddy, contained many tench over 1 lb in weight. One summer the pond all but dried up, and some gypsies nearly cleared it of tench by means of hay rakes, literally raking the fish out of the mud.

This ability to endure droughts is a very useful survival characteristic for a species inhabiting outlying ponds and lakes where the possibility of reinforcement from river-colonies is remote.

Traditionally the best times to fish for tench are early morning and late evening. F. B. has noticed that tench fishing improves considerably when the water level is low – a condition that sometimes ruins sport with other fishes. In the 1950s he caught exceptionally good bags of tench of a beautiful golden olive colour from Elstree reservoir, when the water level was very low; but when water levels were normal he often fished a season through without catching a single tench. Similar behaviour by Elstree tench was noticed by J. J. Manley in the 1870s when he wrote: '. . . and a year or two ago, when the water was very low at Elstree Reservoir, a large number were taken of between 3 lb and 4 lb.'

BAITS

Tench are attracted by the same variety of baits as most other members of the carp family. For the *best* bait we would be hard put to choose between breadflake, crust, marshworms and maggots. Walton reckoned that the tench: '. . . inclines very much to any paste with which tar is mixt'. R. B. Marston, famous editor of *The Fishing Gazette*, once had a very good day's fishing from a freshly-tarred punt. He reported: 'I felt certain then that the tench had been attracted to the spot by fresh tar, and proved it on other occasions, not invariably, but often enough to feel sure that there was no doubt about it.' The Rev. W. B. Daniel felt the same:

The only aid the Compiler has ever experienced from any application *whatever* to the bait, has been by dipping the worm in *Tar* when fishing for Tench.

But now, a dissenter.

A worm well scour'd without the help of stinking tar,
That was her bait and that was best by far,
Tho to my cost I've try'd and certain know,
That Tarr's strong stench hath little here to do,
But kill the worm, but I confess that fishes smell,
Or that my apprehension is but ill,
For I have seen them to my flote and Lead repair,
And gently touch them with insulting care.

JOHN WHITNEY. *The Genteel Recreation: or, the Pleasure of Angling* (1700).

A Tenche is a good fyssh: and heelith all manere of other fysshe that ben hurte yf they maye come to hym. He is the most parte of the yere in the mudde. And he styryth moost in Iune and Iuly: and in other seasons but lytyll. He is an evyll byter. His Baytes ben thyse. For all the yere browne breede tostyd with hony in lyknesse of a butteryd loof: and the grete redde worme. And as for cheyf take the blacke blood in the herte of a shepe and floure and hony. And tempre theym all togyder somdeale softer than paast: and annoynt therwyth the redde worme: bothe for this fysshe and for other. And they woll byte muche the better therat at all tymes.
DAME JULIANA BERNERS, *A Treatyse of Fysshynge wyth an Angle* (1496).

Although groundbaiting is an important aspect of successful tench fishing, *heavy* groundbaiting is not conducive to good sport. The successful tench angler usually prepares his swim gradually over several days before he attempts to fish. H. T. Sheringham put it all in a nutshell: 'The longer and more regularly you bait a pitch before actually fishing it, the more likely are you to catch something when you do begin'. Most tench swims are in or close to weeds. In very weedy water it is necessary to clear a patch, or patches, about 4 yards square.

The best methods for catching tench – as with all fish – depend to a great extent on the conditions found at the waterside. Ledgering is good providing the angler uses tackle of suitable strength. The tench is a powerful fish and usually found close to tackle-breaking weeds. Only a beginner or a fool boasts to his friends when he gets broken by a fish. Good anglers are ashamed of such incompetence.

When float fishing is appropriate the 'lift' method (p. 450) is usually the most effective. It is a method particularly suited to swims that are within easy reach of the bank. Tench frequently advertise their presence in a groundbaited swim by releasing a series of tiny bubbles.

In *Tench* (1971), Fred J. Taylor describes how he and his brothers developed this method of fishing for tench:

'The lift method, as we began to call it, became our basic tench-fishing rig. We soon learned that it was essential to place the rod in a rest after the line was tightened up and to *leave* it there. We fell into the trap of picking up the rod in readiness to strike at the first sign of a 'touch' many times in the beginning, but we found that it was fatal to do so. The moment the rod was taken up, the float keeled over and the rig became ineffective. We had to discipline ourselves to pick up the rod and strike in one continuous movement. We had to practise, practise, practise, but we were soon able to do it blindfold or without taking our eyes off the float. At times one of us would be otherwise occupied and looking somewhere else when the other would simply say "strike!" Without looking or checking we grabbed the rod, struck and caught many fish by word of command . . . !

'We have our few inches of peacock quill attached at the bottom end only to the reel line by a wide tight-fitting float cap.

7 lb tench one-time equal record – caught by the Rev. E. C. Alston from Ringmere at Wretham, Norfolk, on 8th July 1933.

'What do we mean by wide?

'About three eighths of an inch.

'What do we mean by tight fitting?

'So tight that to slide the float up or down the line without first wetting it will cause enough heat literally to melt the line and break it!

'Why does it have to be so tight?

'Because the float setting in lift-method fishing is critical and continual striking tends to pull the line through a loose-fitting float cap and alter the depth.

'How is a lift float tackle set?

'So that the float lies flat while the shot remains on the bottom but cocks nicely as the tackle is drawn taut. This means that the float has to be set a little deeper than the water and the simplest and undoubtedly the most accurate way of doing this is to decide on the size of shot to be used first and trim the float accordingly. With all other float-fishing methods the shot is chosen to suit the float. With the lift method the float is trimmed to suit the shot.

'How is it trimmed?

'With a sharp knife, or better still, scissors, a little at a time, until the weight of the shot causes it to sink slowly.

'Why does it have to sink?

'Because this is the only way you can get a *correct* depth setting in a water where the bottom varies. If the tackle is set too shallow the float will be pulled under and should be slid up until it lies flat on the surface. If it does not cock as soon as the tackle is tightened, the setting is too deep and the float must be lowered. The difference between too deep and too shallow is not a big one but the rig will fish so much better if it is correctly adjusted.

'In the summerhouse swim we often found ourselves chasing bubbles. That is to say the tench bubbles appeared on the surface here, there and everywhere in the swim at different times. Often, to drop a bait in the middle of a patch of bubbles, meant the catching of a fish, but it was important that we should have the depth setting correct each time because a different line of cast often meant that we were fishing in water a few inches deeper or shallower than previously. The sinking lift-float soon gave us the necessary information regarding depth and the rig was quickly adjusted to suit the new conditions.

'For the greater part of the time it was sufficient to set the shot about two inches from the hook and to strike immediately the float lay flat, but there were times when it was necessary to use a little more finesse. It was sometimes essential to set the shot only one inch from the hook and to make the strike while the float was actually in the process of lifting in the water. When you consider, as I have already described, that the rod was never held, but always remained in rests, and that the rod had to be picked up and the strike made during that brief split second, it will be seen that our reflexes became highly developed.'

FRED J. TAYLOR, *Tench*, Macdonald (1971).

They are a firm and good fish to eat;
some cooks stew them in wine, but they
are by no means bad with parsley and
butter. I have seen several tench from six to
eight pounds weight; but there is no great
value set on them here; and in summer a
large one may be had for two or three
pence.

O'GORMAN, *The Practice of Angling*
(Vol. 2, 1845).

COOKING THE TENCH

For the table the tench seems an unlikely fish. But not to the indomitable Michel Duborgel. Here are two recipes from *La Pêche et les Poissons de Rivière*.

Tench à la Poulette

1 tench
½ litre white wine
1 oz flour
2 oz butter
Bouquet garni
Salt and pepper

Cook the cleaned fish in court bouillon and remove the skin. Cut into small pieces. Make a roux with the butter and flour and add the wine. Let this cook for 10 minutes, gently stirring with a wooden spoon. Add the pieces of fish, the bouquet garni, and the seasoning, and let it simmer gently for 10 minutes more. Then blend into this, two beaten egg yolks. Remove the bouquet garni. Garnish with chopped parsley and serve hot.

Stuffed Tench

1 tench
Breadcrumbs
Hardboiled egg
White wine
Chopped parsley
Chopped mushrooms

Split and clean the fish and stuff with a mixture of mushroom, egg, breadcrumbs and parsley. Place in a fireproof dish and cook in oven for 30 minutes, basting frequently with white wine.

28 · The Trout

I state this solemnly. I have never had quite that hushed feeling about the trout anywhere else. And we all felt it. Then one night there was a terrific strike, my rod bent in the dark; it bent, it bent, it bent. . . For you could not allow the fish to run into the rapids immediately below. And then it straightened out. The line came back empty. The fly was gone. I climbed up the bank by the church with the feeling that I was not meant to catch any more fish below the feet of St. Christopher painted on its walls.

I never did.

NEGLEY FARSON, *Going Fishing* (1942).

16 lb 1 oz brown trout taken from Lough Mask by the late William Keal in May 1971.

Brown trout, 12½ lb. This magnificent fish is the largest trout ever taken by a bank angler on fly from Lough Corrib. It was caught by Colonel S. H. Crow, at Oughterard on a Peter Ross in June, 1939, during weather conditions too dangerous for boats to venture out.

28a · The Brown Trout

Salmo trutta fario

Note: It was once the custom to refer to the brown trout as: *Salmo fario*, and the sea-trout as: *Salmo trutta*. This (although seemingly unscientific) had the merit of clarity. Today, on the grounds that there is no discernible physiological difference, taxonomists classify both brown trout and sea-trout as *Salmo trutta*. This is a case of putting bones before behaviour which, although satisfying to the scientist, is irritating to the angler. Although there may be no difference in the way non-migratory and migratory trout are built, there is an enormous difference in the way they behave. This difference in behaviour is of paramount importance, and it demands separate identification. Above all else, it is essential that a writer should make his meaning clear. To discuss the behaviour of a trout (*Salmo trutta*) meaning either brown trout or sea-trout or both, is absurd. With a respect for science, but a greater respect for clarity of expression, we shall use the following classifications:

Brown trout: *Salmo trutta fario*.
Sea-trout: *Salmo trutta trutta*.

We recommend other angling writers to do the same. It will avoid much confusion.

The brown trout (*Salmo trutta fario*) is found almost everywhere. Indigenous to Europe, North Africa and North West Asia, it has been successfully introduced into most outposts of civilization, including Australia, New Zealand, Tasmania, Middle and South Africa, India, North and South America, and Vancouver Island. The criteria necessary for its survival (apart from an adequate food supply) are suitable conditions of water temperature and oxygenation.

Like all its close relatives in the sub-order

of fishes known as the Salmonoidei it possesses seven characteristic taxonomic features. The only two which need concern us here are those familiar to all trout fishermen: the adipose fin, and the pyloric caeca – those worm-like appendages attached to the gut, which help to secrete digestive juices. For the adipose fin no particular function is known.

Salmo trutta fario has such a variation of size and colour that one eminent 19th-century ichthyologist described ten different species in Britain alone. This multiplicity of species is now discredited. A pity in a way, since they had such lovely names: for instance, *Salmo orcadensis* (the Orkney sea-trout); *Salmo ferox* (the great lake trout); *Salmo stomachicus* (the gillaroo), and *Salmo nigripinnis* (the Welsh black-finned trout). It was the great taxonomist, Tate Regan, who first grouped all of these together, and added a load of other so-called species from the Continent.

Because of pronounced *behavioural* differences which directly affect the angler, we have classified the sea-trout as *Salmo trutta trutta*, nevertheless it must be remembered that *physiologically* the sea-trout is an anadromous brown trout wearing its migratory coat. Sea-trout eggs can be fertilized with milt from river-trout, and *vice versa*, and the offspring are fertile. Tate Regan recalls an experiment where members of a colony of sea-trout, prevented from going to sea, subsequently lived and bred in fresh water. He cites a further example of river-trout, exported to New Zealand, which became sea-trout – finding their way to the sea and becoming an anadromous race. This has also happened in several other places; e.g. the Falkland Islands.

Why certain members of a species should migrate to sea, while others of the same species (seemingly with no anatomical difference) should not, is shrouded in mystery. So is the origin of the Salmonoidei. The problem is admirably summed-up by Dr W. E. Frost and Dr M. E. Brown, in their book, *The Trout* (1967):

> The sub-order Salmonoidei includes species which live in freshwater, species which are marine and others which are anadromous (breeding in freshwater and feeding in the sea). The freshwater species, with the exception of *Retropinna* from New Zealand, are indigenous to the arctic and temperate zones of the Northern Hemisphere. The variety of habit among the Salmonoidei is shown by the following British species: the argentines (*Argentina silus* and *A. sphyraena*) are entirely marine; they are caught in deep waters off the west and south-west of Ireland and are sometimes sold in English fish markets. The smelt (*Osmerus eperlanus*) [see p. 285] is a valuable food fish which lives in the sea but comes into estuaries to spawn. The salmon (*Salmo salar*) spawns in freshwater and spends the first two, three, or four years of its life in freshwater but then migrates to the sea from which it returns to spawn in freshwater. The trout (*Salmo trutta*) generally lives in freshwater but may feed in the sea. The British chars (*Salvelinus alpinus*) are entirely freshwater but in Scandinavia fish of this species may be anadromous. The British whitefish: the gwyniad, the schelly, the powan, the pollans and the vendace (all species of the genus *Coregonus*) [see p. 312] are entirely

freshwater and each species inhabits only one or a few lakes.

This gradation in habit from entirely marine through estuarine and anadromous forms to entirely freshwater species raises the question of the ancestry of the whole group – are the freshwater forms more primitive and the marine forms more advanced or vice versa? There are two possible explanations for the present state of affairs. The ancestor could have been an entirely marine fish which developed the habit of laying its eggs in estuaries and then became more and more adapted to freshwater so that it bred farther and farther upstream until it lost the habit of returning to the sea even to feed. On the other hand, the ancestor could have been an entirely freshwater fish, living and breeding in freshwater, which began to forage in estuaries and then in the sea and at first returned to freshwater to breed but then bred in estuaries and finally bred in the sea, losing all connection with freshwater.

But whatever its origin, the trout is now the favourite *game* fish throughout the world. In Britain, although the roach attracts more anglers, the trout undoubtedly attracts more words. About no other species has such a wealth of writing accumulated, some of it the most beautiful and memorable in the whole range of angling literature.

Also, you must not use this aforesaid artful sport for covetousness, merely for the increasing or saving of your money, but mainly for your enjoyment and to procure the health of your body and, more especially, of your soul.

DAME JULIANA BERNERS, *A Treatyse of Fysshynge wyth an Angle* (1496).

Of all British fish species the trout is the most accommodating. It is tasty, easy to catch, fights well and can be taken on a wide variety of baits and lures by almost every known method of angling. Of all methods, however, fly-fishing is the most graceful.

Unfortunately, by over-enthusiastic devotees and others who follow blindly in their wake, fly-fishing has also been described as being the most 'sporting' method; other methods being considered less 'sporting' or, sometimes, even 'unsporting'. This is a pity, since it has created a form of snobbery: a sense of false values.

In modern angling literature the terms 'sporting' and 'unsporting' are in constant use. They are words that flow easily from the tongue and from the pen. But what do they mean? There are many legal, but widely differing, methods of angling. Is it reasonable to suppose that some are more creditable than others?

We think not. And since it seems to us that an analysis of angling 'sportsmanship' is long overdue, we propose, briefly, to discuss the matter and try to arrive at a satisfactory definition of the word: 'sporting'.

Most anglers go fishing to enjoy themselves. Whatever their secondary motives – to catch a meal; to win a prize; to impress their wives or friends – their primary object is pleasure. Each angler has his favourite method or methods of fishing – perhaps because he enjoys handling the tackles involved, or because they are best suited to his temperament, or (most probably) because he finds that they catch him more fish. Whatever the reason, however, provided he does not interfere with anyone else's pleasure, he should be free to catch fish by any legal method he chooses, and be thought neither more nor less of a 'sportsman' in consequence.

But all too often anglers are not free to fish as they choose. On many waters open to the public, they find themselves hedged about with restrictions. Occasionally this is due to exigency; more frequently, however, some of the methods anglers would like to use are forbidden simply because they are considered 'unsporting'.

How has this come about?

First of all, the biggest mistake any angler can make is to be too successful. The 'Brotherhood of the Angle' – a concept much beloved by angling writers of a by-gone age (may they rest in peace) – is unfortunately a myth. Human frailty exists in all men, whether they are financiers or philanderers, artists or anglers. And in angling, as in business, art or love, jealousy is seldom absent. Regrettable though it may be, some anglers cannot bear to see another angler catching more fish than they are catching themselves. And if his success derives from the use of an unusual method – even though it be merely a variation on an old theme – then the presumptuous innovator can be sure that the 'sporting' aspects of his method will very soon come under attack. Indeed, on some fisheries the objectors, if they make sufficient fuss, may even succeed in getting the method banned.

It is pointless to rail at such behaviour. The grizzlers have always existed and will always exist, and one would be naïve to think that anything can be done to change them. Nevertheless, although they cannot be changed, they can be controlled. And should be. But they seldom are.

On a reservoir or any other water open to the public, provided a suitable limit is imposed and that *all* fish caught are counted as part of the limit, it is absurd to object to any angling method on the grounds that it is too successful. If a trout angler possessed of some new magic can take his limit from a lake in half an hour, why on earth shouldn't he – if that is what gives him pleasure? Is another angler, using a more conventional method to be congratulated simply because he takes longer to achieve a similar catch?

It is worth observing that the right fly, properly fished, is often the most killing lure of all; so that if angling methods are to be banned because they are too deadly, then fly-fishing should be one of the first!

Needless to say, there is always the lout who, whatever method he uses, is prepared to exceed his limit, or throw the small trout back and go on fishing. But this sort of behaviour seldom goes unnoticed for long. If it meets with the penalty it deserves – no more fishing tickets – there cannot be many anglers who will risk it.

But for one reason or another the lists of forbidden fishing methods grow, and one of angling's supreme pleasures – experiment: trying other methods when one method fails – is diminished in consequence.

Those noodles who ban such methods as fishing a static fly, spinning, casting a shooting-head, or fly-trailing from a boat, seem to have forgotten *why* people want to go fishing. If anglers enjoy trailing their flies behind a boat instead of waggling their rods about, why in heaven's name shouldn't they trail them? What harm is it doing, and to whom? If they enjoy casting 40 yards to catch fish instead of catching them at their feet, why shouldn't they be allowed their shooting-heads and line-rafts? If they get pleasure from fishing a static fly, or dapping, or float-fishing, or ledgering, for that matter, then let them do it. *Give them their own areas of water to do it in.* Then they will not interfere with anyone else, and no one will interfere with them. In other words, everyone will enjoy his fishing to the full. And that, surely, is what the 'sport' of fishing is supposed to be about.

The greater an angler's pleasure and good fortune, the greater should be the satisfaction of the fishery authorities who derive an income from him. If they are doing their job properly and have got their figures right, there should be a sufficiently large surplus stock of fish to balance the number of tickets they sell: fish that the ticket-holder should be allowed to catch in any legal way he pleases – provided, of course, he fishes only where he is entitled to fish, takes no more than his limit (if he reaches it) and doesn't get in anyone else's way.

Note: It is of course quite impossible to please everybody, and we hasten to point out that the fishery authorities are by no means always to blame. The attitude of some anglers leaves one with a feeling of stunned incredulity. The following gem is taken from a letter of 30th June, 1971, written by Richard Walker to Tom Rawling.

'Just how competitive some of these chaps are was well illustrated by an incident in the fishing lodge at Hanningfield a couple of years ago, when the bag limit was increased from six to ten fish temporarily. Two chaps were talking about this, both of them condemning bitterly the increase in the bag limit. When I asked them what they were grizzling about, one replied: "Why, it makes it nearly twice as hard to take your limit."!'

There are, it is true, a few places run by enlightened men who have their values right and the benefit of the angler firmly at heart, but their example is all too seldom followed. Many fisheries are clogged with pettifogging restrictions bred from the notion that certain methods of fishing are more 'sporting' than others, and that, in consequence, certain species of fish should be caught only in certain ways. It is an attitude that has its roots in ignorance.

A freak example of this is the salmon beat restricted to 'fly only' – as though there were some special merit in fishing for a salmon with a feather as opposed to, say, a float. It seems to be a direct hang-over from the concept, equally weird, that it is more 'sporting' to catch a trout on wet-fly than on spinner; or on dry-fly than on wet-fly; upstream rather than downstream.

On what grounds can such claims be made? Are these supposedly superior methods more difficult? More humane? Less obstructive to other anglers?

Fishing the fly is in every sense a highly rewarding method of catching a salmon; but in conditions of low, clear water, to fish the worm is not only more effective – since, for one reason, it causes less disturbance – it is more difficult. Indeed, the dexterity involved in low-water worming suggests that some of the more vociferous 'fly-only' men may be trying to make a virtue of necessity.

Much the same may be said of those anglers who, whatever the water conditions, use nothing but a spinner – priding themselves on being better 'sportsmen' than those who fish the prawn, although entirely without experience of fishing this much-maligned bait.

The case of the dry-fly trout fishermen is also worth attention. The dry-fly men use a floating artificial because they derive more satisfaction from catching a trout on a close imitation of the fly on the water than on a 'chuck-and-chance-it' fly, or a spinner, or any other bait or lure. It entails stealth and observation, and at least an elementary knowledge of entomology, a subject which is in itself fascinating.

In their enthusiasm, however, some of them make the mistake of thinking that their method of catching a trout is superior to all others.

When one considers the wealth of literature that surrounds this branch of angling, the view is hardly surprising. Nevertheless, it is quite illogical. Casting a dry-fly is certainly a more charming method of fishing than casting, say, a maggot – if only because it is less messy – but this does not make it a *superior* method. And in terms of pleasure, the delight of watching a dry-fly dancing down the stream does not for *all* anglers surpass the fascination of a float.

With an irony that the banned and frustrated reservoir fly-trailer may appreciate, the 'holier-than-thou' attitude adopted by some trout anglers is based on a curious fallacy. The dry-fly, which gradually became popular during the latter part of the 19th century, was acclaimed not because it was considered more 'sporting' than the wet-fly, or the blow-line, but because it was more practical. As that growing band of Victorian fly-fishermen soon discovered, it caught more fish.

By the end of the 19th century the method had become firmly established and the very words 'fly-fishing' began to exert a strange influence. Irrespective of the species to be caught, the fly-rod became the 'sporting' tool of the middle and upper class angler who tended to regard anything else as being slightly suspect. Spinning tackle (other than for salmon), ledger tackle and the humble float stayed mostly with the artisan on a somewhat lower level.

There were, of course, anglers who realized only too clearly the absurdity of such artificial distinctions; men of understanding and experience, such as that fine writer, Hugh Sheringham, who summed it all up so well during his address to The Piscatorial Society in 1909:

> There are few members of the Society who would not go happily to fish with dry fly, to spin for pike, ground bait for roach, wait in patience for carp, long-cork for chub, flog for salmon, or rake for gudgeon with enthusiasm in any case, provided that fate so ordained. We may individually prefer one form of fishing to another, but collectively we despise none, if only it aims at the capture of good fish in a manner that befits the good sportsman.

> As we get older our habits tend to get set, and it may be that we do not all retain the fine careless rapture of youth over the catching of any fish in any way. But it is certain that a keen angler is at heart an all-round angler, sympathizing with all branches of the sport, even though he does not practise them. Personally, I would counsel a man who wanted to get the most out of his fishing life never to outgrow or give up the variety of its interests, to keep his roach rod in action as well as his split cane, to remember that what gave him so much joy in youth may still give him joy in middle age.

This is as true today as it was then. All the same, there are many anglers who, seemingly ignorant of the history of fly-fishing, harbour vague notions of fly 'purity' and couple it with the ultimate in terms of 'sportsmanship'.

This strange cult, which has survived two world wars and exists even today, appears in the most unexpected quarters. It is responsible for those innocents who speak disparagingly of 'wet' fly or lure fishing, or spinning, or ledgering, or trotting, or trailing; who think that 'coarse' fishing is really coarse; who question whether the use of a maggot on a fly at night is a 'sporting' way of killing a sea-trout. (If we are to equate what is 'sporting' with what is humane, the sea-trout should be killed as quickly as possible. For this purpose a small bomb is ideal. But the pleasure in freshwater fishing comes from hunting with rod and line. Obviously, we must compromise in our definition of what is 'sporting'.)

Like the killing of any other animal the killing of a fish is a matter of individual conscience which every fisherman must rationalize. *A dead fish remains a dead fish however it is killed.* To suppose that there is more merit in killing it on an unadorned fly rather than on a fly with a maggot attached is as ridiculous as supposing that simply because a fly-rod is involved, the use of fly-maggot is any more creditable than the use of a worm, or a dock-grub, or a shrimp, or a sand-eel, or a spinner, or any other legitimate lure fished with a fixed-spool reel.

Clearly, all legal methods of angling are of equal merit. The vice or virtue in any form of fishing lies not in the method but in the man. It is the way a method is used; the way an angler behaves that can be termed 'sporting' or 'unsporting'.

Before starting to fish, an angler should ask himself two questions:

1. Am I interfering with a fellow angler's pleasure?
2. Am I giving myself a reasonable chance of landing a fish if I hook one?

If the answer to the first question is 'No', and to the second 'Yes', then by our definition the angler is a sportsman – whatever method he may be using.

What is 'a reasonable chance of landing a fish'? Every angler must answer that for himself, but he will not find it difficult if he accepts the following dictum:

To be broken by a fish is an angling disgrace. It is almost always the fault of the angler.

Although all methods are of equal merit, all tackles are *not*. Here, bearing in mind our humane/sporting compromise, there is a distinct division.

Thames trout, 14 lb 10 oz. caught at Molesey weir in May 1883 by J. R. Faulkner. It is now part of the Piscatorial Society's collection on view at the 'Contented Plaice' restaurant at Kingston.

The use of tackle that is too thick is unprofitable but not unsporting. The use of tackle that is too thin, while equally unprofitable, undoubtedly *is* unsporting. A fish will simply refuse the former, but swim away towing the latter.

The angler who boasts of fishing fine 'to give the fish a chance' exposes himself as being stupid, and insensitive to the fate of the animal he hunts, since his notion of 'sportsmanship' is to allow the fish a vastly better chance of escaping with a hook in its throat and a length of line trailing behind it.

The *sportsman* knows that if he uses tackle too weak he is likely to be broken. If he uses tackle too strong he is unlikely to hook a fish. His compromise is to use the strongest tackle that will enable him to attract, hook and land a fish in the conditions existing at the time.

Thus: by our definition *sporting* tackle (whether fly, float, ledger, spinning, trailing, trolling or trotting) is that which gives an angler the best chance of catching *and landing* a fish.

This, we think, echoes Sheringham's words and '. . . aims at the capture of good fish in the manner that befits the good sportsman.'

It is sad to report that as we go to press an attempt is being made to introduce into Britain an American system of assessing the merit of a catch. This system encourages an angler to fish for big fish with light tackle: the heavier the fish, the lighter the line, the greater the merit. For certain species the line is measured in threads. Thus, to catch a large fish on three thread line is adjudged a more praiseworthy feat than to catch a fish of

For two anglers to share a rod is the most civilized approach to the sport of salmon or trout fishing, and can be applied equally well to certain aspects of coarse fishing. Ghillying for the other man when it is his turn to hold the rod allows an angler to relax and observe what is going on around him. This is of particular importance to the novice. In addition to learning the 'do's' and 'don't's' of angling technique from an experienced companion, he will acquire some understanding of his environment. Time spent in observation of the water and its wild life is never wasted (Photograph: David Jacques).

the same size and species on a line of four threads. And so on.

Such thinking can only bring angling into disrepute. The climate of opinion in Britain today is becoming inimical to field sports, and a growing number of people are opposed to the killing of wildlife for pleasure, fish included. That they have not yet thought out a convincing argument for prohibiting the sport of angling is no reason to suppose that they are not doing their best to conjure one up. To provide these people with a case so obvious as the American System is an act of folly.

It would be of benefit to the future of angling if the concept of 'sportsmanship' were to be re-thought, on the lines we suggest. In the meantime, if those gentlemen advocating the American System must raise their voices, let them make it clear that they speak for themselves alone. Better still, let them take fresh thought and shut up altogether.

Almost everyone is now-a-days a 'piscator'. The *Fanatico*, about Easter, goes off as busy as the cockney on his *n*unter, when bound to Epping. He generally takes a great many things, and kills a few fish. The old angler takes a few things, and kills a great many fish. . . . When fish are well fed is the time to see who is, and who is not, an angler. About ninety in a hundred fancy themselves anglers. About one in a hundred *is* an angler. About ten in a hundred throw the hatchet better than a fly.
PETER HAWKER, *Instructions to Young Sportsmen* (1814).

One wet but amusing morning was occupied in playing to the gallery, not of set purpose indeed, but unwillingly.

The gallery consisted of Fairford bridge, and it was occupied at starting only by the youngest inhabitant, who could not get his head over the parapet, and therefore did not matter . . .

It took me quite a long time to insinuate the fly under the bridge at all, and the youngest inhabitant was reinforced by several of his friends before the feat was accomplished.

Their rather cynical amusement was turned to respectful exclamations when the ginger quill rose hooked and landed one of the three-quarter pounders. The fame of this capture got abroad probably, for the gallery began to fill up, and the next fish was landed more or less in the public eye. Then misfortunes began. A fish was hooked, played for a little and lost. The fly hit itself against the bridge several times in succession. After that a really fine cast sent it right into the depths of the bridge. A 'plop' louder than any followed, the tightened fly provoked a heavy plunge, and the fly came right away. Of course, the frequent dashing against the bridge had broken the barb. A new fly was put on and promptly lost in the chestnut trees behind. Pity began to be expressed on the faces of the spectators. Interest was admissible, admiration was tolerable and even grateful, but pity was too much and could only be avoided by flight.
H. T. SHERINGHAM, *An Open Creel* (1910).

The majority of today's reservoir trout fishermen have been weaned on compound-tapered glass-fibre rods and shooting-head lines. This picture shows eight trout taken by F. B. during Grafham's first year on a built cane rod with 30 yards of Kingfisher *silk line. It is a reminder that reservoir trout fly-fishing extends back to the late 19th Century, when a built-cane rod and silk line reigned supreme.*

It is the birds and other creatures peculiar to the water that render fly-fishing so pleasant. Were they all destroyed and nothing left but mere fish, one might as well stand and angle in a stone cattle-trough.
RICHARD JEFFERIES

FLY-FISHING

Nearly five hundred years ago, Dame Juliana Berners talked of:

'A lyne of one or two herys, batyd with a flye.'

She also referred to another method of fishing, with a *dubbed* hook – which relates to a simulation of the natural insect rather than the insect itself.

But this wasn't by any means the first reference to fly-fishing. The Roman poet, Martial, born in the year 43 A.D., spoke of fish being taken on a fly – whether natural or artificial is not clear.

The first writer who specifically mentioned fishing with an *artificial* fly was Aelian, in his book of Natural History, written about 200 A.D.

I have heard of a Macedonian way of catching fish, and it is this: between Beroea and Thessalonica runs a river called the Astraeus, and in it there are fish with speckled skins. . . . These fish feed on a fly peculiar to the country, which hovers on the river. When a fish observes a fly on the surface it swims quietly up and gulps the fly down. Now, although the fishermen know of this, they do not use these flies as bait . . .

Note the use of the word 'bait'. Obviously, dapping was no mystery 1,200 years before Dame Juliana.

They do not use these flies as bait, for if a man's hand touch them they lose their natural colour, their wings wither, and they become unfit food for the fish. But the fishermen get the better of the fish by their fisherman's craft. They fasten red wool round a hook, and fix on to the wool two feathers which grow under a cock's wattles, and which in colour are like wax. Their rod is six feet long, and their line is the same length. They throw their snare, and the fish, attracted and maddened by the colour, come straight at it – thinking from the pretty sight to get a dainty mouthful.

Well – unquestionably, these fellows were using an artificial fly. And it is interesting that by their choice of red wool they certainly thought the fish were colour conscious. Aelian seems to have been in no doubt that the fish were 'attracted and maddened by the colour'.

To what degree fish can distinguish colour is still uncertain, but most fish, except the shark, can see *some* colour. Examination of the nerve cells has shown that the shark's eye lacks colour-discriminating visual cones, and has only visual rods – which distinguish between light and dark. The eyes of all other tested fishes possess both rods and cones.

All this has been established by recent scientific research. But as Aelian's writing shows, the discovery of colour vision in fishes is by no means new.

Fly-fishing techniques, however, have come a long way since those far-off Macedonian days of the six-foot rod and line.

It is true of fly-fishing, more perhaps than of any other branch of angling, that no sooner have you made a flat statement than you have to qualify it.
MAURICE WIGGIN

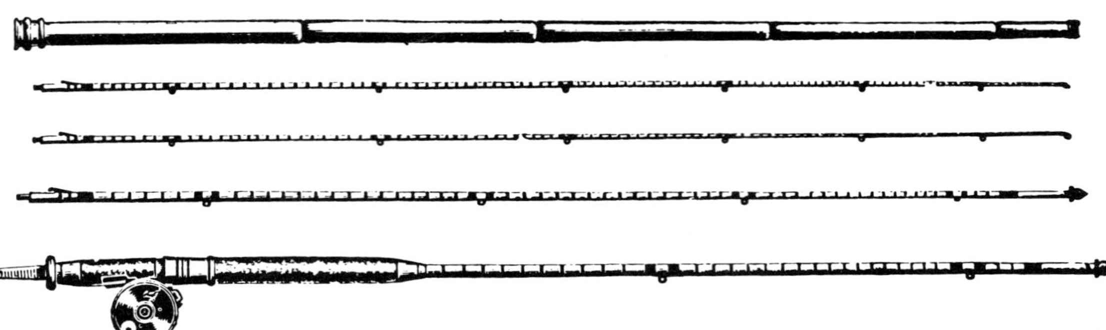

This illustration of the 'Houghton' dry fly rod is taken from the 1909 edition of Hardy's Angler's Guide. *The rod was offered in 5 lengths: '9½ feet, 10 ft, 10 ft 3 in., 10½ ft and 11 ft, in three pieces, two Tops, Cork covered Handle, Patent Lock-fast joints, Patent Reversible combined Spear and Button, "Bridge" Rings, Agate or Revolving Steel Gold Plated Top and Butt Rings – Close tied – with Bamboo Top Case – Weight 8½ to 11 oz – 5 Guineas.'*

The Hardy Perfect *fly reel was aptly named.*

Hardy's 10½ ft Houghton was one of the finest fly rods ever made; ideal for brown trout dry-fly fishing; sea-trout night fly-fishing; low water greased-line fly, and upstream worm-fishing for salmon. (H. F. has used the same Houghton for over 30 years. In addition to a large number of brown trout, it has landed several hundred salmon and several thousand sea-trout.) Present-day glass rods are lighter and in many ways more efficient, however, and for the modern fly fisherman we recommend the following:

1. 'Greased-line' (or floating-line fishing) for salmon: Bruce and Walker 13 ft 4 in. 'Cordon Bleu'.
2. Sea-trout night fly-fishing: Bruce and Walker 10½ ft 'New Era'.
3. Reservoir fly-fishing: Hardy 9 ft 3 in. Richard Walker 'Superlite'.

The Hardy Princess *fly reel is typical of modern lightweight fly reels. By means of cage construction some models incorporate rim control. Other modern fly reels have a 2½ to 1 gear ratio that gives faster line recovery.*

An 18th-Century 'Engine' for Making Tapered Fly Lines

Time was when each angler made up his own lines. The following notes appear in the Sir John Hawkins (1754) edition of *The Complete Angler*.

I would recommend an engine lately invented, which is now to be had at almost any fishing-tackle shop in London; it consists of a large horizontal wheel, and three very small ones, inclosed in a brass box about a quarter of an inch thick, and two inches in diameter; the axis of each of the small wheels is continued through the under-side of the box, and is formed into a hook: by means of a strong screw it may be fixed in any post or partition, and is set in motion by a small winch in the centre of the box.

To twist links with this engine, take as many hairs as you intend each shall consist of, and, dividing them into three parts, tie each parcel to a bit of fine twine, about six inches long, doubled, and put through the aforesaid hooks; then take a piece of lead, of a conical figure, two inches high, and two in diameter at the base, with a hook at the apex, or point; tie your three parcels of hair into one knot, and to this, by the hook, hang the weight.

Lastly, take a quart or larger bottle-cork, and cut into the sides, at equal distances, three grooves; and placing it so as to receive each division of hair, begin to twist; you will find the link begin to twist with great evenness at the lead, as it grows tighter, shift the cork a little upwards; and when the whole is sufficiently twisted, take out the cork, and tie the link into a knot; and so proceed till you have twisted links sufficient for your line, observing to lessen the number of hairs in each link in such proportion as that the line may be taper.

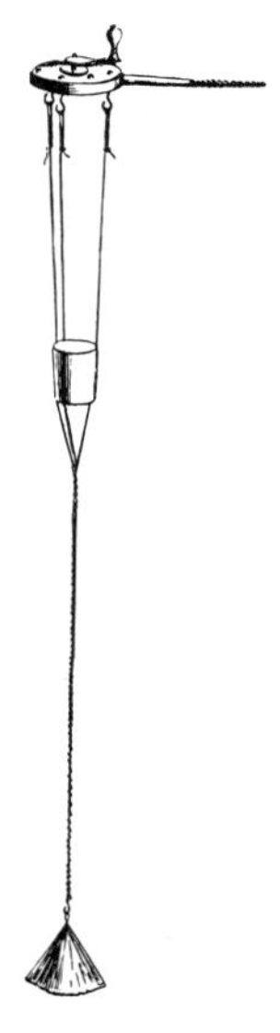

The 'engine'

Fly Lines

Many anglers are confused by the different systems that are used for designating the size and weight of fly lines.

The first system consisted of numbers which referred to oil-dressed silk lines. These indicated the thickness of the line but because all the lines were made of the same materials, the thickness also served to indicate the weight.

Conversion Table

AFTM Number	Letter system Floating line Double taper	Letter system Floating line Weight forward	Letter system Sinking line Double taper	Letter system Sinking line Weight forward	Silk line Double taper	Silk line Weight forward
1					00	
2					0	
3					1	
4	HEH					
5	HDH	HDG			2	
6	HCH	HCF	HEH		3	2
7	GBG	GBF	HDH	HDG	4	3
8	GAG	GAF	HCH	HCF	5	4
9		GAAF	GBG	GBF		
10		G3AF		GAF	6	5
11						
12					7	

Because a simple number could only designate a single thickness, an alternative system was devised which used letters instead of numbers. Different letters meant different thicknesses and therefore, a tapered line could be described in terms of both its thin and thick ends. A double tapered line might be designated, for example, HEH or GBG.

This was satisfactory until plastic coated lines having different densities became available. Obviously, a sinking line, that is one that has a heavy coating, will be thinner for a given weight than a floating line having a lighter or less dense coating.

In choosing the right line for any fly rod, it is the *weight*, not the thickness, that matters.

Because of this, the American Association of Fishing Tackle Manufacturers devised a system of letters combined with numbers that state all you want to know about any line. In this system, the *first two letters* tell you what kind of line it is; that is, whether it is double-tapered (DT) or forward-tapered (WF) (weight forward).

The *number* designates the weight of the first 30 ft of the taper; and the *last letter* tells you whether the line floats or sinks.

Let us take for example a line designated WF8S. This is a forward-tapered, or weight forward (WF) line of medium to heavy weight (as designated by its number 8). That it is a sinking line is shown by the letter 'S'.

A double-taper floating line of the same weight would be designated DT8F.

There is no relationship between the old systems of numbering and the new system – the AFTM system, named after its originators. The old systems referred to *thickness*, and the new system refers to *weight*. Modern plastic-coated lines have a wide range of different thicknesses for a given weight because some are floaters and others are sinkers with different sinking rates. To produce a table of equivalents would only cause confusion.

A double-taper floating line designated DT5F is the same *thickness* as a double-taper medium sinker designated DT7S; but the sinker would be much heavier than the floater. If the floater happened to be the right weight for a given fly rod, the rod would be badly overloaded if you put the sinker on. The right sinker for any rod has the same number as the floater: in this case DT5S; but it will be a good deal thinner than the floater.

Most good fly rod manufacturers nowadays specify what *weight* of line suits a rod best but, remembering that the AFTM designation refers to the first 30 ft of the taper, it will be realised that this information about what line suits a rod is based on the assumption that the angler will be doing most of his false casting with 30 ft, of line out beyond the tip ring. There may be reasons why the angler will want to use a greater or a lesser amount of line beyond the tip ring in his fishing. For example, if he is regularly fishing a small river where he need not cast far, he may decide that he will do most of his casting with only about 24 ft in the air. Conversely, if he is fishing a larger river, he may wish to aerialise more than 30 ft; perhaps 36 ft, or even 42 ft.

In that case, he will find it useful to know that each step in the AFTM numbers is equivalent to about 6 ft of line. In other words 30 ft of No 7 weighs the same as 24 ft of No 8 and the same as 36 ft of No 6 or 42 ft of No 5. For best casting results, therefore, you should choose a fly line of an AFTM number that suits your rod when you have got out the amount of line with which you do most of your casting, in practical fishing.

You can switch from one line to another, with the same rod, if you fish a number of different waters. You may, for example, choose a No 7 for your rod when you are fishing a small brook and change to a No 5 if you use the same rod to fish a wide river, because in the latter case you will be aerializing much more line than you would in the former. In both kinds of fishing the *weight* of line that you will do most of your casting with, will be about the same.

Fortunately, most modern fly rods are fairly tolerant of line weight, so you don't have to be *too* fussy. Nevertheless, our advice is to forget all about the old systems which refer only to a line's thickness and adopt the new AFTM system. Once you have found which AFTM number suits your rod, you will know that whatever kind of line you may buy in the future, be it floater, sink-tip, neutral density, slow sinker, medium sinker or high density, you can ask for the same number in the tackle shop and be sure of getting a line that your rod will handle successfully.

Were I to select the professions among the members of which I have met the best men, and the most skilful anglers, I would certainly name the army and the law. I mean the highest branch of the latter; as for the attorneys, with many honourable exceptions, they are an incorrigible race. Indeed I have rarely seen any of them who could angle at all, perhaps, only one; and he was a sinister biped (left-handed). They are, for the most part, devoted to worldly gain; and, as Giles Daxon used to say, will never give a direct answer to a question.

Few merchants are good anglers.
O'GORMAN, *The Practice of Angling* (Vol. 2, 1845).

The Wilson Fly-Retriever

(At last – a use for those little metal cylinders in which cigars are sold.)

This little gadget – an invention of that splendid fisherman, Brigadier G. H. N. Wilson – should live permanently in the tackle bag. It consists of a crook that can be lifted on the rod point to obtain a hold on a branch in which one's hook or fly is caught.

The crook is strapped on to the empty cigar cylinder with adhesive tape. A suitable length of light, strong cord is tied to the crook, with which to pull down the branch. For this purpose a piece of parachute cord is ideal.

1. Put the cylinder with crook attached on to the rod tip.
2. Reach up with your rod and place the crook over the offending branch.
3. Remove the rod and put it safely out of the way, stripping line off the reel in order to do so.
4. Take hold of the cord and pull down the branch.

It is surprising how easily a fly can be retrieved from seemingly inaccessible branches.

The crook should be light enough to be lifted vertically on the rod tip, but strong enough to take the strain of pulling down the branch. Friction is increased by winding a little adhesive tape round the bend of the hook, which prevents the crook from sliding down a branch when pressure is applied. This tendency to slip can, of course, be countered by the direction of the pull and by intelligent selection of the place where the

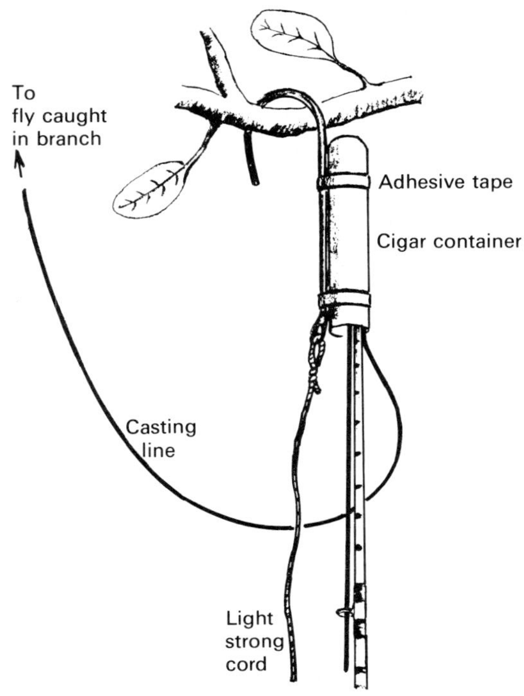

Fig. 28.1. The Wilson fly-retriever.

crook is put over the branch. If possible, place it just above the junction of a lateral (see Fig. 28.1).

This equipment can also be used to retrieve a hook, fly or spinner from certain underwater snags, when clarity of water, strength of current and other circumstances permit.

Brigadier G. H. N. Wilson. Note the simple but practical method of carrying and fastening a landing net. (See also p. 398).

Trout flies seen against the light – as they must sometimes appear to the fish (Tied and photographed by Gerald Berth-Jones).

Brown trout, 12 lb 10 oz, caught by Major H. Warrender on the Test below Middle Bridge at Romsey in 1898.
The town of Romsey is on seven streams one of which runs through the butcher's shop. In the old days offal from the shop used to be tipped into the stream and where this stream met the mainstream many large trout lurked – including this one.

There are trout in my river whose attitude,
Is one of the blackest ingratitude;
Though I offer them duns,
Most superior ones,
They maintain a persistent Black Gnatitude.
ANON.

And let your garments Russet be or gray,
Of colour darke, and hardest to discry:
That with the Raine or weather will away,
And least offend the fearefull Fishes eye:
JOHN DENNYS, *The Secrets of Angling* (1613).

Brown trout, 11 lb 12 oz. This perfectly proportioned trout was taken from Ham Mill Pool on the river Kennet by E. M. Mayes on 24th June, 1894. The fish measured 28¼ inches long. (Photograph by permission of the Piscatorial Society).

The first Fish you catch, take up his belly, & you may then see his stomach; it is known by its largeness and place, lying from the Gills to the small Guts; take it out very tenderly (if you bruise it, your labour and design are lost) and with a sharp knife cut it open without bruising, and then you find his food in it, and thereby discover what bait the fish at that instant takes best, flies or ground baits, and so fit them accordingly.
COLONEL ROBERT VENABLES, *The Experienc'd Angler* (1662).

But Dame Juliana had beaten him to it:

When you have taken a grete fysshe, undo the maw and what ye find therein, make that your bayte, for it is your beste.
A Treatyse of Fysshynge wyth an Angle (1496).

DRY-FLY FISHING

For a few words on this subject we can do no better than quote our friend, David Jacques, renowned both as an entomologist and as an exponent of the art of chalkstream dry-fly fishing:

'The belief that dry fly fishing was invented by a company of Southern gentlemen to make the capture of a trout more difficult in order to display their superiority over less distinguished anglers is amusing but fallacious; the cult spread and eventually ousted all other methods for the simple reason that on the rivers concerned it proved to be the easiest, the most elegant and the most successful means of catching trout (on a fly) yet discovered. In fact, it was not a discovery; it was a natural progression from an earlier routine, for as early as 1676, Charles Cotton, in his addendum to *The Compleat Angler*, described the basic principles of the dry fly, as applied to fishing with a blow line. He made it quite clear that the fly, natural or artificial, should be fished at the top of the water, and only "if the wind be stiff you will of necessity be compelled to drown a good part of your line to keep the fly on the water." Presentation in those days depended almost entirely on the strength and direction of the wind, although by manipulation of the rod and by change of position an angler was able to some extent to direct the fly to a desired destination. The great advance in the art of the dry fly was due to, and came with, the invention of equipment that permitted the unerring placement of the fly where desired, wind or no wind. Indeed, under the new order, wind, instead of being a necessary aid to fly fishing, became an impediment.

'Of course, there is a presumption that the dry-fly fisher knows his business, for if not, he would be better off flicking his arbitrary or favourite flies, wet or dry, here and there in either river or stillwater until some credulous trout, fooled by the motion of the fly, decides it is worth eating. Dry fly fishing however, postulates precision, whereby an individual trout is invested, reconnoitred and eventually presented with a close imitation of the fly on the water, or likely to be on the water, at the time. (The expression 'exact imitation', implying a human ability to usurp Nature's monopoly, merely derides the tongue that uses it.)

Midsummer on the Test. David Jacques surveys the water.

'The fundamental skills required for fishing the dry fly are in the main no different from those required for all angling. They are; sober dress, inconspicuity, circumspection, fine tackle and so on. But to these must be added an ability to cast a fly without drag, and to recognise the natural fly on the water.

'Casting is a mechanical art, and this can be acquired, though some anglers are more adept than others. The avoidance of drag is obtained by casting a loose line and by intelligent selection of the spot from which to cast.

'The mainspring of dry-fly fishing, however, is first recognition and then imitation of the fly on the water, a feat not as difficult as it sounds. This has been advocated by the Masters throughout the centuries with a degree of consensus that overshadows the minority contrary opinions, however eloquently voiced. Even today, the words of the scholar Moses Browne, written 250 years ago, illumine the spirit of the dry fly and of the puristic ideology that accompanies it, as revealed in the works of Cotton, Ronalds, Halford, Francis, Kingsley, Grey and many others:

Yet thus at large I venture to support,
Nature best followed best secures the sport,
Of flies the kinds, their seasons and their breed,
Their shapes, their hue, with nice observance heed.

'In stating that insect recognition is not as difficult as it sounds, I exclude strict entomological identification, for which a microscope is essential. Normal recognition of insects at the riverside, even by an expert entomolgist, is of type, not of species, and this is all the angler needs for his purposes. For instance, it would be pointless to separate the four different types of Pale Wateries native to the Test into their various species, for they may all be represented by the same artificial. In like fashion, the six or seven Olives can be represented by two or three patterns, and the scores of Sedges by the same number. Trout are influenced by appearances only, not by anatomical differences, and the angler must adjust his policy accordingly.

'Some confusion might arise at dusk, when the fishing is fast and furious and the fly in demand not easily determined. At such times a long-handled plankton net can provide a solution to the problem, for with it one can lift off the water, either from the bank or from a low bridge, any insect floating down and match it with an artificial from stock. The use of the plankton net need not be restricted to dusk, but may profitably be used at any time of the day to capture insect specimens for later study. And it is no overstatement to predict that this may lead to a pastime as fascinating as fishing itself.'

Surveying Lough Corrib from the road above. A blazing hot day, cloudless sky and dead calm water: not hopeful conditions for fly-fishing. Nevertheless, artificial mayfly dipped in Permaflote accounted for five good trout with another lost. This may not sound dramatic; but the weather was such that six dapping boats came in with only one trout between them. Permaflote rendered the fly unsinkable and on this occasion it could be fished at much greater range than the natural insect. Furthermore, it could be made to move on the surface without dipping under.

Permaflote

During the late 1960s, being acutely conscious of the shortcomings of the various waterproofing liquids sold for keeping dry-flies dry, Richard Walker began experimenting with a view to producing something better. He was assisted by Arnold Neave, of Hitchin.

Eventually, they arrived at a formula whose waterproofing qualities were greatly superior to anything previously tried.

The result is Permaflote – in our opinion

the best dry-fly floatant ever produced. A fly dressed with Permaflote is unsinkable.

There follow instructions for tying mayflies, given by Richard Walker in a letter to F.B. The new 'soak-up' dressings take advantage of this advance in the technology of waterproofing fly-dressing materials. (See plate on p. 293.)

'Here are the mayfly patterns complete with tying instructions. I expect the flies will get rather flattened in the post but you can easily restore them by holding them in steam from a boiling kettle.

'You will see that I have used two different kinds of material for the sub-imago body and I honestly don't think it makes much difference, if any, as far as the preference of the fish is concerned, but I think the feather fibre soaks up more "Permaflote" and you might therefore find it better. However, a professional fly dresser might very well take the opposite view, since the raffine body is somewhat easier to tie, though it must be wound on while thoroughly damp.'

'You will probably find that these four patterns will cope with practically any situations you might discover but if I have time I will tie and send you one or two more, since if one's fly is refused it is always nice to have an alternative to which to change.'

1. *Nymph*
   Hook, no. 10 or no. 8 long shank down-eyed. *Not* ultra-fine wire.
   Tails, short, pheasant tail fibres. The butts are used to make the two dark bands near the rear end of the abdomen.
   Body and thorax, cream ostrich herl, 7 or 8 strands to make a fat body.
   Wing cases and legs, pheasant tail.
   Weightings, tie in 3 or 4 layers of lead foil on hook shank before commencing the dressing.

2. *Sub-imago* (dun)
   Hook, as nymph.
   Tails, pheasant tail, butts used to make dark bands.
   Body, very pale buff turkey tail fibres, plenty so as to produce a fairly fat body.
   Wings, two broad cock hackle points, dyed green, set upright.
   Hackles, one brown partridge, one pale ginger cock.

3. *Imago* (spinner)
   Hook, as above.
   Tails, pheasant tail dyed sepia.
   Body, ivory coloured turkey tail fibres, fat.
   Wings, rusty badger cock hackle points tied flat.
   Hackle, dark natural red cock.

4. *Special mayfly for heavy hatches*
   Hook, as before.
   Body, as sub-imago.
   Hackles, one speckled duck feather, rather long in fibre, one green-dyed cock hackle, 1 hot orange hackle, shorter in fibre than the others.
   Tails, pheasant tail.

5. *Alternative*
   Body of sub-imago can be pale straw-coloured raffine ribbed with pale brown silk, instead of feather fibre.

Top, left: *A Test carrier. Such streams may be tiny, but the fish* (centre) *can be very big.*

Bottom: *Mr Denis Bridge, fishing a Test carrier with weighted nymph on floating line. Many artificial nymphs of today bear little resemblance to the natural insect. Some – like those pioneered by the late Major Oliver Kite – are simply different sizes of bare hook with copper wire wound round the shank just below the eye. Trout can often be induced to take such an unlikely artificial when it is moved rather faster than the speed of a real nymph. The reason for this may be that the faster speed helps to conceal the true nature of the lure, or, as Richard Walker suggested, it may be due to 'attraction through exaggeration'. Many animal species are attracted by exaggeration; e.g. a herring-gull will incubate an oversized dummy egg in preference to its own; the oversized gape of the young cuckoo so stimulates the feeding responses of a small song-bird that it continues to feed this huge interloper seemingly oblivious of the loss of its own ejected chicks; males of a certain species of butterfly prefer an artificial female four times the natural size, whose wings flap ten times faster. And there are many other examples. Of course, one can think of numerous examples in angling when exaggeration does* not *attract. Nevertheless, it is an interesting hypothesis which offers the thoughtful angler a fascinating new line of experiment and research.*

On a Cumberland beck.

A Trout Stream

To a casual observer a trout stream seems empty and lifeless, save for an occasional hatch of fly appearing mysteriously above the surface, or the rare glint of a fish. But underneath the surface, among the stones on the bottom and the weed beds, the water is teeming with life: a host of tiny creatures, each of them going through its various metamorphoses in sympathy with the season.

The trout react immediately to every change in this flux of underwater life, and the knowledgeable fisherman reacts in turn. His understanding of insect growth and behaviour guides him in his choice of fly. Much of his success – certainly his pleasure – comes from a study of freshwater insects and the plants that harbour them, for they control the behaviour of the fish that rely on them for food.

At times during a hatch of duns, trout, often large, may be seen questing about near the surface in mid-stream and taking the nymphs which are ascending from the river-bed as they find them, generally breaking or 'humping' the surface when they effect a capture. And occasionally trout, when in the height of condition, may be observed hovering in the fastest part of the stream, not moving from one spot, and intercepting just below the surface the nymphs on their way to hatch, and at times doing so without breaking the surface.

It will thus be seen that the occasions most favourable to the angler fishing to individual selected fish are those when he is taking the mature and, for the moment, practically inert nymph, on its way to hatch.

As a matter of fact, it does not seem to have been realised for many years after the advent of the dry fly, what a large proportion of the rising trout under banks, and indeed in the open (other than bulging) is to nymphs on their way to the surface to hatch, with the result that many a fish so rising has been vainly hammered by anglers with floating flies.

G. E. M. SKUES, *Nymph Fishing for Chalk Stream Trout* (1939).

Skues, the originator of nymph fishing, tied patterns of nymphs which were almost identical with modern artificials.

There is not a lovelier sight (*pace* Ramsbury and Hurstbourne Priors in buttercup time) in England than Blagdon from the Butcombe end at sundown, with the tiny town straggling up the steep hillside like a Bavarian village, the red roofs of the houses peeping out of the thick orchards (with never a Methodist Chapel to shock the artist's eye) and the evening sunlight setting the windows of the old church aglow and flushing with purple pink the glassy surface of the lake. There is a stillness here that belongs to no other valley. You can hear the 'plop' of the big trout far out, half a mile away. You can talk to your friend across the water without ever raising your voice, and hear the scream of his reel in the blackness, and Blagdon is seven miles round, and he may be half the length of the lake from you.

But the dominant impression in my mind is of the lovely colour of the evening light upon the valley as you face it looking east. It has a crimson velvet glow which hangs like Aurora on the meadows and makes the shores and the scolloped hills burn with fires. It is Devonshire clay here, and the whole landscape warms pink and deepens to purple black as the sun sinks lower.

I know, too, that there was once a witch in the valley, and that they drowned her when they let the water in; and one night as I grope my way home in the dark I shall stumble on Hansel and Gretel asleep on the grass in a mist of white angels, with the myriad million stars of the milky way and the golden lights of Blagdon shining on their heads and winking in the watery glass at their feet.

HARRY PLUNKETT GREENE, *Where the Bright Waters Meet* (1924).

TROUT FISHING IN STILL WATER

Although we realize that to teach the art of fly-casting by means of words and pictures is almost impossible, there are two aspects of it we wish to discuss. First, the technique of casting the shooting-head – a method which, in some quarters, has become unpopular because of the disturbance it can cause in the hands of an unskilful angler.[1]

1 The other technique – the steeple cast – is shown on pp. 307–8.

While considering how to go about it, we discovered that the joint pen of Richard Walker and James L. Hardy had already dealt expertly with the matter in *Hardy's Guide to Reservoir Angling*. This is the most helpful work of its sort that we have read, and with kind permission we reproduce a part of it together with some notes on how to fish various reservoir flies. The accompanying illustrations are the copyright of Scientific Anglers Inc.

The following sequence of illustrations are the copyright of the Scientific Anglers

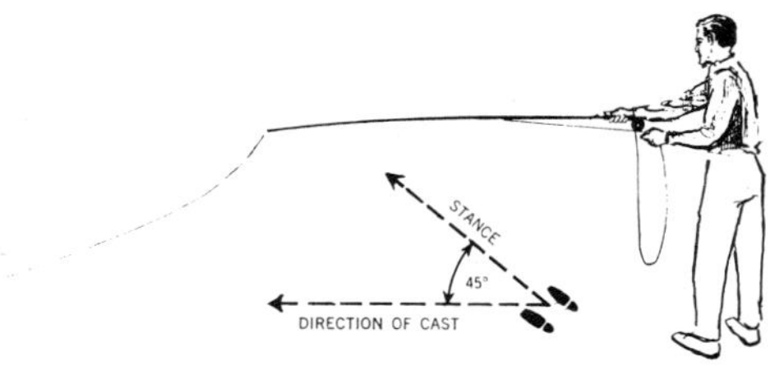

Correct position in which to start casting

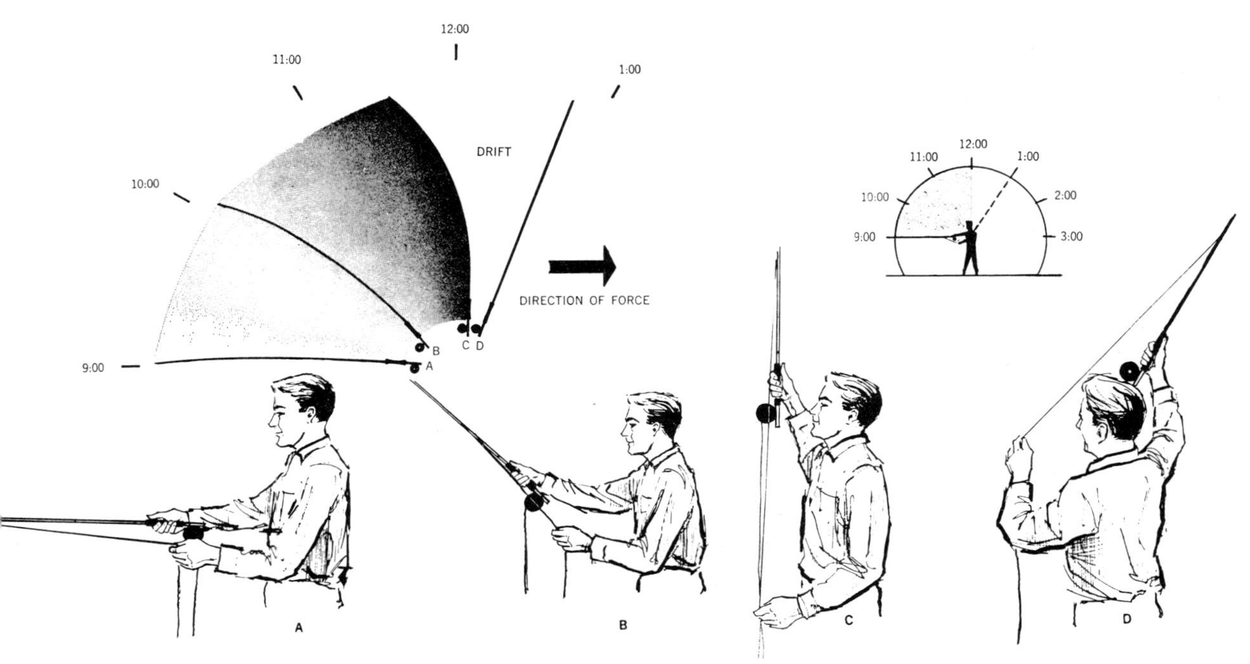

Fig. 28.2. Casting the shooting head (continued overleaf).

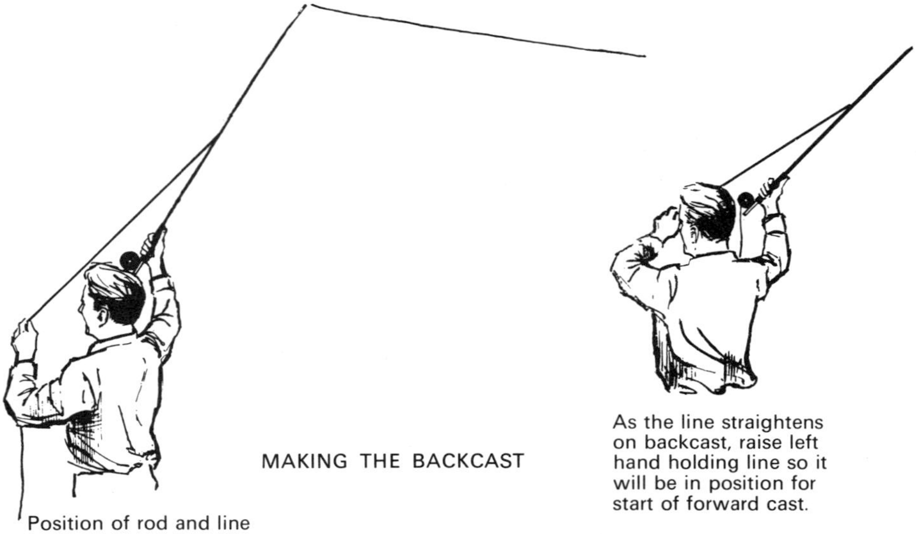

Position of rod and line at conclusion of good backcast.

MAKING THE BACKCAST

As the line straightens on backcast, raise left hand holding line so it will be in position for start of forward cast.

C B A

THE FORWARD CAST

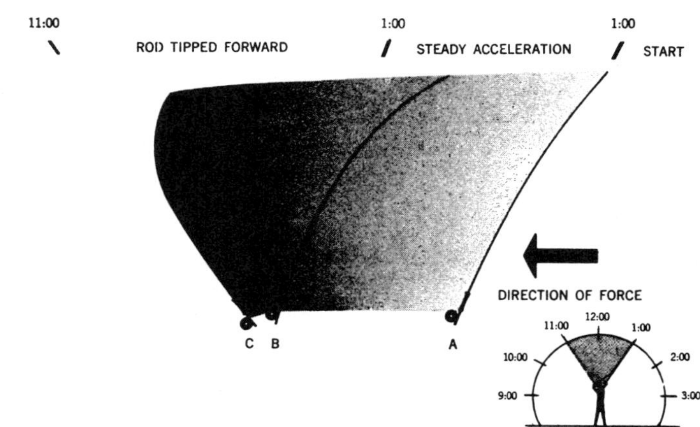

CASTING THE SHOOTING-HEAD

Very few anglers in the U.K. cast the shooting head correctly. In consequence, this method of fishing has acquired a bad name in certain places. The fault lies not with the line but with the caster. It is he who causes the disturbance. A competent caster can lay a shooting head as lightly on the water as any other type of line.

Level or double-tapered lines can be cast only so far. The length of line which can be shot is limited, so is the length which can be false cast. The solution is to use a different type of line such as weight-forward. With this line the back cast is always the same length, no matter how far forward the cast goes. Only the heavy belly portion is false cast; the *rear* taper will be just outside the rod tip but the weight concentrated in the first 30 ft of line, and because the shooting line is smaller in diameter, much more line can be shot.

The shooting head is really only a sophisticated weight-forward line with the shooting line replaced by monofilament which is lighter and shoots through the rod rings with ease. Nobody complained about weight-forward lines when they were marketed 70 years ago, so why fuss now?

Other things being equal, the faster a fly is started on its way, the further it will go. Consequently the knack of distance casting is primarily one of imparting maximum velocity to the line. To do this the technique must be altered and the double-haul method of casting employed. This means that velocity is achieved by pulling the line with the left hand as the rod reaches maximum speed in both the back and forward casts.

Only with monofilament and shooting head line can full potential be realised.

The best position for a right-hand caster is with the feet comfortably separated and angled somewhat to the right of the direction he intends to cast. This will put the left foot forward, making it easier to watch the back cast over his shoulder.

False cast in the usual way until the backing knot is out of the reel. Now strip off 25 or 30 feet of monofil. If you find it kinked from being wound tightly on the reel, straighten it with hard pulls – between hands, four feet at a time. Continue false casting until the knot is about three feet beyond the end ring and let the line fall on the water.

Next, since making a good fishing cast depends on making a good back cast *first*, let's concentrate on it. The back cast movement, when picking up line from the water is up and back. This means up and back with rod *and* arm, not merely with the rod.

(Following a false cast, with the line higher out in front, the back cast is more a horizontal movement. Normally angled only slightly upward, it is made very much the same as the forward cast, save in the opposite direction).

Reach out towards your extended line with both hands at waist height, backing up a few steps to remove slack if necessary. The rod should be pointed straight down the line, the right wrist cocked downward. The left hand, out beside the reel, should hold the shooting line firmly.

Now start arm and rod up and back,

accelerating rapidly. The back cast is made with the elbow and shoulder; the wrist remains locked in the position previously described.

As the rod moves from horizontal to vertical, the rod hand moves from out in front, waist high, to a position somewhat above and behind the right shoulder. The left hand, still holding the shooting line firmly, comes towards the body.

By the time the rod reaches the eleven o'clock position, the line will be coming towards you in the air. Bring the shoulder into play to move the entire rod back about 18 inches. At the same time, pivot the elbow until the rod is vertical and stop it dead. The stop is accomplished by tensing forearm, wrist, and hand, then relaxing them instantly.

During the final movement of the rod, pull the line sharply with your left hand. This is the first half of the double-haul. It will send the line singing out behind. Now let the rod drift back to one o'clock. Raise your left hand, still clutching the line tightly, up near your right shoulder.

With a perfect back cast, you will feel the line tug against the rod. When all the line is out straight behind, start the forward cast. The rod, in one-o'clock position, is behind your shoulder. Push it forward briskly, *still in this position.* Push it as far forward as you can reach. Then, and not before, tip it ahead, faster and faster, pushing on the grip with your thumb.

Simultaneously with this movement, which is called the 'turnover', pull the line sharply with your left hand. The combination of turnover and left-hand pull gives the line the greatest possible velocity. Precisely at the completion of both, with the rod approximately at ten o'clock, stop it dead by tensing the muscles, then relaxing them. Release the monofil.

The shooting taper – well named – will shoot out like a bullet. The monofil will hit the reel with a jerk, and it will be obvious that you would have cast much farther, had you stripped off more line in the first place.

Don't do it! In fly casting, like every other activity requiring co-ordinaton, form is all important. Practise until you can make a perfect back cast every time, watching it over your shoulder. Practise moving the entire rod, and the double-haul. And let the forward cast come up hard against the reel.

But practise only a few minutes at a time. Weary muscles don't respond. Instead of working steadily for an hour, sit down occasionally and analyse what you are attempting to do. Accomplishment is easier with understanding.

A narrow arc of rod rotation results in the line going out in a shallow U-shaped loop essential for both distance and accuracy. A wide arc in which the rod is swung from 9.30 to 2.30 makes a deep loop with which distance is impossible and accuracy a matter of luck.

In addition, making sure the line is straight before starting the forward cast eliminates popping off flies and snapping the line like a whiplash. No fly line can long endure this punishment, yet many anglers ask their lines to do it by holding the butt in one position and swinging the tip farther and farther as they strive futilely for more distance. And since a rod brought too far back inevitably drives the line into the ground, they start the forward cast before the back cast has straightened. This causes the snapping that ruins their lines.

Now, after several practice sessions in which you moved the *entire rod*, making perfect, high-level back casts and forward casts that came up hard against the reel, you are ready to strip off more line and cast farther. And here – we can predict with certainty because we've watched it hundreds of times – you are going to fall flat. Instead of releasing one of the perfect false casts you have been making – and watching your fly sail out 100 feet – you are going to put a little extra muscle into the final effort.

So instead of sailing out fast and high, your fly will come to a halt and fall about 60 feet away. Why? Because you temporarily forgot form and relied, instead, on brute strength.

Remember form – fast, straight back cast; fast, straight forward cast; moving the entire rod, turning it over and pulling the line simultaneously at the conclusion of both. And hold to a narrow arc of rod rotation, even though the butt may move six feet and the tip much farther.

Have a friend watch and tell you when you bring the rod back too far – a much more common error than tipping it too far ahead, although you may do that, too. Remember – narrow arc, shallow loop and more distance; wide arc, deep loop and less distance. Move the entire rod, accelerating from fast to faster on both the back and forward casts.

Once you get the hang of casting a deep or shallow loop at will, you will be able to angle either the back or forward cast up or down as you see fit. And you will realize that the line can move only in a straight line – the line in which force is applied. Left, right, up, or down, it goes only where the rod sends it.

Knowing this, you will be able to tilt the arc of rod movement to control the angle of your cast. And you will soon discover that for maximum distance on a calm day, or with the wind, your forward cast must be angled slightly upward, just as a rifle barrel must be angled well above the horizontal to send its bullet to maximum range. To do this, of course, the back cast must be aimed slightly lower. Conversely, when you are casting against the wind, you will get the best distance by aiming the forward cast lower and holding the back cast high.

Now for some errors you are bound to make. The first is what is known as 'creep'. Instead of keeping the rod far back in the one o'clock position until the back cast pulls against it, you begin to edge it forward as soon as the back cast is made. As the result, when you start to make the forward cast you can use only half the rod movement, apply only half the energy, and your cast goes only half as far.

Another very common error, the cause of so-called 'wind-knots' in the leader, is tipping the rod forward before you push it ahead. Bring the rod, in one o'clock position, from behind your shoulder to as far forward as you can reach, accelerating rapidly, *then* tip it over towards the target.

You may find yourself hauling line too

soon. While a haul at any time helps – just as letting the line slip through the rings kills a cast – for maximum line speed, and distance, the haul must be made simultaneously with greatest tip speed. This is during the final, fastest rod movement of both the back and forward casts.

You will also forget that the back cast requires just as much power and takes just as long to straighten as a forward cast of equal length. Watch your back cast. When the back cast is perfect, the forward cast makes itself.

Don't lower your hand as you bring the butt of the rod forward on the fishing cast. Instead, keep it high, as though you were pushing a weight along a shoulder-high shelf. Remember, for long casts the force must be applied to the line in a single plane. To do this, the rod butt must also move in one plane.

And finally, as you begin to gain proficiency and can make cast after cast of more than 100 feet, you will discover that after you have fished awhile your casts get shorter. Try as you will, you can't improve them. This happens to all of us. We try too hard. We begin to rely on strength, rather than correct form. Relax and use less muscle. As if by magic, your fly will sail out 20 feet farther on the next attempt.

One of the most common faults seen around the English reservoir banks is the undue amount of false casting. As soon as a good back cast has been achieved, the forward delivery should be made. Often anglers go on and on false casting, becoming more and more tired, and shoot the line following a very ragged back cast.

How to Fish Reservoir Flies

There have always been arguments among flyfishers about whether the choice of fly pattern or the manner of presentation is more important, but few would disagree with the view that the correct fly, correctly presented, is likeliest to catch trout.

In reservoir trout fishing, working each pattern in the right way is of great importance. When imitations of actual insects are in use, there is no better way of learning how to fish them than careful observation of the insect. Make your artificial move as nearly as possible in the same way as the real insect.

For example, Sedge flies of the larger kinds scuttle along the surface after hatching. After moving a few feet they stop and rest. Pull your floating imitation along the surface. You may have to pull it faster than the real insect to make it rise on its hackles and skim along nicely. Do this by raising the rod from horizontal to about 50 degrees to the surface of the water, pulling the line with the left hand at the same time. Then lower the rod and recover the slack. Takes may come during the pull or the pause. Repeat until it is time to re-cast.

Midge pupae hang just below the surface. Unless there is bright sunlight, grease the leader to within an inch of the fly. Cast, and move the fly in tiny jerks with long pauses.

A corixa swims up to the surface steadily. Let the artificial corixa sink nearly to the bottom, then bring it up in a long slow pull. When it is near the surface, give it plenty of time to sink again.

Ephemerid nymphs of still water flies like

A reservoir trout angler of the 1970's: Paul Thomas, casting into the breeze on Grafham Water.
Tackle: *Hardy 9 ft 3 in. R. W. 'Superlite' rod. 11 yards of No 8 quick-sinking shooting-head line, needle-knotted to 100 yards of 20 lb* B.S. *monofilament main-line.* $3\frac{3}{8}$ *in. Intrepid reel.*

The line-bucket, slung in front, holds the slack line that accumulates as nymph or lure is worked in at varying speed towards the rod. The landing-net – a Hardy Superlite – stands well clear of the back cast, but ready to hand.
(Photograph: T. Pontone)

the Lake Olive, Pond Olive, Sepia Dun and Claret Dun move in short darts near the bottom and over weed beds until their time comes to hatch, when they swim steadily up to the surface. When no flies are seen hatching and trout are not visible, fish the artificial nymphs deep with short jerks. If flies are hatching, let the artificial sink deep, then draw it up steadily.

Fancy flies fall into two classes, those that are fished fast and those that are fished slowly. The Black and Peacock Spider is one that kills best when fished slowly, either in very slow draws or in tiny jerks. The popular Worm Fly should be retrieved slowly and steadily; the Barney Google in short, slow pulls.

Streamlined versions of old favourites like Peter Ross, Dunkeld and Butcher should be drawn quite quickly, as should more modern dressings like the Sweeney Todd and other hairwings. Sometimes it pays to draw these flies as fast through the water as can be easily managed and this is certainly true of what are usually called 'Lures', i.e. multi-hook streamers. However, when moving any of these flies fast or at medium pace, it often pays to vary the retrieve with pauses of about five seconds. Often, when re-commencing the retrieve, a trout will be found to have taken the fly. It is important to remember to strike firmly when this happens.

Polystickles and other fry-flies should be fished to move in the same way as sticklebacks and coarse-fish fry; small darts, pauses and occasional long pulls. A smooth steady retrieve is not desirable, though it does succeed occasionally.

The kind of line chosen plays an important part in the behaviour of the fly. For slow-moving imitations of insects the floating line is usually necessary, and to fish deep a long ungreased leader is needed, with plenty of time being given to allow the fly to sink. Floating lines may also be used to fish fancy flies, lures and Polystickles, casting cross-wind and allowing the line to be blown round in a bow, towing the fly along just below the surface. Otherwise these flies are best fished on sinking lines. The faster you want to move the fly and the deeper you want to fish it, the faster sinking should be your line. Big hairwing flies and multi-hook lures will often catch trout, when used with an ultra-high density line, in conditions where other combinations of line and fly would fail.

A Polystickle used with a heavy line will sometimes allow one to fish into a wind too strong to allow any other combination, the Polystickle being heavy and having low air-resistance. Often conditions dictate fly and method; you cannot fish a deep nymph, or a midge pupa just beneath the surface, on a floating line in high waves and a strong adverse wind.

Above all, the reservoir trout fisher should avoid acquiring a stereotyped style of retrieve. Instead it should be capable of almost infinite variation. It may take as long as five minutes to retrieve some of the slow-fished flies, less than twenty seconds to retrieve some that need fast movement.

Time allowed for sinking is important and in this, a watch with a second hand helps. If you want to fish near the bottom, keep

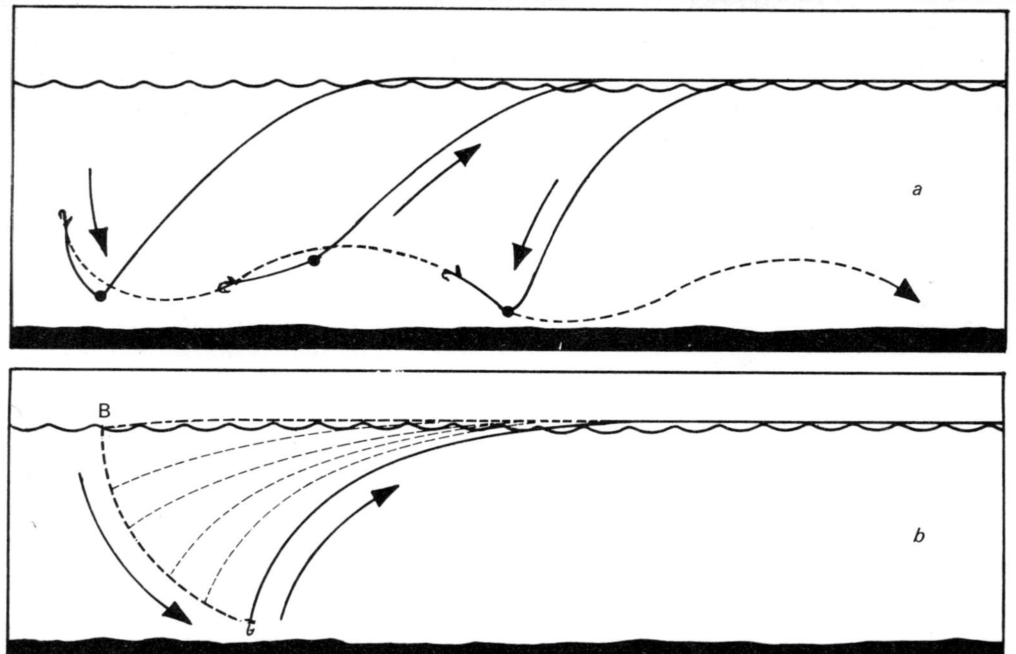

Figs. 28.3.a (top) *and 28.3.b* (bottom).
Stillwater nymph fishing.

adding to the sinking time you allow your fly, until you actually touch bottom. Then subtract a few seconds from the time allowance on subsequent casts.

Remember there are nearly always more trout feeding near the bottom than anywhere else. By all means fish at the surface or close below, if you see many trout moving there, but if not, fish really deep. It is not unknown for trout to feed at midwater, but it is certainly uncommon. Flies near the surface or near the bottom account for many more trout than those fished at intermediate depths.

Think well before deciding which line, which fly and which kind of retrieve are most likely to succeed in the conditions you find, and then give your choice plenty of time to prove itself. Changing flies, lines and depths every few minutes will catch few trout; but when a change is quite obviously necessary, don't be too lazy to change not only the fly, but, if necessary, the line and leader as well.

Nymph fishing

Fig. 28.3 shows a technique of nymph fishing with a floating line and a split-shot on the leader. (A dropper can be used if required, above the split-shot.)

Although not easy to cast, this sink-and-draw style of fly-fishing – in reality nothing more than a form of old-fashioned trolling – is sometimes a highly successful ploy which can be tried when no trout are showing on or near the surface. Weather conditions: dull, windy, cold. Falling barometer. Poor hatch of fly.

Nymphs are very sensitive to weather conditions. A sudden change of temperature and barometric pressure may induce a hatch of fly or cause a hatch to cease with equal rapidity. On a sunny day, when weather is soft and warm with a rising barometer, flies are likely to hatch. The following method of fishing nymph is preferable under these conditions (see Fig. 28.4).

The nymph is cast to B and allowed to sink to the bottom. A turn or two of fine wire round the hook shank will assist quick sinking. The nymph should be drawn up towards the surface with a steady continuous movement, to simulate the hatching insect.

Sedge fishing at dusk – causing a wake

After hatching, large sedges tend to move across the surface of the water leaving a V-shaped wake. It is *not* a continuous movement. A sedge will scutter for a few feet, then stop and rest.

The artificial fly should be worked across the surface in a way that simulates this behaviour. Scutter, pause. Scutter, pause. Scutter, pause. Trout may take when the fly is moving or while it is at rest, but the best taking time is just as it starts to move forward again after a period of rest.

The fly should be worked right in almost to the angler's legs. In the half-light, trout will sometimes take only a rod's length away.

Pause Pause Pause

Scutter Scutter Scutter Scutter

Fig. 28.4 (above). *Sedge fishing : plan view of water surface.*

Below: *Brown trout, 6 lb 4 oz, caught by Paul Thomas on a 3 in. Black Lure fished just below the surface. It took late in the evening, when fish were feeding on perch fry dying of 'perch disease'.*

Leaders for Reservoir Fly-Fishing

The experienced reservoir trout angler, never quite satisfied with the range of professionally tied leaders available, invariably makes his own to suit a particular method or location[1]. The less experienced angler, perhaps fearful of putting his trust in a home-made product, uses shop-bought leaders – often choosing the wrong type.

We suggest that excellent results can be obtained if a shop-bought continuous-taper Platil dry-fly leader is modified by the addition of securely tied pieces of level Platil Strong nylon and/or pieces of level Platil Soft nylon.

1 There are, of course, some thoroughly reliable tapered leaders available in the tackle shops. Nevertheless it is important that the novice knows how to make them should the need arise – and it frequently does!

Richard Walker, utilizing the good qualities of both knots, has devised two basic leaders that will serve the reservoir fly fisherman for practically all his needs. He uses a blood knot at the thick end of the leader – where a neat knot will help to reduce air resistance – and a water knot both at the fine end of the leader and where droppers are tied in.

The needle knot is used at all times to attach leader to line (see p. 408).

Mention of tying lengths of nylon together raises the question of knots. Until recently, few fly fishermen questioned the blood knot's supremacy. But now, practical tests have established that the *water knot* (the oldest knot in angling history) is first choice (see p, 404). Although slightly fatter, the water knot is stronger than the blood knot.

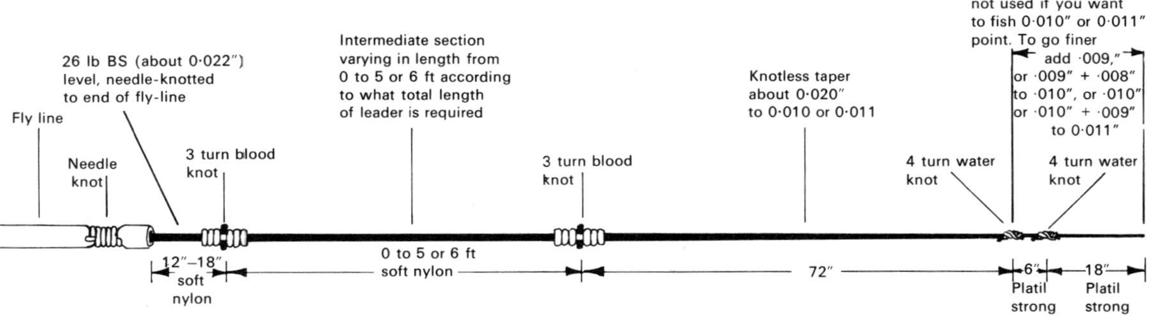

Fig. 28.5. Richard Walker's reservoir leaders for single fly or lure (above) *and* (below) *for more than one fly.*

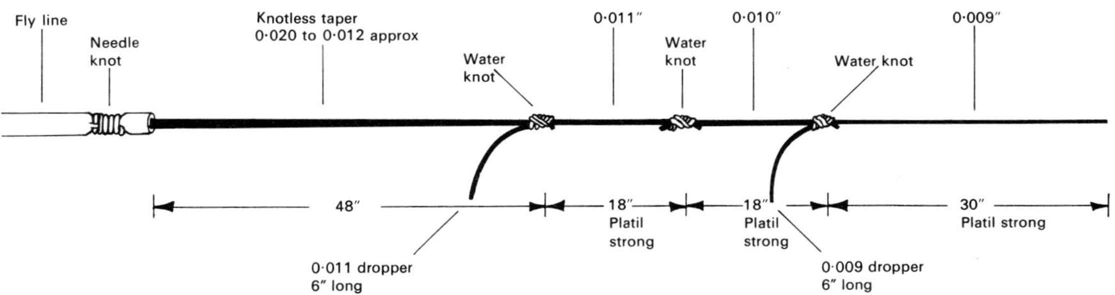

BOAT FISHING

Conventional methods of fishing from a boat on large lakes and reservoirs mostly involve drifting, which makes really deep fishing almost impossible, even with sinking lines.

It is usual to fish two or three flies, though on waters such as Loch Leven, it is common to use as many as four. On southern reservoirs, most anglers content themselves with two. With traditional fly patterns, a favourite team consists of Peter Ross at point, Mallard and Claret in the middle and Butcher on the bob. On southern reservoirs, especially in the evening, an Invicta can be tried at point and a Red Midge Pupa higher up the leader.

The most common method is to drift with the boat's beam at right-angles to the direction of the wind, the drift rate being slowed by means of a drogue. The anglers sit facing down-wind, casting ahead and retrieving at a rate that allows them to keep in touch with their flies.

The retrieve is usually terminated by raising the rod and causing the nearest fly, the 'bob', to dance on the surface for a few seconds. The longer the rod, the lighter the line, the longer this can be made to happen. Since long casting is not necessary a combination of long rod and light line has advantages. But straight down-wind casting is not very efficient, as it covers less water, gives the fish (which tend to head upwind) an unattractive view of the flies, and increases the tendency to pull the fly out of a fish's mouth. Consequently it is better to cast at an angle to the direction of drift, so that the flies are drawn partly across the wind.

This can be done rather better if the boat drifts with its fore and aft axis in line with the wind direction and its occupants casting on opposite sides. This technique is a very old one and used to be known as 'fishing the fall'. With sinking lines, deep fishing is improved if the anglers cast across and slightly downwind and then allow the boat to 'drift through', so that the flies are caused to swing crosswind and inwards behind the boat. Of course, floating lines can be used in the same way, and the method is especially suitable for fishing hairwing and streamer flies of fairly large size.

For some curious reason, this method is barred at Grafham, where it is described as 'side-casting.'

Most of the earlier works on lake and loch fishing advise drifting over water not more than 8–12 ft deep. This may be good advice where natural lakes are concerned, but it is far from true of reservoirs, where trout are often to be found feeding in water up to 70 ft or more in depth. The best opportunities usually occur when there is a moderate breeze and what are known as 'slicks' – long 'lanes' of calm, oily-looking water in line with the direction of the wind and with rippled water on either side. Trout are found in the calm water close to the ripple or on the edge of the ripple itself. When they are feeding on midge or sedge pupae their rises are easily seen, and casts can be made to individual fish.

In such conditions it often pays to abandon drifting, drop anchor and let the fish move upwind towards the boat. Sedge or midge pupae are the fly patterns most often required,

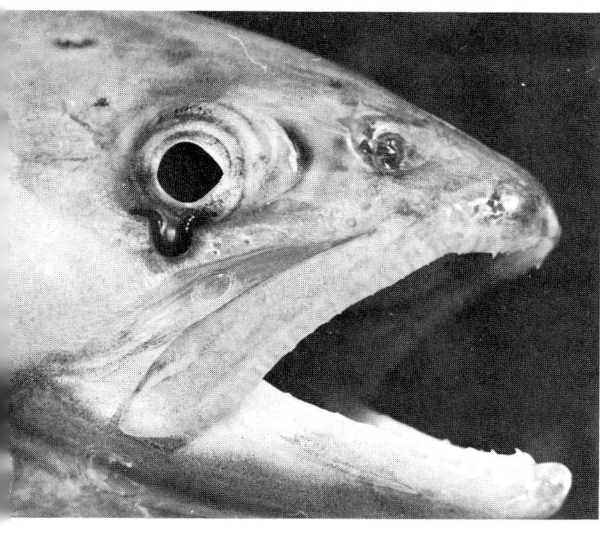

The condition of a trout often depends on parasites, such as the leech which, being a blood-sucker, may cause anaemia. This fish was caught in Lullingstone Lake by G. Berth-Jones. In his experience, trout are more likely to be leech-infested in waters with extensive areas of muddy bottom.

but at times floating sedges or crane-fly imitations can be deadly, as can imitations of ants, beetles, black gnats, hawthorn flies, drone flies and other creatures that may be blown on to the water.

When ephemerid flies such as pond olives and lake olives, are seen hatching, the appropriate nymph can be tied on the point with an imitation of the winged dun on the dropper. The dry fly is much neglected by stillwater trout-fishers, but it is well worth keeping a few Daddy-long-legs, big Sedges, and Drone Flies in one's box, and using them whenever fish are seen eating the natural insects on the surface.

Fishing from a boat in a considerable wind and wave can be very productive. The movement of the boat makes it difficult to keep in touch with the flies, but the wave effect on the line moves them even when the angler is out of touch.

The secret is to fish with a short line and tighten whenever you see the slightest sign of a fish even within several yards of where you think the flies are. You sometimes get a side view of a trout in a wave, as if it were in a glass case. Assume that any trout you see has your fly in its mouth, and tighten at once. You may be surprised to find how often you have hooked the fish.

For really rough water a fairly large Worm Fly on the point and a smallish Red or Black Midge Pupa on the dropper make a good combination.

A method which can be very effective at times is to cast a tandem lure as far as possible, and strip it back at high speed. The same applies to trailing a lure behind a moving boat. But although such methods are certainly not unsporting they can become very dull, since little skill is required to fish them. We suggest therefore that the novice angler keeps them in reserve and uses them only when more interesting methods fail.

Cross Wind Fly-Fishing

(A method of still water fly fishing from a boat for brown trout, rainbow trout and sea-trout.)

Note: Success at this type of fishing depends almost entirely on the way the boat is handled.

Reservoir trout fisherman usually fish two to a boat and manage without the services of a professional ghillie. Almost invariably they restrict themselves to drifting downwind or casting from the boat at anchor – methods which permit both of them to fish at the same time. We suggest that angling companions who are prepared to think in terms of the total 'boat-catch' rather than their individual catches, should try taking it in turns to handle the boat so

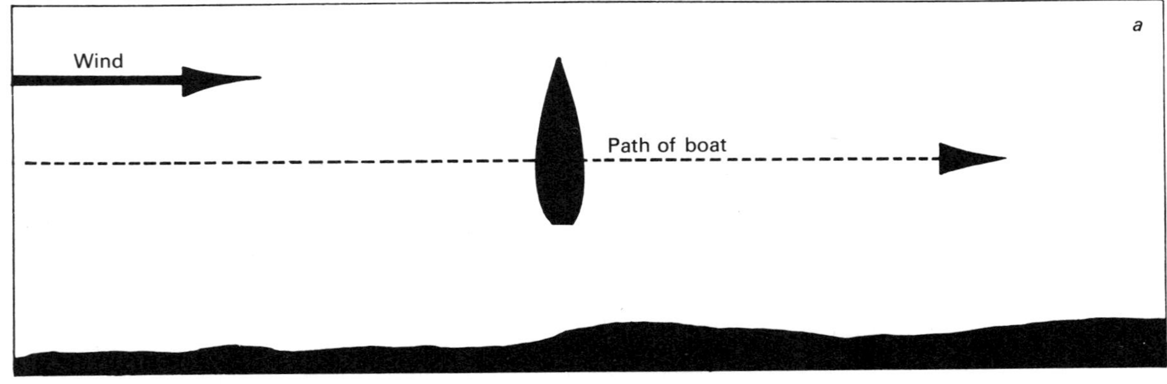

Figs. 28.6.a (above) *and 28.6.b* (below).

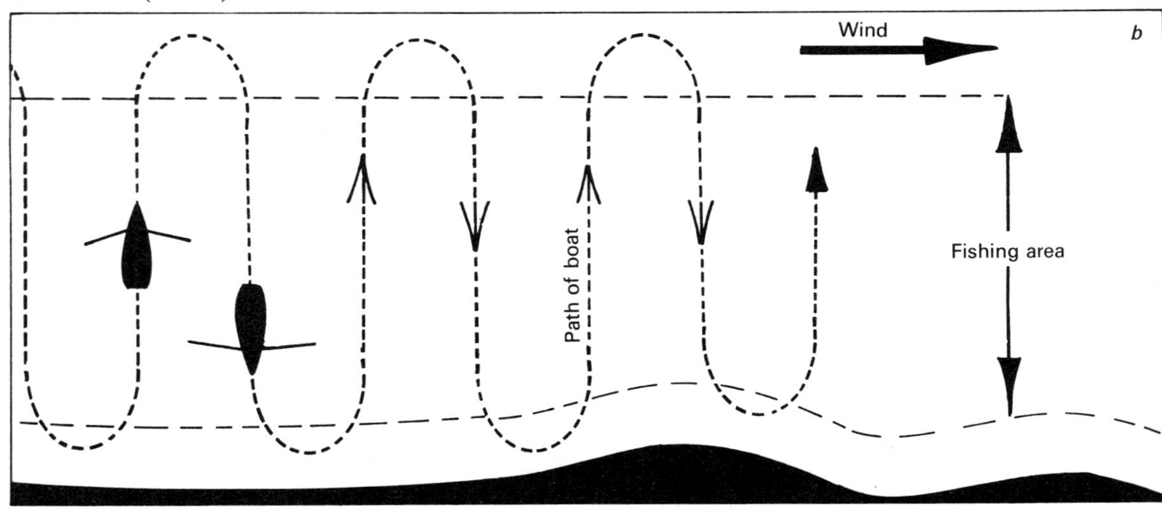

that cross-wind fishing can be practised. It is the deadliest of all still water fly-fishing methods. Needless to say, both sinking-line and floating-line techniques should be tried.

The usual method of fly-fishing from a boat in still water is to motor or row to the upwind end of a fishing area and then drift straight downwind (Fig. 28.6.*a*). The flies are cast ahead of the drifting boat and worked back towards the angler. An oar is used only to keep the boat broadside to the wind, or to avoid shallows.

A very much more profitable method is to fish to and fro along a zig-zag path *across* wind (Figs. 28.6.*b* and 7). The course of the boat varies in relation to the shore according to the wind direction.

Note: The lee shore of a lake is nearly always the most productive.

When two rods are fishing (Fig. 28.8), the stern rod (A) should fish with a sinking line and cast as far as possible to B. As the boat moves forward across the wind he allows his line to sink, until (from position C) he fishes his flies round the arc CD.

The bow rod uses a floating line and casts a shorter distance to F), then concentrates on keeping his bob-fly skimming along the trough of the waves to G; the tail-fly fishing just under the surface.

When a 'hot-spot' is reached, the boat is held in position for a time so that the area can be thoroughly covered.

It is essential that the oarsman should know the best fishing areas and be able to manoeuvre the boat at just the right speed; checking and holding it in position when a 'hot-spot' is reached. For fishing these 'hot-spots' it is better to keep to the oars rather than drop anchor, since skilful handling can keep the boat on station, broadside to the wind.

Fig. 28.7.

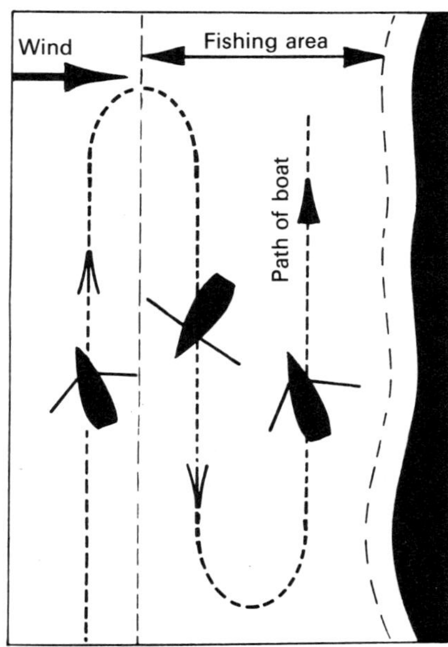

Fig. 28.8.

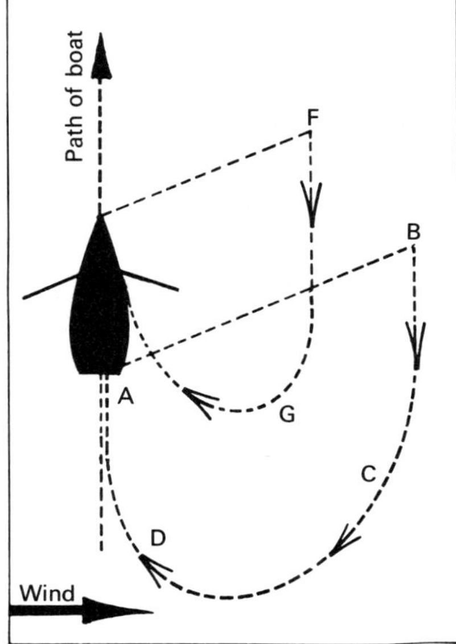

The Static Fly

That trout will occasionally pick up a fly that is lying inert on the bottom is well known. Many anglers have cast out their lines and rested their rods while taking a drink, or eating their lunch, and then found that a trout has obligingly attached itself. Only recently, however, has it been realized that in some circumstances it pays to fish a static fly deliberately.

The method is very simple. You cast out, using a sinking fly line, and allow everything to fall to the bottom. If fishing from a boat you must be securely anchored, and it is best to use a shooting-head and to cast far enough to allow all the fly-line to lie on the bottom – that is, have at least six or seven yards of monofil backing beyond the top rod-ring.

It is important to choose the right place to fish the static fly, and the criteria to observe are:

1. The penetration of light.
2. The nature of the bottom.

The static fly does best on a bottom of gravel or sand, where there is little or no weed growth in depths of from 8 to 15 feet. Short of careful investigation of depth and weed growth, it often pays to try a static fly in parts of a lake where large numbers of sedge flies are seen to be hatching.

The pattern of fly seems relatively unimportant. Trout can be caught on imitations of midge pupae, sedge pupae and the nymphs of dragonflies and water beetles, as well as on Muddler Minnows, Polystickles and Rasputins, and even on traditional

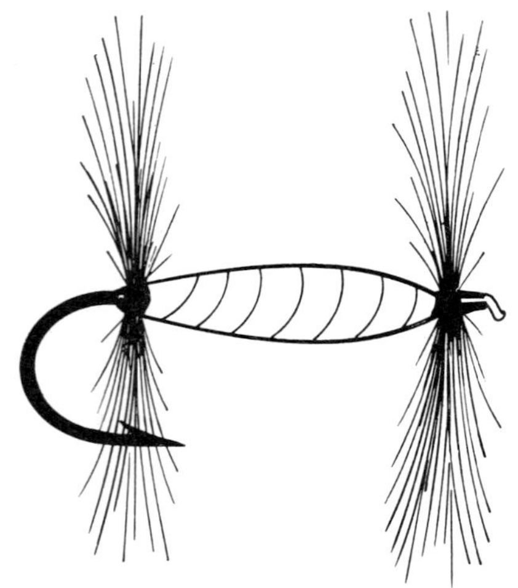

Fig. 28.9. Fore-and-aft Glowstickle (above). *Rasputin* (below).

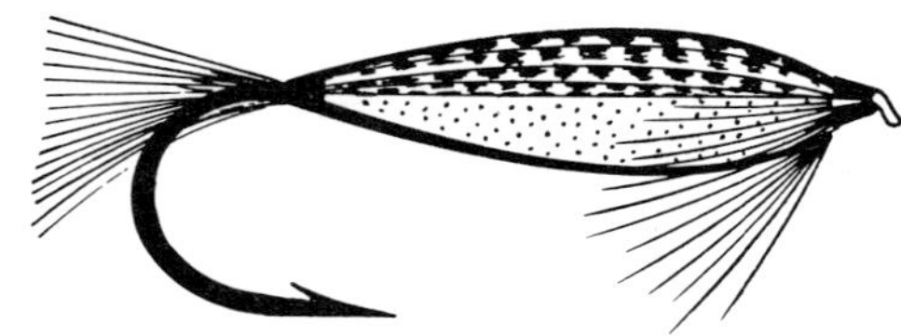

dressings like Invicta, Dunkeld and Butcher and, doubtless, many others. Given such catholicity on the part of the trout one may do well to use a fly that has mechanical advantages and there are two dressings that are particularly successful: the Rasputin and the Fore-and-aft Glowstickle (see illustrations).

The Rasputin has a body of fine-textured expanded polyethylene and is therefore buoyant. It is fished on a Hi-D fly-line (fast sinker) with a very short leader. We have succeeded with as little as four inches, twelve inches is the limit.

The Fore-and-aft Glowstickle can be fished on a normal length of leader. This makes it more convenient to use if the static-fly is given a short trial as a change from normal fly-fishing. It consists of a cigar-shaped body made of luminous plastic strip wound over an underbody of floss, with a pale buff or cream cock hackle, long in fibre, wound at both head and tail. The hackles support the fly when it has sunk and prevent the hook point from catching bottom debris.

Other fore-and-aft dressings in which luminous plastic is replaced by a body of peacock herl, pheasant tail fibres, or white polythene strip, also succeed.

Although the possibility of doing so cannot be discounted, a rainbow trout has never yet been caught on a static fly. Perhaps other anglers have done this without mentioning it. If so, we have never heard of it. The real value of the static method is its ability to catch large brown trout that have become exclusively bottom feeders. These are fish that can never be caught by surface, or near-surface, fishing. To catch them with the static fly adds an extra fillip to more conventional methods.

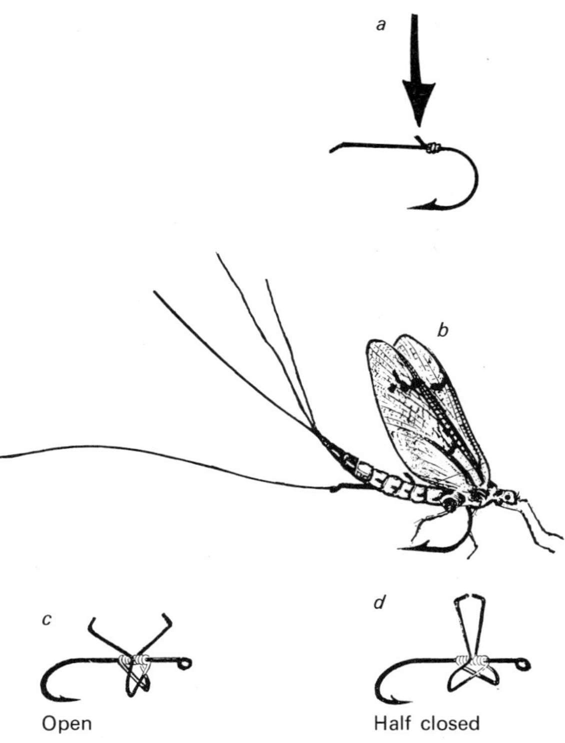

Fig. 28.10. Hooks for dapping. The 'Ayrbro' dapping hook (c and d), fitted with a small spring clip, permits the mounting of a live insect without damaging it. The hook is of the Limerick pattern, made in sizes 6–14. Mayflies, daddy-long-legs and grasshoppers are the most popular dapping baits.

Dapping for Trout

Dapping can be carried out with most species of large fly and beetle, both natural and artificial, but it is usually confined to the natural mayfly, the daddy-long-legs (or crane-fly) and the grasshopper.

A long, light (but not too whippy) rod is essential, 14–16 feet in length.

Any sort of fly or centrepin reel that will carry sufficient reel-line of the appropriate strength will do. To the reel line, ten or twelve yards of floss blow-line is attached.

A 6 ft nylon leader is attached to the blowline. This should not be too fine, since the dap can attract the biggest fish in the water, and sometimes they are very big – especially in some of the Irish limestone loughs such as Corrib and Mask.

To the leader is tied a single hook, fine wire, wide gape, size 10–12. This should have a tiny bristle fastened to the shank with a few turns of the finest tying silk (Fig. 28.10.*a*). Its function is to prevent the fly from slipping once it has been hooked into place. In effect this is similar to the bristle tied on a hook to hold a worm in place (see p. 439) but is tied nearer to the bend of the hook.

Dapping.

The point of the hook is inserted at the side of the thorax just below the wings and pushed right through the insect, so that the tiny bristle emerges and holds the body in place (see Fig. 28.10.*b*).

The boat is set on a drift broadside to the breeze. By raising his rod the angler allows the fly to be carried out with the wind. It should sit naturally on the water, or skim lightly across the surface. As much of the leader as possible should be kept clear of the water – hence the need for a long rod.

When a fish takes the fly the rod point should be dropped at once. The golden rule is: *don't strike.* Give the fish time to go down with the fly for several feet without feeling any resistance whatsoever. As the line straightens out, tighten by raising the rod – and the fish should be hooked.

Note: A good breeze with a fair ripple on the water is very necessary. Dapping in a dead calm when the water is flat and glassy is virtually a waste of time.

THE FIRST CAST OF THE DAY

There have been many accounts of big trout hooked with the first cast of the day, but the best we have ever read is by a little-known American author, William Burroughs, in *Locusts and Wild Honey* (1884), a book written with great charm and feeling.

'It was a dull, rainy day; the fog rested low upon the mountains, and the time hung heavily on our hands. About three o'clock the rain slackened and we emerged from our den, Joe going to look after his horse, which had eaten but little since coming into the woods, the poor creature was so disturbed by the loneliness and the black flies; I, to make preparations for dinner, while my companion lazily took his rod and stepped to the edge of the big pool in front of camp. At the first introductory cast, and when his fly was not fifteen feet from him on the water, there was a lunge and a strike, and apparently the fisherman had hooked a boulder. I was standing a few yards below engaged in washing out the coffee pail, when I heard him call out:

'"I have got him now!"

'"Yes, I see you have", said I, noticing his bending pole and moveless line. "When I am through I will help you get loose."

'"No, but I'm not joking," said he. "I have got a big fish."

'I looked up again, but saw no reason to change my impression and kept on with my work.

'It is proper to say that my companion was a novice at fly-fishing, he never having cast a fly until this trip.

'Again he called out to me, but deceived by his coolness and nonchalant tones, and by the lethargy of the fish, I gave little heed. I knew very well that if I had struck a fish that held me down in that way I should have been going through a regular war-dance on that circle of boulder-tips, and should have scared the game into activity, if the hook had failed to wake him up. But as the farce continued I drew nearer.

'"Does that look like a stone or a log?" said my friend, pointing to his quivering line, slowly cutting the current up toward the centre of the pool.

'My scepticism vanished in an instant, and I could hardly keep my place on the top of the rock.

'"I can feel him breathe," said the now warming fisherman, "just feel of that pole."

'I put my eager hand upon the butt and could easily imagine I felt the throb or pant of something alive down there in the black depths. But whatever it was it moved like a turtle. My companion was praying to hear his reel spin, but it gave out now and then only a few hesitating clicks. Still the situation was excitingly dramatic, and we were all actors. I rushed for the landing net, but being unable to find it, shouted desperately for Joe, who came hurrying back, excited before he had learned what the matter was.

'The net had been left at the lake below, and must be had with the greatest despatch. In the meantime I skipped from boulder to boulder as the fish worked this way or that about the pool, peering into the water to catch a glimpse of him, for he had begun to yield a little to the steady strain that was kept upon him. Presently I saw a shadowy, unsubstantial something just emerge from the black depths, then vanish. Then I saw it again, and this time the huge proportions of the fish were faintly outlined by the white facings of his fins. . . . I had been a fisher from my earliest boyhood. I came from a race of fishers; trout streams gurgled about the roots of the family tree, and there was a long accumulated and transmitted tendency and desire in me that that sight gratified. I did not wish the pole in my own hands; there was quite enough electricity overflowing from it and filling the air for me. The fish yielded more and more to the relentless pole, till, in about fifteen minutes, from the time he was struck, he came to the surface, then made a little whirlpool when he disappeared again. But presently he was up a second time and lashing the water into foam as the angler led him towards the rock upon which I was perched, net in hand. As I reached towards him, down he went again, and taking another circle of the pool, came up still more exhausted, when, between his paroxysms, I carefully ran the net under him and lifted him ashore, amid, it is needless to say, the wildest enthusiasm of the spectators.

'"What does he weigh?" was the natural enquiry of each; and we took it in turns "hefting" him. But gravity was less potent to us then than usual, and the fish seemed astonishingly light.

'"Four pounds," we said, but Joe said more. So we improvised a scale; a long strip of board was balanced across a stick, and our groceries served as weights. A four-pound package of sugar kicked the beam quickly; a pound of coffee was added; still it went up; then a pound of tea, and still the fish had a little the best of it. But we called it six pounds, not to drive too sharp a bargain with fortune, and were more than satisfied. Such a beautiful creature, marked in every respect like a trout of six inches. We feasted our eyes upon him for half an hour. We stretched him upon the ground and admired him, we laid him across a log and withdrew a few paces to admire him; we hung him against the shanty and turned our heads from side to side as women do when they are selecting dress-goods, the better to take in the full force of the effect.

'He graced the board or stump that afternoon, and was the sweetest fish taken.'

COOKING THE TROUT

Baked Stuffed Trout

1 trout
2 tablespoonsful butter

Stuffing:	Sauce:
Stale bread	*1 oz butter*
½ stick celery	*1 oz flour*
1 shallot	*1 teaspoonful capers*
Parsley	*1 teaspoonful lemon juice*
Salt and pepper	*⅓ teaspoonful anchovy essence*
	Salt and pepper

Make stuffing by grating bread, shallot, celery, parsley and mixing together with salt and pepper.
Clean, scale and dry the fish and fill with stuffing. Sew up.
Melt butter in a baking dish, put in fish and bake in a moderate oven for about half an hour, basting frequently.
Take fish out and keep hot.
Make sauce by heating butter, sieving in the flour and cooking for a few minutes. Strain in the liquor from the baking tray. If insufficient, make up with hot fish stock or milk. Stir until boiling and smooth, then add capers, lemon juice, anchovy essence, salt and pepper.
Pour over fish and serve.

Oven-Cooked Trout and Bacon

Clean and dry the fish.
Wrap each fish in a slice of bacon.
Place fish on a rack inside a roasting tin.
Cook in a hot oven for about twenty minutes.
Serve with extra slices of bacon and slices of fried bread.

28b · The Rainbow Trout

Salmo gairdneri

From 1885, for some years, shipments of rainbow ova were sent every winter from U.S.A. to hatcheries in Great Britain, but by 1890 quantities of eggs were also coming into this country from Herr Jaffe, who had been very successful in breeding rainbows in his hatchery at Osnabruck. Doubtless a a certain number of fish were later distributed amongst a few owners of pools and lakes throughout England, yet it was not until about 1898 that there is any record of them being introduced into our waters in any substantial numbers. From that date onwards, many clubs and riparian owners purchased supplies from the English fish farms. Amongst them was King Edward VII who had some placed in the lake at Buckingham Palace, where, in 1903, Lord Denbigh took one on a fly – the first rainbow ever to be caught on rod and line in the heart of London.
A. COURTNEY WILLIAMS, *Angling Diversions* (1945).

The rainbow trout is native only to north-west America, from the Bering Sea in the north to California in the south. But since 1880, on account of its fine sporting and culinary qualities, it has been exported to nearly every country in the world, at least to those that can offer cool clean rivers, lakes or reservoirs.

In its native waters – like our own brown trout which varies from sea-trout and slob trout to gillaroo etc. – the rainbow exists in those differing forms which enable it to exploit the varied habitats of salt, estuarine, and freshwater. An anadromous variety (breeding in freshwater and feeding in the sea) is known as the steelhead. Another rainbow variety lives in lakes and spawns in the feeder-streams. Yet a third spends its whole life in its natal river, while a fourth, known as the coastal rainbow (equivalent to our native slob trout), is an estuarine feeder and a river spawner.

The ancestry of these varieties is open to speculation since some strains spawn in the autumn (Shasta type) and some in the spring (Irideus type).

The rainbow trout has managed to breed successfully in a few British rivers; for instance, the Buckinghamshire rivers Chess and Misbourne, and in the Derbyshire Wye.

Enquiries in 1971 carried out by F. B. for Dr W. E. Frost's rainbow trout survey on behalf of The Salmon and Trout Association, indicate that the breeding colonies of Chess and Misbourne rainbow trout have become extinct. According to the keeper of the Chenies fishery on the river Chess, the original strain of rainbows gradually died out as a result of bad river conditons during the period 1945–70. This was due partly to drought conditions in the headwaters brought on by a lowering of the water table, and by sewage effluents and low water conditions in the middle reaches. Since the

So perfect is the shape of these two fish (above) *that they look like spring salmon – but see the tell-tale spotting on the tail fins. Each was the best of a bag of rainbow trout taken by Peter Thomas and F. B.*

Compare tail of rainbow (below left) *with that of brown trout* (below right) (Photographs: Roy Shaw).

Rainbows caught on a Muddler Minnow, an unlikely yet successful reservoir lure. A Muddler can be seen inside the mouth of the right-hand fish.

demise of the original stock it has been noticed that newly introduced eight to ten inch rainbows flourish for one season only. Those fish that escape capture in their first year go thin or 'disappear' – in all probability, die.

There has always been a certain reluctance to accept the presence of rainbow trout in Britain; but this chauvinism in defence of our native brown trout is beginning to wane, as more and more fishermen become aware of the rainbow's accommodating feeding habits, fighting prowess and culinary virtue. Nowadays an increasing number of stillwater fishery owners and managers prefer to stock with rainbows rather than with browns, in order to enjoy the economic advantages that accrue from a faster growing and more disease-resistant species.

To stock a river with rainbows is quite another matter. There is no doubt that instant trout fishing on the 'put and take basis' can be created in rivers small enough to be provided with an efficient downstream fish-barrier; but without a barrier the fish will migrate downstream and be lost. This tendency to move downstream could be caused by a migratory instinct. This is said to be endemic in our rainbow stock, since it is derived from the mixing of migrating and non-migrating strains.

In its habits the rainbow differs somewhat from the brown trout. It is a gregarious fish – often swimming in shoals, whereas the brown trout is essentially territorial having its own feeding territory which it will attempt to defend.

From our own observations we have

noticed that, like river brown trout, reservoir brown trout continue to feed after dark, whereas reservoir rainbows do not. It would be more strictly true to say that we and our friends have continued to catch brown trout well after dark, whereas we have not succeeded in catching a single rainbow in the same circumstances.

Reservoir rainbows, at least those of up to about 2 lb, are more persistent plankton feeders than brown trout. The fact that rainbow trout can stand a higher temperature range than browns may have a bearing on their feeding habits. We have noticed that rainbows will sometimes provide good sport in the middle of a hot summer day, a time when we would expect little response from brown trout. The reason for this could, quite simply, be a matter of appetite. Perhaps the fast-growing young rainbow trout needs more sustenance than the morning and evening hatch of insects can provide, so that it is forced to augment its diet with plankton. For this reason alone it would become more available to the fisherman.

It is known that the normal four-year life cycle of the rainbow is shorter than that of the brown trout. It is not surprising, therefore, that where both species thrive and where figures are available the recovery rate for rainbows is better than that of browns, since the rainbow is at risk from predators, disease and the ravages of winter for a *shorter* period. But the fact that it has to eat more food during its short life to sustain its faster growth must also put it at *greater* risk from the fisherman.

Peter Thomas with a brace of fine rainbows.

There is no need to explain to any fisherman that the difference between a basket with a brace of fish in it and a basket containing none at all is an absolute, not a relative difference. Eight and ten brace of fish may be about the same thing, but between two fish and nothing no sort of comparison is possible.
ARTHUR RANSOME.

The spectacular fight of the rainbow trout. This $2\frac{1}{2}$ pounder in Hanningfield Reservoir jumped seven times before it was landed.

28c · The Sea-Trout

Salmo trutta trutta

The last catch of my game-fishing season in 1963 was a 7 lb bull-trout. It came from the Whitby Esk, on 26th October. Some may wonder what difference there is between a trout and a bull-trout. This problem has been bothering anglers and biologists ever since we became interested in the types of fish in our rivers. All that the biologists can tell us is that the sea-trout and the bull-trout are exactly the same – biologically. What our eyes tell us is that they look entirely different.
ERIC HORSFALL TURNER (from a letter).

Sea-trout fishing is neither a branch of brown trout fishing nor of salmon fishing, *it is a sport entirely of its own.*

Since a surprising number of anglers fail to realise this, and as a consequence lose many opportunities of catching sea-trout, a few words on the subject may be helpful.

First of all, the fish itself.

The early life of the sea-trout is so similar to that of the Atlantic salmon (already described) that for the purposes of this book there is little point is dealing with it separately. Sufficient to say that like the salmon the sea-trout is born in fresh water where it spends the first two or three years of its life, going through the stages of alevin, fry and parr, finally assuming a silver coat, and, as a smolt, migrating to sea.

The full story of the sea-trout's life at sea is not known. It has been said that sea-trout travel little further than their local estuaries, but catches made by fishing vessels and fishery research stations indicate that the distance is substantially greater. From recoveries of tagged fish, journeys of several hundred miles have been recorded.

Whatever distance it travels, however, the sea-trout (like the salmon) goes to sea in

Sea-trout, 13 lb. Taken on Sunk Lure by H. F.

order to feed and grow, and while at sea it feeds avidly. Although its tastes are catholic its diet most probably consists mainly of small fish. (The stomach contents of a catch of sea-trout made by a fishery research vessel in the North Atlantic consisted entirely of fish.) The fry of herring and mackerel almost certainly contribute to this diet together with sandeels and sparling.

In most sea-trout rivers there are two main runs of adult fish each season: the summer run, which starts as early as April or May in some rivers, but not until June or early July in others, and the autumn or 'harvest' run which comes up in September. The biggest fish run early and late in the season. The shoals of young sea-trout – known as herling, finnock, whitling or sprod according to the district – begin to appear in the bottom pools towards the end of July.

As many fishermen have discovered to their cost, sea-trout are extremely shy. Whether they have an actual sense of taste is arguable, and no-one is certain over exactly what range of the spectrum they are sensitive to colour (although they are certainly colour conscious), but there is no doubt that their vision is unusually acute, and that being sensitive to vibration both from movement on the bank and in the water they are easily frightened. Disturb one fish and alarm quickly spreads through a shoal, even though other fish in the shoal can have no knowledge of what has caused the disturbance.

All fish possess otoliths, or earstones, which are located in the back of the brain. These not only assist a sense of balance but, as they are able to register vibration, form part of the warning system that transmits danger signals to the brain. A sea-trout responds readily to the very low frequencies, but not to the high frequencies. It will remain unaffected by an angler's conversation, but can become alarmed if he treads too heavily on the bank.

The point is academic, however. Conversation may not affect the fish, but it will certainly affect the fisherman. Nothing destroys concentration so effectively as chatter, and concentration is of vital importance to successful fishing. Lack of it is one of the main reasons for fishing failure.

Sea-trout that reach their destined pools during a spate seek shelter for a time from the turbulence and force of the current in the slacker water beside and underneath the bank, in little bays, or on the edge of some back-eddy. As the level of the water falls the fish swing out into the stream and lie in shoals, the larger fish in front, on beds of firm gravel or small shingle usually about two thirds of the way down a pool. Here there is a smooth unbroken flow of water which contains a steady supply of oxygen.

Fresh fish often carry sea lice on their bodies for several days. These lice usually drop off after 48 hours or less in fresh water, but in some instances may stay on for as long as five days. The female louse (see p. 185) carries two long string-like 'tails' or egg-sacs. These fall off very quickly after entry into fresh water, so that lice with these 'tails' intact are evidence that a fish is very fresh run indeed.

A sea-trout that has been for some time in the river takes a lure less readily than a fish fresh from the sea. This is probably because the longer a sea-trout lies in the river the less susceptible it becomes to the sensation of hunger.

While in fresh water waiting to spawn, a sea-trout eats very little – for the very good reason that in many rivers there is very little for it to eat. Many rivers which accommodate runs of sea-trout are clear, rocky, acid, barren spate rivers that hold only a tiny proportion of the food which would be necessary to support a sea-trout population with normal appetites. While in the sea the fish feed greedily. Few rivers can supply such meals.

During their sojourn in fresh water following their return from sea, sea-trout (like salmon) have no need for food. The supply of nourishment in their tissues is sufficient both to sustain them during a long fast, and to provide for the developing spawn. This is not to say that sea-trout eat no food at all while in the river, but there is a very great difference between the taking of occasional food items and *feeding*. If 'feeding' is defined as: *the taking of nourishment in order to sustain life*, then the sea-trout, like the salmon, is a non-feeder in fresh water.

This point is of the utmost importance to the fisherman, in particular to the fly fisherman.

There are two fundamentally different forms of approach to sea-trout fishing:

1. That the fish on their return from sea remain *active* feeders.
2. That the fish do *not* remain active feeders (in the sense already defined).

The fisherman who favours the first approach will take a bag of sea-trout only at certain times and under certain conditions. He will be fishing a fly which is intended to simulate the natural fly on the water. When the hatch is over and fish have gone down he will lose hope, pack up and go home.

The fisherman who adopts the second approach has always a chance of catching fish. While taking advantage of any hatch that may materialize, he will know this to be merely a passing phase. When the fish are down he will change to a completely different form of lure and technique and continue fishing – with every hope of success. By no means every angler understands the significance of this. Still in existence, it seems, is a group of noodles who believe that the earth is flat. Small wonder that anglers still exist who believe that sea-trout and salmon are regular freshwater feeders.

Chances at sea-trout are all too often missed because the angler is informed that

'The food situation is the decidedly dominant influence in the habits of the sea-trout'. Or, 'The sea-trout has a big appetite and is an aggressive feeder'!

While in the sea the sea-trout is certainly an aggressive feeder, its habits undoubtedly dominated by the search for food. But on its return to the river to spawn, nothing could be further from the truth.

Again, it has been said that '. . . rivers which hold large populations of migratory fish have to contain correspondingly large amounts of natural food'. And again, this is nonsense – simply because they *don't*. The fast, quick-rising, acid, spate river which rises and falls six or eight feet in as many hours, can seldom support more than a tiny population of diminutive brown trout in addition to supplying the needs of salmon and sea-trout fry. The *adult* migrants populating a single pool in such a river would require more food during one summer's day than the river could supply in a year – if the fish were eating the meals to which they have become accustomed at sea. But of course they are not. Nor have they the appetites to do so. Were it otherwise they would, by preying on their own young, have eaten themselves out of existence long ago.

Naturally, not all sea-trout waters present the same picture. Sea-trout that run into those food-rich lakes contained between river systems will take considerably more interest in food than their counterparts found in a spate river. In rivers which contain a plentiful food supply, sea-trout can sometimes be seen taking nymph or rising to a hatch of fly. But the reason for this interest in food is not because the fish have suddenly acquired an appetite, but because the food has suddenly appeared in front of them. Broadly speaking, the sea-trout's interest in a food item (or, for that matter, the angler's lure) is similar to that well known mountaineer's interest in his mountain – *because it is there*!

If it is not there the sea-trout will make little or no effort to search for it. In many rivers sea-trout stop hunting for food from the time they run from the sea, to their eventual return from the spawning redds. Sometimes, however, if a worm or a maggot or a spinner or a feathered lure is put in front of them they will take it. And the reason why they do so is very probably because of habit – the feeding habit they have indulged so recently and so avidly at sea.

It would be folly to expect sea-trout behaviour to conform to an exact pattern in all rivers. The behaviour of many species of animals depends largely on environment, and the sea-trout is no exception. *For generation after generation fish return to the rivers that bred them. This is so consistent that populations of migratory fish in rivers only a few miles apart undoubtedly follow slightly separate lines of evolution.*

Nevertheless, sea-trout, like salmon, are equipped to endure a long fast while in fresh water; and although their behaviour may vary according to their environment, very few, if any, can (by the terms of our definition) be called *feeding* fish.

This is the difference between the river behaviour of sea-trout and brown trout. The

Sea-trout, $2\frac{1}{2}$ lb, caught at night by H. F. while fishing with F. B. in a Donegal sea lough, June, 1970. The small fish underneath is a sparling, Osmerus eperlanus, *taken from the sea-trout's throat immediately after capture. In spite of having its mouth full, the sea-trout took the sunk lure also (see p. 296) pictured. A graphic example of sea-trout behaviour when feeding in salt water.*

Note: *Readers familiar with H.F.'s book* Sea-Trout Fishing *may be interested to know that the sea-trout pictured above was caught in the very same place as the sparling-gorged fish described on p. 16 of the book. An exact repeat performance – eighteen years later!*

difference between the river behaviour of sea-trout and salmon is that while the salmon tends to take a lure mainly by day, the sea-trout tends to do so mainly by night.

Thus, the concept of a non-feeding fish which is more active by night than by day, and which takes a lure or bait because of habit rather than hunger and necessity, is a very sound basis from which to start thinking about how to catch sea-trout.

In the Night usually the best Trouts bite, and will rise ordinarily in the still deeps; but not so well in the Streams. And although the best and largest Trouts bite in the Night (being afraid to stir, or range about in the Daytime) yet I account this way of Angling both unwholsom, unpleasant and very ungentiel, and to be used by none but Idle pouching Fellows . . . as for Damming, Groping, Spearing, Hanging, Twitcheling, Netting, or Firing by Night, I purposely omit them, and them esteem to be used only by disorderly and rascally Fellows, for whom this little Treatise is not in the least intended.

JAMES CHETHAM, *The Angler's Vade-Mecum* (1681).

SEA-TROUT BY NIGHT

The sea-trout madness is not quite so widespread as the salmon madness already described. But what the sea-trout lunatics lack in number they make up for in degree. Salmon men, after all, are merely trying to

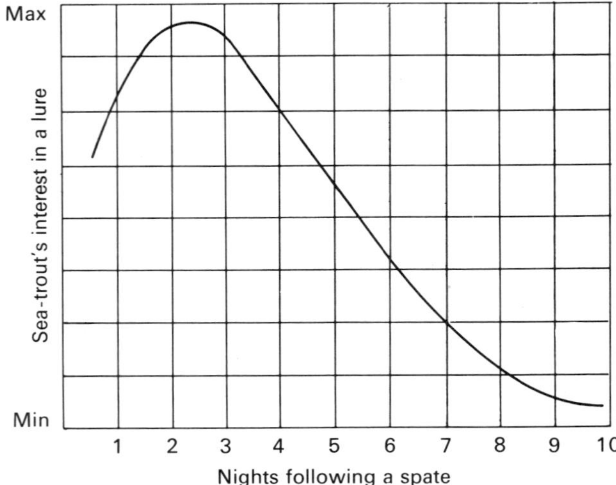

A graph roughly predicting sea-trout behaviour.

tempt non-feeding fish to take something which vaguely represents food. But the sea-trout men are not only trying to hook fish most of which have little or no appetite, they frequently elect to do it at night – and on very dark nights, at that.

Sea-trout can, of course, be caught on a variety of baits and lures at any hour of the day, and many are. But loch fishing apart and with the exception of a few rivers which particularly suit daylight fishing, most sea-trout taken on fly are caught between the hours of dusk and dawn. For a small band of anglers, sea-trout on the fly at night represents the very cream of freshwater fishing.

Night fly-fishing is a difficult sport and, naturally, it is not to everybody's taste. Indeed, anyone who does not derive a deep delight from spending long hours in the darkness with only the wind and water as his companions, should abandon any serious thought of it. It is, however, a rewarding sport, for unless the river is in spate and coloured there is no night of the season when sea-trout cannot be caught.

This is a view that is at variance with much that has been written on the subject. Many writers are of the opinion that sea-trout night fly-fishing is a chancy sport, worthwhile only in certain favourable conditions, seldom profitable after midnight and that many blank nights can be expected: an opinion that is founded on ignorance, both of sea-trout and of the best flies (or lures) with which to catch them.

Apart from the occasional very big fish that remains apart from its fellows in its own carefully guarded lie, sea-trout tend to herd together in shoals. And although during the hours of darkness they will accept a degree of disturbance which they will not tolerate during daylight, mass alarm affects them just as it does porpoises, herring-gulls and other group species. For this reason, if for no other, the angler should cultivate stealth.

No matter how suitable his tackle and lures, no matter how skilfully he may cast, it is all pointless if the fish have fled. He must learn to think and act like a hunter, to move quietly both in and out of the water; he should know where sea-trout are lying, or are likely to be lying, and above all he should understand at least *some* of the reasons why he fails to catch them.

There are anglers who arrive on a river bank in herds in broad daylight, thunder about against the skyline, wade in among the lies, thrash their lines across water from which every fish has vanished – and at the end of a fruitless hour make the night hideous with their wailing.

Starting to fish the fly too soon in the evening is one of the most common sea-trout fishing faults and probably results in more missed opportunities than any other. Unless the water is rippled or sufficiently cloudy to obscure the angler and to 'absorb' the splash of his line, *it is a golden rule never to start fishing until well after the sun has set.*

Provided the water is fished stealthily, one pool is ample for a night's fishing. If a second pool is available, all well and good, for if they are small pools they will fish the better for being given a rest from time to time.

When pools are well stocked with fish there is little to be gained by rushing about from place to place. If the angler has a good holding pool at his disposal to fish as he likes, he will do best to stay where he is. He knows he is covering plenty of fish. If sea-trout are not taking in his pool they are unlikely to be doing so elsewhere. Better by far to become intimate with that piece of water, set up two rods and try the many variations of lure and technique available.

The exception to this occurs early in the season when the main sea-trout run has yet to come and fish are spread very thinly throughout the beat. Then, mobility is more important than variety of method, and the best chance of taking fish is to choose one method, use one rod and cover as much water as possible.

Quite irrespective of any hatch of fly, there are three main taking periods: at dusk; about an hour or so after midnight, and during the hour of daybreak. The angler who packs up after the dusk 'rise', thinking the fish are down for the night, deprives himself of many chances, not least being the chance of catching a *big* sea-trout. Oddly enough, more big fish can be caught after than before midnight.

During the first period, when sea-trout are active and will take a fly that is swimming close to the surface, the angler will do well to fish a 'Medicine' on floating line. When fishing a fly high it is best to fish it fast; but since all lures are intended to represent living animals – usually (though not always) little fish – they should rarely be fished at speeds which would be impossible for animals of that size to attain.

Sometimes, sea-trout remain active all through the night. On these occasions the same fly can be fished, and an exceptional bag taken. But such nights are rare. A typical night usually starts with a taking period lasting perhaps, from 45 minutes to an hour and a half. After this the fish usually stop taking and 'go down'. Quite suddenly the river seems utterly lifeless, the fly swings across the pool untouched, and it is at this point that so many anglers lose heart and go home.

Unless they have to be up early in the morning, or have no relish for late night fishing, they are almost invariably wrong. The fish are certainly down, and the chances are they will stay down, but if the angler has the recommended lures and presents them correctly he can enjoy opportunities of catching fish throughout the night. He will, however, have to make considerable changes in technique.

Now that the fish are inactive, a lure must be offered to them in such a way that it can be taken with the minimum of effort. This means that it must be sunk close to the bottom and manoeuvred so that it swings round in front of a fish's nose *as slowly as possible*. And on most nights unless it is fished in this manner very few sea-trout will be caught.

Knowing this, the experienced angler will have equipped himself with the appropriate tackle: hence the second rod, set up ready with Wet-cel line and Sunk Lure.

It is important that the principles of Sunk Lure fishing should be clearly understood. The angler who thinks that it consists merely of sinking the lure is deluding himself. A lure or fly will fish correctly only when its longitudinal axis forms a direct continuation of the leader and line. It is, then, the *line* that maintains the position of the lure close to the bottom.

The line must be fully sunk. A Sunk Lure is intended to represent the impression of a small fish; but fish, however small, do not swim on a steady course at a constant depth with their heads poking up towards the surface. A floating or semi-floating line will prevent the lure from swimming on an even keel and will tend to lift its nose as soon as it is moved.

The use of a weighted lure is of value only in a strong current. But when the water is slack it is impossible to fish a heavy lure slowly enough, and it is in the slacker, deeper water that most sunk line fishing at night is carried out. True, the lure must fish deep, but it must also fish slowly *without losing its trim.* For this reason, a light iron or mount is more effective than a heavy one.

Everything relating to the Sunk Lure applies equally to fishing the small Double, or maggot on the Secret Weapon – often a deadly method of catching sea-trout late at night. In both cases, the secret is to fish deep and slow.

Another lure which should be tried at regular intervals during the second period is the Surface Lure (see p. 298). This was exchanged for the Medicine on the first rod as soon as the first period ended, and now stands ready for use. Indeed, it is now that it has its greatest chance of success. For reasons unknown, a sea-trout that declines a fly fished just under the surface, or a sunk fly or maggot bounced off its nose, will sometimes rise furiously to a lure which is dragged across the surface.

That the period when the fish are down and sunk line fishing is in operation should be suitable for surface fishing seems paradoxical. But on most nights – at least early in the season – it is never really dark until after midnight, and darkness is all-important for the Surface Lure.

Just beyond daybreak the Surface Lure is exchanged for a small Medicine, which can be fished well into daylight.

During the magic hour of sunrise most sea-trout fishermen, exhausted after an all-night session, are drinking a 'nightcap' and watching the sky catch fire behind the hills.

A pity, really. Now in the cool of the morning there is a splendid chance of hooking a salmon . . .

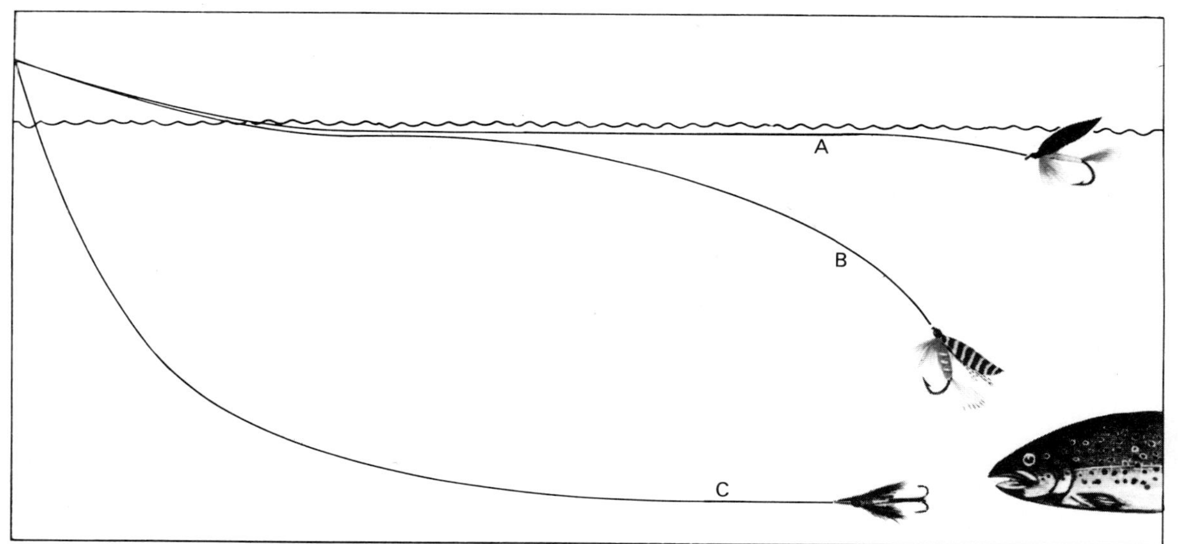

Fig. 28.12. Principles of floating and sunk line techniques; for sea-trout.
A. Floating line technique; fly on horizontal axis – correct.
B. Weighted fly fished on floating line – wrong for sea-trout night fly fishing. Can be used for sea-trout in daylight if the fish are showing interest in a hatch of fly; otherwise good technique for fishing nymph for brown trout.
C. Sunk line technique; fly on horizontal axis – correct.

Fig. 28.13 (below). *Points of difference between a sea-trout* (top) *and a salmon* (bottom).

POINTS OF DIFFERENCE BETWEEN SEA-TROUT AND SALMON

1. Sea-trout's tail, relaxed (straight). Salmon's tail, relaxed (forked).
2. Sea-trout's tail, stretched (convex). Salmon's tail, stretched (straight – but notice the two 'horns').

It can be seen from Fig. 28.13 that a sea-trout's tail is straight or 'square', whereas a salmon's tail is forked. If the salmon's tail is stretched, it, too, will be more or less straight, whereas the sea-trout's tail is convex (see dotted line No. 2). Also, the salmon's tail has two distinct 'horns' which are absent from the tail of a sea-trout.

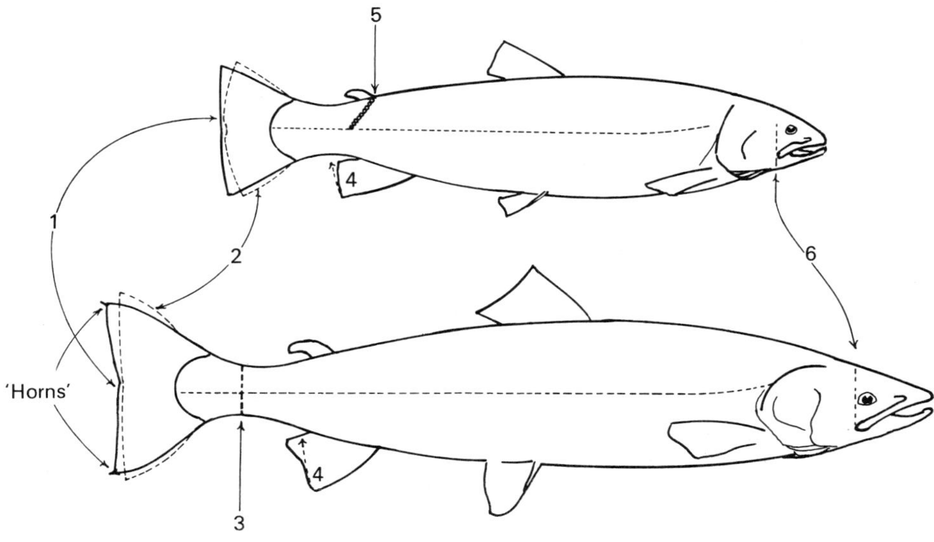

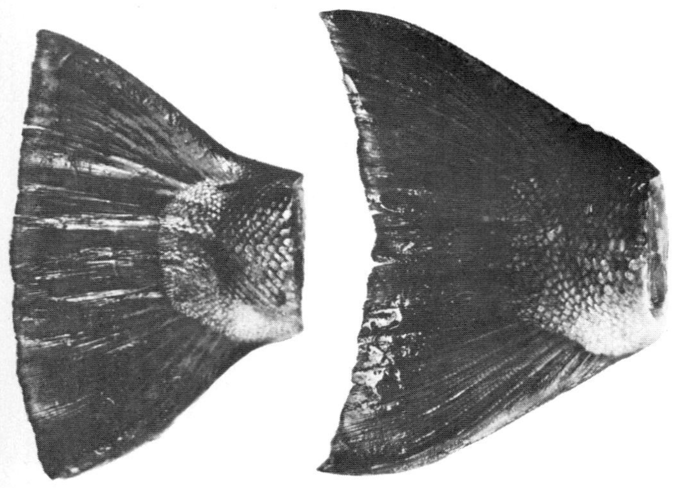

Left: *Tail of 11¼ lb sea-trout.* Right: *Tail of 13½ lb salmon.*
Although the trailing edge of a small sea-trout's tail is forked, this fork becomes less and less pronounced as the fish increases in weight.
At 4 lb to 5 lb the tail becomes square. Upwards of about 8 lb, the tail is convex.
A salmon's tail is concave.

3. Sea-trout's caudal peduncle, deep.
   Salmon's caudal peduncle, narrow.

The base of a salmon's tail (the caudal peduncle) has a pronounced 'wrist'. It is this 'wrist' that enables an angler to tail a salmon, either with a mechanical tailer, or by hand (see p. 209). The sea-trout's broader-based tail has no 'wrist'. Hence, a sea-trout should always be netted or beached, never tailed.

The significance of the 'wrist' on the salmon's tail is referred to in Scandinavian tradition, as quoted by William Radcliffe:

> Loki, fleeing from the pursuit of the gods whose anger he had provoked, had the wit and the time to transform himself into a salmon. Then and in this guise would he have surely escaped, had not Thor caught him by the tail. . . .

Unfortunately for Loki he chose the wrong species! Had he turned himself into a sea-trout he would almost certainly have escaped. The sea-trout's tail would have slipped through even Thor's mighty grasp.

4. When closed, the *outermost ray* of the sea-trout's anal fin is nearest to the tail.

When closed, the *innermost ray* of the salmon's anal fin is nearest to the tail.

The heads of the arrows (No 4) show the relative positions of the outermost rays of the anal fins when in the closed position.

5. Sea-trout scale count: 13–16, usually 14.
   Salmon's scale count: 9–13, usually 11.

The scales are counted from the front edge of the adipose fin backward and downwards to the lateral line.

6. Sea-trout. The extreme end of the maxillary bone extends beyond a vertical line drawn from the hindmost edge of the eye.

Salmon. The extreme end of the maxillary bone is on a level with the hindmost edge of the eye.

Opposite: *A beautiful sea-trout 'run'. The foliage on both banks has been carefully undercut, to form a sort of tunnel. The shadow and shade afforded by the upper branches remain unaffected, but every inch of the water can be covered with a fly. No branches trail low across the river. Once the night fly fisherman has determined the exact length of line needed, he can cast with confidence and put his fly within inches of the opposite bank.*

SEA-TROUT FLIES

A fish caught on a home-made fly is a greater satisfaction to the fisherman than one which has been tricked by a fly bought in a shop. Why? Because it better satisfies the fisherman's instinctive desire to re-create conditions in which he depends on himself alone in his voluntary contest with nature. There is no hostility in this contest.
ARTHUR RANSOME.

With a little practice any angler can soon learn to tie himself more successful flies than those offered for sale, most of which are too small and too neat. Sea-trout think little of colour, neatness and a polished finish. Like salmon, they prefer something rather drab and straggly and thoroughly well chewed.

One point must be made clear, however; presentation of the fly is all-important. No fly, whatever its reputation, will kill fish if it is not fished correctly. About which, more later.

In common with most flies and lures, a variety of exotic materials may be added to the sea-trout fly, and if the confidence of the angler depends on their addition they should, of course, be included. But simplicity is the key-note of success. The purpose of a lure is to entice, and a simple, sparsely-dressed lure will entice more effectively than one which is heavily dressed. And in this context it is necessary to emphasize that *almost all sea-trout flies are simply – lures.*

It is easy to allow fly dressing to become a complicated and esoteric art. The novice, faced with a list of fly dressings, may well despair not only of the mechanics of construction but the cost and difficulty of obtaining the supposedly vital materials.

It is all nonsense. An angler should forget the name a fly has been given, think merely of what he wants the fly to look like and use the most practical materials at his disposal. It is the size, shape and presentation of the fly that matter.

Opposite: *A–F: H.F.'s lures for sea-trout fishing at night. These lures were taken at random from H.F.'s fly-box. All have caught fish.*
A. Sunk Lures (see p. 296).
B. Secret Weapon (see p. 302).
C. Worm-fly (see p. 305).
D. Small double (see p. 305).
E. Surface Lures (see p. 298).
F. Medicines (see p. 294).

G. Flies recommended by Richard Walker for powan fishing on Loch Lomond (see p. 316).

H. Lough Neagh pollan flies, after the dressings described by 'Hi-Regan' (see p. 322).

Bottom row *(not to scale): Richard Walker's mayflies (see p. 253).*
1. Nymph; 2. Sub-imago; 3. Raffene-bodied sub-imago; 4. Special, for heavy hatches; 5. Imago.

A
A
E
F
H
G
B
C
D
I
F
1
2
3
4
5
MADE IN ENGLAND
1
2
3
4
5
6

There are few rivers that do not possess some special fly patterns which, it is claimed, hold magic properties. Sometimes, indeed, they may, and if the locals catch fish on them so should the visitor. But he should not regard them as the only flies worth trying. Many local anglers are inclined to be conservative both in their choice of flies and methods of fishing.

The flies (lures) we describe have proved their worth many times on many different rivers in the face of general failure. Any angler who fishes them correctly should seldom experience a blank night.

Note: Since the thickness of the leader, or leader 'point' in the case of a tapered leader, depends on the type of lure being fished, suggested leader sizes have been given in pounds breaking strain for ordinary Platil monofilament nylon.

The Medicine

(Leader: 8–10 lb).
Dressing: Wing: Wigeon, teal or brown mallard.
Hackle: Blue.
Body: Silver.
Sizes: 3, 4, 5.

Since in many rivers adult sea-trout seldom show an active interest in food, the angler's object is to *tempt* the fish and stimulate their feeding responses by presenting them with a lure that is tenuous and tantalizing.

A great variety of flies and lures will serve this purpose, but one that we can recommend, in the beaten way of experience, is the Medicine. This is a general purpose fly: good at night in clear water, and during the day when the river is in spate or slightly coloured. (It is also a very good grilse fly – ideal for fishing the streamy, broken water at the neck of a pool).

It should be tied in sizes 3, 4, 5, on the lightest low-water salmon hook procurable. The features of a good sea-trout fly of this type – one that is intended to stimulate a little fish – are simplicity and slimness. A slim-line dressing on a low-water hook with silver painted shank provides just that.

When sea-trout are taking well at dusk, in fairly streamy water, we have found nothing to beat the Medicine. A tube-fly often gives good results, particularly in streamy water, but in our experience the wide bend of the low-water hook loses fewer fish than the smaller treble of the tube-fly. Except in very strong water, a double-hook of this size is too heavy, and too bulky. The single hook undoubtedly gets more offers.

The Medicine can, of course, be fished effectively all night, provided both floating line and sunk line techniques are used. But generally speaking, the night fly-fisherman will get better results *after midnight* by using Sunk Lure, Surface Lure or Secret Weapon – especially if conditions become difficult: sharp drop in temperature, ground mist, bright starlight, distant thunder, etc.

A bag of sea-trout taken on the Medicine during the 'first period', between ten-thirty and midnight, by H. F.

The Falkus Sunk Lure

The Sunk Lure is good for both sea-trout and salmon. In clear water it is a most effective night fly-fishing lure for sea-trout of all sizes–and especially good for hooking the really big fish. H. F. has taken a number of sea-trout over 10 lb on this lure at night (one is pictured on p. 282), in addition to the occasional salmon. Indeed, this is the only lure we know that will catch salmon with any consistency late on dark nights. It has done so in six different rivers. It is also a successful daytime salmon lure for sunk line spring and early summer fishing.

The Sunk Lure seldom fails to catch fish. Except on those occasions when the river is in spate, and coloured, the night-fly-fisherman armed with this lure should experience few blank nights. Its particular merit is to attract fish late on – usually after midnight – when so often the fish have 'gone down' and are refusing conventional flies. Provided the night is dark enough, it will even catch fish when the river is at dead summer low. It will also take fish when the water is running high but clear after successive spates – never good conditions for catching sea-trout.

It should be fished slowly on a sunk line.

A weighted lure is often recommended for sunk line fishing. This is a fallacy. It is not a heavy lure that fishes best on a sunk line, but a light one. The object of sunk line fishing for sea-trout (and salmon, for that matter), is to fish the lure as slowly as possible. A heavy lure, or one that is tail-heavy, defeats this purpose.

It is on the way in which the *line* is fished that the behaviour of the lure depends. The line must be completely sunk.

A fish is usually hooked on the tail hook. The advantage of having two hooks set well apart in tandem on a *flexible* mount is that when the fish turns and runs, the top hook often secures a hold in the underside of the fish's jaw – effecting a double hold. If the tail hook comes away (which frequently happens with a big fish early in the season owing to the way it takes a lure at this time of the year) the fish is still held by the top hook.

Construction

1. Put a seating of tying silk half way along the shank of a sneck bend hook.
2. Loop the nylon (22–24 lb B.S.) round the hook and bring both ends out through the eye. The thickness of the nylon used will depend on the size of the hook and the intended length of the lure. It should be stiff enough to support the tail hook without drooping. *Note.* The lure can be made in lengths of 2–3 in. The standard length recommended for sea-trout night fly-fishing is $2\frac{1}{2}$ in.
3. Whip the nylon to the shank of the hook.
4. Bring the longer strand 'B' through the eye of the top hook and back along the shank. Cut off strand 'A' level with the eye of the hook.
5. Whip the nylon to the shank of the hook, taking care to maintain equal tension in the two strands. Put extra turns of tying silk round the hook at 'D' to provide maximum strength at this point.
6. Whip part of the link at 'C'.

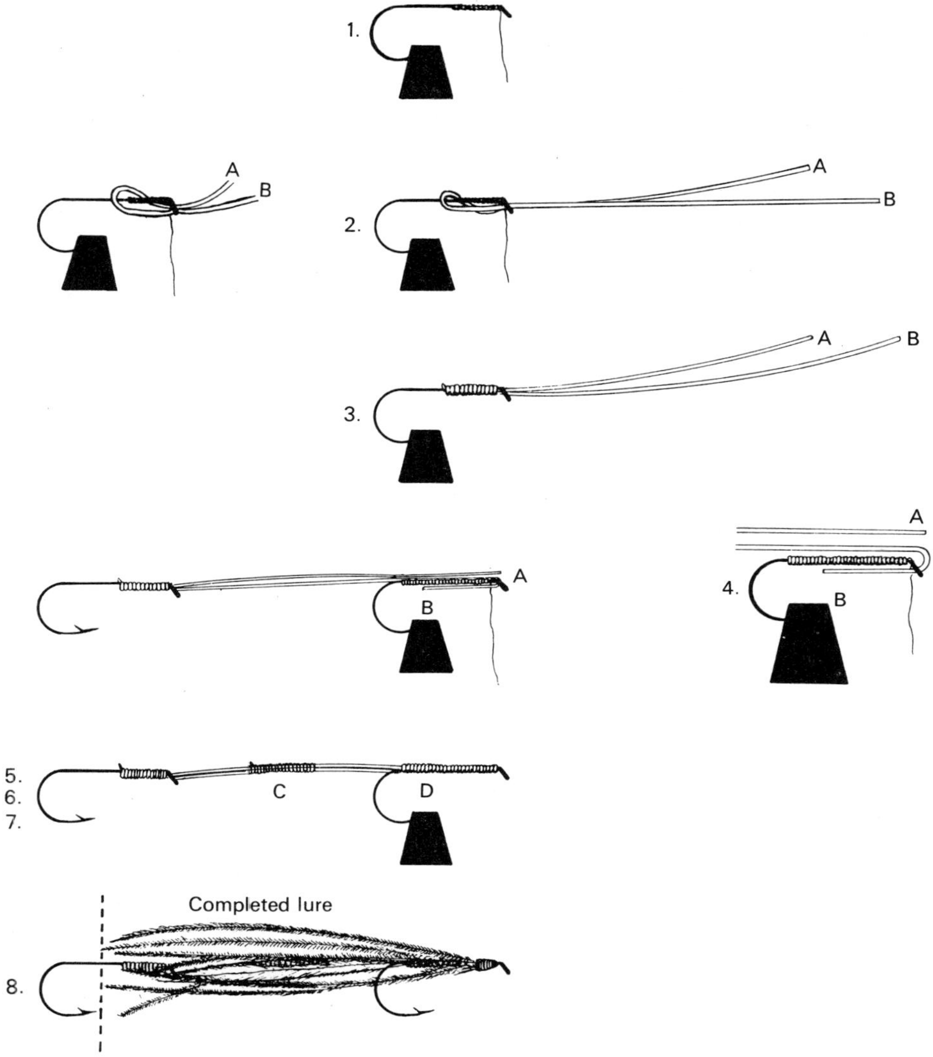

1.

A B

2. A B

3. A B

A B

4. A B

5. 6. 7. C D

Completed lure

8.

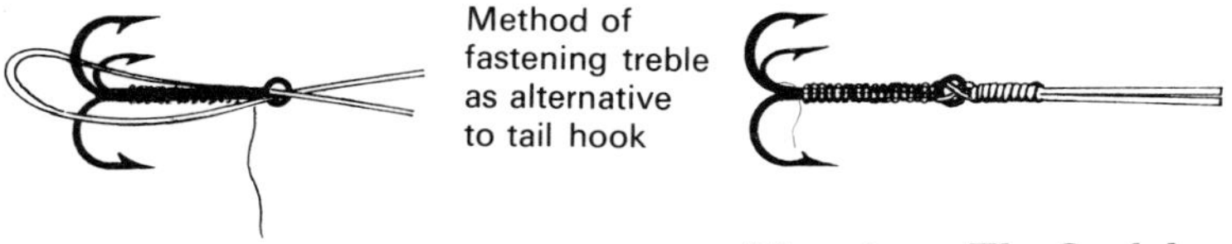

Method of fastening treble as alternative to tail hook

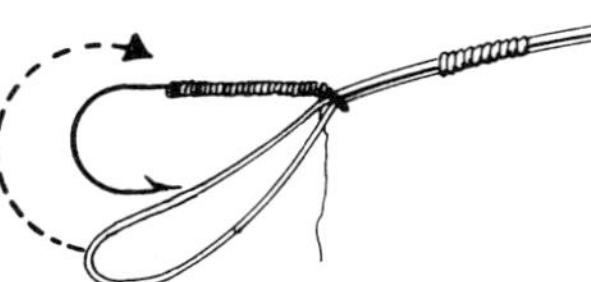

Method of replacing tail hook. Cut whipping and loop nylon through eye of new hook

Fig. 28.15. The Sunk lure.

Dressing: A blue hackle feather along either side of the mount with some strands of peacock herl overlaid. The dressing should not extend beyond the point of the tail hook. Fish on leader of 12–14 lb. B.S.

7. Varnish mount. Then coat with silver paint.
8. Apply dressing. It is important that the tail of the dressing should not extend past the point of the tail hook.
9. Touch off the head of the lure with red varnish.

Note. Do not overdress the lure. A tenuous dressing is much more effective than a thick, bushy dressing. Two blue hackle feathers, one tied either side, with a few strands of peacock herl on top is the standard dressing. This provides excellent results with both salmon and sea-trout.

Needless to say, the dressing can be varied to suit the whim of the fisherman.

For salmon fishing, a small treble is recommended at the tail. The single hook is better for hooking sea-trout.

On no account fail to bring the longer strand 'B' through the eye of the top hook and back along the shank. This method of construction makes it virtually impossible for the mount to 'draw'.

In very strong water, some lead wire wound round the shank of the *top* hook will help the lure to fish deep, and still work attractively.

The Surface Lure

On a dark night, no matter how low the river, the drag caused by a floating lure or a big dry fly moving across the surface of the water can provide a deadly attraction for sea-trout (and, incidentally, for brown trout, too). Although the Surface Lure is of use *only in darkness*, it gives an angler the chance of hooking a really big fish, and no night fisherman should ever be without one.

The principle underlying its attraction is different from that of any other type of fly or lure. Indeed, the technique of fishing it is the antithesis of all customary methods of fly fishing. When an angler is fishing in daylight, the 'V' shaped drag caused by his fly or lure skidding across the water is something he is careful to avoid; but when fishing at night with Surface Lure it is precisely this drag he is trying to create (Fig. 28.17).

Obviously, in order to produce drag, the lure must be kept on the move. If, when fished across a current, the line is allowed to go slack, the lure will begin to drift downstream and drag will cease. Similarly, if in slack water the angler stops stripping in line the lure will stay motionless, instantly losing its attraction. *It is the wake of the lure, not the lure itself that attracts fish.*

The lure *must float.* Provided it does so and provided it causes a wake, almost anything of reasonable size and shape will catch fish. A piece of cork trimmed to size will serve admirably. A length of quill plugged with cork can also be used; but a cork lure, being slightly heavier, is easier to cast – certainly into a breeze.

The leader should be attached a short distance from the nose (as shown). This keeps the lure cocked up slightly as it moves across the water and helps to prevent if from being dragged under. If the lure dips beneath the surface, drag ceases immediately and the lure becomes ineffective.

Strangely enough, the success of the Surface Lure varies considerably from season to season. Some years it catches a great number of sea-trout, in others very few; even so, it is capable of attracting the biggest fish in the pool – on a night when all other methods have failed.

Construction

1. Trim a wine cork to the desired size and shape, or cut and plug a length of goose quill (Fig. 28.16.*a*).
2. Prepare a mount in exactly the same way as described for the Sunk Lure (p. 296), using either an eyed or an eyeless treble on the tail (Fig. 28.16.*b*).
3. Whip the mount to the cork or quill body (see arrows, Fig. 28.16.*c*) and varnish.
4. Colour is unimportant, but, if desired, the whole thing can be given a coat of silver paint.
5. Dressing, too, is unimportant. But *when the silver paint is dry*, two 'wings' can be attached (Figs. 28.16.*d* and *e*). These are by no means essential for catching fish, but have the merit of increasing the angler's confidence and making the lure more stable in the water (Fig. 28.16.*f*). Any small dark feathers will do.

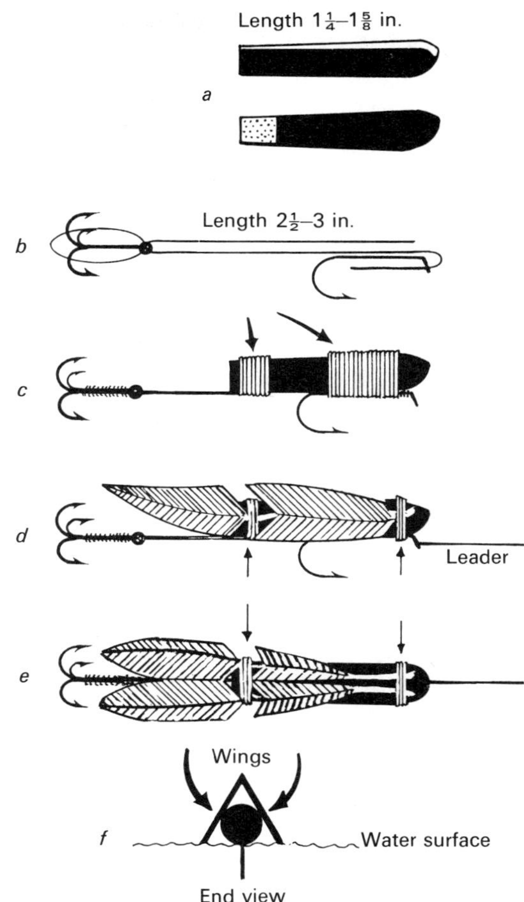

Fig. 28.16. The Surface Lure. Fish on a leader of 10–12 lb B.S.

Fishing the Surface Lure

A still, warm, cloudy night is best, without moon or stars, but no conditions are hopeless. Provided the night is dark enough (as a rough guide the wake of the lure should not be visible to the fisherman), sea-trout will take the Surface Lure at any hour. The most likely period, however, is between one and three in the morning. The best places to fish are unrippled runs, and pool tails where the water flows in a steady glide. All holding water is worth trying so long as the surface is calm enough for the lure to leave a wake.

During every cast, the lure must be kept skimming across the surface right up to the moment of recovery. It is not unusual for a fish to follow for some distance and take only

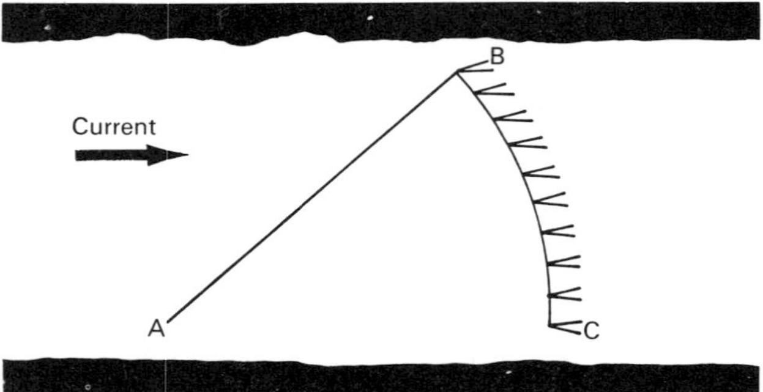

Fig. 28.17. If a dry fly is cast across a river from A to B it will immediately start to swing round on the arc BC and drag against the current, leaving a 'V' shaped wake. It is this drag that the dry-fly fisherman is most careful to avoid. At night, however, a dragging fly can be very attractive.

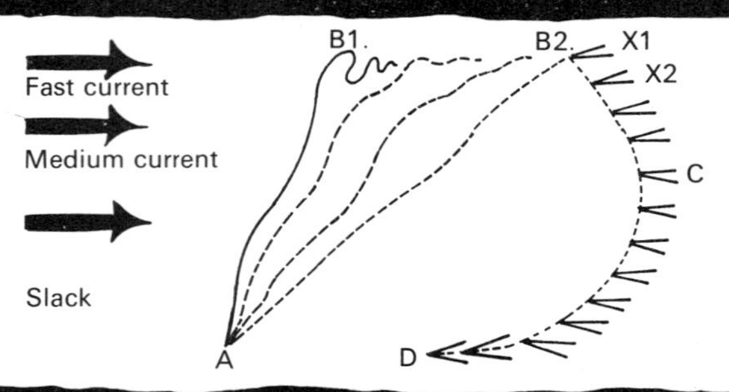

Fig. 28.18.

as the lure is actually leaving the water, but if at any time the lure falters and loses 'life', the fish will have nothing more to do with it.

A large Surface Lure is not an easy object to cast with a light trout rod. However, once this difficulty is overcome the tactics are simple enough.

When fishing down a 'run' or a pool tail (see Fig. 28. 18), cast a loose line from A to B.1, and then flick out a little more slack. Allow the lure to *drift* downstream with the current for three or four yards. At B.2 the slack will take-up and the line tighten on the lure – which will immediately form a pronounced 'V' and begin to swing round on the arc B.2, C. Let it continue to fish round to C, then work it quickly and steadily towards you to D. Fish will take anywhere between B.2 and D, usually at X.1 and X.2. Sometimes however, a fish will make a dash at the lure just as it is about to be recovered, so it is essential that the speed of the lure should not decrease between C and D. If anything, it should increase.

It is important to remember that a fish will ignore a Surface Lure which is drifting with the current. It is only when the lure comes to 'life' and begins to swim against and across the current that a fish's predatory instincts are aroused. To take advantage of this is the reason for casting a loose line from A to B.1. This sudden 'coming to life' of the lure at B.2 (see Fig. 28.19), is very attractive.

As the current tightens the line and the lure suddenly whips into action, a fish will often react by rushing straight at the lure and seizing it fiercely – a most exciting moment.

This ruse may sometimes induce a fish to take after it has risen to, but refused, the lure at some other point of the cast. Mark the position of the fish and move slightly downstream. Then, cast above the fish and let the lure drift down, checking it at the right moment and swinging it round over the fish's nose.

To attempt to fish the lure with a sticky line is a waste of time and effort. A considerable amount of line has to be shot at every cast, and this is impossible unless the line is running smoothly through the rod rings.

It is an advantage to use a heavier line than usual. It will help to punch the lure out against a wind, and to shoot the five or six yards of slack line which accumulate during the final 'work-in' – especially when fishing still water.

In normal conditions use a leader of eight or nine feet; but if there is a head wind put on a heavier, shorter leader of not more than five or six feet.

In moonlight, or at dawn, fish fine. Sometimes, fish will take in the half light – but only if you fish a slender, delicate lure on a fairly light leader.

In conditions of disturbed water, fish a tubby lure which causes sufficient drag to overcome the surface ripple. Generally speaking, use a larger lure on a 'run' than when fishing the smooth water of a pool tail.

Not infrequently one is faced with a piece of good holding water which is beyond casting range and impossible to cover by normal methods – an overgrown 'run' or glide, (see Fig. 28.20), where depth of water, trees, bushes or other obstructions prevent the fisherman from going further downstream. Fish in these difficult pieces of water can be covered satisfactorily by carrying out the following procedure with a floating line and a much longer leader from line to lure than normally used.

Wade out to A, and let the lure drift downstream along the edge of the current by stripping off line. Work the lure in zig-zags across the stream – as shown by the dotted lines in the diagram – by holding the rod parallel to the water on either side of you, at arm's length if necessary, and controlling the

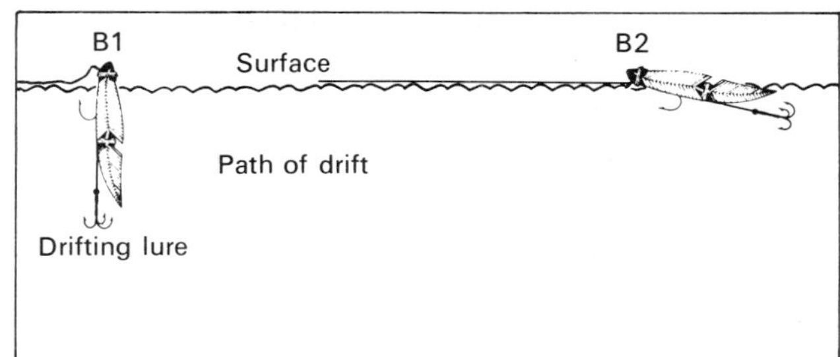

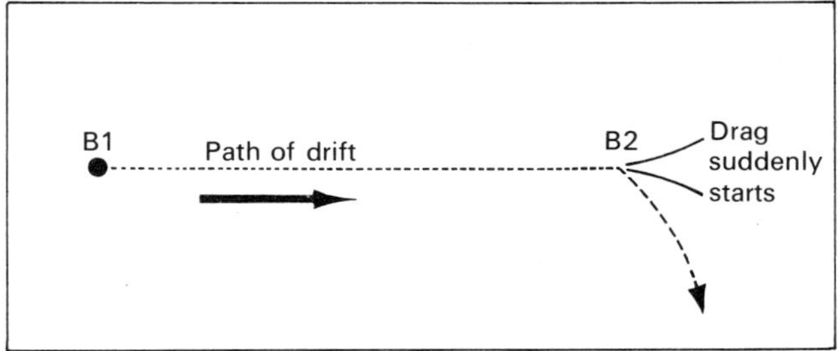

Fig. 28.19. B.2 shows the point at which the lure 'comes to life'.

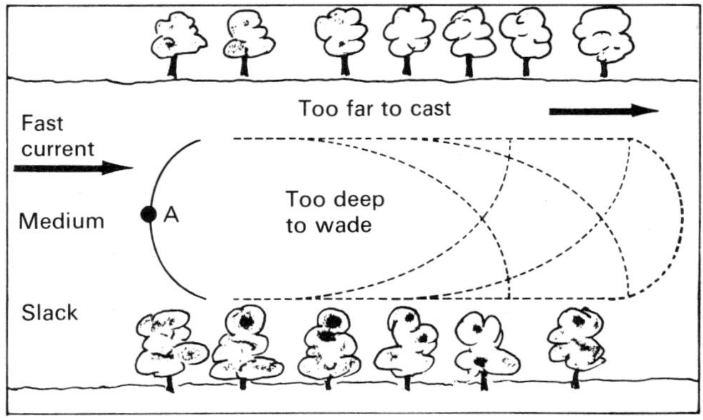

Fig. 28.20.

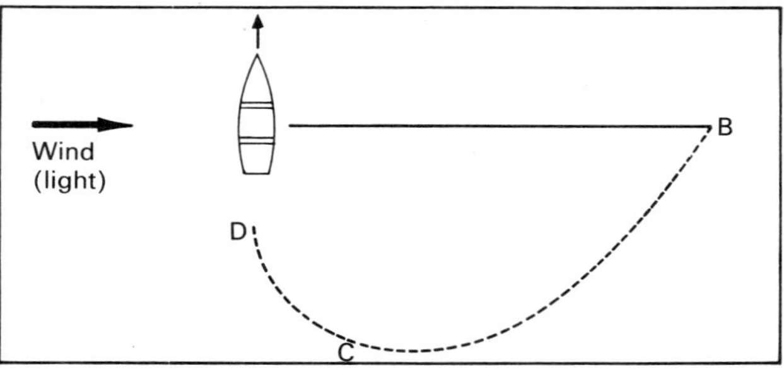

Fig. 28.21. Boat fishing with the Floating Lure.

length of line by means of a coil in the non-casting hand.

Try 'hanging' the lure in the stronger parts of the current, and vary the path of the lure sometimes by drawing it upstream in the slacker water by the bank underneath over-hanging branches.

If fishing by night from a boat in still water, (see Fig. 28.21), the boat should be rowed slowly and quietly at right angles to the direction of the wind – which must not be strong, or there will be too much ripple.

Cast to B, and allow lure to swing round to C, its wake being caused by the forward movement of the boat. Work in from C to D. Fish take at any point of the cast.

You can of course take fish by trailing the lure, but this method has one serious disadvantage: in the darkness long distances may be covered towing a streamer of weed behind the lure. This wastes a good deal of time and exhausts patience.

Wherever you may be fishing, on no account allow the lure to slow down or stop at the end of a cast. When recovering, preparatory to casting again, do so with a steady, easy movement, speeding the lure up over its last yard or two of cast and bringing it straight up off the water.

A word of warning: the Surface Lure is not the easiest lure to cast, especially in anything of a wind. Any angler who has not previously fished it is advised to practice casting it in daylight.

If you put a Cod-bait or Gentle, either natural or artificial, but Natural better, at point of your Dub-fly Hook, they will take the Dub fly better, especially the Salmon Smelt.

JAMES CHETHAM, *The Angler's Vade-Mecum* (1681).

The Sea-Trout Secret Weapon

There are times when the combination of fly and maggot can be a very successful method of catching sea-trout at night. The conventional lure is a small fly tied on a single hook, with one or more maggots impaled on the bend of the hook.

When a sea-trout takes with gusto this arrangement is quite satisfactory, since (together with the maggots) the hook is taken inside the fish's mouth.

But sea-trout do not always take in such an obliging manner. Sometimes, using the very front of the mouth, a fish will give the maggots a little tweak (Fig. 28.22.*a*) and then let them go again (rather in the same way that a salmon will nip a prawn). It usually occurs when rain is imminent, or when the night turns cold in the small hours.

A fish behaving like this cannot be hooked on conventional tackle because the hook is never inside its mouth. All the angler feels is a series of infuriating little tugs. Although he may strike until his arm aches, his only reward is a slack line.

The sea-trout Secret Weapon puts an end to all this. Now, when a sea-trout tweaks a maggot (Fig. 28.22.*b*) it finds itself lip-hooked by the tiny treble which lies astern of the main hook.

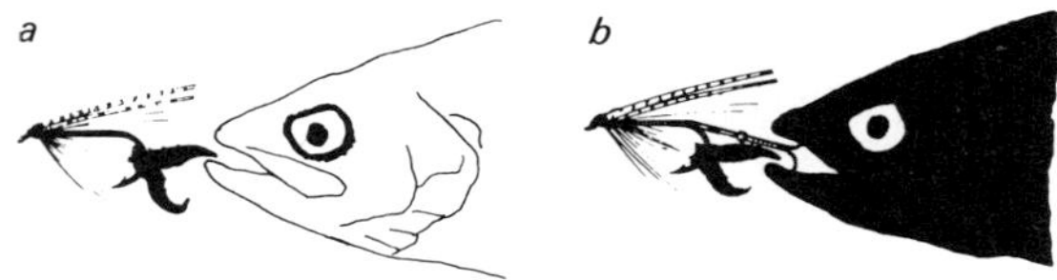

Fig. 28.22. The Secret Weapon. Fish on leader of 5–6 lb B.S.

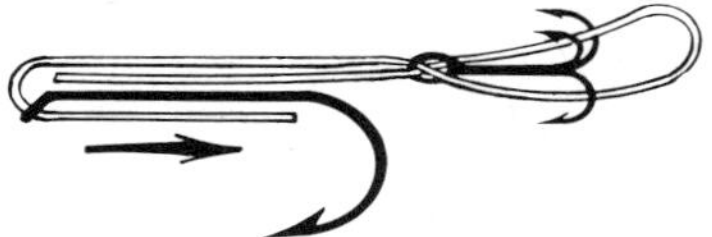

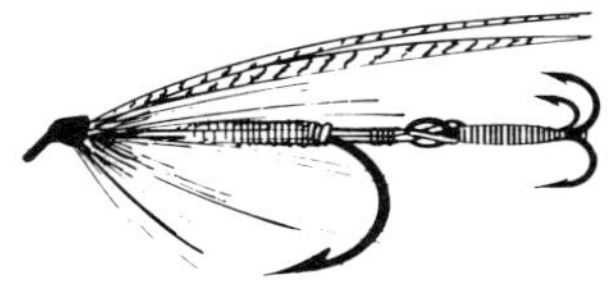

Fly/maggot fishing often provides good sport late at night when sea-trout have 'gone down'. In these conditions fish are not inclined to race about in pursuit of a lure. To ensure the best chance of its being taken, therefore, the Secret Weapon must be placed right in front of their noses. To achieve this it is fished *very slowly* on a quick-sinking, smooth-shooting sunk line.

Fishing the Secret Weapon is delicate work and very exciting. To avoid damaging the maggots a special form of casting action should be developed. It is quite impossible to describe this cast, other than to say that it should be as 'soft' as possible, without jerkiness, all slack line being shot first time with no false casting.

When they are in a tweaking mood, fish are likely to be very lightly hooked through the skin of the lip. Great care must be taken when playing them. The tension of the reel should be slackened and the fish handled as though on cotton.

Construction

1. Lay a seating of fine tying silk along the shank of a size 14 or 16 treble.
2. Loop a short length of 12 lb B.S. nylon round the treble and bring both ends out through the eye from opposite sides.
3. Whip the nylon to the shank of the treble.
4. Whip the two strands of nylon together just above the eye of the treble.
5. Bring one strand of nylon through the eye of a size 8 Hardy 'Perfect' hook and back along the shank. Cut off the other strand level with the eye of the hook. *Note:* It is very important that the distance between treble and hook is not too great. As a guide, the eye of the treble should be level with, or even slightly inside, the bend of the hook.
6. Whip the nylon mount to the shank of the hook, taking care to maintain equal tension in the two strands. Put extra turns of tying silk round the hook at the end nearest the treble to provide maximum strength at this point.
7. Varnish mount.
8. Apply dressing. Brown hackle, fluffed out, with a sparse 'wing' of brown mallard.

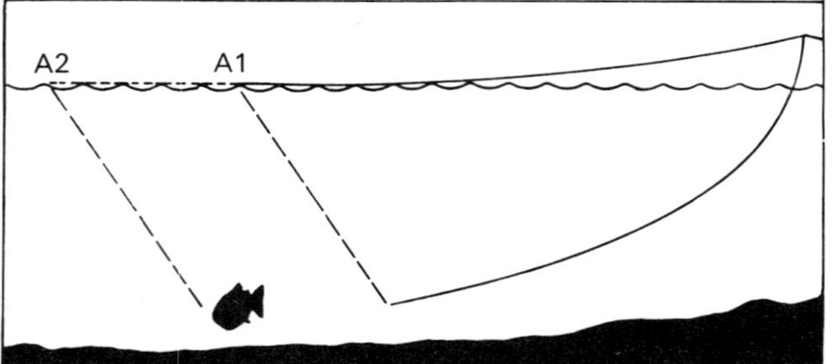

Fig. 28.23. When night fishing it is important to remember that a sunk fly or fly/maggot cannot be put in front of a fish merely by casting to A.1. (see diagram), the distance the fish is from the rod, due to line sag. To allow for this, an extra distance must be cast – to A.2.

9. Varnish head of lure.

Avoid neatness in the dressing. The overall effect should be a small brown straggly-looking creature. It is a fiddly thing to make, but gloriously rewarding on the river in the small hours of a summer night.

Note: An example of re-discovery (see p. 486). The sea-trout Secret Weapon was designed by H. F. during a frustrating night's fishing in August, 1962 (sixteen offers, three fish landed). The prototype was tied the following afternoon and fished later that night. Result: eleven offers, nine fish landed. Here was success. Here was an original type of lure: a new idea.

Not so. W. H. Lawrie had designed a lure on similar lines nearly 20 years earlier.

Like so many other examples quoted in this book, H. F.'s sea-trout Secret Weapon was a re-discovery of an angling principle originally discovered by the author of *Border River Angling*. By kind permission, we print the following extract.

'But, as every angler of experience knows very well, there are nights, apparently perfect in regard to weather and water conditions, when trout appear to be 'rising short', or, as it is personally believed, to be devoting attention to the maggot alone. Nothing is more annoying than constant failure to hook the author of repeated half-hearted offers, very often a good fish. On such occasions it is usually recommended that the line be shortened, and this is good advice up to a point, but does not greatly remedy matters. In an attempt to solve the problem the writer designed a hook which, while in no way interfering with dressing facilities, would

Fig. 28.24. Reproduced from Border River Angling.

greatly increase the probability of secure hooking. It has proved so successful in seasons past that the ordinary hook has now been abandoned entirely. The illustrations explain the idea, and it will be noted that the hackle effectively conceals the small hook.

'The original consisted of two separate hooks, a size 16 being whipped to the usual night iron, dressing then being tied on as usual, but, as the idea has proved so successful, further efforts were made to perfect the design and double hooks were substituted for the single iron. It will be appreciated that any trout which is taking the maggot and disregarding the fly has little chance in avoiding the large hook(s).'

W. H. LAWRIE, *Border River Angling* (1946).

The Worm-Fly.

(Leader: 7–9 lb).
Dressing: Hackles: brown or black, hen.
Body: Peacock herl.
Length: $1\frac{1}{4}$–$1\frac{1}{2}$ in.

This is a very good lure for sea-trout fairly late in the season, say on a late August night. A twist or two of green fluorescent silk showing through the body dressing of peacock herl *seems* to be effective; but whether its inclusion really makes any difference is questionable.

The Size 12 Double

(Leader: 5–6 lb)
Dressing: Anything dark and drab.
Length: $\frac{1}{2}$–$\frac{5}{8}$ in. (size 12 double-iron hook).

This little fly will sometimes work wonders when sea-trout are in a tweaking mood and being finicky. It is difficult for a fish to tweak such a tiny fly without getting hooked (although some manage to do it!). When the angler has no opportunity, or inclination, to fish with maggot the little double provides a good substitute for the Secret Weapon. The double iron is very effective. Fish taking it are usually well hooked.

Note: This size of double iron, suitably dressed, is just right for a salmon on a summer evening in dead low water.

Other Night-Fishing Hints

If he uses them properly, the lures we recommend should give an angler good service on most sea-trout rivers. He will, however, need certain items of tackle.

Recommended tackle requirements for a night's sea-trout fly-fishing.

Two rods. One set up with floating line, the other with sinking line.
A case of lures.
Some spools of nylon of different thicknesses; or, better, a case containing a selection of leaders ready looped and cut to length.
A landing net.
A 'priest'.
A bag for carrying fish.
A torch.
A pair of scissors.
A bottle of midge repellant.

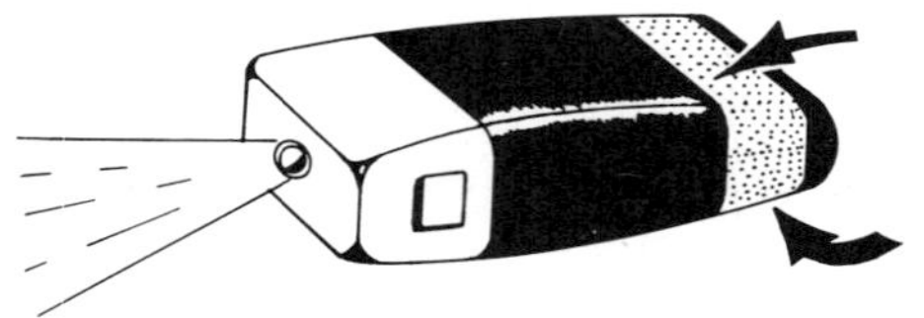

Fig. 28.25.

Flashlamp

Some sort of torch is essential at night. Needless to say, it should never be flashed on the water you are fishing. When you re-tie a fly, or unravel a tangle in cast or line, keep well back from the river.

The best place for a flashlamp when you wish to use it is in your mouth. This leaves both hands free and the light can be directed exactly where you wish; so that a light, slender-bodied torch is the best.

To enable the teeth to maintain a grip, wrap a piece of Elastoplast round the base of the torch (see arrows).

A cap with a red filter which fits on the end of the torch is useful, for it protects your night vision.

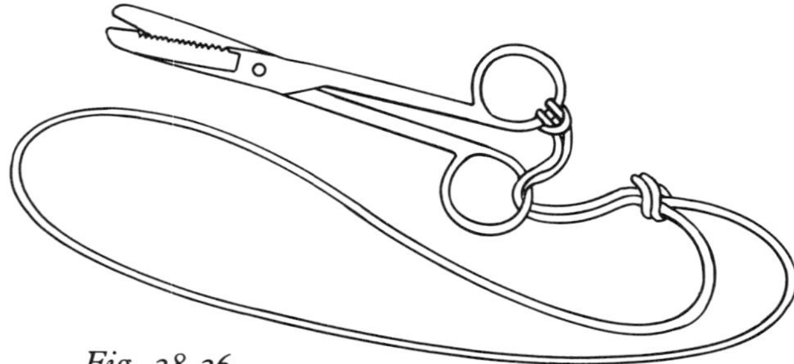

Fig. 28.26.

Scissors

Scissors are an invaluable aid on the river bank. To avoid dropping them in the river or in long grass, especially at night, fasten them with the method shown and hang them round your neck. Allow them to hang down inside your fishing coat. Blunt ended scissors prevent any danger of injury.

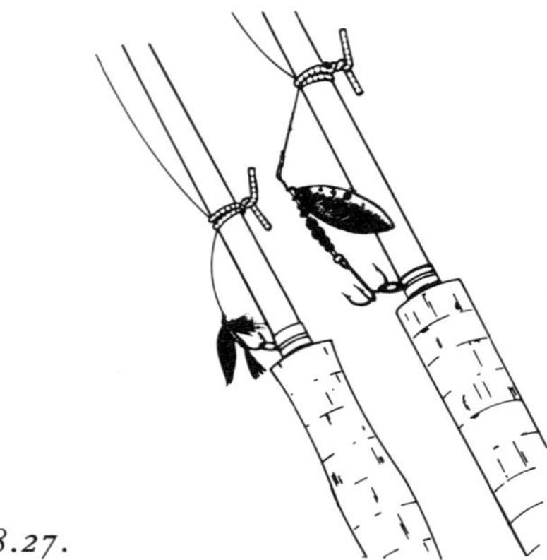

Fig. 28.27.

Rod carrying

Another little dodge, useful whenever a mounted rod is being carried, but especially at night, is the 'Pipe-Cleaner Safety Catch'. A pipe-cleaner twisted round rod and leader, as shown, prevents a fly or a spinner from escaping and blowing into bushes or tree branches. It is also a good way of keeping leads or floats from flapping against the rod.

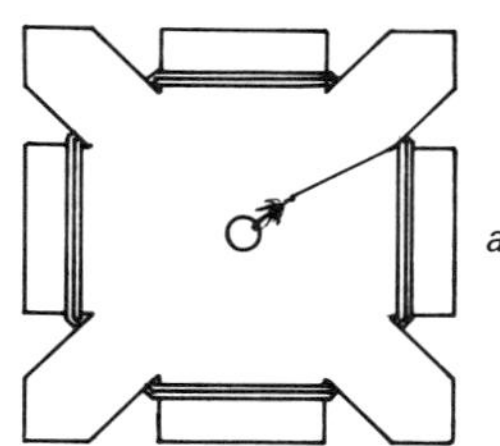

Fig. 28.28.

Leader carriers

Some fishermen prefer to carry spare leaders with flies attached, in which case a serviceable carrier can be made for nothing from old Christmas and Invitation cards. Eight 'V' shaped cuts are made in the card, which is trimmed to the appropriate size (Fig. 28.28). It can just as easily be cut in circular shape to fit inside a tobacco tin (Fig. 28.*b*). The fly is hooked into a hole in the middle.

Fig. 28.29.

Two loops

A very simple and neat method of joining casting line and leader. Useful for the night fly-fisherman, since it facilitates the changing of a leader in the darkness. The loop whipped in the end of the casting line should be renewed at the start of each season.

Below: *A simple, inexpensive but thoroughly practical fishing shelter. It is set with its back to the prevailing wind, and fenced against farm animals. A rain shelter of this type is of great value to the sea-trout night fly-fisherman. Here he can sit out the heaviest shower in comparative comfort. During periods of really heavy rain, fishing is usually poor, but it can be very good immediately the rain stops. Sea-trout often take furiously at night just after a thunderstorm has passed by, or during the intervals between heavy showers.*

The steeple cast

One of the most useful of all methods of casting. It is of particular value to the night fly-fisherman who is wading with a line of high bushes behind him.

Above: *Position at start of back-cast.*

Below: *The cast is made with very fast acceleration. The rod raised with a stiff arm straight up above the head (continued over page).*

Above: *Position at top of back-cast. The line has been sent curling high in the air over the bushes.*

Below: *Start of the forward cast.*

Note: Nowadays, a novice has the opportunity of expert angling instruction at the waterside. From our own experience, we can recommend the course at Grantown-on-Spey run by that fine angler, Arthur Oglesby.

The Falkus 'finger-ring' figure-of-eight retrieve

Having made a cast, anglers use various methods to 'work' and recover their flies. The most common method is to strip the line in and let it fall. There are times, however, when this technique is unsuitable.

1. In a strong wind.
2. When the angler is wading in a current.
3. When the slack line may become entangled with undergrowth.

In these cases, the line is gathered in tight coils inside the non-casting hand by what is known as the 'figure-of-eight' retrieve.

The conventional method is to draw the line straight from the butt ring, as shown in Fig. 28.30.*a*. A far better method is shown in Fig. 28. 30.*b*. Here, the line is drawn *not* from the butt ring direct, but from a ring made by thumb and forefinger of the casting hand.

Having made a cast, grasp the rod only by the 3rd, 4th and 5th fingers of the right (or casting) hand and pass the line over the crook of the index finger (*c*). Drop the thumb until it touches the ball of the index finger. Thumb and index finger now perform the role of an extra rod ring.

Take hold of the fly line *behind* the thumb with thumb and index finger of the left hand (*d*) and draw about 4 inches of line through the 'finger ring'.

Grab the line with the remaining fingers

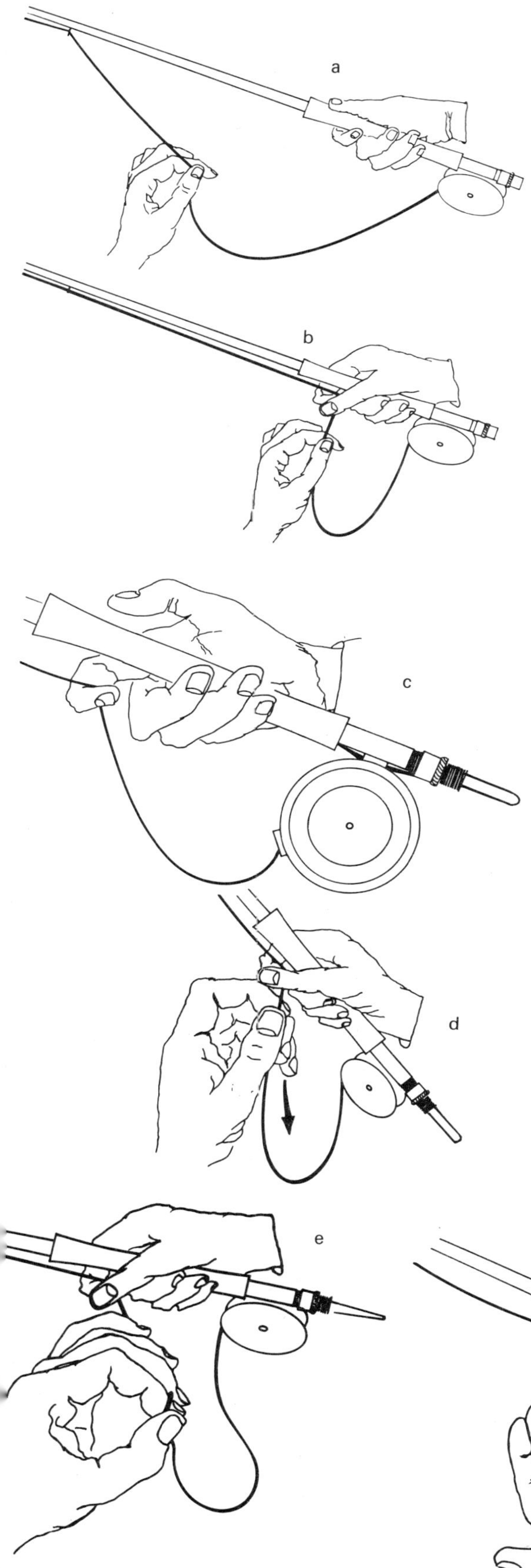

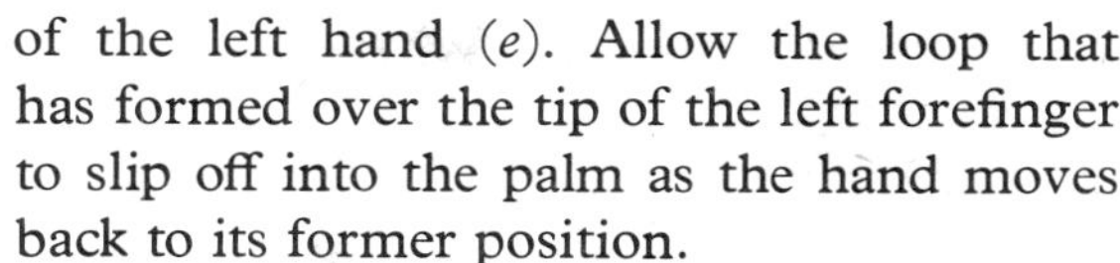

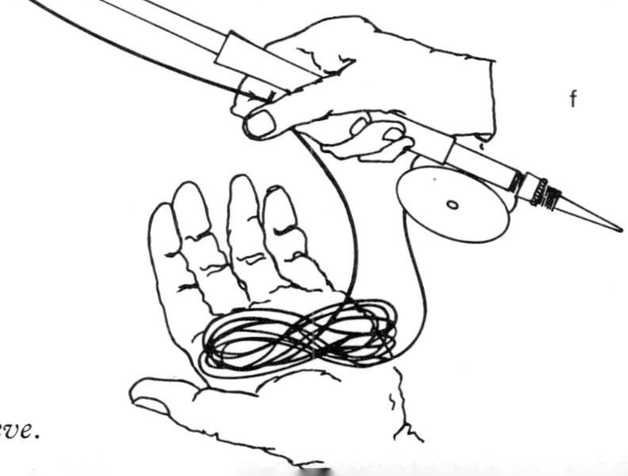

of the left hand (*e*). Allow the loop that has formed over the tip of the left forefinger to slip off into the palm as the hand moves back to its former position.

Repeat the procedure over and over again, with the wrist pivoting in a smooth figure-of-eight movement. It is important to keep the hands very close together; indeed, the angler should be conscious of his left little finger brushing his right thumb with each backward stroke.

Gradually, as the fly is worked in towards the angler, coils of line are gathered up in the left hand. The gathered line is shown in Fig. 28.30.*f*, with the hand displayed in an open position. This has been done purposely to reveal the coiled line. In practice, the hand merely opens sufficiently to grab each succeeding 'bite' of line.

The advantages of the 'finger-ring' figure-of-eight over the conventional method are considerable.

1. It is much easier to perform.
2. It is faster, and thus permits greater variation of fly speed during recovery.
3. When a fish is hooked, the line is under immediate control. One has simply to exert pressure with the right forefinger and trap the line against the rod butt.

Note: The figure-of-eight retrieve is made much easier (as indeed are all methods of retrieve) if the rod butt is kept anchored firmly against the groin. For this reason, it is advisable to fish with a rod that has a short extension below the reel.

a b c d e f

Fig. 28.30. The figure-of-eight retrieve.

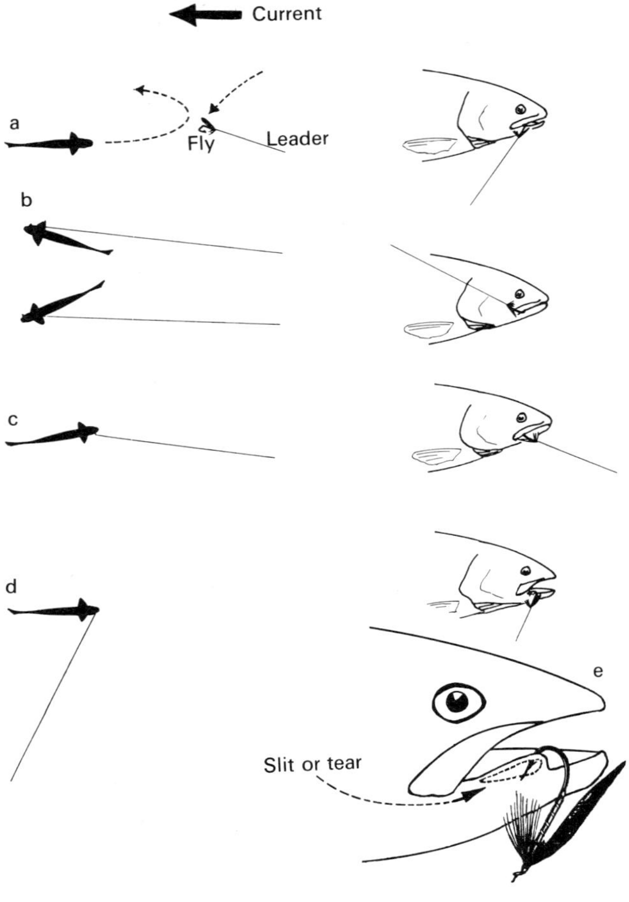

Fig. 28.31.
(a) *A sea-trout fresh from the sea intercepts and takes the fly. He turns away. As he does so, the fly hooks him at the back of the jaw in the 'scissors' – in this case on the righthand side.*
(b) *The fish runs hard downstream for a short distance, the shank of the hook working to and fro against his jaw as he zig-zags about.*
(c) *He turns and starts to come back upstream.*
(d) *He swims steadily past you. This is where you want him; but by now there is a big slit torn in the soft flesh at the corner of the mouth. If he suddenly turns towards you and jumps on a slack line you are very likely to lose him: the hook will simply fall out of the slit.*
Remember: *As the fish jumps don't drop the rod point and allow the line to go slack. Unless it is a big fish and likely to break the leader,* raise the rod and keep a tight line.
(e) *View of the fish's mouth showing slit or tear.*

Although its flesh hardens rapidly in fresh water, the mouth of a sea-trout newly arrived from the sea is very soft. Many fish hooked early in the season are lost not because they are badly hooked or through any fault of the hook itself, but through this tenderness of the flesh. Normally the best hold is in the 'scissors' at the angle of the jaw. With many early fish hooked in this position, however, pressure on the hook while a fish is being played causes a slit to be torn in the thin flesh at the corner of the mouth. (See illustration.) A momentary slackening of the line, especially when a fish is jumping, allows the hook to lose its hold. It is said that the hook tears out. Sometimes it probably does. But more often than not it simply *drops* out. Examination of a fish from whose mouth the hook has come away on landing frequently gives evidence of this.

Unless very fine tackle is being used, or the fish is exceptionally large, it is a good rule when playing a sea-trout *never to drop the rod point as the fish jumps.* Instead, it is

This superb carving of an 8 lb sea-trout (peal, sewin, mort, or white trout) was made by Mr Griggs, proprietor of John Cooper and Sons (see p. 22). It was the only wood carving that he ever attempted. F.B., the owner of the carving, has often wondered whose fish it was that served as the model.

better to *increase the pressure* as the fish leaves the water. This is contrary to all advice usually given on the subject, but the reader who has the confidence to try this ploy will find that he is landing a much higher proportion of early season fish.

If a friendly millionaire were to offer me any white trout lake in Connemara I would choose Clogher. Always I pushed out from its shores with a feeling of anticipation and excitement. It has given a basket in half a gale and in complete calm. There was no telling where fish would rise best, or whether they were going to be large or small. Often disappointed, I never ceased to hope for the day which I felt was due to me, when morning and afternoon, all over the lake, along shores and shallows, butt and islands, the big fish would be moving and I should bring *such* fishes back. It never came.

T. C. KINGSMILL MOORE, *A Man May Fish* (1960).

An enchanting book of trout, sea-trout and salmon fly-fishing in Ireland.

COOKING THE SEA-TROUT

1 sea-trout 2–3 lb.
Clean and fillet the fish.
Coat with oatmeal.
Fry in fairly hot bacon fat. Turn when golden brown.
Serve with slices of bacon and fried bread, and slices of cold tomato.
or
Several small sea-trout cooked with cucumber or almonds.
Clean the fish.
Melt some butter in a pan. Add a tablespoonful of olive oil.
Add cucumber rings. Fry for approximately one minute.
Add the fish. Fry slowly until almost cooked, then crisp the skins by increasing heat. Lift out and place on a hot dish.
Clean pan. Add fresh butter. When butter bubbles, add fresh cucumber rings. Cook for about one minute, then pour the lot over the fish and serve.
Note: Also delicious with almonds instead of cucumber, but cooked in the same way.

Knowing little about the finer points of cooking we were puzzled by the addition of olive oil. The gracious Chatelaine of Cragg informs us that this helps to prevent the butter from burning.

29 · The Whitefishes

Coregonidae

THE HOUTING

Powan, Gwyniad and Skelly

THE VENDACES

Vendace, Pollan

As the years pass and angling continues to increase in popularity, it seems strange that there should be sport-fish of the highest quality that are seldom if ever fished for – the whitefishes. Since these represent an angling resource of great potential, a discussion of their history and biology may help to stimulate interest in a rare but fascinating branch of angling.

The salmon, trout, charr, grayling and whitefish found in British waters are related fishes. They belong to the order Isospondyli, one of the most primitive orders of the Teleosts (the bony fishes). Teleost fishes first came to prominence during the Cretaceous period, about 100 million years ago. Significantly, the Teleost fossil fishes found in the Cretaceous rocks resemble the modern herring.

The closeness of the relationship between salmon, trout, charr, grayling and whitefish is further exemplified by the inclusion of whitefish in the same sub-order; Salmonoidei. This sub-order is represented by a number of genera, and it is at generic level that the fishes become separated. The salmon and trout belong to the genus *Salmo*, the charr to the genus *Salvelinus*, the grayling to the genus *Thymallus*, and the whitefishes to the genus *Coregonus*; all have the characteristic adipose fin, a small fleshy boneless fin situated on the back of the fish between dorsal fin and tail.

Until recently the genus *Coregonus* was represented by a considerable number of species. The common ones recognized in Britain were (with the exception of the marine houting) all freshwater fishes and included powan, pollan, vendaces, gwyniad and skelly. These were all regarded as distinct species.

Nowadays however, opinion among taxonomists is divided as to whether certain of these whitefishes should be recognized as different species, sub-species, or varieties of the same species. The matter remains to be settled. In the meantime, we have followed the classification given by Alwyne Wheeler.

In Wheeler's book *The Fishes of the British Isles and North-West Europe*, the freshwater houting, *Coregonus lavaretus*, includes those

Powan, 11¼ oz, caught by F.B. on Loch Lomond in February 1968.

fishes previously known as powan, gwyniad and skelly; and the vendace, *Coregonus albula*, includes those fishes previously known as vendace (various) and pollan.

Distributed throughout the northern hemisphere are many other whitefish not indigenous to the United Kingdom. Most are freshwater fish, and even the marine members of the family enter rivers for the purpose of spawning.

The freshwater houting and the vendace are probably surviving remnants of migratory stocks, part of which became isolated during a period when glaciation affected the northern land masses of Europe, Asia and North America. The remarkable diversity of the whitefishes which gives rise to a whole catalogue of visual and taxonomic differences among numerous isolated populations without creating new species, may be due to the relatively short period of stabilization since glaciation, the inference being that the shaping hand of evolution will one day consolidate varieties into species.

POWAN

Coregonus clupeoides clupeoides (Loch Lomond, Loch Eck)

The powan is a herring-like fish. So like a herring in fact that in 1802, when first described in a scientific journal, it was given (by Lacépède, a Frenchman) its specific name *Clupeoides*, 'herring' in the Gallic tongue. Its distribution is confined to two British lakes: Loch Lomond and Loch Eck.

In summer, powan seek their food (plankton) near the surface. This habit gives rise to a peculiar characteristic known as 'finning'. At times large shoals of Loch Lomond powan swim so close to the surface that their dorsal fins are out of the water. Shoals thus engaged give a patch of otherwise calm water a disturbed look; and, strange to record, a patch of wind-rippled water, a smooth look.

Of great interest is the comment by Ian Wood, in his book *Loch Lomond and its Salmon*, that although visiting anglers cast their flies like mad among the 'finning' powan, mistaking them for rising trout, only three powan have to his knowledge been taken on the fly in 20 years.

In a somewhat confused account of the powan published in 1838, Dr Parnell noted that a few powan had been taken on the fly '. . . bait they have never been known to touch.' A strange statement when one remembers that in powan stomachs he found items such as '. . . small tough red worms' and '. . . a quantity of gravel which the fish had probably accumulated when in search of the larvae.'

Recent research has proved that in addition to grazing on plant life and foraging for insect larvae in submerged weed beds, powan feed actively on the bottom – particularly during the winter months. Professor Slack, head of the Glasgow University research team presently studying the flora and fauna of Loch Lomond, has caught several powan on worm baits. Moreover, the one-time record powan was caught on fine ledger-tackle.

Powan spawn in January on gravelly shallows. Science has revealed that the young powan disappear from these shallows in spring, shortly after hatching, and are never seen again until they are at least two years old. Considerable efforts have been made to obtain young fish, but so far without success. For years it was thought that the myriads of fry frequenting the shallows in early summer were young powan. Nevertheless every sample caught by Professor Slack's team proved to be roach.

Not surprisingly, the powan has a reputation for being mysterious. Nor is this reputation diminished by the discovery of a few powan specimens which are possessed of a supernumerary fin. This extra fin is usually found on the fish's back, just behind the head.

Thoughts on Powan Angling

At one time there was a ready market for powan. Nowadays, it seems, the economics of marketing fish would not support, as it once did, the cost of bringing over a team of professional pollan-netters from Ireland. That powan are no longer taken in their thousands by professional netsmen should encourage the angler. There is, moreover, little chance of his catching undersized fish – since these are not to be come by at all!

The curious coarse fisherman may like to know if he could catch powan using one of his deadly coarse-fishing methods. We think that he could, or at least that he could in winter, when the powan are bottom feeding. We would suggest the use of link-ledger, or swimfeeder techniques with maggot or small worm as bait.

Rather than ledger indiscriminately, we would select a deep swim within comfortable casting range of the bank – our selection depending to some extent on information derived from local boatmen who know something of the powan's movements.

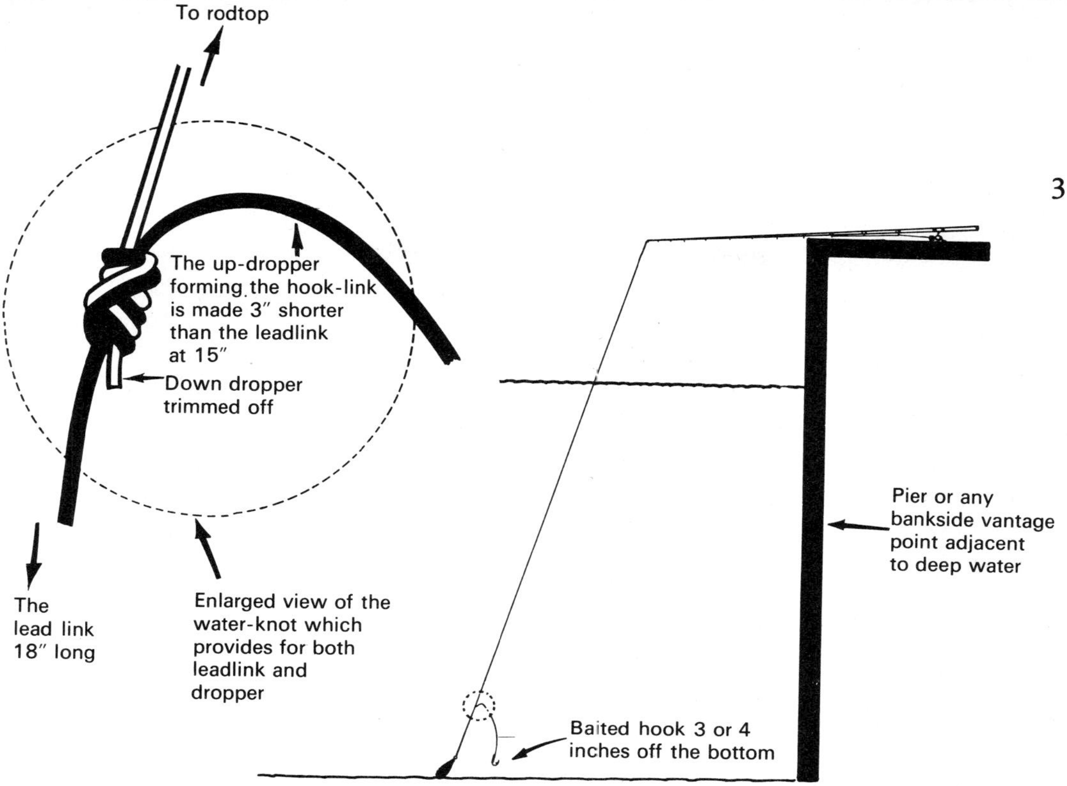

Fig. 29.1. The Loch Lomond winter deep-water powan paternoster.

Prior to fishing we would give the swim a thorough and heavy ground-baiting with chopped worms, maggots and pieces of turf. This would be done in the hope that the turf would provide a landmark for the roaming shoals of powan, and the groundbait an inducement to stay in the swim. In a few days, if our swim were well chosen, we would expect powan to be preoccupied with our offerings, and to fall readily to the hookbait.

It has been said that powan are poor fighters. Like many other snap judgments on the fighting qualities of fish, often made by anglers least qualified to judge, this one is quite wrong. We believe that when anglers 'discover' the powan and fish for it with reasonably fine tackle – either fly or bait – they will soon recognize the true qualities of this sporting whitefish.

Fishing for roach livebait near Balmaha, F. B. caught an $11\frac{1}{4}$ oz powan (once the British rod-caught record) on suitably light tackle – and thought he had hooked Loch Lomond's biggest roach!

When cured of a mania to catch a fifty-pound Loch Lomond pike, F. B. intends to concentrate on powan and charr. For powan he will trail a tiny fly, or nymph, behind a boat that is allowed to drift with the breeze. The fly will be tied to a number sixteen or eighteen hook, and the leader will be the merest gossamer ($1–1\frac{1}{2}$ lb B.S.). The line will be a floating (bubble) line, and the rod an ultra light brook fly-rod. With this tackle (if he is fortunate enough to drift through a shoal of powan) he looks forward to enjoying sport-fishing as good as any to be had in Britain.

Loch Lomond powan grow to a length of

18 in. and a top weight of about 2 lb. A rod-caught two-pounder would be a wonderful achievement. What more could any fisherman wish for? Well, he could wish for his catch to be worthy of cooking in wine. And his wish would be granted, for the powan is delicious to eat.

Very few powan have ever been caught on rod and line largely because very few anglers have ever tried to catch them. Nevertheless, powan-angling holds great possibilities; it also presents a considerable challenge, since almost nothing is known about it. We thought it would be interesting to ask our friend Richard Walker to speculate on how he would set about catching one of these elusive little fish.

'Speculation is held to constitute one of the attractions of angling. Where powan are concerned, it is the only course open to me, because I have never caught one, nor have I ever seen one caught on rod and line.

'I can therefore only speculate about ways and means of catching them on a basis of what the books say about their food, and on the appearance of the fish, since I have been able to examine dead specimens.

'The authorities say powan are plankton feeders, and that they also feed on the littoral shallows, upon insects of various kinds. Certainly their mouths and digestive systems seem adapted to such a diet. Their mouths and indeed their faces bear a remarkable resemblance to those of grayling, the only noticeable difference being the larger eye of the powan. The shape, the scales and the general feel of the two species are also similar and I think the angler can regard the powan as a kind of stillwater grayling, with advantage to his choice of angling methods.

'I am pretty confident that if I could get within easy casting range of a shoal of feeding powan, I could catch them readily. I should use a fly rod, a long nylon leader tapered to about 2 lb B.S., and an artificial nymph or midge pupa chosen to imitate such natural insects as I could capture and identify on that day, dressed on hooks from size 14 to 18 to match the size of the insects found.

'Very successful dressings for insects of these kinds have been evolved for catching rainbow trout from reservoirs. Such trout are largely plankton feeders, as examination of stomach contents has shown. I am confident that these dressings, mainly of chironomid larvae, would also catch powan.[1]

'Various ephemerids, including Pond Olives, caenis and a rather large insect resembling a small mayfly[2] are common on Loch Lomond and I surmise that imitations of these, used when the natural insects were seen, would also account for powan.

'I do not think that choosing the right artificial fly and fishing it with the right motion are the real problems. Much more important is the problem of putting the fly where a powan can see it.

'In fly-fishing for trout on lakes and lochs, the methodical covering of likely areas usually brings some sort of success because trout, be they brown trout, sea-trout or rainbow-trout, are pretty widely distributed.

1 See powan flies, p. 293.

2 Siphlonurus lacustris.

A series of drifts with the boat will be fairly sure to put the angler's flies within sight of at least some of the fish. Powan, however, seem to move in densely-packed shoals covering a relatively small area. An angler might drift about on a big loch, like Lomond, all day for years without ever coming within casting range of a powan shoal.

'With my friends, I have covered miles and miles on Loch Lomond, day after day, and have only twice seen shoals of powan. On neither occasion did I have a fly rod fixed up.

'In order to catch powan, I think it would be advisable to seek all possible information about the areas they frequent from local people, especially the commercial salmon and sea-trout netsmen; and then to move the boat slowly about in these areas, keeping careful watch for shoals of powan, both visually and with a suitably-arranged echo sounder, set up with its transducer looking ahead instead of downwards.

'Powan shoals have a habit of coming to the surface which they break with their dorsal fins and upper tail lobes. This is known locally as "finning" and is easy to observe, even in rough weather.

'Very few powan have ever been caught on rod and line, but that need occasion no surprise, since anglers on Lomond do not try to catch them and do not employ tackle that is very likely to catch them accidentally. Local men fly-fish only for salmon and sea-trout, using for the most part flies that are large and leaders that are stout by ordinary sea-trout fishing standards, the idea being, I suppose, that if a salmon is hooked, an event for which they constantly hope, they will have a fair chance of boating it. When one considers the odds against such flies being cast where powan are, and also the odds against a powan taking a traditional wet fly on a size 8 hook, tied to 8 to 12 lb nylon, one can readily see why the capture of powan is so rare.

'There are lots of grayling in the river Tweed, but not many are caught on salmon and sea-trout flies, though they can readily be caught on tiny nymphs and fine leader points, as I have proved in practice often enough. Grayling and powan are, as I have explained earlier, remarkably similar.

'I expect that, like grayling, powan could also be caught with maggots or worms on float tackle; indeed F. B. caught one on a maggot off Balmaha pier. In dealing with a powan shoal located out in the loch, however, I would expect fly-fishing methods to be more successful, since they would cause less disturbance than float and shot, and would allow an artificial to be fished only an inch or two below the surface. That is the method I would choose, until experience proved me wrong.'

GWYNIAD

Coregonus clupeoides pennantii
(Lake Bala)

SKELLY

Coregonus clupeoides stigmaticus
(Haweswater, Ullswater, Redtarn)

The gwyniad of Lake Bala, Wales, and the skelly of Haweswater, Ullswater and Red Tarn in the English Lake District, are

Skelly, netted in February, 1972, from Haweswater, Cumberland. Two other lakes in the Eden catchment area: Ullswater and Red Tarn, also hold skelly. The skelly (Coregonus stigmaticus), *the powan* (Coregonus clupeoides) *and the gwyniad* (Coregonus pennantii) *are now considered to be one species:* Coregonus lavaretus (Photograph: E. Ramsbottom).

similar fishes; together with the powan they are collectively described as the freshwater houting, *Coregonus lavaretus.*

The gwyniad once swarmed in Lake Bala, but in 1803, according to Yarrel in *British Fishes*, the introduction of pike reduced their numbers considerably. The Ullswater variety, the skelly, was at one time netted by the local inhabitants. Unlike the charr of Windermere, which was preserved in butter, the skelly was preserved in salt. Like the Welsh gwyniads, the Ullswater skellies are now scarce.

The existence of skellies in Ullswater was first mentioned in 1686. John Watson, in his book *The English Lake District Fisheries* (1899), recorded its decline. Watson found an interesting reference to the skelly in Clarke's *Survey of the Lakes*: 'The skelly is remarkable for this, no bait has ever been found which they will take.'

Watson brightens the picture, however, by telling us that he caught one in Haweswater on the fly.

It is interesting to note that once again the growing domination of another species is advanced as the reason for the decline of a whitefish. On this occasion, Watson blamed an increasing perch population for the decline of the Ullswater skellies. If the perch were indeed responsible they seem to have derived no benefit. In Elizabethan times they were recorded as growing to a weight of 5 lb, whereas the Ullswater perch of today are very small indeed.

VENDACE

Coregonus vandesius vandesius
(Mill Loch, near Lochmaben)

Coregonus vandesius gracilior
(Derwentwater, Bassenthwaite)

The vendace of Mill Loch near Lochmaben (a town in Dumfriesshire), together with the vendace of Derwentwater and Bassenthwaite, are so closely related that they can be considered, with the pollan, as varieties of the same species: *Coregonus albula.*

Lochmaben vendace have had a long and unique association with fishermen. At one time this silvery, herring-like little fish (they rarely exceed nine inches) was the centre of activity of a small exclusive group of gentlemen who formed themselves into a vendace club. It was their practice to meet

Vendace, netted in February, 1972, from Bassenthwaite Lake, Cumberland. The Cumberland vendace (Coregonus gracilior) *is closely related to the Lochmaben vendace* (Coregonus vendesius). *Nowadays (1972) taxonomists consider these and certain other British whitefish to be varieties of one species:* Coregonus albula (Photograph: E. Ramsbottom).

each July, net with sweepnets, and enjoy a great vendace feast.

In time the club became defunct. A second club, although bigger and more democratic, met the same fate. By the time

Francis Dummitt Dundas (1972). (See next page).

Dr P. S. Maitland, who took this extremely rare picture (below) *of a Lochmaben Vendace* (Coregonus vandesius), *estimates that only about 3,000 members of the species survive in their last known habitat – Mill Loch. He hopes to disperse the species by introducing it to other suitable waters in south-west Scotland. Maitland has already introduced Powan fry into another Scottish loch and seen these fish grow to spawning size.*
Note: *The projecting* lower *jaw is characteristic of the vendace. A projecting* upper *jaw is characteristic of the powan.*

the third club was formed (1910), the stock of fish was small and the club's annual catch was a mere half-dozen. Today, the 'club water', the beautiful Castle Loch, is empty of vendace. Fortunately, they still survive in nearby Mill Loch.

It is likely that the extinction of vendace in Castle Loch was due to a gradual change of character in the fish's environment. The present eutrophic nature of the water (rich in dissolved nutrient salts), favours roach and bream; whereas the previous oligotrophic nature (poor in dissolved nutrient salts) favoured the vendace. If the disappearance of Castle Loch's beloved little whitefish is really due to the changed character of the water, it will almost certainly have been brought about by the introduction of sewage effluent – even though this may have been strictly controlled.

Castle Loch, once famous for its vendace. The last vendace known to have been caught in Castle Loch on rod and line was taken with worm tackle near the tennis courts in 1937 by Francis Dummitt Dundas (see photograph on p. 319).

Pennant records the local belief that vendace were introduced into Lochmaben waters by the ill-fated Mary, Queen of Scots, when she visited the castle in 1565.

Braithwaite, in *Salmonidae of Westmorland* (1894), mentioned the vendace and noted the resemblance to the gwyniad (skelly) of Ullswater insofar as they swim in large shoals, retire to deep water in warm weather, and rarely take the angler's bait. The vendace, he claimed, often rises to the surface like a common herring '. . . making a similar noise by their rise and fall to and from the surface.'

Describing the netting of vendace in the early 19th century, Sir W. Jardine, in *The*

Edinburgh Journal of Natural and Geographical Science, wrote: 'They are most successfully taken during a dull day and sharp breeze, approaching near to the edges of the loch, and swimming in a direction contrary to the wind.'

POLLAN

Coregonus pollan pollan (Lough Neagh)
Coregonus pollan altior (Lough Earne)
Coregonus pollan elegans (Lough Derg, Lough Ree)

The pollan is generally associated with Ireland's Lough Neagh, although other varieties of pollan occur in Loughs Erne, Ree and Derg. The pollan once so abundant in Ree and Derg, became rare after the Shannon was drained in 1845. Lough Neagh, the largest British lake, has a long history of commercial pollan fishing. Thompson, the Irish naturalist who described the pollan in *History of British Fishes*, recorded a catch made in 1834 of over 17,000 fish with four draughts of the net.

Tate Regan, in *British Freshwater Fishes* (1911), states that the staple food of the pollan is plankton; although insect larvae, shrimps, small bivalves and *the fry of other fishes* are also taken (our italics). To digress for a moment, we should like to point out the fallacy of thinking that fish differentiate between their own fry and the fry of other species: it leads to the common mistake of calling certain species (or specimens; e.g. large brown trout) 'cannibals'. At times, *all* fish will eat smaller fish–trout included.

Mill Loch. A lovely piece of water which still holds vendace.

Lough Neagh pollan. This fish was $11\frac{1}{2}$ in. long and weighed 9 oz. Dr D. Cragg-Hine of the Fisheries Research Laboratory, Coleraine, Co. Derry very kindly arranged for this fish to be caught and photographed to enable us to complete the series of Whitefish photographs.

Pollan Fishing

Writing in 1886, 'Hi-Regan' [Capt. J. J. Dunne], an authority on Irish fishing, made it clear that the capture of a Lough Neagh pollan was an ambition worthy of the best angler. To his everlasting credit he left us this dressing for a pollan fly: 'A very small silver-bodied gnat, hackled at shoulder; with blue-tip and a tiny ring of blue chatterer *and the whole disfigured with a gentle*.' (Our italics.)

It seems that Hi-Regan's informant was a practical angler who killed his pollan either on this fly (see p. 293) or on the 'wasp caddie – sunk and drawn up gently from the bottom.'

Pollan grow to about 13 inches in length. Although a weight of about $2\frac{1}{2}$ lb has been recorded, a fish of this size would be exceptional.

The bank angler should have good chances to take pollan, for they are known to come into the shallows not only during spring and summer but when the autumn is far advanced. Thompson gives the spawning season as November and December. Judging by the results of netting, the pollan is very far from being generally distributed throughout the lough.

According to Thompson, the favourite resort of Lough Neagh pollan is between six-mile water and Shane's Castle. We suggest that the area around Ram's Island would be a good starting point for an angler, for it was here that the record haul of pollan was taken.

A Viking Inheritance?

In South West Scotland and North West England, or more particularly in the country bordering the Solway Firth, certain species of fish are given quaint names. These include 'sprod', 'smelt', 'herling', 'mort' – which refer to sea-trout – and 'skelly', which is of particular interest since it describes two different species of fish.

Around the border town of Carlisle, 'skelly' refers to the chub (*Leuciscus cephalis*). South of Carlisle, in the heart of the Lake District, 'skelly' means the whitefish (*Coregonus lavaretus*), an inhabitant of Haweswater, Ullswater and Red Tarn. Even Frank Buckland, the famous 19th-century naturalist confused 'skelly'-chub and 'skelly'-whitefish. This is not surprising since whitefish are found in Ullswater and Haweswater, and chub are found in the rivers that flow out of these lakes. Occasionally, both species come 'face to face'. Dr Heysham, in

Hutchinson's History of Cumberland, wrote: 'A few of them ('skellies'-whitefish) sometimes leave Ullswater, go down the river Eamont into the Eden, and now and then a solitary one is taken below the bay of Armathwaite.' This is right in the middle of the chub water.

Where does the name 'skelly' come from? Yarrell, *British Fishes* (1839), thought that the 'skelly'-whitefish was so named on account of its large scales. So did that noted ichthiologist C. Tate Regan, although in *British Freshwater Fishes* (1911), he referred to 'conspicuous' scales rather than large scales.

J. J. Manley, in *Fish and Fishing* (1877), suggested that 'skelly'-chub was a corruption of 'skully' or 'skull', since the specific name for the chub is *cephalus*, from cephalic: pertaining to the head, a reference to the size and breadth of the chub's head.

Referring to the tributaries of Ullswater in *The English Lake District Fisheries* (1899), Watson wrote: 'The chub occurs in some of them, and on account of its scales it is invariably called "skelly" by the natives.'

It is of course possible that 'skelly' is a corruption of 'scaly', but we do not think it likely.

'Skalle', pronounced 'skelly' by the Danes, is used in Denmark to describe the roach (*Rutilus rutilus*) and since the Solway area was settled by the Vikings (Danes, Norwegians and Swedes) in the 9th and 10th centuries, it would be reasonable to suppose that the word has survived practically unchanged in both languages like many other Viking words and place names.

The word 'mort', used by Cumbrians to describe large sea-trout, is used in Sweden (spelt mört) to describe an entirely different species of fish. Astonishingly, once again, it is the ubiquitous roach.

The word 'pickerel', used as the diminutive for pike in England during the middle ages, was taken by early British settlers to North America and used to describe similar fishes later identified as entirely different species: chain pickerel (*Esox niger*), redfin pickerel (*Esox americanus americanus*), grass pickerel (*Esox americanus vermiculatus*) and walleye (*Stizostedion vitreum*).

How likely it is, then, that the early Viking settlers in the Solway area used their native words to describe fishes that were *similar* (but not necessarily identical) to the fishes of their own lands. Roach, chub and whitefish are all silvery, herring-like fishes. Could it not be as simple as that?

30 · The Zander

Stizostedion lucioperca

The zander is a member of the Perch family (Percidae) which includes the common perch (*Perca fluviatilis*) and the ruffe (*Gymnocephalus cernua*).

It is an eastern European fish that has been widely introduced into western Europe. It was first introduced into Britain in 1878 (at Woburn), other introductions followed in 1910, 1947 and 1950. Now (in 1971) the zander is a breeding British species notably at Woburn, Leighton Buzzard, and Claydon Lakes, as well as in parts of the Fens and the Great Ouse river system.

Zanders, like all the perches, are carnivorous. Indeed when adult they are almost entirely fish-eaters. As a species they favour large lakes and large slow-flowing rivers. Generally, angling methods are the same as those used for pike, although concessions in the form of smaller baits and lighter breaking strain lines, are made to the zander's smaller size.

Most British zander fishermen have a poor opinion of the zander's fighting abilities when compared with those of the pike. Since few British anglers kill zander, they are unlikely to discover that the zander's delicious flavour compensates for its lack of gameness.

A reluctance to kill fish for food is common among British coarse-fish anglers. Their eastern European counterparts like to fish for the table as well as for sport. Since the zander is very susceptible to injury, and may die as a result of captivity in a keepnet, the zander fisherman may just as well kill his catch and eat it. Mortality due to angling is unlikely to make serious inroads on the zander population. The zander's fecundity

5 lb zander caught by Ken Sutton; Woburn Abbey lake, 1958.

Record zander – weight 15 lb 6 oz – caught by William Chillingworth on 21st February 1971, while fishing the Great Ouse relief channel, Downham Market, with a large roach livebait on float/paternoster.

is remarkable; a 25-inch hen fish has been known to produce 685,000 eggs.

The name pikeperch, sometimes given both to the zander and the walleye is a misnomer. The European zander (*Stizostedion lucioperca*) and the North American walleye (*Stizostedion vitreum*) are closely related. Both species display the 'family crest' of the Perches – the spiked dorsal fin, and both possess large pike-like canine teeth. The combination of these features has led anglers to believe, quite erroneously, that zander and walleye are crosses between the pike and the perch. They are not.

According to Alwyne Wheeler (*The Fishes of The British Isles and North-West Europe*) there is no breeding population of walleye in Britain.

Ways and Means

31 · Chance and Mischance

WEATHER

Wenyng the ffissher suche fisshe to ffynde;
Than comyth there a noyous north west wynde
And dryveth the ffisshe into the depe,
And causeth the draught nat worthe a leeke . . .

(PIERS OF FULHAM, *c.* 1400).

Here ye shall wyte in what weder ye shall angle, as I sayd before ina derke lowrynge daye whanne the wynde blowyth softly. And in somer season whan it is brennynge hote thenne it is nought. From Septembre unto Apryll in a fayr sonny daye is ryght good to angle. And yf the wynde in that season have any parte of the Oryent: the wedyr thenne is nought. And whan it is a grete wynde. And whan it snowith reynyth or hayllyth, or is a grete tempeste as thondyr or lightenynge: or a swoly hote weder: thenne it is noughte for to angle.'

DAME JULIANA BERNERS, *A Treatyse of Fysshynge wyth an Angle* (1496).

Fishing is an unceasing expectation and a perpetual disappointment.

THOMAS DE QUINCEY.

All windes are hurtful if too hard they blow,
The worst of all is that out of the East,
Whose nature makes the Fish to biting slow,
And lets[1] the pastime most of all the rest;
The next that comes from countries clad with Snow,
And *Articque* pole is not offensive least,
The Southern winde is counted best of all,
Then, that which riseth where the sunne doth fall.

JOHN DENNYS, *The Secrets of Angling* (1613).

ANGLING LUCK

It is one of the charms of angling that, occasionally, success is not exclusive to the skilled angler. The novice can catch fish on his first outing – if he is lucky. It does not happen very often, but it happens.

Such a feat sets angling apart from most other games and sports. One would hardly expect a novice batsman to score fifty in his first innings, or a novice clay-shooter to break twenty-five straight at skeet. Of the greatest importance to his peace of mind, however, is the angling beginner's ability to

1 Lets = Hinders.

rationalize this unexpected moment of success – when, in the face of intense competition, *his* rod lands more fish than any other.

The point is illustrated by the following example.

A novice, having joined a fishing club and experienced blanks on two previous trips, is now taking a third coach trip with his club. Luckily he draws an early number, which puts him at the head of the column of anglers winding along the river bank. Motivated only by fancy our novice stops at a certain swim. By chance he chooses to ledger-fish the swim with cheese-paste bait – perhaps because he is still too squeamish to use worms and maggots!

In reality he has the best swim in the whole section and, which is more, the swim is full of chub. On this particular day the chub respond to cheese before all other baits, and the only way to get at them properly happens to be with a ledger rig. So our novice has a field day.

Also in the group is a skilful angler who would have chosen the same swim for certain very definite reasons. Had he been given first chance he would have stopped at the same place, and from experience concluded that it could be fished properly only with a ledger rig. He would have known that chub were a likely prospect since, prior to the trip, he had taken the trouble to enquire about the water. His sample of baits would have included cheese-paste by design, since he is aware of the excellence of cheese as a chub bait. With the minimum of experiment he would have started to take chub on the ledger with cheese-paste – and undoubtedly he would have netted a larger bag of fish.

It takes little thought to put this example of the fortunate novice in true perspective: for him, other good days will be few until he has reinforced the element of luck, which is common to all, with some hard-won experience. At the same time the incident underlines one of angling's major attractions: the beginner is always in with a chance. It is, after all, not impossible that the coveted first 4 lb roach could be caught by a novice – at his first attempt!

A Disastrous Day

Out we went again, with two flies, nor had we made many turns, when my beautiful rod got a drag, that made every loop in it sing, and I had firm a most enormous spring fish. We, as usual, made for the shore, my beast leading quietly until I got in, when I set about butting it in prime style; away he went down and across for a considerable distance, then doubled against the stream, and began to get slack; I wheeled up very quickly, until the weight came on my 'multiplier', and then one yard I could not get up. At this time, a malignant grin passed over the stern phiz of Kean. I made another effort to wheel up, with all the force I could employ, when smash went the multiplying machinery. I then dragged down the line quickly through the loops, and had my fish under the bow of the rod, but he came to the surface, ploughed across the current, took the line on his back, and away he went. My line ran

Have pity on these holy maidens fair,
Resigned unto the Lord they bear their Cross.
Forbidden when they lose a fish to swear,
Or by a hair's breadth to exaggerate their loss.
DAVID JACQUES

out fairly for a time, but at last hitched in the loops, two or three of which gave; the line would not run; it twisted up, my rod snapped in the butt, about a foot and a a-half from the wheel, and my brute got off, taking about forty yards of line. He was one of the largest salmon I ever saw.

'I knew', said Kean, 'what the multiplying wheel would do. . . . Well, sir, we have another rod, and I advise you to put up the fly you killed the large salmon at Castle Troy with.' . . .

To it we went, and . . . I soon after got hold of a very nice fish, about fourteen pounds weight, got to shore, and managed him well. While I was playing him, a Captain Cotter came to the bank, attended by about a half score of dogs, grey-hounds and pointers. He was a great angler, but had been disabled by a wound in a duel with Richard Harrison, which arose out of a difference about the right of fishing a stream. . . . Well, we got in the salmon with some difficulty, the gaff having slipped out of the handle, and the fish was getting out again, when all parties hastened to intercept him; the rod was thrown down, the dogs got entangled with the line, the hook was broken in the salmon's jaw, the line snapped in three or four places, and, to crown all, the rod smashed nearly in pieces. Here followed confusion, cursing, swearing, kicking dogs; damning, openly and mentally, our visitor and his companions . . .

In what I have written thus hurriedly, though there is much of mere detail, there is also warning instruction.
O'GORMAN, *The Practice of Angling* (Vol. 1, 1845).

. . . a blank fishing day does not necessarily mean an unenjoyable (or uneventful) one . . . to capture something of the calm philosophy of Izaak Walton is just as important as the ability to kill a large number of fish.
A COURTNEY WILLIAMS, *Angling Diversions* (1945).

PISCATOR: Oh me! he has broken all; there's half a line and a good hook lost.
VENATOR: Aye, and a good trout, too.
PISCATOR: Nay, the trout is not lost, for take notice, no man can lose what he never had.
IZAAK WALTON, *The Compleat Angler* (1653).

We feel there is a flaw in Piscator's argument. But there is certainly no flaw in Barry Welham's magnificent 6 lb 13 oz brown trout (above).

Twenty-Five Ways of Losing a Fish

Since the dawn of angling wild-eyed men have babbled of great fish hooked and lost. The literature is filled with stories of leviathans sometimes seen, sometimes unseen, that have escaped the record books. And yet in so many cases the loss could have been avoided if the angler had given a little more thought to the matter *in advance*; if he had spent just a little more time and care examining the water he was going to fish, and the tackle he was going to fish it with. Time and again one's admiration of an angler's skill in hooking a fish is tempered by his stupidity in losing it.

Here for your consideration are 25 ways of losing a fish. They are compiled from experience. For each of them, except the first, the angler is mainly responsible – and even the first is not wholly free from suspicion. (There are of course other ways of losing a fish, but these will do to be going on with).

1. *Hook loses its hold*

Unless the angler has mistimed the strike (in which case it is his own fault if the hook secures a poor hold), this is the only valid excuse for losing a fish. Once the angler has tightened on a fish nothing more can be done to improve the hold. If the fish is poorly hooked the chances are it will come off before it can be landed. Luck will always play a part in angling, and before he goes fishing the novice should realise that, through no fault of his own, he is destined to lose[1] a proportion of the fish he hooks. To bewail such losses and allow them to upset him will simply reduce his confidence and concentration and detract from his future chances. He should, however, be quite certain that the loss of a fish *is* due to plain chance – and not to his own carelessness.

1 Piscator notwithstanding!

2. *Unsound tackle*

No 'plain chance' about this. It is clearly the angler's fault. Every item of tackle should be overhauled and tested before fishing starts. Above all it should be remembered that to buy cheap fishing tackle is nearly always false economy.

3. *Hook failure*

(a) *Broken.* A broken hook is due either to poor casting or to poor quality metal. In both cases the angler is at fault: in the former for clumsiness, in the latter for not testing the hook.

(b) *Straightened.* A lot of fish are lost because a hook straightens out. Most modern hooks are suspect, trebles in particular. Every hook should be tested before use.

4. *Knot slips*

Another cause of misery. And whose fault is it? No one should go fishing who has not learned to tie *and to test* the right knot for the job in hand.

5. *Failure to re-tie hook or fly*

Impatience is usually the reason for this. A hook or fly should frequently be re-tied, and always after a big fish has been landed.

6. *Wind knot*
Wind or no wind, 'wind' knots appear in a fly leader as though by magic. They considerably reduce the breaking strain of nylon. The only way of avoiding a smash is by frequent inspection of the leader, especially at night.

7. *Broken by fish*
This may be due to unsound tackle, or clumsiness, or the fish running into weed or round a snag. Whatever the reason, anyone who allows a fish to break him deserves to lose it. It is almost always the fault of the angler. All water should be examined before fishing starts. When the position of a snag is known a fish can usually be 'walked' away from it. The time to get on terms with a fish is the moment it is hooked. To wait until it has run halfway down a pool or gone to ground or into a weed bed, before doing anything constructive, is the fault of many anglers on hooking a fish. Few people seem to know how to 'walk' a fish, or even that a fish *can* be 'walked'. (For details of this, see p. 213.)

8. *Fishing too fine*
Could have come under previous heading, but deserves special mention since there is an unfortunate type of angler who boasts of fishing very fine and 'giving the fish a chance'. He is a fool. There is nothing in the least sporting in giving a fish the chance to escape taking with it a hook in its gullet and a length of nylon. A fish will refuse tackle that is too coarse and strong. It will break and swim away with tackle that is too fine. The sporting angler, knowing that he must use something in between, chooses the strongest tackle that will enable him to hook and land the species he is fishing for in the conditions existing at the time. *There is seldom any excuse for being broken by a fish.*

9. *Reel jams*
This is due either to bad maintenance or lack of attention while fishing. To put the butt of a fly rod down into dry earth or sand often results in the reel becoming clogged. An extension to the rod butt helps to prevent this. It is a good habit (especially in the darkness) for an angler to place the rod butt on top of his foot. Another reason for a reel jamming is when tight coils of line bite down on loose coils underneath. A line should be stripped off and re-wound before fishing starts, and after a big fish has been played.

10. *Leader knot jams*
If, when a fish is being landed, the line is wound in too far – so that the knot joining leader and line jams in a rod ring – a sudden rush often enables the fish to break free. The use of a needle knot (see p. 409) avoids this altogether. If a figure-of-eight knot is used (see p. 411), the angler should make sure that the leader is not too long for the rod.

11. *Striking too hard*
The most likely moment for a break is just as the fish is hooked. But striking consists of tightening on a fish, not giving it a great jerk.

12. *Holding a fish too hard*
Apart from the strike this is the quickest and most certain way of getting broken. A fault common among novices who, when they hook a fish, cannot bear to let it get further away from them. The only time a running fish should be 'held' is when the line (or backing) is almost exhausted, or when the fish is heading for an obvious snag: perhaps the middle arch of a bridge. But the fault lies with the angler for allowing the fish to get into a position from which a disastrous run is likely. In most cases, prior action (such as 'walking' the fish) can prevent it. The angler should *never be taken by surprise*. The successful landing of any fish depends on careful thought before a line is put in the water.

13. *Rod top caught in branches*
This can happen very easily when a bushy run is being fished for sea-trout at night.

14. *Trying to land a fish too soon*
A very common mistake. The angler has shortened line and, with net or gaff extended, hauls the fish towards him. The fish obligingly comes almost within reach; then, frightened by the sight of the fisherman, turns and dashes away in alarm. The reel fails to respond quickly enough or a handle gets hooked up, or the line knot jams in a rod ring and the leader snaps . . . *Wait until the fish has turned on its side.* Even so, an angler should not use a landing net like a child catching tadpoles. A fish is not scooped out, but lifted out. The angler should conceal himself by crouching as low as possible, then sink the net to the bottom so that the fish cannot see it.

When the fish is lying on its side, *and not before*, it is drawn steadily in, and the net raised to encircle it. (See p. 396. Also *Lost at the gaff*, p. 210.)

15. *Leader cut by gaff stroke*
Very easily done. (See p. 210.)

16. *Leader nipped in joint of landing net*
A miserable business which can happen with a folding net, especially at night.

17. *Nylon line or leader burned with cigarette end*
This is hardly likely to happen to a non-smoker. It once happened to H.F. when landing a large salmon–hence its inclusion.

18. *Fish knocked off hook by gaff or net*
This might be called the 'willing helper syndrome'. Invariably the bystander, anxious to help in landing a fish, goes into action too soon. Except in emergency, it is advisable for an angler to land his own fish. Then if it gets knocked off the hook he has only himself to blame.

19. *Line/backing splice draws.* (See comment on p. 404.)
No fly fisherman should ever allow anyone else to splice his fly line and backing for him. If the splice draws he loses not only the fish but the line as well. If he does the job himself and tests it thoroughly it will *not* draw.

A needle knot is preferable to a splice if monofilament backing is used.

20. *Hole in landing net*
Very irritating, but sheer carelessness. Having, as the angler thinks, been netted the fish sets off with renewed vigour and leaves the angler trying to play it through the hole. Usually results in loss of fish; sometimes a broken rod tip.

21. *Hole in keep net*
Really!

22. *Failure to cope with fish making off downstream*
Occasionally a fish is in danger of being lost because it makes a fast run downstream, with the angler unable to follow. This can be disastrous, but if he has plenty of backing (as he *should* have) and keeps his head, the angler is always in with a chance.

Only when the fish has run out all the line and backing is the situation hopeless; and in this instance the angler is wise to hold the fish *before* the last turn of backing has left the reel, otherwise he may lose the lot; fish, fly, line and backing – and doubtless his temper as well. By holding the fish in time (but after it has made a long run) he may turn it, or at least he may save his fly line and backing.

It has been said that an angler can stop a fish running downstream by stripping line off the reel. He can't! Line cannot be stripped off quickly enough to affect a fast-running fish. This method of bringing a fish back upstream can, however, be used to good effect when a salmon, having gone some distance downstream, *has stopped and is lying there.* Now, if line is stripped off, a belly will form below the fish. The fish will soon feel the pressure of this bag of line from behind, and begin to swim upstream towards the rod.
The slack line method can also be used effectively when a fish is *beginning* to tire and is below the angler, stemming the current. But the danger of losing a fish downstream is greatest when the fish is very tired, because then it is unable to resist being carried off tail first. When this happens, no amount of slack line hanging below it will make it move upstream, for it is exhausted.

Think about all this before fishing starts, *not after a fish has been hooked.*

23. *Hook caught in landing net*
This loses a lot of fish. It happens when a fish is being landed on multi-hook tackle; fly leader with bob-fly and dropper; Stewart or Pennell tackles; spinning flight; prawn, livebait or deadbait mounts; quill minnow with flying treble, etc. As the fish is drawn to the net a hook attaches itself to a mesh, and the fish – now held tantalizingly just outside the net's rim – can be brought no farther. At this point it usually stages a rapid recovery, wrenches the hook out and departs.

24. *Fish jumps back again*
Every now and then a fish, having been landed successfully, slips out of the angler's hand, or slithers down a bank, and regains its freedom. A desperate business which (however unlikely it sounds) happens to most of us sooner or later. If a fish has to be handled when the angler is in or close to the water it should be knocked on the head while

still in the net. Otherwise it should be taken well back from the water's edge. For notes on beaching a salmon, see p. 211.

25. *Thieves*

Even when landed and killed a fish is not always safe. Rats, cats, mink, otters, badgers and pigs have all been known to snitch fish from a river bank. Never leave a fish lying out on the grass. Always hang it up out of reach, or put it away in a bag.

Note: Plastic bags are not recommended for use in hot weather.

An oil painting by H. L. Rolfe (circa 1850). Later in his career, Rolfe, who was one of the greatest fish painters of all time, was commissioned to paint a picture for Mr Mundella as a testimonial for sponsoring the Bill protecting certain freshwater fishes by means of a close season. The Bill became an Act of Parliament in 1878.

32 · Rods and Reels

Since angling is the art of deception, tackles should be chosen primarily to deceive the fish rather than please the fisherman. But because few fishermen can concentrate for long when using tackle not entirely to their fancy, best of all is the tackle which both deceives and pleases.

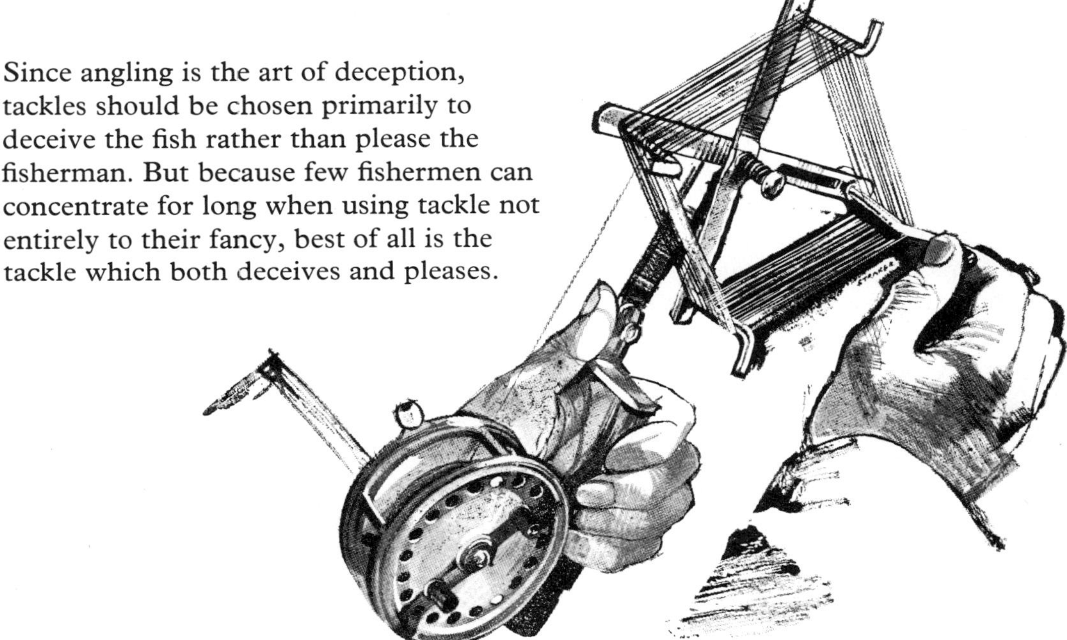

How many rods of evil structure have been fabricated. How many wheels have been constructed on foolish and vicious principles; how many lines badly prepared; how many casting-lines odiously knotted; how many hooks ill-turned and round-shanked, to the evident discomfort of the fly tier, ill formed appearance of the fly, and missing of the fish!
O'GORMAN, *The Practice of Angling* (Vol. 1, 1845).

Always go to a tackle dealer who is an angler and whom you can get to know personally. He knows that the regular satisfied customer is the mainstay of his business, and it is therefore in his interests to see that you have the right tackle for the job, the best value for money, and conscientious after-sales service. I wouldn't buy a box of split shot unless I knew the man who was selling it.
RICHARD WALKER.

HISTORY AND DEVELOPMENT OF RODS

Tackle development through the ages was painfully slow. It took about 4,000 years to advance from a *tight* line – that is, a line tied to the end of the rod – to a *loose* line, which slipped through a rod ring, or rings. (For misuse of the term 'running-line' see p. 458.) Even in mediaeval times there are no pictures which indicate the presence of a top wire ring.

It is probable that a line which could be drawn in or let out through a rod ring came into use in Europe[1] some time during the 16th or 17th centuries, although it was not until Barker's *Art of Angling* (1651), that anything like a *reel* is mentioned. He talks of a 'wind', but it is not easy to understand exactly how it worked. Izaak Walton mentions the fishing 'wheele' – again with scant detail. Even in the 17th and 18th centuries, when reels of a sort were available, most anglers fished with tight lines. The accepted drill on hooking a big fish was to throw the rod into the water and hope to retrieve it later, when the fish had played itself out.

But although the choice of tackle was limited, early anglers were no fools when it came to presentation. Plutarch, writing 1,900 years ago, says:

> Choose a rod which is slim, for fear lest if it cast a broad shadow it might move the doubt and suspicion that is naturally in fishes.

And on the choice of a line he says:

> Take order that the hairs which reach to the hook should seem as white as possible, for the whiter they be the less they are seen in the water for their conformity and likeness to it.

Nevertheless, whatever the cunning of those early fishermen, their tackle remained (for thousands of years) a stick with a horsehair line tied to the end of it.

1 A form of fishing reel had been invented by the Chinese several centuries earlier (see p. 350).

The earliest representation of angling, circa 2,000 B.C. From P. E. Newberry, *Beni Hasan*, Pt. 1, Pl. 29.

Origin and Materials

According to William Radcliffe, in his classic book *Fishing from the Earliest Times* (1921), all four methods of fishing: spear (harpoon), net, hand-line and rod, were being employed by the ancient Egyptians in about 2000 B.C. Indeed, at about this time the fishing rod is depicted in actual use – the first representation of angling with rod and line known in the world.

Judging by the height of the angler portrayed in the mural, the rod then in vogue was five or six feet long, and *tapered.* Furthermore, since the fish is being lifted from the water by its mouth, one may assume that the fisherman has not snatched it, but caught it on a baited hook. He is, without doubt, a true angler; the first on record. But what was his rod made of?

Naturally-grown fibrous materials have always been used in the making of fishing rods, and it is likely that the earliest rods were fashioned from papyrus reeds growing beside the Nile. Even up to modern times, the reed has endured. In the late 1950s, the best match rods were still being made from Spanish reed. But in the meantime, of course, a great variety of wood and other substances had found their way into the manufacture of fishing rods.

Gervaise Markham, writing in 1614, advocated the use of special materials for different parts of a rod. His list included ground-witchen, sallow, beech, hazel, poplar, cane and whale-bone. Great care was taken to ensure the proper action in a rod. For the upper length of a 'ground' (or bottom-fishing) rod, Colonel Robert Venables, author of *The Experienc'd Angler* (1662), prescribed cane, into which was fitted a finer piece of blackthorn, into which was fitted an even finer piece of whalebone.

By the 19th century the most popular materials were ash, greenheart, hickory, cane and lancewood. Cuban lancewood, which was considered the best, was reserved for middle and top joints. White ash and hickory were used mainly for butt joints.

Thomas Stoddart, in *The Angler's Companion to the Rivers and Lochs of Scotland* (1847), had this to say:

> Lance-wood is closer grained and somewhat heavier than hickory. It is a native of Cuba and other West India islands. For top-pieces, it is reckoned invaluable, possessing a spring and

From Hardy's Angler's Guide *1909.*

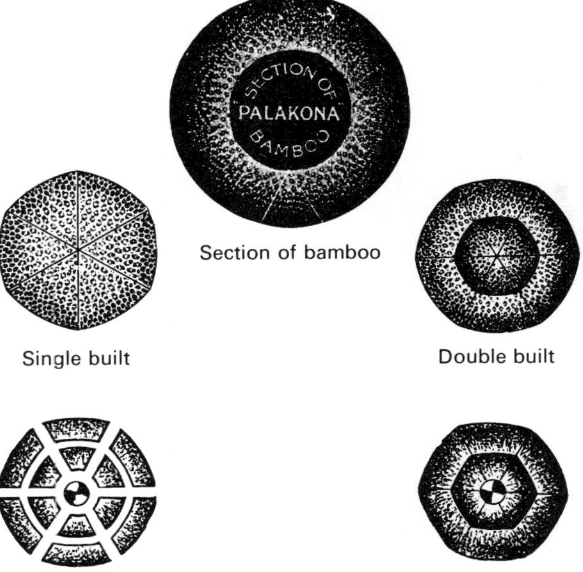

Section of bamboo

Single built

Double built

Double-built steel centre before cementing

Double-built steel centre after cementing

consistency, together with a capability of being highly wrought and polished, not found in any other wood. The great objection to lance-wood is its weight and consequent tendency, when used as a top-piece along with different woods, to injure or discompose the just and desirable balance of the rod.

(That 'just and desirable balance': what a delightful phrase, written with true feeling for the rod that should 'come alive' in the hand.)

Hickory was the first wood to fall out of general favour – although it was still a rod-maker's first choice for the handle of a big-game rod until as late as 1960.

Greenheart remained popular. Most of it came from British Guiana. If the green-heart timbers were carefully selected, rods could be made up that were both strong and elastic while remaining unaffected by water. Greenheart was, and still is, a highly suitable rodmaking material. Treated with keen tools, it files, scrapes, turns and planes very well.

It has been said that although the idea of split-cane rods originated in Britain during the early part of the 19th century, the first serious attempt at constructing rods from lengths of bamboo, split and glued together, was made by Samuel Phillippe, of Easton, Pennsylvania, between 1846 and 1850. It seems, however, that William Blacker, the English rodmaker, was running him neck and neck. We quote from his *Art of Fly Making* (second edition, 1855):

The beautiful rent and glued-up bamboo-cane fly rods, which I turn out to the greatest perfection, are very valuable, as they are both light and powerful, and throw the line with great facility. The cane for these rods must be of the very best description, or they will not last any time. They will last for years if properly made, and of course the fisher must take care of them; they are best when made into pocket rods, in eight joints, with all the knots cut out, and the good pieces between each knot rent and glued up; these may be had in my shop of as good a balance as a three-joint rod, most superbly made of the lightest brazings. They make capital perch and roach rods with a bait top added to the extra fly top, with bored butt to hold all. These rods can be made to suit a lady's hand for either boat or fly fishing.

Even when allowance is made for Blacker's salesmanship, it seems probable that his split-cane rods had been in production for a number of years. In Stoddart's book of 1847, already mentioned, we find:

. . . rod-makers are now in the habit of constructing the top-lengths, partly of lance-wood and partly of bamboo. The bamboo portion consists of a thin slit or slits detached from one of the jointed divisions of the cane. This is rounded off and otherwise cut and planed, so as to admit of being accurately glued on to the lance-wood section of the intended top-piece, the parts thus annexed being afterwards strengthened by a wrapping of waxed thread and coatings of varnish.

Although used only for a part of a rod and seemingly glued on to a lancewood core, this is undoubtedly what is known as 'split-cane', and it is almost certain that Blacker, working on his own, had started to follow the matter to its conclusion (a full-length rod) during the 1840s.

In his introduction to the 1921 edition of Alfred Ronalds's *The Fly-Fisher's Entomology*, Hugh Sheringham had this to say:

The development of rod-building was materially advanced by the discovery of the merits of bamboo for the purpose, the said bamboo being rent into sections, shaped, and then glued together and whipped. Split-cane rods are as a matter of fact much older than has been generally thought, older indeed than the dry fly, older even than Ronalds' *Fly-Fisher's Entomology*, which was first published in 1836. The earliest reference to them seems to be in a curious little book, *Fishes and Fishing*, by W. Wright, 'surgeon aurist to her late Majesty Queen Charlotte', which was published in 1858. In it he relates how in the year 1805 Wright was introduced 'to an old Welshman, named David Williams, whom Mr H. had drilled into making rods according to his plan; this Williams was acquainted with Clark, the unrivalled maker of glued-up bamboo fly-rods; the most excellent of all rods. I obtained about ten sticks of the proper cane, and Williams induced Clark to make one for me, and another for my friend Mr L.'

Which brings us to the start of the 19th century, and possibly the latter part of the 18th![1]

But although the date of the first split bamboo rod may be in doubt, it is certain that by about 1870 the hand-built 'split-cane' rod, made up from strips of baked Calcutta bamboo, was in fairly general use. During the next decade rodmakers began to improve rod-joints, rod-rings and reel-fittings. Rods could now be had in single or double-built split-cane, with or without steel centres. Greenheart rods were still fashionable, chiefly on account of their lower cost – although some anglers preferred them (and still prefer them) irrespective of cost. In 1896, Alexander Grant, inventor of the famous 'Grant Vibration' rod, cast the remarkable distance of 56 yards with his 20 ft greenheart fly rod.

Nevertheless, although greenheart was still used for fly rods, and East India cane, whole bamboo, and reeds were still used in the manufacture of extra-long float-fishing rods of up to 22 ft, split-cane gradually superseded all other materials in the manufacture of good quality fly rods, spinning rods and medium-length float fishing rods.

It was probably the considerable reduction of weight for the same degree of power that

1 In his delightful book, *Angling Diversions* (1945), A. Courtney Williams writes: 'Briefly, built-cane seems to have been invented in China, first applied to fishing-rods in England, and thereafter jointly developed by manufacturers in England and U.S.A.

'Who first thought of splitting bamboo into strips and then gluing them together so as to obtain the full strength of the cane by eliminating its hollow centre, is likely to remain a matter of conjecture. It is, however, certain that it did not originate in either England or U.S.A., but most probably in China. It seems to have been generally overlooked that the art was known in that country nearly 3,000 years ago. In the book of *Tchouang-Tseu* (950 B.C.) an explanation is given as to how to build split-cane "rods", glued and bound.

'Similar "rods" are also mentioned in the *History* of *T'chou* and *T'au* (350 B.C.) Book 7, Chapter 71, which is now based in the National Museum in Paris.

'It is true that in both cases the "rods" are mentioned as being used by water-carriers to transport pails on their shoulders, but even though they were not fishing rods, the essence of the idea was there.'

finally made split-cane supreme. The lightness of this material enabled women (other than Amazons) to take up the sport of angling.

Bamboo from the Tonkin region of China had been found to be the best cane for rodmaking. In 1925, a machine was devised to cut and plane the six triangular sections of bamboo which together made up a built-cane section. Hitherto, this job had been done by hand, and it is interesting to note that when machines replaced the men who had previously split the Tonkin poles with a knife, the term 'split' cane was no longer used. Rodmakers now referred to their material as 'built' cane.

Since 1945, developments in rodmaking have been spectacular: hollow-built cane rods; rods made from drawn-steel alloy tubes, and from aluminium alloy tubes (a failure, due to metal fatigue); rods of solid glass structure, or fibre-glass tubes. The eclipse of natural fibrous materials has begun, and it is likely that very soon man-made materials will replace all others in rod manufacture.

The decline of traditional rodmaking materials would have come sooner had most of the early glass rods not been of such poor quality glass and design. Design was poor at first because glass was treated as a substitute for cane. Being an entirely different material it requires special design treatment. Unlike the early days of glass, when many of the tubes were made outside the tackle industry, progressive manufacturers today produce their own blanks, and so control design and development.

In time, the best fishing rods will have no preferred planes of bending because their wall thicknesses will be controlled with more accuracy. When the full possibilities of the symbiosis between glass fibre and carbon fibre are realised, it will be possible to add the stiffness factor to a fishing rod to order. Rod tapers will be compound, and so calculated as to ensure perfect balance – the 'just and desirable balance' that Stoddart wrote about; the kind of 'feel' that one associates with a best London sidelock shotgun.

It is possible that the fisherman of the future will view our built-cane rods with amusement. But although he may find the mechanics of fishing much easier, he will probably find the fish just as hard to catch.

FUNCTION

A fishing rod is a tool. It has four functions.

1. *Presentation.* A rod is an extension of the arm. By helping the angler to place his bait or lure inside the fishing area it increases his casting potential. Any lure can be presented by hand, after a fashion – even a fly. A rod simply makes this presentation very much easier. A beach hand-line fisherman, using the old east coast technique, can cast his line for 60, 70 or perhaps even 80 yards. But if the fish are upwards of 100 yards out, he will have poor sport unless he uses a beach-casting rod with modern technique. With the help of a rod a bait can be cast further than it can be thrown. A rod helps to reach fish.

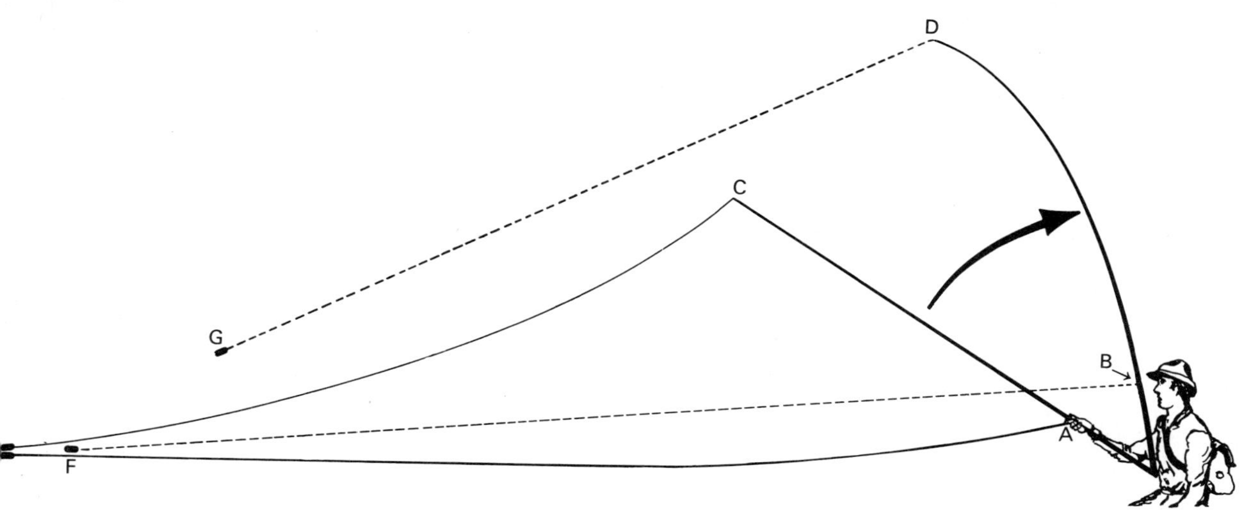

Fig. 32.1.

2. *Attraction.* A rod helps to control the lure all the time it is in the fishing area. For instance, when the line is 'mended' during 'greased-line' fishing for salmon. Thus, it helps to attract fish.

3. *Striking.* A rod improves the efficiency of the angler's arm and thus helps him to hook fish. A rod is not only an extension of the arm's mechanical function. The diagram makes this clear. If an angler with a hand-line holds the line at A and raises his arm to B, the baited hook (resting on the bottom eight yards away at E) will move only eighteen inches closer to him at F; whereas if he holds a $10\frac{1}{2}$ foot rod and again moves his hand from A to B, the rodtip will move from C to D, and his baited hook from E to G, a distance of five feet seven and a quarter inches – four times as much as it did previously.

By relating distance to time, we may infer that the time taken to complete a strike with a $10\frac{1}{2}$ foot rod is only a quarter of the time taken with a hand-line. A 14 foot rod would further reduce this striking time (in other words, improve the *strike transmission* speed). Strike transmission speed, therefore, increases directly with increased rod length.

There is, however, another design factor to consider: stiffness. A completely stiff rod is not a practical proposition, but in terms of strike transmission speed such a rod would be ideal.

4. *Control.* When a fish is being played, the rod and reel take the strain of the line off the angler's fingers. To a certain extent the rod acts as a shock absorber. What is more important, it helps to keep the line clear of the water and free from obstructions. Thus, it helps to control and land fish.

Choice of Rod

It follows that since a fishing rod is a tool designed for pleasure an angler will derive most pleasure from choosing a rod that is most suitable for the job in hand. It is seldom the size of the fish that governs this choice. If leader and line are strong enough, the biggest salmon can be landed in unobstructed water on the smallest trout rod. Conversely, the smallest trout can be landed on the biggest salmon rod. Nevertheless, it would be as foolish to use a small trout rod for spring salmon fishing as it would be pointless to use a big salmon rod for trout fishing.

What normally governs the choice of a rod is the method of fishing, the weight of the bait, or lure, and the distance it has to be cast. A salmon 'fly' fisherman fishing in early spring with a sunk line and a three-inch leaded tube-fly, will need a powerful 14–16 ft double-handed rod to present and control his lure effectively. He can fish the same water for salmon in May or June with a ¾ inch tube-fly on floating line, using a 9–10 ft single-handed trout rod – and probably will. It is his *approach* that dictates his choice of rod, not the size of the fish. Using a shooting-head, the reservoir trout angler with no obstructions behind him can cast his 30–40 yards with an 8½–9½ ft rod. The sea-trout fly fisherman, wading in the darkness down a bushy run needs a 10–11 ft rod to steeple-cast with rhythm, although the distance he casts may be no more than 15–20 yards.

Generally speaking, a long rod (upwards of 12 ft) has a special if limited application. It is useful to the game fisherman when he wishes to keep as much line as possible out of the water; for instance, when playing a fish on a long sunk line. Also, to the beach fisherman when it keeps his line out of the first few breakers, thereby reducing false bites. The coarse fisherman uses a long rod for an altogether different reason.

Paradoxically, he uses it when he wants to float-fish in deep water at *close range*. The long rod enables him to keep rod-tip, float and hook in a straight line, or very nearly, thereby eliminating slack and helping him to strike more effectively.

Since the need to keep rod-tip, float and hook in a straight line is essential for quick striking, long rods (of up to 22 ft) are invariably used for *short range* float fishing. As a swing, rather than a cast, is all that is needed for short range work, long-rod anglers reject the flexible rod (since they do not need its superior casting qualities) in favour of a stiff rod, which gives them the quickness they require for their wristy strike.

In the hands of a competent angler, ideally the stiffer the rod the better for striking a fish, and the better for playing it. (A rod that is too supple and bends nearly double when a fish is being played is of little use for keeping the line out of the water, or controlling the fish when it is near to, or under, the angler's bank – where fish are frequently lost.) It is for *casting* that a compromise must be found between extremes of flexibility.

Medium length rods of between 9 and 12 ft are the most versatile rods of all. Most of them are flexible throughout and have what is known as an all-through action: that is to say, an action designed to withstand the strain of casting. Fly rods, spinning rods, ledger rods, and float-fishing rods are included in this group.

The first aspect that the designer of a casting rod must consider is the casting *weight*. No strain on the rod will be more severe than that imposed by casting. It is

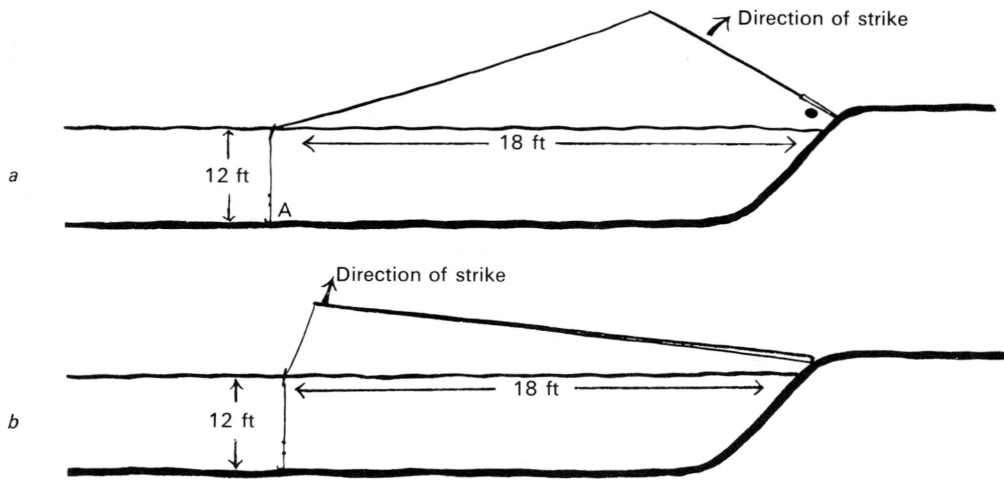

Fig. 32.2.a (top) *and 2.b* (bottom).

only with 'Big Game' rods, and boat rods, and sometimes with match rods that this is not the first consideration. Big game and boat rod breakages invariably occur during the playing of a fish, whereas most breakages in casting rods occur during casting – albeit through bad technique. Match rods, especially those made with Tonkin cane, or Spanish reed, are usually broken when misused as casting rods.

Medium length rods are ideal for long range float-fishing in shallow or medium depth water. They are essential for float fishing at long range in very clear streams and rivers where long-trotting has to be done to avoid frightening the fish.

Medium length all-action rods are suitable for ledgering at long range at any depth. Long range ledgering, and long-trotting (when stretch and sag slow down the transmission speed of the strike to the hook), require a good flexible rod action to cushion the strain of the protracted forearm strike needed to secure a good hookhold.

A short rod makes it difficult for an angler to lift his line clear of bushes and other obstructions, or to control a sunk line. With a short rod it is impossible to keep a fish away from obstructions close to the angler's bank. Except when used for boat fishing, short rods are inferior to medium length rods in almost every aspect, and should be avoided.

The following examples show a few situations that anyone other than a fly fisherman has to deal with. If the novice understands the principles involved, he will be able to choose the best tackle and technique for fishing at any particular range and depth.

In Fig. 32.2.*a*, a roach angler, using a 9 ft rod, is float fishing at a point some six yards from the bank in a swim that is 12 ft deep. In these circumstances, a strike that induces 12 inches of rod-tip movement, merely *flattens the angle* between the rod-tip and bait at A. There are 4½ ft of slack line to be taken up before the hook can begin to penetrate. Hence, for many bites, very few fish will be hooked.

In Fig. 2.*b*, an angler float-fishes the same swim with an 18 ft roach-pole. This time a wristy strike that induces 12 inches of rod-tip movement will give immediate hook penetration, since there is almost no slack line. This style of fishing requires a stiff rod that will transmit the strike to the hook at maximum speed.

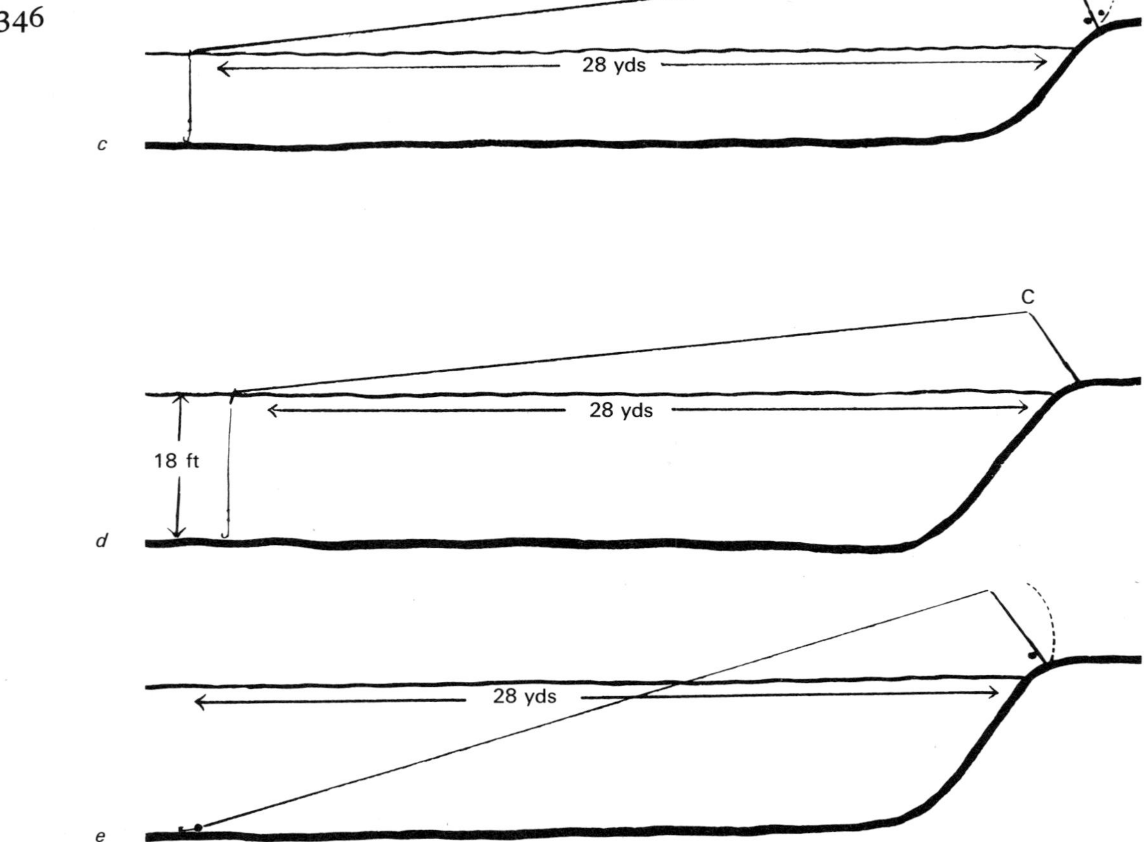

Fig. 32.2.c (top), *2.d* (middle) *and 2.e* (bottom).

In Fig. 2.*c*, an angler using an 11 ft rod fishes a shallow swim some 28 yards from the bank. In these circumstances, the long fore-arm strike provided by an all-action rod is required to overcome nylon sag and stretch.

In Fig. 2.*d*, an angler using a 14 ft rod float-fishes a swim 18ft deep, at a point some 28 yards from the bank. Here, a strike with even a 6 ft rod-tip movement will hardly move the hook at all. With so much slack line ($13\frac{1}{2}$ ft) float fishing is quite impossible (unless a fish hooks itself!)

The answer to this problem is: ledger fishing (Fig. 2.*e*), because it almost eliminates the slack line and takes the strike direct to the hook.[1]

Once again, a long strike movement – provided by a medium length all-action rod – is required to overcome the considerable amount of sag and stretch that is always associated with fishing at long range.

1 There is always a certain amount of slack, since line always tends to sag below an imaginary line drawn direct from rod-tip to lead, and forms what is known as a catinary curve.

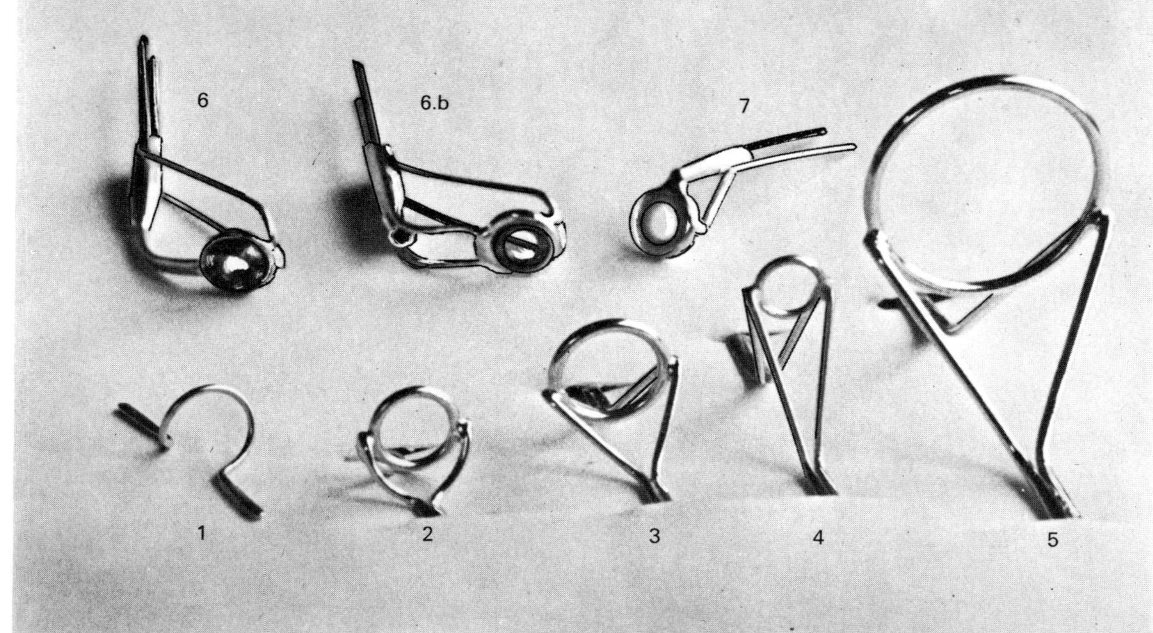

Rod rings (see text below).

So shalt thou have always in store the best,
And fittest Rods to serve thy turne aright;
For not the brittle *Cane*, nor all the rest, I
I like so well, though it be long and light,
Since that the Fish are frightened with the
least Aspect of any glittering thing, or
white . . .

JOHN DENNYS, *The Secrets of Angling* (1613).

ROD-RINGS

Before purchasing a new rod too few anglers give enough thought to the design and quality of rod-rings. Only the best should be used. Needless to say they are expensive, since they are made with great care from expensive materials, but over the life-time of the rod their cost will be handsomely repaid.

Before buying a rod (and you won't get the best unless you pay for it) make sure that all intermediate wire rings have been chromed to resist wear. Any other finish is suspect, unless the material used (e.g. tungsten-carbide) is harder than chrome. Also, make sure that all the rings have been smoothly finished and jointed – otherwise the line will gradually suffer damage that may lead to its breaking when you are into a good fish.

Since no single pattern of rod-ring is suitable for all fishing rods it is not surprising that anglers are faced with a bewildering choice of patterns. Nevertheless, the few patterns we describe cover the needs of freshwater anglers.

1. *The 'snake' ring.* An intermediate ring, ideal for fly rods: strong, light and unobtrusive.

2. *The 'cradle' ring.* The most popular intermediate ring for medium and heavy spinning and ledger rods.

3. *The semi-stand-off intermediate ring.* Ideal for medium length float rods and 'Avon' type rods, and light spinning rods designed to cast very light baits for trout or perch. It is more susceptible to damage than

the cradle ring, but less susceptible than the delicate, high 'Bell's Life' ring (4).

The importance of stand-off rings is that they reduce 'line-stick' and 'line-slap' – both enemies of casting efficiency, particularly when it comes to casting light baits. A wet line *sticking* to the underside of a rod increases the inertia that the casting stroke has to overcome, and a wet line *slapping* against the underside of a rod increases the amount of drag.

4. *The high 'Bell's Life' intermediate ring.* The classic pattern for dressing a float-fishing rod. With this type of ring, 'line-slap' and 'line-stick' are almost entirely eliminated. Other points being equal, rods fitted with these high stand-off rings will cast very light floats (or leads) farther than rods fitted with any other pattern of ring. They should be hard chromed. The wire used in their construction should be stiff. Sad to say, many ring-makers use soft wire which is an abomination (as most coarse-fishermen know to their cost) since the long support legs on this type of ring are easily damaged.

5. *Butt or 'gathering' ring.* For many years anglers and rod-makers alike have been convinced that a large butt-ring was a vital feature on any rod used with a fixed-spool reel. This conviction has been based on the belief that coils of line coming off the spool in spiral fashion need to be 'gathered' by a large ring before they will 'pour' smoothly through the smaller-diameter intermediate rings – just as liquid has to be gathered in a funnel before it can be poured into the narrow neck of a bottle.

It all seems very plausible. We have thought the same. Experience, however, teaches otherwise. Tournament casters are now convinced (and who should know better?) that *two smaller-diameter butt-rings* placed within one inch of each other are more effective.

6. *The 'stand-off' end ring.* This complements the 'Bell's Life' intermediate rings. It is usually furnished with an agate or 'jewelled' centre. Although a good jewelled-centre is more groove resistant than most metals, we suspect that a good tungsten-carbide ring is better still. (Unfortunately, most rod-makers insist on dressing rods the way they *think* anglers want them, rather than the way it *ought* to be done: the *best way*.) There is also a 'stand-off' end ring, similar in design to the previous one, but screw-threaded to take a swingtip (6.*b*).

7. *Standard end-ring.* This is made in many sizes to fit all types of rods other than those fitted with stand-off intermediate rings. Again, the best standard end-rings are made of tungsten-carbide, although jewel-centred end-rings are more popular. Jewelled rings should be inspected regularly for cracks or rough edges. Failure to notice a crack will result in a broken line, and a lost fish.

All good end-rings are fitted with a tube as well as two tangs. The tube accommodates the extreme tip of the top joint and the tangs (once they are covered with binding) help to even-out the bending strain that would otherwise be concentrated at the wide end of the tube – where there is an unavoidable cutting edge.

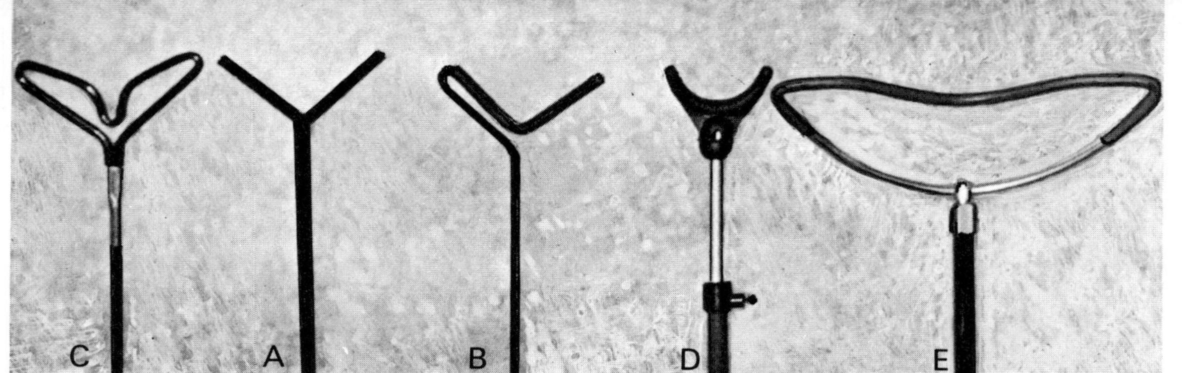

ROD-RESTS

A. The cheapest rod-rest available. It is simply a superior forked stick.

B. A joinless rod-rest slightly superior to type A, lighter and less likely to break.

C. An ideal rod-rest for the angler who ledgers for carp and other fish that are allowed to run with a bait without hindrance until the strike is made. The rod is supported by the top of the 'V' – which allows the line to slip out through the rod rings without being trapped against the rod-rest, as it may be with the 'forked-stick' type of rest.

D. A telescopic rest fitted with a rubber fork. The height adjustment, similar to that of a shooting-stick, is a useful feature. To make full use of his rod length while ledgering, the angler re-fits the rubber fork at right angles to the shaft (see diagram opposite). This enables the rod-rest to be set over the water while maintaining the fork in a vertical plane.

E. The Sheffield 'match' rest is a favourite among competition anglers. The wide rubber fork facilitates a quick sideways strike – sometimes a most useful feature when speed of strike is all-important.

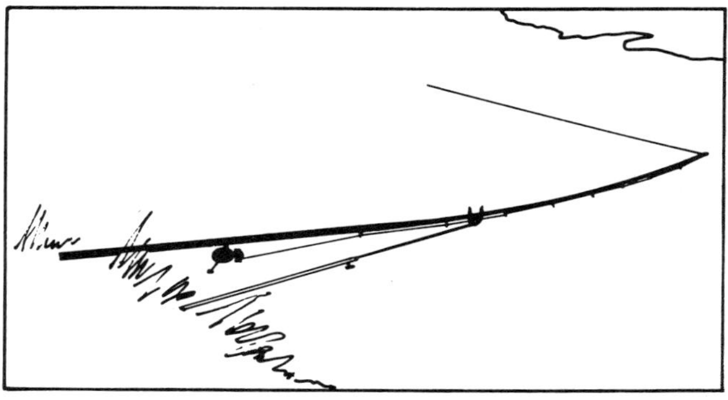

There may have been many attempts to design a rod-rest suitable for use on ground too hard for the spike of a conventional type of rest. The best so far is the 'Wilson Universal' (below). *All the joints can be swivelled and locked, both to provide adjustment on sloping ground and for easy packing.*

REELS

I must say that I totally detest, abhor, and repudiate all click wheels, lock wheels, and multiplying wheels . . .

A multiplying wheel is not worth a farthing for anything but small fish. You cannot get up a weight without breaking your machinery, or dropping your rod to the water. I have had sad experience of this kind of wheel, of which I may hereafter speak – having spoiled the work and lost an immense salmon through its means.
O'GORMAN, *The Practice of Angling* (Vol. 1, 1845).

It seems likely that the reel originated in China. Chinese printed illustrations depict a type of fishing 'wheele' several centuries before the first mention of its use occurs in English angling literature. We are grateful to Dr. Joseph Needham, of Gonville & Caius College, Cambridge, for the following picture and quotations from *Science and Civilisation in China*.

A minor invention of the windlass type which is in all possibility Chinese is that of the reel on the fishing-rod . . . Lodge noticed that such a reel was shown in a painting by Wu Chen (+1280 to +1354) still conserved at the Freer Gallery in Washington . . . But it is not the oldest example, for the painter Ma Yuan, who flourished towards the end of the +12th century (*c.* +1195), also shows one . . . We even have from this same period printed illustrations in Chinese culture. The *Thick Climbing* (Holy Lections from Indian Sources), printed between +1208 and +1224, prefaces each of its Buddhist moral stories with a wood-block picture, and in at least two of these (Nos. 34 and 54) we may see fishermen using rods with reels.

An Armenian parchment Gospel of the +13th century also seems to show a reel, though less clearly . . .

Turtle fishing – from San Tshai Thu Hui *(+1609). This piece of Chinese tackle seems strangely similar to the fishing 'wheele' described by Izaak Walton in 1655 (see p. 351).*

Since many accounts relating to early mentions of the reel in English literature are confusing and inaccurate, we append a simple chronology.

First mention of the reel: Thomas Barker, *The Art of Angling* (1651).

Repeat mention of the reel: Thomas Barker, another edition of *The Art of Angling* (1653).

First mention of the reel in relation to salmon fishing: Izaak Walton, *The Compleat Angler* (2nd edition, 1655).

Second mention of the reel in relation to salmon fishing: Thomas Barker, *Barker's Delight* (1657).

First mention of a 'spring' fixing rather than the 'pin and hole' fixing for the reel: Thomas Barker, *Barker's Delight* (1657).

First illustration of a reel: Colonel Robert Venables, *The Experienc'd Angler* (1662).

Barker's book of 1657 is really a further edition of *The Art of Angling*, re-named *Barker's Delight, or The Art of Angling*. In it he repeats his earlier description of 'trowling-with-a-reel' for pike. He also makes another mention of the reel in relation to salmon fishing, introducing the 'spring' fitting which allowed an angler to vary the position of the reel on the rod butt. He headed this section: 'I will now show you the way to take a salmon', and continues:

> The first thing you must gain must be a rod of some ten foot in the stock, that will carry a six foot top pretty stiff and strong, the reason is, because there must be a little wire ring at the upper end of the top for the line to run through, that you may take up and loose the line at your pleasure; you must have your winder within two foot of the bottom to go on your rod made in this manner, with a spring, *that you may put it on as low as you please*. [Our italics.]

The need to have the reel low down on the rod was presumably to facilitate double-handed casting.

Izaak Walton, too, mentioned the use of the reel, winch or 'wheele' for salmon fishing, in *The Compleat Angler* (2nd edition, 1655):

> Note also, that many use to fish for a Salmon, with a ring of wire on the top of their Rod, through which the line may run to as great a length as is needful when he is hooked. And to that end, some use a wheele about the middle of their rod, or nearer their hand, which to be observed better by seeing one of them than by a large demonstration of words.

(From this it seems likely that Walton's own experience of a 'wheele' was somewhat limited. Nevertheless, it represents one of the earliest mentions of the fishing reel; second only to Thomas Barker's.) *Note:* In *The Arte of Angling* (1577, author unknown), there is an interesting remark; Piscator says:

> My master that taught me to angle could not abide to catch a ruffe; for if he took one, either he would remove or *wind up* and home for that time. [Our italics.]

Now, what did he mean by that? Did Piscator's master wind his line up round his rod, or on to a frame or line-winder, or was this a reference to an early reel? If so, it is certainly the first in English literature, preceding Barker's by seventy-four years. Although not impossible, it seems unlikely. One cannot be dogmatic about the origin of 'wind up', but from what we can gather nobody is aware of any usages earlier than those given in the Shorter Oxford English Dictionary. The first recorded use (*c.* 1205) of 'wind up' referred to the hoisting of sails.

The old fishing reels we show, dating from 1650, come from the collection of Ken Sutton (above), *to whom we are indebted for much of the information in this section.*

Early metal reels. The pins fitted into a hole in the rod handle.

Top: *Spring clips to hold the reel securely on the ash or hickory poles used as rods succeeded the earlier 'pin' fastening. Some of the spring clips were bound with leather to give a better grip.*

Bottom: *One of the earliest multiplying reels. Reels of this type were in use as early as 1780*

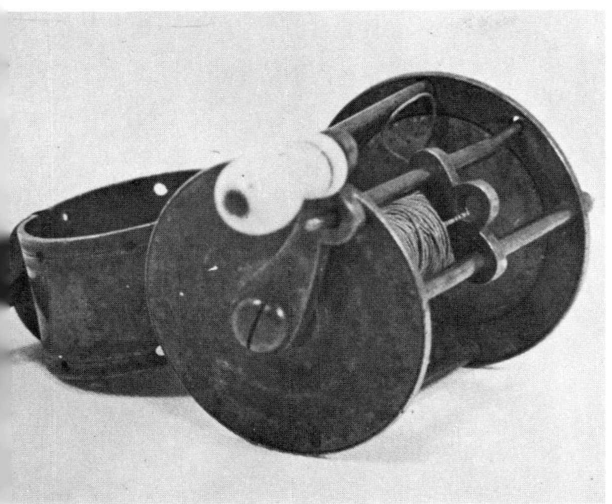

This early brass clip reel has a sliding pin which locks the handle, and a harbour for the hook when the reel was not in use. The small holes in the rim of the clip fastening are needle holes for stitching leather around the clip.

A very heavy eighteenth century salmon fly reel, made of brass with an iron handle. Some of these reels weighed as much as two pounds. The needle holes in the reel seating are for the leather padding.

It is subsequently met relating to 'winding up bottoms' where it was often used in the figurative sense: 'to sum up or conclude'. One finds: 'to winde up all in a short conclusion' in 1583 (which is close to the publication date of *The Arte of Angling*). In modern parlance, Piscator probably meant that his master would 'pack up and go home'.

All the very early brass reels had slender spindles, rarely more than a quarter of an inch in diameter, with spool diameters between one and two inches. As early as 1734 they were being advertised in London, and it is surprising that so few have survived.

The methods used in fastening the reel to the rod give the all-important clues to the age of reels: first the pin fastening through the butt of the rod (c. 1650 to 1700). Next, the spring-clip fastening and the spring-clip bound with leather (c. 1657 to 1880).

The modern reel seating, consisting of one or two sliding rings on the rod-butt, may appear to be a fairly simple engineering idea, but it has to be remembered that to hold the reel firmly the rings have to be on a slightly resilient surface such as cork, and cork handles were not in use until much later on.

Cholmondeley-Pennell, in his book *Fishing* (1885), wrote: 'Some reels are – or used to be – fitted with a circular clasp underneath... With butts such as are now the fashion however, sloping rapidly away from the handle, these fastenings have naturally become obsolete.' So it can reasonably be assumed that the spring-clip, or 'circular clasp' as Pennell called it, was in use until about 1880, and that, in addition to multipliers, there were reels with ratchet checks and brake devices.

The early multipliers had a fairly short period of popularity. According to Hofland, writing in 1839, 'The multiplying reel was formerly much used, but from its liability to be out of order, a plain reel, without a stop is now generally preferred.'

But even in Hofland's day, reels were still made of brass. In the same book, *British Angler's Manual*, he wrote: 'A winch, or reel . . . is generally made of brass but I have seen them in Scotland made of wood, where they are called pirns.'

From 1800 onwards, salmon and trout reels were larger in capacity and spool size. Some weighed as much as 2½ lb. They were then being used with greenheart rods and the combined weight of rod and reel must have taxed our great-grandfathers' stamina.

By then the sliding reel seating was in use, but because of the weight problem and the smooth greenheart rod-butts these old fly reels had a series of small holes drilled down each side of the reel 'shoe'. This was to enable the angler to stitch a piece of leather to the 'shoe' to achieve a tighter fit when the sliding rings were drawn over it. In the latter half of the 19th century, brass was combined with wood in some beautiful old salmon reels. Many of these have survived. Farlows were making them up to the turn of the present century.

John Ray's fixed spool reel.

From about 1850 onwards, the Nottingham type centre-pin reels, mostly made of mahogany, found popularity. The better models were 'star-backed', i.e. reinforced with crossed strips of brass. The larger wooden reels, which found equal popularity with sea fishermen, were known as 'Scarborough' reels – and still are.

Rods, and the materials of which they were made, influenced the design of the fishing reel until the present century, but it was lines rather than rods that popularized the biggest changes in reel design. Alfred Holden Illingworth, a Yorkshire cotton-mill owner, had developed the fixed-spool reel into a remarkably workmanlike instrument before 1920, and Hardy Brothers made some beautiful fixed-spool reels in the succeeding years, but it was only when nylon monofilament line became available, cheaply, in the late forties that the fixed-spool reel began to find popularity. So long as lines were made of plaited silk, the fixed-spool reel was never widely used.[1]

The first clumsy centre-pin reel, the first multiplier and the first patented fixed-spool reel were all British. Sophistication in reel design has been added to by many nations, but the pioneer inventiveness was British. One might wish that Britain had been clever enough to take financial advantage of it.

Most anglers believe that Illingworth invented the fixed-spool reel. John Piper, however, has discovered a much older model and photographed it. This is what he has to say:

History has it that Illingworth invented the fixed-spool reel, circa 1905, after watching high-speed bobbins in action at a Lancashire cotton mill. Be that as it may, this model is unquestionably of fixed-spool design and was produced some years earlier. It was made by John Ray of Belfast in 1890 and today forms part of Mr McGovern's collection at the Melvin Hotel, Garrison, Co. Fermanagh.

Ownership of reels that are thoroughly reliable should be the policy of all sensible anglers. A good reel is essentially functional in design and made of materials that ensure a lifetime's wear. The ten reels displayed in the composite picture are some of the best reels made during the modern era. All of

[1] H. F. remembers float-fishing for perch with a fixed-spool reel over 40 years ago, and casting what seemed a prodigious distance to an audience of local anglers on an East Anglian river.

We are grateful to Mr Charles Bowen of Jacksonville, Illinois, for details of this seemingly modern multiplying reel. It was, in fact, made in 1883 by Benjamin F. Meek & Sons of Louisville, Kentucky. It has a gunmetal body with spiral gears, jewelled bearings and a take-down frame – all modern features. It represents a brilliant American development of a discarded British invention.

We cannot trace the inventor of the multiplier, but there is no doubt that it was a part of the 18th century British tackle dealer's stock-in-trade. In 1760, Simon Ustonson, of London, advertised: '. . . the best sort of multiplying brass winches, both stop and plain . . .'.

This particular reel belongs to the Rev. E. C. Alston.

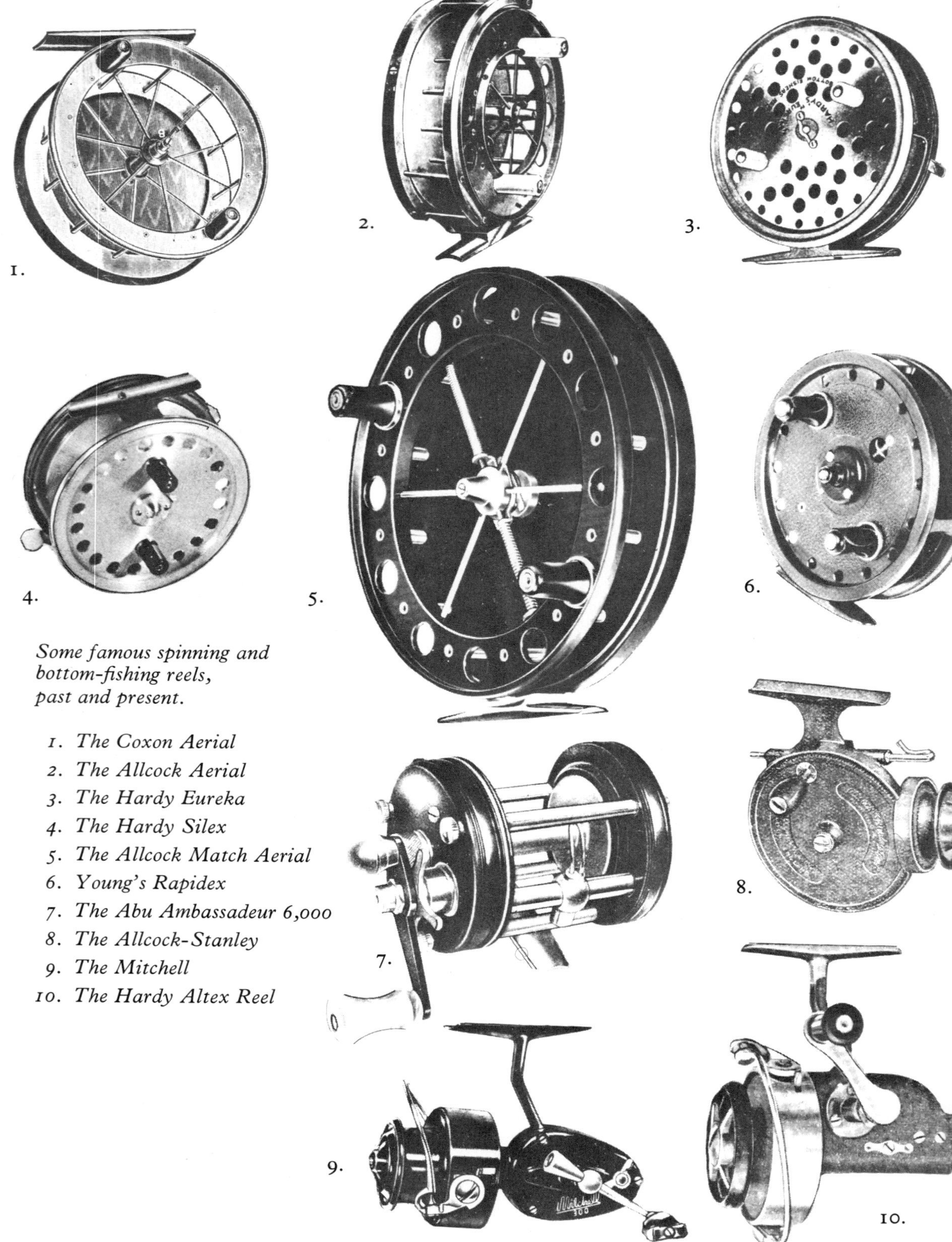

Some famous spinning and bottom-fishing reels, past and present.

1. *The Coxon Aerial*
2. *The Allcock Aerial*
3. *The Hardy Eureka*
4. *The Hardy Silex*
5. *The Allcock Match Aerial*
6. *Young's Rapidex*
7. *The Abu Ambassadeur 6,000*
8. *The Allcock-Stanley*
9. *The Mitchell*
10. *The Hardy Altex Reel*

The drum and spool of a cage-construction centrepin reel: The Hardy Silex.

them, with the exception of the Allcock *Stanley*, can be recommended for modern use.

Allcock's *Aerial* reels were the most famous spinning reels of all time. Nowadays, although seldom used for spinning, they are very good for trailing, pike livebaiting and deadbaiting.

The Allcock *Match-Aerial*, made specifically for float fishing and long-trotting, is the latest reel to carry that famous name. Like its predecessors it is superbly made.

Lacking the four line-guards (possessed by all reels built with cage construction) the *Match-Aerial* is more difficult to control than its stable mate the *Rapidex* – one of the few long-trotting reels of recent manufacture with cage construction.

The Hardy *Silex* spinning reel, too, has a cage construction, which allows easy rim control and minimizes the chances of loose coils coming off the reel in the event of an over-run.

Another centre-pin reel with cage construction was the Hardy *Eureka*, probably the finest reel for long-trotting ever made. *Eureka* reels are no longer manufactured, but were built to last and many are still in circulation.

The *Ambassadeur 6000* multiplying reel has become more popular than any other multiplier during the 200 or so years that multipliers have existed. It is an excellent reel for all forms of pike fishing, and the first choice of most British anglers who spin for salmon.

The Allcock *Stanley* reel was the first cheap fixed-spool reel available to British anglers. Although possessed of one devil of a fault (it kinked the line) it gave all anglers the chance of fishing 'fine and far off'.

The Hardy *Altex* fixed-spool reel was the first reel to incorporate all the known refinements of this type of reel – with the exception of a roller-pickup. Notably, it possessed the bale-arm fitting – a feature which most other fixed-spool reels were to incorporate.

The standard *Mitchell* fixed-spool reel has received world-wide acclaim for spinning, ledgering and float fishing. Strangely, this deservedly popular fixed-spool reel lacks the roller-pickup that the highest possible standards demand.

33 · Hooks and Lines

FISHING LINES (NYLON)

Of all modern tackle developments it is in the excellence and variety of lines that an angler may find some slight consolation for the damage that industry has done to his fishing waters. Our angling forefathers restricted to horsehair would have given almost anything for the lines that we can purchase to-day for a few shillings.

With the exception of fly lines (see p. 243) the most popular line material is nylon monofilament. Many anglers may be surprised to learn that although there are many different brands of nylon there are very few different 'makes'. Nylon is produced by a few large chemical combines whose products are spooled-up for a host of smaller companies.

An angler's allegiance to one brand of nylon and his antipathy to another has often amused and sometimes embarrassed F.B. in his capacity as tackle dealer when he has known both brands to be one and the same nylon.

Before the days of the *Trade Descriptions Act* some brands of nylon were marked up at less than their true strength – with the result that some anglers were impressed if, say, it took a five pound pull to break a line marked 3 lb. B.S. Other brands of nylon were marked up at *more* than their true strength which impressed anglers with the *fineness* of that particular brand when compared with other brands.

The only way to compare the relative strength of different brands of nylon is to test them on a spring balance, first making sure that all samples to be tested are of the *same diameter*. (The gunmakers' balance marketed by Messrs. Parker-Hale and used for testing trigger-pulls on shotguns is ideal for testing the breaking strain of fishing lines because it records the pressure at the moment of the line's fracture.)

Strength in relation to diameter although important is not the only quality to look for in a line. Limpness, for example, is a quality that is preferred for multiplying reels. Limp nylon can be laid neatly and tightly on a small diameter drum and is less likely to spring off and cause overruns.

Stiffness in nylon leaders is a quality appreciated by the fly caster. It helps him to lay the leader down in a straight continuation of the fly line. Although it is always difficult for a fly caster to get full turnover on his cast in the face of a head wind, stiff nylon assists him in his efforts.

A nylon less elastic than the average is

We do not know when the first mechanical horsehair-line-twister was invented, but very finely twisted horsehair lines were in use at least 1,800 years ago. Plutarch (circa 170 A.D.) commended the hairs from a stallion as being longest and strongest, and those of a mare least because of a weakness due to her urination.

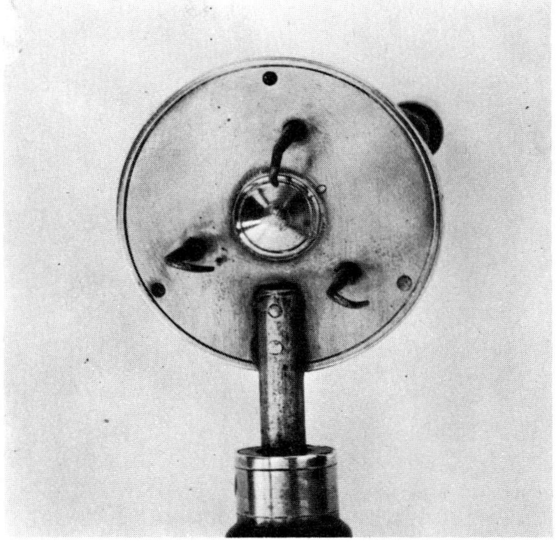

The little machine we reproduce, by courtesy of the Reverend E. C. Alston, is probably early 19th century.

useful in the hands of an expert angler, since a line with limited elasticity transmits the power of a strike with greater speed and impact. This lack of stretch however, reduces the safety margin of the line to the extent that an inexperienced angler may well suffer more frequent breaks when striking.

Many anglers are convinced that certain so-called 'strong' nylons break easily compared with their normal equivalents. In fact the deadweight strength of a 4 lb B.S. 'strong' nylon is the same as the standard 4 lb B.S. product, but due to its limited elasticity it is less able to withstand the dynamic force of the strike. The difference between deadweight strength and dynamic force can be illustrated in the following manner. A 12 stone man leans against a door with all his weight.

A double line-winder (18th century). The tube on the left contains a spindle holding spare binding silks and twines. (Photographed by kind permission of J. Milbourn).

Nothing happens, the door resists the dead-weight (or pressure) of 12 stones. Taking a few steps back the same 12 stone man throws himself at the door (applies a dynamic blow) and the door bursts open.

In the matter of choosing between 'standard' nylon and 'strong' nylon we advise the novice to buy 'strong' nylon of *exactly the same diameter* as he normally chooses for any particular style of fishing, and thus take advantage of its higher strength. He should not (as many have done to their cost) purchase a 3 lb 'strong' line to replace a 3 lb 'standard' line. The former will not be able to 'cushion' a strike to the extent that the angler expects from a normal 3 lb line.

Braided nylon lines, though quite popular when they replaced braided silk lines, have not retained their popularity because for most methods of angling monofilament nylon has proved superior. Nevertheless, 'hot-stretched' braided nylon has remained popular with salmon fishermen owing to:

1. Its low elasticity, which helps to set a hook into a fish at long range.
2. Its suppleness, which makes for ease of handling on a multiplying reel. (Braided nylon is, of course, unsuitable for use on fixed-spool reels).

Braided nylon also has the great advantage of *buoyancy*. This makes it first choice for livebaiting and deadbait float-ledgering.

The last few yards of a nylon line suffer considerable wear and tear during the course of a day's fishing. As a result its strength may be considerably reduced. At least five yards should be cut off before the angler tackles up.

Continued removal of line lowers the line level on the spool. With a fixed-spool reel the line must be 'set up' to proper level again – either by increasing the amount of backing, or by fitting a new line.

Putting Line on a Fixed-Spool Reel

Most fixed-spool reels will carry considerably more monofilament nylon line than is needed in actual fishing. The addition of backing to, say, a 100 yards of casting line is a useful economy.

For maximum casting efficiency, the line level on the majority of fixed-spool reels should be fractionally less than $\frac{1}{8}$ in. below the lip of the spool. In cases where the spool's rim has an extra-wide radius curve the line level should be fractionally more than $\frac{1}{8}$ in. below the lip.

Over-filling the spool will cause tangles. Under-filling will reduce casting range.

To ensure correct filling, carry out the following procedure:

1. Wind not less than 100 yards of new line on to the empty spool.
2. Join line to backing.
3. Wind backing on top of line until the correct level is reached, then cut off.
4. Reverse line and backing. This can be done either by running it off the spool across a field (or round and round the garden) or by winding on to another reel and thence on to a second reel. (Old centre-pin reels are useful for this job.) The end of the backing is now uppermost.
5. Tie end of backing to spool and wind on. The line will now finish up on top of the backing and the level will be exactly right.

Discarded Nylon – a Warning

It is said that the 8th-century Chinese philosopher, Chang Chih Ho, spent most of his time fishing, but used no hook – since his object was to enjoy fishing without actually catching fish.

We do not of course suggest that our readers should go all the way with Ho. But we *do* suggest that angling would be a grim pleasure if the catching of fish were everything, and the angler could find no time to study his surroundings. Quite apart from the fact that the man in sympathy with his environment becomes the best fisherman, an awareness and understanding of the wild life that keep him company at the waterside can lend another dimension to his fishing and provide a deep and lasting enjoyment.

Angling would be immeasurably poorer without the flash of the kingfisher or the heron's harsh croak. Although they are not often seen by day, the otter and the fox tread the river bank at night, and so does the badger and the water vole and the stoat and the squirrel and a host of other creatures. These are the angler's companions, with whom he shares the waterside. They deserve his attention. If he cares to use his eyes he will see the tracks and signs they leave, and 'read' stories of their nocturnal activities which are as fascinating as anything the waterside has to offer.

By learning to read these stories an angler will sharpen his powers of observation and deduction. As a result he will become a better hunter and so, in the end, a better angler.

It is well for an angler to remember his waterside companions – especially when a nylon leader is changed or a tangle is cut away. Lengths of nylon left lying about get wrapped round legs, bodies and wings of wild creatures, causing the most horrible mutilation.

Alas, all too many anglers are guilty of this thoughtless and barbaric behaviour.

DON'T DO IT.

Never leave yards of discarded nylon lying about.

When you wish to dispose of a length of nylon, wind it round two fingers in a small tight coil, and then cut the coil with your scissors. This reduces it to a bundle of tiny pieces that cannot possibly get wrapped round anything. Or take it home and burn it.

Grisly evidence of what can happen when nylon is left on river banks . . .
(Photographs: *Angling Times*)

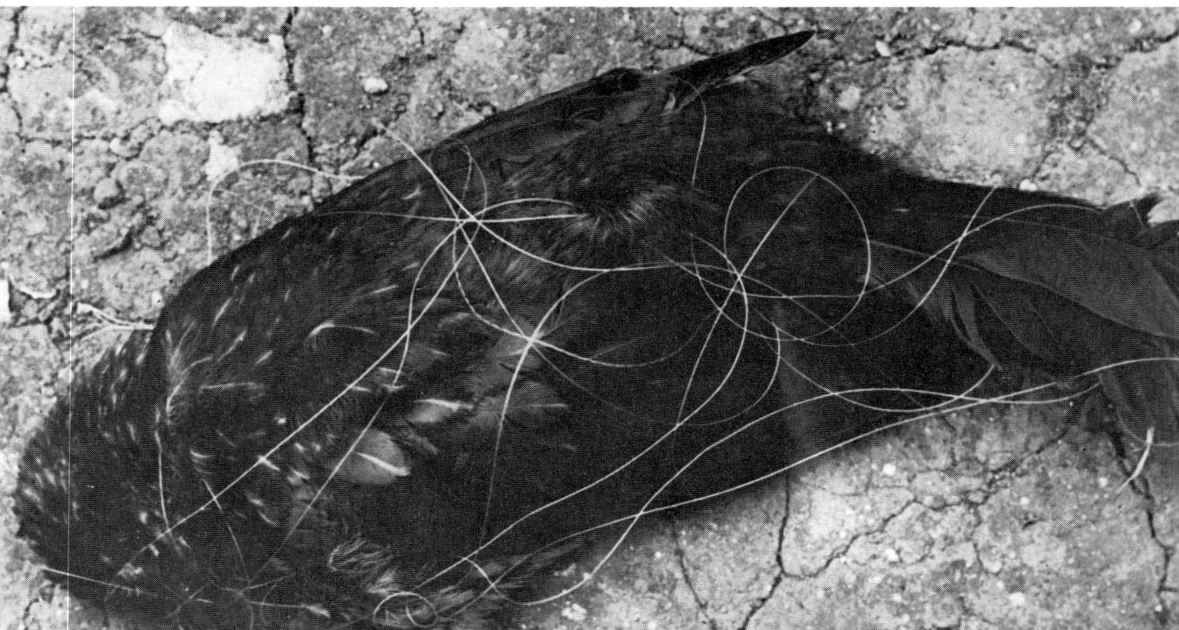

. . . and on the sea shore.
(Photograph: Lawrence Schaffer).

Fig. 34.1 (below). *Wind unwanted nylon round two fingers in a small, tight coil, and cut it with your scissors.*

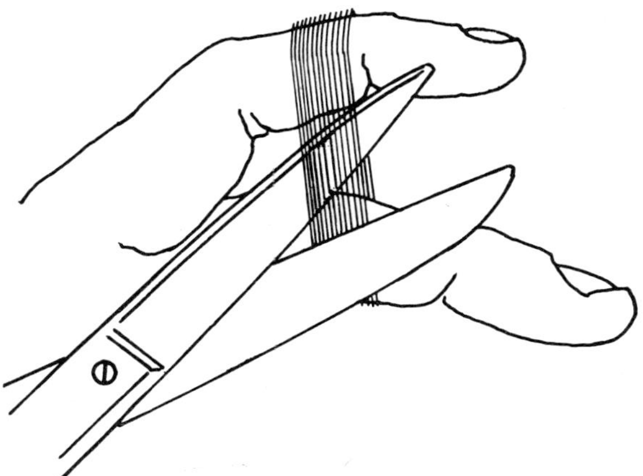

FISHING HOOKS

Left: *Harpoon head made from red-deer antler. The original, the best example we have seen including those found in the caves of France and Spain, is in the Stewartry Museum at Kirkcudbright. Such was the tackle of the British salmon-fishermen thousands of years ago* (Photograph: Maxwell).

Right: *A Mesolithic bone fish-hook found at Risga, reproduced by permission of the Hunterian Museum, Glasgow.*

Some Early Tackle

At the end of the last Ice Age, some 9,000 years ago, north Britain was still an inhospitable place for man. J. G. Scott, curator of The Department of Archaeology at Glasgow Museum, author of *South-West Scotland*, writes:

> . . . it must have been as hunters that man first came to south-west Scotland. . . . Probably they began by exploring by water, along the coasts and into the sea-lochs and rivers.

Kirkcudbright, at the mouth of the river Dee, and Risga by Loch Sunart, Argyllshire, are two of the places known to have beer settled by these Mesolithic or Middle Stone-Age men. From the evidence, it seems likely that they hunted seals, gathered shellfish and fished for a living. In 1895, William Pearson, fishing for sparling in the Dee opposite Cumstoun House in Kirkcudbright, dredged up a barbed harpoon (opposite) fashioned by one of those ancient hunters. Since the Kirkcudbrightshire Dee was once a prolific salmon river, it is likely that the harpoon was lost in an attempt to spear a salmon.

The bone fish-hook (opposite, right) was probably used for sea-fish or pike. It is interesting to note that H. Godwin (*British Maglemose Harpoon Sites,* a paper in *Antiquary,* vol. 7, pp. 36–38, 1933), found pike remains together with harpoon heads at a peat site near North Atwick in Yorkshire, proving that pike were hunted in Britain in Mesolithic times.

On Mesolithic dwelling sites in Kunda, Estonia, and in Sweden, pike remains have been found still adhering to the spear-points on which they were originally impaled. It is possible that those Mesolithic men of Kirkcudbrightshire once fished for pike in Loch Ken, home of Britain's most celebrated pike – the 72 lb Kenmure Monster.

This is a hook with an eye in the shank. It is another Scotch invention, and as to its usefulness may be placed on a par with the newly invented mode of breeding salmon.
O'GORMAN, *The Practice of Angling* (Vol. 2, 1845).

Hook Points

For some anglers hook-sharpening becomes almost a fetish. They will test the point of a hook by drawing it across their thumbnail. If it sticks in the nail, all well and good. If not, it is honed until it does stick. The assumption seems to be that the sharpest hook provides the best hold.

All too often this is a fallacy.

While a very sharp point will undoubtedly help to hook leathery-mouthed fish such as carp, it certainly won't in the case of bony-mouthed fish such as salmon, pike, brown trout and sea-trout. For fish such as these the hook should have a sound point, but it should not be honed to razor sharpness. A hook that is too sharp will stick temporarily in the first piece of bone it strikes, giving only a very brief hold. It should be sharp enough to penetrate gristle easily, but blunt enough to *slide across a bony surface* until it comes to the gristle.

Most game fishermen carry a carborundum stone to touch up their hook points from time to time. It is a false practice. Unless a hook has lost its point altogether, the carborundum should be used to take some of the sharpness *off*, rather than put it *on*.

It is interesting that a very early angling writer, John Dennys, was well aware of this fundamental principle. In *The Secrets of Angling* (1613), he writes of a hook:

His Shank should neither be too short nor long,
His point not over sharpe, nor yet too dull . . .

This excellent piece of advice was not appreciated. William Lauson, who edited a later edition of *The Secrets of Angling* with his own notes (c. 1620), criticized Denny's line about the hook:

He means the hook may be too weak at the point, it cannot be too sharpe, if the metall be of good steele.

But, like writers who have echoed him ever since, Lauson was wrong. A hook *can* be too sharp – and often is.

Bronze Age spade-end or broken eyed hook (c. 500 B.C.) *found at Grays, Essex* (Photograph: Verulamium Museum).

Hook Patterns

A hook is generally recognised by the shape of its bend. The commonest types are shown in Fig. 34.2.

1. The Round bend.
2. The Crystal bend.
3. The Limerick bend.
4. The Kirby bend.
5. The Sproat bend.
6. The Sneck bend.
7. The Kendal round bend.
8. The Round bend (deep throated).
9. The Model Perfect bend.

The various parts of a fish hook are named:

A. Barb
B. Bend
C. Throat or Bite
D. Gape
E. Shank
F. Eye or Spade
G. Regular wire section
H. Forged wire section

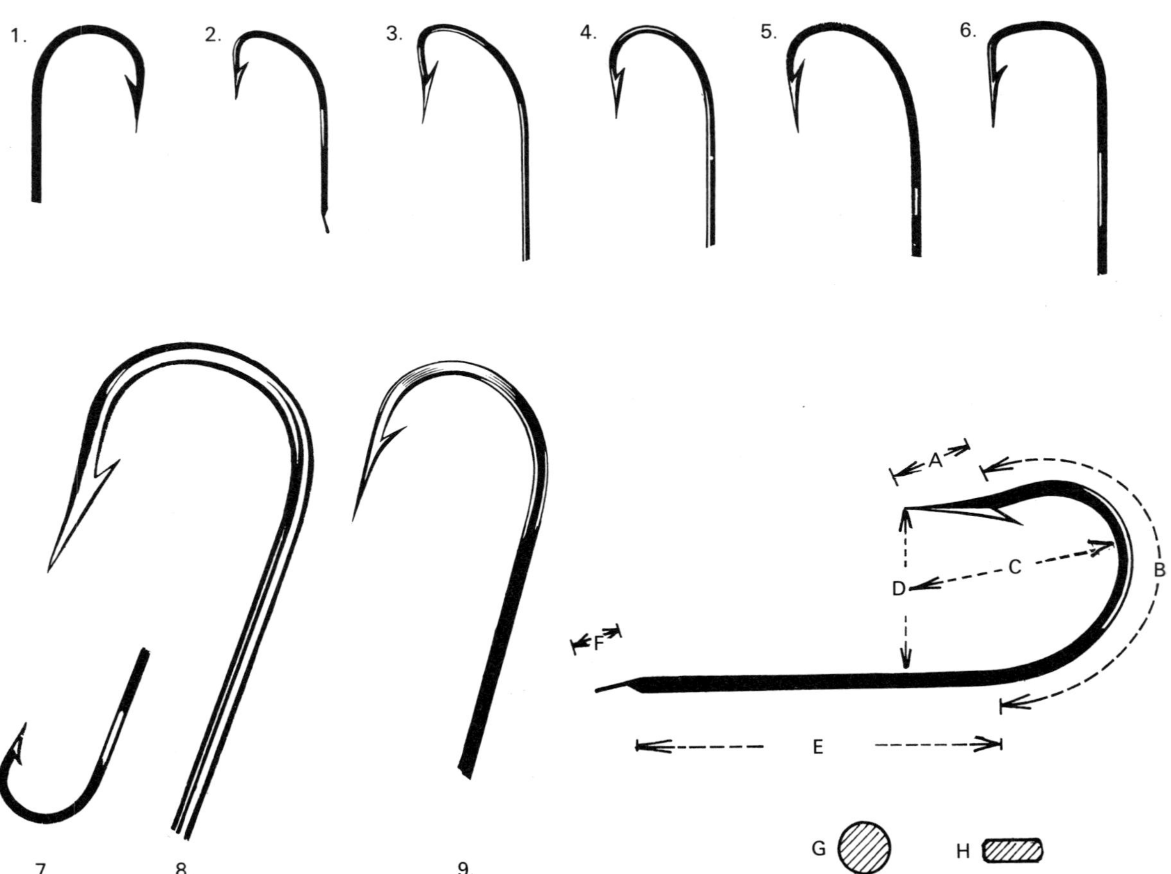

Fig. 34.2. Hook patterns.

Most British anglers recognize the size of a hook by reference to the Redditch Scale. The hook guide depicts a series of hooks (natural size) with the appropriate Redditch Scale numbers. Nowadays for convenience many odd number sizes are left out of a

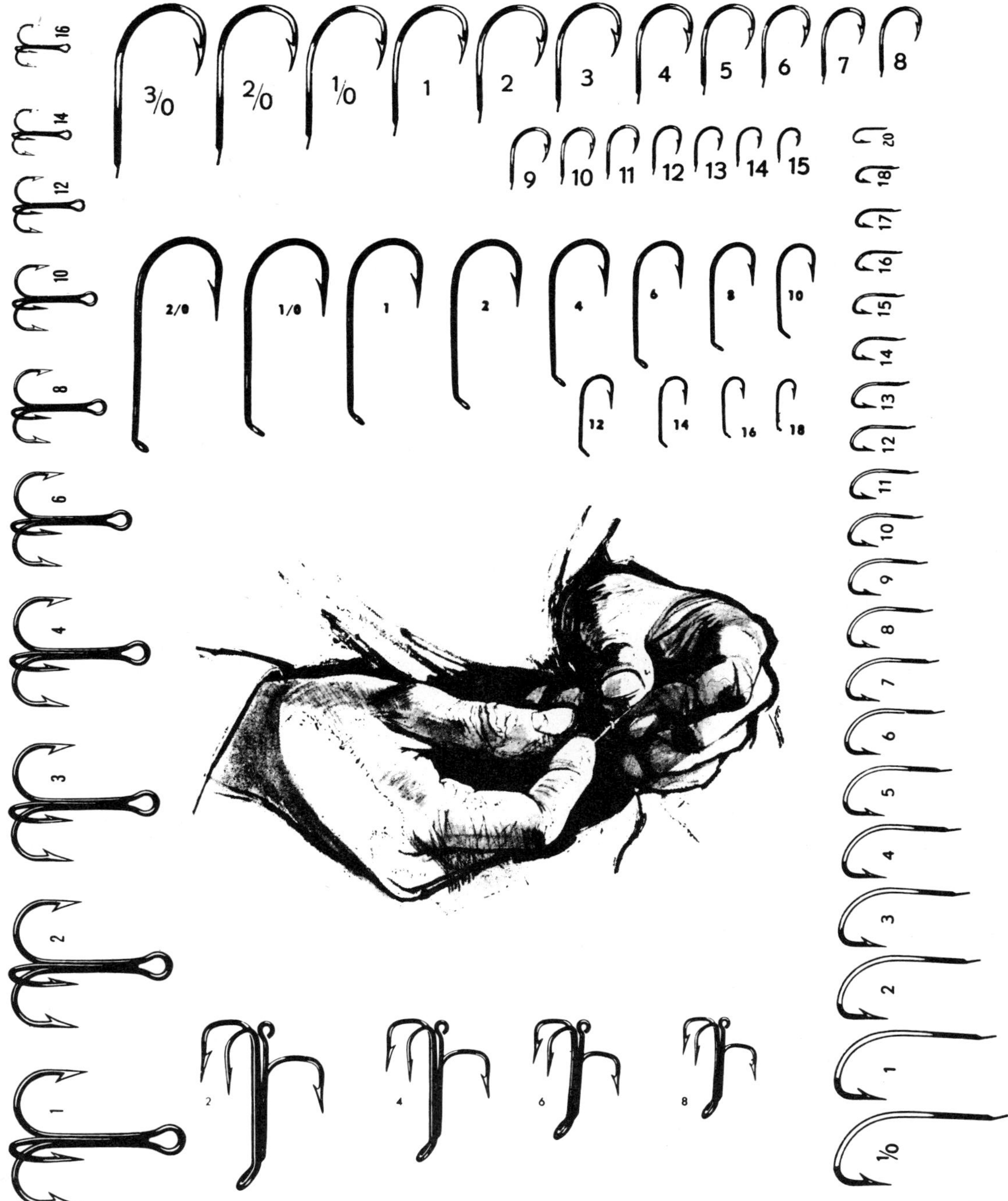

Fig. 34.3. Hook sizes.

manufacturer's range of hooks. To avoid confusion we have purposely ignored that bane: the New Scale.

The treble-hook series: sizes 1–16, are eyed Round-bend trebles. In our opinion this is the best of all the treble-hook patterns for hooking and *holding* fish.

The Crystal bend series of hooks sizes 1/0 to 20, is the most popular in Britain. It is principally the coarse fisherman who buys the Crystal hook, either snooded, whipped to lengths of nylon, or loose in a spade end form (as shown). These hooks are normally gilt finished, although an alternative bronze finish is usually offered by the makers.

The Crystal bend, while perfect for roach and bream, is not strong enough for the more powerful tench, carp, barbel, sea-trout and salmon. For these fish the hollow-point round-bend hooks, sizes 15 to 3/0, are the best. These hooks are forged reverse-barbed with curve-in points and have a blue finish. Sizes eights and tens in this series are almost universal in application – for they will hold any fish that swims in British inland waters. Obviously a larger hook would be first choice for salmon or pike. The sliding hooks, shown at the bottom, are Ryder hooks. These are not usually obtainable from a tackle shop – unless the purchaser buys them incorporated in a Jardine snap-tackle.

The eyed Round-bend hooks, sizes 18 to 2/0, are well designed, strong hooks. The most famous brand in this category is the Allcocks Model Perfect hook – known throughout the world. Anglers should take special care when ordering Model Perfects as the manufacturers' sizes for this hook, are two sizes up on the Redditch scale. For example if size 10 Redditch scale are required – order Model Perfect size 12.

Elementary Hook Design

The design of hooks always involves compromise. Usually, any advantage gained by design changes is offset by some disadvantages.

Consider the hook shown in Fig. 34.4.

Directly the point P starts to penetrate, the line of pull is in the direction of P–E. It is not, as one might suppose, in line with the hook-shank no matter what form of attachment of line to hook is used.

EPA is the angle at which the hook starts its penetration. As the hook penetrates, this angle decreases, until at B (the furthest point from E) the maximum penetration is achieved. Greater depth of penetration than this is impossible.

The greater the angle of penetration (EPA) the more force is required to make the hook penetrate. This angle can be reduced by lengthening the shank in relation to the gape, but an increase in shank length over a certain amount reduces the suitability of the hook for some kinds of bait, fly, or lure. Also, when a load comes on any hook that has been set in a fish the shank tends to bend. The longer the shank, the greater this tendency will be. This can be compensated for by increasing the thickness of the wire, but the thicker the wire, the greater the force needed to make the hook penetrate.

Practical experience indicates that a hook whose total length is from 2 to $2\frac{1}{2}$ times its

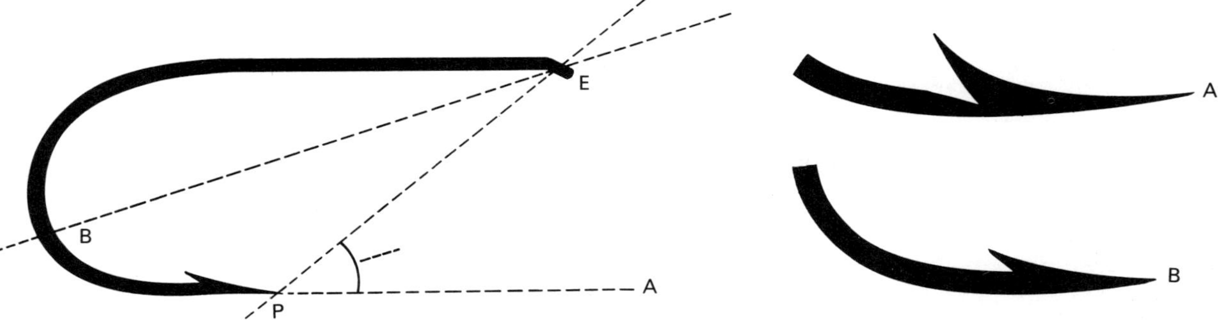

Fig. 34.4. Hook design.

Fig. 34.5. Design of point and barb.

gape, and whose point is parallel to its shank, is a good compromise for most kinds of fishing.

The design of the point and barb is also important and there are few hooks that are not deficient in this respect. Fig. 34.5 shows two hooks A and B with deliberately exaggerated points and barbs.

In A the barb impedes penetration. It has been cut too deeply; it is turned up too much; it is too far from the point. This hook will have to penetrate a long way before the barb is covered. The hook is weakened by the reduction in thickness brought about by cutting the barb. Almost all hooks available have these faults to some extent.

In B the hook has a small barb, needing only a shallow cut, set nearer the hook point and at a small angle that makes for easier penetration.

Only a very small barb is needed to prevent a hook from coming out. The barbs on most hooks do more to prevent them going in than to stop them falling out. When fish get rid of hooks, it is usually due to the hook never having gone in over the barb. The force that an angler can apply in striking is surprisingly small.

If manufacturers would provide hooks with shorter points, and smaller barbs less steeply sloped, fewer fish would be lost.

Hookmakers are often remiss in the matter of hardening and tempering hooks. Hook-wire is made of straight carbon steel with the following heat treatment process. First the hooks are hardened by heating and quenching. In this state they are very brittle indeed. Secondly, the brittleness is reduced by tempering. This consists of re-heating the hooks to the correct temperature, much lower than that used in the hardening process, and again quenching, in water or oil.

If this is correctly done, a satisfactory compromise is obtained between a hard, stiff, but easily broken hook, and a soft, flexible, easily bent hook. In practice this compromise is achieved far less often than anglers would like and at the time of writing really good hooks are very difficult to obtain.

Together with nylon monofilament and the reel, the eyed hook takes its place in history as one of the great angling inventions. It became popular during the latter part of the nineteenth century, and it is a sobering thought that the old eyed hooks of years ago were stronger and more reliable than many that are manufactured today. Apart from the angler's incompetence, it is the *hook* that is responsible for most big-fish losses – and this in an age which boasts a 'scientific' approach to angling. The modern fly fisherman can double-haul his shootinghead forty yards, but many of the hooks he casts are inferior to those in use 100 years ago.

It would seem unnecessary to stress that all tackle should be kept in good order. And yet the main reason why large fish so often break free (a constant topic of conversation when anglers meet) is because a hook is seldom replaced until it is lost on the bottom, or in weed, or in the fish itself!

Before using old hooks and tackles the angler should remind himself that a big fish imposes a greater strain on his tackle than a small fish. Quite simply, *it pulls a damn sight harder*!

Remember: the loss of a fish, whatever its species, due to breakage of any kind is almost always the fault of the angler.

34 · Floats and Bite Indicators

History does not record the first appearance of the float. Exactly when and how this little appendage found its way on to an angler's line is a matter of conjecture, but it certainly happened a long time ago. Since that far-off day evolution has had its way with the float, as it has with all other items of fishing tackle, and the modern angler finds himself confronted with a multiplicity of float design which to the uninitiated must be baffling in the extreme. But whatever its style, be it long, short, round, fluted, slender, tubby, coloured or transparent, a float has four basic uses:

1. It acts as a bite indicator.
2. It suspends a bait at a given depth, or allows a calculated length of leader to rest, or drag, on the bottom.
3. When aided by current or wind it carries a bait to the fishing area.
4. It acts as a casting weight. A float, of course, contributes to the total casting weight at all times, but (apart from the hookbait) it becomes the sole casting weight when the chosen method of fishing requires an unshotted leader.

Float patterns are legion, and the angler's choice of float depends on his intended

The first illustration of a float appears in Dyalogus Creaturarum Moralizatus – *a Latin book published in 1480; cf. Turrell's* Ancient Angling Authors *(1910).*

De lucio et trincha Dyalogus quadragesimusquartus

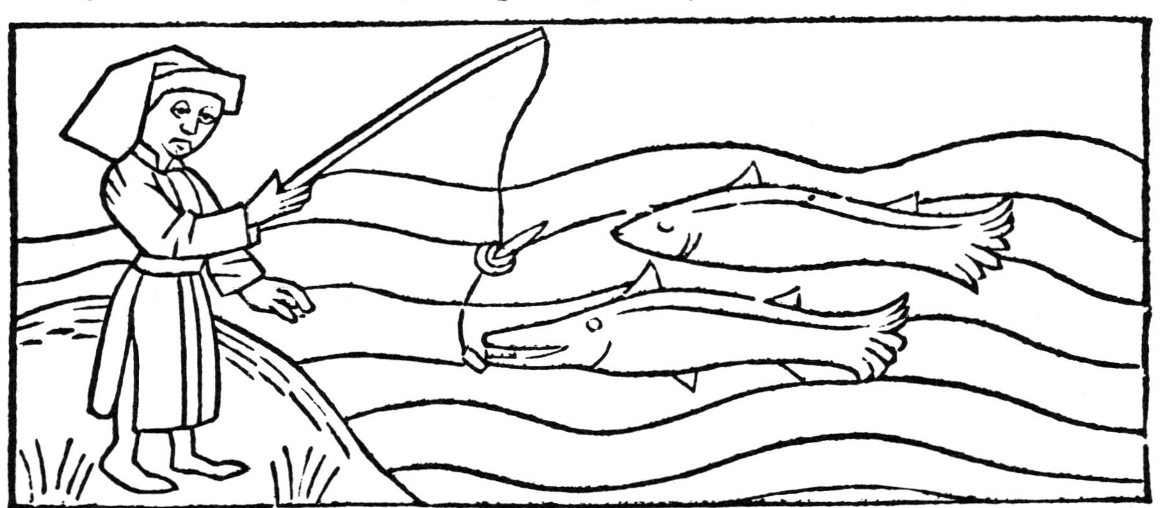

Piscator quidam piscabatur Vnde escam inhamatam

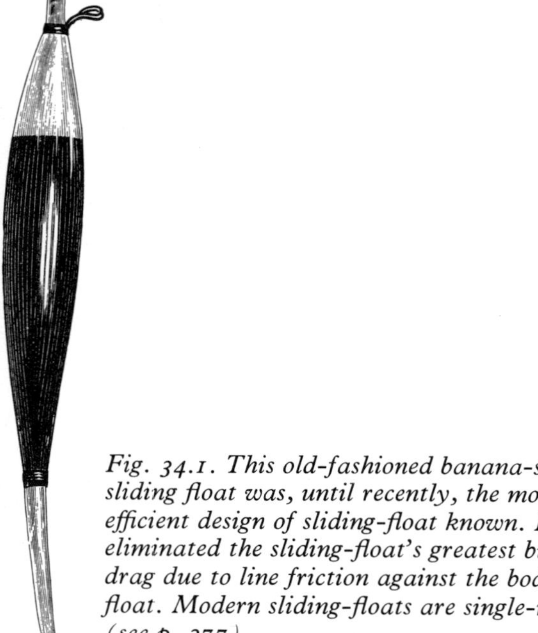

Fig. 34.1. This old-fashioned banana-shaped sliding float was, until recently, the most efficient design of sliding-float known. It eliminated the sliding-float's greatest bugbear – drag due to line friction against the body of the float. Modern sliding-floats are single-ringed *(see p. 377).*

method of fishing and the prevailing conditions of light, weather and water. Generally speaking, when an angler wants to make a longer cast he puts on more lead. This extra lead demands a more buoyant float to support it, so perhaps one may think of a float in terms of its shot-carrying capacity. But although shot-carrying capacity is related to the float's volume, the same volume can be represented by almost endless combinations of length and girth.

In normal conditions when choosing from a number of floats, of different shape but roughly equal buoyancy, the most *sensitive* float is the best choice. A fish may become suspicious and drop a bait when it feels the resistance of a tubby float. The float designer, knowing this, puts a premium on slimness. A compromise, however, is obligatory with any float designed to carry a heavy shot load, otherwise its length would become excessive. Water conditions, too, dictate the shape of a float. In low, clear, water a long float tends to 'rub the backs' of the fish and frighten them. In fast, swirling, water a slim float is likely to be sucked under from time to time, whereas a short bulbous float will ride more smoothly and give fewer false bites.

There is a tendency for the unskilled angler to leave too much of his float showing. A fish will sometimes take a bait firmly but pull the float down very little. If a float dips half an inch when a full two or three inches are exposed above the surface, the bite often goes unnoticed. A float that dips the same distance when only half an inch was showing goes out of sight, and the bite is noticed instantly.

The colour of a float is important if only for the confidence it inspires. A reed-stem-green or yellowish brown are probably the best underwater colours, since these represent the colours of natural flotsam. The suggestion that a float should be painted white or blue to match the background of the sky has little substance. To the fish a float is a solid object and will be seen as a dark silhouette as it passes overhead.

Brightly coloured floats are likely to 'flash' during their passage through the air. (For this reason, both authors of this book have rejected white fly lines in favour of brown or green lines.)

There is no 'best' colour for the visible part of a float. Choice of colour depends on the prevailing light. There is, however, one colour combination that serves well in any light.

The part of the float that shows above water when the float is properly trimmed with shot should be painted in three equal bands of colour: orange at the tip, then white then black. (See Fig. 34.2.) A coloured float-cap is then placed on the appropriate band.

Few anglers can justify the multitude of floats that haunt their tackle bags. Yet they are justified in carrying them, for one day an unusual float pattern may meet the demands of an unusual situation. Walker admits to having carried a rather comical looking float around with him for ten years before he found an appropriate use for it. This particular float – which had a plastic vane fitted to its base reminiscent of the paper flight used on darts – finally justified its existence at Tring Reservoir in a force eight wind which blew any normal float on its side.

Fig. 34.2. Richard Walker's choice of colours for the visible part of an antenna float (left) *and a normal float* (right).

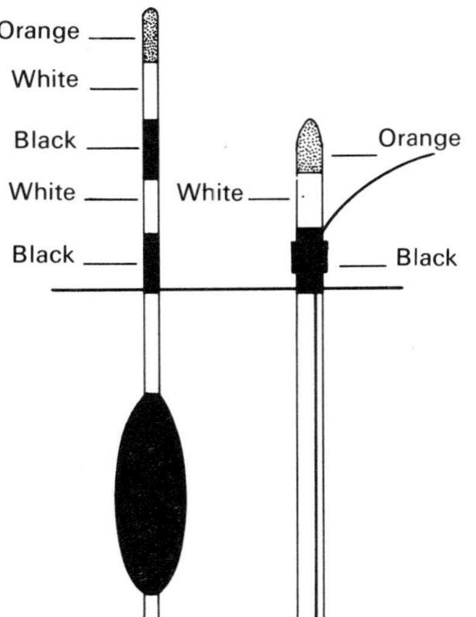

Design and Function

The ease with which a sensitive porcupine quill float slides under the water when pulled down by a biting fish can be described in terms of the float's *hydro-dynamic* qualities.

The reason why a fluted float moves downstream against an upstream wind better than any other float can be described in terms of the fluted float's *hydro-static* qualities.

It is, of course, quite unnecessary to remember these technical terms, but it *is* necessary to understand that they relate to two fundamentally different aspects of float behaviour. In the first example the float has been moved by a fish. In the second it has been moved by the water.

We believe that although most anglers 'know what they like' when it comes to choosing a float, many of them do not have a thorough understanding of float design, so that when selecting a float for a particular purpose they often fail to make the best choice. It might be helpful to look at the random displays of floats shown on p. 374, and consider the relation of design and function.

A. The common porcupine quill float. The best natural float procurable. It can be obtained in a number of different lengths, with varying buoyancy, to suit a wide variety of fishing conditions – from canal fishing with a single dust shot, to long-trotting on the Hampshire Avon. The porcupine quill is very strong, and its natural water-proof qualities allow it to retain its shot-carrying

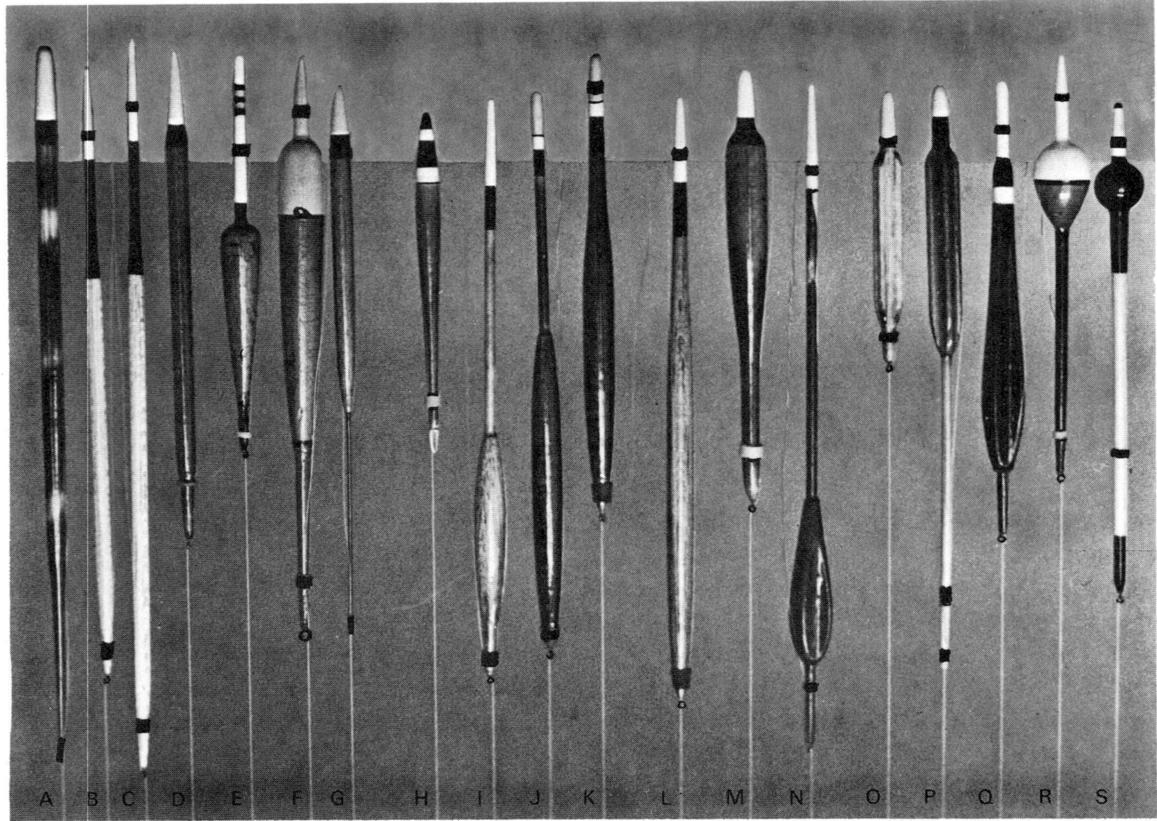

Some characteristic design features of modern floats.

capacity all day if need be (some floats absorb so much water that periodical adjustment of the shotting is necessary). The inherent slimness of the porcupine quill, together with bird quills such as crow, puts it in a class of floats whose sensitivity has only recently been matched by manufactured floats.

B and C. Two examples of the 'wind' float (the larger one, of course, will carry more shot). This is an excellent pattern: a veritable iceberg of a float. Just a slim balsa stem (or antenna) shows above water, but underwater there is a long parallel balsa body of large shot-carrying capacity. As its name implies, this is a good float to use in windy conditions. It will be seen from the diagram that, despite the float's total volume, the wind has little to act upon. There are many floats that achieve the same end as the wind float. All of them come under the general heading of 'antennae' floats.

D. The standard balsa float. Of medium length and thickness, it can carry a reasonable load of shot (considering its volume) because it is made from balsa wood. The exposed part of this float is thicker and therefore more visible than its counterpart on the wind float. This makes it a better proposition for long casting or long-trotting.

E. Some years ago this type of float was made in the south Midlands and called the

'Roach-Ideal'. It is a good float for a lively stream because of its shallow draught. Its draught can be reduced still further if the length of stem above the cork is reduced by a half. Such a model, but with a slightly slimmer body, is F. B.'s favourite all-round float.

F. The conventional sliding float which has served generations of anglers. The line, instead of passing under a float cap before going down through the bottom ring, as with fixed floats, runs through a metal ring that sticks out of the side of the float on a level with the plimsoll line, thence through the ring on the submerged tip.

One snag with this type of slider is the loss of sliding efficiency due to friction of the line passing over the body of the float. To overcome friction, relatively heavy shotting has to be used. As a consequence the float often has to be larger than an angler would otherwise wish.

In the late 1950s, Billy Lane – a Midland tackle-dealer and master angler – discarded the upper ring and replaced the large bottom ring (which hitherto had been big enough to take a 50 lb B.S. line!) with a ring just big enough to allow a 3 lb B.S. line to slip through. These simple but all-important changes made the sliding float popular throughout coarse fishing circles. With Lane's type of sliding float (I and J), friction is almost entirely eliminated since the line no longer passes over the body of the float.

With such a fine ring a small stop-knot suffices. Young anglers skilled in the use of modern sliding floats may be surprised to learn that their fathers and grandfathers often tied floatcaps or matchsticks to their lines to act as stop-knots, even though a stiffish piece of gut would have worked perfectly well.

Austin Clissett, another Midland tackle dealer and master of the sliding-float technique, has some interesting comments on the make-up of a sliding rig:

> I make rings for sliders from fine stainless steel wire; just a couple of turns around a sewing needle. A piece of nylon of about 5 lb breaking strain is used to form a stop-knot, and I always take the precaution of tying two knots to make sure I do not lose the depth. A single stop-knot can slip as it passes through the rod rings. Tying a stop-knot on the bank can prove awkward on a windy or wet day so I always tie my twin knots on the reel line at home. I use the 'needle' knot – the same knot that is used to tie spade-end hooks – and leave half inch 'tails'.

Lane's original sliding float was designed for use in deep, slow-moving rivers – waters too deep to fish with a fixed float rig in conjunction with the favourite 12 or 13 ft match rod. Clissett and others subsequently realized that the advantage of a sliding float is not confined to deep-water fishing. Clissett, describing his match-fishing successes on the river Welland said:

> The reason I used a slider on the Welland had nothing to do with depth. You could have fished it just as easily with a fixed float because it's a comparatively shallow river. The advantage of the slider was that it did not impede the strike; you could hit your fish without having to drag the float a yard out of the water.

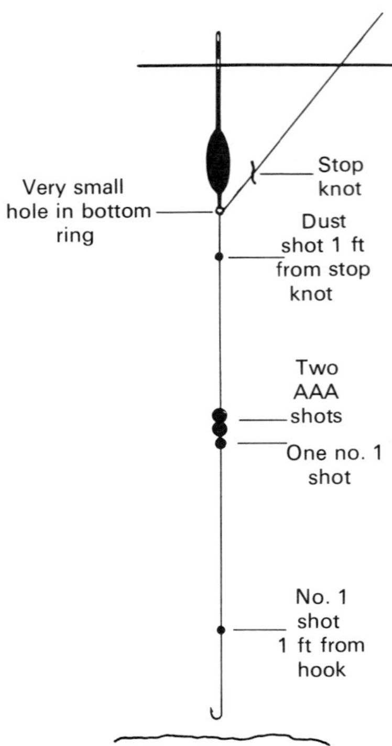

Fig. 34.3. The Sliding Float, as described for the Welland by Austin Clissett.
Note the distance between the dust shot and the stop-knot – about a foot – just enough to permit a clean strike and sure hooking.

In situations where a sliding float is essential (e.g. deep, slow-moving rivers), the dust shot should be removed. This leaves the sliding float free to move between the main bunch of shots and the stop-knot. In practice it has been found beneficial to bunch the heavier shots on the leader midway between hook and float, and any small shot or shots between the hook and the heavy shots.

This method of shotting facilitates casting. It also gets the bait down to the fish quickly, thus increasing the amount of time that the bait is available to the fish. During the very last part of its fall, however, the bait is able to sink slowly and naturally. This natural movement often induces fish to take the bait before it is finally suspended (unnaturally) on a tight line. When fish take a bait in this way the match angler describes their behaviour as 'taking on the drop'.

G. Because of the weight of its wire stem this float is semi self-cocking. Although only a shot or two is required to make it cock fully, it can still be cast a good distance because of its total 'load'. This can be an advantage if an angler wants to cast a long way and still have his bait sink gently in order to accommodate fish that will only take 'on the drop'.

H. Because of its shallow draught and diminutive size this float causes minimal disturbance when it is being retrieved over the heads of easily disturbed fish. Accordingly it is a useful float for fishing clear streams in normal water conditions. A smaller version of this float carrying one BB shot is F. B.'s favourite float for trotting a single maggot to a shoal of wary sea-trout in low-water conditions.

I and J. Billy Lane sliding floats. (See section F.)

K and L. Casting into wind is easier if a float carries the lead – or at least some of the lead needed to make it cock – inside its body. Floats so leaded are known as 'zoomers'.

Zoomers can be used as fixed floats or (without the floatcap) as sliders.

M. Peter Drennan's chub float. Peter Drennan is one of Britain's best float designers. This particular float, although carrying a huge load of shot, is not as clumsy as the so-called 'Avon' floats. Drennan has scaled down the old Avon float without sacrificing its shot-carrying capacity, by using a more buoyant material – balsa. In addition, the Drennan float has a shallower draught – which makes it less likely to frighten fish in shallow runs.

N, O, P and Q. These are versions of the famous fluted float. We cannot do better than quote Fred J. Taylor on this subject. Nobody has described it more succinctly:

> It has been said that the fluted shape offers less resistance to a taking fish than a conventional round-bodied float, but this is not strictly true. Where the fluted float scores is in trotting downstream against an upstream wind. This I think was the purpose of its original design, as outlined by the late Major Smalley, its inventor.
>
> A non-fluted float will not move downstream against a strong wind, but a fluted one will. The reason is the much greater surface area of the float to the current. The round-bodied float offers a stream-lined shape to the current and the current passes round it. The fluted float offers at least one of its concave depressions to the current and is therefore moved along by the flow of water which cannot pass round it.

R. The float that most boys buy the first time they visit a tackle shop. A shorter-stemmed version – the grayling float – is a design classic. Its bulbous body prevents its being sucked under in a lively gurgling stream.

S. A slightly more sophisticated version of float R. In our opinion this float would be improved if the lower stem were shortened to within half an inch of the body. The short-stemmed version would be less inclined to be sucked under by the stream, and in shallow runs would not 'rub the backs' of the fish.

A Note on Pike Floats

When livebaiting for pike with float tackle it is necessary to relate the buoyancy of the float to the power of the livebait. If the float is too small, an angler is not always able to tell whether a pike or the livebait is pulling his float under. But to use an undersized float is the lesser of the two evils: the greater evil is to fish with a float that is too large for the bait. To appreciate this it is necessary to understand what happens when a pike takes a livebait.

Having struck from ambush (usually from below) and grabbed its victim, the pike does one of two things: it either returns to safe cover, or sinks slowly back to the depths from which it originally struck. In either case the victim is held sideways across the pike's jaw, and crushed in a vice-like grip until the shock of its wounds prevents any chance of escape.

The float, of course, has been pulled under. But during the period when it is holding its victim, the pike lies motionless. When a pike is motionless it is very delicately balanced in the water and the extra buoyancy of a large float will affect its equilibrium. A large float will bring a small pike head-first towards the surface again. A big pike is not likely to be brought up in the same way, but its suspicions are likely to be increased rather than diminished by the buoyancy pull of an over-large float.

As a general rule, if an angler sees his float re-surface after a take and the livebait disgorged, he can be pretty sure that his float is too large.

Note: It is not known whether the pike's habit of maintaining a grip on a live victim and making no attempt to swallow it until shock has taken effect, is learned or innate behaviour. There is, however, no doubt at all that a deadbait is swallowed much sooner than a livebait. This is a point of great importance to the deadbait angler who wishes to return his pike relatively unharmed. If he waits too long before striking, his bait – and hooks – are likely to be right down in the pike's stomach.

A Nylon Float-Ring

Fishing floats usually have a wire bottom-ring, whipped on with silk thread. Manufacturers have tried to make these rings with nylon monofilament, only to find that the nylon tends to pull away from the whipping.

This can be prevented by crimping both ends of a 2 in. length of 15–20 lb B.S. nylon with a pair of heated pliers (using a cigarette-lighter flame), before whipping the crimped ends to the base of the float and varnishing.

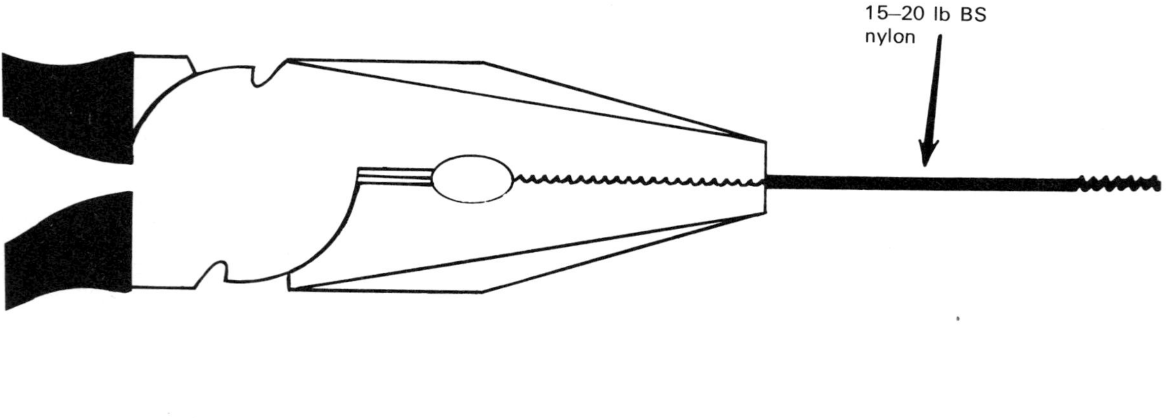

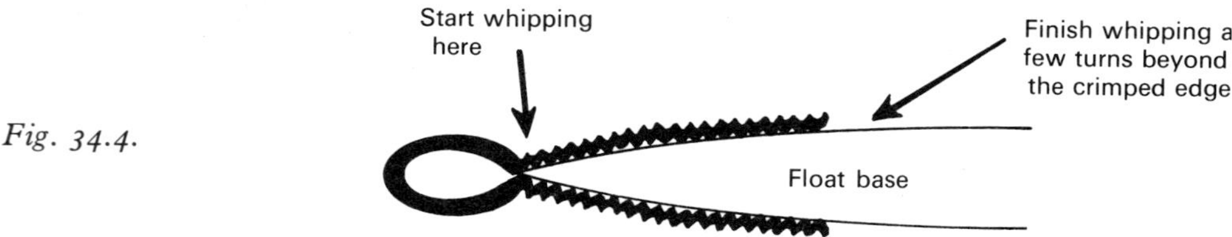

Fig. 34.4.

BITE INDICATORS

There are three basic types of bite indicator: tactile, auditory and visual. An angler can *feel* a bite, he can *hear* a bite and he can *see* a bite. An example of each is as follows:

1. *Tactile.* The touch-ledger.
2. *Auditory.* The peg-bell.
3. *Visual.* The float.

Indication by touch is the classic method used by the boat angler at sea. He holds the line taut with his finger tips and *feels* for the bite. Barbel and chub anglers in particular make use of the same principle and call it touch-ledgering. Salmon fishermen depend on extreme delicacy of touch when they fish the moving worm (although some fishermen, either from snobbery or ignorance, are disdainful of this skilful salmon fishing technique).

The line can be tensioned by the rod alone; or (better) the rod can be held in one hand while the line is gripped between thumb and forefinger of the other hand. Apart from the lips, wetted finger-tips are more sensitive to touch than any other part of the body.

Auditory bite indication in the shape of the peg-bell has long been the pier and beach angler's delight. More recently, Richard Walker produced for the freshwater angler in general, and for the carp angler in particular, an electric bite-alarm.

For the ledger fisherman, bite indication until recent years was a simple matter of keeping an eye cocked for the slightest movement of the rod-top or doughbobbin. Nowadays, the principle of the visual bite indicator is being adapted to numerous

Top: *Touch-ledgering.*

Bottom: *Touch-ledgering a deadbait for pike.*

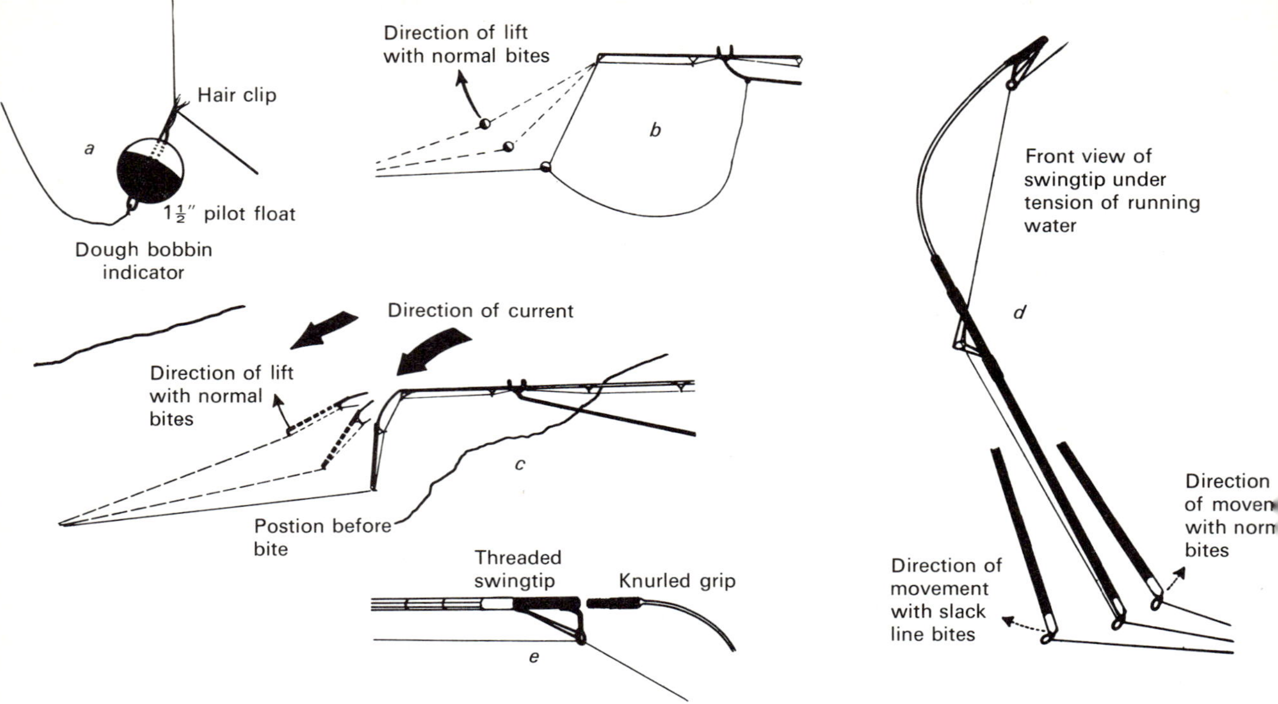

Fig. 34.5. Bite indicators.

systems: slack-line fishing, swing-tipping, quiver-tipping and spring bite-indicator fishing are examples.

As its name implies, the doughbobbin can be made from a dollop of breadpaste or dough. A more durable version can be made with other materials (Fig. 34.5.*a*).

Some five feet of nylon connects the base of the indicator to the front of the rod-rest (Fig. 34.5.*b*). The angler makes his cast, takes up the initial slack, lays his rod down in the rests, walks to the front and clips the bobbin on to the mainline between ten and forty inches from the top ring. He then releases a few turns of line from the reel. These turns are taken up and tensioned by the weight of the bobbin. The amount of line released by the angler – and tensioned by the bobbin – is the amount of line that can be taken by a fish before it feels the resistance of the rod.

The doughbobbin method of bite indication offers:

1. An immediate visual warning of even the most tentative bite.
2. Time for a bite to develop – while the fish takes up the slack.
3. Time for the angler to 'read' the bite – again, while the fish takes up the slack.

Two super modern versions of the doughbobbin are made by Hardy Bros. These are called the *Dobob* and the *Glowbobbin* (Fig. 35.9). The *Glowbobbin* is provided with the best line release clip that we have seen. It also has a screw-capped body which allows shot to be added, so that an adjustment can be made for different current strengths.

Readers may be surprised to hear that the doughbobbin principle has been incorporated in a bite indicator for at least 300 years. There is a perfect description of it in

Fig. 34.6. The doughbobbin rig. As used in the year 1662.

Robert Venables's book *The Experienc'd Angler: or Angling Improv'd,* first published in 1662:

Some use to lead their lines heavily, and to set their cork about a foot or more from the end of the rod, with a little lead to buoy it up, and thus in violent swift streams they avoid the offence of a flote, and yet perfectly discern the biting of the fish. [Fig. 34.6]

In spite of the extreme sensitivity of the doughbobbin rig – and in our opinion there is none better – it is easy to see why it has never been popular with the match-angler. Running up and down to fix on a dough-bobbin would be judged a criminal waste of time. The match-angler largely ignored ledgering until Mr Jack Clayton, a celebrated Boston tackle dealer, created his now famous swing-tip.

Mechanically, the swing-tip and the doughbobbin are the same; but the swing-tip is an ever-precious time saver. Fig. 34.5.*c* and Fig. 34.5.*b* illustrate the similarity between the two systems. Fig. 34.5.*d* shows the swing-tip in action over a streamy run, and displays the expected tip movement with normal and slack-line bites.

Sometimes this movement will be the merest twitch; at other times a dramatic swing. Delicacy of movement applies more particularly to roach bites – for which the swing-tip was originally designed.

It should be remembered that the swing-tip is only a bite indicator, and will not compensate for inferior terminal tackle or technique. Care must be taken when setting up the rodrest position for swing-tipping. Swing-tip movement should always be at right angles to the wind, otherwise the more subtle tweaks (which at times may be the only bites) will go unnoticed.

When angling in strong winds, take care to shield the swing-tip and the line. Make the best use of natural cover; if necessary, use some form of artificial shield. Arrange for the swing-tip to hang near to the water, since air currents close to water are usually less turbulent.

One of the better swing-tip productions is illustrated in Fig. 34.5.*e*. This is the neatest way yet devised for connecting swing-tip to rod. This design allows a swing-tip to be removed at a moment's notice, so that an angler may, if he wishes, quickly change to float fishing. The only drawback is a tendency for the tip to unscrew itself. This defect could easily be eliminated if the nose of the top ring projected about a quarter of an inch – sufficient to allow a piece of valve rubber to be slipped over the joint.

Cheap imitations are less efficient than Clayton's original swing-tip, and the angler is advised to choose the best he can afford.

Generally speaking, it is better to swing-tip from the front rodrest while maintaining a grip on the rod. In circumstances where two rests are used, the layout should ensure that the hand is free to hover over the rod butt, so that a quick strike can be made.

Together with the swing-tip and the electric bite alarm, the spring bite-indicator represents the best of the post-war bite-indicator gadgetry. It is an extremely versatile instrument. It can be used in any ledgering situation where the ground is soft enough to take the stick. For normal ledgering the rig is set up as shown in Fig. 34.7.

There are times, however, when an angler needs to make full use of his rod length. On these occasions, a spring bite-indicator fitted to a 5 ft bankstick allows the rod to be rod-rested right over the water (Fig. 34.8.*d*).

The main advantages of the spring are as follows:

1. An angler is left free to choose a rod for its normal functions of casting for and playing a fish, without having to consider how well it can signal a bite.
2. An angler can remain seated, since there are no bits and pieces to fit up after each cast.
3. A slack-line bite is plainly registered.
4. It will accommodate variations in current strength to a remarkable degree.

Directions

To get the best results from the indicator, set up two rodrests. Cast out, take up the slack, and then lay the rod down in the rests.

Push the spring bite-indicator stick in the ground, so that the 'dodger' on the spring comes up under the line and tensions it about ten inches or so from the rod-tip (the tension of the line actually depresses the spring, see Figs. 34.8.*a* and *b*). Note that the 'dodger' should always be pointing in the direction of the current flow.

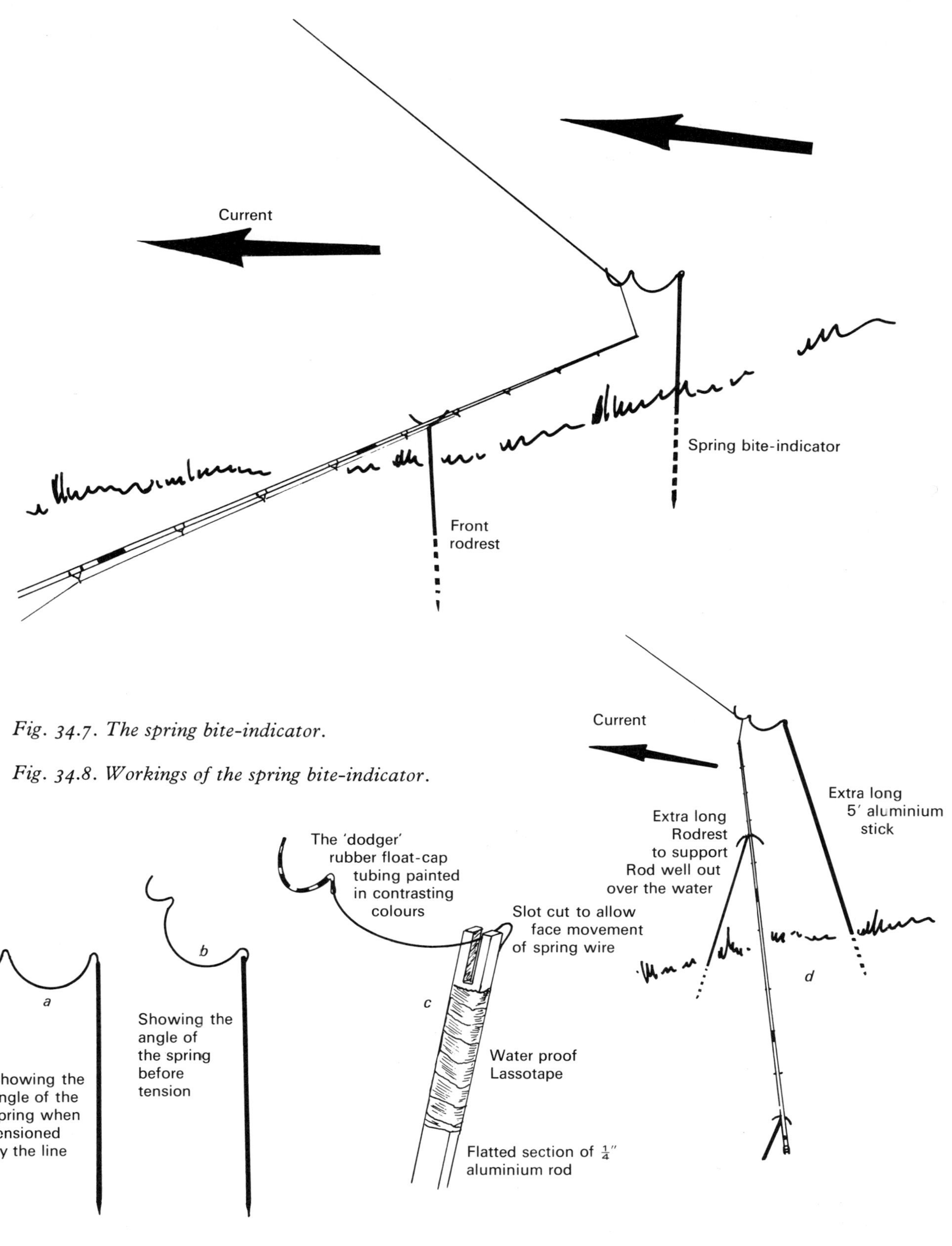

Fig. 34.7. The spring bite-indicator.

Fig. 34.8. Workings of the spring bite-indicator.

There is a commercial spring bite-indicator available, but for the angler who wishes to make his own we give the following instructions:

Take a 30 in. flat or round sectioned piece of quarter-inch aluminium rod. Cut a slot down from the top about ½ in. deep (Fig. 34.8.*c*).

Take a 16 in. length of SWG spring-steel wire; bend one end round half a circle of 1¼ in. radius, and bend the next section round half a circle of 2¾ in. radius.

The remaining straight section of wire is lashed on to the back of the aluminium rod with water-proof 'Lassotape'.

See that the wire comes through the slot so as to obtain lateral support.

See that the finished angle of the spring is as shown in Fig. 34.8.*c*.

Cover the small half-circle (the 'dodger') with float-cap rubber, and paint it with contrasting colours. Choose the colours as if you were choosing them for a favourite float: it is the 'dodger' that you will have to stare at for long periods.

Having discovered that the doughbobbin has been in use for hundreds of years, we looked closely for historical mention of the swing-tip. We were not disappointed. Strange to relate, this too is by no means a modern invention.

In the appendix of the third edition of a little book published in 1805, there is a description of *The Elastic or New Invented Superficial Float for a gentle Stream or Still Water Angling*.

On its cover, the book carries the following title: *Nobb's Art of Trolling*. On the inside page, however, we find a different title: *The Angler's Pocket-Book: or Compleat English Angler: containing all that is necessary to be known in that Art. Also Nobb's Celebrated Treatise on the Art of Trolling.*

Fig. 34.9. Ledgering after dark with a 'Glowbobbin' bite indicator.

Nobbes (this spelling of his name is given in Westwood and Satchell's *Bibliotheca Piscatoria* (1883)), the so-called 'father of trolling' (which he was not), published his celebrated book *The Compleat Troller, or The Art of Trolling* in 1682, and had no hand in the writing of the Appendix in the 1805 volume.

Although no author's name appears in the book other than Nobbes's it seems reasonable to conclude that the swing-tip was invented by the unknown author of *The Angler's Pocket Book.*

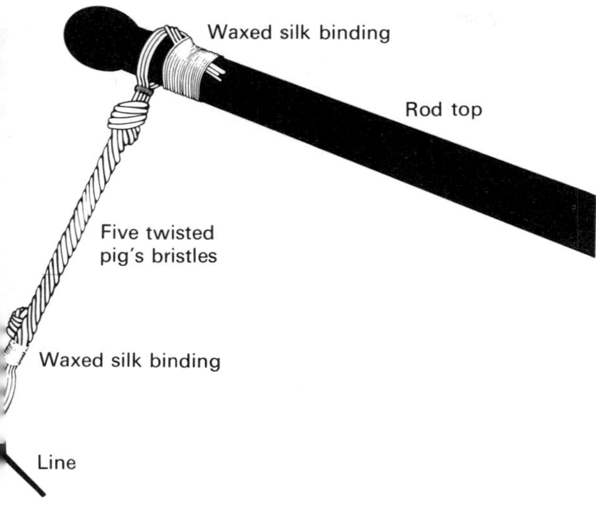

Fig. 34.10. The earliest known swingtip first described in 1805.

Because the author recommends the swing-tip primarily for bream fishing in still or slow waters, and because the first edition of the book was published in Norwich, we suspect that the author was a fensman. Be that as it may, here is his description of *The Elastic or New Invented Superficial Float* (the earliest recorded swing-tip):

Take five, six or more Pigs' Bristles, tie them together near the extremity of the thin end; bind as much of them with waxed silk as will make a loop about the size of a small ring of a trolling rod; twist the Bristles together with your finger and thumb, and tie the other ends, or they will untwist, leaving about an inch or more untied, that they may lay neat round the tip of your rod; divide the ends which are not tied, into two equal parts, placing the tip of your rod in the middle; bind them tight with waxed silk crossways, fastening the surplus as near the extremity of your rod as possible, observing that the Float stands out horizontally, so that the loop hangs down towards the water, as in the Print.

This Float must not be made too stiff or you will not see when you have a bite, nor too weak, if it is, the weight of shot to your line will bend it, and will likewise prevent you seeing a bite; therefore to avoid either extreme, it must be made only stiff enough to remain quite horizontal as already explained; and this may be regulated by the number of shot, in the same manner as the common float, to make it stand higher or lower as the angler pleases; but above all it must remain quite horizontal to retain its elasticity.

Now your float is compleat and fastened to your rod, pass the loop of your line through the little loop of your float, and over the other end of your tip, and draw it tort, as you do when your tip has a common loop to it, when you begin to fish, let your line sink gently; you will feel when the shot touches the bottom, as it will give your float a visible check; then raise your line a little, that the bait may be near the bottom, but not touch it; when you have a bite, this float will have the same motion as the common float, although out of the water.

Among the many advantages this new float has above the common one, are these:

Your float will never frighten the fish; small fish will never play with it; nor will it disturb the water. In rough weather when you cannot see the common float, this remains unmolested; and if your line is long enough, you may fish a whole day without plumbing the depth. Amongst weeds you will find it answer beyond your expectation. When you strike, the rod, line, and fish has but one motion; but with the common float there is three if your line is long; the first motion is your rod, second the line, and third the float and fish, if the first motion has not frightened him away; but with this new elastic float, your line is infallibly perpendicular from the tip of your rod to the bait, and of course there can be but one motion when you strike, as the float is no impediment, it being one piece with the rod. Besides these advantages, with practice, you will find many more too tedious to mention. No float can equal this for Roach angling.

Instead of a loop, you may make a round knob of silk near the extremity of the float, of the same shape and size, as the knob at the end of a common rod, and fasten your line to it in the same manner.

For Smelt and Bleak fishing, this float will be found most useful, as well as at all mid-water angling.

Angling 'Signals'

Unlike the participants in most other sports, anglers improve (or *should* improve) with age. Their rate of improvement depends on:

(a) The amount and range of their angling experience.

(b) The ability to draw the right conclusions from that experience.

(c) A thirst for any information that will extend their knowledge of angling.

Since this book is something of a catalogue of thoroughly tested tackles and techniques, it is in category (c) that we hope to be of assistance. At the same time we should point out that the difference between success and failure often depends on some tiny variation. Accordingly, we advise that whatever rig and method an angler chooses, *final adjustment must always be made at the waterside.*

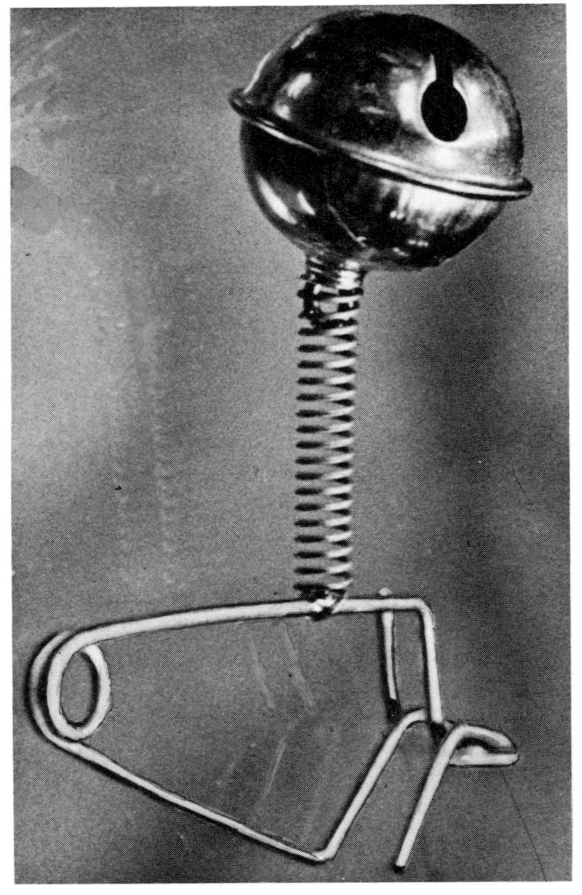

The rod bell (much beloved of sea anglers) is at least 250 years old. It was recommended as an aid to ledgering by Robert Howlett in his Angler's Sure Guide *(1706).*

An angler becomes aware of the need to make some adjustment through signals sent by his float, rod-tip, lure or bait, or by changing conditions of weather and water. The ability to receive and understand these signals, and know how to act on them, separates the expert angler from the rest.

35 · Miscellaneous Tackle

SWIVELS

The swivel is an underrated but essential piece of tackle.

Most swivels are made of brass and, in accordance with tradition, have a natural or a bronze finish. Recently, however, two types of swivel, made of rustless bright wire, have become popular. One is known as a 'diamond-eye' swivel, the other as a 'diamond-eye link' swivel. Both versions are small, strong and efficient.

A swivel's primary function is to minimize line kink, but it can also be used as a link between separate parts of a rig. For instance, a wire leader is seldom joined direct to the mainline. Instead, a swivel is interposed, and the line and the leader are fastened to opposite ends. Sometimes a 'link' type swivel is preferred, to facilitate a quick change of tackle.

The most efficient swivel is the ball-bearing swivel (Fig. 35.1). Unfortunately, this swivel, unlike the barrel swivel (Fig. 35.3), is not offered in a series of graded sizes. The comparatively high cost of the ball-bearing swivel tends to discourage the novice, but we unhesitatingly recommend it to anyone who wants to spin for his fish – whether trout, sea-trout, salmon, pike, perch or chub.

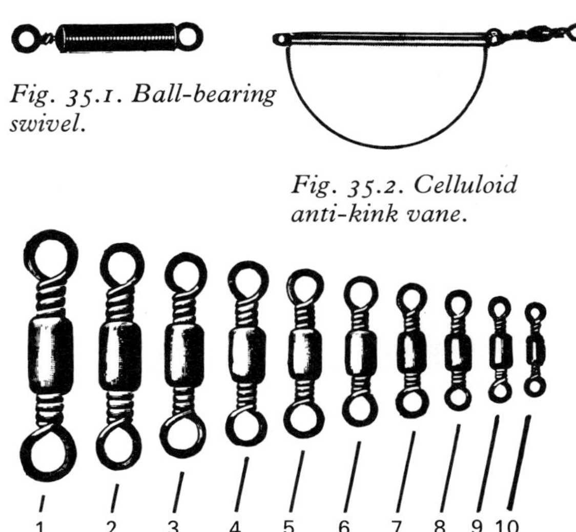

Fig. 35.1. Ball-bearing swivel.

Fig. 35.2. Celluloid anti-kink vane.

Fig. 35.3. Barrel swivels (actual size).

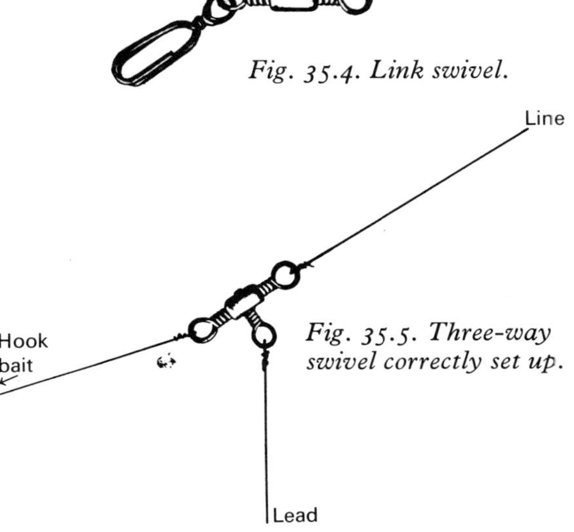

Fig. 35.4. Link swivel.

Fig. 35.5. Three-way swivel correctly set up.

Fig. 35.6. Hardy's 'Diamond eye' swivel is an old favourite. It is made in two patterns: a link version, and plain (as illustrated). The makers claim that the Diamond eye swivel is superior on two counts:

1. *Friction is reduced to a minimum.*
2. *Attachment to the swivel is central with the bearing. We think this pattern is superior to the more popular box and barrel swivels.*

Fast revolving baits often overload a barrel swivel. Even a ball-bearing swivel cannot keep up with the revolutions caused by retrieving a spinner in a heavy current. In these circumstances, a swivelled, celluloid anti-kink vane (Fig. 35.2), or an anti-kink lead (see p. 389) is essential. A swivel with anti-kink lead is efficient when deep water is being fished, but in shallow water the celluloid anti-kink vane is better.

Three-way swivels are popular for paternostering (see p. 387). When using them, however, it is important that the bait link (the link that takes the strain if a big fish is hooked) is tied *opposite the main-line link*. The *middle* eye of the three-way swivel should always be used for the lead link. Failure to observe this rule will eventually result in a lost fish – due to fatigue fracture. This is caused by the right-angle in the swivel being constantly strained to an obtuse angle, and as constantly bent back again by the angler.

LEADS

Split shot to regulate the rate of the worm downstream are usually considered indispensable by the angler; but, except on rare occasions, impeding the motion of the worm is objectionable, and for the following reasons:– A worm thrown into a stream would be carried down by the current and turned round in every eddy; and as this is the way in which trout are accustomed to see worms coming down stream, every deviation from it is calculated to excite their suspicion . . .

The alleged reasons for shotting are, that the worm travels more slowly, affording the trout plenty of time to seize it, and that it reaches the bottom. Now, as to the first assertion, the best rate for the worm to travel at is undoubtedly the natural one, and if the trout wish to seize it, they have always plenty of time to do so. To the second reason we attach some importance; it is natural for the worm to be near the bottom. But it is not in deep water that the worm-fisher must look for sport; and in water not above a couple of feet deep, the worm will reach the bottom very quickly without any assistance; and even should it not, the trout will rise to seize it, frequently jumping at it as they would at a fly . . .

Besides giving an unnatural motion to the worm, sinkers are highly objectionable in other respects. They are constantly hanking below stones, and occasioning the angler a great deal of annoyance and loss of time. With them also the angler gets over the ground at a much slower rate than when his worm comes down almost at the same rate as the stream. This opinion about sinkers is held by almost all the best worm-fishers; and some Tweedside adepts never use them under any circumstances.

So wrote W. C. Stewart, one of the greatest worm-anglers of all time, in *The Practical*

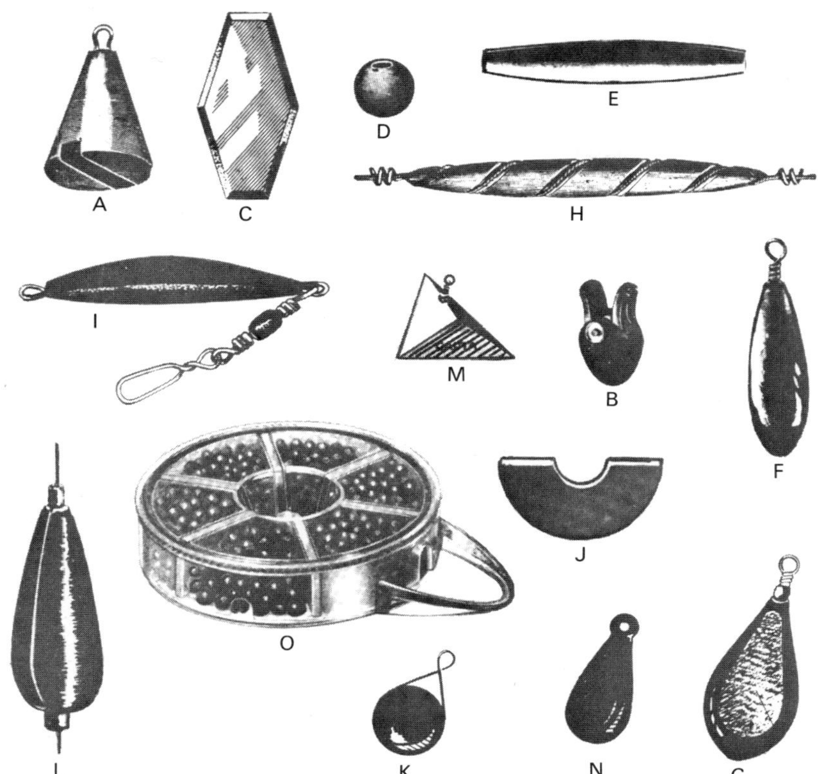

Fig. 35.7.

Angler (1857). And how right he was. But he referred specifically to fishing the moving worm. For many other baits and methods, split-shot and leads are obligatory. The following are those in general use.

The obvious function of a fishing lead is to sink and, if necessary, anchor the bait. Many leads, however, have auxiliary functions and are often designed with this in mind.

A. The traditional plummet. As its name implies, it is used to measure the depth of a swim.

B. The modern plummet. Originally of French origin, this consists of two spring-loaded cups centrally hinged. Pressure on the two 'ears' opens these cups sufficiently to allow a baited hook to be dropped inside. When the pressure is released, the cups close over the baited hook.

Before the traditional plummet can be used, the bait must be removed. The modern plummet avoids this delay.

C. The coffin lead.
D. The drilled-bullet lead.
E. The barley corn or barrel lead.
F. The Arlesey bomb.

} Ledgering leads.

The Arlesey bomb, though not invented by Richard Walker, was re-designed and popularized by him in the early 1950s. Walker produced this design of lead especially for long distance casting so that he could reach the big perch that were almost out of casting range in Arlesey Lake, Bed-

Fig. 35.8.a.

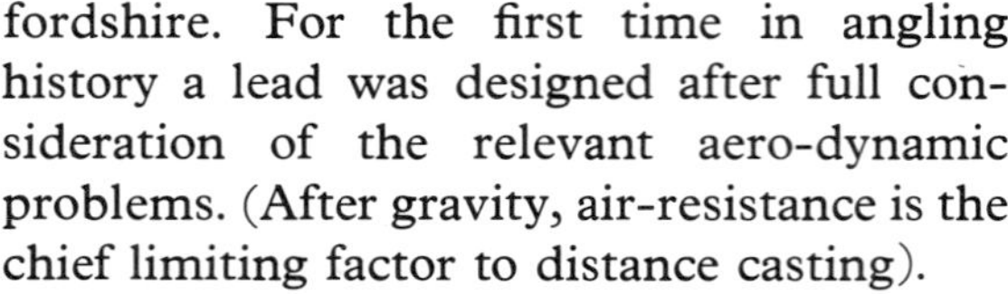

Fig. 35.8.b. Anti-kink lead is fixed to the line end *of the swivel.*

fordshire. For the first time in angling history a lead was designed after full consideration of the relevant aero-dynamic problems. (After gravity, air-resistance is the chief limiting factor to distance casting).

The Arlesey bomb will not tumble in flight. As a result it is less likely to foul line and tackle during its passage through the air. The built-in swivel prevents kinks developing in the line. On the bed of a lake or a slow-moving river, the Arlesey bomb stands nearly upright. This is a useful design feature, since it helps to keep the line clear of mud.

The Arlesey bomb is very useful when bait and lead are required to bounce and roll over the bed of a river. The swivel almost entirely eliminates the chance of the lead kinking or fouling the line.

G. Arlesey bomb with flattened sides. This is a useful lead to use in medium or fast rivers when an angler wishes to anchor his bait rather than have it move downstream. The more bulbous shape reduces casting range but improves anchoring efficiency.

H. The Jardine lead.
I. The Wye lead.
J. The half-moon lead.
K. The Hillman lead.
} Spinning leads

The Jardine is a quick-change lead which can be put on a leader, or removed, without the tackle having to be broken down.

The Wye lead, too, can be removed easily if placed between two link-swivels (Fig. 35.8.*a*). It is a more secure lead than the Jardine – which has a tendency to fall off.

Both Wye and Hillman are good leads for spinning, since they are both useful anti-kink devices.

The Hillman, also a quick-change lead, is used with a swivel (Fig. 35.8.*b*).

The half-moon is a useful lead for light spinning. It is the favourite lead of the fisherman who spins for trout and sea-trout, or salmon in low-water summer conditions. It is particularly useful for fishing in comparatively shallow streams, where a very light lead that also acts as an anti-kink is required.

L. The Catherine lead. Another quick-change lead. For the angler who wishes to dead-bait (with or without a float) and to use a lead, this is the best lead for the job.

The Catherine lead is slotted; so is the tapered hollow plastic peg that runs through its middle. This allows passage for the line through both slots into the bore of the plastic peg. Once the line is inside, the plastic peg is revolved ten degrees to close up the inner slot. Finally, the tapered peg is pushed tight into the lead – which is now free to be moved up and down the leader until located in the desired position by means of a stop-knot.

A pike picking up a dead bait is free to take line through a Catherine lead without moving the lead and without feeling its resistance. There are times when a fish may be sufficiently circumspect for such sensitivity in a rig to be important.

Note: The pike angler who fishes with float tackle usually fits a Jardine lead, although a barrel lead is preferable since it is more secure. A barrel lead can be moved up and down the leader once a stop-shot is fitted.

M. The Capta lead. It is a lead of quite modern design. It has leech-like qualities because of its streamlined shape and will stay where it is on a river bed when heavier leads would be swept away. It is an inferior casting lead.

N. The paternoster or pear lead. This, like the Arlesey bomb stands nearly upright on a river bed.

O. The split-shot dispenser. A useful piece of equipment so long as an angler is able to purchase a refill of *any* size that gets used up.

Split Shot

Good quality split-shot should be made of *soft* lead and should be nearly bisected by the cut that forms the split. Only if the lead is suitably soft can a shot be removed from the line and used again. With large shot (see largest shot arrowed in Fig. 35.9) it helps if the leading edges are trimmed to form a 'V' entry to the split. This 'V' entry gives the fingernail greater purchase and facilitates the easy removal of shot from a leader without the need of a special tool.

Split-shot of any nominal size should be uniform in weight. This uniformity of weight is very important. It allows an angler to pre-determine the number of shots that a float will carry, thus eliminating the need for experiment at the bankside. All floats can then carry the owner's mark with the guarantee that the nominated number of shots will cock the float nicely.

Reference to the Shot Chart (where the shots are actual size) will allow anglers to calculate shot loads by weight.

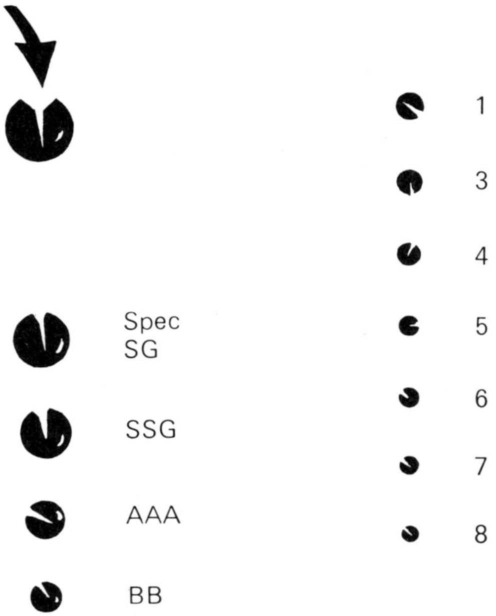

Name or Number	Pellets per ounce
Special SG	11
SSG	15
AAA	35
BB	70
1	100
3	140
4	170
5	220
6	270
7	340
8	450

Fig. 35.9. Shot chart.

NETS

Lastly, you shall have a little fine wanded Pebbe to hang by your side, in which you shall put the Fish which you catch, and a small round net fastned to a poales end, wherewith you may land a Pike or other great Fish . . .
GERVASE MARKHAM, *The Pleasures of Princes* (1614).

Having uneasy doubts about all folding gadgetry – whether landing nets or chairs – I prefer a solid outfit. My idea of a landing net is something simple and strong, with a great big wide mouth. Do-it-yourself enthusiasts can construct a net frame with laughable ease from a length of thick fencing wire, and a stout ash stick . . . if the rim and upper part of the handle is covered with a coat of silver paint it will show up nicely in the darkness.
HUGH FALKUS, *Sea-Trout Fishing* (1962).

I've seen plenty of fish lost because the net was too small but never a one lost because the net was too big. . . . Anglers grudge paying a good price for a first class landing net before they've lost the fish of a lifetime because the net proved inadequate. Afterwards they express different opinions.
RICHARD WALKER.

Landing Nets

The first hint of a landing net is to be found in one of the earliest fishing books printed in the English language: *The Arte of Angling*, published in 1577.[1] The author is unknown, but the book was printed at the *Sign of the Falcon* in Fleet Street by Henry Middleton, and sold at his shop in St. Dunstan's churchyard.

In this didactic volume – which was probably the model for Izaak Walton's *The Compleat Angler*, published 76 years later – Piscator (the skilful angler) is teaching Viator (the pupil) the ways of fish and the ploys of fishermen. Piscator hooks a good perch and, after playing it out, tells Viator to lie down on his belly, hold the bank with one hand and take the fish with the other by putting his forefinger into the gills and his thumb into its mouth.

As soon as the perch is landed, Viator, aglow with this sudden and unexpected justification for his presence, not unnaturally asks: 'How would you have done if I had not been here?' In a lengthy reply, Piscator tells his pupil that it had been his intention to fish the swim for roach, and, in accordance with that intention, had brought only roach gear with him. He finishes thus: '*I . . . left one of my tooles at home for hast, whiche if I had brought I could have landed him without your help*.'

1 Or so we thought. According to A. Courtney Williams in *Angling Diversions* (1945), the first record of a landing net is to be found on one of the Leptic Magna mosaics of the first or second century A.D., which were discovered in 1933, in Tripoli. 'The picture depicts two Roman anglers, one baiting his hook, the other in the act of landing a fish; he is holding his 7 ft rod high above his shoulder in his left hand, whilst with the other he guides the fish towards his net.' As A. C. W. also points out, the triangular type of landing net was no modern invention; it was first described by Frère Francois Fortin, in *Les Ruses Innocentes* (1660).

From this it is evident that a landing net (or something similar) was implied.

In the same little book (which we consider one of the most *practical* volumes of instruction among all the early fishing books) is a description of a piece of equipment used in the 16th century for snatching pike, and which evolved into the 20th-century salmon fish-tailer (illustration H, overleaf).

. . . he will be haltered, [caught with a noose] and some men use that way very oft to kill him, for hee will lie glaring upon you, as the hare or larke, until you put the line with a snittle [noose] over his head, and so with a good stiff pole you may throw him to land.

A long-handled net enables the angler to reach a fish from a high bank.

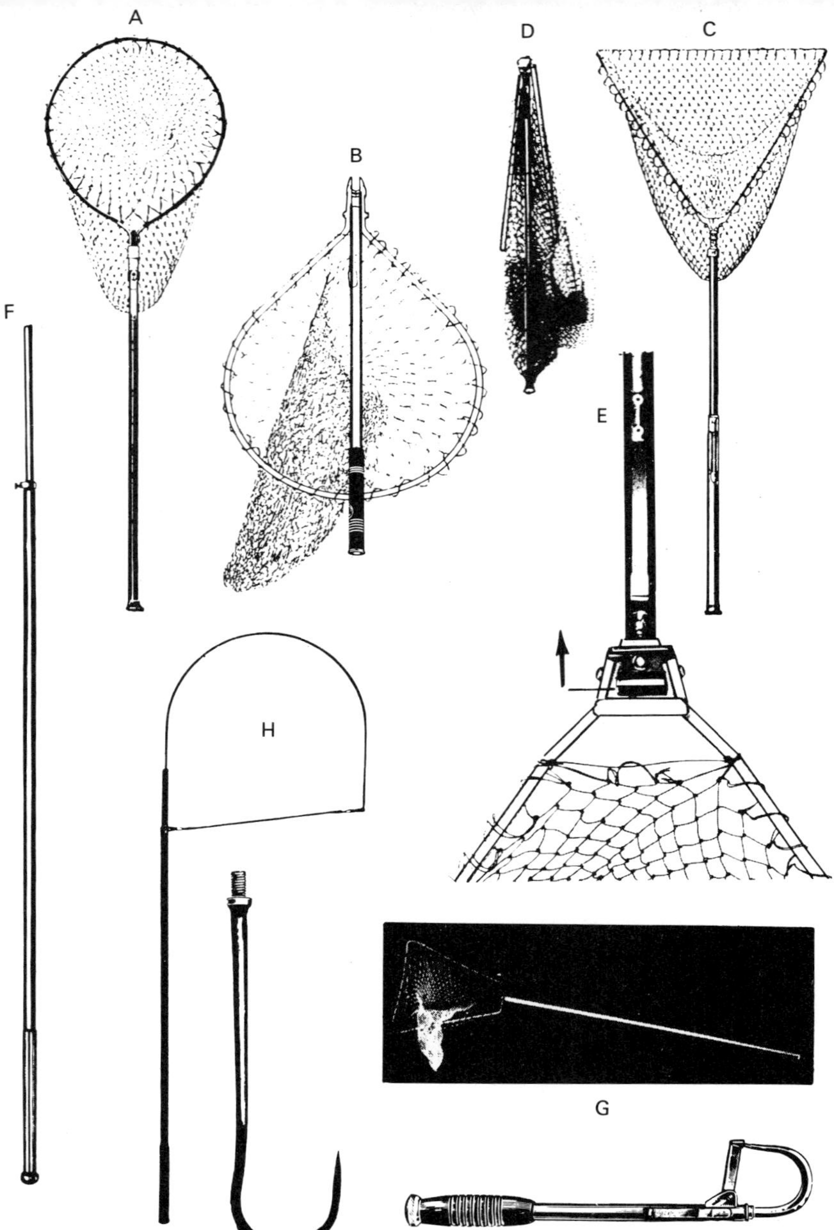

Modern Types of Landing Net

A. A flick-open folding net of classic shape.

B. A similar type, folded down ready to be clipped on to a carrying ring.

C. A triangular-shaped net with telescopic handle. This type enables the angler to reach further, when he wishes, without the awkwardness of a permanently long handle. The triangular shape has a special function and is primarily a net for use in shallow water. It is, moreover, non-tilting when rested on the riverbed before a fish is drawn over it.

D. The same net folded down.

E. The pull-bar in close-up, the arrow

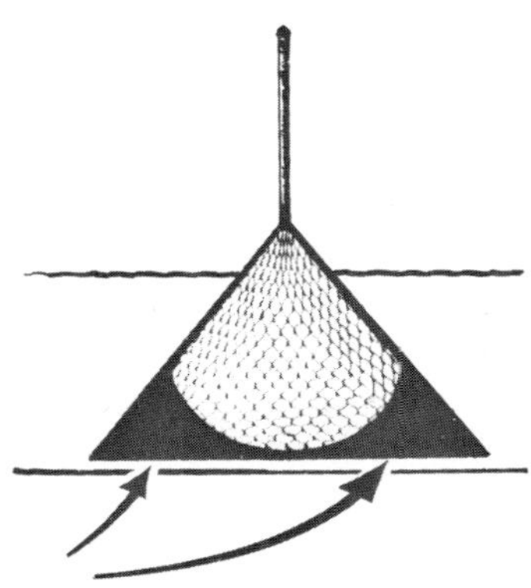

The two corners of a triangular net cut off possible escape routes for a fish being landed in shallow water (see the shaded areas in diagram).

indicating the direction of pull needed to fold the net. Also shown is the type of spring steel clip that is usually fitted to the net handle. The clip fastens on a ring fitted to an angler's belt or harness.

Note: This type of folding net easily becomes detached from its carrying ring when an angler kneels down. Often the loss of the net remains unnoticed until, having hooked a fish, the angler gropes for his net – in vain . . .!

F. An 8 ft telescopic alloy landing net handle. This is standard equipment for many match-anglers. The match-angler must be prepared for any eventuality: perhaps to fish into a swim separated from him by reeds or boggy ground, or from a high bank.

G. The triangular frame landing net favoured by most coarse fishermen. It is used in conjunction with the 8 ft handle shown, or with the telescopic handle already described.

Remember: a small net will accommodate only a small fish. The owner of such a net is faced with the prospect of never being equipped to land the fish of his dreams. *Don't economize.* Buy a good big net to start with.

With a big fish safely in the net, the angler (Ken Taylor) has shortened his grip of the net handle, so that he can lift the fish clear of the water (Photograph: Richard Walker).

Netting a Fish

It is surprising how inexpert many anglers are with a landing net. A net is never used on a fish in the manner of a butterfly net. Nor is it used to 'dig' the fish out of the water. It is used as a trap. And, as with all traps, it *must not be seen.*

A fish, when it is tired *and not before*, is drawn over the waiting net – which is completely submerged except for the handle end. When the fish is over the net, the net is raised to encompass it. Once the fish is safely inside the net the rod can be put aside, since the net frame will need extra support (from the angler's rod hand) if the fish is a heavy one.

When the fish is lying on its side, the net is raised to encompass it.

The fish is unhooked while still in the net, well back from the waterside.

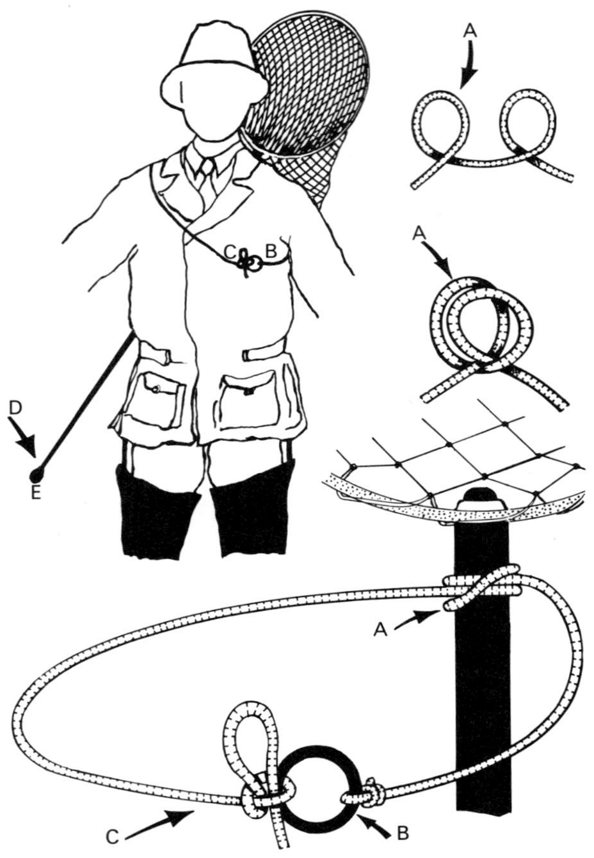

Fig. 35.10. A simple method of carrying a landing net.
A. Clove hitch round net handle.
B. Metal ring.
C. Slip knot.
D. A piece of lead sheet tacked round the end of the handle enables the net to be used as a wading staff – useful when fording a river.
E. A rubber pad on the butt of the handle reduces noise when the net is used as a wading staff.

Keepnets

A keepnet is a receptacle for keeping fish alive. An angler should choose a net that will house the size and number of fish he hopes to catch. All nets should have a fine mesh (gudgeon or even minnow mesh). This makes them suitable for housing small fish as well as big fish. All keepnets cause some pectoral and tailfin damage to fish. Fine mesh helps to reduce this damage.

A keepnet should be able to accommodate the longest fish an angler is likely to catch. It should be able to lie in the net in the normal horizontal position. Good nets are rectangular so that a number of fish of the same length can lie side by side. This shape of net allows the fish to face the stream in a natural position.

Round keepnets are bad because large fish are bent round in the shape of the net. A keepnet should have a long neck that can be used as a delivery funnel for the fish. This will eliminate the need to raise the net out of the water each time a freshly caught fish is put in.

The part of the net that houses the fish (the large rectangular or square section) should be fitted with a stretcher. This will eliminate the chances of the net failing to open out, if it gets caught on an underwater obstruction.

A keepnet should be fitted with a rope and a bankstick-fitting so that it can be dangled to its plimsoll line even from a very high bank position (see diagram).

Nylon is the most popular material used for net manufacture. Its rotproof qualities and therefore its economy appeals to the

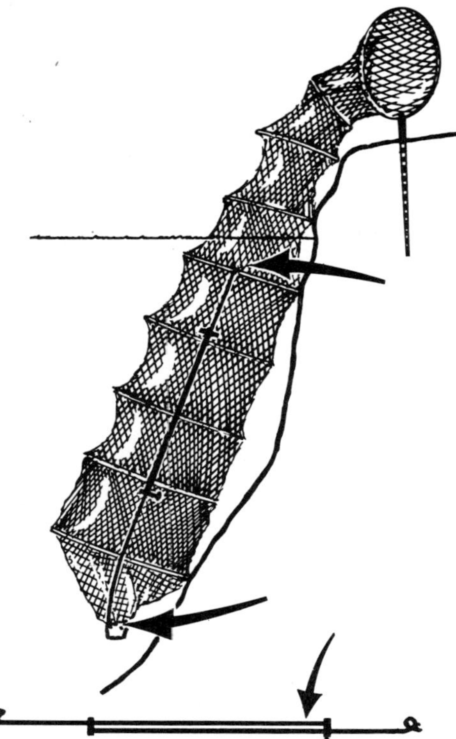

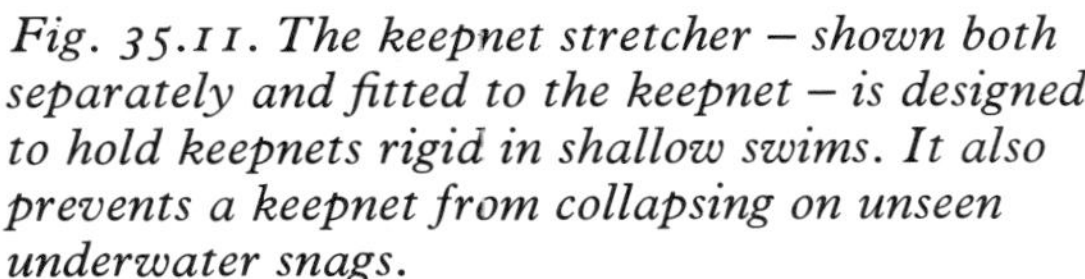

Fig. 35.11. The keepnet stretcher – shown both separately and fitted to the keepnet – is designed to hold keepnets rigid in shallow swims. It also prevents a keepnet from collapsing on unseen underwater snags.
Fitting instructions. *Fit the ringed end of the stretcher on to the 4th or 5th frame-wire (counting from the bottom) and place the hooked end on the wire handle at the bottom of the net, (that part of the handle that is threaded through the net). After loosening the wing-nut, the stretcher is expanded to the appropriate tension and the wing-nut is re-tightened.*

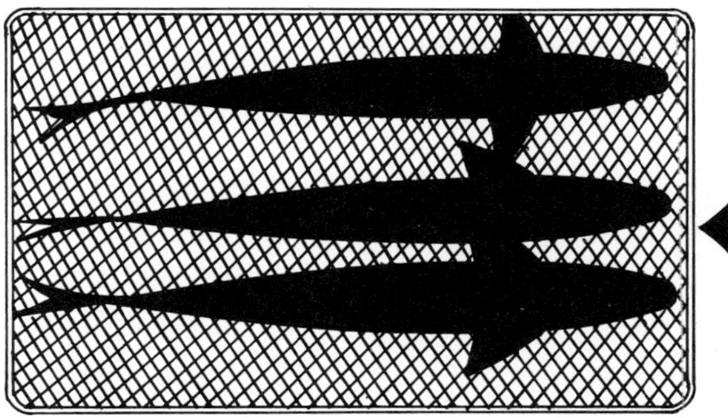

Round keepnets (top) *are bad for large fish, which get bent round in the shape of the net – like this catch of barbel.*

The rectangular net (bottom) *allows fish to keep their noses to the stream and lie in a natural position.*

angler. Nylon, however, is a killer material. The hard knots on a nylon keepnet do much more damage to a fish than the knots on a flax net. It is not the fault of the net manufacturer: anglers insist on nylon nowadays. However the new (1972) *knotless* mesh nylon keepnets reduces the damage to fish by 90 per cent.

F. B. who has had considerable experience as a match angler,[1] always carried two keepnets, one of which was held in reserve in case of a field day. The second net was also useful in the 'roving match' once popular in the south of England. It allowed the angler to

1 F. B. once held the record bag of dace taken in a match: 251 weighing 64 lb.

rove without taking the bulk of his catch about with him.

If an angler can allow himself the luxury of fishing in one swim and hanging his keep-net in another – he should do so even if it necessitates carrying the fish a dozen yards to the net. It is possible that disturbance caused by fish in a keepnet is communicated to other fish and deters them from feeding (at least it seems to deter the big ones!).

The reader who thinks this unlikely should remember that thousands of highly skilled match anglers fish every week-end – and rarely catch a two pound roach between them during the whole season. Yet the waters they fish yield a number of two pound roach when all is quiet. Although of course there are other reasons why big roach are not caught on match days, it is almost certain that the main reason is water disturbance.

DISGORGERS

No angler can avoid the occasional hooking of undersized fish. Such fish are protected by legislation, but there is little point in introducing special size limits under which fish may not be killed, unless the angler takes special care when removing the hook. All too often, undersized fish hooked, unhooked, and returned to the water, die as a result of being roughly handled.

For removing hooks from the throats of small fish, the 'V' Prong (Fig. 35.12) is the disgorger in common use. This is to be deplored, since the 'V' Prong is both brutal and ineffective.

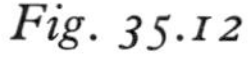

Fig. 35.12

The Cross-Cut Slotted Disgorger

A vastly better instrument is the Cross-cut Slotted disgorger (Fig. 35.13). We cannot, alas, discover the name of its inventor and so cannot give him due credit. We can, however, assert that his invention is the most humane and efficient disgorger available today for use on small fish, and must already have been responsible for saving a great many lives.

There are two patterns. One has a narrow slot and is designed to disgorge hooks whipped to nylon. The other has a wider slot and is designed for use with *eyed* fly or bait hooks and spade-end hooks.

Directions

Hold the hooked fish and tension the line coming to its mouth (Fig. 35.13). Let the line drop in the cross cut before turning the disgorger 90° in the direction of the fish's mouth. The line now runs right through the

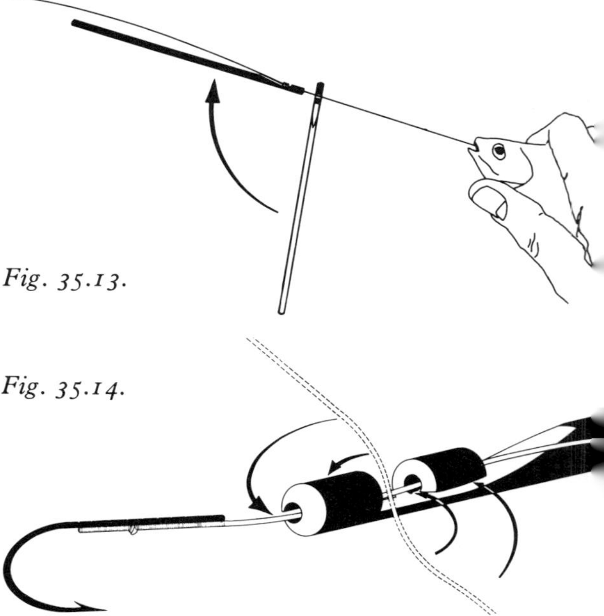

Fig. 35.13.

Fig. 35.14.

disgorger. Slide the disgorger down the line into the fish's mouth until the nose of the disgorger creeps over the shank of the hook and touches the bend.

Now that the shank of the hook is retained by the disgorger a further push frees the barb, and the hook can be withdrawn.

Fig. 35.14 shows the design of the disgorger in close-up. It also shows the position of the angler's leader before and after it has been located in the disgorger.

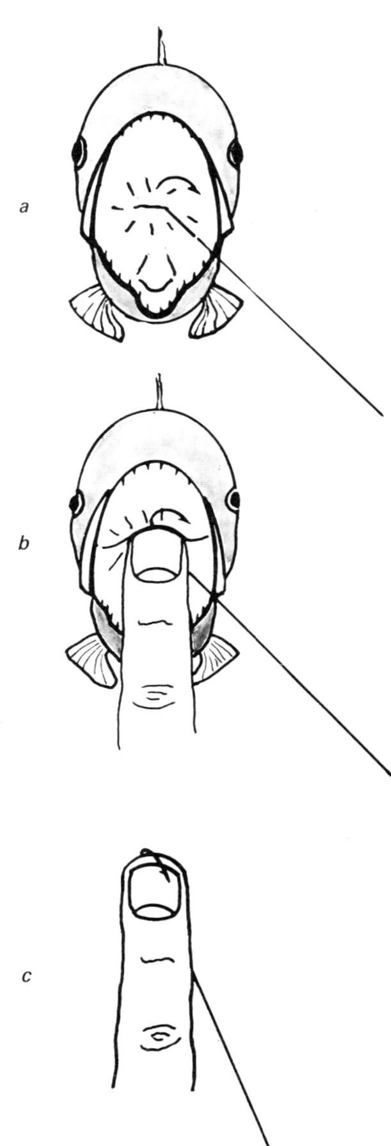

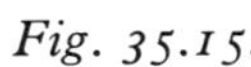
Fig. 35.15.

The Finger Disgorger (for game fish)

If you have no disgorger handy when a fish has swallowed the hook, don't break the leader. Your finger will serve as a substitute.

Fig. 35.15.*a* represents a view down the fish's throat. The hook is right at the back of the throat.

1. Having made sure the fish is dead, slide your forefinger down the leader into the bend of the hook (Fig. 15.*b*) so that the point of the hook is on the fingernail.
2. Push your finger further down the fish's throat, taking the hook with it, and then ease backwards – still keeping the point of the hook on the fingernail and keeping the leader taut with the other fingers. The hook will come out as shown in Fig. 15.*c*.

Care must be taken to avoid ripping the back and sides of your finger on the fish's teeth. If you intend to make a habit of unhooking fish in this way, wrap your forefinger in adhesive tape.

The Buller Pike Gag and the Baker 'Hookout' Disgorger

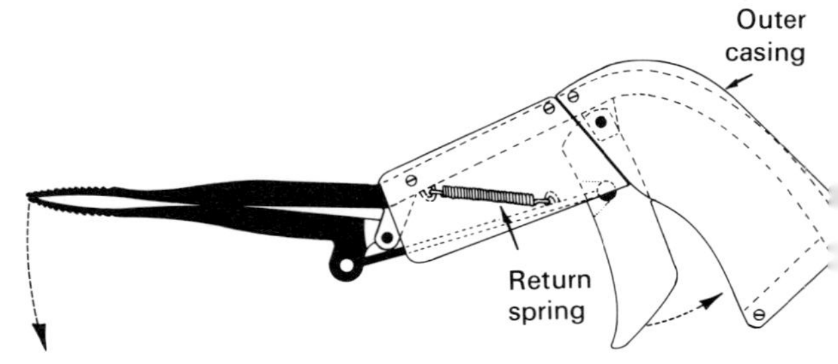

Fig. 35.16. The Buller pike gag.

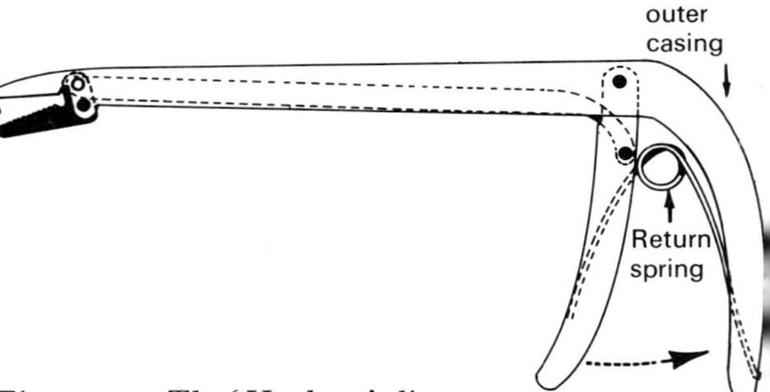

Fig. 35.17. The 'Hookout' disgorger.

Giving quarter to a pike is rather a novel idea. Traditionally, pike have been treated brutally simply because of their reputation and brutish appearance. But times have changed. Nowadays the pike fisherman seldom wants to kill all the fish he catches. He keeps one for the table, perhaps, and tries to return the others unharmed.

We write 'tries to' advisedly, because to return a pike to the water unharmed is not as easy as it sounds. The hook is usually embedded behind rows of razor-sharp teeth and the angler is faced with the problem of removing it.

Almost invariably this unhooking operation is performed with the aid of the conventional gag and disgorger, both of which should long ago have been confined to some angling museum. The gag has to be pushed sideways into the pike's mouth and then screwed round a full ninety degrees before it can function properly as a gag. Inevitably, the forked ends – *set nearly two inches apart in the closed position* – tear through the skin and bone of the pike's jaw. It is extremely difficult to use on a live fish reluctant to open its mouth. Even after a pike has been knocked on the head, the forcing open of its jaws with such a tool can be a hazardous operation, and many an angler has the scars to prove it.

The disgorger (like the gag, of Victorian origin) offers an angler the opportunity to inflict the maximum injury, for with it he can hack, stab, slice, wrench and slash – and indeed it is very difficult to avoid doing so. It is just possible for an expert to gag a pike and disgorge a hook with these infamous tools, but the majority of anglers use them at the risk of injury both to the pike and to themselves.

The Buller gag (drawn to show the working principles for anglers who wish to make one for themselves) changes the whole picture. This gag can be slipped between a pike's clenched jaws and open them instantly to the required extent. While pressure is maintained on the trigger of the gag with one hand, the other hand is free to handle the disgorger. This disgorger, the 'Hookout' it is called, is produced by an American company. It is both efficient and humane, and will remove a hook from a pike's mouth in a few seconds.

The photographs show a treble hook being extracted from the throat of a 15 lb Loch Lomond pike caught on ledgered dead-bait. The authors have done a great deal of fishing together, for many species of fish, in many places. They have found the Buller gag and the 'Hookout' disgorger to be as effective in salt water as in fresh.

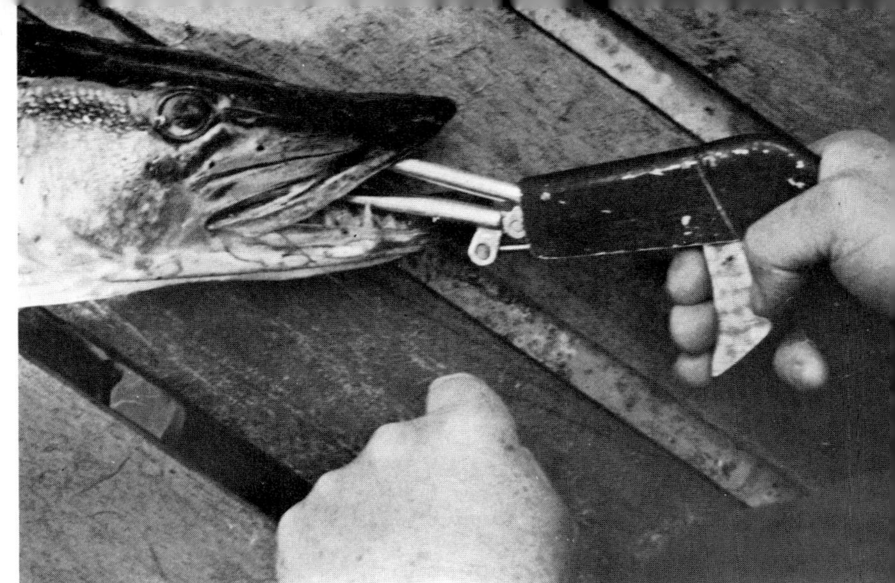

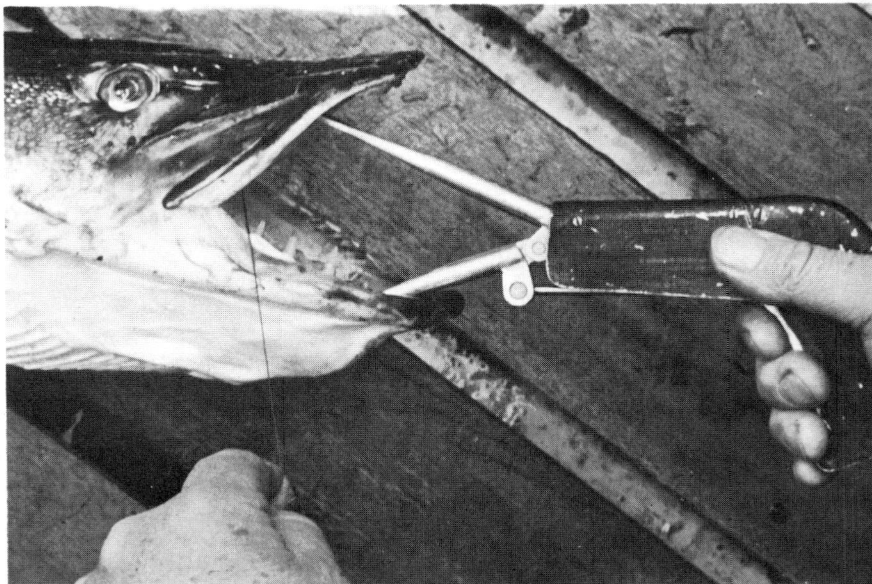

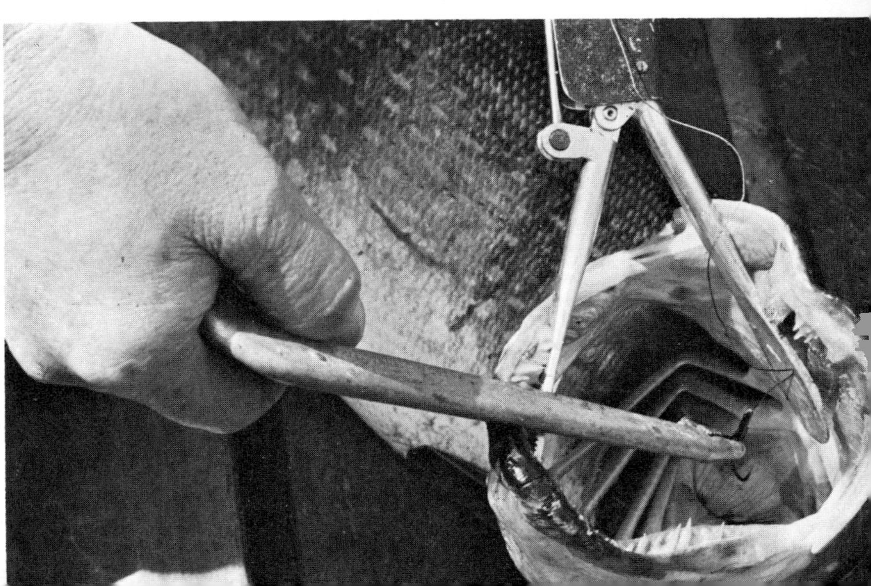

36 · Knots

Never allow some well-meaning friend to assemble your tackle for you. Never, never, never. *Always* do it yourself. Then if a rod-ring has been missed, or there is a turn of line round the rod and the line won't shoot (most irritating at night, when you can't see what is happening); if the reel falls off when a fish is running; if a knot slips in the best fish of the season – you have only yourself to blame.

A knot is a very personal matter. When buying a new fly line never let anyone splice on the backing for you or tie the backing to the reel. A salmon fly-fisherman of our acquaintance lost thirty yards of new Wet-cel line, plus a huge springer, because the backing splice (although professionally tied) drew as he was playing the fish.

Such grisly misfortune may happen only once, but that is once too often. First, get an experienced angler to show you the right way to assemble your tackle and tie the knots you need, and then – *do it all yourself.*

Tying knots in nylon monofilament – a caution

Always lubricate nylon, by moistening in the mouth, before tightening a knot and carefully snugging it down. Moistening the nylon overcomes friction and helps to 'set' the knot.

The Water Knot

From time to time all anglers need to tie two lengths of nylon together. If one of the lengths is conveniently short (a few yards) we recommend the water knot. It is also an excellent knot for tying a made-up leader containing one or more droppers.

Hold the ends of the nylon together so that they overlap some 10 in. (6 in. if a dropper is not required) as shown in Fig. 36.1.*a*. Bring the paired thumbs and index fingers together (Fig. 1.*b*) until a loop springs into place (Fig. 1.*c*). For this, the right hand should be held slightly closer to the body than the left. Grip the loop with the left thumb and fore-finger, as shown in Fig. 1.*d*.

Free the lengths of nylon held in the right hand and make an overhand knot by pulling the end through the loop from behind (see arrow in Fig. 1.*d*). Make two more turns. At this point the picture in Fig. 1.*e* will emerge. Take the ends of the nylon between thumbs and index fingers and pull tight. The resultant knot will then form as shown in Fig. 1.*f*.

In our experience this knot will survive all other popular knots when pulled to

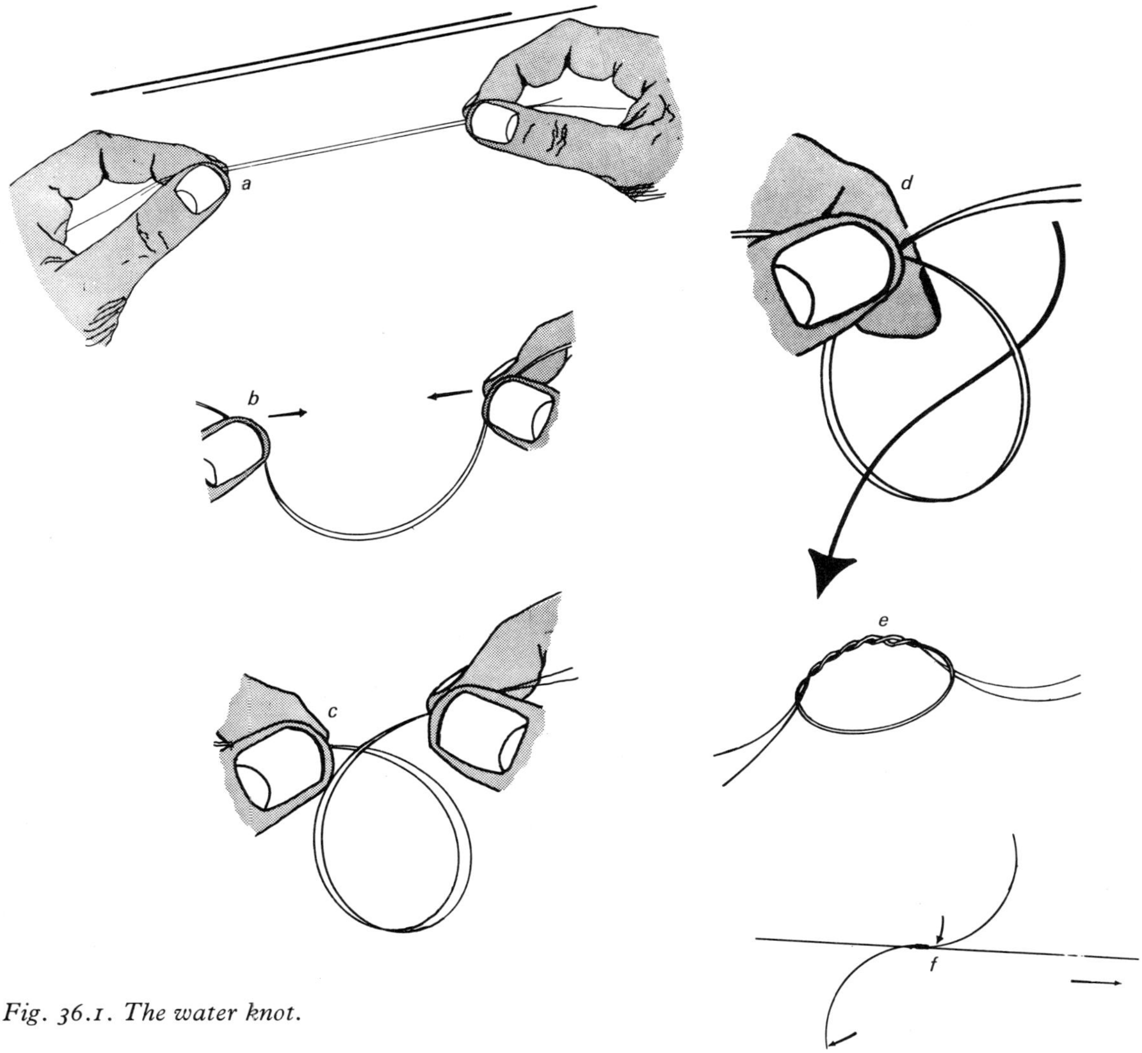

Fig. 36.1. The water knot.

Fig. 36.2.a.

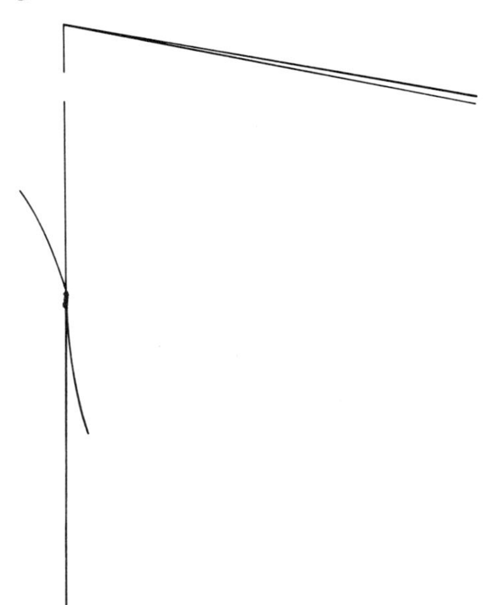

Fig. 36.2.b.

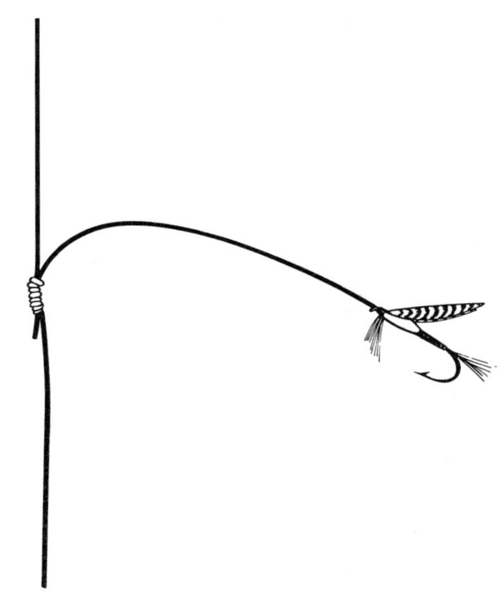

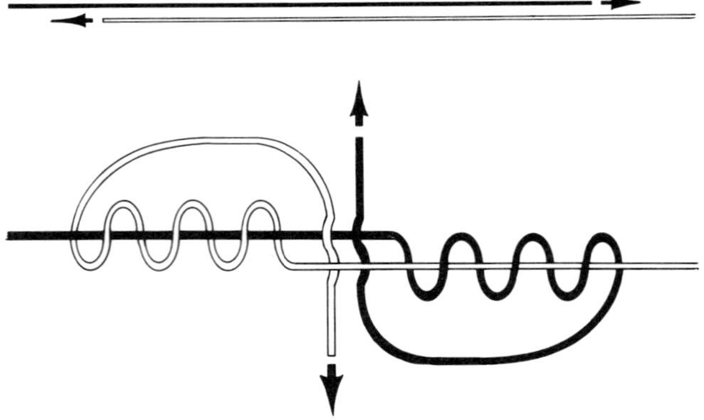

Fig. 36.3. Three-turn blood knot, for joining two thicknesses of nylon. The blood knot has only one advantage over the water knot: it is less bulky (see leaders for reservoir angling, p. 267).

breaking point. Tied with two turns, it was first described by Dame Juliana Berners in *A Treatyse of Fysshynge wyth an Angle* (1496) – the first printed work on angling. Nylon, a slippery material, requires an extra turn – as shown in the diagram.

When the knot is used for making a dropper, the fly is fastened to the stalk which runs towards the rod (Fig. 36.2.*a*). So tied, the lie of the dropper opposes the pull of the line, and the fly will tend to stand out from the leader, as shown in Fig. 2.*b*.

For made-up, tapered, nylon leaders for greased-line salmon fishing, or for sea-trout or brown trout fishing, this is the best knot. Many salmon fishermen miss chances of catching fish because they do not change their leader thickness when they change the size of fly. A small fly tied to thick nylon will attract few fish – even though the size of the fly is right for the prevailing conditions. This is not because the salmon is afraid of the nylon, but because the fly is not 'working' attractively. The thickness of a salmon leader point should suit the size of the fly it carries. If the greased-line fisherman goes down from, say, a size 6 hook to a size 8, or size 10 hook, he *must* go down in nylon thickness if the smaller fly is to appear attractive.

Exactly the same principle applies to the trout fisherman.

Apart from its strength, the ease of tying a water knot puts it ahead of all others at the waterside. A foot and a half of lighter nylon to suit a smaller fly can be added to a leader in a matter of seconds.

Tying on a Spade-End Hook (method A)

Most anglers who attempt to tie on spade-end hooks for the first time are possessed by a sudden fit of parsimony. Fearful of wasting a few inches of nylon, they try to use the minimum amount. This makes the task much more difficult than it need be. Also, it tends to waste time. Time is much more valuable than nylon.

Hold the hook, point up, in the left hand. Fold back a generous six inches of nylon (Fig. 36.4.*a*).

Grip the nylon against the shank of the hook (Fig. 4.*b*). For ease of tying ensure that the line coming to the left hand is kept under tension.

With the right hand, take the free end of the nylon round and round the shank, securing each turn by dropping the second finger of the left hand (Fig. 4.*c*).

After completing six or seven turns, pass the end of the nylon through the loop (Fig. 4.*d*).

While maintaining a grip with the left hand, pull the mainline in the direction of the arrow until the knot pulls tight (Fig. 4.*e*).

Slide the knot along the shank until it reaches the broad spade end. Give the mainline nylon a final tug with the right hand, while resisting this pull from the the opposite end by holding the nylon stub between the teeth. Finally, trim off the nylon stub.

When tying tiny spade end hooks (sizes 16, 18, 20), it is difficult to operate the securing finger properly unless the tyer has very small hands. Catch each loop, as it is laid, with a pecking motion of the left thumb and forefinger.

Tying on a Spade-End Hook (method B)

In our opinion, this method is superior to method A. It produces a reliable, neat, shank-hugging knot which is no more difficult to tie than the other; indeed, in poor light it is easier. It can be used prior to a fishing trip for snooding-up spade-end hooks to lengths of nylon, or at the waterside for tying a hook direct to the mainline.

Put a three-and-a-half inch diameter loop in the end of the line (or, in the case of snooding, at one end of a length of nylon), leaving a two-inch overhang.

Lay the loop along the shank of the hook

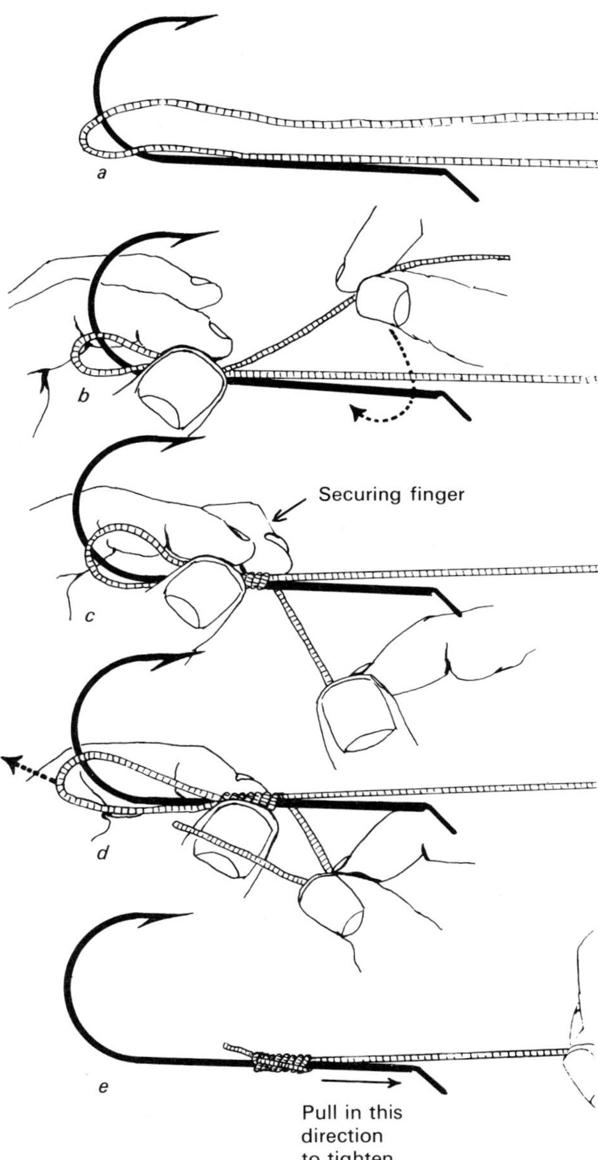

Fig. 36.4. Tying on a spade-end hook (method A).

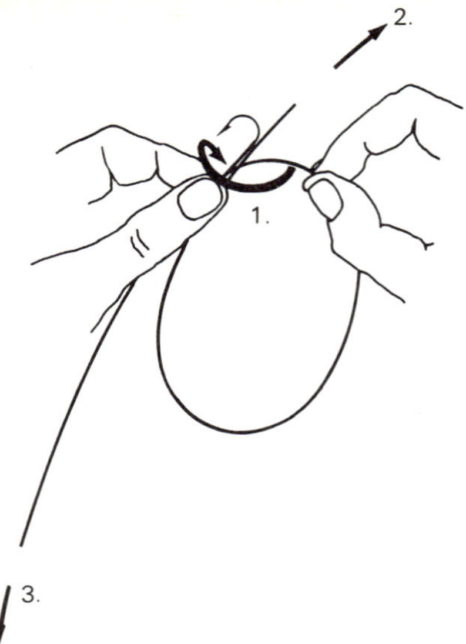

Fig. 36.5. Method B.

(see diagram), gripping the nylon against the shank with thumb and index finger of the left hand.

With the right hand, start to wind turns clockwise round the shank in the direction of arrow No. 1—*keeping each turn hard up against the left thumb.*

Make eight or ten turns altogether, taking care not to wind these on too tightly.

When the last turn is made, pull the end of the nylon in the direction of arrow No. 2; gently at first, then firmly.

Since the knot forms on the shank some distance from the spade-end, it must be slid close up to the spade before being snugged down. This is achieved by pulling on the line in one direction (arrow 3), while pulling on the end of the nylon in the opposite direction (arrow 2).

The spade-end knot is equally effective for tying an eyed hook to the mainline, the bulge forming the eye of the hook being treated as the spade-end. If hooks with upturned or downturned eyes are used, the mainline nylon is passed through the eye before the knot is tied. But in the case of a *straight-eyed* hook the eye is by-passed, and the hook treated exactly as though it were a spade-end hook, otherwise it will stick out at an angle to the line.

The Needle Knot

Over the years, various methods of attaching a leader to a fly line have been devised. None has been completely satisfactory. Short-comings in traditional methods become acute when an angler uses a leader which is longer than his rod. The lumpishness of the join impedes the smooth flow of the line through the rod rings. Prior to the needle knot, the changing of a leader often meant careful knot picking and re-tying.

From an idea which originated in America and was passed on to him by Don Neish, Richard Walker developed a knot known as the needle knot, so-called simply because it was tied with the aid of a needle. It was used successfully during the first year of fishing on Grafham Reservoir.

The knot has these advantages:

1. It is very strong.
2. It passes easily through the rod rings, and allows the use of a leader which is much longer than the rod.
3. There is no wake on the surface caused by a bulky knot when the fly is retrieved.
4. The centres of the leader and the fly line are exactly in line.

With a needle that is some ·003 in. to ·005 in. thicker than the nylon, perforate the end of the fly line so that the point comes out at the side of the line about $\frac{1}{8}$ in. to $\frac{3}{16}$ in. from the end. Leave the needle stuck in the line with about a quarter of an inch of the point emerging.

Apply the flame of a match or lighter to the eye end of the needle, until the line starts to bend.

Take the flame away and blow the needle cool.

Remove the needle.

Take approximately 2 yards of 24 lb B.S. nylon and point one end of it. This is done by cutting the nylon obliquely with a razor blade.

Pass this end of the nylon into the hole at the end of the fly line and out at the side. Pull a length of it through and take four or five turns round the fly line. Bring the end back and lay parallel (Fig. 36.6.*a*).

Take a turn in the opposite direction to the turns already made (Fig. 6.*b*).

Lay on the other turns – taut, but not too tight. Continue until all original turns are uncoiled (Fig. 6.*c*).

Snug down and tighten the knot. Cut off loose end of nylon (Fig. 6.*d*). Varnish over knot, and also apply varnish to the end of the fly line where the nylon emerges.

As a refinement a taper can be built up with tying silk, and then varnished (Fig. 6.*e*). This is not strictly necessary, but it allows a smoother passage of the knot through the rod rings. Alternatively, the end of the fly line can be frayed in advance to create a smooth taper, and finished off with tying silk. An ideal varnish for this purpose is 'Vycoat'.

Now that two yards of heavy nylon has been attached to the end of the fly line (one yard is better for river work), a suitable tapered leader can be added, either with a blood knot or a water knot (see p. 405). This two-yard section will last for several seasons. If not greased it acts as a sinking tip on a floating line, and ensures a good turn-over when cast. The section between the heavy nylon and the fly can be anything from one to three yards.

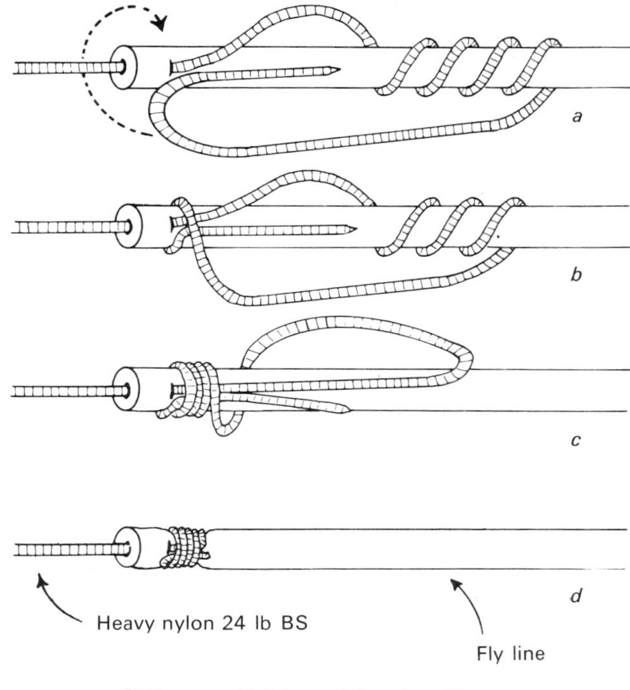

Fig. 36.6. The needle knot.

Variants of the Half-blood Knot

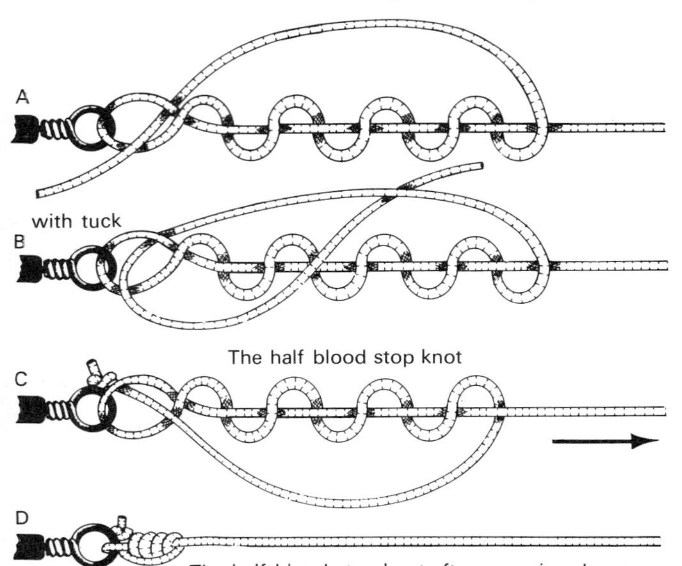

◁ *Fig. 36.7.*

The Turle Knot

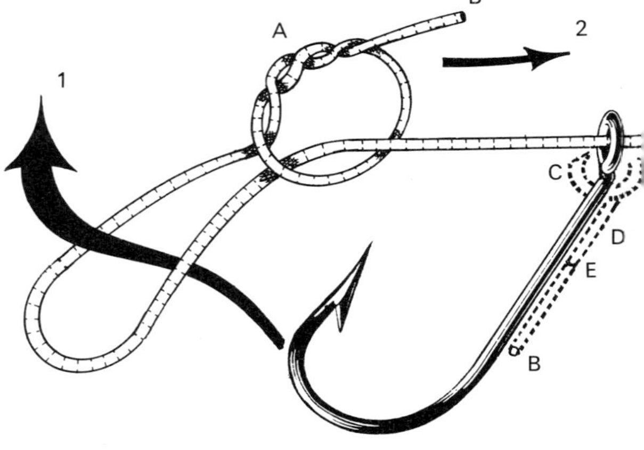

Fig. 36.8. Turle knot.

The half-blood knot (A) or half-blood tuck knot (B) is used to tie nylon to hook, swivel or lead. It is *not* suitable for tying *braided terylene* or *braided nylon*. For these materials a hangman's jam knot should be used. (See p. 416.)

Notes on the Half-Blood Stop Knot

Pass the nylon through the eye of the swivel, then put a simple overhand knot in the end of the nylon before tying the half-blood as in C. Hold the stop-knot against the eye of the swivel before tightening in direction of arrow. The knot tightens as shown in D. Des Brennan, Ireland's famous sea angler, prefers this type of knot to any other. (His own version requires the nylon to be passed *twice* through the eye of the swivel.)

The turle knot (Fig. 37.8) was first described by R. B. Marston, editor of the *Fishing Gazette*. It is a secure knot that grips the shank of the hook, and is probably the dry fly fisherman's first choice for tying a dry fly to a leader.

1. Tighten knot A.
2. Pass hook/fly through loop in direction of arrow 1.
3. Draw loop up to eye of knot in direction of arrow 2.
4. Hold end B. inside loop, parallel to shank of hook, and draw loop tight round hook just below eye (dotted line C).

End of nylon (B) should now lie along hook (dotted line D).

5. Cut off end leaving short stub (at E).

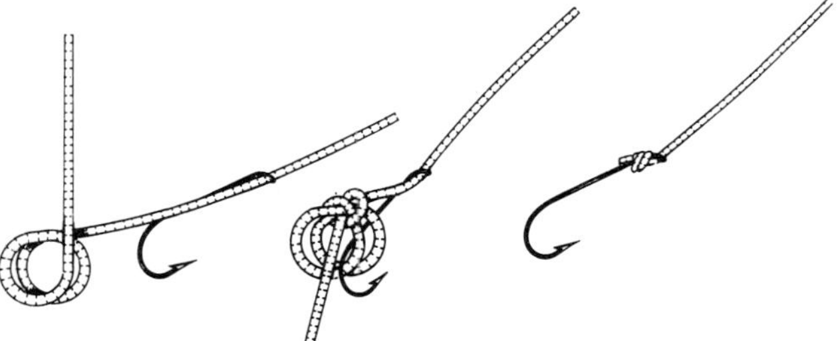

Fig. 36.9. The two-circle turle knot.

1. Thread hook or fly, and slide up cast out of the way. Make first circle 6 to 8 inches from the point; overlay the second circle.
2. Holding the circles with the thumb and forefinger, tie a slip knot as shown. Tighten the slip knot and push the end of the monofil, and then the hook or fly, through the two circles.
3. Pull on standing part, and circles – close one after the other. See that circles close round neck of hook or fly.

Figure-of-Eight Knot

Although the needle knot (p. 409) is undoubtedly the neatest knot for joining fly line and leader, the old fashioned figure-of-eight is sometimes preferable. This is when the angler wishes to make a number of leader changes to suit changes in size of fly or lure.

Such changes can of course be made simply by replacing the 'point' in a made-up tapered leader with one of different thickness, using a blood knot or (better) a water knot. But some anglers, wishing to avoid leader knots – especially when fishing at night – prefer either a knotless tapered leader or a length of level nylon in which a blood bight loop has been tied. (See p. 414.)

Fig. 36.10.

For joining fly line (arrow A) to blood loop in leader (arrow B) the figure-of-eight knot is better than any other: simple both to tie and untie. *Note:* the stalk of the line does not stick out at an angle but lies in the same plane as the leader, thus reducing drag.

Knot for Tying Nylon Direct to a Wire Leader

Because of the meagre range available, most commercial stranded-wire pike leaders are unsuitable for the job in hand. Even so, many anglers are content to use them – rather than suffer the inconvenience of fiddling about with loose coils of stranded wire. Some make up their own leaders with single wire. A few, anxious to use stranded wire for heavy work, make up their leaders by joining the wire to a swivel by means of a soldered or ferruled loop. In this instance, the two ends of the swivel bring wire and nylon together and prevent the nylon from being cut by the wire.

But why use a swivel? At best, its breaking

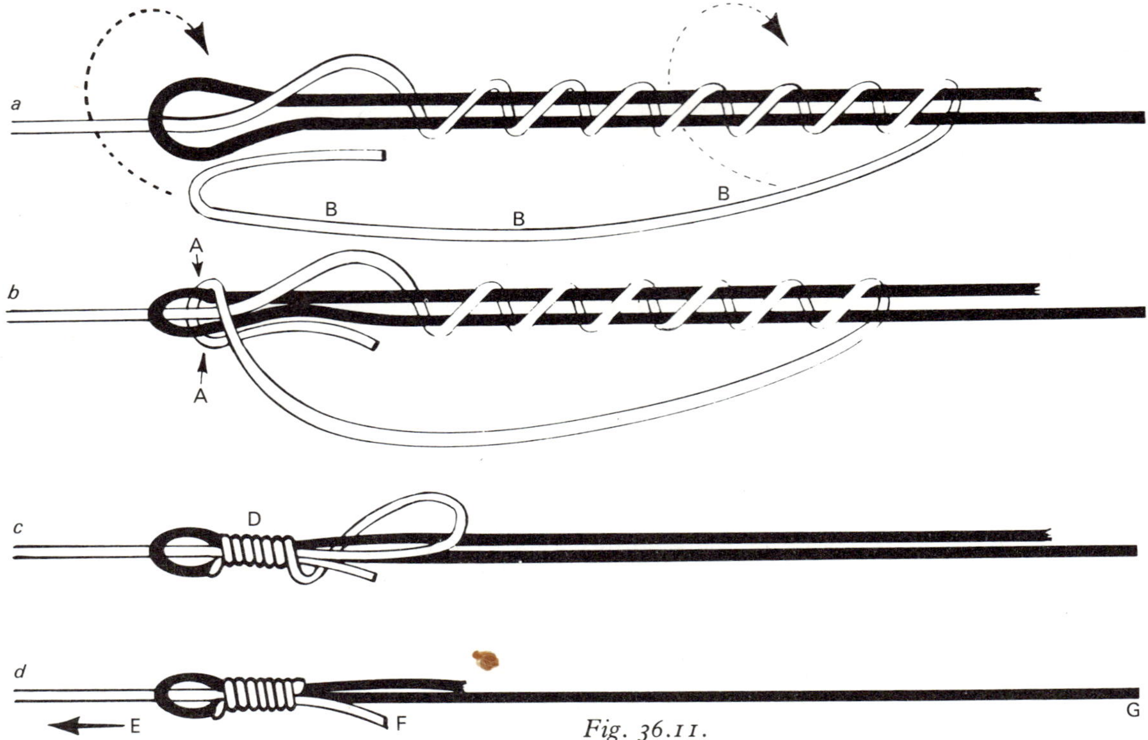

Fig. 36.11.

strength is suspect. In this case, its only function is to serve as a link which joins (yet, in a sense, separates) two unsympathetic materials.

A soldered or ferruled loop, or an unwanted swivel can be avoided by adapting the needle knot described on p. 409.

Make an open loop at the end of a five foot length of stranded wire, by bending back five or six inches (Fig. 36.11.*a*). The wire is shown in black.

Pass the end of the nylon (shown in white) into the wire loop from behind and pull through about twelve inches.

Twist the nylon round the wire for seven or eight turns, then bring back and lay parallel for about two inches (Fig. 11.*a*).

While gripping this parallel piece against the wire loop at AA with the left thumb and index finger (Fig. 11.*b*), take the line BBB round the back of the wire with the right thumb and index finger, as shown by the dotted arrows in Fig. 11.*a*.

By repeating this operation, the original turns gradually uncoil and new coils are formed close to the left thumb at D (Fig. 11.*c*). It helps if the left thumb and index finger grip each new turn as it is completed.

When the coil is complete, pull the nylon in the direction of arrow E (Fig. 11.*d*), until the last loop is pulled in. Snug down and tidy all the loops forming the new coil before tightening the knot by an opposing pull on E and F.

Finally, test the knot for strength by pulling on E and G.

The Grip Knot

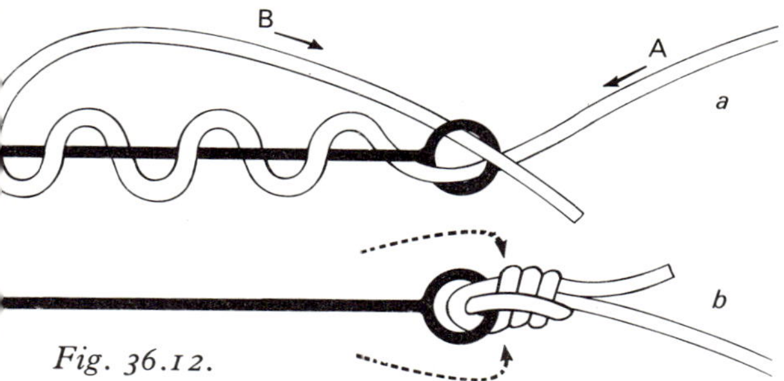

Fig. 36.12.

We are indebted to Mr Westmorland, of Wakefield, for details of a useful knot for tying nylon to eyed hooks, swivels or spinners: the grip knot.

Pass the nylon through the eye in the direction of arrow A (Fig. 36.12.*a*). Take it behind the shank and proceed to wind three loose coils. Make the nylon re-enter the eye from the opposite side to the first entry (arrow B). Pass the coils over the eye (Fig. 12.*b*) before snugging tight.

The double loop through the eye holds the hook with a surprisingly firm grip. Salmon anglers who fish with a bunch of lobworms, will find this knot as good as, if not superior to, any other.

Fly line/backing splice

Crimp end of nylon with pliers, tease out end (last $\frac{3}{4}$ in.) of fly line with needle point

Monofil nylon backing
Crimped end
Fly line
Teased out end

Braided nylon backing
Fly line

Splice tied at A leaving double lengths of tying silk (well waxed) whipped from A to B and back to A then A to C and back to A or with single length of tying silk, whip splice A to B to C and then back to A

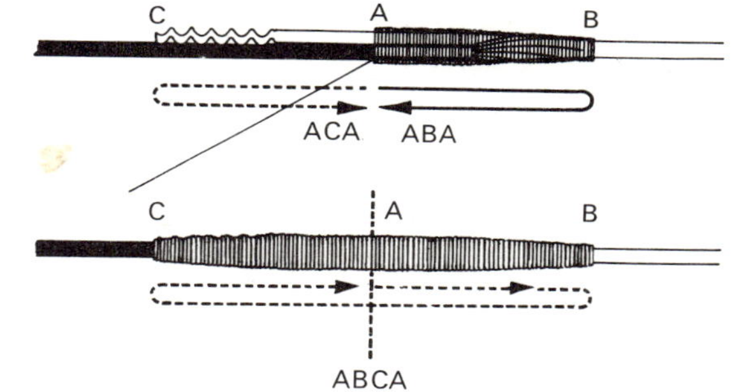

Method of making a whip finish

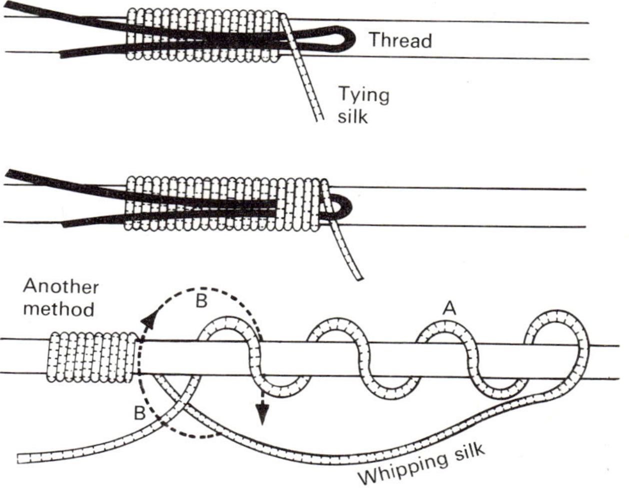

Wind on loose coils A
Wind whipping silk on fairly tightly in direction B

Fig. 36.13.

The Blood Bight Knot

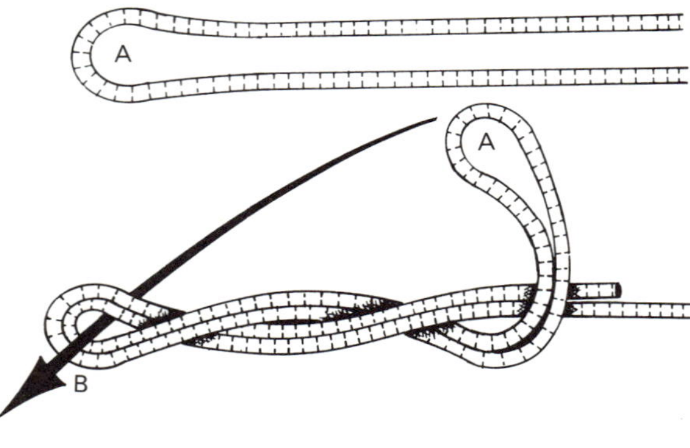

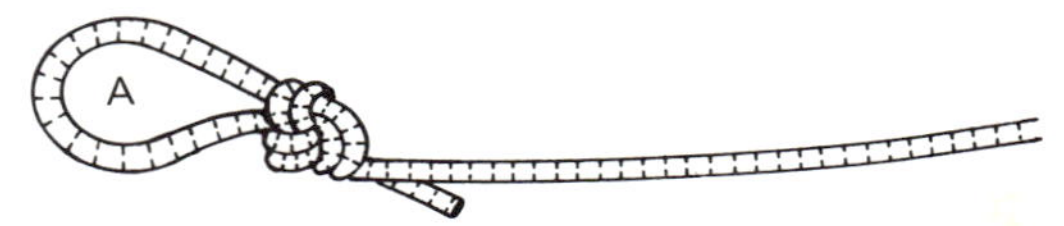

Fig. 36.14.

1. Bend end of cast back on itself to form loop A.
2. Twist loop A round cast as shown to form loop B.
3. Pass loop A through loop B.
4. Pull knot tight and cut off free end.

A loop for a nylon fly-leader. The line is attached to the loop with a figure-of-eight knot (see p. 411).

Finishing a Whipping

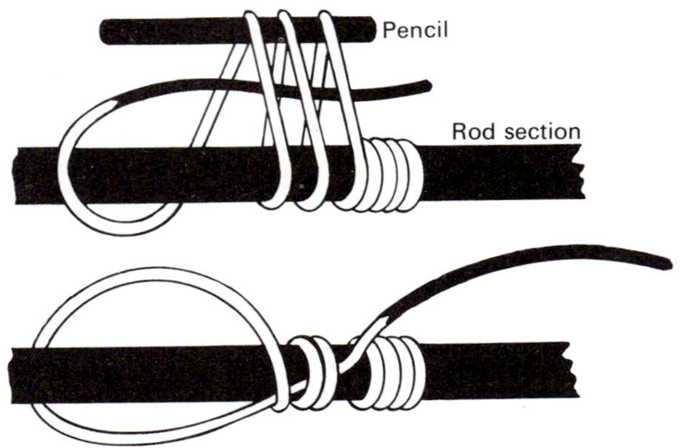

Fig. 36.15.

The best methods of finishing a whipping are those described on p. 413; but the following very simple method will suit the novice and help him to remember how the job is done.

Having come to within four or five turns of the finish of a whipping, hold a pencil in the left hand (the same hand already holds the rod section) half an inch or so above the rod.

Take the last three turns round both pencil and rod section. Pass the end of the tying silk back through the turns. Slip the thumb and index finger of the left hand over the turns and withdraw the pencil with the right hand. Pull the end of the silk gently in the vertical plane until the coils lie against the rod. Snug the coils into position before tightening. Trim off the emergent end of the tying silk. Finally, give the whipping two coats of varnish.

Sliding Stop Knot

For use when fishing a sliding float.

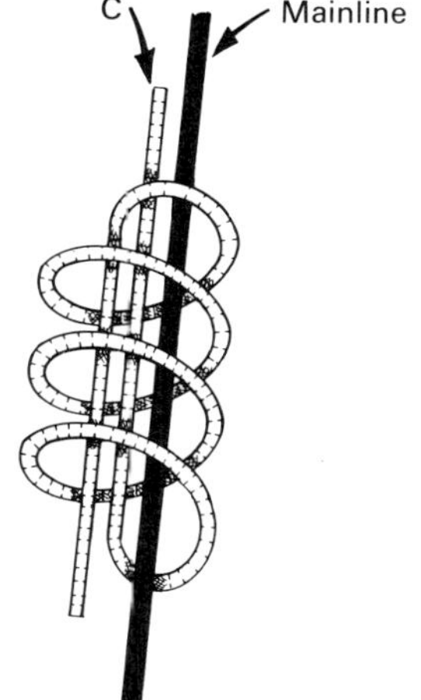

Fig. 36.16.

To tie the stop-knot, lay slip of nylon alongside the main line with the end at point C, then proceed to lay coils as indicated in the diagram. For ease of tying, hold each loop as it is formed between thumb and index finger of the left hand. Pull tight, so that a determined pressure is needed to slip the knot up or down the line. Trim off, leaving $\frac{1}{8}$ in. stub ends.

The Bowline

KNOT SAVES MAN FROM QUICKSAND
[Headline in national newspaper]

'It was then that I remembered my training as a naval rating. I tied a bowline round my waist and was winched out. It was 90 minutes of my life I will never forget.' Police said: 'He is lucky to be alive.'

He *was* lucky. The bowline should have been tied in the rope before the rope was thrown. The trapped man might have had frozen fingers, or been on the verge of unconsciousness and quite unable to tie the knot himself. In which case, the rope would have been useless.

Learn how to tie this knot in case you find yourself in a similar predicament. Never throw a drowning man a rope without first tying a bowline in the end of it. A bowline is a loop that does not slip. So long as the man in the water can get his arms and shoulders through the loop he is safe.

The bowline is the best knot for tying a boat's painter to a ring-bolt.

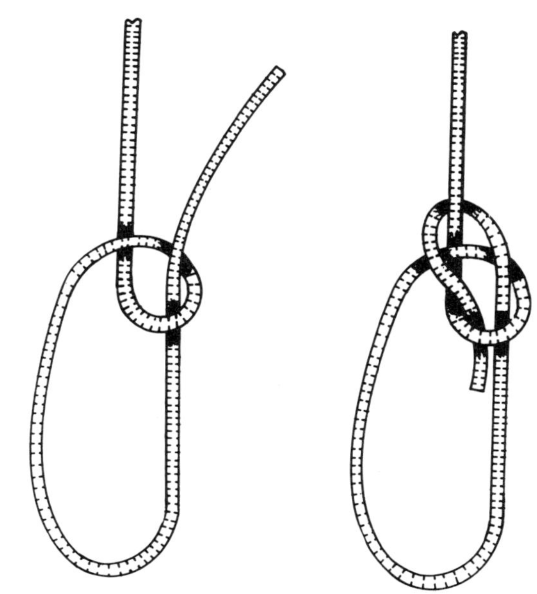

Fig. 36.17.

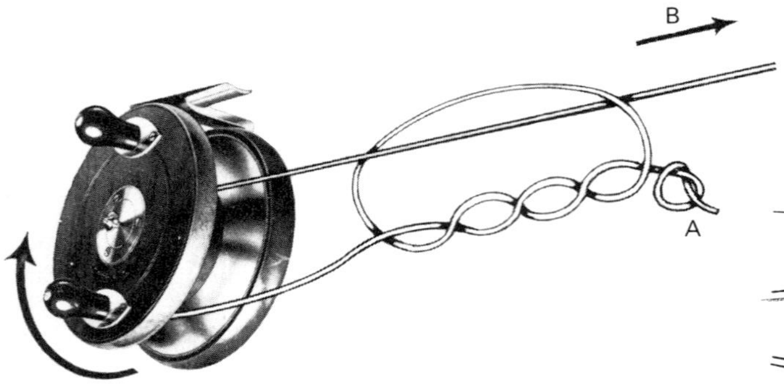

Fig. 36.17. A safe method of attaching a nylon line or backing to a reel. Pull both parts of the knot tight and trim at A. Wet the tightened knot before sliding it back towards the reel. Finally, tighten the line firmly round the drum of the reel by holding the reel handles firmly with left hand and pulling the nylon in the direction of B.

The Hangman's Jam Knot

Elsewhere in this book we have referred to the desirability of using a hangman's jam knot when joining a line of braided terylene or braided nylon to a swivel or tackle. If one of the popular monofilament knots is used on either of these materials (which are of the hollow core type) the line breaks far below the maker's claimed strength, usually an inch or so back from the knot. When such a break occurs it is said to be through 'strangulation'. This is probably because the strands within the braid do not take an equal share of the load.

The pike fisherman, especially the livebaiter, often prefers a braided nylon line because of its good floating properties. In the near future he will probably change to a bubble-type fly line for livebaiting, as this line will float all day without dressing. The bubble line, too, will need to be attached with a hangman's jam knot.

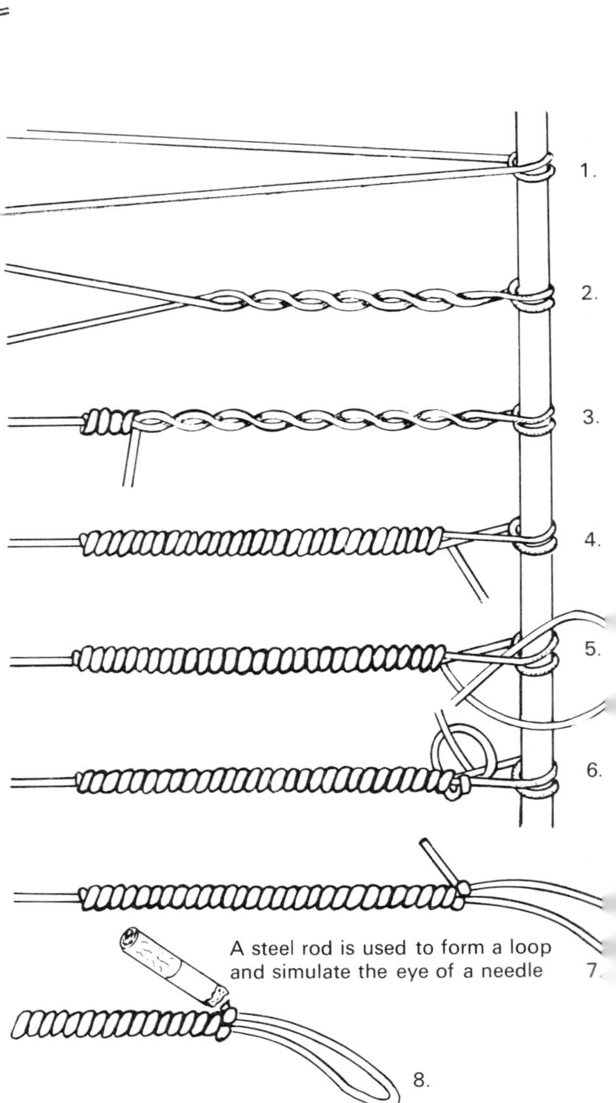

Fig. 36.18.
1 The braided Terylene is passed twice round the rod to form a long loop.
2 A tight wind is made for 2 in. back from loop.
3 Short length is doubled back and bound tightly back towards loop.
4 Tight winding is taken nearly up to loop.
5 A half-hitch is formed on right side of loop to form a jam hitch.
6 The same is done on the left side of loop.
7 This is drawn tight and end cut off.
8 Short fibres where end is cut are fused with a touch of cigarette.

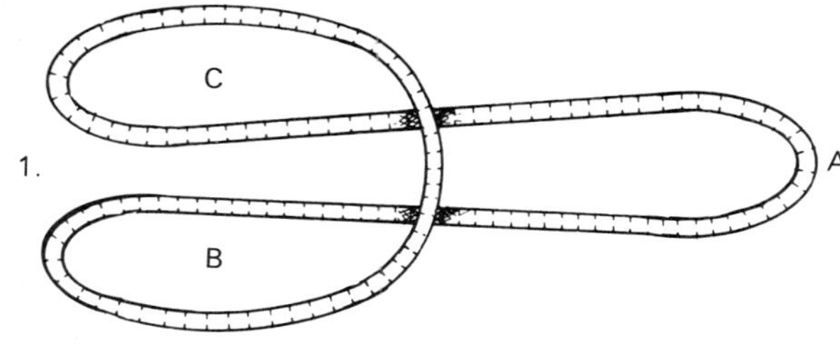

The 'Bucket' Knot

A rather amusing knot for fastening two handles to any container that has a rim or sloping sides: e.g. a jam-jar, or a pail that has lost its handle. It is a knot of special interest to juvenile hunters of the minnow, or anglers who wish to fashion a make-shift portable livebait container from an old bucket.

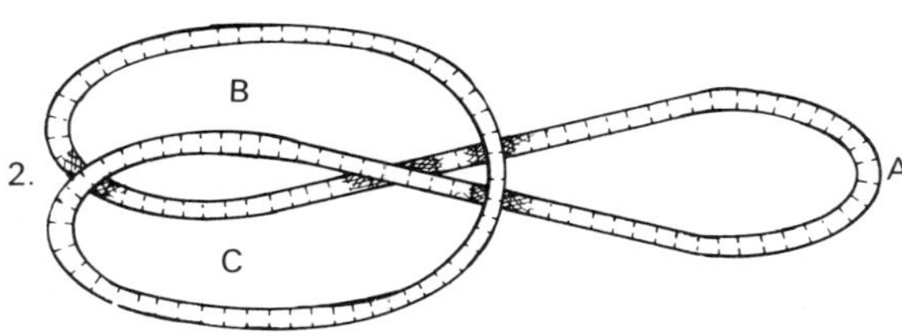

Directions

1. Knot or splice a length of cord at A. and arrange three loops as shown. *Note:* In the completed knot, loop A. will be one of the two handles.
2. Place B over C.
3. Place C over B leaving hole D.
4. Take loop E down through loop A underneath C and B and bring it up through hole D to form the second handle.
5. Bring loops F and G together *underneath the knot* and turn the knot flat on its side away from you. It is important to *flatten* the knot as much as possible, so that the strands are running exactly as shown in the diagram. This can be done by untwisting the turns that have formed in the handle loops. *Note:* The centre of the completed knot will be at H.
6. Bend loop F *backwards underneath and to the right*. Arrange the knot around the centre at H.
7. Place container in hole H and tighten knot.

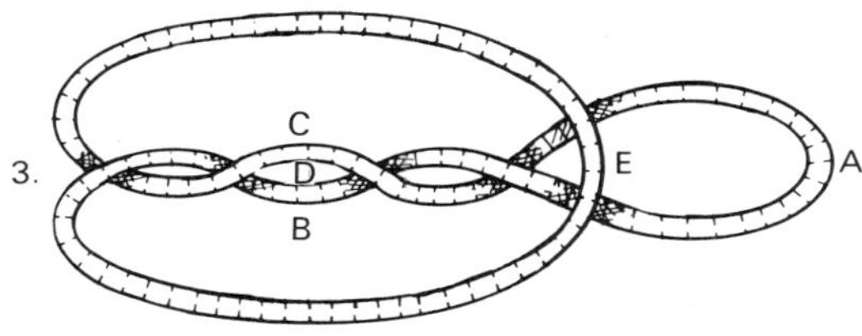

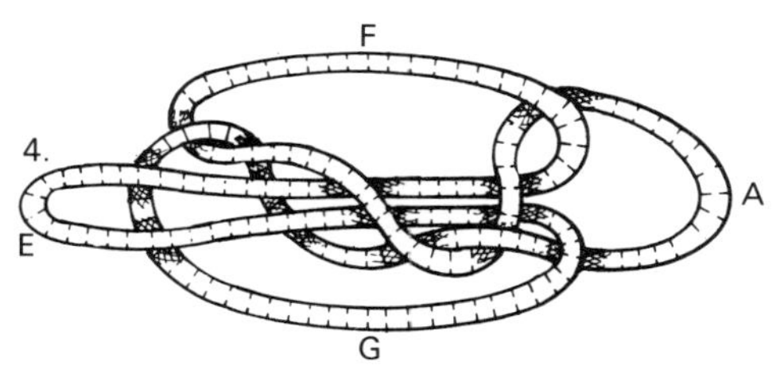

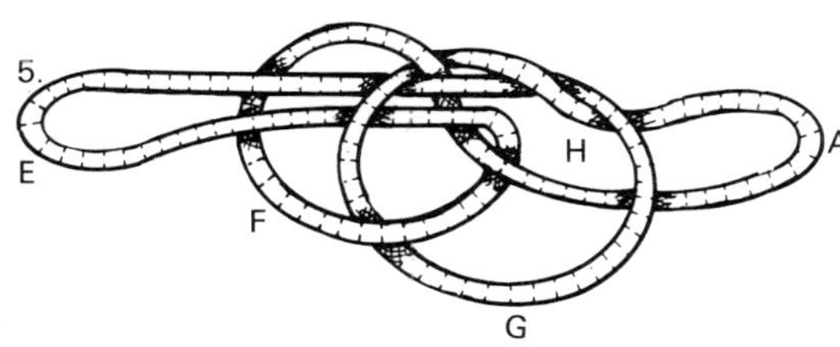

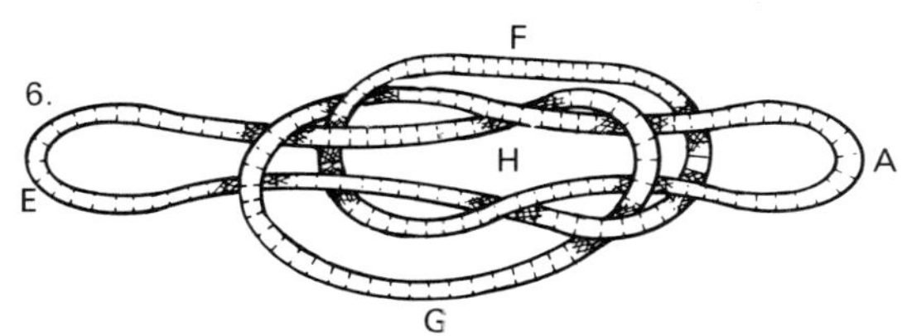

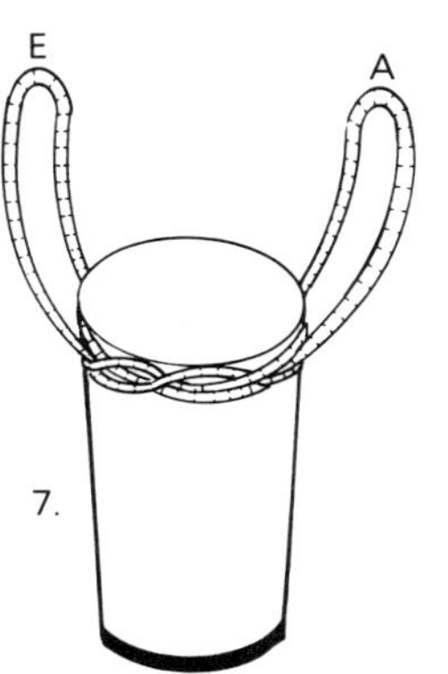

Fig. 36.19.

Knot for Tying Stewart and Pennell Tackles

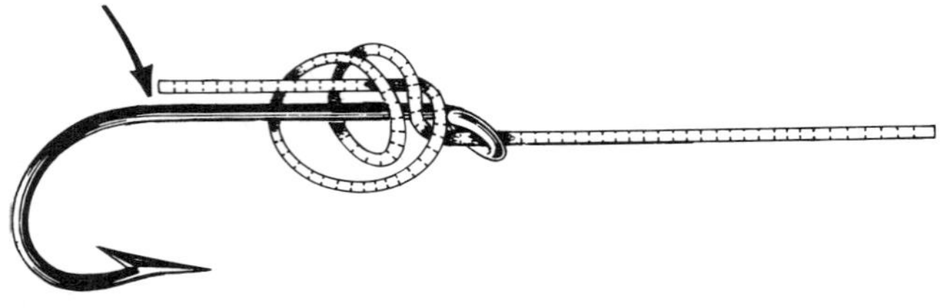

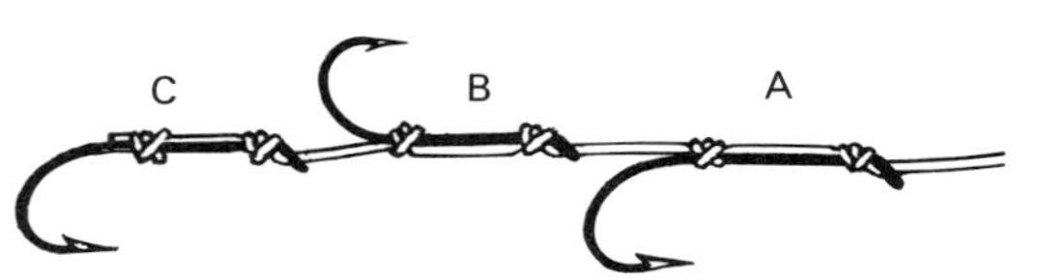

Fig. 36.20. Tie on hook A first, leaving sufficient nylon to tie on B and C.

Make your own Stewart and Pennell tackles. These are simple to tie – indeed they can be made up at the riverside – and will be stronger and cheaper than any you can buy. Use the knot shown in the diagram.

Note: Eyeless hooks whipped to monofilament nylon – as in the bought article – have an unfortunate habit of 'drawing'. Tackles made as shown may break, but they will never draw.

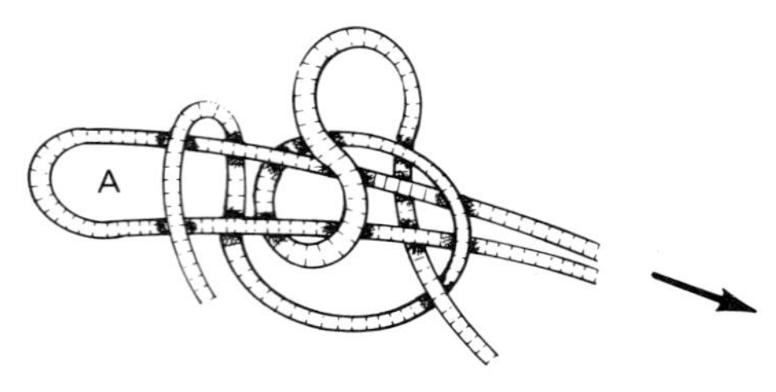

Fig. 36.21. Unravel a tangle by pulling loop marked A in direction of the arrow.

A Tangled Line

The simplified diagram shows a corner of a tangle. Tangles in line or leader are a frequent occurrence particularly at night. *Don't* despair. Most tangles are easy to unravel – once you know the secret. It is this: almost all tangles are caused by *loops* of line getting caught up. (See the loop marked A.) Work round the tangle, freeing these loops. Provided the line is not pulled too tight, there is no tangle that will not unravel in a few minutes. The golden rules are: patience; *don't pull*; find the *loops* and free them one by one. When you have freed all the loops, the tangle will be undone.

An Irresistible Compound

To make all the fishes in a pond to come to thy hand.

Tak Palma Christi and frankandsence, and medel hem togedir, and put hit in a fome clowte, and holde the pouder in thi finger that a gold ryng is upon, and wasch thy hond in every corner of the pont, fisches wolle come to thi honde.

From a MS on vellum, c.1400 – quoted by ROBERT BLAKEY, *Historical Sketches of the Angling Literature* (1856).

Match fishermen care little about the weather. Snug under their umbrellas, like a row of mushrooms, they fish the hours away – intent only on beating the other fellow (Photograph: Angling News Services).

37 · Baits and Baiting

GROUNDBAITING AND GROUNDBAITING DEVICES

There are four ways in which groundbaiting helps an angler to catch fish:

1. It stimulates their appetites.
2. It attracts them into the fishing area.
3. Once they have been attracted into the fishing area, further groundbaiting will keep them there.
4. By providing the fish with easy pickings, groundbaiting tends to dull their protective mechanism and makes them less suspicious of the hookbait – especially when this closely resembles the groundbait, as it almost always should.

Since groundbaiting offers all these advantages, a novice might be forgiven for thinking that it automatically assures him of success. Experience soon teaches him otherwise. Usually the fault lies not in his groundbait but in himself, for like many beginners he thinks that the catching of fish depends on the lobbing-in of great quantities of groundbait.

Consider a river or canal bank crowded with anglers. If each angler satisfies the appetites of the fish in his swim, there will be few if any hungry fish about for anyone to catch. (Bream, of course, require special consideration, since their distribution is erratic and their appetites enormous; but bream are a law unto themselves). Generally speaking, if you are one of many anglers lining a bank, all furiously groundbaiting, you can no more expect to draw fish from a neighbour's swim than he can expect to draw fish from yours.

But if, on the same crowded bank, each angler were to *start off* by groundbaiting sparingly with a light 'cloud' groundbait – which attracts fish without over-feeding them – there would be a marked improvement in the sport.

Groundbaiting is an art, and the knowledge of how to groundbait, when to groundbait, what to use and how to prepare it, comes only from a patient study of a particular species of fish in a particular location.

An example of this is the shallow, clear water of the Kennet and Avon Canal near Aldermaston. A study of this water reveals that most of the best bags of fish consist principally of dace. An angler with a good knowledge of this canal realizes that, in most swims, light or very light groundbaiting gives the best results. If the swim is a shallow one, the dace will respond well to a frequent light sprinkling of maggots, whereas heavy groundbaiting will make them vacate the swim altogether.

Roach, in the deeper swims, will respond to small amounts of 'cloud' groundbait and sprinklings of maggots.

There are plenty of fine chub in this stretch of the canal. They will often fall to bread-baits if a few walnut-sized lumps of bread groundbait are flicked out into the swim from time to time.

Groundbaiting devices

Anglers have ever been gadget-minded; and it is not surprising that attention has been paid to devices which make ground-baiting more sophisticated and precise.

Fig. 37.1 (overleaf) shows a twin-celled plastic pike float. The upper cell is air-filled to provide buoyancy. The lower cell is perforated, to allow a supply of maggots to escape gradually and attract small fish round the livebait – an added attraction for the pike.

Fig. 37.2 illustrates a boat with a polythene bait-delivery tube rigged overside. The tube is designed to deliver groundbait close to the lake or river bed. This gives an angler the opportunity of swimming a baited hook just off the bottom in the middle of a groundbait trail. The bait-delivery tube can be adapted for bank fishing, and the tube combined with a hopper feed.

Fig. 37.3 depicts a bait-dropper. Its object is two-fold:

1. It deposits a load of maggots on to a selected part of the river or lake bed.
2. It carries the groundbait straight to the bottom, without attracting or feeding small and undesirable fish on the way down.

The bait-dropper is an adaptable device which can be used for lift-fishing, laying-on, float-ledgering, or swimming the stream.

Most droppers have a cork fitted on one side to accommodate the angler's hook. This enables the angler to attach the bait-dropper to the end of his tackle without having to 'break-down'.

Fig. 37.3.*a*, depicts the loaded bait-dropper before it hits bottom. Note how the striker releases the contents of the dropper as soon as it touches the river bed (Fig. 3.*b*).

A bait-dropper must be swung out smoothly and easily with the rod, otherwise there is a danger of the groundbait tipping out. Because of this, dropper techniques are associated with close-to-the-bank fishing.

One of the oldest and simplest methods of groundbaiting is shown in Fig. 37.7. A mash of bread/bran (or similar groundbait), with or without a sprinkling of entombed maggots, is 'cupped' round the ledger lead. Although this method is simple in operation, the angler must take great care when mixing his mash. An over-sloppy mixture tends to come off during the cast, or when the lead hits the water; an over-stiff mixture may fail to break up at all.

A natural development of the 'cupping' method of groundbaiting is the springwire (Fig. 37.6). This consists of a fine copper or brass tube soldered to a wire coil. Ledger anglers who fish at long range favour this method, because groundbait of any reasonable consistency readily adheres to a springwire even during the most violent casting.

The springwire can be used effectively in conjunction with float tackle provided the

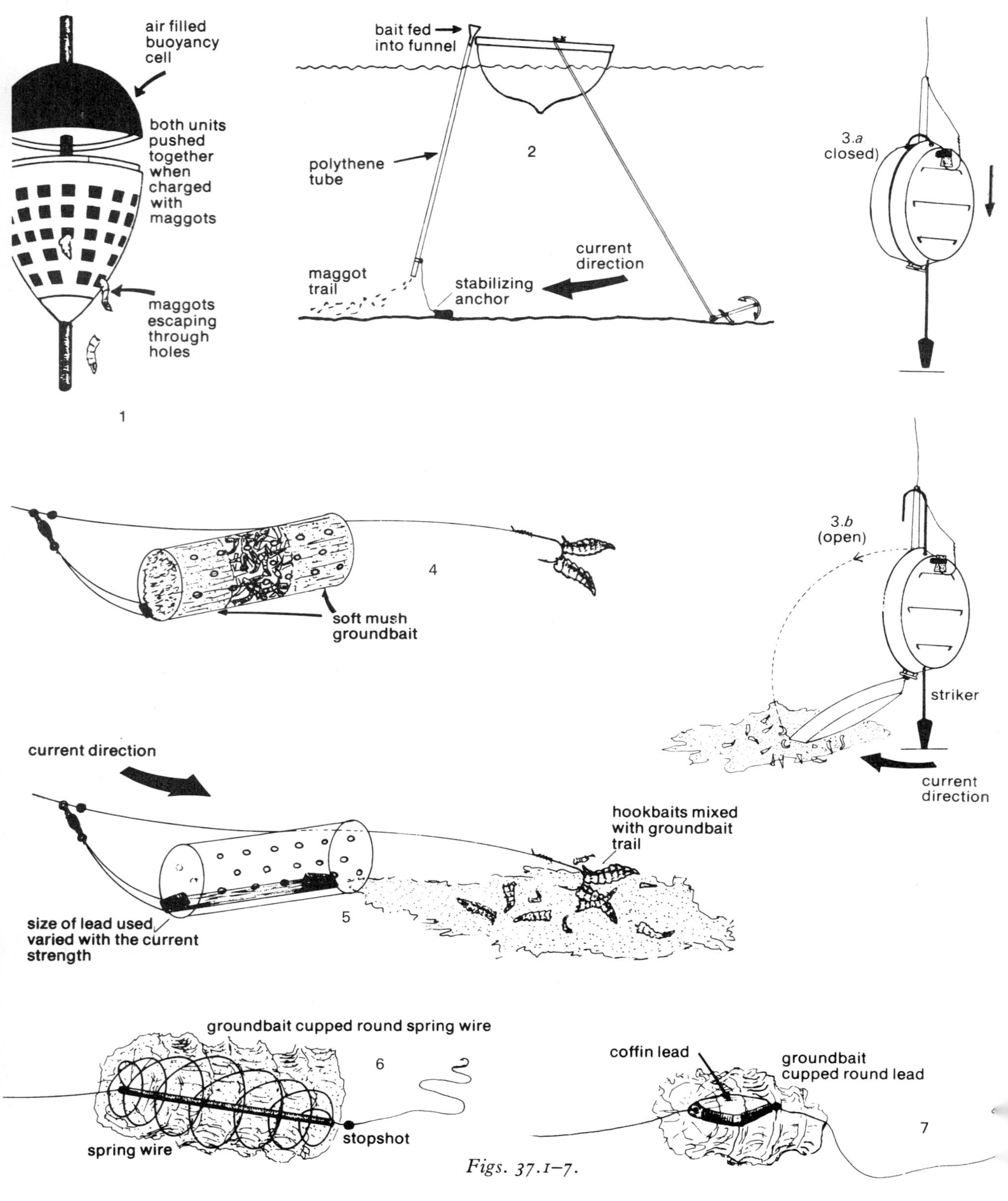
air filled
buoyancy
cell
both units
pushed
together
when
charged
with
maggots
maggots
escaping
through
holes
1
bait fed
into funnel
polythene
tube
2
maggot
trail
stabilizing
anchor
current
direction
3.a
closed)
3.b
(open)
striker
current
direction
4
soft mush
groundbait
current direction
hookbaits mixed
with groundbait
trail
5
size of lead used
varied with the current
strength
groundbait cupped round spring wire
6
spring wire
stopshot
coffin lead
groundbait
cupped round lead
7

Figs. 37.1–7.

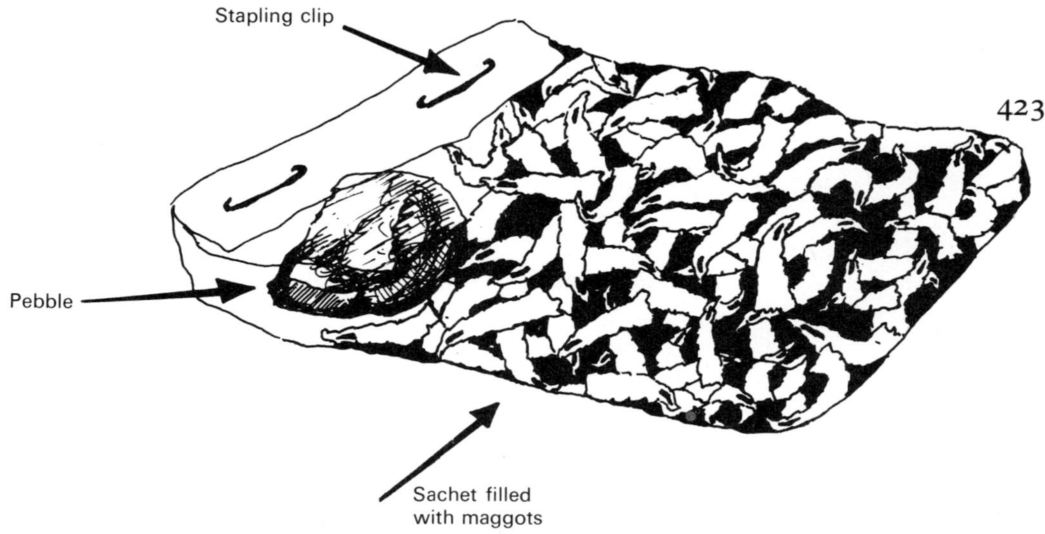

Fig. 37.8. Sachet groundbaiting.

angler is fishing in deep water. The greater the depth, the less the disturbance caused by splash when the bait-loaded wire is cast.

Most anglers have a high opinion of the swimfeeder (Figs. 38.4 and 5). Here is a device capable of depositing (at long range, if necessary) a quantity of maggots straight on the lake or river bed. The maggots, contained within a sandwich of soft mash, are prevented from escaping until the water has eroded the mash and freed them.

Seal one end of the feeder with mash. Fill the middle with maggots, and seal the other end with more mash.

Of all snares, a crust-baited hook pitched on a carpet of similar pieces of groundbait crust is the deadliest for large capricious roach.

The swimfeeder provides a means of getting pieces of breadcrust or breadcrumb straight down to the bed of a river. Without wetting or pressing, the springy nature of the crust ensures a grip on the inside wall of the feeder.

Fig. 38.4 shows one of the best methods of attachment.

Fig. 38.5 shows the action of the stream emptying the feeder, and illustrates the effect of hook baits mixed with groundbaits.

Fig. 38.8 depicts a new groundbaiting device, which is capable of considerable development: a transparent bag of soluble plastic (polyvinyl acetate) made by I.C.I.

Fill the sachet with maggots, and include a pebble to overcome the buoyancy of the trapped air. Staple-clip the end of the bag before throwing it into the swim.

The bag, with enclosed maggots, sinks to the bottom. Within minutes it dissolves—leaving a concentration of maggots on the bed of the swim. The value of putting groundbait straight on to the bottom, before small fish help themselves to it, is obvious.

In still water, the exact position of the groundbait can be marked by including a small quantity of sodium bicarbonate and citric acid in the sachet. As soon as water reaches the mixture, gas bubbles will be generated. These bubbles, rising to the surface, provide the angler with a target at which he can aim his baited hook.

An Ingenious Method

If you will bait a stream, get some tin boxes made full of holes, no bigger than just fit for a worm to creep through; then fill these boxes with them, and having fastened a plummet to sink them, cast them into the stream with a string tied there to, that you may draw them forth when you list. By the smallness of the holes aforesaid, the worms can crawl out but very leisurely, and as they crawl the fish will resort about them.

NICHOLAS COX, *The Gentleman's Recreation . . . 'Collected from Ancient and Modern Authors Forrein and Domestick, Etc.'* (1674).

The Polycone (Maggot) Swimfeeder

Of all swimfeeder designs the polycone is the most advanced. The sharp nose of the cone cleaves the water like the bow of a ship, causing less disturbance than the conventional, blunt-nosed, cylinder-shaped maggot-feeder. When stationary on the bottom, the cone-shaped body creates less drag, and during the strike reduces the stress on rod line.

The feeder can be used either as a ledgering or a float-ledgering device. In both cases the mainline is passed through the hole in the sharp end and out through the hole in the blunt end. A stopshot prevents the feeder from running down to the hook.

The feeder is loaded with maggots by means of a removable cap that fits over the blunt end. When in position on the river bed the maggots crawl out of the holes and are taken by the current in the direction of the hookbait.

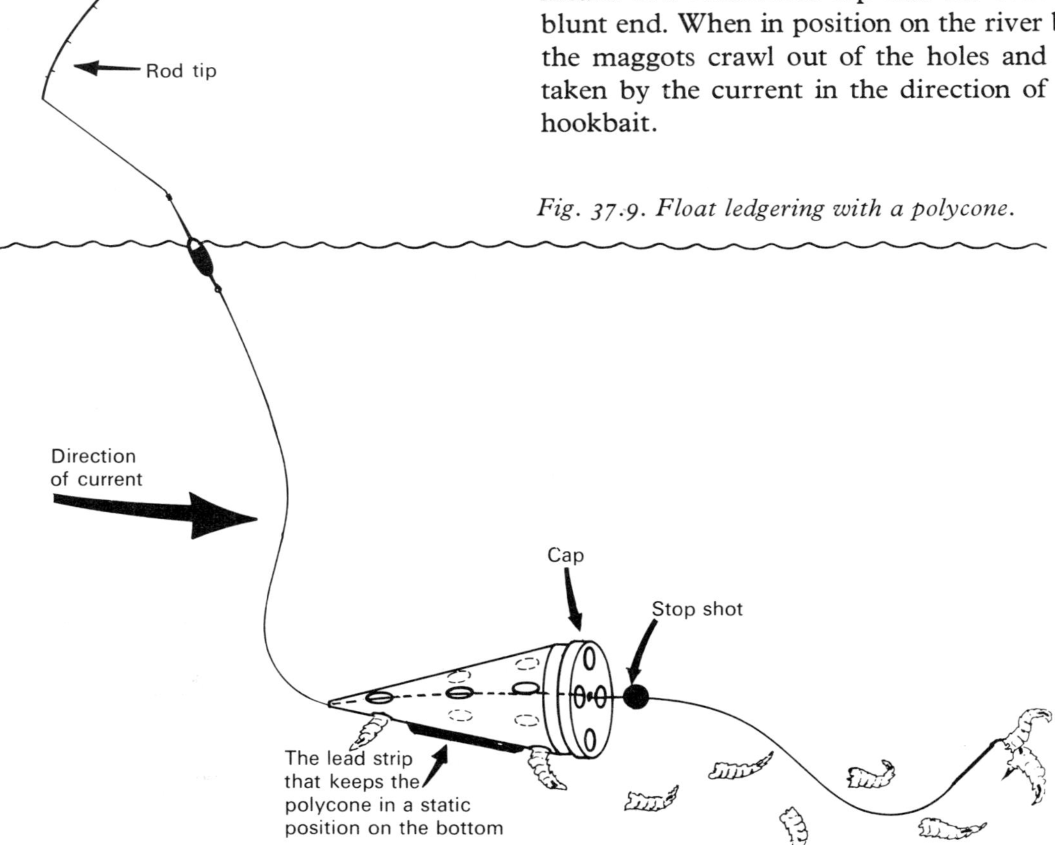

Fig. 37.9. Float ledgering with a polycone.

The Groundbait Marker-Buoy

F.B. writes:

I have used the groundbait marker-buoy method with great success. It has enabled me to have fine sport on days when nearby anglers were hard pressed to catch a single fish. Although I developed the method for ledgering, I have also found it a very useful aid to float fishing – particularly at long range.

The consistently successful angler is the man who gives himself the best possible chance of catching a fish during every fishing moment. Part of his repertoire is the judicious use of groundbait – the purpose of which is to attract fish. But this in itself does not guarantee success. To be effective, his hookbait *must* fall inside his groundbait area otherwise the groundbait will merely tend to draw fish *away* from the hookbait.

Often, however, after throwing out his groundbait an angler becomes uncertain of its exact position, and can no longer ensure that his hookbait always falls in the right place. This is particularly evident when he is ledgering open sheets of water, such as lakes and reservoirs, which are devoid of local landmarks. In waters such as these, the accurate pinpointing of the groundbaited area is very difficult, and becomes progressively more difficult as the casting range increases.

This difficulty is easily overcome. If the groundbait is placed close to an anchored float acting as a marker-buoy, the subsequent positioning of the hookbait can be judged with complete accuracy.

First, ascertain the depth of water at the place you wish to groundbait. Do this by fitting up a float-fishing outfit consisting of rod, fixed-spool reel, 4 lb B.S. line, sliding float, and plummet. The sliding float should be of the modern 'Billy Lane' type with a very small eye for the line to run through. Tie a special sliding stop-knot (see p. 415) on the line above the float. Set the float at the estimated depth and cast out to the desired area. The depth has been over-estimated if the float lies on its side; under-estimated if it disappears. Adjust the stop knot until the float just cocks. The distance between float and plummet now indicates the true depth.

From a reserve spool, cut off a length of 6 lb B.S. nylon which exceeds the measured depth by about two feet. Tie one end to a 2½ oz Arlesey bomb, and the other end to the bottom eye of a medium pike-float. Anchored by the lead, the pike-float will serve as a marker-buoy.

Hold the lead between thumb and forefinger; the top of the float between palm and little finger (Fig. 37.10.*a*). Throw the lead so that it pulls the float out behind it. When the float settles (point E in the diagram) its movement is restricted, since it has been allowed only two feet of spare anchor line.

Fit up a swimfeeder ledger rig (see p. 422). Fill the feeder with groundbait and cast slightly beyond and to one side of the marker-buoy. The moment the feeder hits the water, retrieve it to a point level with the float (area F) and allow it to sink. As soon as the feeder touches bottom, give the rod a fierce pull to eject the groundbait. Retrieve, fill up the feeder and repeat the operation. Twenty minutes of this will ensure that a

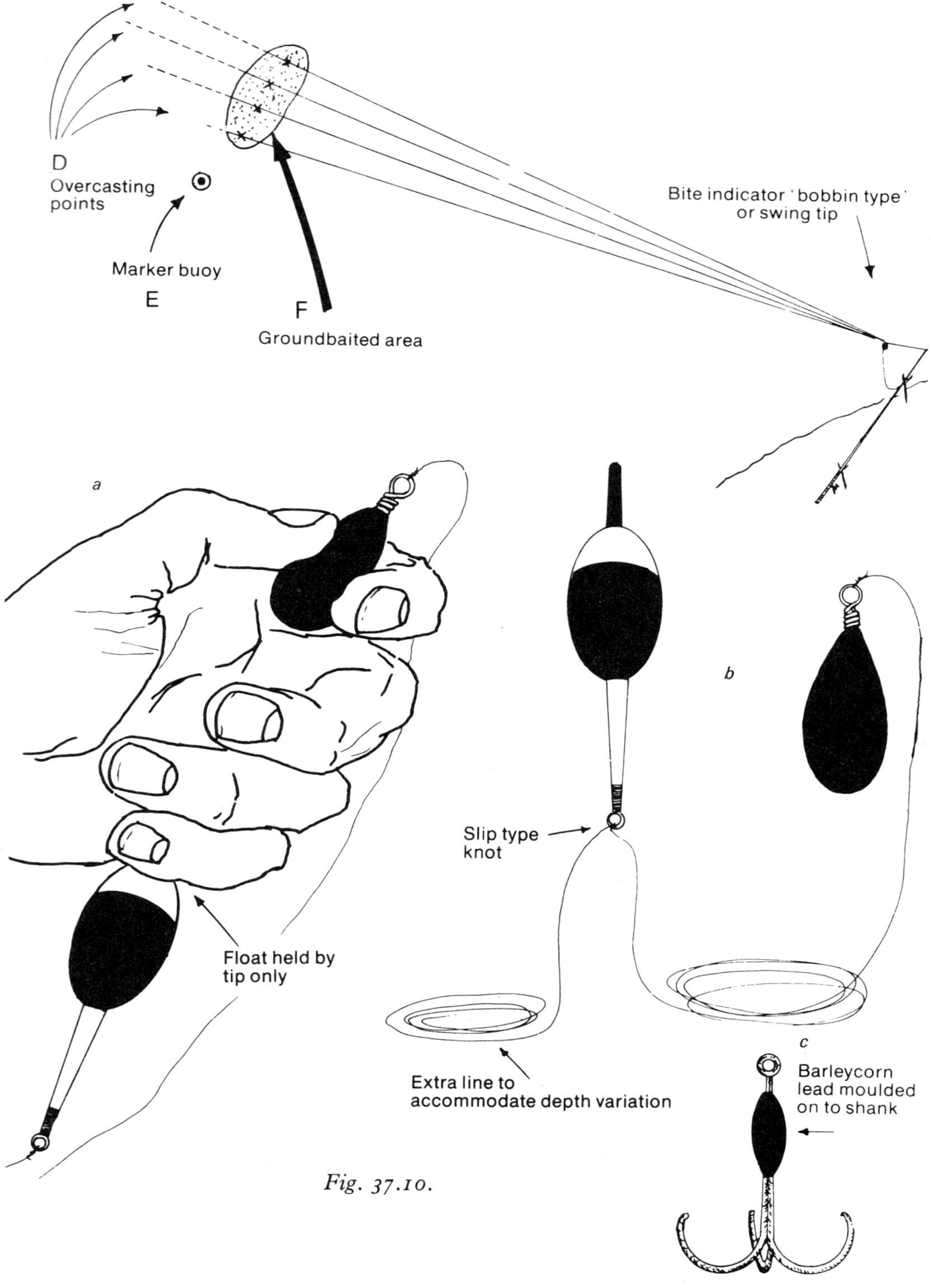
D
Overcasting points
Marker buoy
E
F
Groundbaited area
Bite indicator 'bobbin type' or swing tip
a
b
Slip type knot
Float held by tip only
Extra line to accommodate depth variation
c
Barleycorn lead moulded on to shank

Fig. 37.10.

carpet of groundbait is accurately placed in position.

You are now ready to start fishing. And knowing exactly where to place each cast, you can fish with complete confidence.

The swimfeeder remains with the terminal tackle of the ledger rig. Re-bait it fairly frequently during the first few hours of fishing. This will entail more casting than you might normally expect to do, but if carefully performed, this activity will excite the fish rather than frighten them.

Provided that the groundbaited area is within accurate lobbing range, bream fishermen should augment the supply of swimfeeder groundbait with hand-thrown balls of heavier texture groundbaits: e.g. a bread/bran mixture. Bream have huge appetites and require more substantial groundbaiting than other species.

At the end of the day's fishing, retrieve the marker-buoy with a casting drag (Fig. 10.*c*). The drag can be fashioned from a piece of wire, or from a large treble hook. *Don't* cast directly at the buoy. First walk several paces along the bank either to right or left, then cast across at an angle beyond the buoy. Return to your original position before retrieving, and the drag will catch the anchor line first time.

It is interesting to reflect that in addition to its material advantages, the marker-buoy method of fishing offers a certain spiritual comfort. When lake or reservoir fishing, the angler is easily overwhelmed and dispirited by the great sheet of water which confronts him. With the marker-buoy, a specific fishing area is defined. The angler is no longer casting into a featureless expanse, but concentrating on a piece of water which in his imagination seems intimate and friendly. Far from losing heart, he is made eager by a sense of involvement – for in effect he has created a little 'swim'.

Never Before Heard Of

Then go to Mother Giberts, at the
Flower-de-Luce at Clapton, near Hackney,
and while you are drinking of a Pot of Ale,
bid the maid make you two or three
Penny-worth of Ground-bait, and some
Paste (which they do very neatly, and well);
and observing of them, you will know how
to make it yourself for any other place;
which is too tedious here to insert.

WILLIAM GILBERT, *The Angler's Delight . . . 'the whole Art and Mystery of Clean, Neat, and Gentile Angling, in a far more Plain, and Easie Way, than ever was yet in Print; All from Experience, and not Borrowed from other Books, and many things never before heard of, by most People.'* (*1676*).

As fish are the inhabitants of an element which man cannot live in, and have unlimited motion in the water, with innumerable retreats, it is evident they are to be taken only by stratagem. In rivers, they retire to pits and holes, lie concealed under the roots of trees and in a thousand close places, so that nothing is to be done but by alluring them out of their retreats and bringing them to hand by the art of a skilful workman – and thus they are

sometimes surprised and made prisoners.
GUINIAD CHARFY, *The Fisherman: or The Art of Angling Made Easy.*[1]

Ye can not brynge an hoke into a fyssh mouth without a bayte.
DAME JULIANA BERNERS: *A Treatyse of Fysshynge wyth an Angle* (1496).

(Well, actually ye can – by dibbling it on the surface or getting it to work like a nymph. But these are exceptional rites and of little or no importance to the coarse fisherman, who stands an infinitely better chance of 'alluring' a big roach on breadcrust than on a bare hook.)

HOOKBAITS

Diamond-Shaped Compressed Breadcrust

Sometimes, one angler will catch considerably more fish than other anglers fishing the same water. This may be due to his superior skill with a rod; but angling skill alone is not always the whole story. Attention to detail is the key to angling success, and careful thought and preparation well in advance of a day's fishing ensures an advantage over all other anglers less well prepared. For instance, there are times when an angler will succeed simply because he has the 'taking' bait when others haven't.

If big roach happen to prefer breadcrust to maggots, as they so often do, it is clear that an enterprising angler of even moderate skill who has gone to the trouble of preparing some crusts prior to the fishing trip, will reap the major reward.

In fast water, *compressed* crust (whatever the bait size) has three distinct advantages over normal crust. It survives casting better. It resists the eroding action of the current for a longer period. It obtains a higher bite frequency and a higher ratio of fish hooked in relation to the number of strikes.

Small pieces of crust perform a special duty: they catch middling-sized roach as well as big roach, when this is the aim. They are obviously less selective than large pieces in the sample of roach they produce, but even so the angler is unlikely to be plagued with under-sized fish to the extent that he would be if using maggots.

Diamond-shaped compressed breadcrust baits are prepared as follows:

Take a new, uncut loaf and cut off $\frac{3}{8}$ in. slices of crust from both ends and both sides. Lay the slices on one half of a dampened tea-cloth (Fig. 37.11.*a*) and use the other half to cover them. Put the wrapped slices between two boards and place under a heavy weight (Fig. 11.*b*). Leave overnight. Next morning, remove the compressed slices of crust from the cloth and make a series of parallel cuts every quarter of an inch. Make a second series of cuts, so as to produce diamond-shaped pieces of varying size (Fig. 11.*c*).

Keep the day's supply of crustbaits in a

1 Charfy was a pseudonym. The book was compiled by George Smeeton, printer, of St Martin's Lane, London, and published by J. Dixwell c. 1800. The second edition was published by J. Smeeton c. 1815. It is a verbatim appropriation of *The Compleat Fisherman* written by James Saunders and published in 1724.

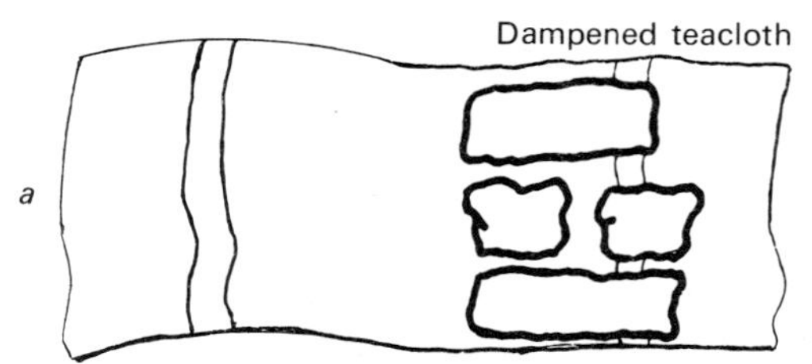

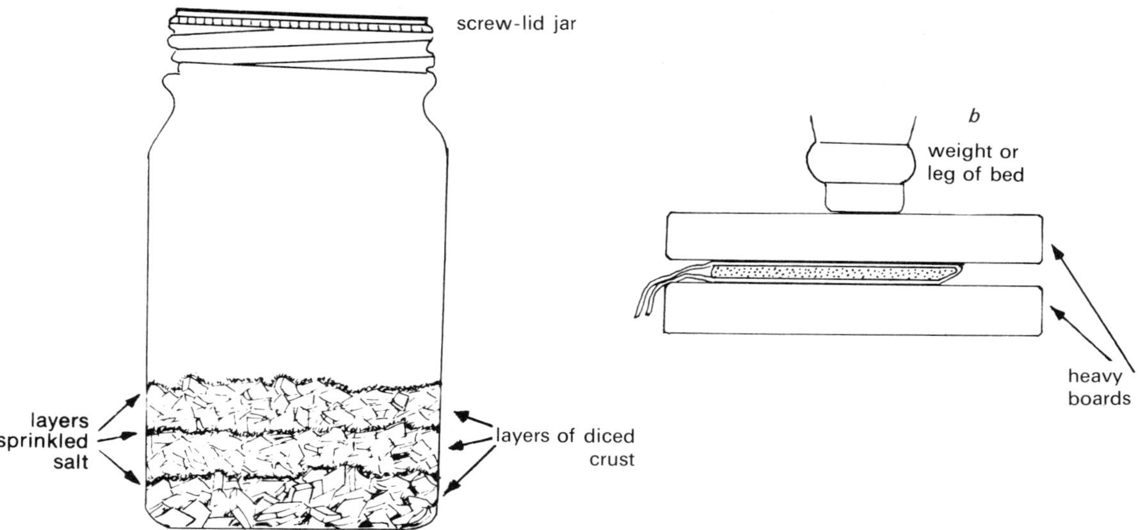

Fig. 37.11.

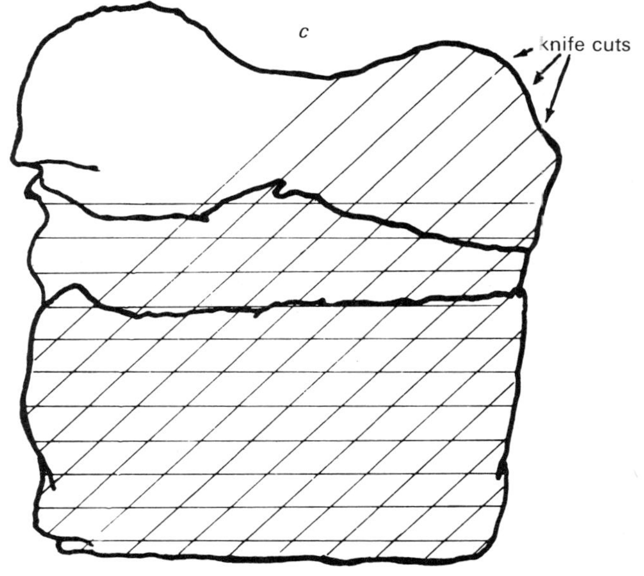

Kilner jar. This retains the moisture content of the bread, and will continue to do so if only a few hookbaits are removed at a time.

A spare supply can be preserved in the following manner:

Spread a layer of crustbaits on the bottom of a Kilner jar and shake a thin sprinkling of crushed salt over them. Add another layer, and again cover with salt. Repeat the process until the jar is filled.

If the crusts are kept in polythene bags, refrigerators preserve them for an indefinite period. Refrigerated crusts need no salt preservative if the polythene bags are properly sealed.

A brace of 2 lb roach taken on ledgered breadcrust from the Suffolk Stour.

Ointments to Allure Fish to the Bait . . .

Take Man's Fat and Cat's Fat, of each half an Ounce, Mummy finely powdred three Drams, Cummin-seed finely powdred one Dram, distill'd Oyl of Annise and Spike, of each six Drops, Civet two Grains, and Camphor four Grains, make an Ointment according to Art; and when you Angle anoint 8 inches of the Line next the Hook therewith, and keep it in a pewter box . . . JAMES CHETHAM, *The Angler's Vade-Mecum* (1681).

Baiting with Crust and Crumb

Although crust will account for larger roach than any other bait, many anglers avoid using it. They suspect that for much of the time they are fishing with baitless hooks. This is understandable. Crust softens quickly, and an angler's suspicions that all is not well down below are seemingly confirmed each time he pulls up a bare hook. It is certainly true that crust is seldom retrieved intact after a long soaking; but even so, an angler using it can be confident that his bait will remain on the hook *until he has a bite, or moves his tackle.*

Softened crust will disintegrate when the hook is jerked, or if a fish gives it an exploratory knock; even a slight touch will dislodge crustbait that has been in the water for some time. Invariably, after striking or after inconclusive bites it is necessary to re-bait.

Successful crust-fishing depends on four

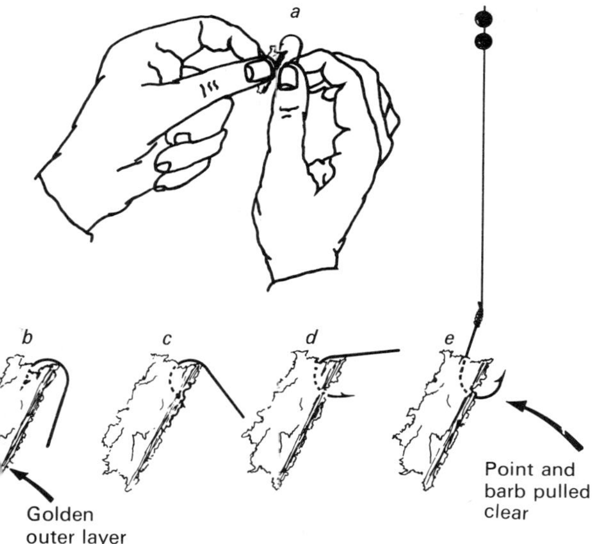

Fig. 37.12. Baiting with crust.

essentials: correct choice of bread; choice of hook; correct method of baiting the hook; and, most important of all, confidence that the bread will stay on until the hook is moved. Clearly, an angler who lacks this confidence will never become a crust enthusiast. In consequence, he will seldom give himself the best chance of hooking a really big roach.

Crustbait should be taken from a new loaf, so that when crust is torn off a fair amount of white crumb remains adhering to it. Only the top and sides of the loaf are used. The choicest crustbaits usually come from the corners which are golden, shining and rubbery. These parts are stored in a sealed tin or a slightly dampened cloth. Crust cracks easily when it begins to dry, and soon becomes almost useless for hookbait. Many good fishing days have been ruined because crust slices were left out in the wind or sun.

A round-bend hook is best for crust fishing; crystal hooks should be avoided. The round-bend cuts the truest arc through the crust, and makes the smallest hole. In addition, it provides a firmer hold.

The hookbait is held white side up (Fig. 37.12.*a*). As the hook penetrates, it is allowed to follow a natural course through the crust. The angler should be conscious of his right elbow being raised as the fingers holding the hook describe an arc. Figs. 12.*b*, *c*, *d* and *e* illustrate the changing angle of the hook as it finds its way through. Only the bend of the hook remains in the crust; the point and barb are left clear.

The baited hook can be tested by swinging it in the air like a conker on a string. If the bait comes off, the crust has been mounted wrongly, or the wrong sort of crust chosen, or the hook is too small. To make assurance double sure, experiment with a baited hook by dropping it into a bowl of water under a running tap. If the crust stays on for a time, you can be confident that it will do so while you are fishing.

The size of the bait varies according to the species the angler is fishing for. Large pieces of crust are more selective than small pieces. This is helpful when the angler wishes to avoid catching small fish. In strong currents, however, it can be a drawback especially when roach are the quarry. Even a big roach has a smallish mouth, and in fast water a good bite indication is often obtained before the roach has had time to take the bait right in. By comparison, pieces

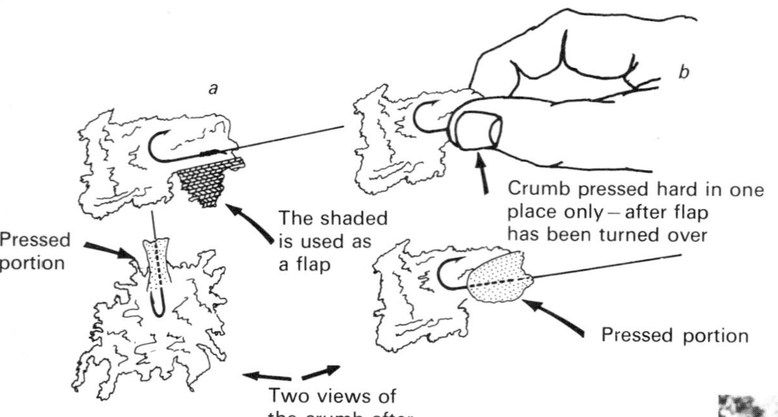

Fig. 37.13. Baiting with crumb (or flake).

of crust two or three inches across can be used effectively for chub.

Crumb

Baiting with crumb (or flake) is another method used by the experienced angler. Once again, a new loaf should be used and great care taken to prevent it from drying out. The secret of crumb fishing is to use bread so new and soft that a single press of the finger turns it almost to paste.

When tearing off a piece of crumb, an angler should remember that the hook needs to reach about halfway down the bait. One part of the crumb is selected as a flap (Fig. 37.13.*a*). With the minimum of handling, the flap is bent over the hook-shank (but not over the bend or the point of the hook), and pressed hard (Fig. 13.*b*). For larger pieces of crumb, eyed or spade-end hooks provide a good anchorage. The smaller the pressed section the better, since the bait should be used in as natural a state as possible.

No attempt should be made to 'tidy' the bait. Its irregular shape is thought to be one reason for its killing properties. Excessively hook-shy fish can sometimes be deceived by bringing the crumb round on both sides of the hook and securing it with a small pinch at the bend.

F. J. Taylor, F. B. – and a lobworm (Photograph: Richard Walker).

The lob-worm is a proper bait for salmon. It is to be found in gardens and churchyards by the help of a lanthorn, late on a summer's evening. In great droughts, when they do not appear, pour the juice of walnut-tree leaves, mixed with a little water and salt, into their holes. It will drive them out of the ground.

RICHARD BROOKES, *The Art of Angling* (1740).

Note: We think little of this method.

Worms

Fly fishing may be a very pleasant amusement, but angling or float fishing I can only compare to a stick and a string, with a worm at one end and a fool at the other.

No one knows for certain who uttered this classic aphorism. It was attributed to Dr Johnson by Colonel Hawker, and certainly there is a Johnsonian ring about it even though no trace of it can be found in his writings. But never mind who was responsible for it, is it valid?

Well – no, it isn't. And the reason is not because angling hasn't got its quota of fools. No, the reason why Johnson (if it was Johnson) made a lemon of it was because he chose the wrong bait. He showed an intuitive understanding of anglers when he put a fool at one end of the string, but an ignorance of angling when he put a worm at the other.

A worm deserves someone rather better than a fool at the other end if its merit as an angling bait is to be shown to advantage. Although, basically, it is easy enough to use and has a universal appeal to novice anglers, it is much more difficult to use *effectively* than any other bait. A worm and a fool simply don't go together.

That the worm is a very popular bait is understandable. There are few species of fish which at some time or another cannot be taken with it. It will catch fish (literally on a stick and a string) even in the hands of a half-wit; but it takes a first-class angler to realize its full potential. To fish it properly demands great skill.

Broadly speaking, angling skill can be divided into two parts:

1. The ability to present a bait or lure in such a way that a fish will take it.
2. The ability to hook and land the fish once it has taken the bait.

It is not difficult to attract the attention of a hungry fish, but to hook that fish is altogether another matter. Many an angling chance is lost through faulty striking. And in no method of angling is the proportion of loss so high as in worm fishing.

It all devolves on the question of when and how to tighten on the fish. When the biting fish is unseen, as it usually is, the subtleties of timing the strike are based on the angler's assessment of two vital matters:

1. The species of fish.
2. The size of the specimen.

The first is more important than the second, since each species has its own characteristic method of dealing with a worm. For instance, the 'taking' differences between, say, salmon, sea-trout, brown trout, eel, chub and flounder, should be well known to any experienced angler. In the lower reaches of some rivers a worm fisher may hook any of these species. He may even hook all of them on the same day. In each case the bite, and thus the timing of the strike, is quite different. And if the angler wishes to fish successfully, either to hook or (in the case of small eels) to *avoid* hooking the fish, he should be able to identify each species from the way in which it takes his worm. He should know this from the feel of the line, or movement of the rod tip. And of course he should be able to do the same with other species.

The *size* of the fish is also important, but perhaps not quite in the way that might be expected. A 3 lb chub may swallow a worm in a second. A 30 lb salmon may take ten seconds, or even longer – as many an angler who struck too soon has ruefully discovered. A large member of a species does not necessarily swallow a worm faster than a small member of that species. The reverse is often the case. As an example: a small sea-trout can and often does swallow a whole lobworm with great rapidity, whereas a big sea-trout will usually bide its time and 'taste' the worm for several seconds before taking it properly.

It is clear, therefore, that although in some circumstances the worm may seem easy enough to fish, it is nevertheless very difficult to fish well. The timing of the strike is subject to extreme variation, and it is the way in which he strikes that separates the good worm-fisher from the rest.

From this it will be appreciated that there is more to worm fishing than a stick, a string and a fool. Indeed, when entering the realm of clear-water upstream worming, we are sometimes moved to wonder at the expostulations of the so-called 'purist', who condemns all worm-fishing out of hand. We have no hesitation in asserting that in terms of angling ability, certain aspects of worm-fishing equal any other form of fishing, fly included.

A man may fish with the worm that hath eat of a king, and eat of the fish that hath fed of that worm.
(*Hamlet*, Act IV, Sc. 3.)

1. The common lobworm; tail-end section oval or flat. Adult lobs are about six inches long when relaxed, not generally found in flower beds or well dug ground; found in more stable ground, e.g. playing fields and meadows.
2. The big blue-headed lobworm; tail-end section round. An adult blue-head, is the only other native worm to match the size of the lobworm; deep digging in rich soils, e.g. in chicken runs, is the only way to collect numbers of them.
3. The small blue-headed lobworm; tail-end section round; about 3–4″ long. The common worm of well dug ground; the most common worm to find its way into an angler's bait can – if he 'digs his own'.
4. The common brandling; noticeable for its 'rugby shirt' skin pattern consisting of alternate hoops of reddish browns and yellows; the worm that anglers associate with a foetid yellow body fluid, and the rich smell of the dung heap.
5. The giltail; a smaller, striped brandling-type worm (but without the yellow hoops of the brandling); 1½″–2″ long but more tapered in the body than the common brandling, and without its unpleasant smell.
6. Marsh worms in a pot. Marsh worms and redworms are very similar in shape and size – 2½″ – 3½″ in length with a practically uniform body thickness throughout. However a marsh worm has a darker and a more iridescent hue than the redworm and is more active: it can actually jump if suddenly exposed to light.

Note: After much enquiry we surprisingly concluded, since worms are so important to agriculture, that in Britain little is known about worms. In our attempts to identify various species we are pleased to acknowledge the help given to us by Mr Sims of the British Museum (Natural History).

1
2
3
4
5
6

Species

Twenty-seven species of earthworms are recorded from the British Isles. The following are those most commonly used by anglers:

1. Lobworm (*Lumbricus terrestris*), also known as dew-worm, rain-worm, twachel, flat-tail, squirrel-tail and (in America) night-crawler.
2. Big blue-headed lobworm (*Allolobophora longa*).
3. Small blue-headed lobworm (*Allolobophora caliginosa*).
4. Brandling (*Eisenia foetida*), the bramble-worm, manure-worm, foetid-worm. The name is derived from the Scottish 'Brannit': meaning a reddish-brown colour as if singed by fire.
5. Gilt-tail (*Denrobaena rubida subrubicunda*), the cockspur, gold-tailed brandling or yellow-tail. There is a delightful reference to the gilt-tail by the 18th-century poet, John Gay:

> Those baits will best reward the fisher's pains,
> Whose polished tails a shining yellow stains . . .

6. Red-worm (*Lumbricus rubellus*). A worm of rich organic soil with high moisture content.
7. Marsh-worm (*Lumbricus castaneus*).

Note: It should be remembered that colour alone is not a good guide to worm identification. Colour varies considerably according to the worm's habitat and food.

Worms can be bought from worm farms or (sometimes) from tackle shops. But many anglers collect their own brandlings from a manure dump, or compost heap, and their lobworms from a lawn at night. Others dig desperately for lobs on the day they need them. This usually indicates a lack of foresight. In fairness, however, it should be stated that some anglers prefer to fish with freshly-dug worms. Although worms straight from the soil are less able to withstand the rigours of casting, they are, it is claimed, more attractive to fish.

Collection

It is not without good reason that the Americans call the lobworm the 'night-crawler'. On damp, dark nights, lobworms can be collected from the lawn or from any field of short grass. They are seldom picked up from dry ground, and never from frozen or even frosted ground. They are reluctant to surface on windy nights; when they do they tend to expose less of themselves above ground. In such conditions they are restless and easily disturbed.

All earthworms are sensitive to vibration and light (except red light), and both of these stimuli result in their retiring deep within their burrows. Only those persons who have observed it can appreciate the astonishing speed at which a disturbed lobworm can disappear down its hole. Whenever possible *a red light should be used for worm collecting at night*, since worms are blind to this part of the spectrum.

The collector should choose a damp, warm night; wear rubber shoes or wellingtons, and move with great stealth. To have the use of both hands is an advantage, and the lobwormer will find it convenient to mount a torch on his head after the fashion of coal miners or surgeons. An alternative method is to hold a small torch between the teeth (as recommended for night fly-fishing, see p. 306).

Frequently only a small portion of worm is visible among the grass stems. It is this short length of worm that the lobwormer searches for when he creeps about. Instantly, it is pinned down by a lightning movement of thumb and forefinger, or by both thumbs, one at either end. Next, the head of the worm is located and held firmly until the worm's peristaltic movement thins its body sufficiently to allow it to be withdrawn gently from the hole. Any attempt to drag a lobworm out too soon is disastrous; invariably it breaks in two. (*Note:* there is seldom any difficulty in locating the head of the worm, since it is always the tail that is in the hole. Sometimes, however, the whole worm is above ground – in which case it is unable to make a speedy escape.)

Redworms are found in old manure sites (fresh manure sites favour the brandling) and under stones and cowpats resting on rich organic soil.

Care of Worms

An Australian worm-farmer, Don Ewers, who breeds the red compost worm, *Eisenia foetida*, has found that when packed in a peat moss and food mixture, the worms will live without weight loss in cartons for between four and six weeks, unless exposed to direct sunlight or left in dead air space.

The worms live in a rich compost which supports 5,000 worms to the cubic foot, a hundred times as many as live in the finest soil.

This mixture is kept between 68° and 75°F, with summer cooling by mist sprays, and winter heating by special feed which generates heat – basically composed of three types of manure, peat moss, lime, gypsum, and a powdered food made of meat meal, sugars, lucernes and wheat.

Amongst the old recipes for *scouring* worms, the putting them into a powder got from a dead man's *Skull*, by beating it to atoms, was deemed *super*-excellent.
THE REV. W. B. DANIEL, *Rural Sports* (1801).

Take the Bones or Skull of a Dead Man, at the opening of a Grave, and beat the same into powder, and put of this powder into the Moss wherein you keep your worms, but others like Grave-earth as well.
JAMES CHETHAM, *The Angler's Vade-Mecum* (1681).

Brandlings

Brandlings should be kept in bulb fibre, or peat, or compost from the actual worm bed – the top layer of compost being used. Brandlings kept in compost that is too moist will attempt to vacate their quarters at night.

Lobworms

The secret of keeping lobworms alive and in good condition is – temperature. They must be kept cool during summer, and insulated against frost during the winter. The ideal

Fig. 37.14. ▷

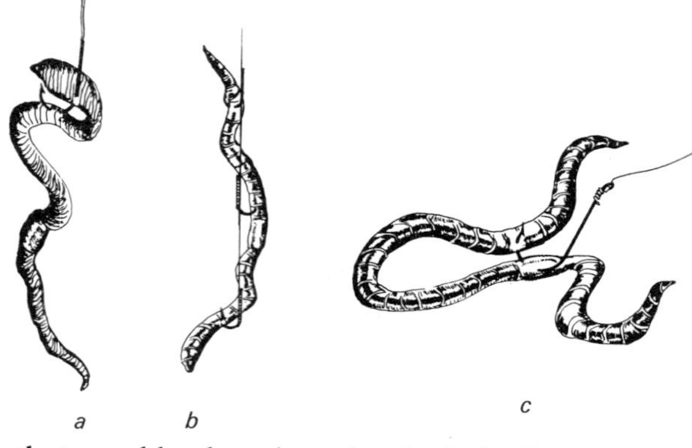

temperature is 33–35°F. Lobworms should be stored in shredded newspaper. They will survive far longer in newspaper than in the usually recommended moss.

Soak and squeeze enough shredded newspaper to fill a biscuit tin. Add worms. Place a piece of damp sacking on top of the newspaper. On top of the sacking put a plastic container full of ice. Have two containers on the go: one in the deep freeze, one on top of the worms. Change them round daily.

For this excellent advice on the care of worms (which we have thoroughly tested) we are indebted to those two great wormers: F. J. and Ken Taylor. Using these methods, which they pioneered, they once kept 200 lobworms alive and well for twelve months. *Note:* The Americans have recently produced an artificial worm-keeping moss. We have heard good reports of this, but have had no experience of it ourselves.

The Stewart 3-Hook Tackle

First described in 1857 by W. C. Stewart in his classic book *The Practical Angler.*

The advantages of this tackle are – that a trout can hardly take hold of the worm at all, without having one of the hooks in its mouth; that the worm lives much longer, and being free to wriggle itself into any shape, is more natural looking and consequently enticing; and lastly, that it is much more easily baited, particularly if the worms are fresh. Its disadvantages are, that it is more difficult to extricate from the trout's mouth; that it requires to be baited afresh every bite; and that the exposure of so many hooks is calculated to scare away some trout that would otherwise take the bait. But, upon the whole, the advantages preponderate considerably over the disadvantages, particularly when trout are biting shy.

For over a century Stewart's tackle has been popular with anglers. It can be purchased ready-made from a tackle shop or it can be made up with three eyed-hooks, together with a piece of nylon of suitable strength (i.e. slightly stronger than would normally be associated with a particular size of hook – so as to accommodate the harder pull that is required to set three hooks, as against a single hook).

It is worth observing that Stewart did *not* straighten the worm out – as it is often depicted – but hooked it so that it hung loosely.

Presentation

Worms can be presented to fish in many different ways. They can be ledgered, float-ledgered, float-fished, trotted, babbed, rolled, paternostered, sunk and drawn, or free-lined either upstream or down. First, however, the angler should give consideration to the various methods of attachment.

If long casting is necessary a worm will need maximum support from the hook. This is best achieved by using a slightly larger hook than would otherwise be required, and

Fig. 37.15. Stewart's original 4-hook worm tackle. This illustration is taken from the first edition of Stewart's book : The Practical Angler *(1857).*

by putting several hookholds into the worm. One end of the worm should be left unhooked – or, as the ancients put it, 'unarmed' – so that it is free to wriggle.

A worm's wriggle is of the greatest importance, for it acts as a signal to a hungry fish, and perhaps stimulates other fish to start feeding. The 'free' end of a worm is important for another reason: it provides an aiming point and, *ipso facto*, a starting end for the fish to take hold of. This ensures that when a worm is swallowed, the hook is automatically facing in the right direction.

A fish taking in fast water often grabs the worm and swings back to its lie before attempting to swallow. In these circumstances the drag caused by belly in the line either frightens the fish and makes it drop the bait, or pulls the bait away the moment the fish opens its mouth to swallow. The 3-hook Stewart tackle helps to overcome this (Fig. 37.14.*c*). This tackle is in effect a lobworming snap-tackle, since it ensures that at least one hook is in the fish's mouth when the worm is grabbed, and allows the angler to strike immediately. For smaller worms the two-hook Pennell tackle can be used.

Lobworms fished on a single hook have a better chance of withstanding the exigencies of casting if hooked in the area of the head rather than the tail (Fig. 37.14.*a*). Brandlings can be mounted in ones, twos, or threes. They remain more active when doubly supported at the $\frac{1}{4}$ and $\frac{3}{4}$ marks (Fig. 14.*c*).

Fig. 37.16. The Pennell 2-hook worm tackle.

Bickerdyke claimed to have invented the two-hook worm tackle (see *Angling for Coarse Fish*, 1899, p. 58). It is Pennell, however, who is given the credit by posterity.

In Bickerdyke's version, the bottom hook is larger than the top hook. His instructions for baiting-up are as follows:

> The two-hook tackle I usually bait up by inserting the point of the large hook about the middle of the worm and threading it through to the tail, then catching the head of the worm on the top hook.

Fig. 37.17.

The sliced-shanked bait-hook

If sliced-shanked bait-hooks are not available whip a nylon bristle (or two bristles) to the hook shank (Fig. 37.17.*b*) to prevent the worm, or worms, from slipping down the shank and bunching-up on the bend of the hook (Fig. 17.*c*). Bunched-up worms often obscure the point of the hook and allow it to be pulled straight out of a fish's mouth on the strike.

The single hook baited with two lobworms

Fig. 37.17.c.

shown in Fig. 37.17.*c* is a suitable hooking arrangement for sea-trout or salmon.

Or you may fasten some bristles under the silk, leaving the points above a straws breadth and half or almost half an inch standing out towards the line, which will keep him from slipping back.
COLONEL ROBERT VENABLES, *The Experienc'd Angler* (1662).

Sixteenth Century Bait-Horn

Note: See illustrations from the title-pages of *The Pleasures of Princes* (1614), Gervase Markham; and *The Experienc'd Angler* (1662), Colonel Robert Venables.

. . . then he shall eyther have a close stopt horne, in which he shall keepe Maggots, Bobbes, Palmers, and such like, or a hollow Cane, in which he may put them, and Scarrabs.
The Pleasures of Princes.

We have gentles in a horn,
We have paste and worms too;
We can watch both night and morn,
Suffer rain and storms too.

Although published in *The Compleat Angler* (1653), these lines are from a poem attributed to J. Chalkhill.

Photograph by courtesy of J. Milbourn.

Markham makes no mention of anything like a reel in *The Pleasures of Princes*. He fished with a tight line, and kept his spare lines on a frame:

His comments on the clearing-ring are explicit:

> Then he shall have some fine smooth board of some curious wood for show sake, being as big as a trencher, and cut battlement-wise at each end; on which he shall fold his severall lines.
> Then he shall have a large ring of lead, sixe inches at least in compasse, and made fast to a small long line, thorow which, thrusting your *Angle-rod*, and let it fall downe into the water by your haire line, it will help to unloose your hooke if it fastened eyther upon weeds or other stones in the water.

Title page of Venables' Experienc'd Angler.

The Riddle of the Rod

The title-page of Venables's *The Experienc'd Angler* (1662), has caused much confusion. The rod on the left has a knob on the butt resembling the modern screw-in rubber button. The rod on the right, however, is fashioned with what seems to be a gun-butt. At least, so it has seemed to generations of anglers. And so it seemed to us – until we realised that Venables's title-page was a *copy* of the title-page from Gervase Markham's book: *The Pleasures of Princes*, published 48 years earlier, in 1614.

The artist who copied Markham's title-page so faithfully (clearly no angler himself) strengthened the line of the supposed rod-gun-butt, making it seem part of the rod. In fact, what seems to be a gun-butt is not part of the rod at all, it is a *bait-horn* – standing *in front of the rod*. Another bait-horn can be seen standing on the shelf, top-left.

The Riddle of the Reel

The frontispiece of Colonel Robert Venbles's *The Experienc'd Angler* also contained the first illustration of a fishing reel, or 'winch' as it was sometimes called. (See above. The reel is enlarged in Fig. 37.18.*a*).

Fig. 37.18.a.

The crudeness of the drawing calls for some textual support to convince the more sceptical reader that it really is intended to represent a fishing reel. This is provided on pp. 44–5 of *The Experienc'd Angler.*

The next way of Angling is with a Trowle for the Pike, which is very delightful, you may buy your trowle ready made, therefore I shall not trouble my self to describe it, only let it have a winch to wind it up withall. For this kind of fish your tackle must be strong, your Rod must not be very slender at the top, where you must place a small slender ring for your line to run through.

Ken Sutton's drawing of the Venables reel (Fig. 37.18.*b*), which was published in *Fishing* (1965), shows what he thought to be the working principle: a barrel turned by a handle; a saddle, and a circular rod clamp. This was a most intelligent reconstruction and is probably very near to the truth. There is, however, one weakness: the way in which the reel is fastened to the rod. We find ourselves unable to endorse the practicability of the circular-sectioned rod-clamp. In our view, the 'clamp' part of Venables's illustration, albeit badly drawn, represents an early pattern of wing-nut that screwed down on a vertical, threaded, reel-support pin which passed through a hole in the rod handle (Fig. 37.18.*c*).

This method of fixing a winch to a rod was described eleven years previously in Thomas Barker's *The Art of Angling* (1651), the first book to mention the reel:

The manner of his Trouling was, with a Hazell Rod of twelve foot long, with a Ring of Wyre

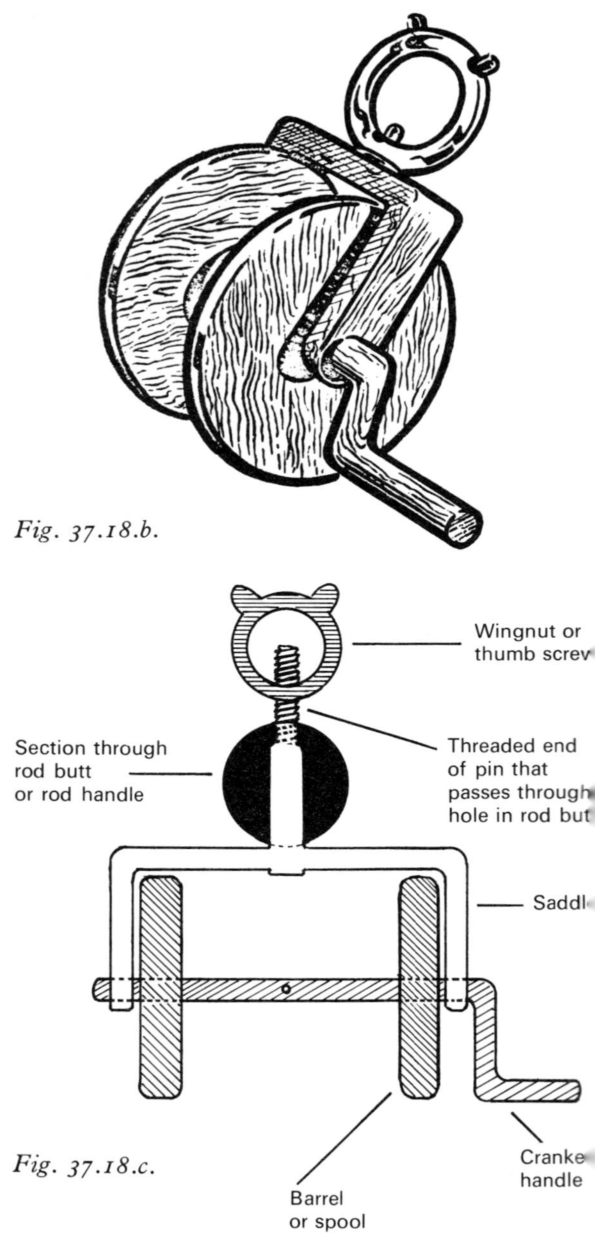

Fig. 37.18.b.

Fig. 37.18.c.

in the top of his Rod, for his line to runne thorow: within two foot of the bottome of the Rod *there was a hole made*, for to put in a winde, to turne with a barrell, to gather up his Line, and loose at his pleasure . . . [Our italics].

Seventeenth century reels of this type are shown on p. 352.

Maggots

Notes on the care of maggots

The life of a maggot – after it has stopped feeding but before it pupates – can be extended by temperature control. For several weeks, maggots can be prevented from turning into chrysalids if kept at a low temperature (i.e. a few degrees above freezing point). An ordinary domestic refrigerator is ideal for this purpose.

The glazed pipe that protects a domestic water supply turn-cock – found in the grounds of most properties with a mains water supply – provides a site that will keep maggots in good condition for months. The bait should be placed in a dried-milk tin (fitted with a string handle) before being lowered down the pipe. The lid of the bait tin should be punctured with tiny holes so that atmospheric humidity and the humidity inside the bait-tin can equalize. (Failure to ventilate a bait-tin may cause sweating, which will spoil the bait.)

If maggots are allowed to get too dry they tend to lose their body liquid. As a result, they shrink in size and their skins become tough. This toughness of the skin makes a maggot more likely to burst when impaled on a hook. To prevent this, add three tablespoonfuls of water to each pint of the sawdust mixture in which the maggots are kept.

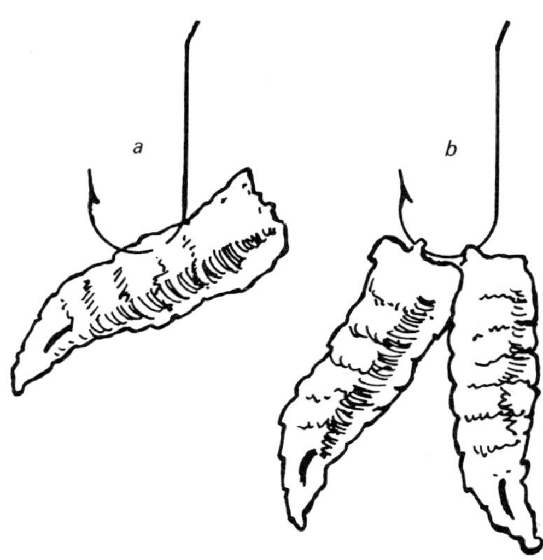

Fig. 37.19.

Baiting with Maggots

Movement is probably the most important element of attraction. When attaching a maggot to a hook care must be taken to ensure that the liveliness of the bait is retained. Use only fine, sharp hooks, and wherever you place the point of the hook make the smallest possible nick into the skin of the bait. If a maggot has a coarse, blunt hook pushed right through its body it will burst and quickly lose its attraction for fish.

There is no 'best' method of attaching a maggot, although the way illustrated in Fig. 37.19.*b*, is usually described as such. The beginner's way (Fig. 19.*a*) is often quite useful as a change method, provided the hook just penetrates the skin.

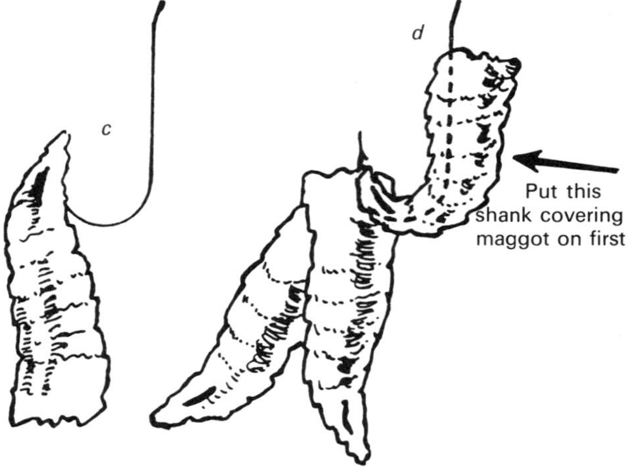

Fig. 37.19 cont.

The method illustrated in Fig. 19.*c*, leaves the point of the hook inside the maggot and provokes intense activity. Indeed, a maggot mounted in this way often turns round and round on the hook like a propeller.

The method shown in Fig. 19.*d*, is the one used by Jack Harrigan, who is an outstandingly good Hampshire Avon barbel-angler. His method of mounting three large maggots hides the hook and presents the barbel with an attractive mouthful.

When fish become shy, try different methods of bait attachment. Vary the number of maggots used on the hook. Try coloured maggots, or chrysalids (casters). Even a tiny change may help to deceive fish that would otherwise be suspicious of the same bait constantly presented in the same way.

A bunch of maggots – deadly bait for a barbel.

Baiting with Stewed Hempseed

When hempseed is stewed it splits open. The usual method of mounting a seed is to push the bend of the hook into this split leaving point and barb exposed (Fig. 37.20.*a*). This is a good method, but it entails frequent re-baiting since the seed is easily removed by a fish.

The point and barb are left exposed in the second method of baiting (Fig. 20.*b*), but this time the point of the hook is inserted into the split and pulled out through the shell.

Mounted like this the hempseed is more secure, so that less re-baiting is necessary; but the position of the seed reduces the

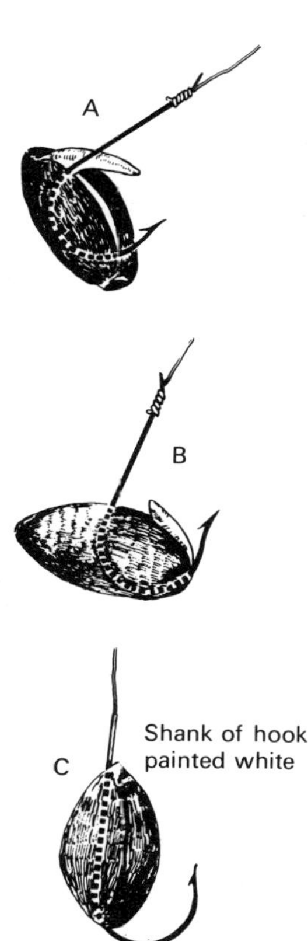

Fig. 37.20.

effective gape of the hook, which in turn reduces the chance of a good hook-hold. Moreover, a fish has a better chance of levering itself off the hook if the hempseed fails to budge.

The third method (Fig. 20.*c*) is very good indeed, but like so many of the best fishing methods it requires a little more time and trouble. Select a large, partly-cooked seed that has not yet split open. Drill a hole through the length of the seed – slightly off centre. Having first cut off the snood-*loop* with which most shop hooks-to-nylon are supplied, pass the nylon through this hole and pull the seed down on to the shank of the hook.

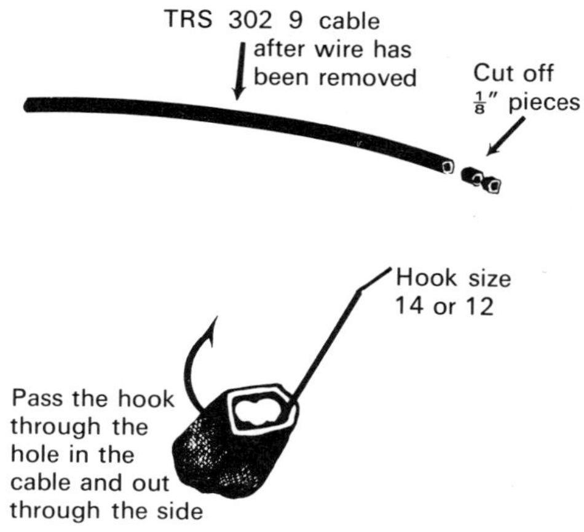

Fig. 37.21.

Cable-Hemp

Some hemp-fishers tire of having constantly to re-bait their hooks. An effective substitute for the natural seed, and one which will stay put, can be made from a small piece of special rubber known as T.R.S. 3029 cable.

For the technical description of this rubber, we are indebted to Mr Bourlet, a London hemp-angler of notable skill.

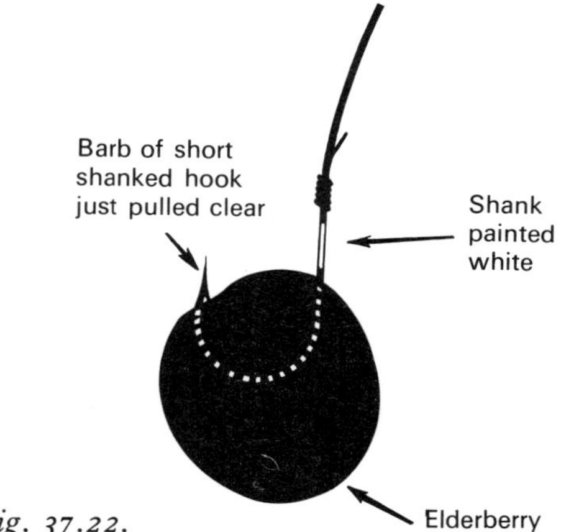

Fig. 37.22.

Hemp and elderberry

If, in a hemp-baited swim, the fish are equally disposed to take a hook baited with elderberry, then use elderberry in lieu of a grain of hemp so as to obtain the advantage of a more enduring bite.

In streamy swims, choose a *medium* float and weight it with a lead coil so that only the tip of the float shows above the surface. Avoid *light* floats. These tend to drift in an arc, since they are more affected by line drag. This drag makes the baited hook move in a most unnatural manner. Fish are suspicious of a bait moving sideways across the line of drift, even though that deviation may, at times, be slight. Very light floats can, of course, be used in still water.

Do not use spade-end hooks or eyed hooks, since these demand the drilling of over-large holes. Use fine wire round-bend hooks to nylon. Prepare the hooks by painting the shanks white. (Dayglo undercoat white is recommended.) This touch of white on the hook simulates the white germ of the seed, which is exposed by stewing.

This method saves constant re-baiting. Although the hook gape is reduced, the effect is less than that of the second method because the seed lies up and down the shank rather than across. Leverage is lessened by the off-centre boring which allows the seed to swivel to its narrow side or up the snood under pressure of a fish's mouth.

To prepare hempseed, soak it overnight in cold water. Next morning, bring the water to the boil and maintain this temperature until the majority of the seeds split open. Wash the seed in cold water; then drain and place in a polythene bag.

If the need to prepare hemp is more urgent, place the seeds in boiling water and simmer until they begin to split open. Most novices tend to over-cook hemp, with the result that the seeds break up when an attempt is made to put them on a hook. Avoid this by keeping an eye on the pot and stirring frequently.

There is one other way of cooking hemp – the lazy way. Put the seeds into a vacuum flask, then fill with boiling water and leave standing overnight.

The best hemp obtainable is Chilean hemp. If you are lucky enough to get some, reserve it for hookbait. For groundbait, use a smaller, cheaper grade of hemp.

A bottle of preserved elderberries should always be included in a hemp angler's tackle bag, for there are days when fish take an elderberry just as eagerly as a hempseed. Such days are rewarding, since fish will hold on to a soft elderberry longer than they will a hempseed, and more fish will be hooked for any given number of bites. Once again, a white-painted hook shank is recommended. Apart from giving the elderberry the 'hemp-seed look', the white paint attracts a fish's attention and makes the bait visible at greater range.

Hempseed is a first-class bait for roach and dace. Sometimes, on hot, sunny summer days, it seems to be the only bait that will get a response. Roach and dace are not the only fish with a liking for this bait, however; chub, barbel and even bream will often invade a baited swim and provide a bonus for the hemp-fisherman.

38 · Float Fishing

The float is pleasing in appearance, and even more pleasing in disappearance.
HUGH SHERINGHAM.

. . . to watch a float is the symbol of all angling, of all that recreates and is contemplative. Ask the man in the morning train if he angles. If he does not he will reply, perhaps apologetically, perhaps haughtily. 'I am afraid,' he will say, 'that I have not the patience to watch a float.' Not, mark you well, 'to flog a stream' or 'dangle a worm', but to 'watch a float'.

Yet, in all angling, there are few things of greater contenting than a float, and a red float (our brother Sheringham has written lovingly of a red float) is to be preferred before any other. What may it not, in certain waters cheerfully bobbing, indicate anon? A three-pound roach? A four-pound perch? A sixteen-pound carp? A twenty-pound pike? A float puts the whole subaqueous world at Fancy's disposal. A float may even foretell the accomplishment of a great trout – and blush no redder for man's subsequent ungrateful ignoring of its acquaintance in the tale of triumph.
PATRICK CHALMERS, *A Fisherman's Angles* (1931).

TROTTING IN FAST WATER

The word 'fast' in the context of running water is a relative term. It could be used to describe the normal current speed of a river like the Hampshire Avon, or it could be used to describe the abnormal speed of flood or semi-flood water in a normally sluggish river like the Thames or the Great Ouse.

Of importance to the angler is the fact that whereas the normal mainstream current in the Avon causes no distress to an Avon fish, the same speed of current in the Thames would cause a Thames fish to vacate its usual mainstream swim and seek a more sheltered one.

An experienced angler instinctively recognizes the maximum current that fish in a particular swim are likely to tolerate. To deal with any reasonable increase of current over the normal flow, he will increase the amount of shot on his line and use a larger float. With a further increase in flow, he will stop fishing the mainstream swim in favour of a more sheltered swim close to the bank.

There are two other important aspects of fishing in normally fast-flowing rivers. These are best illustrated by recounting actual incidents.

A few years ago two anglers were sharing a very fast weirpool swim in the course of a fishing match (Fig. 39.1). Angler No. 1 stood on the bank at the head of the weirpool close to the apron. He faced downstream and trotted his float down the stream, so that after a trot of 20 yards or so his float tripped through the swim in front of angler No. 2, who stood facing out towards the middle of the pool. Because of the nature of the current in the weirpool, both anglers could trot their floats upstream or downstream according to whether they cast into the main downstream lasher, or in the back-eddy which carried the float back to the apron. In practice it was more convenient for both anglers to allow their floats to go up and down the runs together.

At first, when the fish were unwary, both anglers had plenty of bites. After a time, however, the 'apron' angler's sport declined, although angler No. 2 continued to catch fish at the same tempo.

After a few hours of frustration, the 'apron' angler stopped fishing and approached the other for a chat. The object of the visit was obvious: he was seeking an explanation for his failure to continue catching fish, even though he was fishing with a rig similar to his rival's. As the two anglers stood side by side exchanging pleasantries, more fish fell to the second angler's rod, and the fact that his float was not pulled under during these proceedings added to his companion's astonishment.

Quite simply, the 'apron' angler had failed to realise the significance of a slight increase in the speed of the current. Whereas the slacker current in the morning had given the fish time to take the bait 'out in front', as it were, the faster current of the afternoon forced the fish to chase the bait downstream. This change of behaviour on the part of the fish made a great deal of difference to the behaviour of the float. In the morning, when the fish were facing upstream as they took the bait, the float was pulled under by the drag of the stream. Later, when the fish were obliged to turn downstream in order to take the bait, the only sign of a bite was a slight tipping backwards of the float – the result of a small degree of overshooting on the part of the fish as it grabbed the bait (Fig. 38.2). By this time, some hours had elapsed and the fish remaining in the swim had become more circumspect. Indeed they were so suspicious that unless they were struck on the first indication of a bite, the bait was dropped.

Fig. 38.1 depicts the weir and the swim shared by No. 1 and No. 2 anglers. Both anglers trotted their floats continuously round the swim (see fine dotted line). The letters on the diagram represent various species of fish. Although all the species present could be caught in any of the weirpool swims, nevertheless to those who regularly fished in the weirpool a pattern of distribution was always noticeable.

C – CHUB
D – DACE
G – GRAYLING
L.G. – LARGE GRAYLING
R – ROACH
S.T. – SMALL TROUT
T – TROUT

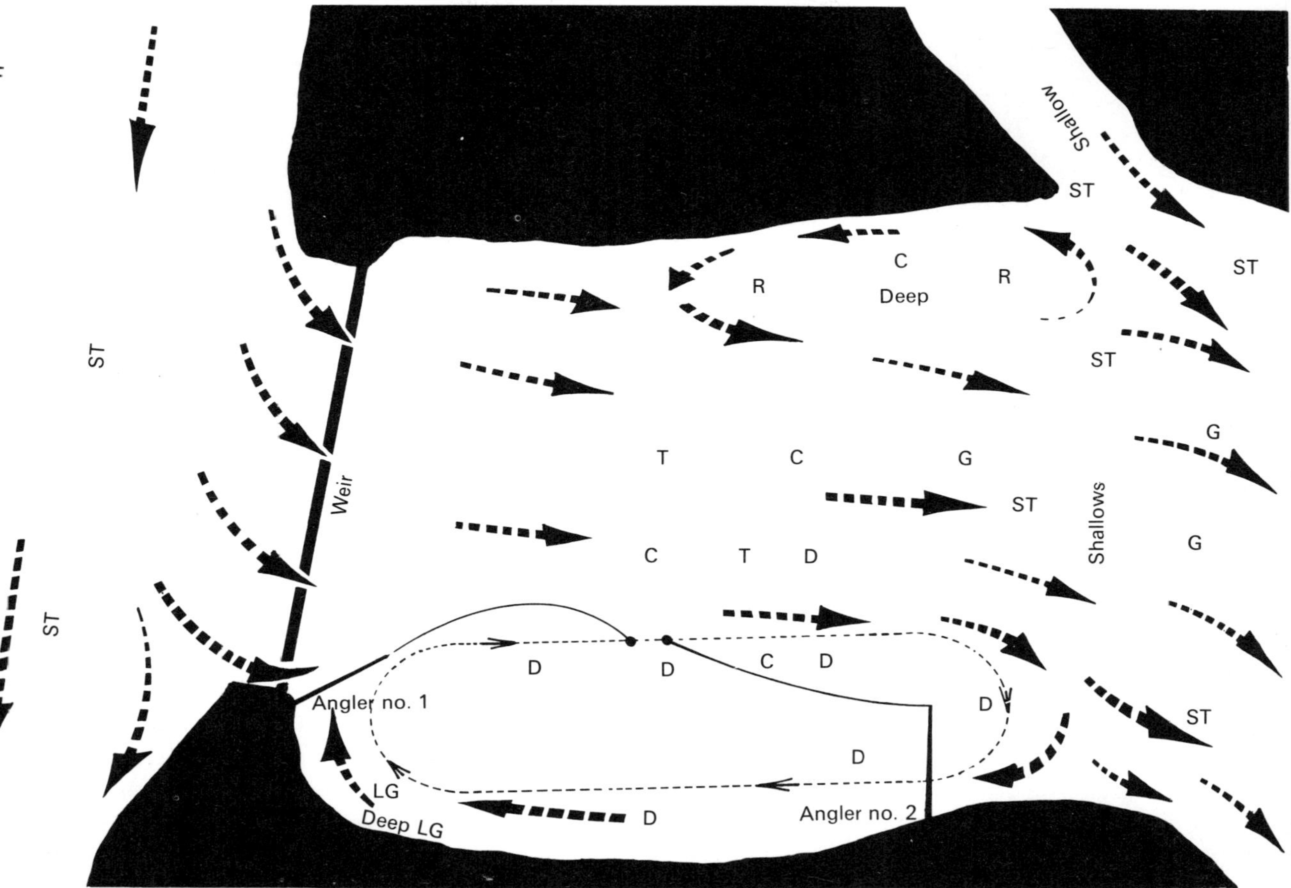

Fig. 38.1. A Hampshire Avon weirpool.

The diagram represents a private weirpool on the Hampshire Avon. If the mainstream part of the diagram (left) was continued to cover the next 50 yards upstream it would include the productive 'armchair' swim so named by famous Avon fisherman Captain L. A. Parker. Parker thought this swim to be the best roach swim on the Avon. It has produced six 2 lb roach for F. B. – all taken on breadcrust.

On the occasion of the second incident, two anglers were float fishing from a punt moored above a fast run. Both were trotting big Avon-type floats down the run so close together as to be almost touching. They were using identical tackle, and yet one angler caught fish after fish while the other caught nothing.

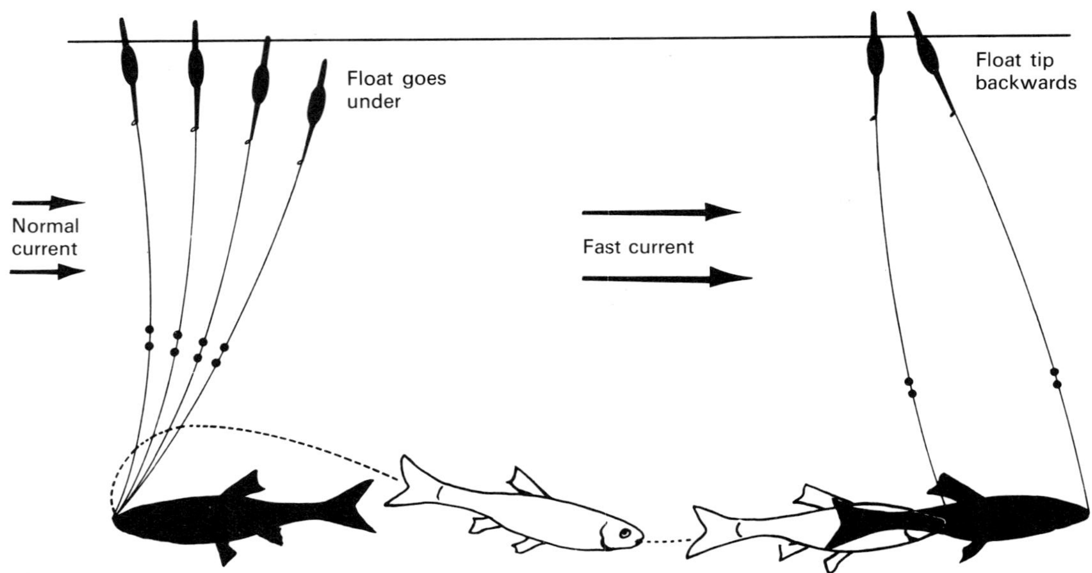

Fig. 38.2. Diagram showing how bite indication can vary with the speed of the current.

Again, the answer, though simple, discloses a fundamental truth. The unsuccessful angler had been making a short cast down to the head of the run, whereas the skilful angler had been overcasting slightly and winding back before letting his float join up with his companion's. From this point onwards, both floats proceeded down the run together. But there was an essential difference between the two methods. The novice's baited hook tripped along the bottom *behind* the float, whereas the successful angler's baited hook *preceded* the float – a killing orientation of tackle caused by overcasting and winding back.

THE LIFT METHOD OF FLOAT FISHING

Judging by their reluctance to use it, some anglers must find the famous 'lift' method a bit of a bogey. Although this method is very old, its popularity suffered a decline until the persistence of Fred J. Taylor brought it back into prominence (see pp. 226–8). Essentially of use in still-water, or a very slow stream, its principal virtue lies in its visual exaggeration of a bite. As can be seen in Fig. 38.3, there is a dramatic movement of the float the moment it is released from tension through the lifting of bait and lead by a feeding fish. When more conventional stillwater methods of float fishing are used, such pronounced bite indication can be expected only when a fish actually moves off with the bait.

The 'lift' method takes advantage of the

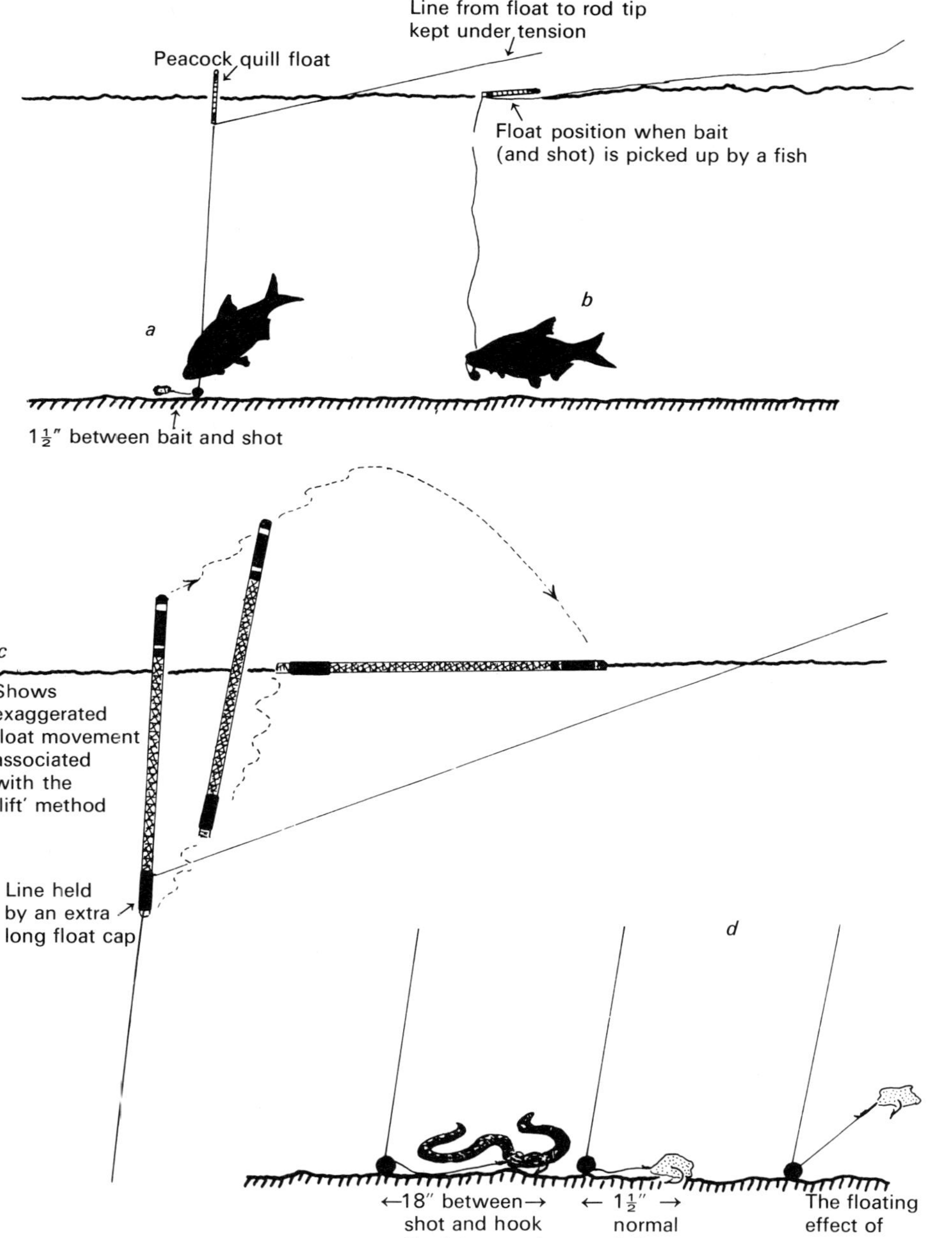

Fig. 38.3. The 'lift' method.

changing postures of a feeding fish. From being nose down and tail up (the near vertical position, see Fig. 38.3.*a*), the fish moves into the horizontal position (Fig. 3.*b*) once it has picked up the bait.

Set the rig up as follows. Attach the float (in this case a purposely overlong piece of peacock quill) to the line by means of a half-inch rubber float band. This attachment should be made at the base of the quill. Set the float somewhat deeper than the depth of the swim. Cast out, and draw the line tight with the rod seated in a rod-rest. After a preliminary cast, trim the peacock quill to a suitable length with a pair of scissors, leaving about $\frac{3}{8}$ in. showing above water.

Put the bait in the same spot each time by swinging out the tackle on a fixed length of line. Lay the rod in the rest while lead and bait are still sinking. As soon as the lead touches bottom, draw the rig tight until the float cocks.

A useful variation using the floating properties of crust is illustrated in Fig. 38.3.*d*. From the diagram it can be seen that the crustbait can be fished a pre-determined distance off the bottom – to keep it clear of algal growth, debris or soft mud.

With worm baits, we recommend a longer length of line between swanshot and hook. This effectively dampens the immediate sensitivity of the rig and allows a fish more time to take a proper hold of the worm before feeling resistance. When lobworms are used, some 18 in. of line between shot and hook is desirable. Damping the sensitivity of the rig does not hide bite-indication completely. A slight trembling of the float is enough to inform the angler that his bait is receiving attention.

With the 'lift' method, it is normal practice to strike as soon as the float lies flat. Conditions prevailing at the waterside, however, must always determine the course of action that an angler should take. Apart from varying the timing of the strike, anglers fishing canals and other waters where extreme delicacy of touch and tackle is required will prefer to use a smaller holding-shot and a correspondingly tiny float.

'Lift' fishing requires long and sturdy rod-rests. Take great care to position them well, for they will in turn determine the fishing area of the float and hookbait. Once this area is established, groundbait it accurately.

THE ADJUSTABLE FLOAT-LINK RIG

Notwithstanding a float's natural uses, and its hundred and one different shapes and sizes, there are (trimmers apart) just two traditional methods of attachment.

1. *The fixed float*. Used when the distance between float and hook is less than the length of the rod.

2. *The sliding float*. Can be used for any depth, but *must* be used when the hook depth is greater than the rod length.

In both methods the float is attached to the mainline and operates somewhere between the rod point and the hook. Although the first method is open to less criticism than the second, neither is entirely satisfactory. The trouble is that unless a float is fished with a very shallow hook depth, or almost directly beneath the rod point (as it is with roach-pole technique) it presents an angler with a problem of great complexity: how to strike effectively.

For a strike to be effective, the pull initiated by the sudden upward or sideways movement of the rod should be transferred instantaneously to the hook. But this is possible only when there is an absence of slack line between rod

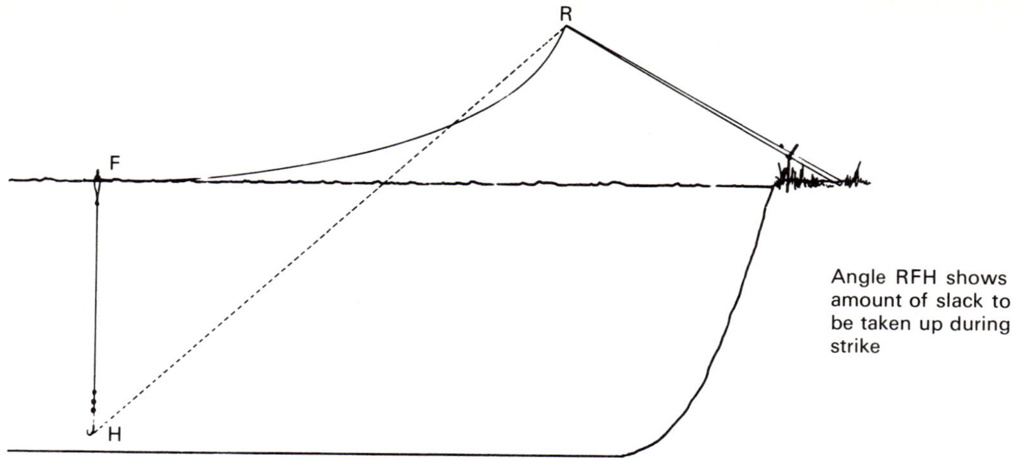

Figs. 38.5 (above) *and 38.6* (below).

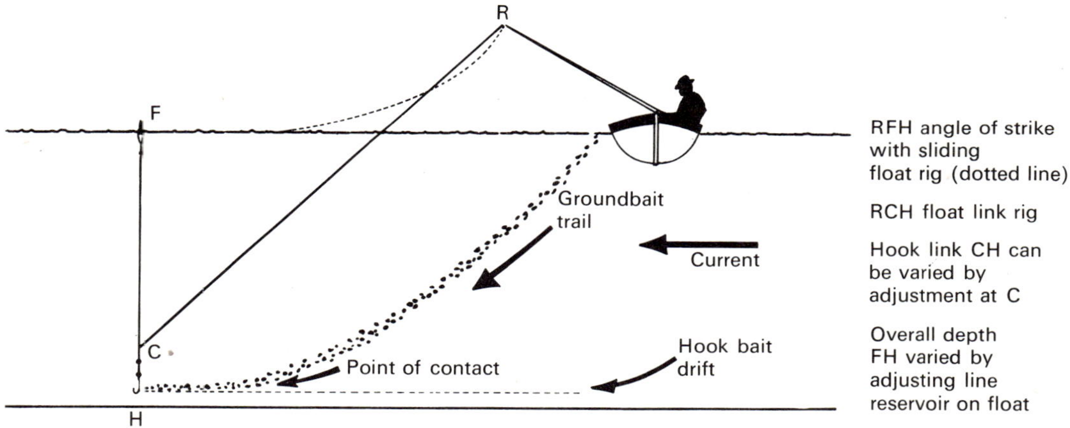

point and hook. With conventional float tackle (Fig. 38.5), the angle between rod and hook represents a substantial amount of slack, which has to be taken up before the effect of a strike is felt. This is the curse of float fishing. The longer the range at which a float is fished, and the greater the depth between float and hook, the more ineffectual the strike. The tightening of the line which precedes an incisive movement of the hook takes too long: it gives the fish time to drop the bait.

This loss of hooking efficiency due to slack line often frustrates an angler who is long-trotting a swim with fixed float. It is even more frustrating when he is fishing deep water with sliding float.

The traditional sliding-float technique is not without value. It permits an angler to float-fish in water of considerable depth. It enables him to cover a lot of ground. And by doing so it undoubtedly offers more chances of catching fish than any other method. *But*, the inevitable slack which accumulates between rod and hook inhibits him from taking these chances. Like those of the long-distance trotter, the sliding-float man's advantages are lost through ineffectual

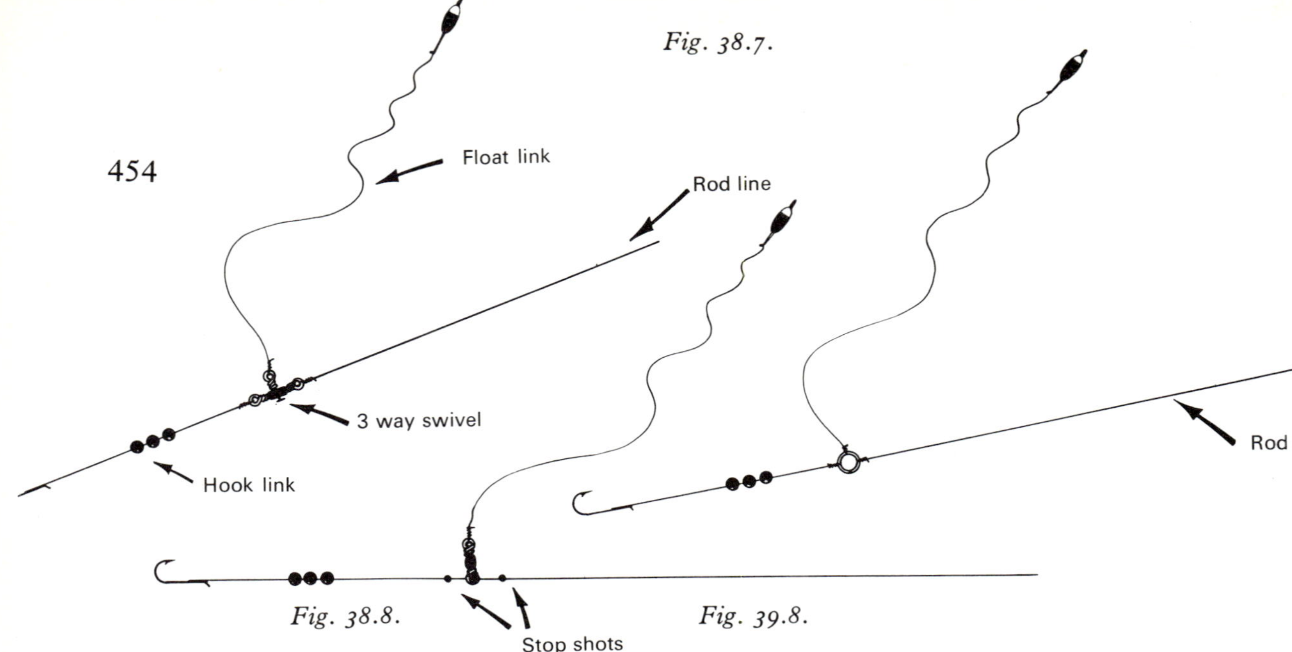

striking; and the ledger angler, with fewer bites but more fish, may be forgiven his gleeful grin.

No matter. Float enthusiasts can take heart. There is a third method of attaching a float: a method which not only sanctions the use of a smaller float and less lead at maximum range and depth, but offers the opportunity of an effective strike. This seemingly Utopian dream achieves substance in the 'float-link' rig (Fig. 38.6).

We have no hesitation in suggesting that this is the most efficient method of float fishing yet devised – certainly in deep water. With the float nicely out of the way on its own separate linkage, the line is straightened between rod point and hook, thus reducing that accursed slack which has always weakened the sting of an angler's strike. Nor is that all. Since the angler is now in direct contact with his hook, loss of power through striking against the float is almost entirely eliminated. By itself, no small advantage.

The full beauty of the method can be appreciated by referring to Fig. 39.6, and comparing the indirect route taken by a line when it travels to the hook via the float.

The rig has another distinct advantage over the sliding float. Virtually any float can be used. A sliding float has to be on the large side to support the extra lead needed to overcome the drag of the mainline pulling at right angles to the eye of the float. Since this drag is non-existent in the float-link rig, less lead and a more delicate float can be used.

Although the float-link method has already been published (by F. B., in an earlier book), it is practised by very few anglers. And yet, with suitable modifications, it can be used for catching a wide variety of both fresh and salt water species, and, compared with other methods, offers spectacular opportunities. It is a particularly effective method of float fishing in any water – whether lake, reservoir, river or sea – which otherwise demands the use of a sliding float.

Two ways of assembling the rig are shown in Figs. 38.7 and 8. In each case the float has its own separate link, which is approximately 3 feet less than the depth of water.

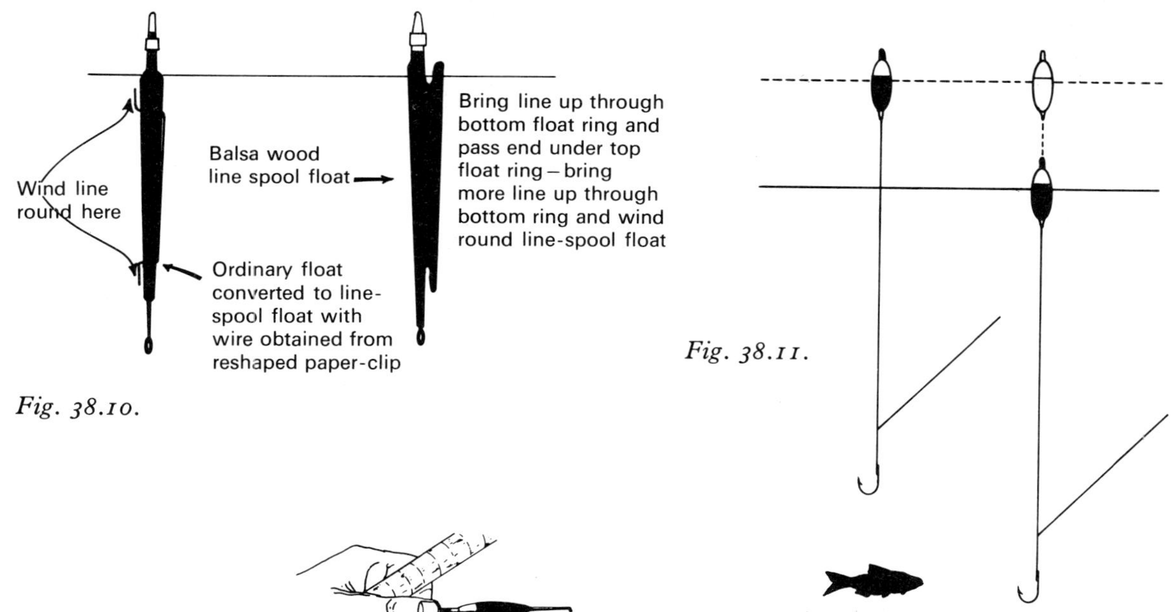

Fig. 38.10.

Fig. 38.11.

Fig. 38.9.

In Fig. 38.7, the hook is attached to a separate link fastened to either a three-way swivel or a split ring. The swivel, or ring, is used only when a wire leader is required for the hook-link.

When nylon will serve for the hook-link, tie the hook direct to the mainline (Fig. 38.8). The float-link slides on a tiny swivel held in the appropriate place by two split shot. This simplifies and strengthens the rig by eliminating unnecessary knots, and allows the length of the hook-link to be adjusted instantly.

Fishing preparations are very simple. First, plumb the depth of water. Supposing this to be, say, 20 ft, cut off 17 ft of nylon from a spare spool. (This can be much lighter than the mainline.) Tie one end to the float and the other to the mainline, using one of the methods already described, leaving 3 feet of hook-link below the join. Balance the float with the appropriate amount of lead.

The bait will now fish on, or just off, the bottom, but can be raised a few inches, if desired, by cutting off that amount from the hook-link.

When casting from a bank, wind up the rig until the connecting link is up to the top ring of the rod. Then, with the float-link dangling in a loop, hold the tip of the float between thumb and index finger of the left hand (Fig. 38.9). The other hand controls the reel. Now, cast in the usual way. As soon as the lead is in flight, it carries the float out of the lightly-gripped fingers of the left (or non-casting) hand. The float, of course, lies flat on the surface until cocked by the lead sinking to its full extent.

A similar cast can be made from a boat when the angler is fishing in still water. In running water, no cast is necessary. The rig is simply lowered overside and allowed to drift away with the current (Fig. 38.6).

Of vital importance to sea anglers is the Buller/Falkus design of float (Fig. 38.10). This device (known as the 'line-spool' float) incorporates a reservoir of link-line, which enables an angler to combat the rise and fall of the tide. The effect of a rising tide is shown in Fig. 38.11. It can be seen at once that float-link trotting in tidal water is im-

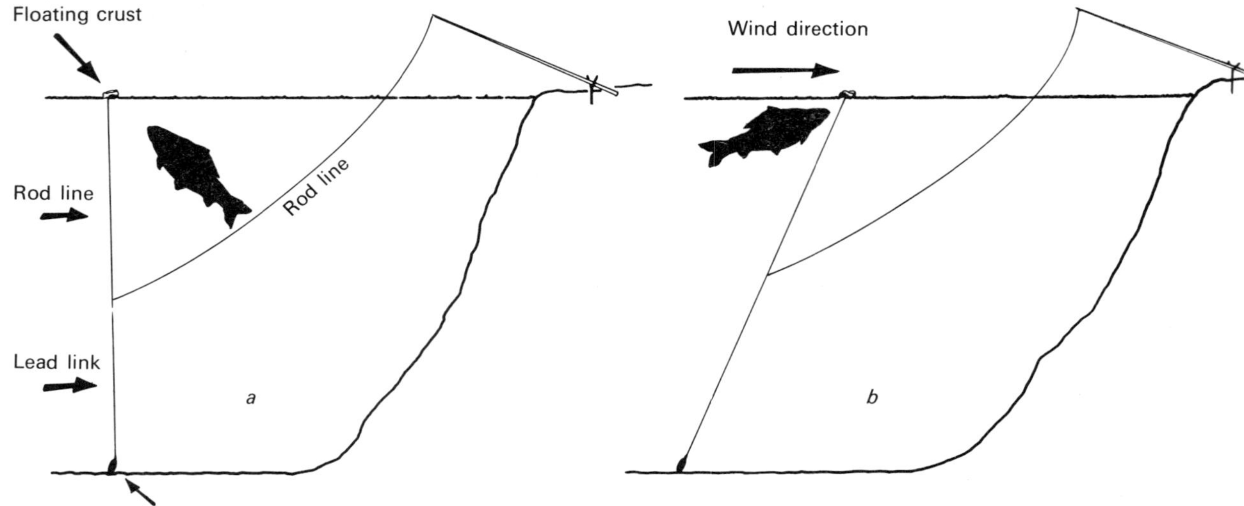

Fig. 38.12. Fishing with anchored floating crust.

practicable without a simple method of regulating the depth at which the bait is fished.

On occasion, a line-spool float is very useful in fresh water. We do not pretend to have exhausted its possibilities. As with all other aspects of the rig, it offers opportunities of experiment and discovery which should appeal to thoughtful anglers.

The rig can, of course, be fished with the help of groundbait (see Fig. 38.6). The angler can be confident that his drifting hook bait will meet the groundbait trail regardless of the speed of the current. This meeting point can be described as the 'point of contact'. At sea, this point will be close to the boat during periods of slack water, but as much as 60 to 70 yards away when the tide is running strongly.

Most bites are obtained at the point of contact, but there are times when feeding fish start to work along the groundbait trail towards the source. If the angler suspects this, he should adjust the rig to fish at a shallower depth – and work it in shorter drifts. The use of a line-spool float makes this link adjustment very easy.

There is a variation of float-link fishing which may interest anglers who fish deep pits for carp. In certain circumstances, the thermocline forms in summer at depths of 15 to 20 feet. It occurs frequently when there are no shallows, and where the pits have deep-cut banks. In these conditions, bottom fishing is most unlikely to be successful.

Baited with floating crust, the float-link rig (fished in reverse) offers splendid chances of catching fish (Fig. 38.12.*a*).

The rig is similar to the one already described, except that the float is exchanged for a crust-baited hook, and the hook for a small Arlesey bomb. The crust-hook is, of course, attached direct to the mainline, with the lead on a separate link. This link should be of very fine nylon. It has only a small lead to cast, and will easily break away from the mainline tackle if entangled in obstructions by a fighting carp.

The small Arlesey bomb not only facilitates casting, but anchors the crust in windy weather (Fig. 38.12.*b*). This is of paramount importance when the rig is fished against an onshore wind. Without an anchor, the crust is blown straight back to the bank.

Since the crust must be encouraged to float, there should be no weight of any sort

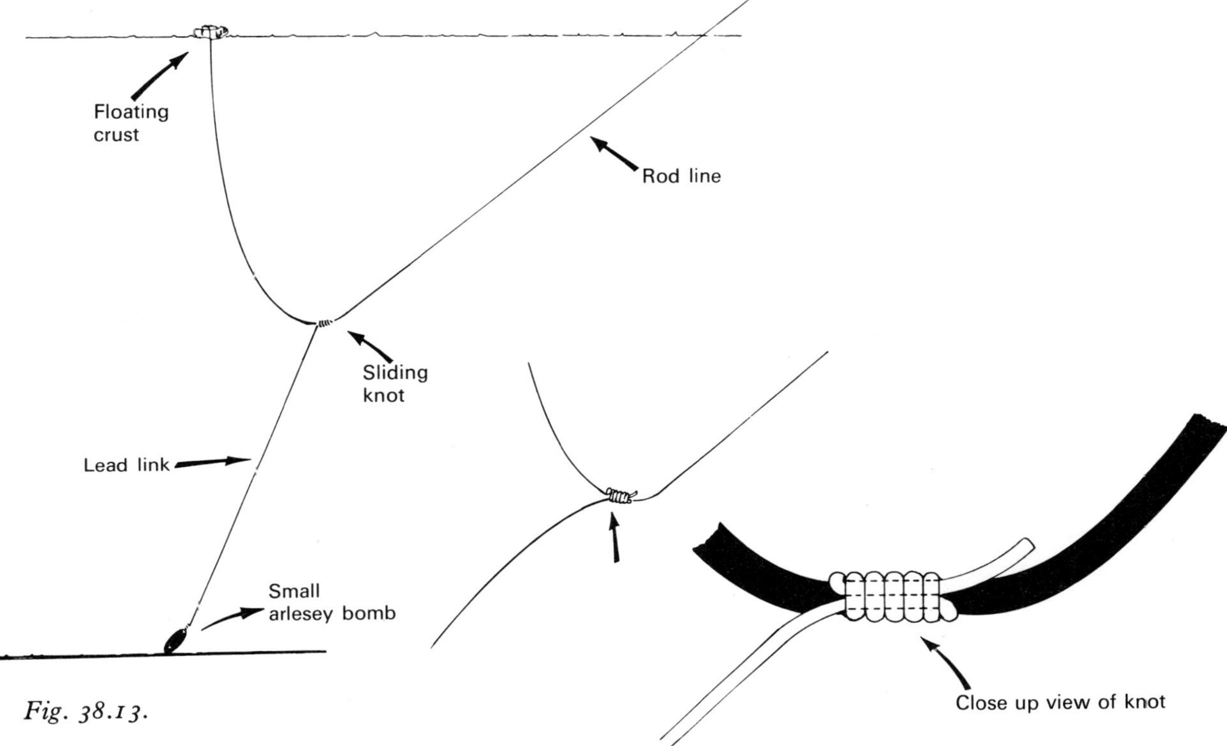

Fig. 38.13.

Fig. 38.14.

between the hook and the Arlesey bomb. Hence, a sliding knot will be found useful for the lead-link attachment (Fig. 38.13). The knot itself is shown in Fig. 38.14.

39 · Ledgering, Float-ledgering and Laying-on

Tis Hope that taketh birds with the snare, fish with the rod with fine Hooks well hidden in the bait.
TIBULLUS.

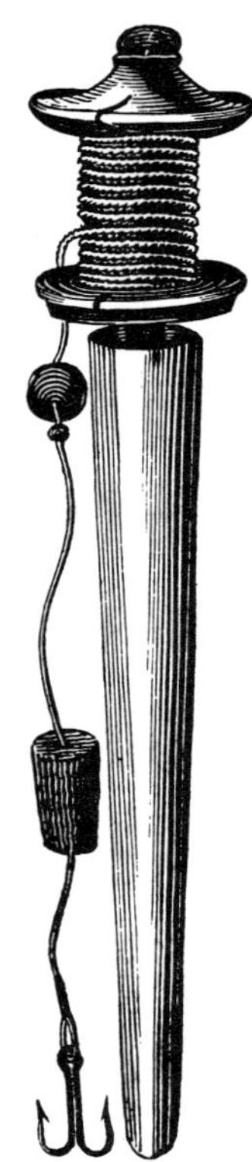

Bank runner (18th century). A type of 'running line'.

THE RUNNING-LINE

It is important to remember that the term 'running-line' was used by early angling writers to mean a line that ran unimpeded through the lead – on the bottom, or (as they put it) 'at ground'. It did *not* refer to a line running through the ring, or rings, of a rod. (Here William Radcliffe's *Fishing from the Earliest Times* is in error.)

Running-line: so called, because it runs upon the bottom; it should be as long as the rod, or nearly so, and strong; about ten inches from the end fasten a small cleft shot, and through a hole made in a small or large bullet, according to the *current*, put the line, and draw the ball down to the shot; to the extremity of the line fasten a *grass* or silk-worm gut, with a large hook.
THE REV. W. B. DANIEL, *Rural Sports* (1801).

Take a . . . small Pistol-bullet, make a hole through it, wider at each side than in the middle; yet so open in every place, as that the Line may easily pass through it without any stop; place a very small piece of Lead on your Line, that may keep this Bullet from falling nearer the Hook than

that piece of Lead, and if your flote be made large enough to bear above water against the force of the stream, the Fish will, when they bite, run away with the bait as securely, as if there were no more weight upon your line, than the little piece of Lead, because the hole in the Bullet gives passage to the Line, as if it were not there.
COLONEL ROBERT VENABLES, *The Experienc'd Angler* (1662).

Your lynes must be plumbid wyth lede. And ye shall wyte yt the nexte pumbe unto the hoke shall be therefro a large fote and more. And euery plumbe of a quantyte to the gretnes of the lyne. There be thre manere of plumbis for a grounde lyne rennynge. And for the flote set upon the grounde lyne lyenge X plumbes Ioynynge all togider. On the grounde lyne rennynge IX or X smalle.
DAME JULIANA BERNERS, *A Treatyse of Fysshynge wyth an Angle* (1496).

Since this passage occurs in the earliest angling book in English, we are taking the liberty of appending a modernized version. It makes the point very clearly:

Your lines must be weighted with lead sinkers, and you must know that the sinker nearest the hook should be a full foot and more away from it, and every sinker of a size in keeping with the thickness of the line. There are three kinds of sinkers for a ground running-line. And for the float set upon the stationary ground-line, ten weights all joining together. On the ground running-line, nine or ten small ones.

LEDGERING

During recent years, on the doubtful grounds that the word is of French origin, angling writers and editors have tended to drop the 'd' in ledger. We prefer the spelling and explanation offered by the O.E.D.

As with many words, the meaning of 'ledger' has changed with the years. 'Ledgering' today means 'fishing at ground'; but in the early 18th-century to fish at ground was 'to lie upon the grabble' – a term long fallen into desuetude. Here is a description of it:

At six inches above the hook, a cut shot is to be fixed, and next to this a small bored Bullet, thus the bullet will be prevented from slipping, and the hook Link have liberty to play in the water. If a Float be used, let it lie flat on the surface; and when you see it move along slowly, and presently stand upright, then strike . . .

So much for lying upon the grabble, which to modern anglers means ledgering or float-ledgering. To the 18th-century angler, however, ledgering meant something very different:

When an angler uses the Ledger Bait in Pike fishing, he fixes it in one certain place, where he may leave it; if he please. For this kind, some living bait is best, as a Dace, Roach, Gudgeon, or a living frog. To apply it; if a fish, stick the hook through his upper lip; then fastening it to a strong line twelve or fourteen yards long, tie the other end of the line to some stake in the ground, or bough of a tree, near the Pike's usual haunt, letting the line pass over the fork of a stick placed for the purpose, suspending the hook and about a yard of line in the water, but so as that when the Pike bites, the fork may give way, and let him have line enough to go to his hold, and paunch.

Nowadays the 'ledger bait' is seldom if ever used – except perhaps by poachers. *Modern* ledgering, float-ledgering and laying-on, however, are highly skilled techniques, and the next few pages are devoted to some of the rigs and methods involved.

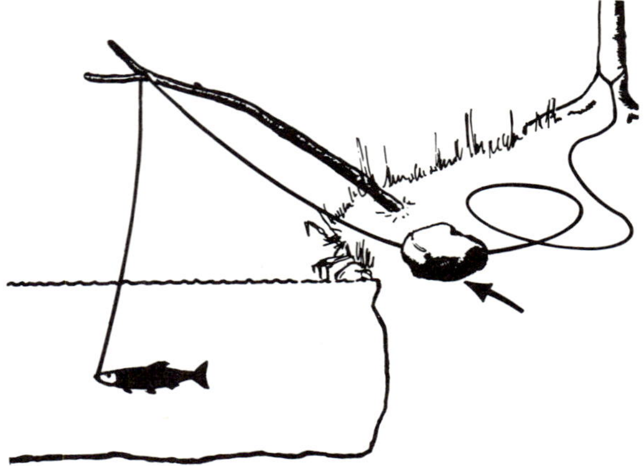

Fig. 39.1. Ledgering as described in 1725. Note the use of a stone (see arrow) to prevent the line from running out before the livebait was taken.

Fig. 39.2. When river ledgering, an 18th-century angler would have found the back eddy a profitable site for his operations.

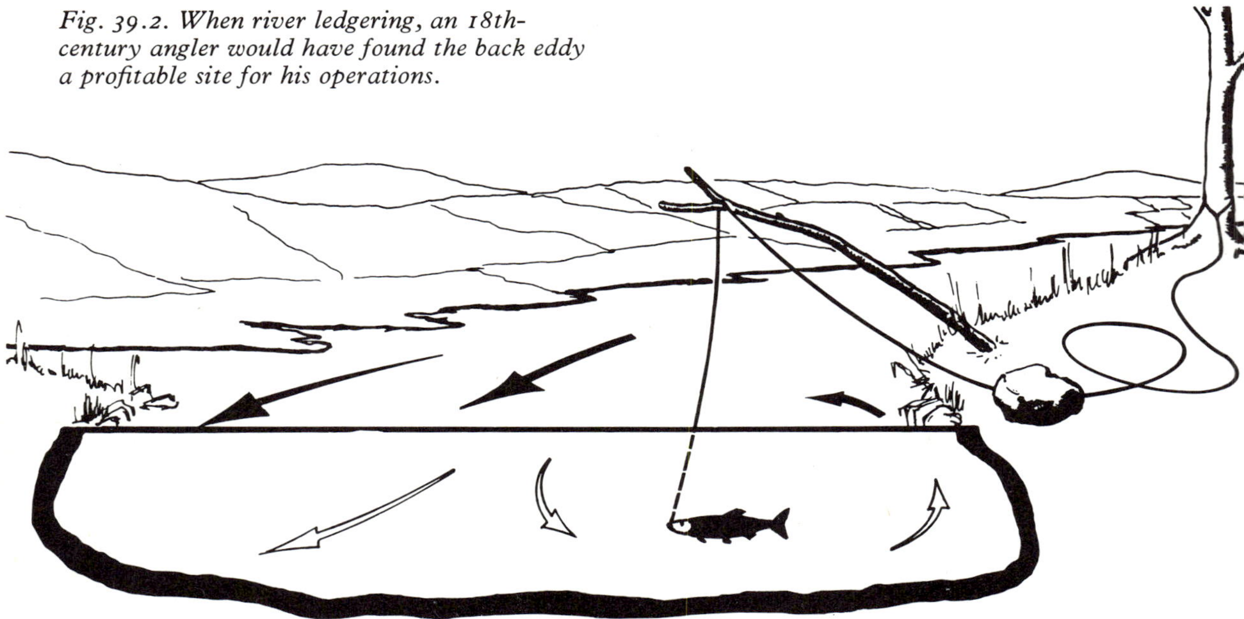

6 lb BS nylon reel line

BB stop shot

18″ of nylon between stop shot and hook

12 lb nylon looped over reel line with swan shots added

Fig. 39.3. The shot-link ledger.

THE VARIABLE SHOT-LINK LEDGER

Compared with the equivalent weight of lead in any other form, this rig is less likely to become fouled or snagged when lying on a softish bottom, or weed bed. Moreover, the addition or removal of one or more swan-shots makes adjustment very easy. This is of great importance to the angler who moves from swim to swim and needs to adjust his lead to suit differing strengths of current.

In ledgering, the calculation of weight can be critical, so critical, indeed, that frequently it makes the difference between success and failure. Converts to the shot-link ledger soon appreciate the delicate means of weight adjustment provided by increments of $\frac{1}{15}$ oz, instead of by traditional leads graduated in quarter ounces. After some small experience most anglers become expert at judging the number of shots required, either for holding the bait still or allowing it to bounce along the bottom.

Prepare a stock of shot-loops holding varying numbers of swan shots, say from two to ten, so that you can start fishing with the loop you think holds the right amount of lead for the prevailing conditions. This will save a lot of fiddling about at the waterside.

Swan shots pulled off a loop can be put into a spare tin, opened at home, and used again.

Whenever angling for particularly shy fish, always try the shot-link ledger in preference to any other. When it hits the water it causes less disturbance than a rig with more concentrated weight.

A barbel on ledgered lobworm.

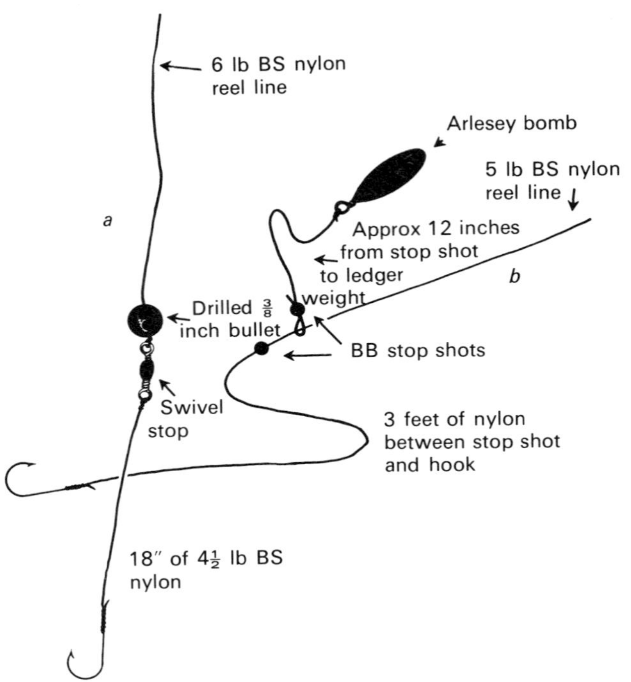

Fig. 39.4. These rigs, together with float/ledger and variable shot-link ledger, are simply variations of the 'running-line' (see p. 458), one of the earliest recorded angling rigs.

F. B. with a $5\frac{1}{2}$ lb sea trout caught on rolling ledger on H. F.'s water.

THE PIERCED-BULLET LEDGER

Although now out of favour, this rig (Fig. 39.4.*a*) has been with us for a long time. Its gravest defect is a tendency to roll. But this 'defect' can be used to advantage, e.g. when there is a need to roll a bait towards fish lying under weed streamers on a bottom of fine gravel. By this means, a direct fish-scaring cast is avoided.

When using this rig, one often suspects that, because of line drag through the lead, a fish is likely to become suspicious and release the bait before giving indication of a bite. Opening up the bore of the lead reduces this line drag and increases the rig's sensitivity.

THE BOMB-LINK LEDGER

The bomb-link ledger (Fig. 39.4.*b*) is a typical variation on the Arlesey bomb theme. The shape of the Arlesey bomb helps with long distance casting. It also prevents the lead from tumbling in flight – which so often causes the terminal tackle to snarl up.

The lead-link is usually attached by means of a swivel, although some anglers prefer to use a barbel bead, or a split ring. The link can vary between one inch and several feet in length. Use a long link when fishing from a high bank over deep water, otherwise excessive 'take-up' of line will be required during the strike.

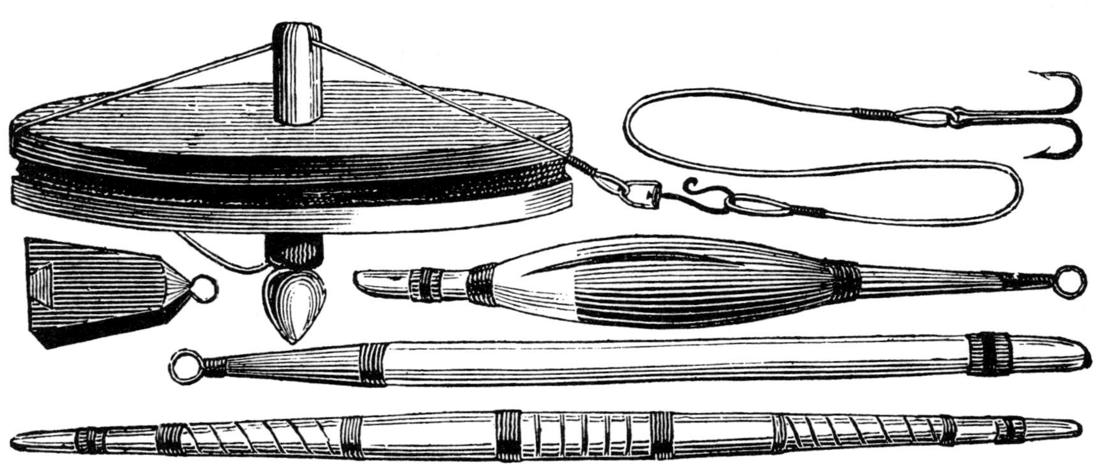

Eighteenth century trimmer, plummet and floats.

FLOAT-LEDGERING AND LAYING-ON

It is reasonable to assume that the use of a float in combination with a ledger rig dates from the earliest days of float fishing. This assumption is based on the near certainty that the earliest float-fishermen, whoever they were, must occasionally have over-estimated the depth of a swim. The effect of such an over-estimation is that float and hook are set too far apart, so that weight, hook and bait rest on the bottom and the float lies flat on the surface. Some ancient angler who failed to adjust his tackle became the first man in history to witness the mesmeric movement of a float that suddenly comes to life before sliding out of sight. He was the first man to fish with a composite float-and-ledger rig. To put it more precisely, he was the first to *lay-on*.

The terms 'laying-on' and 'float-ledgering' may seem confusing, but the difference between them is simple enough. When a *fixed* lead or leads are incorporated in a float and ledger rig, the method is termed 'laying-on'. When a *running* lead is used, the method is known as 'float-ledgering'.

There are two time-honoured precepts of coarse fishing:

1. Fish on the bottom and catch bigger fish.
2. Fish with a float and get more enjoyment from the sport.

It is to these precepts that float-ledgering and laying-on owe their popularity. Bottom fishing and float fishing are combined.

Laying-On

Laying-on (Fig. 39.5.*a*), is usually practised with float tackle that is already rigged for normal float fishing. There are times when an angler, having fished a swim successfully with ordinary float tackle, finds the sport slackening off–even though (he suspects)

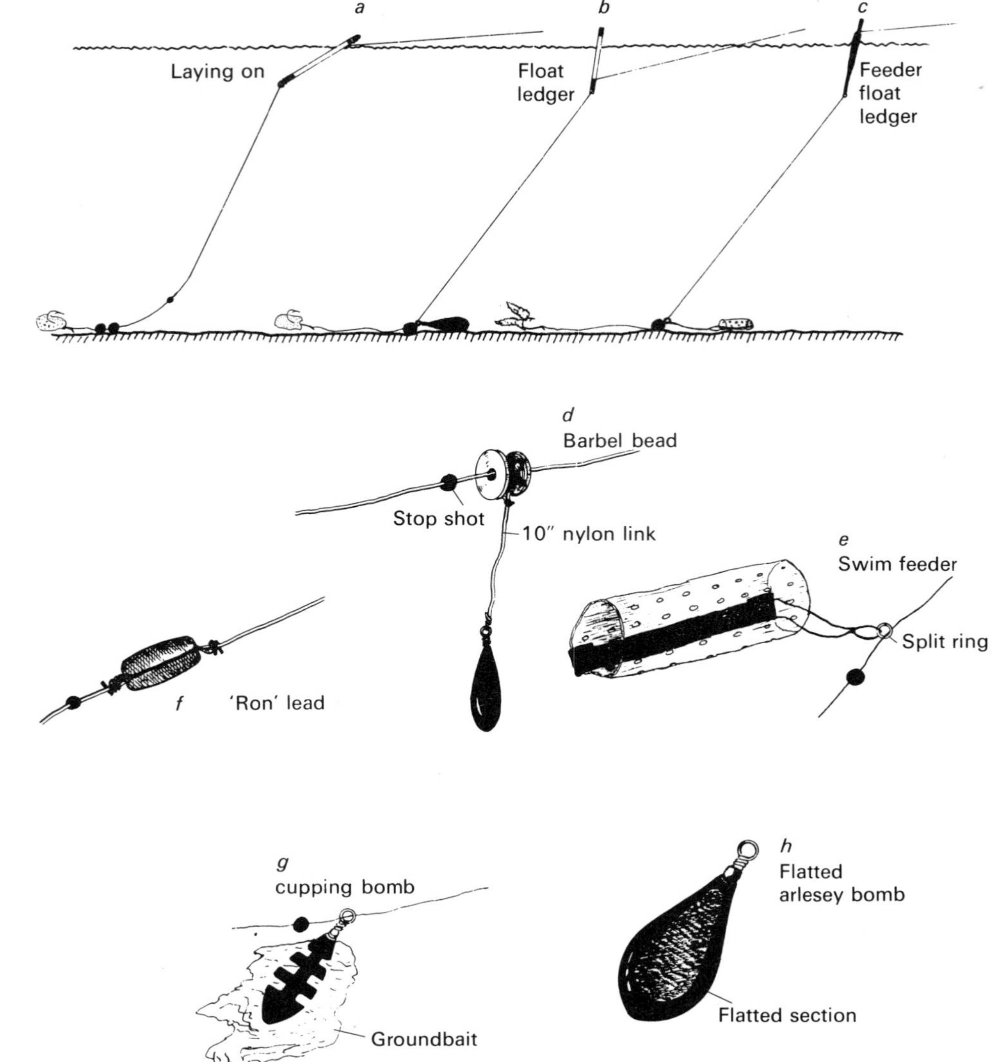

Fig. 39.5. Tackles for laying on (i.e. float with fixed *lead) and float-ledger (i.e. float with* running *lead).*

the swim still holds plenty of feeding fish. In such cases, laying-on is well worth a try. The float is pulled higher up the line so that part of the shotted leader lies on the bottom; the rod is placed between two rodrests, and the float delicately tensioned by the winding-in of a little line. While waiting for fish to find the anchored bait, the angler should groundbait in small doses, making sure that the groundbait finds bottom close to the hookbait.

Fish tend to take a stationary bait quite boldly. Usually there is a preliminary vibration of the float which gives the angler just enough time to grasp the rod handle preparatory to the strike. Sometimes the float slides away; at other times (when the fish picks up the shot as well as the bait) the

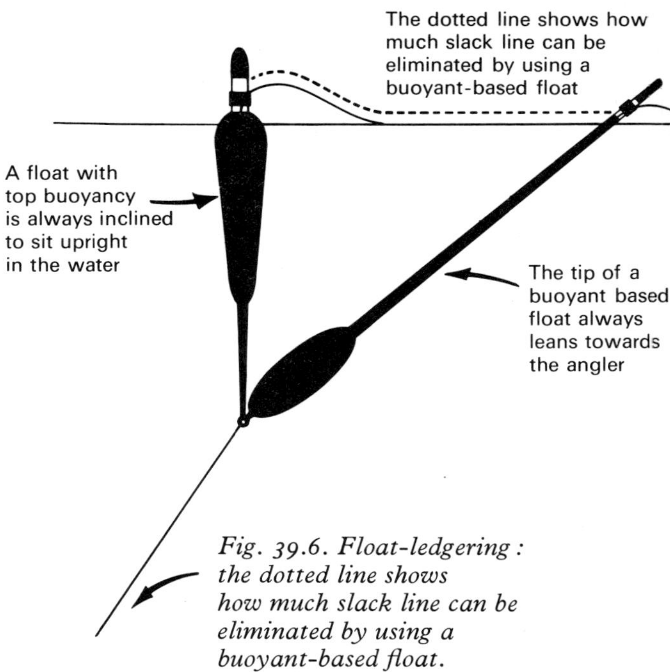

Fig. 39.6. Float-ledgering: the dotted line shows how much slack line can be eliminated by using a buoyant-based float.

float lies flat on the surface. In both cases the angler should strike firmly.

Although primarily a method for fishing still waters or sluggish rivers, laying-on can be profitably employed along the edges of fast water. The rig is cast out and allowed to swing round in the current on a tight line until the lead comes to rest at a point between current and slack. When the float stops its swing, the rod is placed in rodrests with the tip pointing downstream.

Float-Ledgering

Float-ledgering (Fig. 39.5.*b*), as used in still water, is a simple but highly effective method of fishing. If the float is to be attached in the normal manner, i.e. fixed at both ends, it is advisable to use a pattern which is more buoyant at the base. This type of float will lean better than one with top buoyancy, and so help to reduce slack. (Fig. 39.6).

Most float-ledger anglers prefer to attach only the bottom end of the float. This method reduces the float's resistance during the strike. It also helps in another way: an imperceptible movement at the base of a float – caused by a biting fish – is signalled by a big, and therefore easy to see, oscillatory movement at the tip of the float. (The windscreen wiper is an example of this: a small movement at the base of the blade; a very large movement at the tip).

An ordinary float rig can, without being 'broken down', easily be adapted to a float-ledger rig by means of a slip-on lead. For example, the 'Ron' lead (Fig. 39.5.*f*). This type of lead is quickly taken off again if the angler wishes to revert to normal float fishing.

In a fairly strong current float-ledgering can be a deadly method of fishing, but the technique required to float-ledger successfully in fast water is, in our opinion, one of the most difficult of all fishing skills to acquire. It is also extremely difficult to describe, in view of the many small but vital tackle adjustments demanded by varying conditions.

Basically, float-ledgering in medium and fast rivers is a close-range method and is best undertaken with a long rod – the longer the better in most cases. The bait is anchored with an appropriate amount of lead, and the float supported against the flow of the stream by a tight line from the rod tip – which is positioned as close to the float as possible. This is float-ledgering in broad outline, but the all-important tackle adjustments can be learned only on the river bank from a master of this angling technique.

The swimfeeder float-ledger (Fig. 39.5.*c*) shows how a swimfeeder can be used to advantage instead of a lead weight. The benefit of fishing a bait so close to an abundant supply of groundbait can be derived only when fish are not likely to be frightened by the splashing of such a bulky object: for example, in deep water. One method of attaching the swimfeeder is shown in Fig. 5.*e* – although a ten inch nylon link between the split ring and the feeder is generally desirable. The barbel-bead attachment (Fig. 5.*d*) carries a lead (or a swimfeeder) perfectly, via a short nylon link.

A variation of the Arlesey bomb (Fig. 5.*g*) is useful for 'cupping' groundbait round the lead. The secret of successful cupping is to prepare groundbait of a consistency that will enable it to stay in one piece while the lead is cast out, but allow it to break up soon after it has reached the bottom.

Another Arlesey bomb variation (Fig. 5.*h*) has the good design features of the bomb with an additional bottom-hugging quality: the flattened section reduces a tendency to roll.

Note: During their many expeditions together to Loch Lomond, and other lakes, the authors have found float-ledgering with deadbait to be a highly successful method of catching pike.

The float keeps the line clear of the bottom, and thus free from snags; it acts as a bite indicator and, prior to the strike, points the direction in which the pike is travelling – a vital piece of information.

Fig. 39.7. Arthur Cove's method of attachment is shown on the right.

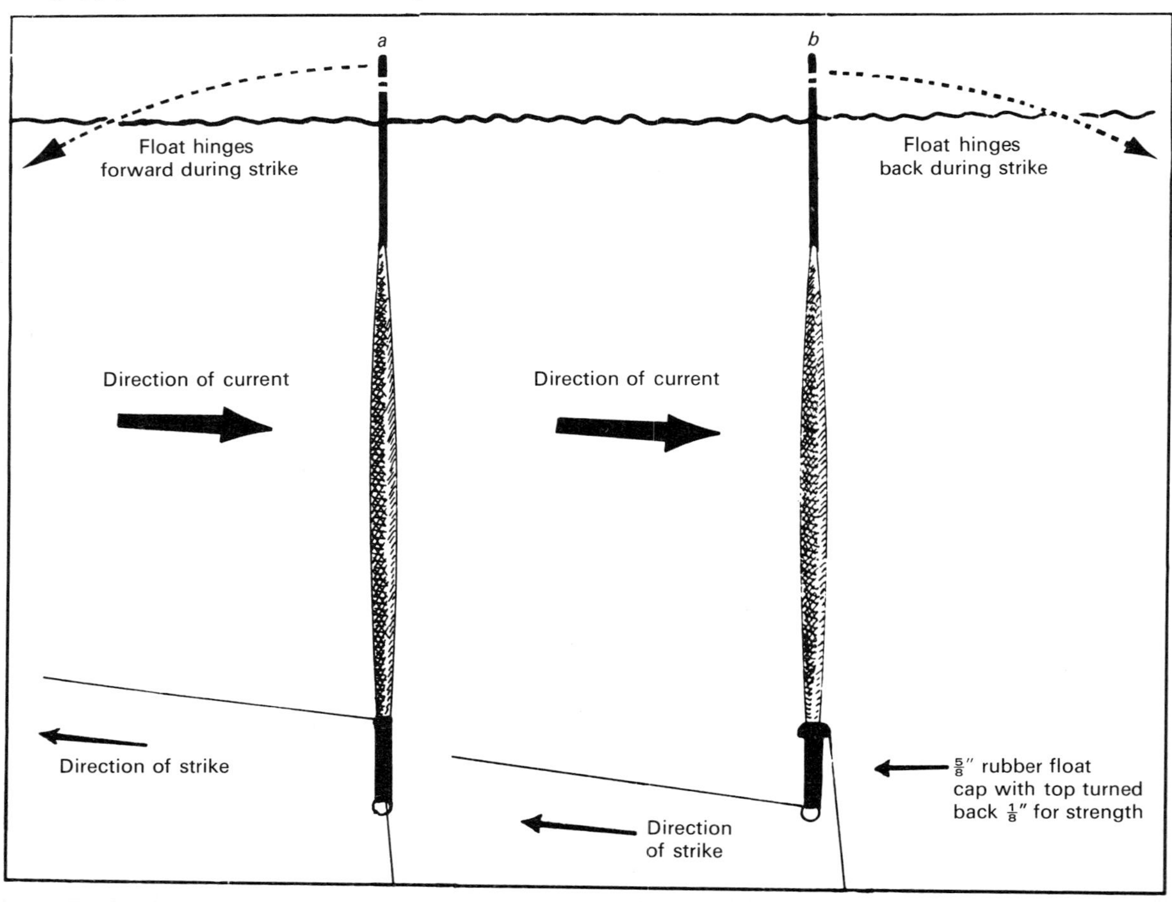

COVE'S REVERSE-SWING FLOAT

Fig. 39.7.*a* depicts a swinging float attached at the bottom end only. This method of attachment provides a sunk line to the float. On windy days this is a great advantage, since it reduces wind drag on the line.

Normally associated with the float-ledger style of fishing, this method is now popular with the match angler who wishes to 'swim' the stream in windy weather. Nevertheless, when a fine line is used, breakage often occurs as the float is struck against the current.

By swinging *with* the current instead of against it, Arthur Cove's ingenious 'reverse swing' float (Fig. 39.7.*b*) reduces the strain imposed by a strike. The line is passed *up* through the bottom float-cap instead of down.

STRET-PEGGING

Stret-pegging is a method of laying-on that can be used in running water at long range without the disturbance of long-range casting. The bait not only covers a wide area but reaches the prime feeding place without breaking surface nearby.

Having set his float deeper than the true depth, by some 12 to 18 in., the angler at A makes a short cast at right-angles across the river to point B, then momentarily holds back his float on a tight line. This holding back of the float induces the shotted leader to sweep the bottom. The float is then released and allowed to travel a yard or two downstream before it is once again held back for a few seconds. Each pause allows the shotted leader and the hookbait to cover fresh

Fig. 39.8.

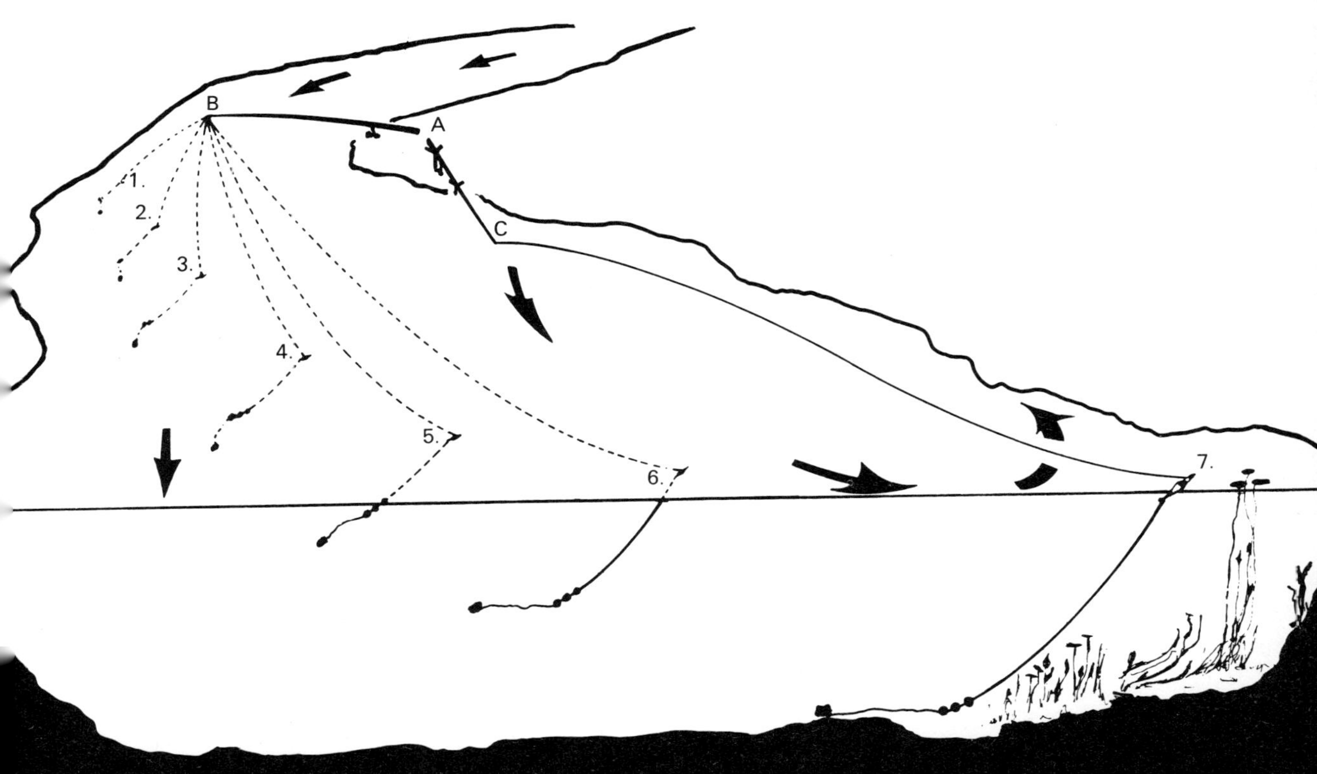

ground, and even rest on the bottom for a moment or two wherever there are little pockets of deep underwater slack.

Gradually, in a crab-like fashion (see Fig. 39.8, positions 1–6), the float moves over towards the angler's bank and ends up considerably farther downstream than when it started, directly below the rod tip at 7. The rod – which up to now has been held at right angles to the stream – is placed in a rod-rest, so that it points downstream and lies as close to the bank as possible at C. This allows the float, bait and shot to make a final quiet approach to the slack water between current and bank.

As soon as the shotted leader reaches the slack it will lie still. It is now that the angler has his best chance of catching the biggest fish in the swim.

Note: So far as we know, nobody has ever mentioned stret-pegging for salmon. And yet, when conditions are suitable, this method of presenting a shrimp is one of the most deadly of all salmon fishing techniques. (See p. 203.)

40 · Paternostering

'The paternoster is a most deadly piece of tackle', said Bickerdyke. 'Except in weir pools, there is rarely occasion to cast out the paternoster for any considerable distance in summer. Indeed to cast it out is a mistake; it should be swung out with the motion of a pendulum.' If we add his third dictum from *The Book of the All-Round Angler* (1888): 'One great advantage of this tackle is that it almost always puts the bait at about the right depth from the bottom, however much the depth may vary', we have summed up a considerable combination of qualities. There is a further and most important quality of the paternoster which escaped the notice of Bickerdyke: by reducing the need for casting to a minimum, an anchored rig has the merit of preserving the livebait.

Even so, the beam and boom paternosters loved by old-time freshwater anglers would, through neglect, have long become obsolete but for the interest shown in them by sea anglers. The modern angler prides himself on a more subtle approach to his sport; he is inclined to treat any form of old-fashioned, crude looking tackle with disdain. But in spite of a clumsy appearance, both these old paternoster rigs were (and still are) very effective indeed.

THE SLIDING BUBBLE-FLOAT PATERNOSTER

The sliding bubble-float paternoster, however, is likely to have more appeal for the modern angler, since it is both effective and suitably streamlined.

The rig is made up with a bubble float, a split ring, a barrel swivel, a three-way swivel, a Hillman lead and an Arlesey bomb. Once the principle of the rig is understood and its various parts remembered, its assembly can be varied to suit different situations.

An important feature of this rig is the bubble float, which can be part-filled with water to provide additional casting weight. The float also provides the structure to which an additional bubble float can be attached, should increased buoyancy be required.

The sliding stop-knot is positioned so as to make the distance between float and lead exceed the true depth by $1\frac{1}{2}$ ft to 2 ft. This latitude accommodates any small variation of depth. The remaining slack is taken up by drawing tight after the cast. The nylon link between the three-way swivel and the lead should be weaker than the mainline; thus, in the event of the rig's becoming snagged, only the lead is lost.

The sliding stop-knot should be made of

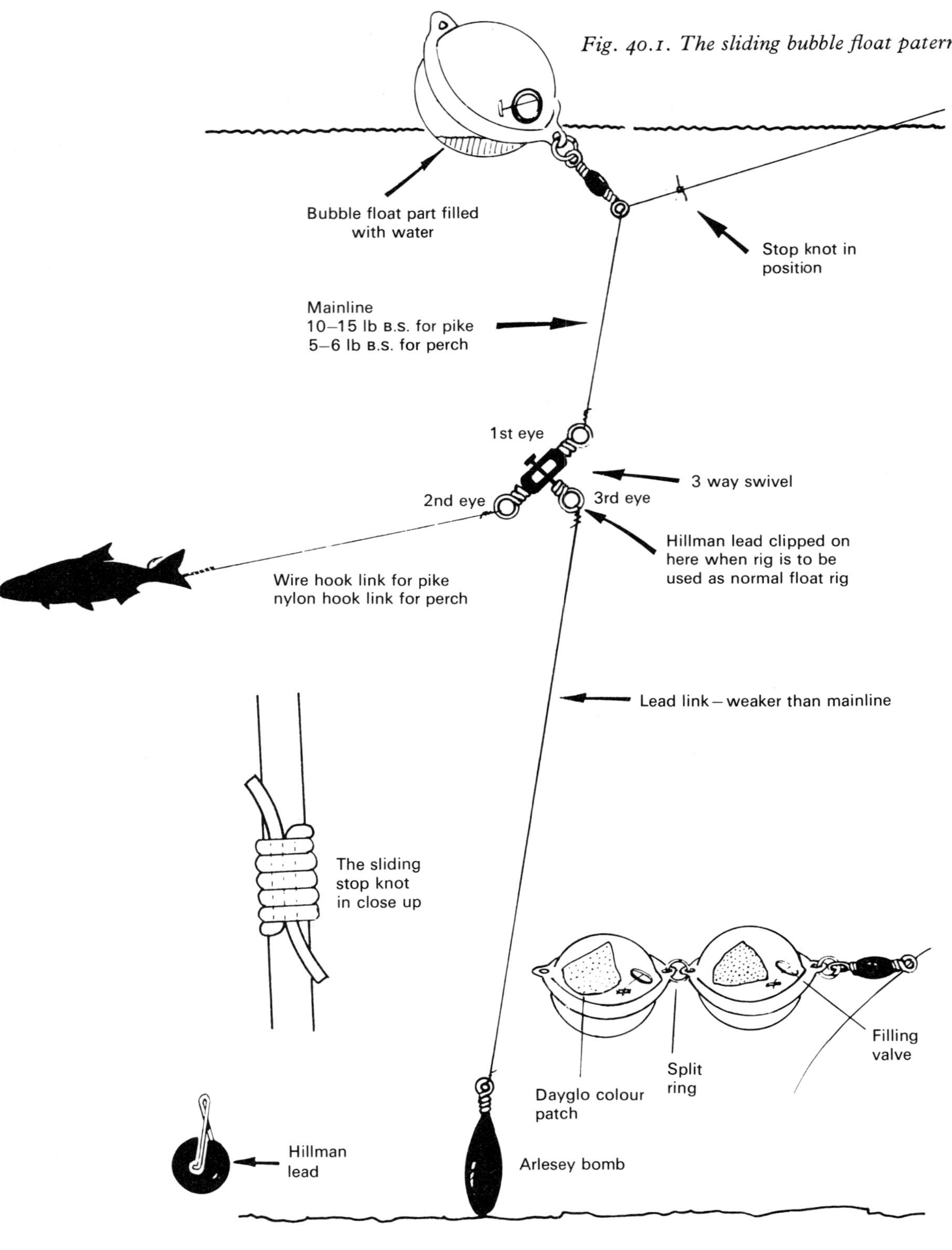

Fig. 40.1. The sliding bubble float paternoster.

Fig. 40.2. ▷

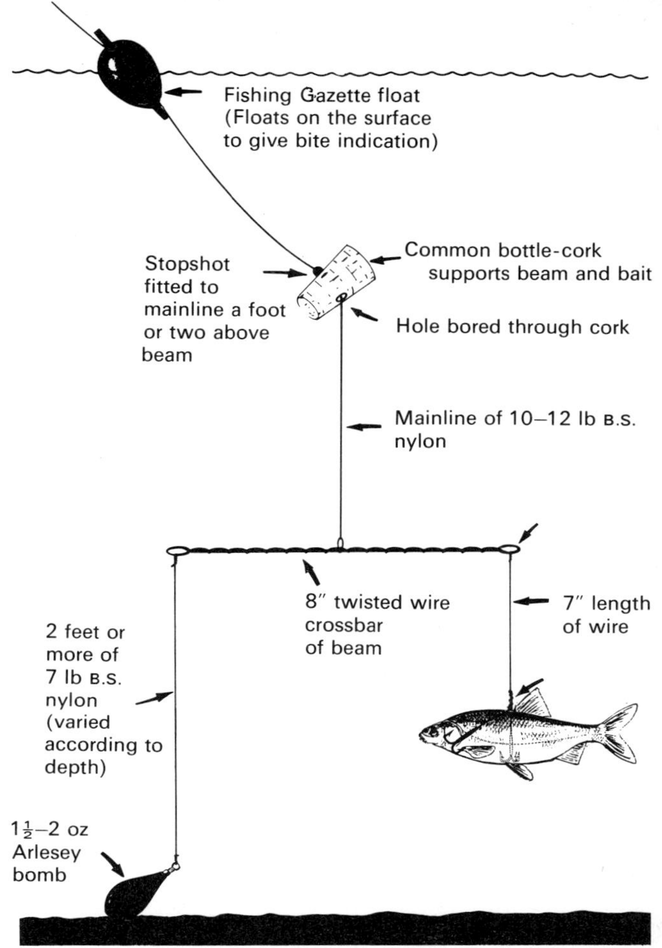

thickish nylon. This will give the stub-ends of the knot that degree of stiffness which will allow them to pass through the rod rings during the cast, but prevent them from passing through the eye of the small barrel swivel attached to the bubble float. Use a spade-end knot, or the knot illustrated in Fig. 40.1. For ease of tying, use a generous length of nylon. When the knot is completed, trim off leaving $\frac{1}{2}$ in. stub-ends.

From the drawing it would appear to be difficult to prevent the lead-link and the hook-link becoming intertwined. In practice, the Arlesey bomb is retained in the left hand until the angler is ready to make his cast. As the rod is projected forward, the lead takes up the front position due to greater air-resistance operating on the bait and the float.

If the rig is no longer required as a paternoster, the lead-link is removed. What remains is, with the addition of a Hillman lead, a livebaiting float rig which has the special merit of being quickly adjustable to suit all conditions and bait sizes. The Hillman lead, available in graduated sizes, is readily clipped on to the middle eye of the three-way swivel. To aid vision, patches of suitably coloured Dayglo paint can be dabbed on the bubble float.

If perch are the quarry, the hook-link should be of nylon; but wire must be used for pike.

COUNT DE MOIRA'S BEAM PATERNOSTER

Numerous beam and boom paternosters have been advocated for pike fishing. This particular rig was described by John Bickerdyke in *The Book of the All-Round Angler* (1888). The description is so clear that we give it verbatim. (The rig has been re-drawn in terms of modern materials):

It is obviously important to have the cork just the right size to support the bait and the wire beam in horizontal position. With this tackle the bait has great freedom, pirouetting round the plumb which anchors it at the proper place and depth. It is altogether so novel, and apparently so complicated, that it is not likely to be viewed with much favour; but the Count de Moira says he kills more fish with it than his friends do on other tackle. R. B. Marston wrote of this tackle: 'You often come across breaks and bays in beds of weeds and reeds which line the bank; they are often too small to try the ordinary live-bait tackle in, because the bait would swim into the reeds at once. It is impossible to keep the bait on an ordinary paternoster at the exact depth, unless you are almost over the spot, and hold the line taut all the time; directly the line slackens, the bait fouls the weeds at the bottom, and might remain there a month without attracting the notice of a fish. With Count de Moira's invention your bait must swim round, *supported* (at any depth you please) by the cork, and anchored in one spot.'

THE STANDING PIKE-PATERNOSTER

Most anglers are familiar with the beach-caster's style of setting his rod up almost vertically with rod-rest. Strangely, the fresh-water angler disdains to emulate him; yet the sea fisher's style, with certain modifications, is perfectly suitable for pike fishing. The standing pike-paternoster, which incorporates this style, has several advantages over most other rigs.

1. It effectively fishes a chosen swim, hole or run, over an extended period without the disturbance of further casting.
2. The vigour of the livebait is not dissipated by frequent retrieving and casting, as it is with other methods.
3. The livebait can be fished at a calculated distance from the bottom, regardless of any variation in the depth of water.
4. The anchored bait cannot foul up the tackle by swimming into weedbeds or other obstructions.
5. There is a close relationship between the number of baits used and the number of pike caught. This saving of baits is no small consideration.

Perhaps the greatest advantage of the standing paternoster is that the bait stays in position until the pike start to feed. This is very different from the usual practice of searching for fish that are already feeding.

It is a contemplative style of fishing, but very deadly. So deadly, in fact, that once they have tried it many anglers regard it as their favourite method. It is, moreover, as effective on great pike rivers like the Dorset Stour and Hampshire Avon, as it is on the still waters of a Tring reservoir.

Choose a rod of 10 or 11 ft that will cast a bait weighing about $\frac{1}{2}$ lb. Avoid all those short, stumpy, stiff rods beloved by generations of pike fishers. The rod should be flexible enough to fish a 12 lb monofilament line. The most important item is a tapered 6 in. steel spike, threaded so as to screw into the rod-butt.

Use a centrepin reel of the Aerial or Silex type. Tie a 1 oz Arlesey bomb to the end of the line and introduce a three-way swivel into the line about six feet up from the bomb. To the second eye of the three-way swivel, tie, via a short link, any preferred type of hook tackle.

Select a swim and cast out the livebait with a long, slowly accelerated swing. As soon as the lead settles, stick the rod-spike into the ground to support the rod in a vertical position (C, Fig. 40.3). Wind in the slack line until it is taut between rod tip and lead. Maintain tension of the line by setting the drag on the reel to support the clutch.

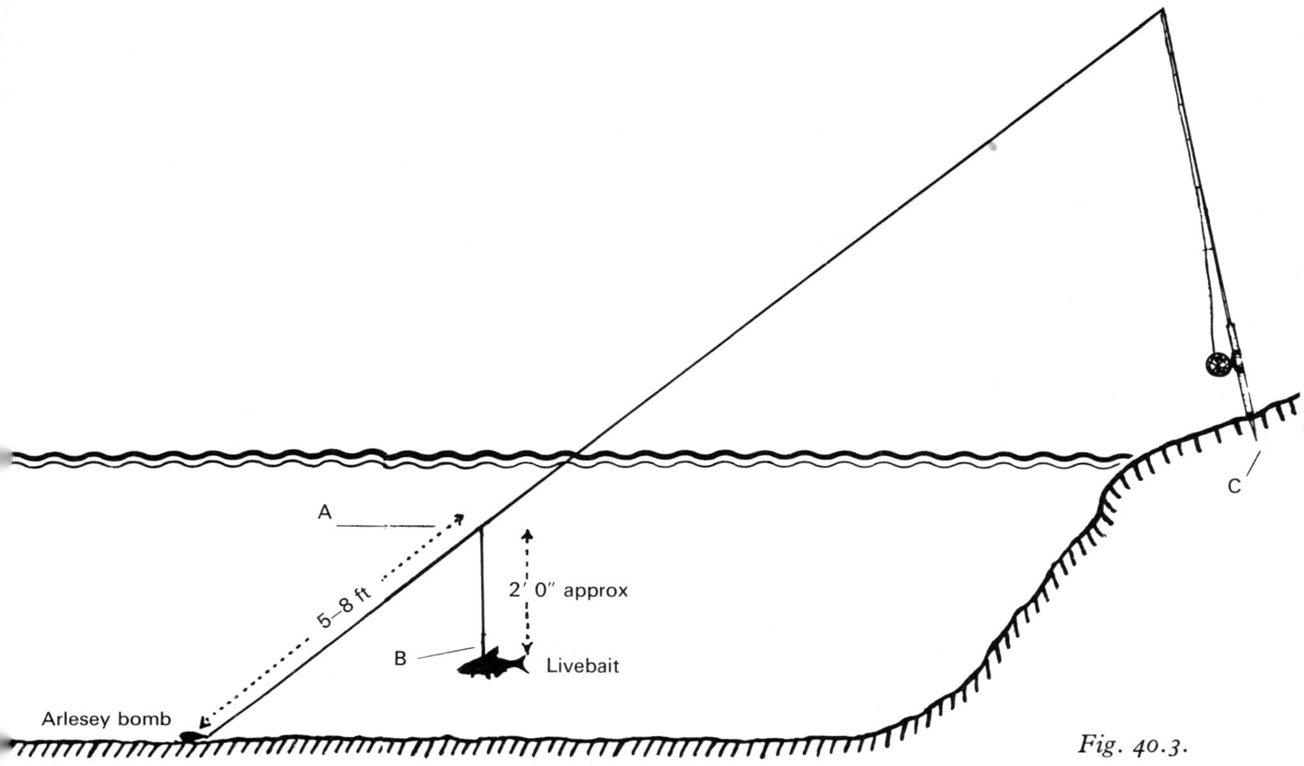

Fig. 40.3.

Note: For very soft ground, or in a high wind, use a beachcaster's tripod rod-rest.

The tugging of a fresh livebait will be shown by movement of the rod tip, but this will soon settle down. Unless the sport is exceptionally fast, there is no need to sit behind the rod in a mood of tense concentration. Carry on fishing for bait if you wish, glancing at your rod tip every minute or two. A pike take is signalled by a characteristic movement of the rod-tip. The difference between this movement and the movement made by the livebait is soon learnt. Sometimes, a pike will grab the bait and take line out in a smooth run, but when this happens the check will immediately give warning.

Fig. 40.4 shows enlarged views of the three-way swivel (A), of the short link which joins the snap-tackle to the three-way swivel (B), and of the steel spike (C) which screws into the rod-butt.

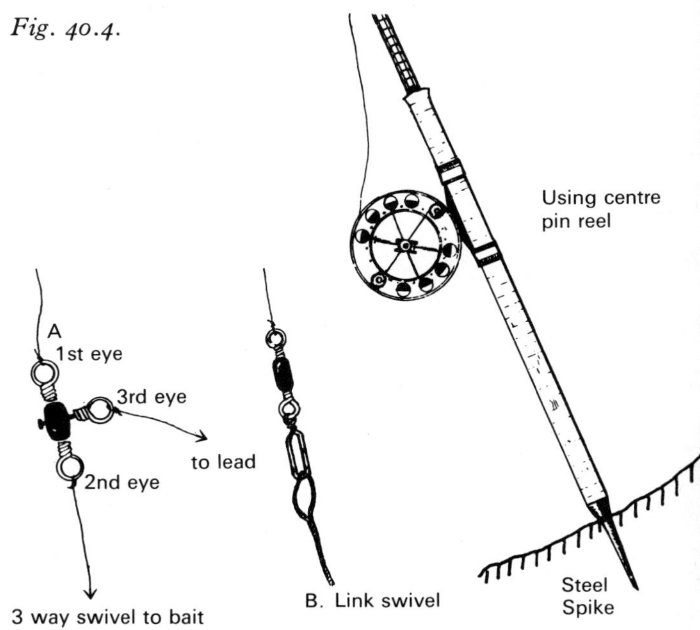

Fig. 40.4.

41 · Trolling and Trailing

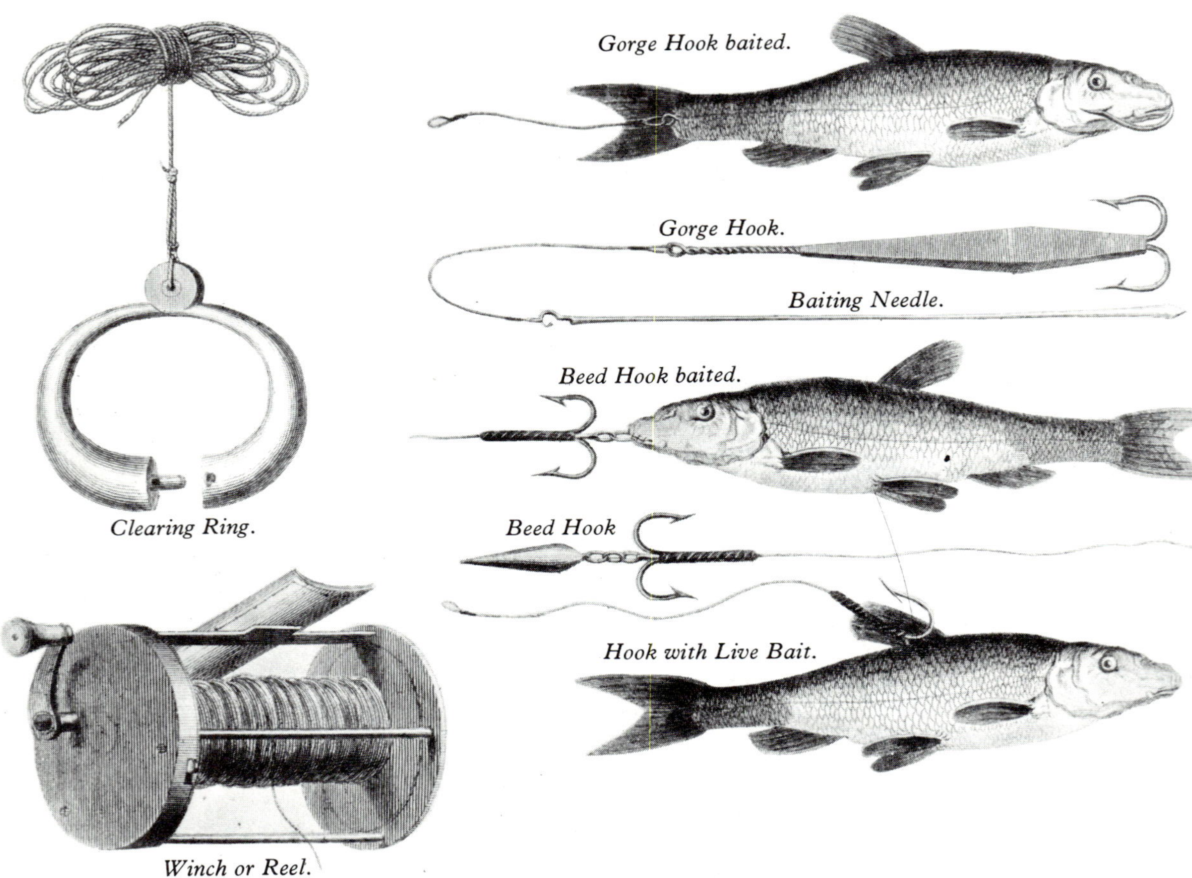

This engraving from The Rev. W. B. Daniel's Rural Sports *(1801) contains the first known illustration of a multiplier reel. It also shows a clearing-ring, used for recovering baits snagged on the bottom.*

Trolling with the Gorge. From T. F. Salter, The Angler's Guide, *1833 (eighth and last edition).*

TROLLING

Since many anglers still confuse 'trolling' with 'trailing' it is necessary to define these terms.

The best definitions of 'trolling' and 'trailing' are given by John Bickerdyke in *The Book of the All Round Angler* (1888):

Dead-baits, when used in pike-fishing, are either arranged so that they spin when drawn through the water, or are placed on trolling-tackle, in which case they do not spin. Spinning baits are either cast out some distance, and drawn back through the water to the angler, or are trailed at the back of a boat. This trailing is often called trolling in Scotland and Ireland, a misnomer which has doubtless caused some little confusion in the minds of anglers. Trolling proper is the use of a dead-bait which does not spin, and is worked with a *sink-and-draw* motion in the water. [Our italics].

Here is an account of trolling published in 1805:

. . . trolling is the noblest branch of Angling, and is performed as follows: the Angler must have a very long and strong rod, with rings, as for Barble, and a winch or reel, properly fastened to the butt-end; a trolling line at least thirty or forty yards long, with a swivel at the end, which receives the loop of the wire that the hook is fastened to; whether a double or single hook, it must be leaded. Thus equipped, begin to troll; let the bait fall in bold at first, close to the shore,

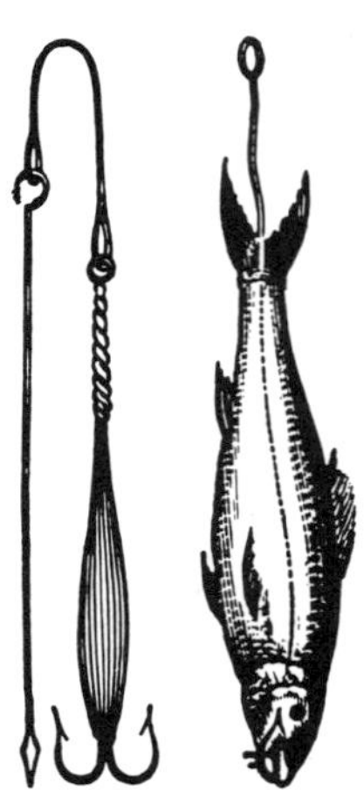

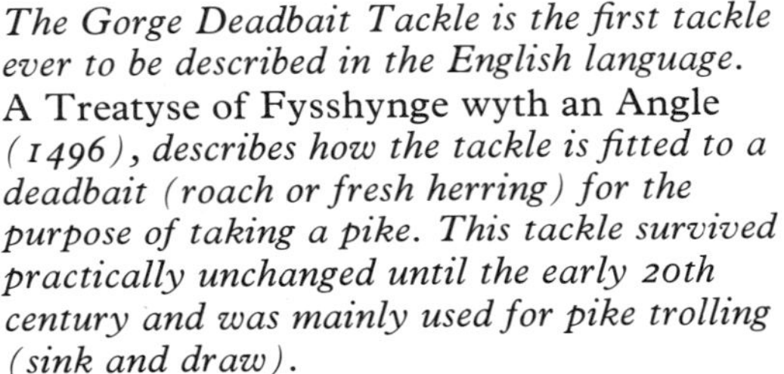

The Gorge Deadbait Tackle is the first tackle ever to be described in the English language. A Treatyse of Fysshynge wyth an Angle *(1496), describes how the tackle is fitted to a deadbait (roach or fresh herring) for the purpose of taking a pike. This tackle survived practically unchanged until the early 20th century and was mainly used for pike trolling (sink and draw).*

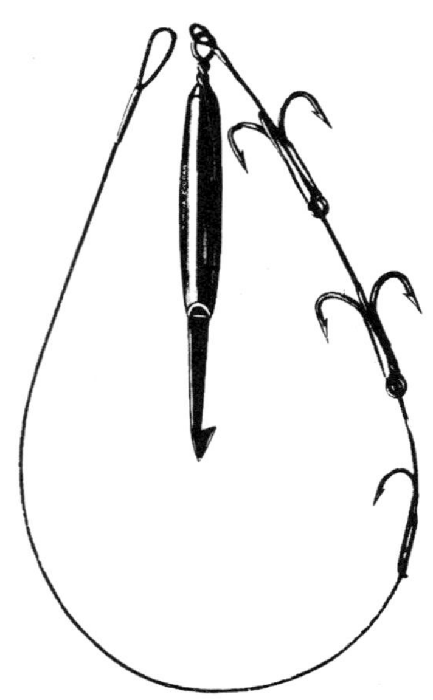

Hardy's Pike Drop-Tackle. This is a simplified version of R. B. Marston's Deadbait Flight, and was produced until quite recently. The spiked lead is pushed down the bait's throat and the single hook pulled right through the narrow fleshy part of the deadbait's tail. A twist of copper wire secures the bait.

if deep. With your right hand hold the rod tight, keeping the top always in motion, by raising and lowering; in your left, hold your line, which keep continually pulling and letting go; this gives the bait a motion as if alive in the water. One gill-fin cut off, improves the motion of the bait. If a pike be near, he darts at the bait, and seizes it with incredible voracity, and runs off to his hole.

ANON. *The Angler's Pocket-Book* (third edition, 1805).

Trolling as described by Alfred Jardine in *Pike and Perch.*

When trolling it is best to fish up stream, and to work the bait down with the current through the weeds. If the contrary way is attempted it will result in many a hang-up in the weeds; besides, there is this advantage in fishing up and bringing the bait down with the stream: it approaches the pike more naturally, and is better seen by them, as (except in gentle currents) they always lie, whether in ambush or not, with their heads up stream, on the look-out for small fish swimming past. It is not necessary to make long casts; in fact, it is better not to do so, for the bait being lifted and dropped almost perpendicularly in the openings between weeds, trolls, or gyrates in a much more tempting way than when drawn slantwise through the water; and as the pike are usually among the weeds or in deep weedy holes, from whence they cannot readily see the angler, it is better to carefully fish all the nearest water than to make long shots with the bait. Raise the bait to the surface every two or three seconds and let it sink head foremost, giving a foot or so of slack line, and then it will have a darting rolling movement as it drops to the bottom. Keep continuing this, and if a check is felt, slacken the line by paying off a few yards from the reel (if none is already unwound), and see that all is clear for a run, in case a fish has taken the bait, which will soon be known by the fish moving off, or by a few fierce little drags at the line; then allow the few minutes that are usually given the fish to pouch, wind up the slack line, give a firm draw with the rod, and play the fish on and off the reel, in preference to dropping the line in coils on the ground.

Not very helpful . . .

Many use to Troule for a Pike; but that is so easie, that I shall not spend time in giving Directions: For it will be far easier learnt; by once going with any Person that understands it, in ones day time, than is possible to be taught by Printed Directions.
WILLIAM GILBERT, *The Angler's Delight*, 1676.

In some places they Troll without any Pole or any playing of the Bait, as I have seen them throw a Line out of a Boat, and so let it draw after them as they Row forward; but that must be a careless and unsafe way, for so they may have Bites and Offers so, yet it must certainly check the Fish so much that he will never Pouch it; I cannot tell what Art they may have at the Snap, though it is very improbable to have any as they go to work, without either Pole or Stick.
ROBERT NOBBES, *The Compleat Troller* (1682).

So far as we know, the earliest description of *trailing*.

TRAILING

There is what may by courtesy be termed spinning, the practice of trailing (it is often erroneously called 'trolling') for big lake trout in Ireland and Scotland. The angler simply sits in the stern of a boat and lets his spinning bait trail thirty yards or more behind while somebody else rows. The tackle and rod must be strong, as a big pike or a salmon is sometimes a possibility. No overwhelming display of skill is demanded of the angler, but the oarsman must know something about the geography of the lake and the nature of the bottom. Trailing may, however, be made something like an art if the angler does his own rowing, and is alone; in fact, *there are few kinds of fishing which demand more promptitude and resource.*
H. T. SHERINGHAM, *Elements of Angling* (1908).

Deep-Water Trailing

As an angling method, trailing is often considered boring and lacking in finesse. But the fisherman who consistently takes good fish from the depths of what appears to be a featureless expanse of water is not, as many people seem to think, haphazardly dragging a bait about. On the contrary, he is being as calculating as the angler who fishes streamy water. His fish are caught by *design*, not accident. A skilful and imaginative angler who uses an echo sounder, and tackle which fishes at a specified depth, gradually builds up a complex and fascinating picture of the loch bottom and the best 'taking' depths. As a result he will, in the long term, catch far bigger fish than the less imaginative angler who moves aimlessly about, never certain of the depth of water or the depth at which his lure is fishing.

In the early 1950s, when F. B. first made the acquaintance of that famous Loch Lomond angler the late Harry Britton of Balloch, he was puzzled by the local method of trailing for sea-trout and salmon. This method, although popular on the loch, was restricted to fishing from a power-driven boat travelling at a uniform speed, tactics which automatically cause the bait to fish at a uniform depth. The only important variables, it seemed, were in the type and size of bait (a fresh-killed natural minnow was preferred), in the choice of locality, and, of course, in the wind and weather conditions.

This choice of fishing depth – or, rather, this self-imposed *restriction* of depth, seemed to F. B. to be unnecessarily inhibiting and in conflict with his own trailing practice. From his experience of charr-trailing on Windermere, where six baits per line are fished at depths ranging from 20 ft to 70 ft, (see p. 44), he had learned the importance of varying the depth at which a bait is trailed. He had noted that brown trout and charr which had deserted the upper levels would sometimes take a bait avidly in deep water. In addition, his experience of trailing different baits for different species on many other waters had made him aware of the need to trail baits at varying speeds in order to find the best 'taking' speed for the day in question. (The best taking speed varies from day to day.)

F.B. writes as follows:

I ventured to suggest to Britton that everyone who fished in the customary Loch Lomond manner was not making the most of his opportunities. When this method of fishing produced a blank, only one inference could be drawn: that on the day in question no sea-trout was interested in taking that particular bait trailed (say) 35 yards behind a boat at 2 m.p.h. at a uniform depth of 2½ ft (the figures are hypothetical, and used merely to illustrate the point). Britton was so impressed with my argument in favour of fishing at different depths and at different speeds that he lost no time in trying out a modified experimental charr-trailing rig himself. It met with immediate success. Alas, since this occurred only a short time before his final illness, he was unable to develop it further.

A disadvantage of the traditional charr-trailing rig (see p. 44) is the heavy lead that forms part of the mainline tackle. This is most cleverly avoided in the *Downrigger* – an American method of deep-water trailing that will get a bait (or baits) down to a considerable depth without the use of lead on the mainline.

Fig. 41.1 shows the working principles of the rig with one or two homespun variations.

The downrigger

To prepare the downrigger, a Nottingham reel of large diameter (A), holding about 50 yards of 60 lb B.S. terylene line, is secured with the usual winch fittings to the back of the rodrest. The last 12 yards are marked at intervals of three feet with tags of wool (B). (Two-inch tags of wool are passed through the braid of the terylene with the help of a

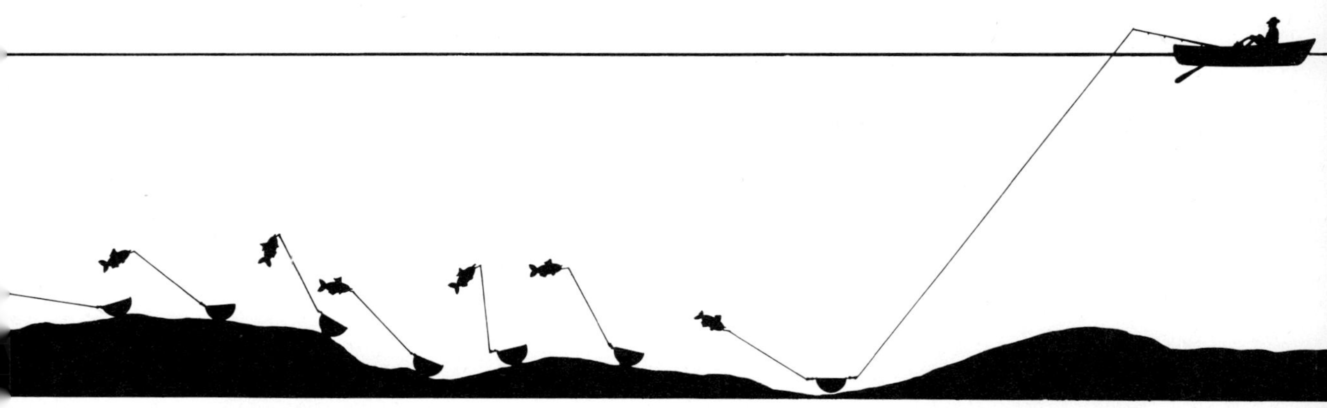

Fig. 41.4. The skid trailing-rig in operation: when the boat is in motion the bait moves close to the ground as soon as the motion stops the bait rises nose first due to the buoyancy of the balsa dowell.

vane made up from one half of a circle of celluloid 6 in. or 8 in. in diameter. As can be seen in the diagram, the line runs along the top of the vane, while the lead is located at the base in the form of a keel. This keeps the vane in an upright position, so that when drawn along the bed of the lake it acts as a skid.

If required, extra lead can be added in the form of swanshots pinched over a loop of nylon and hung from either swivel.

The deadbait is 'loaded' with a suitable piece of varnished balsa dowel which is pushed down the bait's throat. Once the dowel is fitted, an appropriate treble is wired up with 14 lb Alasticum wire. A small celluloid disc is then slipped on to the wire. This prevents the treble from pulling into and damaging the body of the bait (see diagram). The wire is then threaded through the bait with the aid of a baiting needle. A large single hook is slipped on to the emergent wire. Once the hook is positioned to suit the length of the bait it is secured with a few turns of wire. The hook is then pulled through both lips of the deadbait.

Use of the rig is simple and straightforward. The baited tackle is put over the stern of the boat and some 30 yards of line released from the reel. The leaded skid sinks to the bed of the lake and takes the buoyant deadbait to within six feet of the bottom. The first pull of the oars brings the bait wobbling down towards the bottom and, as the momentum of the boat gradually fades, the bait rises again due to the buoyancy of its balsa content. Another pull at the oars repeats the action, and so on.

Kinnear uses mackerel as bait, although he concedes that other baits such as roach or dace are perfectly suitable. He has found that it pays him to dress a number of baits with balsa and hooks prior to a fishing trip. This advance preparation of baits gives him the opportunity to test and, if necessary to correct their buoyancy. This is done in the bath. After which, the baits are wrapped in damp newspaper.

Mask trout caught by Gerry Berth-Jones, weight 10 lb; taken on a Mepps – trailed 40 yd behind a boat (on slow engine tick-over).

lead wire joins the third eye of the three-way swivel to the swivel of the downrigger.

The tackle is now ready for use and the rod is placed in the rest with the *reel-check on*.

If two anglers are fishing together, one watches the rod, or rods, while the other rows the boat. The angler who fishes by himself will find it convenient to use one of the specially designed American trailing electrical-outboard-motors, otherwise he will need to clamp the downrigger rodrest on to the gunwale within reach of the oars. F.B. prefers the use of oars at all times owing to the greater variation of speed which rowing affords, but most anglers prefer to trail with the aid of a motor.

As soon as the boat is in motion the lead-line is slowly released from the downrigger reel (A). Each coloured wool tag that passes the end of the rodrest indicates that the lead is fishing three feet deeper. While line is being released from the downrigger reel the corresponding amount of line is being pulled off the rod reel – which is under the tension of its check.

When the required depth has been reached, the lead line is looped round the handle of the downrigger reel (J).

The angler now knows the exact depth at which his bait is fishing. An echo sounder enables him to make any necessary adjustment to the depth of the downrigger lead to accommodate changes in depth of water, or any shoals of food-fish which the sounder may locate.

Some anglers make a point of tensioning the line until the rod dips slightly (K). Thus as soon as a fish takes the bait and breaks the cotton or lead connecting link (G), the rod straightens, giving immediate bite indication.

Fig. 41.2. The herring magic.

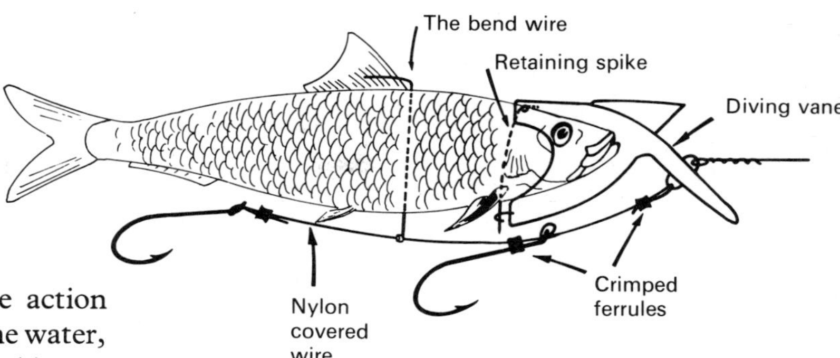

The Nose-Cone Trailing Tackle

Some time ago, while admiring the action of a plug as it burrowed its way into the water, we considered the question of making a natural bait behave likewise. It occurred to us that hitherto any life-like movement given to a non-revolving deadbait had always been imparted by the angler – by means of rod-tip movement, or an irregular retrieve. The well-known 'sink-and-draw' retrieve is an example.

The deadbait trailer is always hard put to get any sort of special action into his bait simply because so much of his time is taken up with the handling of his boat. With the intention of achieving a true *plug-action* on a deadbait trailing rig we set about designing a fibre-glass nose-cone that would (a) fit over the head of a herring, (b) incorporate a plastic diving vane of the type fitted to the majority of plugs.

After experimenting with numerous patterns, we became even more convinced that the nose-cone was a practical proposition worthy of further development.

A chance conversation with a Canadian salmon angler, however, ended our quest for the perfect nose-cone. An American manufacturer with similar notions had anticipated our experiment. After trying out hundreds of different cones, involving thousands of comparative tests, his firm had finally developed a nose-cone that would give a herring deadbait the true plug-action.

This nose-cone is called *The Herring Magic, The Frantic Swimming Actionizer*! Purchasers are exhorted to: 'Fish it fast. Remember, you are simulating real, live, freshly-injured minnows trying to escape (herring, anchovy, sardine, mullet and fresh-water shiners)!'

According to our Canadian informant, the *Herring Magic* nose-cone is used extensively and with great success in the famous 'Salmon Derby' – an annual competition for the biggest salmon, held off the west coast of Canada.

Since angling for salmon in British coastal waters with a trailed herring (or anything else, for that matter) is a waste of time, we suggest that the nose-cone should be used to catch pike. The large lochs of Scotland and Ireland are particularly suited to the trailing method, and we feel confident that if this new rig is used intelligently it will open up new opportunities for pike fishermen. As a result, more big loch pike will be caught than ever before.

Directions

Hold the herring in the left hand. Push the retaining spike into the back of the herring's head. Swing the herring's nose into the cone. Clip the end of the spike (which has penetrated right through the neck of the bait) into its retaining clip. Push the 'bend-over' wire clamp up through the belly of the herring to just behind the gills, and bend the emergent wire back towards the dorsal fin. The bend-over wire supports the hooks and hook trace.

The Skid Trailing-Rig

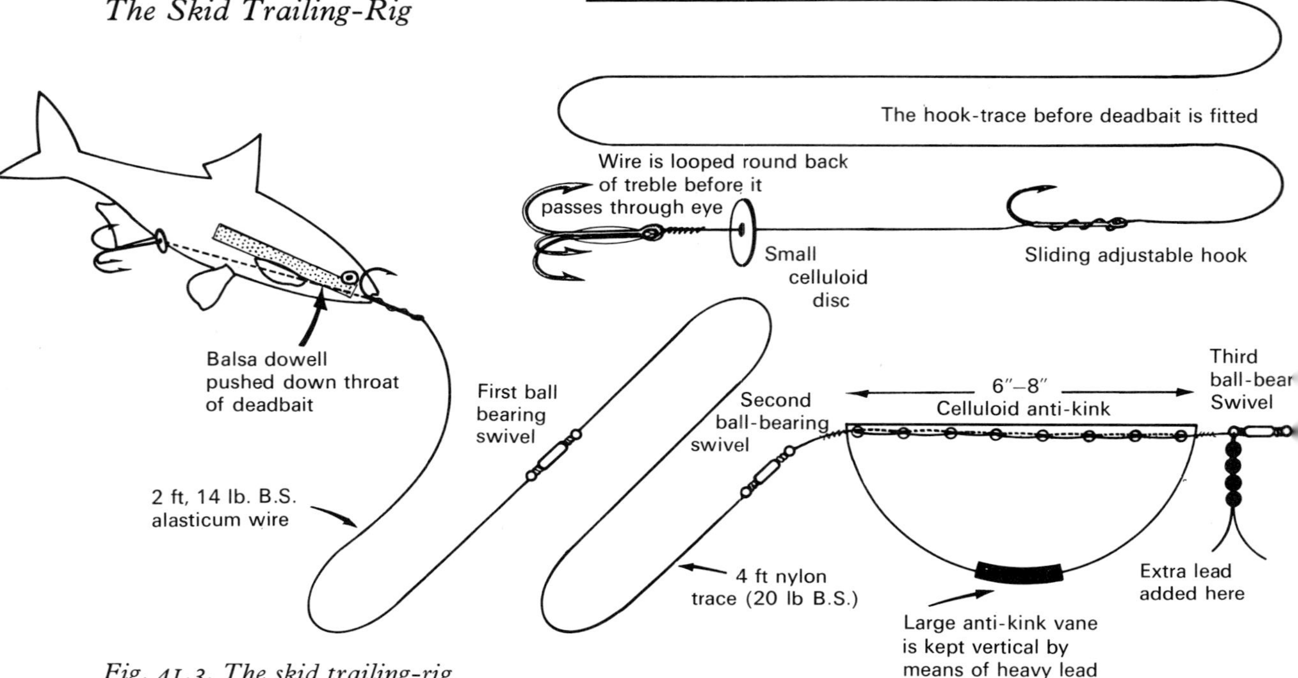

Fig. 41.3. The skid trailing-rig.

This is an improved trailing-rig which was devised in 1965 by pike angler, Colin Kinnear. It represents an advance in an area of fishing which during the present century has been both despised and neglected; indeed, in Britain there have been no significant improvements in trailing techniques since the semi-professional charr fishermen of Windermere developed their unique but killing charr-trailing rig during the 19th-century.

The major problem with trailing in lakes, particularly in the large lakes that occur in the mountainous districts of Britain, is to overcome the difficulty of fishing a measured distance from the bottom where there are so many unseen variations in depth. As Kinnear puts it: 'I have done a great deal of trailing and used to be continually worrying how far off the bottom the bait was. Now I know it is never more than six feet. With this rig, the bait must be faithfully following the contours of the lake bed, regardless of any variation in depth.'

Kinnear uses his new trailing rig not as an end in itself but as a means of finding the 'hot-spots' that are known to exist somewhere in a vast and bewildering expanse of water. Having found a 'hot spot' with this rig, a pike angler can then fish it with more conventional methods.

The basis of the rig is a very large anti-kink

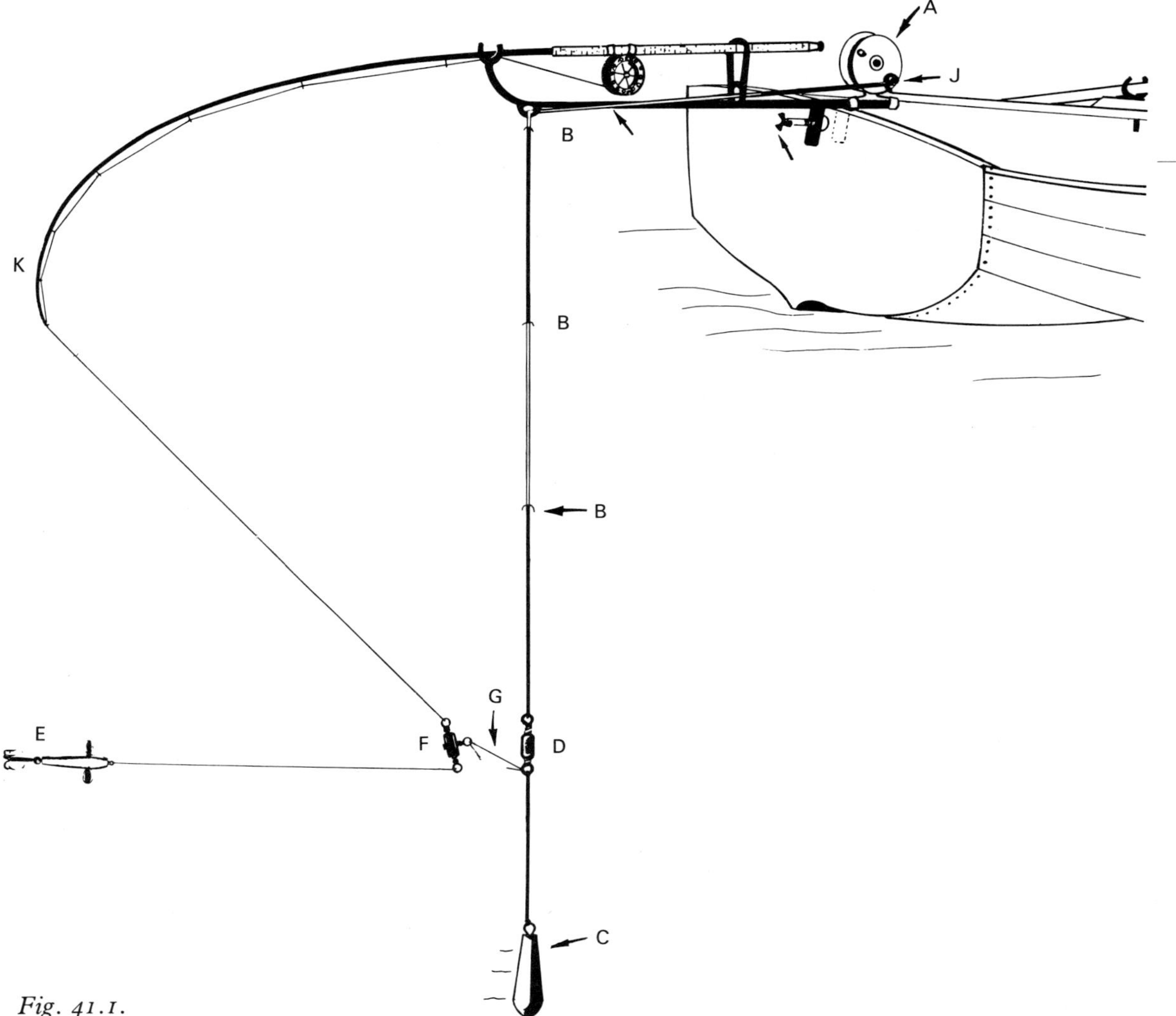

Fig. 41.1.

coarse needle and then tied with a double knot, leaving an overhang of wool on each side. A colour code of wools is used so that an angler can tell precisely how much line is out at any time.)

The line is fed through the rodrest and a 1 lb or $1\frac{1}{2}$ lb lead (C) tied to the end.

Three feet above the lead a swivel (D) is tied into the line.

When the downrigger is ready, sufficient line is pulled off to allow the lead to rest on the back seat of the boat.

The rod, reel and line are now assembled and the appropriate bait (E) attached.

The difference between this tackle and tackle normally used for trailing or bait casting, is that the former carries no lead and includes a three-way swivel (F) in lieu of the usual two-way swivel.

Finally, a link (G) of cotton, elastic or

42 · Spinning and Plug-Fishing

SPINNING

There is an old saying that goes: 'Those who keep their bait in the water catch the most fish.' This is simply not true of spinning. Those anglers who fish selectively and calculatingly and who make every cast a thoughtful measured one, catch most fish. But spinning can so easily become automatic and repetitive; you need spells of rest to rebuild your nervous energy. If everything you know about spinning and the fish you are after tells you it is a waste of time to continue – then stop. Sit down and rest for a while. Otherwise the chances are you will be on your way home, tired and demoralized, just when the fish begin to take.

Time after time I have seen novices catch fish because they were keen and hopeful, when the experienced rod comes back clean because he knew enough to be sure that the fish would be dour, and therefore spent his day flogging away mechanically or sitting on the bank in a hopeless frame of mind.
L. R. N. GRAY, *Torridge Fishery* (1957).

In *The Art of Angling* (1651), Thomas Barker described a new method of trolling for trout with minnow. ('Trolling' then was what is known today as 'sink-and-draw'. A bait mounted on a leaded hook would be cast out, allowed to sink nose first, retrieved for a short distance tail first, allowed to sink again, then retrieved . . . and so on. See pp. 475 *ff*). But Barker, having given instructions for baiting the hook, recommends that *a swivel should be fixed to the line*. This is of great interest. So far as we know it is the first mention of a swivel in angling literature. If the bait was intended to revolve some sort of swivel was obligatory, and it is likely that Barker's was the first reference to *spinning*, as it has become known:

You must alwayes be Angling with the poynt of your Rod down the stream, with drawing the menow up the stream little by little; nigh *the top of the water* [our italics] the Trout seeing the bait, cometh at it most fiercely, so give a little time before you strike.

Izaak Walton defined spinning with great clarity in the 5th edition of *The Compleat Angler* (1676):

. . . and then you are to know, that your minnow must be so put on your hook, that it must run when 'tis drawn against the stream, and that it must turn nimbly . . . the minnow shall be almost straight on your hook, this done, try how it will turn by drawing it cross the water or against

Taken from a cut in T. F. Salter's The Angler's Guide *(8th edition, 1833).*

a stream; and if it do not turn nimbly, then turn the tail a little to the right or left hand, and try again, till it turn quick; for if not, you are in danger to catch nothing; for know, that it is impossible that it should turn too quick.

Walton's first edition (1653) also contained a description of spinning, although not so clear as the one given.

In his 5th edition of *The Experienc'd Angler* (1683), Colonel Robert Venables wrote:

You must have a swivel or turn, placed about a yard or more above your hook; you need no lead on the line, you must continually draw your bait up the stream near to the top of the water.

There is no doubt that this was spinning. The element of sink had been eliminated from the well established method of sink-and-draw, leaving only the draw – which caused a suitably mounted bait to revolve.

But during the 18th-century, spinning a bait seems to have been little practised. Like certain other methods, and items of tackle, spinning fell into neglect until, during the early part of the 19th century it was rediscovered.

Angling literature since the publication of *A Treatyse of Fysshynge wyth an Angle* (1496) reveals many examples of re-discovery. Several are given in this book: the herring dead-bait method of catching pike (p. 115). The swing-tip (p. 385). The water-knot (p. 405). The hook bristle for worm baiting (p. 440). The tapered line (p. 243). A maggot tackle for sea-trout night fly fishing (p. 304). The double fly-hook (p. 191).

Spinning was no exception. T. F. Salter made no mention of a turning bait in the first edition of *The Angler's Guide* (1814). But in his *eighth* edition (1833), he wrote:

> . . . anglers who will take the trouble to add a box swivel to the gorge hook, in the following manner, will find it assist much in spinning the bait and enticing the Jack or Pike to take it.

From this description it is clear that he was adding spin to the action of that old method, sink-and-draw:

> After trying closely, make your next throw further in the water, and draw and sink the baited hook, by pulling and casting the line with your left hand, while raising and lowering the rod with your right, drawing it straight upwards, near the surface of the water, and also to the right and left, searching carefully every foot of water, and draw your bait against and across the stream *which causes it to twirl or spin*; [our italics], and then by its glistening in the water it is sure to attract and excite either Jack or Pike to seize it.

Salter had re-discovered an exciting new method – that had been first described nearly 200 years before!

ARTIFICIAL BAITS PAST AND PRESENT

Artificial baits have a long history. Apart from flies dressed to imitate natural insects, one of the earliest uses of an artificial bait in Britain is described in Izaak Walton's *The Compleat Angler* (1653):

> I have – which I will show you – an artificial minnow, that will catch a trout as well as an artificial fly and it was made by a handsome woman that had a fine hand and a live minnow lying by her, the body of cloth, the back of it of very sad French green silk and a paler green silk towards the belly, shadowed as perfectly as you can imagine, just as you see a minnow; the belly was wrought also with a needle, and it was a part of it white-silk, and another part of it of silver thread; the tail and the fins were made of a quill, which was shaven thin; the eyes were of two little black beads, and the head was so shadowed, and all of it so curiously wrought, and so exactly dissembled, that it would beguile any sharp-sighted trout in a swift stream.

Walton neglected to give angling instructions, so it is not known if he ever used this bait himself. He assured his pupil, however, that an artificial minnow would be 'of excellent use: for note, that a large trout will come as fiercely at a minnow as the highest mettled hawk doth seize on a partridge, or a greyhound on a hare.'

It seems likely that Walton was recounting somebody else's experience, but like all angling optimists, having heard about a super bait, had quickly obtained one for himself.

The use of a *hard* substance for making an artificial bait (in this case for pike) is given in

Nobbes's *The Compleat Troller* (1682). 'Anything that may affect the eye, may be used at snap; some pike will take a piece of hard cheese, or pack-wax, a rasher of bacon, or sheep gut, or *almost anything that is radiant and shining*.' (Our italics.)

After Nobbes there is a gap of 132 years.

The next reference to an artificial bait is in the first edition of T. F. Salter's *The Angler's Guide* (1814).

The shops keep artificial baits for trolling, both of fish and frogs, made of wood, pearl, and also of leather stuffed and painted, and which in form and colour, much resemble nature, but I should never think of using them while there was a possibility of getting a natural one; when they are used, it is with the snap, which I think shows judgement, for surely the most sanguine angler could hardly expect a pike to pouch either wood, pearl, or leather even with the addition of stuffing.

Artificial spinning baits were not in use until much later; in fact, not until the principles of spinning with a natural bait had been established by four writers:

Captain T. Williamson, *The Complete Angler's Vade Mecum*, 1808.

Robert Salter, *Modern Angler* (second edition), 1811.

T. F. Salter, *The Angler's Guide* (eighth edition), 1833.

Colonel P. Hawker, *Instructions to Young Sportsmen* (6th edition), 1844.

A plain spoon, it seems, was the forerunner of all metal artificial baits. The first notice of the use of this type of artificial in British waters is given by Cholmondeley-Pennell in *The Book of the Pike* (1876).

Pennell describes the experience of one of the Duke of Exeter's servants, an incident that happened sometime between 1846 and 1856. While emptying a pail of slops into the river Exe, this servant saw a pike dart out from under the bank and take a spoon that had been inadvertently left in the pail. Being a fisherman, he had a local tinsmith fashion a spoon bait with appropriate hooks.

Subsequently, a sample was given to Pennell – the prototype for baits that were soon to be used by anglers throughout the world.

However, for a still earlier mention of what might have been a spoon-bait see *The Angler's England* by Patrick Chalmers:

'There was a nobleman in Denmark called Lodbroc, and his two young sons were Henguar and Hubba. Lodbroc was fond of fishing and of falconry. Indeed he was fond of all field sports. One day he took his boat and his fishing rods . . . and he pulled out along the coast to make a mixed bag among the islands. But a storm came on and swept Lodbroc and his boat out to sea. . . . In due course Lodbroc was cast ashore on the Norfolk coast, at the village of Redham to be exact.

'King Edmund [King of East Anglia] who happened to be passing Redham and who was fond of fishing and falconry as was Lodbroc, became Lodbroc's friend. Now one day the King's game warden, by name Berne, was advising his master as to the capture of a 30 lb pike which lay off a little holm (or eyot) of Hyckelyngge [or Hickling] Broad. Berne's baits were not good baits, and it was only when Lodbroc produced a lure, one of

The original spoon bait. From Cholmondeley-Pennell The Book of the Pike *(1876)*.

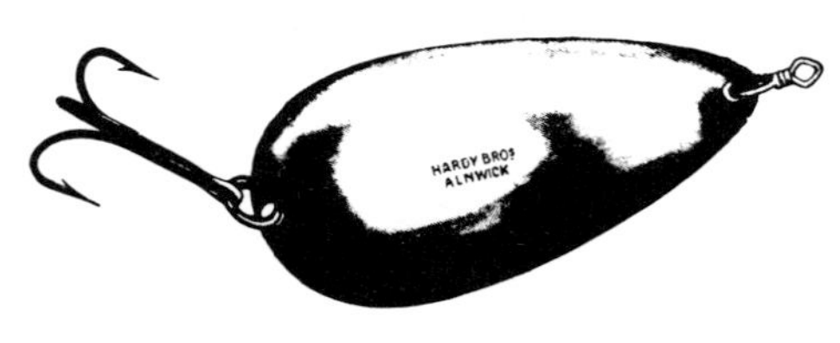

A modern equivalent.

his foreign contrivances ("*a trowling lure of bryte shel*") that the pike came to hand. The King was delighted, but Berne hated Lodbroc for his knowledge of baits.' (Our italics.)

We do not know the origin of this passage, but 'a trowling lure of bryte shel' has the ring of truth about it: it indicates that the modern Scandinavian 'pirk' may be no new invention. Lodbroc's 'trowling lure' could have been an original Norse pirk, used with a 'trolling' (or sink-and-draw) action for cod and other fish.[1].

1 Since writing this chapter on the history of artificial baits we have discovered that the King Edmund of Patrick Chalmers's piece is the King Edmund who was murdered by a party of marauding Danes in the year 870. After death this christian King was canonized Saint Edmund and the city of Bury St. Edmunds commemorates his name and his burial place.
Our discovery suggests that trowling for pike with an artificial lure (sink and draw) with wobble or spin was practised eleven hundred years ago.

A selection of artificial spinning barb (for a description of each see pp. 491ff). (1) The Yellow Belly. (2) The Quill Minnow. (3) The Phantom Bait. (4) The Devon Minnow. (5) The Wagtail Bait. (6) The Leather Eel-Tail. (7) The Slotted Devon. (8) The River Runt Spook. (9) The Kidney Spoon. (10) The Toby Bait. (11) The Mepps Spoon. (12) The Fly Spoon. (13) The Rapala Plug. (14) The Mackerel Spoon. (15) The Jim Vincent Spoon. (16) The Canadian Bar-Spoon. (17) The Colorado Spoon. (18) The Norwich Spoon. (19) The Plain Spoon. (20) The Wooden Devon.

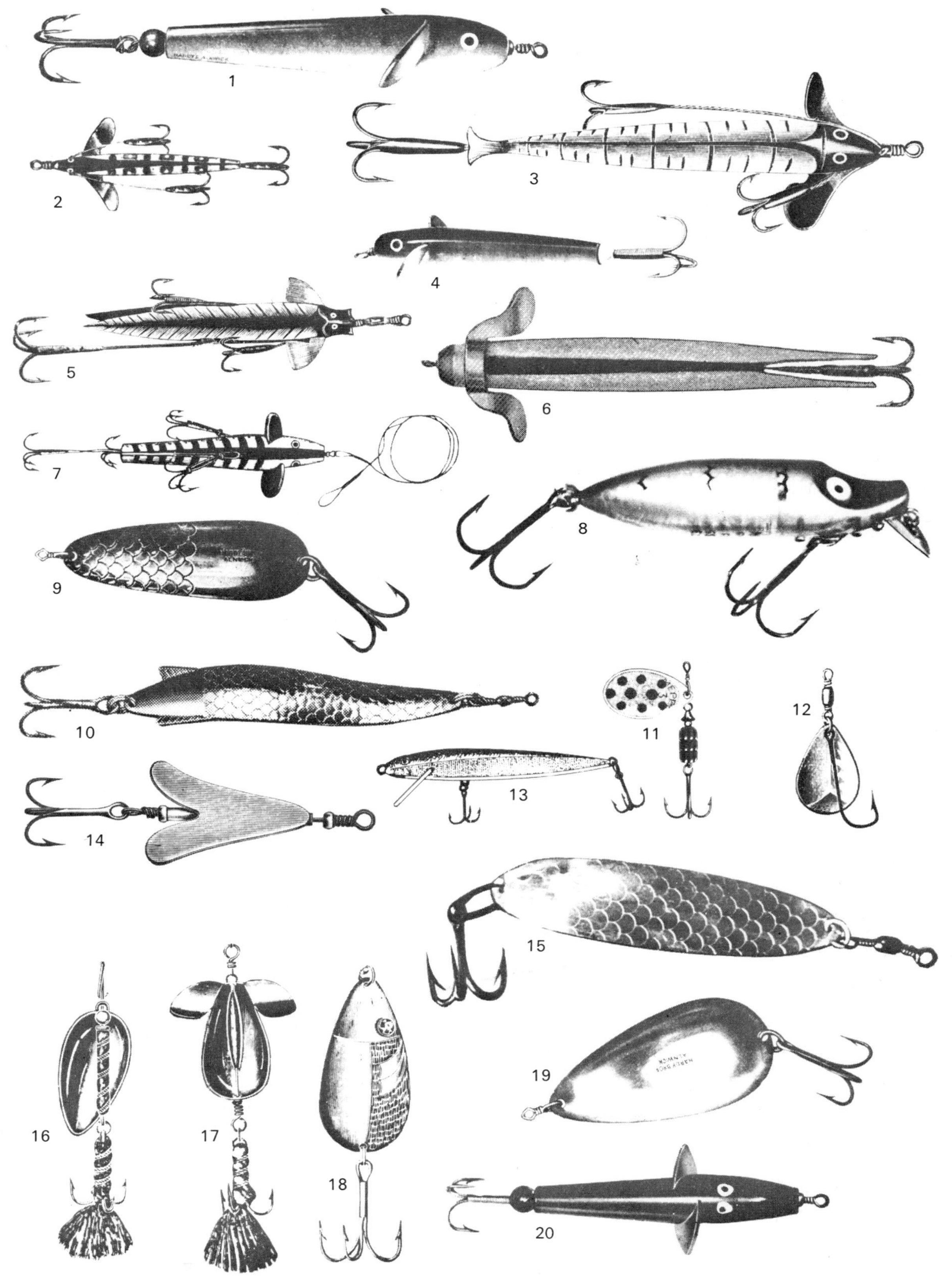
1
2
3
4
5
6
7
8
9
10
11
12
13
14
15
16
17
18
19
20

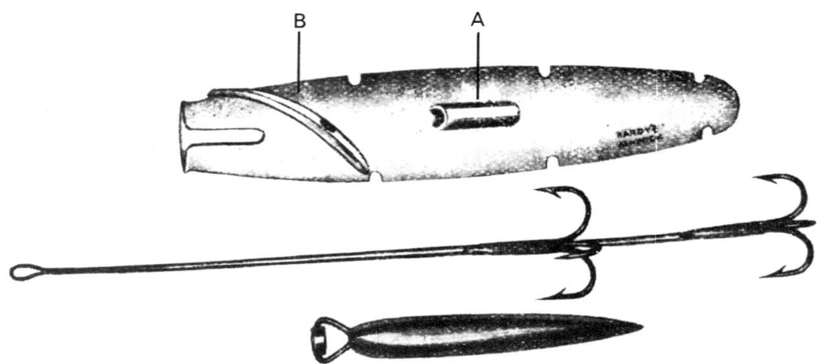

Hardy's improved transparent jacket for spinning natural Baits. Illustration of No. 4 jacket with tackle and lead, exact size.

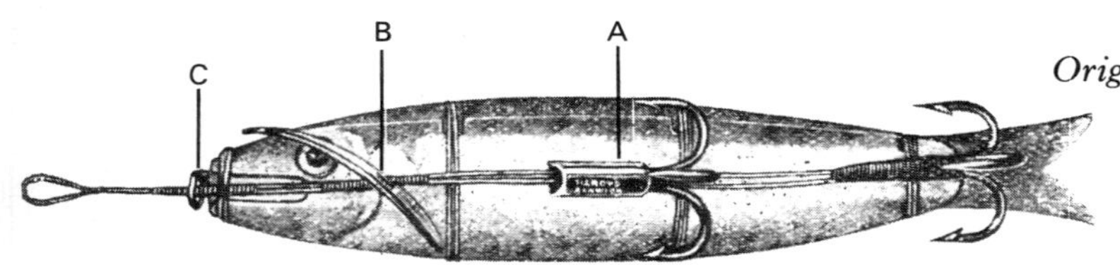

Original scarab mount used with natural sprat.

Illustration is of the No. 4 jacket mounted with a $3\frac{1}{4}$ in. sprat, exact size.
Pull the eye of flight – on which the two treble hooks are mounted through the guide on the side of the jacket A, the hole B in the fin and then through the wire eye of the lead C.

Sizes	Jackets	
No. 1	For baits	*$1\frac{1}{2}$ in. to $1\frac{3}{4}$ in.*
No. 2	,,	*2 in. to $2\frac{1}{4}$ in.*
No. 3	,,	*$2\frac{1}{2}$ in. to $2\frac{3}{4}$ in.*
No. 4	,,	*3 in. to $3\frac{1}{4}$ in.*
No. 5	,,	*$3\frac{1}{2}$ in. to $3\frac{3}{4}$ in.*
No. 6	,,	*4 in. to $4\frac{1}{4}$ in. to $4\frac{1}{2}$ in.*

The wooden brown and gold Devon which has replaced the scarab mounted natural golden sprat. A reliable and highly efficient salmon spinning bait.

1. *The Yellow Belly*

This bait was introduced by Hardy Bros. (c. 1953). It is a very good lure for early spring salmon fishing. Being made of wood it is much lighter than the traditional metal Devon, and can be fished slowly close to the bottom. In the original Hardy version the spinning fins were made from one piece of metal which passed right through the bait, thus ensuring durability – a feature absent, alas, from most modern imitations.

2. *The Quill Minnow*

The direct descendant of Walton's artificial minnow. It is a wonderful brown-trout lure and, due to its lightness, better than the metal Devon when shallow waters are fished.

H. F. writes: 'I prefer to make these baits without the two flying trebles.'

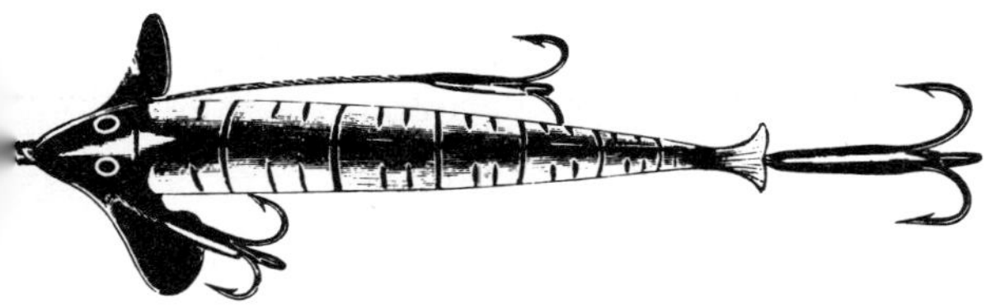

3. *The Phantom Bait*

This killing bait is unfortunately out of production due to high cost – a much lamented loss. The larger phantoms were made of moleskin and accounted for many large pike, including Major W. H. Booth's 37 lb Wye pike (see p. 124). Medium and small phantoms were made with silk bodies. Both materials produced 'soft body' baits that fish were likely to hold on to, thus enhancing the chances of a good hook hold.

4. *The Devon Minnow*

Since the Devon's introduction during the latter part of the 19th century, the total production of its various types must have exceeded any other bait. In spite of changing fashions it is still one of the most popular spinners. Devons are made in sizes varying from ½ in. to 4 in., and in almost every colour or combination of colours. Salmon fishermen usually prefer a blue and silver Devon during the early part of the season when the water temperature is low, and a brown and gold when the temperature begins to rise. During the spring of 1971 (not far from the scene of that historic spoon-dropping incident) F. B. fished the River Exe. Although during the previous days a number of salmon had been killed on blue and silver Devons, Buller and his two companions caught ten fish with brown and gold Devons – after trying the blue and silver without success.

5. *The Wagtail Bait*

Next to the Devon minnow, the wagtail bait has probably accounted for more predatory

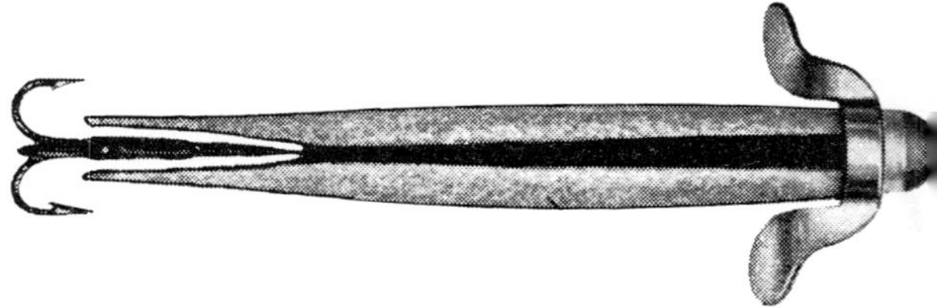

fish in British fresh water than any other bait. William Lunn, famous keeper of the Houghton Club water, considered it the only artificial spinning bait of any use in removing pike from his beloved River Test. According to the manufacturers, its production is no longer economic. In truth, anglers will not pay the price for it, which is a pity. In an era that started during the last century and ended in the 1930s, the wagtail was the favourite bait of a long line of pike anglers – including such famous sportsmen as Payne-Gallwey, Lord Walsingham, Cholmondeley-Pennell, and the Rothschilds – who fished the great limestone loughs of Ireland: Conn, Mask, Derg and Corrib. These loughs were unique: they held huge trout as well as some of the biggest pike in Europe. As natural mixed fisheries they were unsurpassed. Today, only memories of their great pike remain. All of them, with the exception of Derg, have been extensively netted. For anglers (including both authors of this book) who loved those vast elemental lakes this is a matter of the utmost regret; the fascination and excitement of fishing them has almost vanished.

6. *The Leather Eel-Tail*

A development of that famous Irish pike and salmon bait: the natural eel-tail. Generations of Irishmen and visiting anglers have described its deadly qualities. It has a weighted head, the body consisting of two leather strips joined together for two thirds of their length and free for one third. It is usually made in 3 in., 4 in. and 5 in. sizes.

7. *The Slotted Devon*

Now extinct, this bait incorporated a design feature of doubtful merit. It was festooned with three or four treble hooks, presumably in the hope of improving its fish-hooking qualities. In fact, a single treble at the tail secures a more reliable hold. Not the largest, but certainly the most celebrated fish to fall for a slotted Devon was caught by The Reverend Tom Seccombe Gray: a pike of 30 lb. (Gray wrote a very fine account of this incident.)

8. *The River Runt Spook*

It floats at rest, dives a foot or two on retrieve. No imitations have ever surpassed the fish-catching potential of the original River Runt. F. B. writes: 'I am sure the reasons for the River Runt's phenomenal

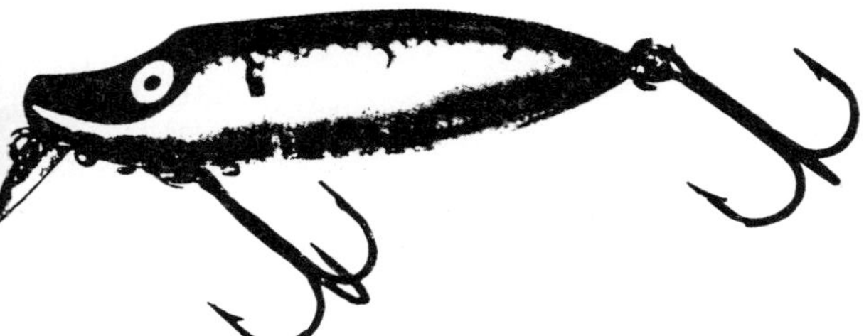

success is due to the fact that the plastic material content of the plug is standardized. With plastic material, once a killing pattern is established after testing in the field, it can be the model for any number of *true* copies.'

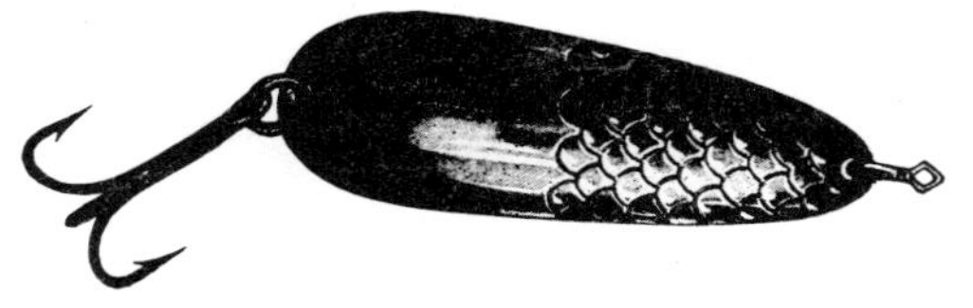

9. *The Kidney Spoon*

The original kidney spoon had a half-scaled copper finish outside and a silver finish inside. It was sometimes furnished with a single treble hook (as shown) and sometimes with a second treble attached by a split ring to the front swivel. The $2\frac{1}{2}$ in. or 2 in. kidney was considered to be one of the best baits for the big salmon of Norway. Latterly, it became more popular when made up as a bar-spoon (like the Canadian-bar). The kidney-bar-spoon has a red tassel and a different metal finish. Unlike the original kidney, it has a chrome finish outside and a red-painted finish inside. The irregular action of this spoon is particularly attractive to pike.

10. *The Toby Spoon*

This bait is very popular at the present time. F. B. recalls a visit to the clubroom of the Vale of Leven Angling Society during the 1969 season. From the large number of rods fitted up with Toby spoons, it seemed that all Loch Lomond salmon and sea-trout anglers – at least, all those who were spinning or trailing – were using this bait. This was in contrast to an earlier visit, in 1957, when the natural minnow was first choice.

H. F. writes: 'In my experience (of spinning for salmon, sea-trout and bass) the Toby spoon is a wonderful attractor, but a poor hooker.'

11. *The Mepps Spoon*

During recent years the fame of the Mepps spinner has spread with the rapidity of a bush fire. It is modelled on a fly spoon or bar spoon action, and its popularity is well deserved. The basic improvement on earlier baits is the provision of a low friction bearing attachment to the blade of the spinner. This allows the blade to flutter even when fished at very low speeds. So far as we know, the best pike to be caught on a Mepps was taken by Richard Barder – appropriately enough the author of *Spinning for Pike* (1970) (see p. 123).

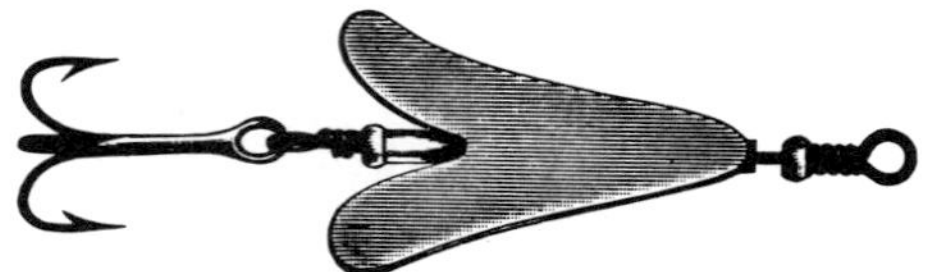

12. *The Fly Spoon*

The fly spoon owes its popularity to a number of features:

(a) It is cheap.

(b) It catches fish.

(c) It continues to flutter attractively when retrieved at slow speeds.

(d) It can be fished conveniently on a fly rod.

kill charr for the visiting Lake District angler better than any other bait (in the absence of the local hand-made charr-baits). There is probably no predatory species of up to twenty pounds or so in weight that has not at some time or another been taken on a mackerel spinner.

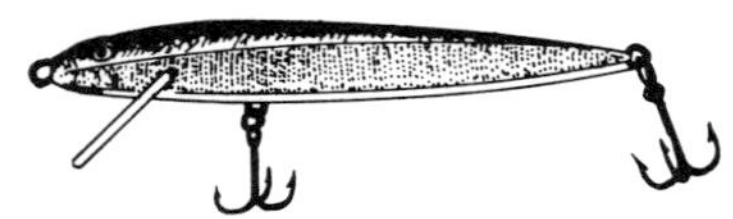

13. *The Rapala*

This Finnish plug bait was the cause of a mild sensation when it was introduced into the U.S.A. Such was the demand for it that the Finnish manufacturers were unable to keep pace; American tackle-dealers hired out baits at so much a day. There was no such reaction to the Rapala in Britain, partly because its introduction came much later – when cheap copies of the bait could be purchased. These baits were inferior fish-catchers and blunted the general enthusiasm. The genuine Rapala is excellent for both pike and salmon.

14. *The Mackerel Spoon*

This cheap, mass produced bait is equally attractive to salt and freshwater fish. It will

15. *The Jim Vincent Spoon*

This famous pike spoon made by Hardy Bros. was named after that master pike angler, Jim Vincent, who had copied an Indian-made spoon which he brought back from Canada. Nowadays made of chromed copper, it was originally made of hard-wood. The modern Canadian equivalent of the Vincent Spoon – also based on the Indian original – is called a William's Wabler. Being a quick sinker, the Vincent is effective in deep water, whereas the Wabler (which is made of light alloy) is a useful shallow-water bait.

16. *The Canadian Bar-Spoon*

The favourite spoon of a generation of successful Dorset Stour pike anglers. Many

a tale of its deadly attraction has been told by men favoured with a day's pike fishing on Dorset's very private Long-Crichel lake.

17 *The Colorado Spoon*
First described in Cholmondeley-Pennell's *Pike and Coarse Fish* (1885), this spoon is a development of an old bait (recommended for perch spinning) known as the Comet bait. It is a popular pike spoon since it possesses all the attributes that pike fishermen look for:
(a) It flashes: the outside is chrome finished.
(b) It has a liberal dash of red about it: the inside is painted red and there is also a red wool tassel.
(c) Its leaded bar provides ample casting weight without the need for extra lead.
(d) It spins well.

18. *The Norwich Spoon*
This spoon is an old favourite of Norfolk pike fishermen. As its name implies, it is closely associated with the Broads. It is finished half-scaled gilt and half-polished nickel on the outside, and half nickel and half red on the inside. It is also furnished with a red glass-eye.

Housing Baits, Plugs and Spinners

There has always been a carrying and storage problem with artificial baits and mounts. If these are kept in tins or boxes, hooks become entangled and there is the ever-present problem of rusting when a wet bait is returned to the box. The American spinner and plug box, with its series of hinged trays honeycombed with individual compartments, solves the first problem, but does nothing to reduce the second – rust!

Nowadays, anglers can buy little hook-hoods (above), in various sizes, to prevent trebles from becoming entangled, and our photograph shows F. B.'s improved, ventilated, spinner box that exposes one tray of baits at a time. The vertical packing of the spinners ensures perfect drainage and ventilation, thus eliminating the problem of rust.

A Devon-type bait presents a special problem since the hook mount is separate from the shell. Overleaf we show the method that we use to keep the component parts married. A simple paper-clip. But how effective!

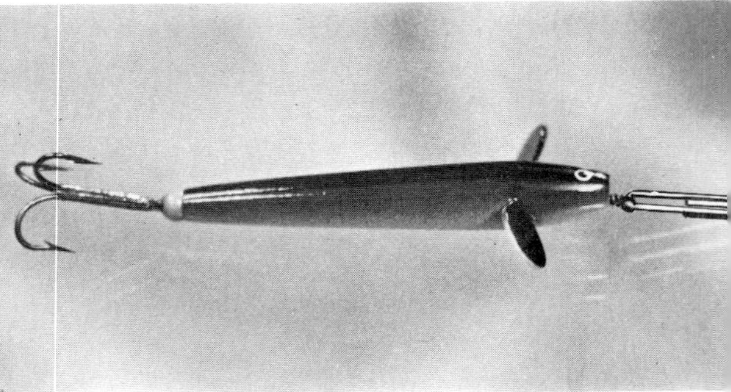

When not in use – use paperclips to keep Devon flights and shells together.

◁ *The F. B. bait-box.*

One thousand artificial baits – a sight that weakens an angler's resolve not to spend money when he visits a tackle shop.

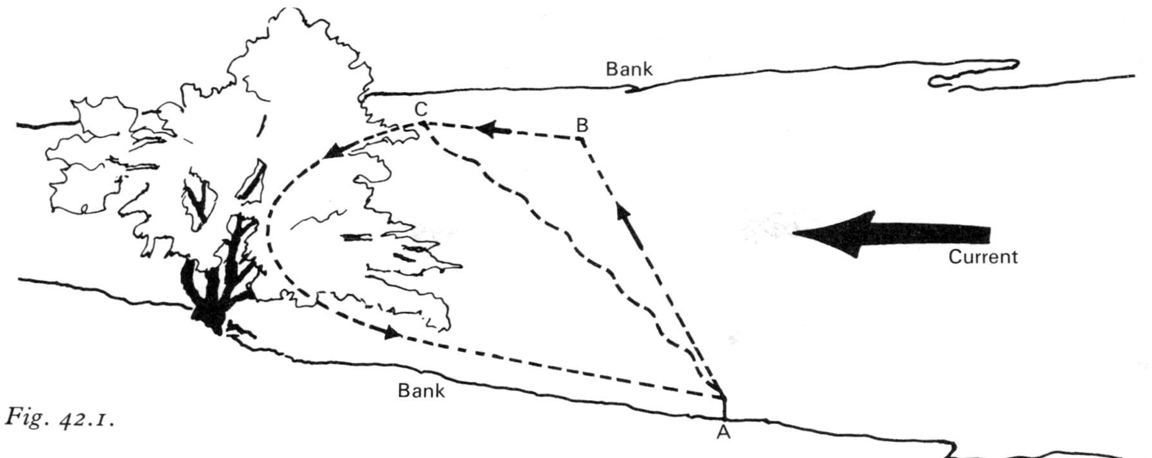

Fig. 42.1.

PLUG FISHING

Plug fishing has numerous advantages over spinning. Perhaps the plug's most important advantage is that it can be fished successfully all through the season, whereas in summer, heavy weed growth often makes spinning impossible.

Areas of weedy water are usually highly productive. Often, they can be covered with a plug that is fished a few inches below the surface.

In fast water, due to its buoyancy, a plug can be fished successfully over a lie that is upstream of the angler. All too often, a spoon or a Devon minnow fished upstream in similar conditions has to be retrieved very fast (too fast to attract a fish), otherwise owing to the speed of the current it falls to the bottom.

A floating plug can be used to cover a difficult lie underneath overhanging tree branches (Fig. 42.1). The angler stands at A, eight or ten yards upstream of the tree. The plug is cast to B, well beyond the branches, and allowed to drift down with the current – the rod being held well out over the water. When the plug has drifted to C, the rod tip is dipped under the surface and the reel given a few quick turns to make the plug 'bite'. Once it is at the right depth, the plug is retrieved with the rod tip still held below water level. The drag of the line will swing the plug in towards the bank and underneath the tree.

Patches of open water in a weedy swim may also be investigated with a floating plug (Fig. 42.2). The plug is cast from A to B just short of the far weed bed. It is made to dive sharply by means of a few quick turns of the reel, then retrieved at normal speed through the extent of the open water. When it reaches C, it is allowed to surface. A fierce pluck retrieves it through the air in the manner of a retrieved fly.

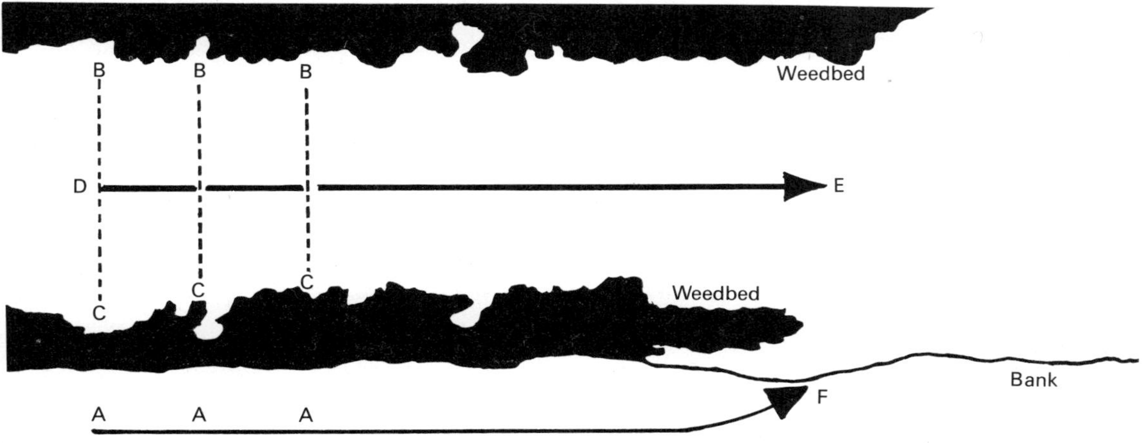

Fig.42.2.

If a fish is hooked, say at D, it is quickly 'walked' to more open water at E, and landed at F. (For notes on 'walking' a fish see p. 213.)

The action of any one design of plug can be varied in three ways:

1. Changing the direction of the cast relative to the stream.
2. Manoeuvring the rod tip during the retrieve.
3. Changing the speed of recovery.

Although American anglers favour a short single-handed rod and multiplier reel for plug fishing, we prefer a fixed-spool reel and monofilament line of about 10 lb B.S., on a rod of not less than 8 ft 6 in. Within limits, the longer his rod the better an angler can control his lure.

The use of leads should be avoided whenever possible.

Frequent inspections of the Alasticum leader should be made for kinks.

We cannot over-emphasize the importance of maintaining an open loop at the point where the plug swings on the leader (see illustration). After a plug has touched weed or been caught on the bottom, this loop should be inspected – and opened again if it has pulled tight.

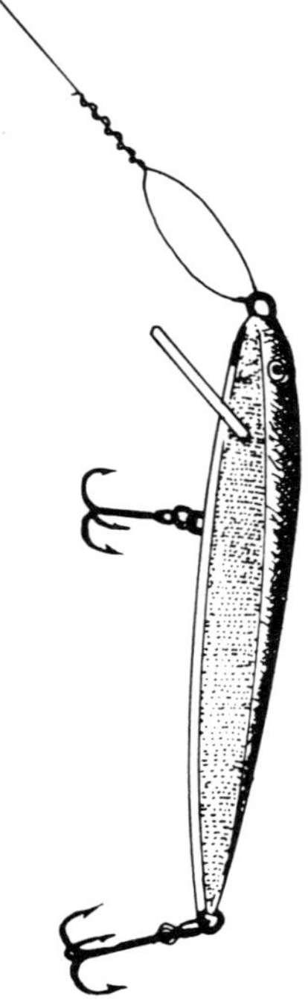

Fig. 42.3. The open-loop method of attaching a plug to an Alasticum wire leader.

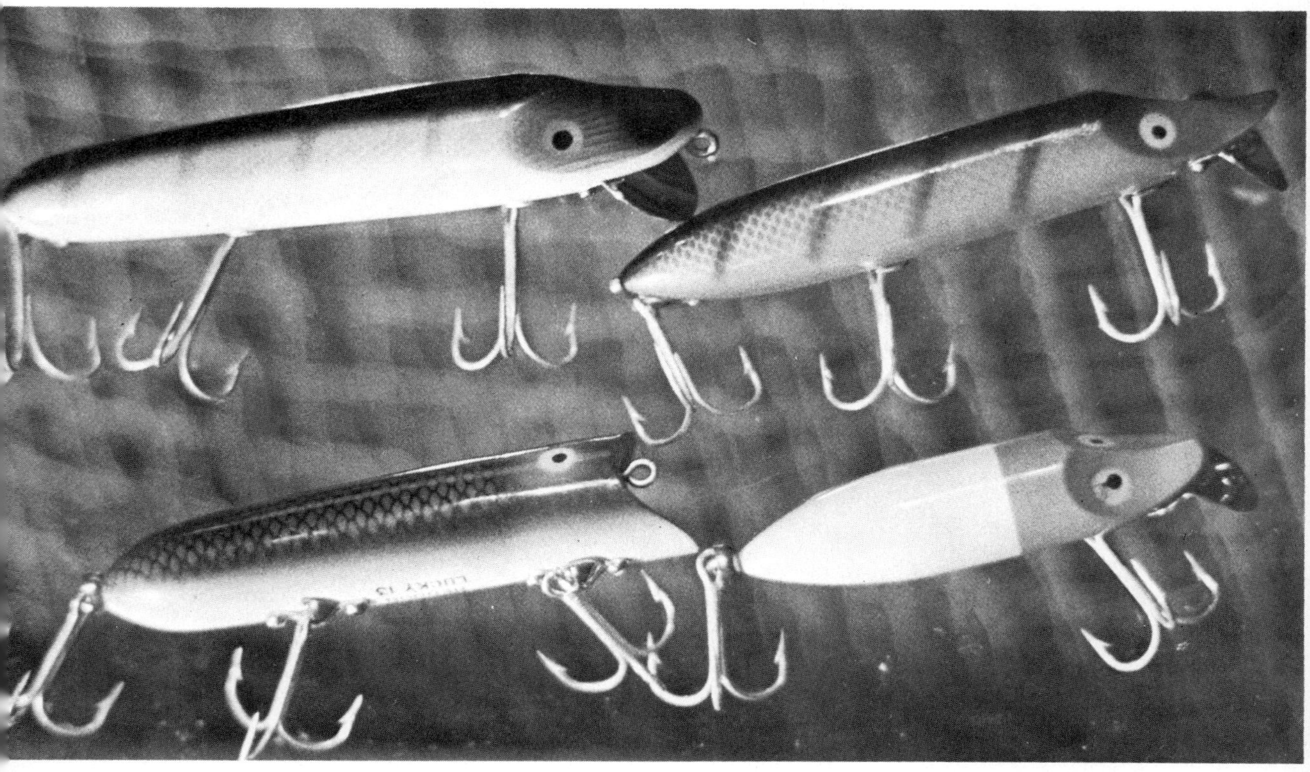

Top left: *The original Heddon Vamp. The first floating/diving lure ever made – a pattern for hundreds of imitative baits. In an age of plastic, this is one of the few baits still made with wood. A great pike plug.*
Top right: *Heddon Vamp Spook. One of the best plugs for pike and muskellunge. It floats at rest, dives about two feet below the surface on retrieve.*
Bottom left: *The Heddon Lucky 13. An old favourite with pike fishermen. A good surface or shallow-diving plug for summer pike fishing.*
Bottom right: *The most famous of all plug baits: the River Runt Spook. It floats at rest, dives a foot or two on retrieve. A great favourite with the Hampshire Avon salmon fishermen in the yellow shore colour. No imitations have ever surpassed the fish-catching qualities of the original River Runt. That this should be so is almost certainly due to the fact that the plastic material of its construction is standardized. With plastic, a killing pattern can be the model for any number of true copies.*

Top: *Heddon Commando. Patent plastic jointed plug having a rear section designed to spin. Once a fish is hooked, the bait slides up the line, making it impossible for the fish to lever itself free against the bait.*
Bottom left: *Heddon Crazy Crawler. This has what can only be described as a 'violent' action. Nevertheless, this very action has given the bait a reputation for attracting big pike. It is essentially a surface lure, which makes it most effective for summer fishing in weedy waters.*
Bottom right: *Heddon Deep Dive River Runt Spook (slow sinker). Note the outsize diving lip. It is the* size *of lip, not the steepness of angle, that achieves a deep dive.*

43 · Fishing Safety

Finally, some notes on personal safety: an all-important aspect of angling, all too seldom considered.

Most fishing accidents result in little more than a wetting. A fisherman gets his boots full, or stumbles and falls unhurt in shallow water. But every so often comes news of a fishing fatality. Someone has lost his balance or been swept off his feet while wading; a loose rock has toppled over; a piece of river bank has collapsed; a boat has capsized . . . a fisherman has drowned.

Accidents such as these can happen very suddenly; indeed they usually do. Within seconds of being safe and sound, the unlucky man finds himself floundering out of his depth. Terrified, he throws up his arms and screams. Two involuntary actions. Both fatal.

Many lives would be saved if people would only think *beforehand* of the correct action to take in the event of emergency.

It is the unexpectedness of most accidents that carries the greatest threat to safety; the shock of a sudden plunge into cold water, followed immediately by panic – panic caused by the thought of being heavily clothed and shod, and out of one's depth. It has been said – and the number of people who believe it is surprising – that if a fisherman wearing waders falls into deep water, his boots will drag him down.

They will do nothing of the sort.

It is quite a simple matter to swim for short distances fully clothed and wearing waders; their weight when submerged is negligible, and although they don't make swimming any easier they certainly don't make it impossible. It is not too difficult to swim fully clothed while carrying a fishing rod. Provided you can swim, no great danger need accompany a tumble into deep water.

In order to enjoy a feeling of security on or beside water – whether river or lake – you should be able to paddle about fully clothed when out of your depth. If you can't, practise until you can, paying particular attention to the back-stroke. Most emergency swimming of this nature is (or should be) carried out on the back.

There is nothing difficult about it. On the contrary, it is really very easy. And it is very, very important, for once you are able to swim on your back you will be armed with confidence, and the thought of falling into deep water will no longer be one of fear.

Remember: *it is panic that drowns most people.*

When the worst happens – perhaps an undermined river bank collapses, or a shingle bottom slides away beneath your feet – and you suddenly find yourself plunging fully clothed, rod in hand, into the deeps – *don't* open your mouth and shout. Pay no attention to those stories of drowning men coming up three times. If you ship enough water first time down, you won't come up at all. So – *keep your mouth shut.*

Provided you don't wave your arms about above your head you will soon bob up again. A living body is very buoyant. (Even if you can't swim, there is sufficient air trapped in your various garments to keep you afloat for several minutes, if you only give yourself half a chance.)

Float on your back. Keep your head lying well back in the water and let your legs come to the surface. Once in this position you can start shouting for help.

If in a river, *don't* try to swim against the current. Let yourself drift downstream, feet first; then it will be your boots that will strike a rock, not your head. Paddle away with your hands and gradually edge in towards the bank.

WADING

The ability to wade deep is an asset to every fly fisherman. But rivers vary enormously. Some are gay, uncomplicated little streams with easily-waded gravel runs and glides. Others are awkward and treacherous, with slimy rocks and deep, sullen pools where a single false step may take the unsuspecting non-swimmer straight over a shallow, sunken ledge – into eternity.

On the river, wading is the most common cause of fishing accidents, and it is probable that those accidents involving the use of body waders form the highest proportion. No denigration of body waders is intended; the point is simply that the higher his waders the deeper the fisherman is tempted to wade, until sooner or later the fatal step is taken. When this happens, the water is not up to his knees or thighs, but his chest, and in all probability he is swept off his feet by the current.

An experienced fisherman who knows his river can tell at a glance where he can wade safely and where he can't. Even so, it is easy to make mistakes. A place quite safe to wade when the river is, say, nine inches above summer level may be impossible after a further rise of two inches. In a lake, a two-inch rise means that your safe wading depth is reduced by exactly that amount; but in the river there are two other factors involved. Two extra inches in the river mean not only two inches of extra depth, but a stronger current.

This added pressure of water against your body increases the water level against your back, and also causes you to lean over at a greater angle against the current in order to maintain a footing – thus further reducing the safety margin of your waders. The combination of these two factors results in a loss of considerably more than two inches.

When wading for any distance downstream, always be sure of the depth of water between the bank and wherever you happen to be. Your path may be along an underwater ridge with deep water on either side, in which case the only possible retreat is

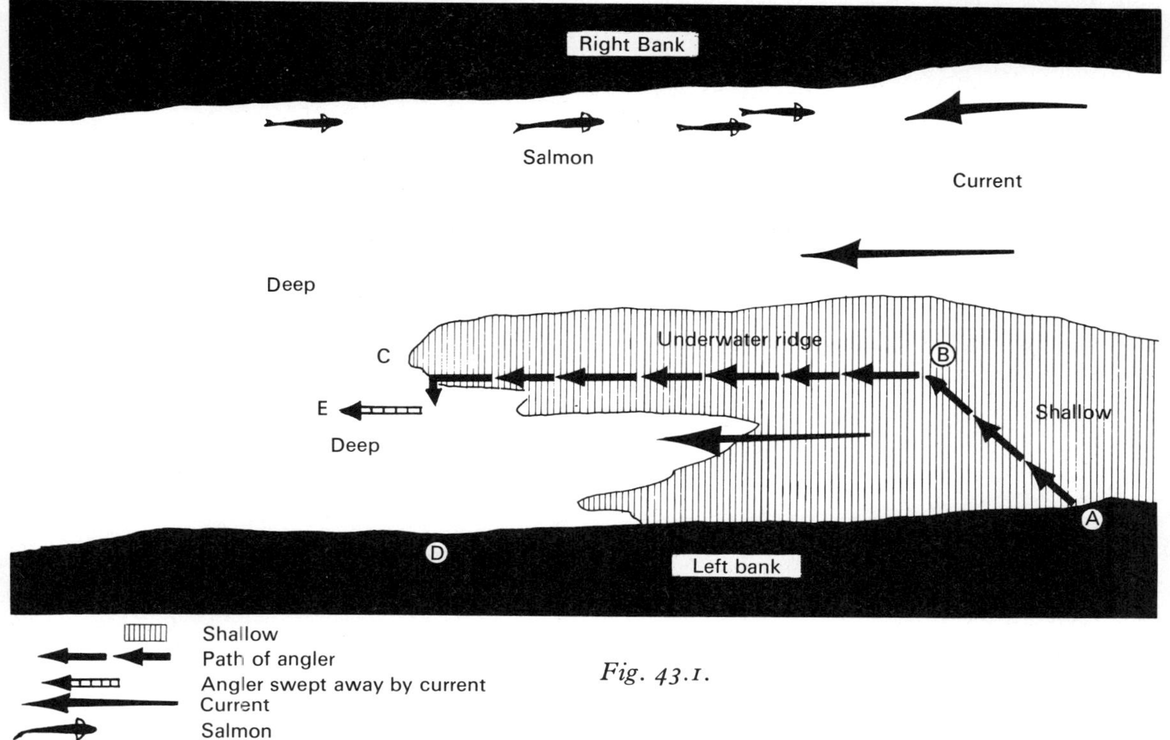

Fig. 43.1.

straight back upstream. Wading against even a weak current is a great deal more difficult than wading with it. Your return will be even more difficult if, while you have been wading downstream, the river has begun to rise.

Such a rise may be entirely unexpected. It is not by any means unusual for a downpour further up the valley to affect the river, although not a drop of rain has fallen in your locality. The early stages of such a rise are not immediately evident to anyone intent on fishing. The water level may creep up unnoticed – until the margin of safety is passed.

Before wading deep, make certain of the pool's underwater contours.

A fisherman wades out from A to B in order to cover salmon lying under the top right bank. Wading along a shallow underwater ridge, he fishes down to point C. There he comes to deeper water and finds he can wade no farther downstream. He is unable to retrace his steps upstream owing to the strength of the current. Not realising he is on the end of an underwater spit he attempts to wade straight in towards the bank along the line C D. Almost at once he steps into deep water and is swept off his feet downstream by the current E. (See photographic sequence, p. 504).

When standing in a current, remember that the water is piled higher against your back than your front, thus allowing a smaller margin of safety than you may think by a casual glance down. As soon as you begin to wade against the current the water will pile up, not only from the added pressure, but the greater angle at which it is necessary to lean.

When wading in a current, *never* step up on top of a submerged rock. It is very difficult to keep your footing when trying to step down again.

We are grateful to our friend, Frank Plum, for his gallant co-operation in photographing the following sequence.

1. A salmon fisherman wading in a strong current on steep shingle . . .

2. . . . takes a step too many.

3. The shingle slides away underfoot; the current sweeps him forward . . .

4. . . . and down he goes, into deep water.

5. This type of accident can happen in any river, whatever the nature of the bottom. Within seconds of being safe and sound you may find yourself floundering out of your depth. It is the unexpectedness of such accidents that carries the greatest threat to safety – the shock of a sudden plunge into cold water; the fear that your waders may drag you down. They will do nothing of the sort.

6. Don't *try to swim back against the current.* Turn on your back *and let the current take you with it. If you cannot swim and hold your rod too, let it go. With line out, there should be a good chance of recovering it later.*

7. Float on your back, head upstream. Kick with your legs, paddle with your hands, and keep your head back.

8. The classic 'safe' position. Head well back. Legs up. Arms outstretched. Once in this position you can start shouting for help.

9. Keep on your back. Float downstream feet first with the current and gradually edge in towards the bank by paddling with outstretched hands.

10. But don't *try to pull yourself up a steep bank out of deep water. The weight of sodden clothes and waders full of water will quickly exhaust you. Resist the temptation to cling on in a hopeless situation.*

11. Keep on down the pool. Head back, legs up. Don't drop your legs to feel for the bottom : a vertical body will sink at once.

12. When you reach the shallows, don't *try to stand up and walk out. Tired, suffering from shock and exposure, you may stumble and injure yourself. Roll over on to hands and knees . . .*

13. . . . and crawl out.

14. Having crawled out on to dry land, don't *immediately get up and try to walk : lie on your back and empty your waders first!*

BOAT FISHING ACCIDENTS

We make no apology for the elementary nature of the following advice. Some anglers who go afloat are astonishingly ignorant of boats and boat-handling and do the most stupid things. Each season we hear of boating accidents that could have been so easily avoided. Here are some 'don'ts'.

When getting into a boat from a landing-stage don't step on the side of the boat, or on one of the seats, or on the bare planking between the ribs. Always step on the floor-boards as near the middle of the boat as possible. Having stepped into the boat, *sit down*.

Don't go out in any boat that is not provided with a baler, a spare oar, and spare rowlocks or thole-pins (whichever are used). If the boat normally relies on an engine, make sure it also has a pair of oars. Don't relax this rule however calm the day. The weather can change with frightening rapidity and in only a few hours a big lake (Lough Mask, for instance) can become very dangerous.

Don't, if you are alone in a boat some distance from the bank on a hot day, succumb to the temptation of going in for a swim – unless the boat is anchored. A sudden breeze may spring up and blow the boat away from you faster than you can swim after it.

Don't try getting from the water into a small boat by clambering over the *side* of the boat (Fig. 43.2.*a*). Pull yourself up over the stern (the blunt end) (Fig. 43.2.*b*).

Before you go overboard for a swim be quite sure you *can* pull yourself back on board. It isn't so easy as it sounds. (At one time or another we have had to assist quite a lot of people who hadn't considered this!)

Don't stand up in the boat without warning the other occupant or occupants. If you are inexperienced, don't stand up at all. If you want to pee, use the baler.

Don't attempt to change places with a companion without first planning exactly, move by move, where each of you is going to position himself.

When the boat is anchored in a strong current, don't move forward too quickly when you go to pull up the anchor. This can be a very dangerous situation. The current, stronger than when you anchored (perhaps in a sea loch), can swamp the boat, if your weight is suddenly transferred too far forward (Figs. 43.2.*c* and *d*). Edge towards the bows very carefully, a foot at a time. If it is doubtful whether you can reach the anchor rope without the bows going under, either wait for slack tide or tie your knife to the loom of an oar or the handle of a landing net, reach forward and cut the rope.

If you *can* reach the anchor rope, don't start to pull it in unless it is running through a fairlead on the bows (see Fig. 43.2.*e*). Keep your hands low down while you pull in the rope. If it comes out of the fairlead the chances are that the boat will swing broadside to the current – with the danger of a subsequent capsize. (See Figs. 43.3.*f* and *g* with explanatory notes.)

If (for whatever reason) the boat fills up and overturns *don't panic*. Keep your mouth shut and try not to swallow any water; you have some thinking to do. If the water is very cold you must quickly make up your

Fig. 43.2. Boat Fishing Accidents.

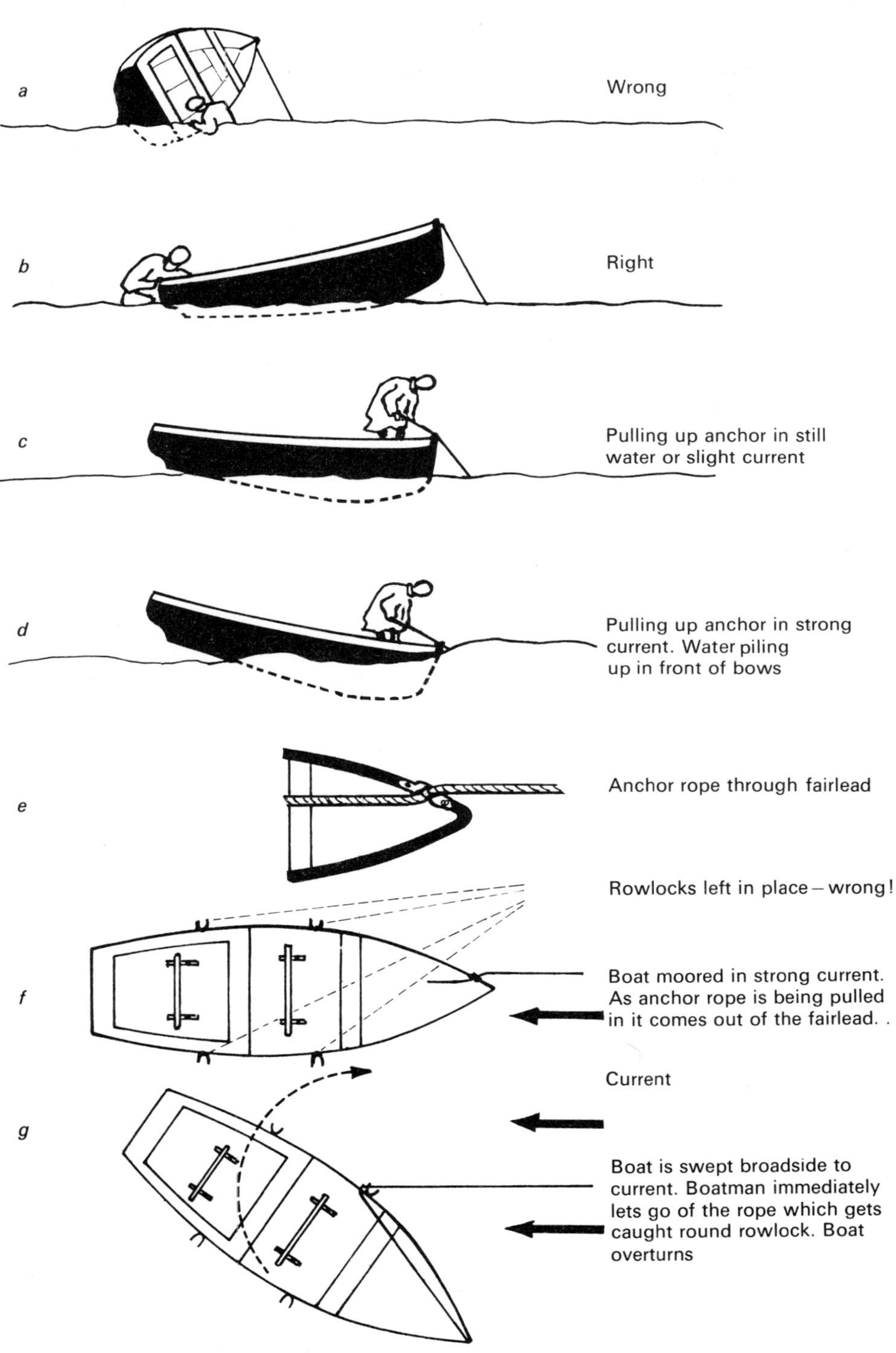

Note. We have witnessed this accident on more than one occasion. *Always* remove rowlocks when not in use

mind whether to swim for the shore or stay where you are and wait for help.

If you know that help is coming you will naturally cling to the oars or the water-logged hull and wait to be picked up. But if you remain motionless in cold water you will soon become numbed, lose consciousness and drown. So – keep moving your arms and legs. Whatever you do, *don't stay still.*

If there is no help forthcoming and you decide to swim for it, the sooner you start the better. If you have only a short distance to go, don't undress. Air trapped in your clothes will help to keep you afloat for a time, and also help to keep you warm. But if you have far to go strip off all your clothes as quickly as you can and get started. When you want a rest turn on to your back, but don't just float, keep your legs and arms moving. Even when you reach the shore, force yourself to *keep moving* until you get help.

Remember: however strong a swimmer you may be it is the *cold* you are really up against.

Top: *A boat angler, fishing with deadbait float/ledger tackle for pike on Loch Lomond.*

Middle: *He casts with perfect balance.*

Bottom: *As the reflections show, there is hardly any extra surface ripple – as there would be if the boat were rocking wildly. But this is not a method we recommend the novice to try, especially when alone and in such a small boat. Unless you are very experienced, when you get into a boat, sit down – and stay down.*
Note: *For all his dexterity, this angler (like those on the following page) loses marks for keeping his rowlocks in position while at anchor. Even in slack water they can be dangerous.*

A 20 lb pike comes to the net. The angler's companion has shortened his grip to the very head of the net handle, while the angler himself leans back to balance the boat and prevent a sudden capsize (Photograph: Angling News Services).

Bibliography

Anon, *The Angler's Pocket-Book* 1805 (third edition).
Anon, *The Arte of Angling*, 1577 (second facsimile edition, 1958).
J. van den Assem, *Territory in the Three-Spined Stickleback*, 1967.

Sir Francis Bacon, *A History of Life and Death*, 1623.
Richard Barder, *Spinning for Pike*, 1970.
Thomas Barker, *Barker's Delight*, 1657 (second edition).
Thomas Barker, *The Art of Angling*, 1651.
Mrs Beeton, *Dictionary of Cooking*, 1872.
Mrs Beeton, *Every-Day Cookery*.
Dame Juliana Berners, *A Treatyse of Fysshynge wyth an Angle*, 1496.
John Bickerdyke, *Angling For Game Fish*, 1889.
John Bickerdyke, *The Book of The All-Round Angler*, 1888 (and a revised edition, 1900).
William Blacker, *Blacker's Art of Fly-Making*, revised edition, 1855.
Robert Blakey, *Historical Sketches of The Angling Literature*, 1856.
George Braithwaite, *Salmonidae of Westmorland*, 1884.
Richard Brookes, *The Arte of Angling*, 1774 (fourth edition).
William Browne, *Britannia's Pastorals*, 1613.
Arthur Bryant, *The Age Of Chivalry*, 1963.
John Buchan, *John MacNab*, 1925.
Frank Buckland, *A Familiar History of British Fishes*, 1873.
Frank Buckland, *The Natural History of British Fishes*, 1881.
Fred Buller, *Pike*, 1971.
William Burroughs, *Locusts and Wild Honey*, 1884.

David Cairncross, *The Origin of the Silver Eel*, 1862.
Patrick Chalmers, *A Fisherman's Angles*, 1931.
Patrick Chalmers, *The Angler's England*, 1938.
Guiniad Charfy (pseudonym), *The Fisherman: or The Arte of Angling made Easy*, 1800.
W. A. Chatto, *The Angler's Souvenir*, 1835 (new edition, 1877).
James Chetham, *The Angler's Vade-Mecum*, 1681.
H. Cholmondeley-Pennell, *Fishing, Pike and Other Coarse Fish*, 1889 (fourth edition).
H. Cholmondeley-Pennell, *The Book of the Pike*, 1865 (and the third edition, 1876).
H. Cholmondeley-Pennell, *The Fisherman's Magazine*, Volume 1, 1864.
Jonathan Couch, *British Fishes*, 1862–65, four Volumes.
A. Courtney Williams, *Angling Diversions*, 1945.
Nicholas Cox, *The Gentleman's Recreation*, 1674.

The Rev. W. B. Daniel, *Rural Sports*, 1801.
John Davy, *The Angler in The Lake District*, 1857.
John Dennys, *The Secrets of Angling*, 1613 (and a reprint, 1883).

E. Ensom (Faddist), *Coarse Fish 'Briefs'*, 1957.
Ephemera (pseudonym), *A Handbook Of Angling*, 1847.
G. A. Escoffier, *A Guide to Modern Cookery*, 1898.

Hugh Falkus, *Sea-Trout Fishing*, 1962.
Negley Farson, *Going Fishing*, 1942.
Francis Francis, *A Month in the West*, 1886.
W. E. Frost and M. E. Brown, *The Trout*, 1967.

James A. Gibbinson, *Carp*, 1968.
William Gilbert, *The Angler's Delight*, 1676.
H. Godwin, *British Maglemose Harpoon Sites*, 1933.
L. R. N. Gray, *Torridge Fishery*, 1957.
Sir Edward Grey, *Fly-Fishing*, 1907 (fourth edition).
A. C. Günther, *The Study of Fishes*, 1880.

R. P. Hardie, *Ferox and Char*, 1940.
James Hardy and Richard Walker, *Hardy's Guide to Reservoir Angling*, 1974.
Barbara Hargreaves (editor), *The Sporting Wife*, 1971.
Lieut.-Col. Peter Hawker, *Instructions to Young Sportsmen*, 1814.
Dr Heysham, *Hutchinson's History of Cumberland* (2 Volumes, reprinted 1974).
Robert Howlett (attributed), *The Angler's Sure Guide*, 1706.

Alfred Jardine, *Pike and Perch*, 1898.

Michael Kennedy, *The Sea Angler's Fishes*, 1954.
T. C. Kingsmill Moore, *A Man May Fish*, 1960.

Henry Lamond, *Loch Lomond*, 1931.
Joscelyn Lane, *Lake and Loch Fishing for Trout*, 1955.
William Lauson, *The Secrets of Angling*, c. 1620.
W. H. Lawrie, *Border River Angling*, 1939 (and another edition, 1946).

J. J. Manley, *Notes On Fish and Fishing*, 1877.
Gervase Markham, *The Pleasures of Princes*, 1614 (and a reprint, 1927).
E. Marshall-Hardy, *Coarse Fish*, 1943.
Charles Marson, *Super Flumina*, 1905.
Leonard Mascall, *A Booke of Fishing with Hooke and Line*, 1590.
A. R. Matthews, *How to Catch Coarse Fish*, 1921.
J. M. D. Meiklejohn, *A New History of England and Great Britain*, 1903.
J. P. Moreton and W. A. Hunter, *Fisherman's Manual*, 1932 (and a third edition, 1965).

Dr Joseph Needham, *Science and Civilization in China*, Volume 2.
P. E. Newberry, *Beni Hassan*, 1893.
G. V. Nikolsky, *The Ecology of Fishes*, 1963.
Robert Nobbes, *The Compleat Troller, or The Art of Trolling*, 1682 (and the third edition, 1805).

O'Gorman, *The Practice of Angling*, 1845 (two Volumes).

Piers of Fulham, *Manuscript poem*, c. 1400.
H. Plunkett Greene, *Where the Bright Waters Meet*, 1924.

William Radcliffe, *Fishing from the Earliest Times*, 1921.
Arthur Ransome, *Rod And Line*, 1929 (also second edition, 1932).
R. V. Righyni, *Grayling*, 1968.
Alfred Ronalds, *The Fly-Fisher's Entomology*, 1836.

Robert Salter, *The Modern Angler*, second edition, 1811.
T. F. Salter, *The Angler's Guide*, eighth edition, 1833.
James Saunders, *The Compleat Fisherman*, 1724.
J. G. Scott, *South-West Scotland*, 1967.
H. T. Sheringham, *An Angler's Hours*, 1905.
H. T. Sheringham, *An Open Creel*, 1910.
H. T. Sheringham, *Elements of Angling*, 1914 (second edition).
H. T. Sheringham, *Fishing Its Cause, Treatment, And Cure*, 1925.
G. E. M. Skues, *Nymph Fishing For Chalk Stream Trout*, 1939.
St John, Charles, *Wild Sports of the Highlands*, 1847 (another edition, 1893).
W. C. Stewart, *The Practical Angler*, 1857.
Thomas Stoddart, *The Angler's Companion to the Rivers and Lochs of Scotland*, 1847 (second edition, 1853).

C. Tate Regan, *The Freshwater Fishes of the British Isles*, 1911.
Eric Taverner, *Salmon Fishing*, 1931.
F. J. Taylor, *Tench*, 1971.
J. Thompson, *History of British Fishes*, 1835.
Niko Tinbergen, *Animal Behaviour*, 1965.
William Turrell, *Ancient Angling Authors*, 1910.

Colonel Robert Venables, *The Experienc'd Angler*, 1662 (and reprint, 1927).
B. Vesey-Fitzgerald, *The Hampshire Avon*, 1950.

Richard Walker, *Still-water Angling*, 1953.
Isaac Walton, *The Compleat Angler*, 1653 (and the fourth Sir John Hawkins edition, 1784).
John Watson, *English Lake-District Fisheries*, 1899.
Westwood and Satchell, *Bibliotheca Piscatoria*, 1883.
Alwyne Wheeler, *The Fishes of The British Isles and North-West Europe*, 1969.
John Witney, *The Genteel Recreation: or, the Pleasure of Angling*, 1700.
Maurice Wiggin, *Fishing For Beginners*, revised edition, 1958.
Maurice Wiggin, *Troubled Waters*, 1960.
Captain T. Williamson, *The Complete Angler's Vade-Mecum*, 1808.
E. B. Worthington and T. Macan, *Life in Lakes and Rivers*, 1951.
William Wright, *Fishes and Fishing*, 1858.

William Yarrell, *A History of British Fishes*, second edition, 1841 (third edition, 1859).

Let's be going, good Master, for I am
hungry again with fishing.
IZAAK WALTON, *The Compleat Angler*.

Index

C

D

E

F

G

H

I

T

U

V

W

X

Y

Z